MW00533206

Prolonging the Agony

How The Anglo-American Establishment Deliberately Extended WWI by Three-and-a-Half Years.

Jim Macgregor
&
Gerry Docherty

Published by:
Trine Day LLC
PO Box 577
Walterville, OR 97489
1-800-556-2012
www.TrineDay.com
publisher@TrineDay.net

Library of Congress Control Number: 2017952755

Macgregor, Jim and Docherty, Gerry.
–1st ed.
p. cm.

Epud (ISBN-13) 978-1-63424-157-1
Mobi (ISBN-13) 978-1-63424-158-8
Print (ISBN-13) 978-1-63424-156-4
1. World War, 1914-1918 -- Causes. 2. World War, 1914-1918. 3. Europe -- Politics and government -- 1871-1918. I. Macgregor, Jim and Docherty, Gerry. II. Title

First Edition
10 9 8 7 6 5 4 3 2

Printed in the USA
Distribution to the Trade by:
Independent Publishers Group (IPG)
814 North Franklin Street
Chicago, Illinois 60610
312.337.0747
www.ipgbook.com

War is a racket. It always has been. It is possibly the oldest, easily the most profitable, surely the most vicious. It is the only one international in scope. It is the only one in which the profits are reckoned in dollars and the losses in lives.

A racket is best described, I believe, as something that is not what it seems to the majority of the people. Only a small "inside" group knows what it is about. It is conducted for the benefit of the very few, at the expense of the very many. Out of war a few people make huge fortunes.

In the World War [I] a mere handful garnered the profits of the conflict. At least 21,000 new millionaires and billionaires were made in the United States during the World War. That many admitted their huge blood gains in their income tax returns. How many other war millionaires falsified their tax returns no one knows.

– Smedley Butler, Congressional Medal of Honour, 1914 and 1919;
Distinguished Service Medal 1919,
Major General United States Marine Corps.

I am making this statement as an act of wilful defiance of military authority because I believe that the war is being deliberately prolonged by those who have the power to end it. I am a soldier, convinced that I am acting on behalf of soldiers. I believe that the war upon which I entered as a war of defence and liberation has now become a war of aggression and conquest ... I have seen and endured the sufferings of the troops and I can no longer be a party to prolonging these sufferings for ends which I believe to be evil and unjust.

– Captain Seigfried Sassoon, War Hero Poet
in an open latter to his commanding officer
on 6 July 1917.

Acknowledgments

We are not the first to openly challenge the official propaganda and lies which were translated by the victors in 1918 into accepted history, the history we have been force-fed in school. For this reason we have to begin our acknowledgements by stressing the debt we owe to writers and historians who challenged the official accounts and provided some of the evidence which helped us unpick the web of deceit woven around the First World War.

Our original publisher at Mainstream, Edinburgh, then headed by the redoubtable Bill Campbell, backed us without question and offered the invaluable advice that we should split our research findings into two parts, with the first, *Hidden History, The Secret Origins of The First World War*, focusing on the causes of the war and debunking the myth that Germany was to blame. By the time this second part, *Prolonging the Agony*, was completed, Mainstream had been taken over by Random House. Bill Campbell's enthusiasm was replaced with studied indifference, despite the clear success of *Hidden History*, translated as it is into German and, shortly, French and Swedish.

There were moments in the early days when it would have been easier to walk away from the project; when it seemed that few wanted to know what had really happened. That these dark moments were completely dispelled is due to the positive reaction to both the book and our blog. The enthusiasm and encouragement from across the globe took us by surprise, and fuelled our determination to expose the truth. Our American publisher at TrineDay, Kris Millegan was absolute in his commitment to getting that truth out. Also in the U.S. our immensely knowledgeable colleague, Peter Hof, stood by our side and made many valuable contributions. Tom Cahill, the American photo-journalist and activist in the US Veterans Against War movement, has championed our work from the start. Mees Baaijen, the Dutch philosopher and writer living in Cost Rica has also frequently added thoughtful considerations and pointers as our work progressed.

In Australia, Greg Maybury, writer and host of the brilliant blog, *Pox Americana*, gave invaluable advice and promotion, while David Jones and his team at *New Dawn* journal have published our Gallipoli investigations and much else. Another Aussie writer, James O'Neil, has been ever helpful as has his name-sake (though no relation), Hugh O'Neil from New

Zealand. We enjoyed the company of both these fine men when they engaged in engrossing discussions with us during trips to Scotland.

Over the last four years German academics, historians, and others have supported our work. None more so than Professor Hans Fenske at the University of Freiburg who contributed important pieces to our series of blogs. Wolfgang Effenberger, author of many fine books, co-edited Sie Wollten den Krieg with Jim Macgregor, and has given us unstinting support. Our German publishers at Kopp Verlag, headed by Jochen Kopp himself, have been endlessly helpful in advancing and developing our message. Indeed the sheer enthusiasm and dedication of his staff at Rottenburg am Neckar, including Jochen Thum, Sasha Renniger, Ute Kopp and Mathias Schultz is deeply impressive. Guenter Jaschke has also given us great assistance in providing and translating Austro-Hungarian and German political and military documents into English.

Another impressive European investigator, Hugo Leuders from Beyond the 1914-1918 Centenary in Brussels, has made important contributions to our research in Belgium and supplied new evidence which supports our investigations into Edith Cavell and Belgian Relief. Hugo is a sharp analyst whose advice we continually appreciate.

The contemporary Irish historian and researcher, Dr. Patrick Walsh, who has written extensively on Irish History and the First World War, has supported our work and added his insight on a number of occasions as has Richard K. Moore, the American writer and political analyst living in Wexford.

Pat Mills, the British writer famous for the immensely popular *Charley's War,* invited us once again to the Edinburgh International Book Festival. In addition to lectures in Edinburgh and elsewhere in Scotland, we have had enthusiastic audiences in Namur, Brussels, Dublin and London. Each time we have been supported by local academics and authors, and would again thank, Hugo Leuders, (Brussels) Nick Kollerstrom, (London) and Anthony Coughlan, (Dublin)

The international nature of our new contacts and associates may be gleaned through the wide-ranging comments and advice from which we have benefitted. These include Mujahid Kamran, professor of physics and former vice-chancellor of the University of the Punjab in Lahore, Pakistan, the widely read author and scientist, and Michel Chossudovsky, Professor Emeritus the University of Ottawa, who has supported us and published our work in Global Research. Contacts from Sweden include Peter Graftstrom and Bjorn Eklund; from France, Pierre Maze of Nouvelle Terre and locally, Patrick Scott Hogg, Dr. John O'Dowd, Richard Edwards and, importantly, our IT mastermind, Sally Blewitt.

There is also a small but important number of academics who have supported our enquiries and aided our research but who prefer not to be named. They are afraid for their positions and futures, have mortgages to pay and families to feed. The heavy hand of censure still sits above those university academics who break from the orthodox establishment view. Your names remain in our hearts.

In acknowledging the various contributions, considerations and corrections through which these talented people have added to our manuscript, we remain responsible for the final product. Any sins of omission or commission are ours alone. Having said which, we want to salute the patience and at times the resilience of the many librarians in Edinburgh, London, Oxford, Brussels and Washington DC who have come to our assistance and helped us find a path through the mass of original sources, records and materials of which they are the guardians. It should be remembered that librarians can only catalogue and preserve the evidence to which they have been allowed access. Our apologies to those we have confronted when documents are missing, torn out or no longer 'available'. T'was not your fault.

Finally a word of thanks to Joan, Maureen and our families who have patiently supported us through long years of research and writing. They have stood by us unquestioningly.

Jim Macgregor and Gerry Docherty
December 2017

Table of Contents

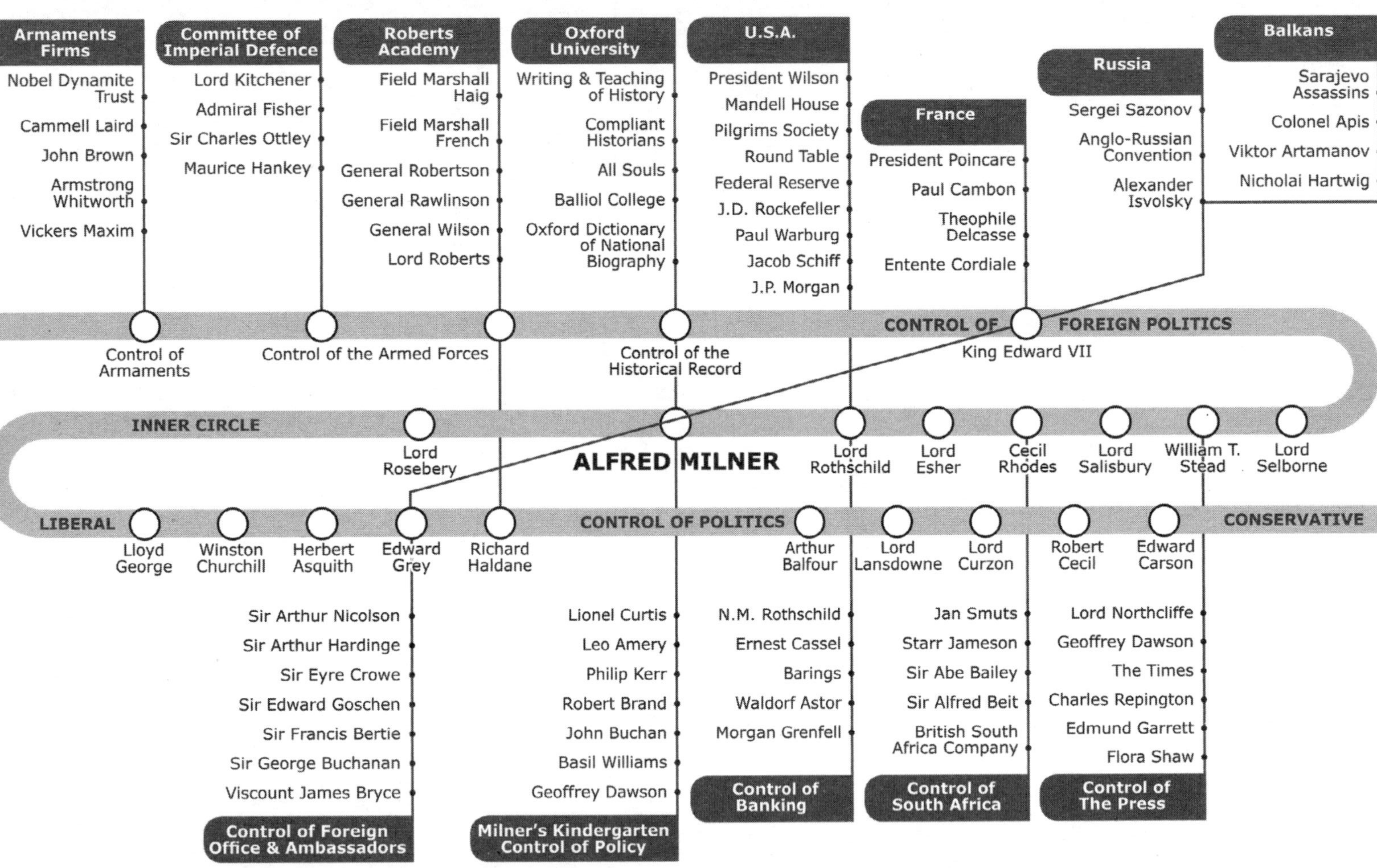
The Secret Elite's Hidden Control & Connections 1891 - 1914
Armaments Firms
Nobel Dynamite Trust
Cammell Laird
John Brown
Armstrong Whitworth
Vickers Maxim
Committee of Imperial Defence
Lord Kitchener
Admiral Fisher
Sir Charles Ottley
Maurice Hankey
Roberts Academy
Field Marshall Haig
Field Marshall French
General Robertson
General Rawlinson
General Wilson
Lord Roberts
Oxford University
Writing & Teaching of History
Compliant Historians
All Souls
Balliol College
Oxford Dictionary of National Biography
U.S.A.
President Wilson
Mandell House
Pilgrims Society
Round Table
Federal Reserve
J.D. Rockefeller
Paul Warburg
Jacob Schiff
J.P. Morgan
France
President Poincare
Paul Cambon
Theophile Delcasse
Entente Cordiale
Russia
Sergei Sazonov
Anglo-Russian Convention
Alexander Isvolsky
Balkans
Sarajevo Assassins
Colonel Apis
Viktor Artamanov
Nicholai Hartwig
Control of Armaments
Control of the Armed Forces
Control of the Historical Record
CONTROL OF FOREIGN POLITICS
King Edward VII
INNER CIRCLE
Lord Rosebery
ALFRED MILNER
Lord Rothschild
Lord Esher
Cecil Rhodes
Lord Salisbury
William T. Stead
Lord Selborne
LIBERAL
Lloyd George
Winston Churchill
Herbert Asquith
Edward Grey
Richard Haldane
CONTROL OF POLITICS
Arthur Balfour
Lord Lansdowne
Lord Curzon
Robert Cecil
Edward Carson
CONSERVATIVE
Sir Arthur Nicolson
Sir Arthur Hardinge
Sir Eyre Crowe
Sir Edward Goschen
Sir Francis Bertie
Sir George Buchanan
Viscount James Bryce
Control of Foreign Office & Ambassadors
Lionel Curtis
Leo Amery
Philip Kerr
Robert Brand
John Buchan
Basil Williams
Geoffrey Dawson
Milner's Kindergarten Control of Policy
N.M. Rothschild
Ernest Cassel
Barings
Waldorf Astor
Morgan Grenfell
Control of Banking
Jan Smuts
Starr Jameson
Sir Abe Bailey
Sir Alfred Beit
British South Africa Company
Control of South Africa
Lord Northcliffe
Geoffrey Dawson
The Times
Charles Repington
Edmund Garrett
Flora Shaw
Control of The Press

Chapter 1

The Origins Revisited

We are lied to. Constantly. We live in a world where fake news has impacted on national elections, plebiscites and referenda to such an extent that the freedom of the Internet has been called into question. This is not a new phenomenon. Governments and historians, official versions of events and records have long been manipulated and falsified to deliberately misrepresent what happened and why.

Each of us faces the difficulty of overcoming cognitive dissonance if asked to accept that the history we learned in school or university is incorrect, inexact or heavily biased. The challenge is greater if invited to consider the possibility that accounts of our past have deliberately been written to mislead, and are outright lies peddled as truth.

We have all read books or watched movies which are "based on true events," but paid for and produced by those with a vested interest in influencing our understanding of what happened. A world-impacting disaster like the First World War provides such an example. How was it explained to you in school or in books you have read? We now know that the catastrophic events of August 1914 were not caused by the shootings at Sarajevo on 28 June when Archduke Franz Ferdinand and his wife were assassinated by a Bosnian student, yet that has been taught for generations and remains the stock answer to the question "what caused the First World War?" Alarmingly, despite all of the evidence now available to us, the myths continue to be repeated.

Read the following, please: "The war began with the assassination of Archduke Franz Ferdinand in Sarajevo on June 28th, 1914...."[1] If we told you this was written by a reputable journalist for the *Irish Times* one hundred and more years after the event, would you be surprised? The story may have gained credence through constant repetition, but it remains a convenient myth.

The question is not why journalists or teachers tell us lies but, more generously, how do they get it so wrong? When our teachers studied at university were they mislead by their professors and tutors? Who directed the sources of "evidence" they used when writing essays or answering exam questions? Whomsoever controls the teaching of teachers, controls the understanding of future generations. If the facts are polluted by propaganda, by suppression and careful editing, limited by the removal or concealment of documents and reports, clouded by rewritten diaries and heavily censored autobiographies promoted by those who made fortunes through the financing of war – then it becomes increasingly difficult to slice through the lies and disinformation to find the truth.

And we in turn have difficulty in disbelieving the lies because these were the certainties on which we have built our understanding. This cognitive dissonance, the disharmony and psychological stress resulting from simultaneously holding conflicting beliefs, leads to an unwillingness to consider alternative evidence. It is hard to admit that what we have always believed is a lie. Realizing that there is a suppressed body of evidence which runs contrary to what we consider the truth, represents for all of us a major step in appreciating that we have been deliberately duped.

This book is the second in a series which introduces readers to a concept that is totally at odds with mainstream history, and very likely to induce cognitive dissonance. The disastrous First World War which began in August 1914 was caused by a small clique of Anglo-American conspirators, who then very deliberately and unnecessarily prolonged it beyond the Spring of 1915 by supplying Germany with food, munitions, oil and money. Their ultimate goal was the complete and utter destruction of the young, burgeoning Germany as an industrial, economic and imperial competitor, and they knew that it would require a prolonged miserable war of attrition to achieve that. They also knew that Germany, surrounded as she was by her enemies, could not sustain a long conflict. Chapter by chapter, we reveal in great detail exactly how the war was deliberately prolonged at the cost of tens of millions of lives.

We also reveal how this clique justified the war they had so carefully contrived, mobilized the establishment which supported them, sometimes reluctantly, and produced a range of highly sophisticated propaganda to win over neutrals, especially in America. As the lies, treachery and duplicity are unmasked, what is left in the wake of this awful war is both shameful and unforgivable. It involves hidden forces on both sides of the Atlantic and persists well past the November 11, 1918 date which traditionally commemorates the final day of war.

If this is the first time you have read about those genuinely responsible for causing the First World War, an overview of our book *Hidden History: The Secret Origins of the First World War* will enable a clearer understanding of the individuals involved and their treacherous intent.

It is important from the outset to repeat that the received history of the First World War is a deliberately concocted lie. Not the sacrifice, the heroism, the horrendous waste of life or the misery that followed. No, these were very real, but the truth of how it all began and how it was unnecessarily and deliberately prolonged has been successfully covered up for a century. A carefully falsified history was created to conceal the fact that Britain, not Germany, was responsible for the war. Had the truth become widely known after 1918, the consequences for the British Establishment would have been cataclysmic.[2]

The Causes, A Brief Synopsis from *Hidden History*

In the late nineteenth century a secret society of immensely rich and powerful men was established in London with the singular aim of expanding the British Empire across the entire world. They deliberately caused the South African War of 1899-1902 in order to grab the Transvaal's gold from the Boers. Their responsibility for that war, and the horror of British concentration camps in which 20,000 children died,[3] have been airbrushed from official histories. The second stage of their global plan was destruction of their major economic rival, Germany.

Falsified history? Secret society? Twenty thousand children dying in British concentration camps? Britain responsible for the First World War? Should you jump immediately to the conclusion that this is some madcap conspiracy theory, please consider the work of Professor Carroll Quigley, one of the twentieth century's most highly respected historians. Quigley's greatest contribution to our understanding of modern history was presented in his book, *The Anglo-American Establishment.* It carried explosive details of how a secret society of international bankers, aristocrats and other powerful men controlled the levers of politics and finance in Great Britain and the United States. Professor Quigley explained that very few people knew about this because the cabal was able to conceal its existence and "many of its most influential members are unknown even to close students of British history."[4]

Carroll Quigley

Cecil Rhodes, the South African diamond millionaire, formed the secret society in London in 1891. As Professor Quigley wrote: "One wintry afternoon in February 1891, three men were engaged in earnest conversation in London. From that conversation were to flow consequences of the greatest importance to the British Empire and to the world as a whole. For these men were organizing a secret society that was for more than fifty years to be one of the most important forces in the formulation and execution of British imperial and foreign policy."[5] No one outside the favored few knew of the society's existence. Members understood that the reality of power was much more important and effective than the appearance of power, because they belonged to a privileged class that understood how decisions were made, how governments were controlled and policy influenced. Party-political allegiance was not a given prerequisite for members; loyalty to the cause of Empire was. They have been variously referred to obliquely in speeches and books as the "Money Power," the "Hidden power" or the "Deep State." All of these labels are pertinent. We, however, have called them, collectively, the "Secret Elite."

The Secret Elite aimed to renew the bond between Great Britain and the United States, spread all they considered worthy in English ruling-class values and bring all habitable portions of the world under their influence and control. They believed that ruling-class men of Anglo-Saxon descent rightly sat at the top of a hierarchy built on predominance in trade, industry, banking and the exploitation of other races. Victorian England sat confidently at the pinnacle of international power, but could it stay there forever? That was the question which exercised serious debate in the great country houses and the expensive cigar-smoke-filled parlors of influence. The elites harbored a deep rooted fear that unless they acted decisively, British power and influence across the world would be eroded and replaced by foreigners, foreign business, foreign customs and laws. The choice was stark. Either take drastic steps to protect and further expand the British Empire, or accept that the new, burgeoning Germany might reduce it to a secondary player on the world's stage. In the years immediately after the Boer War, it became clear that the "Teutonic menace" had to be destroyed. Not defeated, destroyed.

The plan began with a multi-layered attack on the democratic process. They controlled power in administration and politics through carefully selected and compliant politicians inside the major British political parties. British foreign policy was dominated by them from behind the scenes, irrespective of any change of government. The Secret Elite drew into their ranks the increasingly influential press-barons to exercise influence over the avenues of information that created public opinion. More subtly, they controlled the funding of university chairs, and completely monopolized the writing and the teaching of the history of their own time.[6] One early example was the *Times History of the War in South Africa* (the Boer War) written by Lord Alfred Milner's select administrators whom he took from Oxford to reorganize and administer South Africa's recovery. They literally wrote their own history so that it was their version of events which became the accepted "truth." It became the template for the official histories of the First World War.

Five principal players, Cecil Rhodes, William Stead, Lord Reginald Esher, Lord Nathaniel Rothschild and Alfred Milner were the founding fathers, but the secret society developed rapidly in numbers, power and presence in the years before 1914. Influential old aristocratic families that had long dominated Westminster were deeply involved, as was King Edward VII, who operated within the inner core of the Secret Elite. Cecil Rhodes, a mining magnate who made millions in South Africa, had long talked about setting up a Jesuit-like secret society, pledged to take any action necessary to protect and promote the extension of the power of the British Empire. He sought to "bring the whole uncivilized world under British Rule, for the recovery of the United States, for the making of the Anglo-Saxon race but one empire."[7] In essence, the plan was as simple as that. Just as the Jesuit Order had been formed to protect the pope and expand the Catholic Church, answerable only to its own superior general, so the Secret Society was to protect and expand the British Empire, and remain answerable to its leader. The holy grail was control, not of God's kingdom on earth in the name of the Almighty, but of the known world in the name of the mighty British Empire. Both of these societies sought a different kind of world domination but shared a similar sense of ruthless purpose.

William Stead, Rhodes' close associate in the secret society, represented a new force in political influence: the power of affordable newspapers that spread their views to ever-increasing numbers of working men and women. Stead was the most prominent journalist of his day. He had dared to confront Victorian society over the scandal of child prostitution in an outspoken article in the *Pall Mall Gazette* in 1885 and, consequently, the government was forced to pass the Criminal Law Amendment Act. This is what earned Stead his place in Rhodes' elite company. He influenced the general public. He was one of the first journalistic crusaders and built an impressive network of younger journalists around his newspapers, who in turn promoted the Secret Elite's ambitions throughout the Empire.[8]

Stead commented immediately after Rhodes' death that he was "the first of the new dynasty of money-kings which has been evolved in these later days as the real rulers of the modern world."[9] Great financiers had often used their fortunes to control questions of peace and war, and of course influence politics for profit. Rhodes was fundamentally different. He turned the objective on its head and sought to amass great wealth into his secret society in order to achieve political ends: to buy governments and politicians, buy public opinion and the means to influence it. He intended that his wealth be used by Anglo-American elites to expand their control of the world. Secretly.

The third man present at the inaugural meeting of the secret society was Reginald Brett, better known as Lord Esher, a close advisor to three monarchs. Esher had even greater influence in the upper echelons of society. He represented the interests of the monarchy from Queen Victoria's final years, through the exuberant excesses of King Edward VII, to the more sedate but pliable King George V. He was "the *éminence grise* who ran England."[10] Esher wrote letters of advice to King Edward VII almost daily during his eight-year reign,[11] and through him the king was kept fully appraised of Secret Elite business. His precise role in British politics was difficult to grasp even for his contemporaries. He chaired important secret committees, was responsible for appointments to the Cabinet, the senior ranks of the diplomatic and civil services, voiced strong personal opinion on top army posts and exerted a power behind the throne far in excess of his constitutional position. His role of power-broker on behalf of the Secret Elite was without equal.

In the world of banking and finance, of investment and the raising of loans and bonds, the Secret Elite had a most important founding member, Lord Natty Rothschild. The Rothschild dynasty epitomized "the money power" to a degree with which no other could compete. It was all-powerful in British and world banking and considered itself the equal of royalty,[12] even to the extent of calling their London base "New Court." Like the British royal family, their roots lay in Germany.

The House of Rothschild was immensely more powerful than any financial empire that had ever preceded it. It commanded vast wealth. It was international. It was independent. Royal governments were nervous of it because they could not control it. Popular movements hated it because it was not answerable to the people. Constitutionalists resented it because its influence was exercised behind the scenes – secretly.[13] The Rothschilds understood how to use their wealth to anticipate and facilitate the next market opportunity, wherever it was. Their unrivaled resources were secured by the close family partnership that could call on agents placed throughout the world. They understood the worth of foreknowledge a generation ahead of every other competitor. The Rothschilds communicated regularly with each other, often several times a day, with secret codes and trusted, well-paid agents, so that their collective fingers were on the pulse of what was about to happen, especially in Europe. Governments and crowned heads so valued the Rothschilds' fast communications, their network of couriers, agents and family associates, that they used them as an express postal service, which in itself gave them access to even greater knowledge of secret dealings.[14] It is no exaggeration to say that in the nineteenth century, the House of Rothschild knew of events and proposals long before any government, business rival or newspaper.

Bankrolling pliant politicians was another tool. Although he was by nature and breeding a Conservative in terms of party politics, Natty Rothschild believed that on matters of finance and diplomacy all sides should heed the Rothschilds. He drew into his circle of friends and acquaintances many important men who, on the face of it, were political enemies. In the close world of politics, the Rothschilds exercised immense influence within the leadership of both Liberal and Conservative parties. They lunched with them at New Court, dined at exclusive clubs and invited all of the key policy makers to the family mansions, where politicians and royalty alike were wined and dined with fabulous excess. Edward VII was always welcome at the sumptuous Chateau at Ferrières or Alfred de Rothschild's enormous town house when enjoying a weekend at the Parisian brothels. It was in such exclusive, absolutely private environments that the Secret Elite discussed their plans and ambitions for the future of the world. According to Niall Ferguson, the Rothschild biographer: "it was in this milieu that many of the most important political decisions of the period were taken."[15]

Although Rothschild was the epitome of the "money-power," the undisputed leader of the Secret Elite from around 1902 until 1925 was Alfred (later Viscount) Milner. Remarkably, few people have ever heard his name. Professor Quigley noted that all biographies of Milner were written by members of the Secret Elite and concealed more than they revealed. In Quigley's view, this neglect of one of the most important figures of the twentieth century was part of a deliberate policy of secrecy. Alfred Milner, a self-made man and remarkably successful civil servant whose Oxford University connections were unrivaled, became absolutely powerful within the ranks of these otherwise privileged individuals.

Milner was prepared to take the hard-edged action necessary to tackle the problem of Boer control of the gold-bearing Transvaal. A clear solution was required that could not be trusted to a less determined man. He was prepared to give the Empire the leadership it required by confronting the Boers. In 1897, he set out for South Africa on a personal crusade to make it as loyally British as the gardens of England. He would remain there for eight years, cement his role as leader and build a team of brilliant young acolytes to drive the Secret Elite agenda forward over the next 30 years. His mission was absolutely clear: govern South Africa, all of it, remove Boer obstacles to complete British domination and take the Transvaal's gold. Milner knew it would mean all-out war. He also knew that the only way to make such a war acceptable to the Cabinet and British public was to portray Kruger's Boers as the aggressors.

Alfred Milner organized and developed a talented coterie of Oxford graduates inside his South African administration, men who by 1914 held critical positions of power in the City, the Conservative Party, the Civil Service, major newspapers and academia. Carroll Quigley specifically dedicated a chapter in his seminal *Anglo-American Establishment* to this "Milner's Kindergarten,"[16] the men who rose to high office in government, industry and politics. He appointed, trained and developed his chosen men to drive forward the Secret Elite agenda with conviction.

Cecil Rhodes and Alfred Milner were inextricably connected through events in South Africa. Rhodes chided William Stead for saying that he "would support Milner in any measure he may take, short of war." Rhodes had no such reservations. He recognized in Alfred Milner the kind of steel that was required to pursue the dream of world domination: "I support Milner absolutely without reserve. If he says peace, I say peace; if he says war, I say war. Whatever happens, I say ditto to Milner."[17] Alfred Milner grew in time to be the most able of them all, to enjoy the privilege of patronage and power, a man to whom others turned for leadership and direction. If any individual emerges as the central force inside our narrative, it is Alfred Milner.

Taken together, the five principal players – Rhodes, Stead, Esher, Rothschild and Milner – represented a new force that was emerging inside British politics, but powerful old traditional aristocratic families that had long dominated Westminster, often in cahoots with the reigning monarch, were also deeply involved, and none more so than the Cecil family.

Robert Arthur Talbot Gascoyne-Cecil, the patriarchal 3rd Marquis of Salisbury, ruled the Conservative Party at the latter end of the nineteenth century. He served as Prime Minister three times for a total of fourteen years, between 1885 and 1902 (longer than anyone else in recent history). He handed over the reins of government to his sister's son, Arthur Balfour, when he retired as Prime Minister in July 1902, confident that his nephew would continue to pursue his policies. Hence the phrase, "Bob's your uncle." Lord Salisbury had four siblings, five sons and three daughters who were all linked and interlinked by marriage to individuals in the upper echelons of the English ruling class. Important government positions were given to relations, friends and wealthy supporters who proved their gratitude by ensuring that his views became policy in government, civil service and diplomatic circles. This extended "Cecil-Bloc" was intricately linked to the Secret Elite ambitions throughout the first half of the twentieth century.[18]

The Liberal Party was similarly dominated by the Rosebery dynasty. Archibald Primrose, 5th Earl Rosebery, was twice Secretary of State for foreign affairs and Prime Minister between 1894 and 1895. Salisbury and Rosebery like so many of the English ruling class, were educated at Eton and Oxford University. Adversarial political viewpoints did not interfere with their involvement behind the scenes inside the Secret Elite.

Rosebery had an additional connection that placed his influence on an even higher plane. He had married the most eligible heiress of that time, Hannah de Rothschild, and was accepted into the most close-knit banking family in the world, and certainly the richest. According to Professor Quigley, Rosebery liked and admired Cecil Rhodes, who was often his guest. He made Rhodes a privy counselor, and in return Rhodes made Rosebery a trustee of his will. Patronage, aristocratic advantage, exclusive education, wealth: these were the qualifications necessary for acceptance in a society of the elite, particularly in its infancy. They met for secret meetings at private town houses and magnificent stately homes. These might be lavish weekend affairs or dinner in a private club. The Rothschilds' residences at Tring Park and Piccadilly, the Rosebery mansion at Mentmore and Marlborough House when it was the private residence of the Prince of Wales (until he became King Edward VII in 1901), were popular venues, while exclusive eating places like Grillion's and the even more ancient The Club provided suitable London bases for their discussions and intrigues.

These then were the architects who provided the necessary prerequisites for the secret society to take root expand and grow into the collective Secret Elite. Rhodes brought them together and regularly refined his will to ensure that they would have financial backing. Stead was there to influence public opinion, and Esher acted as the voice of the king. Salisbury and Rosebery provided the political networks, while Rothschild represented the international money power. Milner was the master manipulator, the iron-willed, assertive intellectual who offered that one essential factor: strong leadership. The heady mix of international finance, political manipulation and the control of government policy was at the heart of this small clique of determined men who set out to dominate the world.

What this privileged group intended might well have remained hidden from public scrutiny had Professor Carroll Quigley not unmasked it as the greatest influence in British political history in the twentieth century. Everything they touched was about control: of people and how their thoughts could be influenced; of political parties, no matter who was nominally in office. The world's most important and powerful leaders in finance and business were part and parcel of this secret world, as would be the control of history: how it was written and how information would be made available. All of this had to be accomplished in secret – unofficially, with an absolute minimum of written evidence, which is why so many official records have been destroyed, removed or remain closed to public examination, even in an era of "freedom of information."

On his return from South Africa in 1905 Alfred Milner set about preparing the British Empire for war with Germany. In goading the Boers into war, Milner displayed the cold objectivity that drove the cause. War was unfortunate but necessary. It had to be. The very future of the Secret Elite's global ambitions depended on a victorious outcome. Though the Boer war had finally ended in victory, with South Africa's gold and diamonds in the hands of the Secret Elite, it came at a cost greater than the number of lives lost. Britain had fewer friends than ever before. Living in "splendid isolation" had not been viewed as a handicap for as long as no other power on earth could challenge the primacy of British rule.

However, by the beginning of the twentieth century, one European nation was rapidly gaining a position which threatened that dominance. Britain retained its immense global financial power and still ruled the waves in terms of the size of its navy and merchant marine, but industrial leadership and pre-eminence was passing to Germany with a rapidity that caused undeniable concern.

First one British industry then another fell behind German output, capacity or invention. Modern machinery, highly trained technical skills, application of scientific discoveries to production techniques and a will to adapt to the purchaser's wishes were just some of the reasons Germany forged ahead. In 1871, the German fleet consisted of a few sailing vessels plying the Baltic, but by 1900 the situation had changed dramatically, with over 4,000 ships carrying her merchandise across every ocean. In fact, the Hamburg-American shipping line became the largest in the world.

The Foreign Office viewed this competition in shipping much more seriously than rivalry in trade because it was a point of honor that Britannia ruled the waves. In addition, the mercantile navy had always served as a nursery for men of the fighting navy, and the rapid expansion in German naval activity alarmed the Secret Elite. The German chancellor, Theobald von Bethmann-Hollweg, stated that the British "looked upon a Germany that kept on growing as an unwanted and troublesome intruder on the sanctity of British supremacy over the commerce and oceans of the world."[19] They did, so the troublesome intruder had to be confronted.

British industrialists knew but rarely acknowledged that there was also a marked superiority in new German manufactures like organic chemicals and electrical goods. The British press carried bitter stories of the "unfair" tactics of German salesmen spying on British trade practices, pandering to foreign countries and seducing them to the extent of, heaven forbid, translating brochures into their own language. By the turn of the century, German success was being denounced in exaggerated and over-excited terms, but the truth was ever more evident: German industrial expansion had left important sections of the British economy behind.

The Secret Elite did not accept that German economic and industrial success was a just reward for their investment in better education and new technology. Together with its burgeoning industry, and a brand-new merchant fleet that promised future colonial expansion, Germany was also beginning to invest in oil production in Romania and Galicia.[20] This was even more alarming because the Secret Elite knew just how strategically important oil was for future industrial development and warfare. The German threat had to be removed, and war was the only means by which that could be achieved.

As far as the Secret Elite were concerned, there was no need to be squeamish or reticent about war. Britain had never experienced a single year of peace since the start of Queen Victoria's reign, with British forces having fought in over a hundred wars of imperial conquest across the globe.[21] If the Secret Elite were to achieve their great dream of world domination, the first step had to be the removal of the Teutonic menace, the destruction of its economic prowess and restoration of the primacy of the British Empire. The plan presented great strategic difficulty. Friendless in her splendid isolation, Britain could never destroy Germany on her own. For a start, there was no continental foothold, and Britain's strength was her all-powerful navy, not a large army. Diplomatic channels had to be opened and overtures made to old enemies Russia and France. Friendship and alliances were required.[22] This was no mean task since Anglo-French bitterness had been rife over the previous decade and war between them a real possibility in 1895.[23]

Step forward the Secret Elite's most special weapon, Edward VII, whose greatest contribution lay in engineering the much-needed realignments, and addressing the Secret Elite's prerequisite need to isolate Germany. Ultimate responsibility for British foreign policy lay, by precedent, with the elected government and not the sovereign, but it was the King who enticed both France and Russia into secret alliances within six short years. The great armies of France and Russia were integral to the mammoth task of stopping Germany in her tracks. Put simply, the Secret Elite required others to undertake much of their bloody business, for war against Germany would certainly be bloody.

A treaty with France, the "Entente Cordiale," was signed on 8 April 1904, marking the end of an era of conflict that had lasted nearly a thousand years. The talk was of peace and prosperity, but secret clauses signed that same day aligned the two against Germany.

The subsequent convention with despotic, hateful, anti-Semitic Russia would have been totally unacceptable to most members of Parliament and the general public, but was enacted for one purpose, to throttle Germany. They enticed Russia into their web with a promise they never intended to deliver – Russian control of Constantinople and the Black Sea Straits following a successful war with Germany.

One of the most important features of the Secret Elite plan for war was to keep an iron grip on foreign policy. The long-term drive to war had to be imprinted on the departmental mindset at the War Office, the Admiralty and, in particular, the Foreign Office. Governments might rise and fall, but the ultimate objective had to be sustained, no matter the politics of the day. To that end, a permanent Committee of Imperial Defence (CID) was established by Prime Minister Arthur Balfour. This secretive and very exclusive group first met in 1902 as an advisory committee to the Prime Minister on matters of national defence but was re-formed permanently in 1904. It would go on to play a very significant role in bringing about war with Germany in 1914. In addition to Balfour, the only original permanent member of the committee was Lord Roberts, commander-in-chief of the armed forces and longstanding friend of Alfred Milner.

Lord Esher recognized the strategic importance of the CID and the absolute necessity that its work remain hidden and at all times under the control of the Secret Elite. Afraid that a change of government would result in a radical element within the Liberal Party gaining control of the CID, Esher pressed the Prime Minister to appoint trusted agents like Milner, Field Marshal Lord Roberts, and Roberts' up-and-coming protégé, Sir John French, as well as himself, as permanent members. Balfour partly acceded.[24] He sanctioned the appointment of both Esher and Sir John French to limitless tenure in the CID, and at a stroke the Cabinet was literally eclipsed from discussion on questions of military preparedness. Esher's appointment was again of the utmost significance. He ensured that King Edward VII and his successor, George V, received regular secret reports on all CID business. More importantly, he ensured that Secret Elite designs were followed; all hidden from view and, in terms of cabinet government, strictly unconstitutional.

Crucially, the Secret Elite also dominated the highest echelons of the armed forces through Field Marshall Lord Roberts, in what we have termed the "Roberts Academy."[25] The Secretary of State for war may have thought that he held political control over the army, but a small coterie of very powerful senior officers were, first and foremost, loyal to Field Marshal Roberts, friend and close associate of Alfred Milner and the Secret Elite. Roberts had served with Milner in South Africa. He knew Cecil Rhodes well, and was fully committed to the Rhodes-Milner vision of an all-controlling Anglo-Saxon world power. Right up to 1914, Roberts played a highly significant role in selecting and shaping the military high command. Crucially, through Milner and Roberts, the Secret Elite 's political and military strategy was as one. For years they had known of and encouraged the planned great war with Germany, and there would be no dissenting voices in the senior ranks of the armed forces when it finally arrived.

Lord Roberts's key influence lay in placing the principal military personnel within the War Office. Men who had served under him in various campaigns were promoted to the very highest ranks of the armed forces, including John French, Henry Wilson, William Robertson, Henry Rawlinson and Douglas Haig.[26] Their careers were launched on the strength of the little field marshal's support and their acceptance of his self-determined "advanced ideas."[27] To a man, they owed Roberts everything, having been chosen in the first instance in South Africa for their unquestioning loyalty to him and his "vision." In turn, they brought with them their own coteries of loyal personal followers who would form a new army "fit for purpose."[28] That is, the Secret Elite's purpose.

Thanks to Lord Roberts, loyalty of the armed forces was never in doubt, but what of politicians? British democracy, with regular elections and changes of government, was portrayed as a reliable safety net against despotic rule. It has never been this. Both the Conservative and Liberal parties had been controlled since 1866 by the same small clique that consisted of no more than half a dozen chief families, their relatives and allies, reinforced by an occasional newcomer with the "proper" credentials. The Secret Elite made an art form out of identifying potential talent and putting promising young men, usually from Oxford University, into positions in politics that would serve their future ambitions.

The Liberal party won the 1906 general election with a resounding victory. Having taken only 183 seats in 1900, they emerged with 397 Members of Parliament. The public had spoken. It was an overwhelming endorsement of "Peace and Retrenchment." The country was poised for reform. The leader of the jubilant Liberal Party, Henry Campbell-Bannerman's first Cabinet brought a very vocal and popular Liberal into Government, David Lloyd George. This young Welsh firebrand clearly stood out as a parliamentarian of considerable potential. So too did Winston Churchill, who had crossed from the Conservative Party two years before and been re-elected as a Liberal. Here was a Parliament bristling with new faces, keen to bring much-needed reform to Britain, yet even before the oath of office had been taken, arrangements devised through King Edward, Lord Esher, and other members of the Secret Elite ensured that foreign policy remained their preserve. Lloyd George reflected later that during the eight years that preceded the war, the Cabinet devoted a "ridiculously small" percentage of its time to foreign affairs.[29]

Anti-imperialists in the eighteen-strong Liberal Cabinet comprised Campbell-Bannerman himself, Lloyd George and at least five other radicals. But they had been outwitted. Before the demise of the Conservative government in 1905, the Secret Elite selected their natural successors in the Liberal Party: reliable and trusted men immersed in their imperial values. Herbert Asquith, Richard Haldane and Sir Edward Grey were Milner's chosen men, and their rise to prominence was approved by the King. Grey moved into the Foreign Office, Haldane the War Office and within two years Asquith would be Prime Minister. It may legitimately be asked how this small clique of approved imperialists could proceed with such a complex war conspiracy when faced with an anti-war Prime Minister and Cabinet. The straightforward answer is that they kept everyone else completely in the dark about their activities. Although Cabinet members and backbenchers frequently questioned foreign policy, Grey and Haldane repeatedly lied to them. It would be many years before the other Cabinet members learned of the dangerous military compact that had been secretly rubber-stamped in their name. With continuity in foreign policy assured, a complete root-and-branch reorganization of the War Office began in preparation for the coming war with Germany. How the Secret Elite must have laughed in their champagne at the notion of parliamentary democracy.

Grey was surrounded in the Foreign Office by seasoned permanent secretaries like Sir Charles Hardinge and Sir Arthur Nicolson, proven Establishment men who were associated with the Secret Elite. Hardinge was one of the most significant figures in the formation of British foreign policy in the early twentieth century. As a close confidant of King Edward, he traveled widely with him and played an important role in both the Entente Cordiale and the convention with Russia.[30] Sir Arthur Nicolson, later Lord Carnock, who played a similar role in guiding Grey in the Foreign Office, was always at the center at critical moments in Morocco, St Petersburg and eventually as permanent secretary in London. They controlled Britain's diplomatic reach across the world, while Grey fronted and deflected questions in Parliament.

The Foreign Office was the hub of the imperial spider's web, linked through diplomatic and commercial channels to every part of the globe. Its incumbents plotted and planned ceaselessly for the "good" of the Empire and the benefit of the Secret Elite. Grey was the perfect figurehead, but it was Hardinge and Nicolson who turned Secret Elite policy into practice.

In the War Office, Richard Haldane required no minders. He had the vigor, determination and intellect to tackle the mammoth task of reorganizing a military set-up that was soaked in historic tradition and riddled with vested interest. The British Army still offered commissions to the sons of the noble and wealthy. Rank and its privilege were available at a price. Haldane approached his new job in the confident knowledge that he had the complete backing of King Edward, Lord Esher and Alfred Milner. He told the House of Commons on 12 July 1906 that he intended to remold the army "in such a fashion that it shall be an army shaped for the only purpose for which an army is needed ... for the purpose of war."[31]

The navy had a great and historic tradition, but the Secret Elite needed to ensure control from the inside in the same way as the army through Lord Roberts. The man selected was Admiral Sir John (Jacky) Fisher who was perfectly agreeable to the Secret Elite's coming war. While friends in high places were undoubtedly a factor in elevating Fisher to the navy's top job, he was a man of vision who didn't hesitate to instigate revolutionary reforms that made the Royal Navy more effective for the job in hand. He valued ships for their fighting worth, and in 1904, with the German navy still in its infancy, he began a "ruthless, relentless, and remorseless" reorganization of the British fleet. The navy was purged of 160 ships that, in his own words, could "neither fight nor run away" and Fisher replaced them with fast, modern vessels ready "for instant war."[32]

From the beginning of the twentieth century, the Secret Elite indulged in a frenzy of rumor and half-truths, of raw propaganda and lies, to create the myth of a great naval race. The story widely accepted, even by many anti-war Liberals, was that Germany was preparing a massive fleet of warships to attack and destroy the British navy before unleashing a military invasion on the east coast of England or the Firth of Forth in Scotland.[33]

It was the stuff of conspiracy novels. But it worked. The British people swallowed the lie that militarism had run amok in Germany and the "fact" that it was seeking world domination through naval and military superiority. When the war ended and all of the plans and events that had taken place were analyzed and dissected, were there any naval records found of secret German plans to invade England or for the secret building of more dreadnoughts? No. Not one.

Control of politics, the army and navy was not a problem, nor was control of the press. Viscount Alfred Milner understood the role and the power of the newspapers. From his earliest years in the *Pall Mall Gazette* in the 1880s, Milner's personal network of journalist friends included William T. Stead, editor of the *Review of Reviews*, George Buckle and Geoffrey Dawson at the *Times*, Edmund Garrett at the *Westminster Gazette* and E.T. Cook at the *Daily News* and *Daily Chronicle*. Professor Quigley revealed that all were members of the secret cabal.[34] The combined impact of these newspapers and magazines gave the Secret Elite great influence over public opinion by directing editorial policies from behind the scenes, but it was the intimacy between the *Times* and the Foreign Office, the colonial office and the War Office that demonstrated just how deeply this symbiotic relationship ran.

The *Times* was taken over and controlled by Milner's men "quietly, and without struggle."[35] Others might own the newspaper, but Milner ensured that its editorial leadership came from within the Secret Elite's trusted ranks. Members of the innermost circle swarmed all over the *Times*, writing editorials and articles, submitting news and views in line with their agenda. The newspaper could not boast a mass circulation, and it never pretended to be a vehicle for mass propaganda. What Milner and his Secret Elite associates understood clearly was that the *Times* influenced the small number of important people who had the capacity to influence others. It represented the governing class, the elite political, diplomatic, financial, wealth-bearing favored few who made and approved the policies they ordained.

It was part of the process through which the Secret Elite directed policy. They endorsed those elements that met their approval and derided contrary opinion. When, for example, a member of the Secret Elite announced a policy on national defence, it would be backed up in an "independent" study by an eminent Oxford don or former military "expert," analyzed and approved in a *Times* leader and legitimized by some publication favourably reviewed in the *Times Literary Supplement*.[36] Everyone involved in the process would in some way be associated with the Secret Elite, including the writer of the anonymous review.

Lord Northcliffe, the most powerful press-baron, was a valuable contributor to the Secret Elite in their drive to vilify Germany and prepare the nation for war. His ownership of the *Times* and *Daily Mail* allowed them to create the impression that Germany was *the* enemy. A large and influential section of the British press worked to the rabid agenda of poisoning the minds of the nation. If the *Times* was their intellectual base, the popular dailies spread the gospel of anti-German hatred to the working classes. From 1905 to 1914, spy stories and anti-German articles bordered on lunacy in an outrageous attempt to generate fear and resentment.

Every bit as crucial was the hidden preparation for war which the Secret Elite approved and directed. The myth persists to this day that Belgian neutrality was the key reason why Britain declared war on Germany on 4 August 1914. In reality Belgium was never neutral. General James Grierson, director of British military operations and a member of the Roberts' academy and the Committee of Imperial Defence, wrote to Brussels in 1906, advising the Belgian chief of staff that the British government was prepared to put "4 cavalry brigades, 2 army corps and a division of mounted infantry" into Belgium, with the explicit intention of stopping a German advance.[37]

Britain's military link with Belgium was one of the most tightly guarded secrets, even within privileged circles. General Grierson was present with Lord Roberts, Admiral Fisher, Prime Minister Arthur Balfour and the director of Naval Intelligence, Captain Charles Ottley, at the CID meeting on 26 July 1905. They agreed to treat the special sub-committee that would take forward joint planning with French and Belgian military personnel as so secret that minutes would not be printed or circulated without special permission from the Prime Minister.[38] Grierson was tasked to drive forward the links with France and Belgium. On 16 January 1906, he opened official military "conversations" with Major Victor Huguet in France, and on the same day wrote to Lieutenant Colonel Nathaniel Barnardiston, the British Military Attaché in Brussels, advising him that a British Force of 105,000 would be sent to Belgium if a war broke out between France and Germany.[39]

Documents found in Belgian secret archives by the Germans after they had occupied Brussels disclosed that the chief of the Belgian general staff, Major-General G. E. V. Ducarne, held a series of meetings with the British military attaché over the action to be taken by the British, French and Belgian armies[40] against Germany in the event of war. Their plan detailed the landings and transportation of the British forces, which were actually called "Allied armies," and in a series of meetings they discussed the allocation of Belgian officers and interpreters to the British Army and crucial details on the care and "accommodation of the wounded of the Allied armies."[40] Grierson was kept fully informed and approved the joint agreements. Absolute confidentiality was stressed repeatedly. These conversations had to be kept secret, especially from the press.[41]

In 1912, when the likelihood of a European war over the Balkans became a serious possibility, Anglo-Belgian military arrangements were further refined. Secret guidebooks for the British military dated that year contained highly detailed maps of Belgian towns, villages and rural areas. British-Belgian military tactics had been worked out in fine detail, including the role of interpreters, hospital accommodation for the British wounded and more. Military arrangements with Belgium were so far advanced by February 1914 that the rate of exchange for payment of British soldiers fighting in Belgium had been fixed.[42] Britain and Belgium had been deeply involved in joint military preparations against Germany for at least eight years. Belgian "neutrality" was a sham; an excuse to declare war on Germany. Sir Edward Grey knew perfectly well that Belgium would side with Britain, France and Russia against Germany when war was declared. It had long been so arranged.

The American journalist and writer, Albert J. Nock, completely destroyed the notion of Belgian "neutrality." In his words:

> To pretend any longer that the Belgian government was surprised by the action of Germany, or unprepared to meet it; to picture Germany and Belgium as cat and mouse, to understand the position of Belgium otherwise than that she was one of four solid allies under definite agreement worked out in complete detail, is sheer absurdity.[43]

And yet this absurd notion was used to take Britain into war and has been propagated ever since by many historians. Belgium posed as a neutral country in 1914 like a siren on the rocks, set there to lure Germany into a trap, whimpering a pretense of innocence.

Belgium was not the only covert ally which Britain secretly drew into the plan to destroy Germany. Both France and Russia would be required to supply the man-power in wartime since their huge armies on continental Europe provided the essential factor that Britain lacked. It was therefore important to influence the foreign policies in both countries and encourage their Germanophobia. To that end the Secret Elite courted, financed and promoted key agents who would advance their cause. In Russia, Alexander Isvolsky was, first and foremost, their chosen man; in France they backed the Revanchists, Theophile Delcassé and Raymond Poincaré to drive their country to war.

Be clear about this: from the outset, Raymond Poincaré, President of France, knew that he was funded and supported by outside agencies to turn France against Germany. He was fully aware that he owed his political success to hidden forces that financed his rise to power. He sold his soul to the Secret Elite in order to regain Alsace-Lorraine. Poincaré was personally involved in bribing the French press, advising Isvolsky "on the most suitable plan of distribution of the subsidies."[44] Subsidies indeed. It was outright corruption in its most blatant form. French newspaper editors were paid large sums of money to subject opponents to a torrent of abuse. The new Prime Minister of France owed everything to Isvolsky and his controllers. From the start, he carefully fashioned French foreign policy to meet Sir Edward Grey's approval, and it was to the British Foreign Office that he looked for direction.[45]

Alexander Isvolsky's other contribution to the outbreak of war was his malign influence over the Balkan States. It was no accident that he played a significant role in creating perilous conditions there. The Secret Elite used him and their diplomatic and commercial agents in Serbia and Bulgaria to identify prominent individuals and organizations they could influence. Far from being passive observers, the Secret Elite in London made certain that their agents influenced events at every opportunity. Received wisdom acknowledged that by 1912 Serbia was "completely an instrument of Russia,"[46] and in one sense it was. The instructions, the finance and the promises of support all stemmed from St Petersburg to Russian diplomats in Belgrade, a state of affairs that seemed to underscore their commitment to Serbia. In reality, these Russian diplomats were taking their orders from men who we know were controlled by the Secret Elite: Isvolsky and his puppet, Russian foreign minister, Sazonov. Furthermore, the real sources for their slush funds could be traced to Paris and London.

Two conditions had to be met before the Secret Elite could start their war. Firstly, Britain and the Empire had to be made ready. Secondly, in order to heap blame on Germany, she had to be goaded into making the first move. The assassination of the heir to the Austro-Hungarian throne, Arch-Duke Franz Ferdinand, on 28 June 1914, provided the excuse for monstrous manipulation. It has often been cited as the cause of the First World War. What nonsense. On its own it was just one more political assassination in an era of many. The blame rested with a group of Serbian officials who trained, armed and aided the assassins and Austrian retribution was generally accepted as a valid reaction. What we have demonstrated in our book, *Hidden History* is that a chain of command linked the Serbian conspirators, the Russian Ambassador in Belgrade, the Foreign Office in St. Petersburg and the Secret Elite in London. [47] Austria demanded that the Serbian government take specific action against the perpetrators and allow Austrian involvement in the investigation. Serbia refused. Russia, having assumed the spurious role of protector, voiced total support for Serbia.

In London, the Secret Elite purposefully fanned the orchestrated antagonisms into a crisis. When Serbia and Austria squared up to each other in what should have been a localized conflict, Russia, with the full support of London and Paris, began in secret to mobilize her massive armies on Germany's eastern border on 30 July. Everyone was aware that once the general mobilization of an army began, it meant war and there was no turning back. Germany faced invasion along her eastern front, and, as the French army mobilized to the west, the Kaiser repeatedly made valiant attempts to persuade his cousin the Czar to stand down his armies. In the full knowledge that France had promised to join with her immediately, and that Britain, though not openly admitting her collusion, was secretly committed to war, the Czar refused.

On 31 July 1914, Isvolsky sent a highly revealing telegram from Paris to St Petersburg:

> The French War Minister informed me, in hearty high spirits, that the Government have firmly decided on war, and begged me to endorse the hope of the French General Staff that all efforts will be directed against Germany.[48]

France had "firmly decided on war" almost 24 hours before Germany had announced mobilization or declared war on Russia. General Joseph Joffre was straining at the leash. He sent Poincaré a personal ultimatum that he would no longer accept responsibility for the command of the French army unless a general mobilization was ordered.[49] Poincaré did not need much encouragement. At 4 p.m. that day, telegrams ordering the French general mobilization were sent from the central telegraph office in Paris. By that point, Serbia, Austria, Russia, France and Great Britain had begun military measures of one sort or another. Churchill had secretly ordered Britain's entire Grand Fleet to its war stations at Scapa Flow on 29 July.

Germany alone had not yet mobilized.[50] On the afternoon of 1 August, the German leaders gathered at the Kaiser's palace in Berlin. Theobald von Bethmann and Gottlieb von Jagow arrived with sensational news from the German ambassador in London; the British government had just given him a promise that France would remain neutral under a British guarantee. Hugely relieved, the supposedly "war-mongering" Kaiser called for champagne. He sent a telegram to King George: "If Britain guarantees the neutrality of France, I will abandon all action against her."[51] There was no British guarantee of French neutrality. It had simply been a delaying tactic, a ruse to gain time and advantage for the Russians and French.

At 5 P.M., after waiting in vain for twenty-four hours for an answer to his telegram demanding that the Russians stop all military movements on his border, the Kaiser ordered general mobilization. Germany was the last of the continental powers to take that irrevocable step. How does that possibly fit with the claim that Germany started the First World War? Time: 6 P.M., 1 August 1914.

Germany's declaration was an understandable reaction but a tactical mistake. Russia had been mobilizing with the definite intent of attacking her, but Sergei Sazonov had been instructed not to declare war. The vital message oft repeated by Sir Edward Grey to Poincaré and Sazonov was that France and Russia must, as far as possible, conceal their military preparations and intent on war until Germany had swallowed the bait. The British people would never support the aggressor in a European war, and it was imperative that Germany should be made to appear the aggressor. It was akin to bullies goading, threatening and ganging up on a single boy in the school playground, but the moment he had the audacity to defend himself, he would be blamed.

What else could Germany have done? She was provoked into a struggle for life or death. It was a stark choice: await certain destruction or strike out to defend herself. Backed into a corner and forced into a defensive war, Germany was the last power in Europe to mobilize her army. In order to deal with the French who had secretly mobilized to the west, the Kaiser ordered the German army to advance into France through Belgium. He had little other option. Continental Europe was at war.

The Secret Elite watched and waited. Joint preparations for war against Germany had been ongoing between Britain, Belgium, France and Russia since 1905, but had been kept so secret that only five out of twenty Cabinet ministers in the British government knew of Britain's commitments. Sir Edward Grey addressed the House of Commons on 3 August 1914 and promised that no action would be taken without the approval of parliament, yet that approval was never put to a vote. The crux of his argument rested on Belgian neutrality, though he knew full well it was a grotesque charade. The fiction of Belgian neutrality provided the legal and popular excuse for Britain's declaration of war on 4 August 1914. Sir Edward Grey, loyal servant of the Secret Elite, bounced the British Empire into war and no-one questioned him.

Over the last 100 years facts have been twisted and falsified by court historians. Members of the Secret Elite took exceptional care to remove traces of their conspiracy, and letters, telegrams, official reports and cabinet minutes which would have revealed the truth have disappeared. Letters to and from Alfred Milner were removed, burned or otherwise destroyed. Incriminating letters sent by King Edward were subject to an order that, on his death, they be destroyed immediately.[52] Lord Nathan

Rothschild, a founder-member of the Secret Elite, likewise ordered that his papers and correspondence be burned posthumously lest his political influence and connections became known. As his official biographer commented, one can but "wonder how much of the Rothschilds political role remains irrevocably hidden from posterity."[53]

Professor Quigley pointed an accusatory finger at those who monopolized "so completely the writing and the teaching of the history of their own period." There is no ambivalence in his damning accusation. The Secret Elite controlled that through numerous avenues but none more effectively than Oxford University. Milner's men largely dominated Balliol College, New College and All Souls which, in turn, largely dominated the intellectual life of Oxford historians. They controlled the *Dictionary of National Biography* which meant that the Secret Elite wrote the biographies of its own members, striking out any incriminating evidence and portraying the best public-spirited image that could be safely manufactured. They paid for new chairs of history, politics, economics and, ironically, peace studies.[54]

There was a systematic conspiracy by the British government to cover all traces of its own devious machinations. Official memoirs concerning the origins of the war were carefully scrutinized and censored before being released. Cabinet records for July 1914 relate almost exclusively to Ireland, with no mention of the impending global crisis. In the early 1970s, the Canadian historian, Nicholas D'Ombrain noted that War Office records had been "weeded." During his research he realized that as much as five-sixths of "sensitive" files were removed as he went about his business.[55] Why? Where did they go? Who authorized their removal? Were they sent to Hanslope Park, the government repository behind whose barbed-wire fences over 1.2 million secret files, many relating to the First World War, still remain concealed today?[56] Incredibly, this was not the worst episode of theft and deception.

Herbert Hoover, the man who fronted the Belgian Relief Commission and was later the 31st President of America, was closely linked to the Secret Elite. His undeniable role is fully documented in later chapters. He removed incriminating evidence from Europe and dressed his action in a cloak of academic respectability. Hoover persuaded General John Pershing to release fifteen history professors and around 1,000 students serving with the American Forces in Europe and send them, in uniform, to the countries his agency was feeding. With food in one hand and reassurance in the other, these agents faced little resistance in their quest to hunt down official papers which might damage the Secret Elite. They made the right contacts, "snooped" around for archives and found so many that Hoover "was soon shipping them back to the US as ballast in the empty food boats."

The evidence for every statement in this chapter can be found in our book, *Hidden History, The Secret Origins Of The First World War*. In addition, we have been blogging regular articles since June 2014 on what really happened during the war, not the pre-packaged history on which the British government would like us to concentrate.[57] After a century of propaganda, lies and brainwashing about the First World War, cognitive dissonance renders us too uncomfortable to bear the truth that it was a small, socially advantaged group of self-styled English race patriots, backed by powerful industrialists and financiers in Britain and the United States, who caused the First World War. The determination of this London-based Secret Elite to destroy Germany and ultimately take control of the world was responsible for the deaths of millions of honorable young men who were betrayed and sacrificed in a ruthless, bloody slaughter to further a dishonorable cause.

A much fuller explanation of the events detailed in this chapter comprise the body of evidence presented in *Hidden History*. It was our starting point, not a conclusion. In tracing the activities of the men who successfully and deliberately caused the war, it became apparent that a number of contemporary commentators from different fields of action, at different levels of responsibility, complained bitterly that as the miserable years progressed, the First World War was being unnecessarily prolonged. We are not talking about anti-war activists, conscientious objectors or political opponents. Our research brought to light a series of high-level accusations that repeated a consistent message; the war was being prolonging. Deliberately.

Surely this was nonsense. But each and every time we examined the evidence, the claims proved to have substance. The history which emerged is presented here. It is shocking; repulsive and difficult to accept because fair-minded people will not want to believe it. From the day that Britain declared war on Germany – 4 August, 1914 – steps were very carefully put in place to ensure that it would be a long and bitter war of attrition. Bear in mind that the Secret Elite were determined, not simply to win a battle and have everyone home for Christmas , or worse, fight to an inconclusive end. They intended to completely destroy Germany; to break her spirit, ruin her economic prowess and remove her as their greatest rival in Europe for all time. If it could not be achieved in a short decisive war, and Lord Kitchener said immediately that it could not, then every step had to be taken to keep the war going until the enemy was crushed, exhausted beyond recovery.

This is what our record explains. From the moment that the Foreign Office obligated war on Britain and its Empire, the Secret Elite greased the path to eventual victory with a mind-set that sacrificed millions of brave young men to the ultimate objective – dominant control of the civilized world. Their first move provided the flow of limitless funds which enabled Britain to throw caution to the wind knowing full well that war would offer them years of undreamed-of profit. They mobilized the banks, they mobilized the establishment, the church, Oxford and invented an immense propaganda machine. They mobilized the flower of youth and the corridors of privileged learning with equal enthusiasm. The citizens of the British Empire had to be convinced of the just nature of the world war for "civilization," no matter how ridiculous the claim, for there could be no long war without the commitment of the Empire.

Germany had to be supplied with vital resources for war and for survival. Starved of these the German people and the German army would quickly have been forced to capitulate. She was more or less land-locked since her coastline in the North Sea was easily blockaded, and without sufficient food, coal, oil, fodder, ores, gun-cotton, iron and steel, the war would have been brought to an end by 1915. German resistance would have petered out against a background of insufficient armaments and a starving population. Motorized transport, U-boats and airplanes would have ground to a halt without oil. Farm animals would have died where they lay in empty fields without fodder.

The following chapters record exactly how all this was achieved.

Summary:

- The received history of the First World War is a deliberately concocted lie.
- The origins are to be found in England not Germany.
- A Secret Elite of political dynasties, financiers and bankers galvanized initially by Cecil Rhodes, emerged at the end of the nineteenth century determined to establish a new world order based on their perception of the best values of the English upper-class.
- This group, identified first by Professor Carroll Quigley, adopted a three-pronged attack on an unsuspecting Britain by taking control of politics, the press and the teaching of history to advance their cause and cover their true influence.
- Important leaders included Lord Alfred Milner, the man who caused the Boer War, Lord Nathaniel Rothschild, the richest man in the world; leading liberal politicians in Britain, aided and abetted by the press, especially the *Times*, and a cabal in Oxford University, especially All Souls College.
- From 1902 onwards, British foreign policy was focused on the destruction of Germany because the German Empire had emerged as the greatest threat to Britain's economic position as the world leader
- The first step was the unexpected abandonment of isolationism. Britain signed a treaty with Japan and sold her the latest heavy battleships and Dreadnoughts with which the Japanese destroyed the Russian navy in 1905, thus removing the Russian threat to the safety of India.
- King Edward VII played a vital role inside this elite cabal by fronting the Entente with France in 1904 and a secret treaty with Russia in 1906. In both instances the perceived enemy was Germany. Until his death in

1910 Edward toured the monarchical courts of Europe gathering friends and distributing honors and titles to draw European nations into Britain's secret web of allies.

- The army was re-organized and modernized by Secretary of State for war, Richard Haldane, who created a special British Expeditionary Force which trained specifically for the coming war on continental Europe.
- An elite pro-British group in America, "The Pilgrims," gathered strength on the Eastern seaboard and at the same time, links between the British arm of the Rothschild dynasty and the American financiers and bankers, J. P. Morgan increased its influence inside the US government.
- Anti-German propaganda spread fear and resentment in Britain with ludicrous stories of spies and wild allegations that the Kaiser had embarked on a naval race to attack Britain and threaten her Empire.
- Thanks to the direct efforts of King Edward VII, the Russians appointed Alexander Isvolsky as their Ambassador in Paris from where he organized the disruptions in the Balkans which threatened to spark war in Europe from 1912 onwards.
- The emergence of the money-power in America was given added facilities to finance a war through the convenient establishment of a Federal Reserve Board in 1913, which was able to print money and generate funds necessary for a world war.
- Bribes were procured to help Frenchman Raymond Poincaré buy his presidency. Rabidly anti-German, Poincaré belonged to a political group who lived to grasp Alsace and Lorraine back from Germany. He twice visited the Czar in Russia to encourage an attack on Germany which France would immediately join.
- The assassination of Archduke Ferdinand in June 1914, though no big deal in itself, was financed by secret channels from London to St Petersburg to Paris and Serbia. Austria thought she had the open support of all European governments in taking steps against Serbia, but this was orchestrated into a cause for war. Russia turned on Germany and mobilized her immense army.
- France mobilized her army against Germany in secret and Britain, though feigning neutrality, mobilized her navy.
- Realizing that she was about to be attacked by Russia and France, Germany was the last country to mobilize before she declared a defensive war against her European neighbors.
- Sir Edward Grey bounced the British Empire into a war against Germany, with a litany of broken promises and lies to the Britain parliament. Ignorant of secret alliances and promised a democratic vote which never materialized, the British people found themselves at war on 4 August 1914.
- Received historians blamed this war on the Kaiser and Germany. This is untrue.

Chapter 2

The First Victims – The Truth and the People

Once war had been declared, the psychological ground rules changed. No matter the regret, no matter the stupidity, the lack of principle or the risk, the fact of war altered everything. While acknowledging that Britain had nothing to gain, and that "some day we shall all regret it," the *Guardian*'s view on 5 August 1914 reflected the complete about-face that war imposed on a nation's psyche. The new message they delivered bore all the hallmarks of Lord Nelson's call to arms. "Now there is nothing for Englishmen to do but to stand together and help by every means in their power to the attainment of our common object – an early and decisive victory over Germany."[1] Music indeed to the Secret Elite. Once war had been declared, the tipping point of public opinion did as it always has; swung immediately behind the flag of loyalty, duty and national pride, all of which became part of "the cause." There was still opposition to war, but it had little focus. Once the commitment had been sealed in blood through the death of a soldier or sailor fighting for that cause, then most of the nation would rally behind those who died.

Democracy was dead. It fell victim to years of Secret Elite preparations. A raft of emergency legislation was rushed through Parliament, literally on the instant approval of both Houses, with no consideration given to discussion or dissent. As an example of how to curb a nation's freedom without objection, 5 August 1914 stands testament to how democracy can be turned against itself in the name of "protecting the realm." An unprecedented wave of spy-mania was fanned by the introduction of the Aliens Restriction Act which had been pre-drafted by the Committee of Imperial Defence in readiness for war.[2]

Home Secretary, Reginald McKenna announced in the Commons that, "Within the last twenty-four hours no fewer than twenty-one spies, or suspected spies, have been arrested in various places all over the country, chiefly in important military or naval centers, some of them long known to the authorities to be spies."[3] Rumors and spy stories were taken very seriously, and served to remind the public how important it was to curb "freedoms." The government took *carte blanche* power to impose restrictions on those not born in Britain, though, as was explained in the House of Lords, the arrangements were fine-tuned to cause little inconvenience to alien friends, while securing effective and, if necessary, severe control over alien enemies.[4] Alien friends and alien enemies, it sounded like H.G. Wells' *War of the Worlds*.

This was followed three days later, by the Defence of the Realm Act, which, though originally a brief bill of around 400 words, was amended and extended six times over the course of the war to give the government powers close to those enjoyed by a military court martial in a dictatorship.[5] Ostensibly it purported to prevent spying or any action that put in jeopardy the safety of railways docks, and harbors.[6] It too was passed in minutes without discussion, and grew with each amendment to encompass a vast range of restrictions on freedoms.

At the same time, in the House of Lords, the vital interests of the Secret Elite were being presented by Lord Crewe, a man close to their inner circle, as if they were acts of noble benevolence. He announced that "during the last few days, the Government have been conferring at great length with the most important representatives of finance and commerce, including bankers, bill-brokers, the Stock Exchange, discount houses and with virtually every one of the great industries – textile, iron, docks and the rest (he could not for some reason bring himself to say armaments) ... in the interests of the country at large."[7] He added that it would be "business as usual," and that money would be forthcoming to meet the "ordinary needs and concerns of life." Lord Crewe failed to mention that such preparations had been fully discussed at secret sub-committee meetings of the Committee of Imperial Defence since early 1912.

The dislocation of trade, industry, commerce and finance brought about by war, any war, offers an opportunity to those privileged with sufficient forewarning to make indecent profits. The disruption of banking, insurance and the process of trading through bills of exchange and clearing houses could also be severe, and a panic in the stock market or rumor that a particular bank would suffer huge losses, made the early days of war particularly susceptible to a collapse in confidence. The Secret Elite had overwhelming control of the financial sector and had been working for years to ensure that their interests were safeguarded when war was declared. Detailed advice and recommendations had been gathered by the Committee of Imperial Defence in 1911-12 to ensure that the government was ready to protect the money markets in the City of London,[8] which was the inner-sanctum of British banking and housed the registered offices of many Secret Elite associates.

Banks were kept shut by the convenient mechanism of extending the August Bank Holiday in 1914, so that a run on their assets could be avoided. Lord Crewe urged the ordinary citizen to keep his head and avoid panic, promising that there was no reason why any person, rich or poor, should be alarmed by the "momentary difficulty" of war.[9] As far as protection of the nation was concerned, the banks came first. Lloyd George, once the champion of the people, proudly entitled one of the early chapters in his *War Memoirs*, "How We Saved The City."[10] (He really meant, "How I saved the City.") Ponder that fact for a moment. Yes, the government took great powers to itself in the name of the people, but it was the banks and the bankers who benefited from the earliest acts of Asquith's government at war.

Given that the business of the City was dependent on the smooth running of credit, the punctual payment of foreign debtors and bills of exchange, the sudden paralysis of the mechanisms for foreign exchange threatened a default which would have brought the banks to their knees. The solution, one very similar to the Federal Reserve System that was about to be adopted in America, was to announce a moratorium during which the banking, industrial and commercial interests persuaded the British government to "temporarily assume" the liability for over a hundred million pounds worth of bills. In other words, to save the banking system which feared a financial crash, banks were given special protection by acting as agents for the government. Profits were not interfered with, but the government would pick up the bill for any losses, and the ordinary citizen would have to pay for it through taxation.[11] Government provisions like old age pensions, insurance and other liabilities continued to be paid as before, but incredibly, housing rents were omitted from the moratorium.[12] The high-flying bankers and industrialists, the investors and the finance houses were instantly cushioned from loss while the working men and women, who would have to pay for this through taxation, had no automatic protection from future abuse. It was a charter for racketeers.

The Secret Elite knew better than any politician how to protect the wheels of commerce, and it was they, through the Bank of England and the Chancellor of the Exchequer, David Lloyd George, who ensured that the supply of "notes sufficient to meet the currency requirement" was met by introducing £1 notes and 10 shilling notes for the first time. A Currency and Bank Notes Act was followed by the suspension of the Bank Act to allow previous restrictions on banks to be "temporarily" removed.[13] The gold standard of old was effectively amended, and the power to print money was unleashed to the Banks.

With a craft that was even by that time a signature mark of the Secret Elite, the Conservative Lord Lansdowne congratulated Asquith's government on these decisions by acknowledging that the proposals, "have been the result of a careful consultation with the representatives of the financial, commercial, and industrial interests of this country. There can be no doubt that the Government did well ... to satisfy themselves that they were in possession of the best advice which they could procure from the highest authorities in this country, and that they could count upon the support of those authorities."[14]

And where did the best advice come from? Those who would benefit most. Every action sanctioned by the government that day reeked of the self-interest of the Secret Elite. They knew how wars depended on money, its supply and availability, and how important it was to be well prepared for reaping the profits of war.

Despite their every advantage, hoarding was another problem which was caused by the rich. Lloyd George spoke out against the hoarding of gold as early as 5 August, berating the "selfish motives of greed … or cowardice" which was, in his eyes, comparable to assisting the enemies of his native land. Barely three days later, Mr Walter Runciman, President of the Board of Trade, was forced to introduce a bill to stop the unreasonable hoarding of foodstuffs. Faced by evidence from many parts of the country that the greed of "better-to-do" people was causing great hardship to the poorer classes, the government was forced to take prompt action to limit such outrageous behavior. Runciman denounced the panic and greed of the richer community "who have really disgraced themselves by placing long queues of motor cars outside the stores and carrying off as much provisions as they could persuade stores to part with."[15] What an unhappy image. The hungry poor frightened by food-price rises would suffer shortages while the rich sent their servants to buy up as much produce as could be obtained. So much for the spirit of togetherness.

A further curious enigma, which was solved in those opening days of August 1914, was the vacant position of Secretary of State for War. Indeed the position had been covered by Asquith since the embarrassing resignation of John Seely on 30 March,[16] which meant that in the run-up to a World War, he served as both Prime Minister and head of the War Office. One consequence was that in all of the Cabinet discussions about Belgium, France and Russia, Germany and Austria-Hungary, and the growing possibility of war in Europe, the War Office had no individual voice. Why had Asquith failed to appoint a successor to John Seely – sacked after the Curragh incident in Ireland? Clearly his Secret Elite advisors had approved his decision, which on the face of things, appears to be quite strange. No other Cabinet post had been left unfilled during his period in office.

Asquith's problem was embarrassing in that there was no member of his Cabinet who could be trusted with the War Office. He confessed so in writing to his paramour, Venetia Stanley.[17] Everyone who knew that war had been ordained against Germany already held key Cabinet Posts. Churchill at the Admiralty could not be moved. Neither could Sir Edward Grey from the Foreign Office nor Lloyd George from the Treasury. Richard Haldane, Asquith's life-long personal friend and former incumbent, would have been a perfect choice, but Haldane had been unfairly tainted by the press as a pro-German, and his appointment would have caused disquiet.[18] Any in-comer would have had to be briefed about the preparations for war, the work of the Committee of Imperial Defence and the military "discussions" that had been agreed with France. His dilemma was that there was no politician in his government whom Asquith dared trust with such knowledge, and certainly no Liberal back-bencher.

On the positive side of this equation, a vacant post suggested that Britain was completely unready for war. If, in the aftermath of the near revolt of the army over its possible involvement in Ulster, it appeared that the War Office had been downgraded, then Germany would see it as positive proof that Britain was unlikely to go to war.

Although Asquith was tempted to defy public opinion and reappoint Richard Haldane, the Secret Elite inner-core was not. Whatever their previous difficulties over the ending of the Boer War,[19] Alfred Milner considered Field Marshal Herbert Kitchener as the only man with enough driving force for the job.[20] Kitchener should have been at his post in Egypt, but "happened" to be in England in July 1914 to be created Earl of Khartoum and Broome in the county of Kent by King George V.[21] This too was no chance happening. Asquith approved Kitchener's membership of the Committee of Imperial Defence some years before,[22] and Winston Churchill was regularly in contact with him. They discussed the plans that emerged from the CID, and in the week before the outbreak of war, Kitchener and Churchill lunched and dined together "two or three times."[23] Yet Asquith hesitated to break with tradition and appoint a Field Marshal to his Cabinet. Sir Henry Wilson reported the Prime Minister's hesitations to Alfred Milner and his Secret Elite colleagues who were dismayed that Asquith had failed to immediately dispatch the British Expeditionary Force to France. Fearing a weakness that might mortally wound their plans, they approached Kitchener directly and convinced him to go in person to 10 Downing Street and demand a definite appointment.[24]

A newspaper campaign in favor of Kitchener's appointment at the War Office gathered quick momentum. Horatio Bottomley's highly popular and patriotic one-penny weekly, *John Bull* magazine, first suggested that Lord Kitchener be given the post in April 1914, but little more was discussed in public until the morning of 3 August when the *Times* carried an article by Colonel Charles Repington[25] making the same suggestion.[26] On the following day the clamor for Kitchener's appointment was championed by a *Times* editorial which trumpeted public confidence in him and pressed the Prime Minister to make a formal appointment "at least for the term of the war."[27] *The Westminster Gazette* and Northcliffe's *Daily Express* insisted on Kitchener's appointment. Rumors that Asquith intended to return Haldane to the War Office were later denied by him with a caustic parliamentary swing at the critical press;

> The only person – and I should like this to be put on record – whom I ever thought of as my successor was Lord Kitchener, who

> happened, by a stroke of good fortune, to be at that moment in this country, on the point of returning to Egypt ... Lord Kitchener's appointment was received with universal acclamation, so much so indeed that it was represented as having been forced upon a reluctant Cabinet by the overwhelming pressure of an intelligent and prescient Press.[28]

Asquith's bold claims do not hold true in the light of later memoirs. Leopold Amery revealed that Milner had gone so far as to put Kitchener into a taxi to Downing Street to force Asquith into a decision. Kitchener was instructed to tell the Prime Minister that he would return immediately to Egypt unless he was given more important work.[29] As ever the Secret Elite got their man and Asquith was left to reconcile his colleagues to the highly unusual idea of a Field Marshal in a Liberal Cabinet. A War Council was held on 5 August. It comprised select politicians and the top men from the "Roberts' Academy."[30] Lord Roberts himself was present with Kitchener, Sir John French, Douglas Haig, Haldane, Grey, Asquith and, since it was essentially an extension of the Committee of Imperial Defence, Maurice Hankey.[31] Why Lord Roberts, who had retired ten years earlier, was present, has never been explained. Indeed, he was so intimately involved with the Secret Elite that the question was never even asked. This was the Secret Elite War Council, an exclusive cabal of men who had planned the outbreak of war, prepared the nation for war and proposed to run the war. Their task was to crush Germany.

Outside the privileged Downing Street cabal, many thought it would all be over by Christmas. Student volunteers at Cambridge in August, expected to be back for the restart of term-time on 7 October. Even serving officers who were stationed abroad in Gibraltar feared that they would miss the war because they were not part of the British Expeditionary Force.[32] But the assumed simplicity of that task withered before their eyes within two short weeks. The theory that the war would be a brief affair was shot down by Lord Kitchener. At his first cabinet meeting he dominated the room and spoke a truth some found difficult to believe. In staccato sentences – Kitchener was never an orator, nor a politician – he bluntly told the cabinet that the war would not be short, that it would not be resolved by sea-power and that millions of men would have to be involved in the conflict for several years.[33] The politicians sat in silence. Most were stunned by his unexpected prediction and we can only wonder at what point those outside the Secret Elite began to fear the consequences of their inability to stop the warmongers.

When he delivered his first speech in the House of Lords as Secretary of State for War, Kitchener quashed any notion of a quick-fix solution. His terms of service were the same as every man who stepped forward to the colors, for the duration of the war, or for three years, so that "if this disastrous war be prolonged," others "fresh and fully prepared" could step forward and "see this matter through."[34] Kitchener was the inspired choice for whom the empty cabinet chair had been allegedly reserved; but his inspiration had limitations and unforeseen consequences. Though he did not foresee trench warfare, Asquith, Grey and Balfour all talked of Kitchener having "flashes of genius" or "instinct."[35] Kitchener's prediction that the war would be prolonged has been recorded in history as an inspired insight, as though this was the first time such a possibility had been considered. How could it have been? Kitchener had attended the Committee of Imperial Defence, discussed war with Churchill on several occasions and had been specifically chosen by the Secret Elite. They well knew that it would take a prolonged war to destroy Germany. As far as the Secret Elite was concerned, he was decidedly on-message. Three years or more of warfare promised rich and extravagant profits, which, coming from the mouth of the national hero, spoken in cabinet, repeated in the House of Lords and carried solemnly in the press, meant that long-term investment in the instruments of war could begin at once, and would be unquestioned.

Though he had detractors, Kitchener's immediate impact on the British war effort was electric. His immense prestige with the public galvanized the nation in a manner that no other could have contemplated. Margot Asquith reputedly remarked that "if Kitchener was not a great man, he was at least a great poster," and there is absolutely no doubt that in those first weeks of war, it was Kitchener's imposing posture pointing directly at the man in the street which inspired hundreds of thousands of volunteers to join the army.[36]

But Kitchener was dictatorial by nature, distrusting of politicians and schooled in foreign wars far from Europe. He was dismissive of Haldane's Territorial Army which had been previously hailed as a great achievement, and his "bull-in-a-china shop manners and methods" at the War

Office caused Asquith concern. The first bursts of enthusiasm for war encouraged Kitchener. He was the great magnet, and his hypnotic presence on billboards across the nation won the day. In the first eighteen months of the war, 1,741,000 volunteers joined Kitchener's army, and a further 726,000 were added to the Territorials.[37] But an immediate problem soon became evident. How would the weapons of war, the rifles, the heavy guns and shells, the uniforms and the provisions for huge armies, be provided?

Asquith grasped the moment on 6 August by seeking Parliamentary approval for a grant of £100,000,000 "for all measures that may be taken for the security of the country, for the conduct of Naval and military operations, for assisting the food supply, for promoting the continuance of trade, industry and business communications ... and generally for all expenses arising out of the existence of a state of war."[38] He shamelessly intoned a litany of solemn obligations, of duty, honor, and the prospects of European civilization. His claim that "we are fighting to vindicate the principle that small nationalities are not to be crushed, in defiance of international good faith, by the arbitrary will of a strong and overmastering Power," sat ill at ease with Britain's conduct towards the Boer Republics, but did not stop Asquith from eloquently asserting that the principles for which Britain had entered the war were "vital to the civilization of the world."[39] Naturally, his appeal for unprecedented funding was approved by the "opposition" benches, even though the granting of £100,000,000 meant that the government had no reason to seek parliamentary approval for expenditure for months to come, and consequently was freed from democratic accountability.

The Secret Elite, having successfully ambushed the British nation into war, inflamed popular passion by portraying the German rulers as monstrous criminals. They had to take swift action before any other view challenged their stance. Within days of the declaration of war, the British people were confronted by a sophisticated propaganda machine which posed as the voice of reason, based in Wellington House, London. Some of the most famous British academics, novelists and journalists became willing cogs in that machine and, throughout the war, produced a morass of twisted logic, untruths and fictional tales of German atrocities and outrageous designs, which served one purpose; to justify the war both at home and abroad; especially America. As the disillusioned Liberal MP Arthur Ponsonby recorded:

> Facts must be distorted, relevant circumstances concealed, and a picture presented which by its crude coloring will persuade the ignorant people that their Government is blameless, their cause is righteous, and that the indisputable wickedness of the enemy has been proved beyond question. Lies are circulated with great rapidity and the unthinking mass accept them.[40]

Propaganda had many purposes. Its primary aim was to draw neutrals into the Empire's camp, soften their objections and allay their fears. It was a powerful morale builder especially when it successfully justified the reasons for war, and as we have already explained, reassured people that they were fighting a holy war in a noble crusade for civilization. Propaganda is also a vicious master, for it seeps into the unconscious and lasts beyond its intended life-time. Propaganda can become the accepted version of events when it is represented as truth even one hundred years on. Its subtlety may remain poisonous for generations.

The "Preliminary Memoir and Documents concerning the Outbreak of War," otherwise known as the "German White Book," was presented to the Reichstag on 3 August to prove to the German people that their nation was fighting a war of self-defense against Russian aggression,[41] and most Germans accepted that clear understanding. It was translated into English for the benefit of the American people. The diplomatic evidence produced by Germany in August 1914 had to be rebutted, for it revealed a very different story from that presented to the British Parliament by the Foreign Office on 6 August.[42] What really mattered was that neutral nations, among whom America was pre-eminent, believed that the entire blame should be fairly placed at Germany's door.

When questions were asked about the German "version," it was comparatively easy for the British press to discount the "White Book" as lies. Sir Edward Grey did not hesitate to snub the Liberal MP for Somerset North, Joseph King, when he asked that copies of German pamphlets be placed in the Commons Library so that members could assess their collective worth,[43] but obstructing MPs in Parliament was easier than stopping those German pamphlets being distributed in America. Neutral America. Essential America.

It is, however, entirely misleading to imagine that the Secret Elite's propaganda campaign began in late August or early September 1914. It had been raging for years. Fanned by Northcliffe's incessant anti-German rhetoric in articles and editorials in the *Times,* in ridiculous spy stories[44] and repeated diatribes against German "militarism," it was well underway long before the war began. The declaration of war drove propaganda with a higher, more sophisticated intensity above the level of local influence and opinion, to an all-out, no-holds-barred international crusade.

The Round Table visits to America from 1910 onwards, Milner's lecture tour of Canada, the Imperial Press Conference in 1909, all of the trans-Atlantic meetings of the select Pilgrims society in London and New York, laid the foundations for a hugely professional propaganda machine whose first act struck violently at Germany's capacity to compete equally in this critical arena; the war of words. Though the Anglo-American money-powers were increasingly integrated into the Secret Elite, and supported and enabled Britain and their allies to wage war, the American public showed little interest in becoming involved. They were the target audience for most of the outrageous propaganda that flooded across the Atlantic.

Churchill's Admiralty landed the first propaganda blow. In the early hours of 5 August, while most of the world had yet to learn that Britain was at war with Germany, a decision taken by the Committee of Imperial Defence in 1912 was quietly effected. The British Post Office Cable Steamer *Alert*[45] ripped out the first of five German trans-Atlantic cables which ran from Emden on the German-Dutch border through the English Channel and thence to Spain, Africa and the Americas.[46] It was both the first act of censorship and the first act of propaganda in the war.[47] It proved to be a devastating setback for direct communications between Berlin and New York. At that instant in time, on the opening day of the world war, when first impressions set the tone, the most effective instrument for German news and propaganda was closed down. That a cable steamer was immediately in place to dredge up and sever the most important channel for German communications, demonstrated how well-prepared the Secret Elite's Admiralty agents were.

Every advantage in creating that vital first impression lay with them. Indeed, naval censorship of radio messages began on Saturday 1 August, under the control of Rear Admiral Sir Douglas Brownrigg from his office at the Admiralty. His task as Chief Censor of Radio Telegraphy was to monitor all radio messages to ensure that only approved information was passed fit for transmission and to gain early intelligence from merchant shipping. He augmented his clerical staff by "borrowing" men from trusted munitions and ship-building companies, namely Cammell Laird and the Fairfield Shipbuilding Company. Thus, four days before war was declared the Admiralty was able to monitor intelligence from all over the world about the movement of both British merchant ships and "hostile'"vessels.[48] So much for the oft-repeated claim that Britain was taken by surprise and unprepared for war.

Censorship of news was reluctantly accepted by the British press. Initially, they surrendered their right to freedom of information and expression with barely a noticeable whimper. Again it was left to Churchill, who gloried in being the front-man, to make the announcement in Parliament on 7 August. He praised the editors and proprietors who had deliberately turned a blind eye to the discreet preparations for mobilization by the Admiralty and the War Office barely ten days earlier and announced the formation of an all-powerful press bureau under the command of the Secret Elite's legal colossus, F.E. Smith.[49] It's purpose, he claimed was to provide:

> ... a steady stream of trustworthy information supplied both by the War Office and the Admiralty ... which, without endangering military or naval interests, will serve to keep the country properly and

> truthfully informed from day to day of what can be told, and what is fair and reasonable; and thus, by providing as much truth as possible, exclude the growth of irresponsible rumors.[50]

Perhaps the clue lay in the words "as much truth as possible." Out of nowhere, a press bureau was created under the all-pervading arm of the Defence of the Realm Act, which allowed the government to impose very powerful social controls on the population. Freedom to access news about the war that had just begun, was removed. Journalists were not allowed to travel to, and report from, the front line in August 1914, but newspapers were promised absolute accuracy from the War Office and Admiralty liaison officers.

The truth is that the press sold its prestige and degraded its soul by surrendering to government propaganda, in abandoning its critical faculty throughout the war and in willingly taking part in the deliberate deception of the public. Northcliffe and his Secret Elite acolytes dominated the British press to an extent that no national newspaper stood against them. They have much to answer for, even a century later. They carried the slogans, their editors and leader-writers provided the invective, and they gloried in the malice they concocted against Germany. That those who survived the war were misled about its purpose and meanings is, on its own, deplorable, but that millions of fighting men died under the misconception that their cause would have some long-term impact on the future of civilization is surely one of the most poignant of all historic tragedies.[51]

To the upper echelons of the Secret Elite, control over the population, how and what it thought, and what it was allowed to know, was central to their philosophy. Freedom of thought was not acceptable. Dissent was deemed unpatriotic. Their disdain for democracy was raised to a new level. The masses would be told only what the masters allowed. But implementing these draconian measures proved difficult. Fredrick E. Smith, later Lord Birkenhead, was thrust into a new role in charge of the press bureau for which there was no precedent and no experienced staff.[52] He had no previous Cabinet experience, and belonged to the more right-wing school of the Secret Elite. He was closely associated with the Milner/Roberts/Northcliffe group, which favored conscription to the armed services rather than a volunteer force.

Denied first-hand accounts of what was happening in northern France and Belgium from experienced and reliable journalists, the information vacuum had been filled with patriotic nonsense. For approximately three weeks the public were force-fed a series of preposterous stories in which half of the German army had been killed and the others had taken flight. Every day reports boasted that the German soldiers were cowards, and that they ran away at the sight of the bayonet, or surrendered ignominiously. What made matters worse was that the public had been solemnly promised that they would be given the absolute truth through the Press Bureau. The accounts they read about German soldiers virtually inferred that fighting was mere child's play.[53] No-one anticipated a military disaster. The public had been fed a diet of cheerful nonsense that raised high expectations of imminent victory. The *Daily News* produced chatty reports from correspondents "at the front," with stories of "Kippers for Tea," "Toothache in the Trenches," and "The Lieutenant's Morning Tub,"[54] reassuringly encouraging and anodyne in nature, but completely at odds with what was happening in northern France and Belgium. Little wonder many of the earliest recruits harbored a fear that the war might be over before they got to France.

Suddenly the brutal nature of modern warfare punched middle-class Britain in the face over Sunday breakfast on 30 August. The truth was devastating. The first shots fired by the British Expeditionary Force (B.E.F.) in Belgium on 23 August near the city of Mons,[55] gave the B.E.F. a brief sense of superiority, but wave after incessant wave of German infantry bore down on the greatly outnumbered British, who were forced to retreat in the face of the onslaught. On 26 August the B.E.F. fought the famous delaying action of Le Cateau with wonderful courage against an enemy "double their numbers and double their artillery," but lost 8,000 men before continuing the retreat.[56]

Though they battled with consummate distinction, the B.E.F. was confronted by a well disciplined and armed host which in places was three times its size. The retreat, which lasted for thirteen days of unparalleled anxiety covered one hundred and sixty miles, over which the British regulars sustained huge losses. General Sir John French was convinced that the B.E.F., which he described as "shattered," would have to be withdrawn behind the River Seine.[57] He was overruled. Details of this serious reverse were not given to the press until the *Times* received a dispatch from one of its most reliable correspondents in the early evening of Saturday 29 August. It came as a bolt from the blue, and they instantly sought permission to print the story. Surprisingly, the press bureau replied within three hours, removed some minor details and gave permission to print. Confident of their source, and with F.E. Smith's approval, the *Times* carried the news of "a retreating and broken army… a terrible fight… broken bits of many regiments."[58] It was a disaster. The British people were aghast. Had the B.E.F. been destroyed? The effect was stunning. The moment was later caught perfectly by H.G. Wells in his novel *Mr. Britling Sees It Through* (published in 1916): "it was as if David had flung his pebble – and missed!" And it was a Northcliffe exclusive.

The following day the *Times* and the *Daily Mail* "suppressed the articles from their Monday editions."[59] The *Times* revised its position with a damage-limitation editorial to prevent widespread panic and defuse accusations of disloyalty made against it in Parliament. Instead of focusing on the retreat of a "broken army" they turned truth on its head by writing:

> The British Army has surpassed all the glories of its long history, and has won fresh and imperishable renown. It has inflicted terrible losses on the German army and has repeatedly held its own against tremendous odds. Though forced to retire by the overwhelming strength and persistence of the foe, it preserves an unbroken if battered line … [60]

It was an indefensible lie. The B.E.F. was by 30 August retreating south towards the River Marne leaving behind it a trail of broken wagons, tattered, abandoned equipment and rations and piles of supplies dumped by the roadside. Anything else that could ease the marchers' burden apart from their arms and ammunition was left behind.[61]

What the *Times* initially revealed had blown a gaping hole in effective censorship and forced Kitchener to claim that "for every man lost, two more have reached the front." The *Times* rejoiced to receive the assurance that British troops are still facing North with "undiminished strength and undaunted spirits." Another lie. Had the Censor got it so badly wrong in allowing the truth to surface or was there another motive? Outrage at Northcliffe and his flagship newspaper was short lived when it became apparent that the Censor himself had not only cleared the article, but included a comment which Northcliffe duly printed. Convinced that the serious losses sustained by the B.E.F had to be used to rally support for Kitchener's drive for volunteers, Smith approved the article and admitted in Parliament next day that following discussions with Kitchener, he had been asked by him to "obtain recruits for his army." The words he had added to the original dispatch were, "we want reinforcements, reinforcements and still more reinforcements."[62] Smith had briefly breeched his own draconian censorship and for the first time the fear of defeat was used to bolster recruitment.

Meanwhile, the first person to fall foul of the censorship law was a newsboy who was thrown into jail for "calling out false news" on the streets of Edinburgh, the Scottish Capital, on 30 August 1914.[63] False news is not a twenty-first century phenomenon.

From the very earliest days of the First World War, the Secret Elite in London set about fabricating history in order to conceal their guilt and heap responsibility on Germany. Their version is still presented as truth in the present day and regurgitated by generations of undergraduates for the simple reason that it was written by professors at Oxford University, reputedly the greatest academic institution in the world. However, Professor Carroll Quigley revealed that Alfred Milner and his faction had such power and control over Oxford that it was able to completely monopolize the writing and the teaching of the history of their own period.[64] It is a brave or foolhardy person indeed who questions the veracity of history as recorded by the eminent men and women within Oxford's ivory towers.

In the first week of August, as events on the continent were about to explode, many academics who valued their long-standing ties with Germany and German Universities recoiled at the prospect of war with a country which had contributed so much to European civilization. A letter signed by several Cambridge professors and other leading academics was printed in the *Times* on 1 August. It made the following appeal:

> We regard Germany as a nation leading the way in the Arts and Sciences and we have all learned and are learning from German scholars. War against her in the interest of Serbia and Russia will be a sin against civilization. If by reason of honourable obligations we be unhappily involved in a war, patriotism might still our mouths, but at this juncture we consider ourselves justified in protesting against being drawn into a struggle with a nation so near akin to our own, and with whom we have so much in common.[65]

The invasion of Belgium altered the parameters of the debate but there was a still a degree of "pro-German" sentiment which persisted even after the outbreak of hostilities, partly in Britain itself and even more so in neutral countries. The potential consequences alarmed the Secret Elite and their Oxford academic division which supported the war. They retaliated immediately.

The solution was a series of short pamphlets, explaining their version of both the long and short-term causes of the war. But who was to provide the appropriate material? Oxford historians, like their colleagues in other British universities, should have been ill- prepared for the role of semi-official apologists for the British declaration of war in August 1914.[66] Yet through the conquest of Oxford, the Secret Elite quickly mobilized their All Souls battalion which promptly rose to the challenge of justifying the war and vilifying Germany.

In total there were 87 specially commissioned *Oxford Pamphlets*[67] some of which enjoyed a profitable tenth reprint, with translations into French, Italian, Spanish, German, Danish and Swedish. The *Oxford Pamphlets* often contained authentic information to which the authors willingly gave a patriotic interpretation in the guise of an objective analysis. It was all about smoke and mirrors and muddied waters. Make the

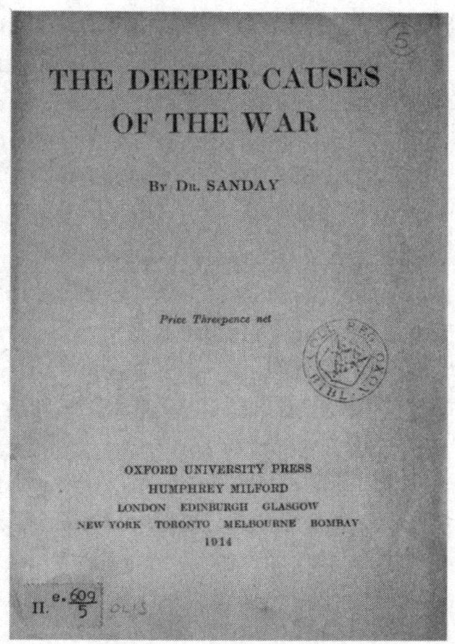

THE DEEPER CAUSES OF THE WAR

By Dr. SANDAY

Price Threepence net

OXFORD UNIVERSITY PRESS
HUMPHREY MILFORD
LONDON EDINBURGH GLASGOW
NEW YORK TORONTO MELBOURNE BOMBAY
1914

populace believe. Convince the alien neutral. These pamphlets stemmed from what was reckoned to be the best brains in Britain. It was the gospel according to the University of Oxford, and the pamphlets, published in London, Edinburgh, New York, Toronto, Melbourne and Bombay could be purchased individually or in sets – at affordable prices.[68]

Alfred Milner's Kindergarten group from his Boer War days waded into the mire of anti-German propaganda with a special war edition in September 1914 entitled, *Germany and the Prussian Spirit,* targeted at the middle- and upper-classes. It dealt in stereotypes, with biased historical background and crudely delineated images of an older idyllic Germany, now dominated by a new ruthless Prussian steel, whose "rapid glacier-torrent" had carried ice into the heart of the old Rhineland.[69] The irony of their message was completely ignored in the British press, and its hypocrisy plumbed new depths. According to the Round Table it was not the business of the state "to mold the general will of its citizens, but to represent it." The accusation levied against Germany was that its people followed absolutely the "paternalism of Prussian Nationalism."[70]

And this from the direct disciples of Ruskin and the heirs of Rhodes, who sought to mold the world into a British Race power-block dominated by English ruling class elites; the very men who privately despised democracy.[71] It is surely instructive that the Round Table's conclusion was that "the ultimate aim of German Imperialism is indeed nothing less than the destruction of British power, the humiliation of England and the partition of the British Empire."[72] In truth the Secret Elite's ultimate aim was the destruction of German power, the humiliation of Germany and the partition of their Empire. They were dressing the Prussians in their own obsessive megalomania for global control. Britain declared war on Germany. France and Russia mobilized first against Germany, but *truth* has long been acknowledged as the first casualty of war.[73]

The list of pamphleteers included; Spencer Wilkinson, First Chichele Professor of Military History at Oxford; W.G.S. Adam, Professor of Political Theory and Institutions at Oxford; C.R.L. Fletcher the conservative, imperialist historian, was in conjunction with Rudyard Kipling in 1911, the author of *A School History of England,* which libeled the Spanish as vindictive, the West Indians as lazy and vicious, and the Irish as spoilt and ungrateful;[74] Henry W.C. Davis, Regius Professor of Modern History, who was called to work in the War Trade Intelligence Department and the Ministry of Blockade, was later editor of the *Oxford Dictionary of National Biography*; C. Grant Robertson, the academic historian, went on to be Vice-Chancellor of Birmingham University. Every one of the above was a Fellow of All Soul's. The Secret Elite inner-core member, H.A.L. Fisher,[75] historian and tutor in modern history at Oxford, had his say on the *Value of Small States* with an academic reminder of the incalculable debt that civilization owed to the smaller nations. He was later promoted by Lloyd George to the post of President of the Board of Education. Gilbert Murray, Professor of Greek at Oxford wrote on the moral question, *How can war ever be right?* He found a suitably acceptable answer.

These myth-makers of history were not restricted to the university. The Oxford Pamphlets were supplemented by journalistic heavies such as Secret Elite member, Sir Valentine Chirol,[76] who from 1897-1912 was foreign editor for the *Times*. His two pamphlets, *Serbia and the Serbs* and *Germany and the Fear of Russia* were basically an accusation that Germany encouraged Austria in order to bring about war. This was typical of the lie that was repeated so often that it became "fact," the more so because it had the stamp of Oxford University's approval. Another powerful figure, Rear-Admiral Sir James Thursfield, a naval historian and journalist, a man close to Lord Fisher, lectured regularly at the Roberts Academy at Camberley, and was the first editor of the *Times Literary Supplement*. His pamphlet, the *Navy and the War* boasted of the silent pressure maintained on Germany by the Fleet, and warned of the dangers of pacifism. And the pro-British American lawyer, James M. Beck, a vehemently anti-German Republican politician, contributed a valuable pamphlet, *The Double Alliance versus the Triple Entente*, whose partisan, pro-British judgment on the conflicting alliances was both welcomed and praised. It amounted to a complete endorsement of Britain's actions.

No-one should underestimate the importance of this quasi-intellectual onslaught. Letters were sent to the Oxford University Press from "war lecturers" asking for more detailed material to help them with their talks. These fatuous pamphlets were seen as the new gospels, the "evidence" that the British Empire was fully justified in taking up arms against Germany. Their capacity to influence opinion in neutral countries, especially the United States, was of even greater importance.

Great care was taken to avoid the impression that the Oxford Pamphlets were part of the propaganda campaign, which is why they were mainly distributed and sold "in the ordinary way of trade."[77] Oxford University Press usually charged between 1 penny and 3 pence per pamphlet and a hardback series could be purchased for one shilling in 1915. Naturally the pamphlets were hailed for their authenticity and the *Saturday*

Review wrote that "these little books are easily the best books of the war; accurate, quietly written, full of knowledge and unspoiled by vainglory or bitterness."[78] Well, little changes. Oxford histories still rely on positive reviews from Oxford alumni.

We should remember Professor Quigley's admonition that no country that values its safety should allow a small secret cabal, by that we mean the Secret Elite, to exercise complete control over the publication of documents, over the avenues of information that create public opinion and then monopolize the writing and teaching of history.[79] This was precisely what was happening. Virtually every British contributor to the *Oxford Pamphlets* was in some way linked directly or indirectly to the Secret Elite and their grand design. The "truth" was defined by them and for them.

In September 1914 the British Foreign Office authorized a War Propaganda Bureau under Charles Masterman at that point, chancellor of the Duchy of Lancaster, a minor position in Asquith's government. Asquith's prime objective appears to have been to keep his paramour, Venetia Stanley fully informed of events, often secret events, while keeping the British public in dutiful ignorance. After the Cabinet meeting was informed that the War Propaganda Bureau would be set up in secret, he wrote on 5 September to his beloved: "The papers I see are crying out (not without reason) for news, of which they have had precious little all this week. I am just going to tell Winston to repeat his feat of last Sunday, and to dish up for them with all his best journalistic condiments the military history of the week. K (Kitchener) is absolutely no use for this kind of thing and has an undisguised contempt for the 'public' in all its moods and manifestations."[80]

So much for the steady stream of trustworthy information which Asquith's government had promised. How many of the young men who answered Kitchener's call would have done so had they known the contempt he bore for the general public?

In advance of the announcement of his appointment, Masterman held two conferences on 2 September and 7 September 1914 to organize and co-ordinate the official propaganda directed at foreign opinion. The first was with prominent literary figures, the second with journalists and publicists. Masterman took over possession of the Buckingham Gate premises occupied by the National Insurance Commission, better known as Wellington House. Work was conducted in absolute secrecy. Masterman was convinced that his targeted opinion leaders would be unwilling to commit themselves wholeheartedly if they knew the source of their information.[81] Even members of the Cabinet did not know about his department.

The most famous literary figures of the day signed up to what amounted to the paid publication of their novels and short stories. It was little more than a free lunch for the well-fed. Distinguished writers like H.G. Wells, Arthur Conan Doyle, G.K. Chesterton, Sir Edward Cook and Hilaire Belloc were amongst the literati who penned articles, tales and stories specifically aimed at spreading British propaganda, especially in America. Naval Intelligence, for the two were often kept apart, called on the additional services of Rudyard Kipling, Joseph Conrad and Alfred Noyes.[82] The master-craftsman of this literary propaganda was none other than Alfred Milner's private secretary from the Kindergarten years in South Africa, John Buchan. His career in propaganda and military intelligence blossomed magnificently from 1916 onwards when, as Milner's trusted appointee, John Buchan, a member of the Secret Elite[83] linked them to the heart of the British intelligence community.[84] More on this later.

Masterman's task was neither straightforward nor easy. Conflicting views between allies, and military criticism of and from French High Command was somewhat fraught at times. It all had to be handled with great care and the whole business of propaganda moved swiftly into the new media of pictures, photographs, film and newsreels. Propaganda grew from a cottage industry into an international business in its own right. Its aims remained intact; promote the great cause of the allies and damn the evil actions or intentions of the enemy. Its reach expanded into new quarters of the globe. By 1916, Masterman had to open a department of Muslim affairs, such was the growing importance of India, Persia, Egypt, Turkey and the Middle East.[85]

Too many organizations, departments, sometimes even individuals became involved in propaganda, to the extent that no-one seemed to have clear control of what had grown into a monstrous beast. Duplication of effort and inter-departmental jealousies became debilitating. Effective propaganda required continuity, creativity and speed of action.[86] This was what the Secret Elite wanted. Lord Robert Cecil, as parliamentary under-secretary at the Foreign Office, and a member of the Secret Elite,[87] represented them at a crucial inter-departmental conference on 26 January held at the Home Office. Matters degenerated into a bitter row between the war and Foreign Offices, but it was Cecil who triumphed. The Foreign Office assumed the lead role in a wholesale reorganization of propaganda which saw all the other departments bend the knee and appoint a liaison officer to supply the Foreign Office with relevant information. But Cecil's victory was temporary, for the Foreign Office proved inflexible in a theatre of war where flexibility and creativity were invaluable pre-requisites.

The Central Committee for National Patriotic Organizations was yet another organ of the mass investment in propaganda. The two men responsible for this were directly linked to the Secret Elite. George W. Prothero was closely associated with the Cecil family and Alfred Milner[88] while Henry Cust was a protégé of William Waldorf Astor, a member of the inner-circle of the Secret Elite.[89] He had edited the *Pall Mall Gazette* and was associated with Arthur Balfour, George Curzon, Margot Asquith and Alfred Lyttelton, often referred to as "The Souls." With Prime Minister Asquith as their honorary president, they organized lectures, patriotic clubs, rallies in the major cities and in country towns to counteract any opposition to the war. In addition they targeted individuals from neutral countries, using a tactic of direct personal approach to enlist sympathy and support for the war. Distinguished men and women agreed to play their part in this with the result that foreign acquaintances, colleagues, business associates and fellow workers across the globe were sent propaganda material directly to their homes and work-places. More than 250,000 books, pamphlets and other publications were sent abroad through this agency during the war.[90] By 1916, they had used 250 speakers to conduct 15,000 meetings. Students from neutral countries and British nationals abroad were exploited in a similar manner.[91] They flooded the libraries in industrial districts with 900,000 leaflets and distributed a similar number to schools. Children too were also a frequent target for Masterman's people at Wellington House.92 Propaganda is no respecter of age.

Secrecy was demanded from all who served in Wellington House. In the first two years of the war some of the civil servants initially transferred from their posts at the national insurance commission to propaganda work, left. They were replaced at the higher levels with Milner's men, James Headlam-Morley and Arnold J. Toynbee, both members of the Secret Elite,[93] and a new Balliol man, Lewis Namier. Wellington House was well organized in its international set-up with sections based on a geographic or linguistic basis like Scandinavia, Italy and Switzerland. Masterman worked in tandem with the Belgian legation on propaganda, and his office generally acted as the ministry of propaganda for Belgium in the early months of the war.[94] The foreign press was studied in detail on a daily basis, and the department kept files on public opinion in all neutral countries. Specific "stories," most of which was concocted nonsense, were directed to the appropriate country to maximize impact. The greatest priority was always the United States[95] and it continued to be so at every level, until America joined the war.

Americans were welcomed with open arms. Press correspondents and distinguished visitors were courted shamelessly to express support for Asquith's government or changes in government policy. Special correspondents were sent to America to glean first hand information about public opinion in the United States, and, when necessary, counter opposition to British policy. They liked to keep it personal, person to person, using banking, business, academic, journalistic and even family ties to bolster support for Britain and the Allies. Few were better connected through all of the above-mentioned agencies, than the Secret Elite.

The Anglo-American bond proved to be an unassailable asset to the British and Allied cause, and did much to help spread the propaganda. In Washington, the German military attaché, Franz von Papen claimed that a conference was held in the New York offices of J.P. Morgan as early as 23 August 1914 to seek ways to promote and endorse British propaganda in America. Von Papen wrote that they adopted a policy to color the American press and duly appointed English editorial writers on forty U.S. newspapers.[96] Naturally Morgan and his powerful companies supported the allies. He was after all closely associated with the Rothschilds and the Secret Elite, and had been chosen as their sole nominated representative for buying munitions and organizing loans for Britain, from which he was making a fortune.

Sir Gilbert Parker, head of the American department at Wellington House,[97] explained how the British government went about its business in America to promote the Allied cause. Three-hundred and sixty newspapers in the smaller states were supplied with an English newspaper which gave them a weekly review of the war from the British and French perspective. Important Americans were encouraged, he did not say how, to write articles for the local press, and eminent professional Americans received personal correspondence from their British counterparts, "beginning with university and college professors."[98] His mailing list contained the names of over 260,000 prominent Americans.

The French historian and politician, Gabriel Hanotaux wrote an illustrated history of the war of 1914 in which he interviewed Robert Bacon, a former US Ambassador to France and ex-Morgan partner. Bacon stated categorically:

> In America ... there are 50,000 people who understand the necessity of the United States entering the war immediately on your side. But there are 100,000,000 Americans who have not even thought of it. Our task is to see that the figures are reversed and that the 50,000 become the 100,000,000. We will accomplish this.[99]

It proved to be no idle boast. Newsreel propaganda in cinemas became increasingly common as the war progressed. Every possible method was used to connect the man in the street; cinema, pamphlets, advertising, photographs, illustrated news, novels and interviews. The mass media had become a weapon of war,[100] and America was its prime target.

Of the milestones in the propaganda war aimed at the heart of America, the most devastating was the Bryce Report, the *Report of the Committee on Alleged German Outrages*[101] which examined the conduct of German troops in Belgium, the breaches in the rules of war, and the inhumanity perpetrated against the civilian population. Lurid stories of German atrocities came first-hand from the many Belgian refugees who fled to Britain in August and September 1914 and filled newspapers of every political hue. None howled louder than the Northcliffe stable. On 12 and 17 August the *Daily Mail* railed against "German Brutality," including the murder of five civilians corroborated by sworn statements from "witnesses." Coming as it did when news from the front was scarce, such damning stories caught the public imagination and set it on fire. On 21 August, Hamilton Fyfe, a Northcliffe journalist who had served on the *Times,* wrote of "sins against civilization."[102] A sensational list of accusations filled the columns of the *Times* and the *Daily Mail* including the maiming of women and children, the bayoneting of wounded soldiers, women with their breasts cut off, nuns raped, and with sickening surety on 18 September a photograph was published purporting to be that of an innocent Belgian father holding the charred stub of his daughter's foot.[103] Backed by the evidence of civilian Belgian refugees and of British servicemen, these stories were spread across the world and did enormous damage to the German cause. Members of Parliament called for an official inquiry and a committee of the most eminent men in the realm was appointed on 15 December 1914 by Prime Minister Asquith.

Belgian resistance to the German invasion in August 1914 was stubborn and brave. The Garde Civique (Civilian police) was certainly deployed in Louvain; innocent people lost their lives.[104] The *Daily Mail* correspondent, A.T. Dawe followed the German army in its drive from Aix-la-Chapelle to Brussels and reported that some of the civil population, urged on by the Mayor and Belgian officials, rained machine gun bullets on the German trains as they approached the station, and the church of St. Pierre, which overlooked the railway, was turned into a veritable fortress.[105] Sharp-shooters fired on German infantry from upper-floor windows and the street by street defense of towns and villages seriously threatened the invasion timetable. Reprisals followed, of that there was no question, but British newspapers outdid each other in reporting these as gross atrocities with mutilated and murdered children, ravished innocent women, executed priests and nuns, and indiscriminate heinous crimes against nature itself.

Let us be absolutely clear. There were atrocities. The burning of Louvain, Andenne and Dinant was brutal. When they invaded Belgium in 1914, the German high command expected to sweep through the country with very little opposition. The German army was many times larger and stronger than the Belgian army, and the Germans thought that any resistance by Belgium would be futile. The strength of Belgian resistance came as a surprise, and disrupted the German timetable for their advance into France.[106] This in turn led to exaggerated suspicions among German commanders of Belgian civilian resistance. The Germans responded harshly to all perceived acts of resistance. By the time the German army marched through Brussels on 20 August, its progress had been disgraced by a savage and at times indiscriminate severity against the civil population. In several villages and towns, hundreds of civilians had been executed. Many buildings were put to the torch. Priests thought guilty of encouraging the resistance were killed. The essential German objective was to ensure that they did not have to leave a strong force to guard their lines of communication or an exposed rear by a policy of Schrecklichkeit,[107] literally, terror. The atrocities were shocking and cannot be excused, but the manner in which they were grossly exaggerated beyond credibility stands testament to the power of propaganda.

The chairman of Prime Minister Asquith's official inquiry, Viscount James Bryce, had from 1907-13 been Britain's most popular ambassador to the United States, a personal friend of President Wilson, twice the principle guest of the Pilgrims of America and from 1915-17, President of the British branch of the Pilgrims. He was assisted by three eminent lawyers and H.A.L. Fisher, the historian and member of the inner-circle of the Secret Elite,[108] who at that point was Vice-chancellor of the University of Sheffield. The final member, Harold Cox was editor of the *Edinburgh Review* and proved somewhat difficult to control. He was not one of the "group."

The Committee was specifically asked "to consider and advise on the evidence collected ... as to outrages alleged to have been committed by German troops during the present war" and to prepare a report for the government on the conclusions they drew from the evidence.[109] The impression given was that this illustrious committee of very experienced and trustworthy gentlemen had examined 1,200 witnesses from whose evidence around 500 statements had been included in the report along with extracts from thirty-seven diaries taken from dead German soldiers and eye-witness reports from British soldiers. This was simply not the case. Witnesses spoke to no member of the Commission.

The process was as follows. In September 1914 the Prime Minister requested that the Home Secretary and the Attorney General collect evidence of accusations of inhumanity and outrage carried out by German troops in Belgium. Most of the accusations came from Belgian witnesses, some military, but most civilians from the towns and villages through which the German army had advanced towards the French border. More than 1,200 depositions had been taken, not by, but under the supervision of the Director of Public Prosecution. The work involved "a good many examiners" who had some legal knowledge but no authority to administer an oath. This had been going on for "three or four months" before the committee was appointed.[110] The task they were given was to sift through thousands of pages of testimony, given freely, but not under oath, and decide what should or should not be included in a final report. While they were able to speak with and "interrogate" the "lawyers" who took down evidence from the witnesses,[111] they were not allowed contact with any witnesses themselves.

Harold Cox was particularly displeased with the arrangement. He wanted to re-examine some of the witnesses and forced Bryce to allow the committee to question the legal teams involved in taking the depositions. Indeed, without his intervention, the preface to the report would not have mentioned the fact that they had not spoken to a single witness in person. Almost every account that was put on record had already appeared in the national newspapers but by being included in the final report, they gained authenticity. The esteemed gentlemen had read the "evidence" and confirmed its veracity. The quasi-legal nature of the Committee, the trappings of procedure and due process, the presence of an eminent Judge, Sir Frederick Pollock, the wording which talked of corroboration of evidence, lawyers, cross-examination, testimony, the Courts of England, the British Overseas Dominions and the United States, witnesses and conviction[112] allowed the report to assume the status of a profound judgment from the High Court of Judiciary. It was nothing of the sort.

The conclusion read as the charge sheet of ultimate villainy. It was designed to. The decision of the pseudo-court to which Germany had no appeal, was that in many parts of Belgium deliberate and systematically organized massacres of the civil population, accompanied by many isolated murders and other outrages had taken place. That in the conduct of the war innocent civilians, both men and women, were slaughtered in large numbers, women violated, and children murdered. Looting and the wanton destruction of property were deemed to have been ordered by the officers of the German Army and they determined that elaborate provisions had been made for the systematic burning and destruction of towns and villages at the very outbreak of the war.

They pronounced that this destruction had no military purpose. They asserted that the international rules of war were frequently broken, particularly by the use of civilians, including woman and children, as a shield for advancing forces exposed to the fire, to a less degree by killing the wounded and prisoners, and in the frequent abuse of the Red Cross and the White Flag. Every charge was "proven" guilty. In the penultimate paragraph the committee declared that all the charges were "fully established by the evidence."[113] The only trapping that was missing from this judicial pantomime was the black cap. And the world believed, though not one word was actually heard from the witnesses.

The Bryce Report was a propaganda coup of the highest order. It was translated into 30 languages and dispersed across the globe by every British propaganda service. In the United States, the *New York Times* of 13 May 1915 ran Bryce's "verdict" on three full pages, over twenty-four columns, with pictures and unequivocal headlines. A measure of their clear success may be derived from the opening passage which began by stating that: "Proofs of the atrocities by the German armies in Belgium – proofs collected by men trained in the law and presented with unemotional directness after a careful inquiry are presented in the report ... headed by Viscount Bryce, the famous historian, formerly British Ambassador at Washington."[114] He was hardly famous as a historian, but certainly very popular in the United States; a shrewd choice indeed by the Secret Elite..

With headlines that screamed "German Atrocities Are Proved" and "Premeditated Slaughter in Belgium," "Young and Old Mutilated," "Women Attacked, Children Brutally Slain, Arson and Pillage Systematic," "Countenanced by Officers," "Wanton Firing of Red Cross and White Flag," "Prisoners and Wounded Shot," "Civilians Used as Shields," the *New York Times* could hardly have bettered itself in supporting the Allied cause.

However, the American Irvin Cobb, in Belgium in 1914 as a correspondent for the *Saturday Evening Post,* wrote:

> I had been able to find in Belgium no direct proof of the mutilations, the torturing and other barbarities which were charged against the Germans by the Belgians ... fully a dozen seasoned journalists, both English and American, have agreed with me, saying that their experiences in this regard had been the same as mine.[115]

Another American, lawyer Clarence Darrow, was similarly skeptical. In 1915 he visited France but was unable find a single eyewitness who could confirm even one of the Bryce stories. Increasingly unconvinced of the allegations that had apparently been substantiated by Bryce, Darrow announced he would pay $1,000 to anyone who could produce a Belgian or French boy whose hands had been amputated by a German soldier. He found none.[116]

War, any war, harbors atrocity, it goes with the territory. It must never be excused, but it happens. Far from Belgium the massive Russian army was invading East Prussia. The civil population in the region offered no resistance, but of the 2 million plus inhabitants, more than 866,000 were driven from their homes. Some 34,000 buildings were burned to the ground, 1,620 civilians murdered, and over 12,000 were sent to Russia as prisoners.[117] None of these atrocities were ever reported in the British or American press. Who cared, they were mostly Germans after all.

The original basis for the atrocity stories from Belgium came in the first weeks of the war between 4 August and the start of September when raw German conscripts were met head-on by patriotic Belgians, military and civilian. Bryce recognized that "the invaders appear to have proceeded upon the theory that any chance shot coming from an unexpected place was fired by civilians."[118] No-one challenged that hostages were taken, buildings destroyed and groups of ordinary citizens executed.[119]

Nor can it be denied that a number of priests and teachers were executed or deported. Joseph, Cardinal Mercier, Archbishop of Malines, the most senior and powerful of the Belgian Catholic hierarchy quickly emerged as the national figurehead for the embattled population in occupied Belgium. He used his many contacts within the world-wide College of Cardinals to pressurize the German governor von Bissing to have his priests released from internment. Mercier wrote openly of the "massacre of 140 victims at Aershot"[120] and stated in a letter to his German counterpart, Cardinal Felix von Hartmann of Cologne, dated 28 December 1914, that he "was personally acquainted with hundreds who have been victims ... and am in possession of details that would make any fair minded man shudder."[121] However, when he in turn was asked by the German governor to produce evidence concerning the alleged outrages committed against nuns, Mercier refused on the grounds that it would be too upsetting for nuns to be questioned, and much of what he had heard was given to him in due confidence. Governor von Bissing concluded, "it is enough to state now that neither your Eminence nor the other Bishops can provide any proof based on facts."[122] But the stories of the rape of Catholic Belgium ran and ran.

Propaganda is so much more potent when laced with some truth. The rumors, opinions, exaggerated accounts and barrack-room stories were dignified by Viscount Bryce and his team as a true record. If we could refer back to the "evidence" they used then perhaps the skeptic might be convinced. Unfortunately the names and addresses of all of the witnesses whose depositions were so carefully catalogued by lawyers have disappeared, as have the depositions. We don't know how objective the questioning was or how many statements were the product of leading questions. We do know now that a great quantity of evidence was based on second- or third-hand information. In H.A.L. Fisher's biography of Viscount Bryce, the Secret Elite historian claimed that the main body of the report had not been disproved, and each story should be considered true until proven false. Was the burden of proof against the German soldiers not the responsibility of Bryce and his committee? We will never know. Although they were originally placed in the vaults of the Home Office for safe-keeping, all of the proceedings of the inquiry were subsequently destroyed. But the damage done to the reputation of the German army, the subsequent increases in enlistment in Britain and its worth in terms of American public opinion was priceless.

Though rarely ever mentioned, there was arguably a more despicable level of propaganda hurled at the masses from the pulpits of justification. If the Church of England was "the Conservative Party at prayer."[123] the most senior prelates and professors of divinity who headed that Church represented the Secret Elite in conclave. Promoted and championed by inner-circle powerbrokers like the Earl of Roseberry, the men who in August 1914 hailed the "Holy and Righteous War"[124] owed their allegiance to God, All Souls, Oxford and the Secret Elite, though not necessarily in that order. They chose their role to justify the war, to explain the meaning of the war, to maintain morale on the home front and to remind the public that the primary obligation of young men was to enlist.[125] In other words, it was Germany's fault, Britain had to save civilization, the war had to be seen through no matter the sacrifice and it was every man's duty to serve.

Before examining the role of the Church of England from 1914 onwards, we should understand that its political power rested both with a select section of the chosen hierarchy and with the Prime Minister and senior members of the House of Lords who appointed them. Control of the Church had once rested with the Crown but had been slowly transferred to Parliament between the fifteenth and seventeenth century. The Prime Minister appointed bishops, though they had to be approved by a "cathedral chapter" or council of high church officials,[126] a strange anachronism given that a Presbyterian such as Campbell-Bannerman, or the Welsh non-conformist, Lloyd George, were involved in the process of election.

The Church of England was the religious preserve of the middle and upper classes, with its ministry drawn from university graduates, traditionally from Cambridge and Oxford.[127] In the very class-conscious world of pre-war Britain, it aimed to place an educated gentleman in every parish church across the kingdom[128] which aligned well with John Ruskin's philosophy of a ruling class oligarchy, but alienated many working class Christians. Indeed, the vast majority of Anglican churchmen were openly hostile to trades union and labor movements and they feared the social unrest which was assumed to accompany them.

On the eve of what might have been the first general strike in England, William Randolph Inge, the Dean of St. Paul's, summed up the alarm felt by his associates when he "denounced the unions as criminal combinations whose leaders deserved to be executed as rebels against society."[129] This was the same Dean Inge who profited from the war while extolling it as God's work. His lucrative shareholding in Vickers Ltd. was not unusual. A roll-call of Bishops who invested in armaments firms like Vickers Ltd., Armstrong-Whitworth Ltd. John Brown and Co., included their Lordships of Adelaide, Chester, Hexham, Newcastle and Newport. [130]

There can be no question about the Secret Elite pedigree of the most important Anglican clerics in August 1914.[131] Cosmo Gordon Lang was recruited from All Souls by Lord Rosebery, and enjoyed a meteoric rise through the ranks of the church. Lang became the suffragan (assistant) Bishop of Stepney from which comparatively lowly post he shot to the Archbishopric of York in 1908. At the invitation of Prime Minister Herbert Asquith, it took Lang a mere 18 years to rise to the second most esteemed office in the Anglican Church. He decreed that the war was "righteous"[132] and was supported in this by all of his fellow Bishops. Another influential cleric, the Dean of Durham, Henley Henson was similarly an All Souls man. His *War Times Sermons*, published in 1915, extolled the Allied cause and by 1918 he was controversially installed as the Bishop of Durham and therefore became a member of the House of Lords.

When war was declared the Oxford Dons amassed an extensive 87-pamphlet assault on every aspect of learned justification to "prove" German guilt. This was met by a heartfelt cry from German theologians to American newspapers that a systematic network of lies emanated from Britain to blame Germany for the war to the extent that they denied the right of Germans to invoke the assistance of God. Ah, there we have it; God was an Englishman. The pamphlet, "To Christian Scholars of Europe and America; A Reply from Oxford to German Address to Evangelical Christians by Oxford Theologians" published on 9 September 1914, was a perfect example of the extent of Secret Elite influence. They immediately enlisted 14 theologians at Oxford, including five professors of divinity, to write the pamphlet dismissing the claims from German theologians as nonsense. The Oxford "Divines" condescendingly admonished the Germans for failing to study the events that led up to the war and concluded, "Will not the Christian scholars of other lands share our conviction that the contest in which our country has engaged is a contest on behalf of the supreme interests of Christian civilization."[133] Consider the arrogance and self-glorification of this argument. Oxford Professors claimed that Germany had no right to ask God's blessing on the war, that German academics had failed to study the true causes of the war or the political "utterances" of their own countrymen, while stating that Britain and her Empire were fighting for the "supreme interests of Christian civilization." The supreme interests for which British soldiers were sacrificed were those of the bankers, financiers, armaments producers, politicians and charlatans who comprised the Secret Elite.

A commonly repeated theme among Anglican leaders was exemplified in a sermon given by Cosmo Lang in October 1914. Archbishop Lang alluded to the German philosopher Nietzsche and the common British interpretation of his writings to conclude that "might makes right." He insisted "there could be no peace until this German spirit had been crushed" and thus paradoxically appealed to "friends of peace… to be supporters of our war."[134] Note the language. German spirit had to be crushed; not beaten, crushed. It is interesting to note that those who took a stance against the war were few in number and drawn from "an important cluster of socialists, Liberals [and] philosophical pacifists," while there was virtually a total lack of resistance to the war by any vicar of the Church of England.[135] Indeed not. Time and again church leaders denied the very basis of Christian teaching, discarded the tenet of man's conscience and denied that objection to the war was an acceptable stance for any Christian. They followed the Bishop of Oxford's blunt message: "I do not hold the views of those who are seeking exemption to military service on the grounds of conscientious objection to war under any circumstances."[136] Amen.

In a spirit of reconciliation and humility there is great cause for the Church of England to reflect on its behavior during the war, and apologize. Not since Jesus was betrayed in Gethsemane has Christianity been so willfully sold out.

In addressing the Anglican Bishops and senior clergy at Church House, Westminster in February 1915, the Archbishop of Canterbury stated the old justification that he did not "entertain any doubt that our nation could not, without sacrificing principles of honor and justice more dear than life itself, have stood aside and looked idly on the present world conflict."[137] He was repeating, almost word for word, Sir Edward Grey's statement of 3 August 1914. The concept of a Christian duty to fight was virtually universal among the Anglican clergy. Few if any said otherwise from within the ranks of the Church of England. Given such unanimous support for the war by even the most liberal of Anglicans, it is not surprising that the pulpit became an adjunct for the recruiting office. The Archbishop went so far as to state that it was their sacred privilege to bid men "to respond ungrudgingly to their country's call."[138]

Ponder these words for a moment. Young men, sitting in quiet country churches or great Gothic cathedrals were exhorted to go to war, to do their duty, to accept the sacrifices. Their emotions were constantly battered by sermons drawn from the Old Testament that extolled the wrath of an avenging God. How did they feel when the pastoral shepherd dropped the mantle of Christ the Peacemaker and became a bitter recruiting sergeant? Priests and Pastors would often stress duty and equate fighting for Britain and the Empire with fighting for Christ.[139] Others railed against cowardice. The master of St. Catherine's College, Cambridge said of those who refused to volunteer:

> It is a pity that we cannot brand that sort of man "Made in fear of Germany." Would to God we had known when they were born that they would eat our bread and grow and live amongst us, trusted and approved, and yet cowards. We need not have prayed and worked for them.[140]

Can you imagine hearing your own brother or son described in such outrageous terms? With what sense of self worth would a young man be left, who internalized these damning words? It was moral blackmail of a nefarious kind. But the most outrageous proponent of the "virtuous war," the prelate who stepped well over the line of Christian decency, was the Bishop of London, Arthur Winnington-Ingram. He was an Oxford man who worked hard for the poor in the East End of London and was consequently popular with the people of Bethnal Green. With the blessing of Lord Salisbury in 1901, Winnington-Ingram was appointed to the Bishopric of London and enthroned at St Paul's Cathedral where he remained for thirty-eight years.[141] He was one of the most outspoken and patriotic advocates of the war, beloved by the War Office and the Admiralty, who feted him on his visits to front line troops and naval installations.

Bishop Winnington-Ingram on steps of St Pauls

Winnington-Ingram claimed to have added ten thousand men to the armed services with his sermons and other recruiting crusades. He made no estimate of how many died or were maimed needlessly because of his work for God and country. As Bishop of London, he never shrank from the enthusiastic endorsement of the righteousness of the war and the British cause and the important role the Church of England must play in the whole affair. His favorite text was; "better to die than see England a German province." In return, he was given the second highest award for chivalry for his war service by King George V who appointed him Knight Commander of the Victorian Order. [142] Winnington-Ingram's pronouncements veered from the obnoxious to the banal. Speaking at a "Rally without Shame" at Westminster Church House in February 1915, he said that the Church had to foster and increase the fortitude of the nation; to comfort the mourners and inculcate a happier and brighter view of death.[143] What did that involve? Cheer up, your only son is dead? Don't get too upset; it was all in a good cause? His concept of comforting the mourners did not extend to the enemy. It was an odd kind of Christianity. Winnington-Ingram will long be remembered for words of a very different kind. After a year of war, the Bishop called for the men of England to:

> … band in a great crusade – we cannot deny it – to kill Germans. To kill them, not for the sake of killing, but to save the world; to kill the good as well as the bad; to kill the young men as well as the old, to kill those who have showed kindness to our wounded as well as those fiends who crucified the Canadian sergeant, who superin-

tended the Armenian massacres, who sank the Lusitania ... and to kill them lest the civilization of the world should itself be killed.[144]

Apologists have claimed that these words have been taken out of context, but it is difficult to imagine any context at all in which they could comfortably sit. Dress these words any way you can but they will still reflect a blood-thirsty crusade against Germany. Winnington-Ingram went further by adding, "as I have said a thousand times, I look upon it as a war for purity, I look upon everyone who dies in it as a martyr."[145] British, of course; one can only assume that Germans went to Hell. This is a theme he returned to time and again. He wrote in his sermons, "this nation has never done a more Christ-like thing than when it went to war in August 1914 ... the world has been redeemed again by the precious blood shed on the side of righteousness."[146] In words that have been repeated to spur the modern-day jihadist, Bishop Ingram invoked the God of war.

He was also ready to absorb every word of anti-German propaganda and repeated stories of atrocities without caution. His reference to the crucified Canadian soldier was one such myth that circulated early in the war. It was a vicious lie wrapped in fear and loathing to inspire vengeance. Propaganda was an important source for the tales of unforgivable German wickedness the Churches were willing to perpetuate. Clergymen of all faiths became both participants in and victims of propaganda. Many Anglican ministers found it hard to believe that civilized Germans could be responsible for the atrocities claimed in the initial stories. However, the burning of Louvain and especially the university library, and the horrors of the Bryce Report were all instrumental in changing their minds. Once their faith in German civilization had been breached, nearly every atrocity story in circulation was accepted and transmitted to their flocks.[147] They took their texts from a different Bible, one written by the propagandists at Wellington House or an unnamed journalist from the Northcliffe stables.

Perhaps the last word should go to Brigadier-General F.P. Crozier, who wrote: "The Christian churches are the finest blood-lust creators which we have, and of them we made free use."[148]

Summary.

- Democracy in Britain was dead. An Aliens Restriction Act and the Defence of the Realm Act, immediately gave sweeping powers of control to the government.
- Acts of Parliament prepared by the Committee of Imperial Defence in 1911-12 were rushed into law. Banking and finance was given pride of

place and the Bank holiday was extended to protect the stock market. Paper money was printed for the first time.

- The Prime Minister did not appoint any member of his cabinet or the Liberal Party to the vacant post of Secretary of State for war, because he could not trust them with the truth about the causes of the war.
- Appreciating the value of his public persona, the Secret Elite decided that Lord Kitchener, who 'just happened ' to be in London at the time, should be appointed. Alfred Milner physically put Kitchener into a taxi to 10 Downing Street to confront Asquith.
- In his first speech to the House of Lords, Kitchener warned that a war would not be short-lived. He talked of a minimum of three years.
- A sophisticated propaganda machine swung into action to justify the war.
- Censorship was meekly accepted by the British press. The public were effectively misled until news of the retreat from Mons was leaked by the Northcliffe press in order to stress the need for recruitment and reinforcements.
- The Secret Elite mobilized their academic forces at Oxford University to produce 87 specially commissioned pamphlets to justify the war. Many were aimed at America.
- The myth makers of history included authors and journalists. In September 1914 a War Propaganda Bureau was set up secretly. It used H G Wells, Arthur Conan Doyle, G.K. Chesterton, Hilaire Belloc and John Buchan.
- Americans were shamelessly courted. In late August 1914, J.P. Morgan influenced the appointment of English editorial writers on forty U. S. newspapers.
- 360 newspapers in smaller States were supplied with weekly reviews of the war from a British and French perspective. 260,000 prominent Americans were targeted with personal correspondence directly from Britain.
- The mass media became a weapon of war and America was its prime target.
- The first major propaganda onslaught came with the publication of the *Bryce Report on Alleged German Outrages* (in Belgium). Bryce was chosen to lead the so-called investigation because he was a popular former ambassador to the United States. It was a propaganda coup.
- American correspondent Irvin Cobb and the lawyer Clarence Darrow unmasked many of the wilder, most offensive claims, but the damage was done.
- The Church of England indulged in a despicable level of propaganda from the pulpits, while many of their senior churchmen held shares in the armaments industries.
- The Bishop of London was the most outrageous. He called war a great crusade, 'to kill Germans, to kill the good was well as the bad...to kill them less the civilization of the world itself should be killed.'
- The Church of England has never apologized for this disgusting behavior.

North Sea
UNITED
KINGDOM
Trent
Thames
London
Portsmouth
Strait of Dover
Amsterdam
The Hague
NETHERLANDS
Ems
Weser
Antwerp
FLANDERS
Brussels
Liege
Meuse
Düsseldorf
Lys
Boulogne
Lille
BELGIUM
Somme
Amiens
ARGONNE
LUXEMBOURG
Mosel
Le Havre
Reims
Verdun
Metz
Seine
Marne
Paris
Nancy
ALSACE
VOSGES
Rhine
Strasbou
Rennes
Mulhouse
Belfort
Basel
Loire
Besancon
Nantes
REPUBLIC
OF
FRANCE
Bern
SWITZERL
JURA
Vienne
Rhone
Geneva
Clermont
Lyon
MASSIF
CENTRAL
MARITIME ALPS
Turin
Dordogne
Bordeaux
Rhone
LES CEVENNES MTS
Genoa
Garonne
400 km
Toulouse
Marseilles
PYRENEES
ANDORRA
Mediterranean Sea

Chapter 3

The Scandal of Briey

As the European crisis moved towards the planned conflict at the end of July 1914, General Joffre, Chief of the French General Staff, acted quickly to bring their forces up to wartime strength along the Franco-German border in advance of the declaration of war. Troops were ordered to remain ten kilometers behind the frontier lines to limit German awareness that the build-up had begun. On 31 July, angered by apparent dithering, Joffre sent President Poincaré a personal ultimatum to the effect that he would not accept responsibility for the command of the French armed forces unless a general mobilization was declared.[1]

Joffre was straining at the leash. He had the advantage but by 1 August, feared that the Germans might secretly mobilize. A few minutes before 4.00PM that very day, the French government acceded to his wishes and declared a general mobilization of its army. All Europe understood that mobilization meant war,[2] and both Russia and France had started the process before Germany made a move. They were not to be caught unawares. Yet four days later, on 5 August 1914, the German army literally walked unopposed into the northeastern border district around Briey, the most invaluable source of iron ore and coal for France's own production of munitions. Prime Minister Jean Viviani later spoke bitterly of Briey's abandonment, blaming the difficulties faced by France in the production of armaments during the war on "la non-defense de Briey."[3] He blamed the failure of the army high command to secure the priceless region as a pre-requisite for victory; they vehemently denied the allegation. Who then determined that the entire Briey basin should be allowed to fall into German hands on the first days of the war?

The iron mines of Briey-Thionville lie south of the Ardennes forest and to the east of the small French city of Verdun. This ore-rich countryside straddled the borders of France and Luxembourg before the Treaty of Frankfurt ceded Alsace-Lorraine to Germany in 1871. A glance at a mineral map of the area would immediately demonstrate the strategic importance of this relative backwater. The major iron smelters for both France and Germany sat literally along their mutual border. In 1913, of the thirty-six million tons of iron ore produced in Germany, twenty-nine million tons came from this area alone. Across the border, in the department of Meurthe-et-Moselle, 92 per cent of French iron ore was sourced that same year in and around Briey.[4] In terms of strategic importance for the production of weapons for modern warfare, the Briey basin was the prime site in Europe. Everyone who understood the armaments business knew this.

Those who understood the business best, who organized, sold, purchased, traded and manipulated the world's munitions' industries, who formed an exclusive cartel, who dominated the multi-million pound merchandise of death which crossed all political and national boundaries, knew full well that control of the Briey basin was absolutely essential to the German war effort. Without the continuing supply of these essential ores from Briey, Germany could not have sustained a long war. By 1916 major French newspapers including *L'Echo de Paris, L'Oeuvre, Le Temps* and the *Paris-Midi* were united in the belief that the single, most effective way to bring war to a standstill was to stop German iron and steel production in and around Briey.[5] It was public knowledge.

Military voices including General Verraux, joined with elected politicians like Senators Henry Berenger and Fernand Engerand in the clamor to forcibly shut down the smelters and mines of Briey and neighboring Joeuf. Yet somehow, men wielding greater power overruled the military and ignored the outcry from the public and the press. The reader may find it difficult to accept that while hundreds of thousands of young French soldiers were being sacrificed at Verdun, some brief kilometers away, the great furnaces at Joeuf and Briey lit up the night sky with angry red foreboding, forging the iron and steel that would kill those who came after them.[6]

The importance of the Briey basin to German success between 1914-1917 cannot be understated. A secret memo from the Association of the six largest German industrial and agricultural manufacturers to Chancellor Bethmann-Hollweg on 20 March 1915 included a warning that if the iron ore production from Lorraine was interrupted, the war would virtually be lost.[7] Even though the memo was later publicly exposed by the French Iron and Steel Association in September 1915,[8] no action was taken to grasp back this invaluable mineral-laden territory. The *Leipzige Nueste Nachrichten* of 10 October 1917 stated that, "if, in the first days of the war, the French had penetrated to a depth of twelve kilometers in Lorraine, the war would have been ended in six months by the defeat of Germany."[9] By their reckoning, a seven-and-a-half mile attack in the first days of August 1914 literally could have ended the war by Christmas.

In December 1917, the German Association of Iron and Steel and the Association of Metallurgists warned that any withdrawal from the Briey basin would pose "a dreadful peril" to Germany's chances of winning the war. They saw it as their good fortune that the French had not been able to destroy the factories, smelters and forges on both sides of the border around Briey because without those resources the war would have been over in a matter of weeks "to our disadvantage."[10] Evidence was repeatedly produced from both France and Germany that clearly established the strategic and economic importance of the Briey basin to victory on the Western front. Nothing happened. It was as if Briey and Thionville had been issued with a special exemption from the war that raged around them.

An inquiry into the Briey affair was set up after the war. The military commanders were adamant that it was not their fault. Marshal Joffre, in a categorical statement to the Briey Commission, insisted that it had been impossible to defend Briey "either by fortifications or by a blanket coverage."

He was supported by General Ferdinand Pont who confirmed with equal certainty that it was impossible to defend Briey on the frontier and protect Verdun behind it without running serious risks. Their faith in a short successful war may well have blinded them initially, but as events unfolded, and Briey was literally abandoned to the Germans, and left intact, the failure of the French commanders to take effective action became an issue in itself. One story put about in defense of the military, was that the general order given by Prime Minister Viviani on 31 July 1914, that all troops should withdraw ten kilometers from the German border, brought about the unintentional abandonment of Briey, Joeuf and the basin area. The story was proved a lie by no less an authority than Adolphe Messimy, then Minister of War. In a deposition to the Briey Commission he made it clear that although he instructed Joffre to respect the ten kilometer withdrawal, he also gave him very specific permission to work within that measure if there was strategic necessity or if ten kilometers was too far from key points. Five or six kilometers distance was sufficient under these circumstances and the military GHQ was given license to establish a line between villages that were barely four or five kilometers from the border.[11] The French army was poised at a target barely three miles away – and left it intact. Messimy stated on record that he had personally seen maps and documents which carried this authority to local commanders. In any case the argument was very short-lived, for Viviani's order to withdraw to a nominal ten kilometer distance from the frontier was rescinded on the afternoon of 2 August.[12] The "non-defense" of Briey had deeper, more sinister, roots.

No attempt was made to defend Briey or destroy it before it fell into enemy hands. Such an incomprehensible decision should have merited a flurry of high-level resignations, yet no-one accepted the blame. During the post-war commission investigating the "catastrophe" of Briey,[13] Joffre insisted that the basin constituted a very small part of the overall defense strategy, which few could fully comprehend without all the facts at their fingertips.[14] It was a card often played in the aftermath of the war when difficult questions were raised by journalists or ex-servicemen seeking answers to decisions that clearly prolonged the wretched war.[15] Joffre's stance was safeguarded by the astonishing revelation that on 1 September 1914, an absolute directive had been issued by the general staff at GHQ that plans, orders and written instructions issued since the start of the war had to be systematically destroyed. Military strong-boxes were emptied and records burned. No inventory was kept. What was left in the War Ministry's archives, the detritus haphazardly garnered from unclassified remnants and bits and pieces of documentation that hardly amounted to evidence, made historical research of what the Minister of War termed "this obscure period," extremely difficult.[16] How very convenient.

Such obfuscation helped protect military careers and hide the truth about who was ultimately in charge. The greater enigma of Briey in August 1914 stemmed from the inaction of the French army. Units were formed into a group known as the Army of Lorraine, but for whatever reasons, it did not make a move on Briey. The records which survived the cull show that it was established on 19 August specifically to retake Briey, brought together on 21 August, but was dissolved on the 25th without firing a shot. Uncertainty reigned over who was in command of this specific element of the French 3rd Army, and whether or not orders were sent appropriately. In the confusion of battle many mistakes were made by both sides, but the evidence later presented to the Commission showed that the French could have won a great victory whose consequence would have changed the course of the war had the Army of Lorraine retaken Briey on 25 August. Instead it was disbanded.[17] The French politician Fernand Engerand, Depute for Calvados, called it the "phantom army."

One argument put forward in support of the military decisions was that the defense of Paris took precedence over Briey in that short time-frame. This doesn't explain why the French ignored such vital targets as the forges in Thionville in the opening days of the war, or why they failed to destroy both Thionville and Briey to thwart Germany in gaining possession of mines and smelters in the years that followed.

The loss of Thionville would have brought a rapid end to the war because Germany simply couldn't continue without the minerals needed for armament manufacture.[18] Laying waste to town and country to deny any comfort to an enemy has always been a recognized tactic by an army in retreat. If the French military were not aware of it, they had learned nothing at all from Napoleon. But they were not destroyed. Nor were Briey and Thionville ever effectively bombed or bombarded by artillery or aircraft between 1914-1917.

How could this possibly have happened? Military commanders, soldiers in the trenches, journalists, Senators and Deputies in the French Assembly, even Prime Minister Viviani and key officials of the Third Republic knew about the economic and strategic importance of the Briey basin. Thionville alone boasted 28 mines and 8 factories and smelters and the east bank of the Moselle river provided Germany with 48% of its total iron output.[19] Proposals that direct action be taken to bombard Briey and Thionville to oblivion were made repeatedly, even at Cabinet level. It was a perfectly feasible proposition, but never carried out. Why?

Pierre-Etienne Flandin was elected to the French Parliament in 1914. His credentials were impeccable, coming as he did from a family steeped in the conservative right wing of French politics. He held several senior ministerial posts in the 1920s and 30s before becoming Prime Minister in 1934. His testimony, given in January 1919 is even more remarkable. An accomplished aviator himself, Flandin went to the military headquarters in Souilly a few days before Christmas 1916, to speak personally to General Adolphe Guillaumat who commanded the 2nd French Army. He gave the General a detailed plan of the Briey/Lorraine basin with the principal factories and foundries clearly highlighted, and as a consequence, Joeuf was bombed some days later.

It proved to be a singular sortie. General Guillaumat was immediately instructed to desist from this initiative by GHQ, which reserved the right to make such decisions. Outraged, Flandin claimed that the top military officials at GHQ knew what was going on in the Lorraine basin and knew of the "huge interests" which were concerned with its exploitation. Flandin spelled out the message. Not only had Germany exploited the natural resources for twenty-seven months, "without being disturbed," but, and this is absolutely significant, "there was therefore a method of shortening the war, and this method was neglected for more than two years."[20] Here from the mouth of a Depute destined to be the Prime Minister of France, comes proof-positive that the continuation of iron and steel production in Briey was sanctioned by unnamed "huge interests" and came at the cost of utter misery for millions of men and their families in a war that was deliberately prolonged.

A more politically sensitive officer, General Malleterre, discussed the issue of Briey and Thionville with both the French General Staff and the Secretary-General of the Comite des Forges, Robert Pinot. The agreed solution was that the mines and smelters be blockaded. They advocated that the railway stations should be bombed so that the precious material could not be transported to armaments factories elsewhere in Germany. This ingenious scheme would have left the iron and steel works untouched.[21] Ineffective though it proved, the "blockade" was partially adopted and, as General Gabriel Malleterre predicted, failed to achieve any meaningful result. But why did he seek permission from the Comite des Forges, the French association of Master Forgers, the steel-producing collective monopoly which exclusively controlled the production of iron and steel across France? Why was the army obliged to have permission from the munitions manufacturers?

The answer found voice in the French Assembly after the war. On 24 January 1919, Eduoard Barthe, a socialist member of the Chamber of Deputies who represented the French section of the Workers' International, made the following statement:

> I declare that, either owing to the international solidarity of heavy industry, or in order to safeguard private interests, orders were given to our military commanders not to bombard the factories of the basin of Briey exploited by the enemy during the war. I declare that our aircraft received instructions to respect the blast-furnaces which were smelting the enemy's steel.[22]

Astonishing, unbelievable, incomprehensible. Words fail to capture the implication of this public statement. Eduoard Barthe clearly stated that ultimate control of both government and military decisions lay at a level above Prime Minister Viviani, his Cabinet, or General Joffre, Marshal Ferdinand Foch and the French general staff. So who was calling the shots? Barthe compiled a dossier which was suppressed by the French government. It included references to Lloyd George and the armaments dealer, Basil Zaharoff, and claimed that they agreed that it would be senseless to destroy industrial plant and end up after the war with derelict factories and mass unemployment.[23] Iron and steel production across Europe was granted special protection from strategic destruction by powers beyond the understanding of the common man, but what was the Comite des Forges and what power did it wield? Who was in a position to decide the fate of the Briey basin? Clearly not the elected politicians or the professional military command.

The Comite des Forges represented a powerful group of iron and steel producers whose links with the French government were so dominant that the two were often as one. Imitating the American business practice by which major manufacturing companies acted together in monopolistic collusion, the Comite des Forges harmonized its prices and liaised with other international iron and steel groups which completely dominated the world market. The Comite was the epitome of the capitalist power structure in France.[24] It bound together individual iron and steel companies by strict agreements on quotas and prices.

The Comite neither sold nor produced products. It acted in a far more subtle manner, retaining political, strategic and economic influence by means of elected politicians and well financed propaganda. The Comite des Forges had no subsidiaries, though its members paid annual dues to the central treasury based on the size of their output and number of employees. Under the leadership of the President of the Comite this power-bloc controlled all of the major iron and steelworks in France through regional committees in Loire, Nord, l'Est, Miniere d'Alscace-Lorraine, Forges de Lorraine and Champagne. It controlled regional and national press. It influenced the French Foreign Office at the Quai d'Orsay and many top level national politicians emerged from these lairs in later years.[25]

Its first President was Eugene Schneider, a director of the Creusot Company, Depute for Saone-et-Loire and at one point, Minister of Agriculture and Commerce. He grew rich on the monopoly gained from the French government to supply armaments and railway construction material.[26] The French navy purchased its armor plate from Schneider Creusot which became a market leader in naval artillery.[27] Eugene Schneider was also a director of the Credit-Lyonnais and a founder of Banque de L'Union Parisienne. A mutually supportive blueprint for success emerged from the turn of the century where arms firms, government ministers and banks collaborated at the highest level to win foreign orders and maximize profits. [28]

Before the war began, the Comite des Forges appointed Francois de Wendel as its president, the man dubbed by the socialist leader Joseph Caillaux as "the symbol of the plutocracy." He embodied every aspect of the industrial elite in France. Elected Deputy to the National Assembly, acknowledged as a *maitre de forges* (iron master) from a dynastic line of iron and steel producers, Wendel became a Regent of the Banque of France and worked closely in conjunction with his great ally, Edouard de Rothschild.[29] Coming from a family which suffered the embarrassment of being torn in two when Lorraine was ceded to Germany in 1871, Francois was deeply anti-German and a strong supporter of Raymond Poincaré and his Revanchist party.

His father, Henri Wendel remained behind in the annexed section of Lorraine as a subject of the new German Empire in order to keep control of the family's extensive industrial interests. Indeed he quickly reoriented his political loyalties and was elected to the Reichstag as a Representative for Lorraine from 1881-1890. In like vein his cousin Charles sat in the Reichstag from 1907-1911. Thus the Wendel family retained its political and economic interests on both sides of the border, with Francois in the French National Assembly and his father and cousin in the Reichstag. Together they owned the mines, factories, plants and smelters in Briey and Thionville.

The Wendels dominated French iron and steel supplies. With the Germans given unchallenged ownership of the Briey basin in August 1914, there was precious little left for the industry in France. Although the Comite des Forges was permitted to import 19,0000 tons of metal per month from Britain, nothing moved for seven months. At which point a tried and tested method was imported into the system. Just as the British appointed J.P. Morgan as their sole agent for all purchases from the United States, so the French government decided to approve a single agent to purchase the importation of iron and steel; it was Francois de Wendel's brother, Hubert. In addition, the military attaché in London responsible for overseeing the purchasing agent was de Wendel's brother-in-law, General de la Penouze. It only got worse. In the ministry of munitions in Paris, responsibility for checking these vital imports rested with a director of the Comite des Forges's bank[30] who was given the rank of captain and raised to the position of general secretary of the Commission of Woods and Metals.[31] When accusations were made of speculation and profiteering in the iron and steel industries towards the end of 1915, they were referred to the Committee of Markets at the Chamber of Deputies and duly investigated by its most experienced member, Francois de Wendel. Three years later the Chamber of Deputies was still waiting on the report.[32]

Can there be any wonder why both during the war and at the end of that terrible conflict the Wendels were accused of using their immense power to protect their vast mineral assets at Briey and Thionville? The mineral rich Briey basin extending to the east bank of the Moselle around Thionville was their personal fiefdom. They owned it, they ran the great mines and factories, they represented the people both in the French Assembly and the German Reichstag, they patronized the Catholic Church and owned the local newspapers. From 1906, Francois Wendel subsidized *L'Echo de Lorraine* and the family controlled *Le Journal de Debats*, a loss-making political journal which was sent free to every teacher in Wendel's electoral district.[33]

When in 1919 bitter accusations were raised against him in the French National Assembly, and in particular the charge that he had blocked the destruction of the Briey steelworks, Francoise Wendel haughtily dismissed them. He cited a list of generals who claimed either not to have had the technology capable of such long-ranged destruction, or who considered the target inappropriate as a military objective.[34] Accusations that the Comite des Forges had paid a pliant journalist to write an article in *Le Temps* in 1916 were rejected on the basis that according to Francoise Wendel, President of the Comite itself, it did not have a publicity fund. This was truly an outrageous claim since the Comite controlled whole swathes of the press. The story written by Max Hoschiller suggested that the destruction of the Briey complex would not substantially weaken Germany, a ridiculous claim that flew in the face of every other assessment.[35]

Unsurprisingly, the Regent of the Banque de France, President of the Comite des Forges, Deputy of the National Assembly and international associate of the global munitions family, a friend and colleague of the Paris Rothschilds and long term supporter of President Poincaré survived these attacks relatively unscathed. The verdict of supportive historians was that "none of these claims about a Wendelian conspiracy were ever substantiated."[36] The reader must make her/his own decision as to what can be defined as corroboration when key documents are missing or destroyed and the wealth of the Wendel family is given a higher priority than the lives it cost. But such a focus on one family, one example, no matter how pertinent, could deflect the spotlight away from a greater influence.

Francoise de Wendel asked a very pertinent question during a debate in the Chamber of Deputies on 1 February 1919. Why had the Germans not bombed the French coal mines in the Pas de Calais and destroyed the last main source of coal in France? The Pas de Calais lay only 15 kilometers from the front lines and could easily have been blasted from long-range or from Zeppelin bombers; after all they had traveled 120 kilometers to bombard Paris. Wendel claimed that such attacks were far more complex than people imagined.

For Gustave Tery, the socialist journalist, it was a moment of horrific revelation. Wendel had unwittingly opened a can of worms. Tery suddenly realized that if the French had destroyed Briey the Germans would have reciprocated by bombing the Pas de Calais. That neither side did so signified an agreement at a very high level to protect these industrial complexes, so crucial for a long war. Gustave Tery was not the only one stunned by the implication. At that moment he heard a colleague burst out, "By George, they were in cahoots!" He admitted, "it made me shiver."[37] It should make us all shiver.

French newspapers joined in the clamor, demanding explanations, but *Le Matin,* a conservative daily newspaper, suggested that the decision was a matter of military convention; one simply did not attack such targets.[38] Few were duped by this ludicrous suggestion. There had clearly been a secret agreement between the belligerents which would have remained so had not the French Deputies stirred public outrage. The basic question was, who was responsible for the undeniable immunity given to coal mines, iron, steel and chemical plants whose destruction could have stopped the war in a matter of weeks?

Deputy Edouard Barthe stepped forward in the French Assembly on 24 January 1919 and formally and unequivocally stated that either the international armaments industry, or influential and powerful private interests, had ordered the French military high command not to destroy Briey even though it was undeniably being exploited by the enemy. Barthe confirmed that the air force had been ordered to respect the blast furnaces in which the enemy steel was being made, and "that a general who had wished to bombard them was reprimanded."[39]

Yet no-one was brought to court. No company director was charged with complicity with the enemy. The abandonment of Briey to the German army was a scandal which was never resolved. The Wendels survived the opprobrium thrown their way by the socialist press. There was no concrete evidence. Nothing could be proved.

In trying to understand the extent of the power and influence asserted by international armaments conglomerates, the evidence from Briey offers an example of the power they exerted to control and extend the war. Politicians were in their pocket. Occasionally, they acted as politicians themselves. Newspapers protected their interests. They included in their ranks bankers and financiers who operated across the boundaries of political nationalism. Top military staff acceded to the demands issued through their appointed agents so that no-one knew precisely who ultimately made the decision or gave the instruction. Not just in France or Germany. Inside this shadowy world, the British Secret Elite furthered their ambitions and increased their influence. Many benefited personally from the enormous war profits but the ultimate objective remained paramount; the destruction of Germany as an imperial rival through a long protracted war. Briey's "non-defense" captures one instance of how that was achieved.

The Briey scandal also helps us understand how "hidden powers" operated within one national boundary, in this instance, France. They forbade military strikes against their own industrial interests, and allowed supplies vital to the continuation of war to flow unhindered. But this is only one layer in the exercise of control. Armaments were a global business organized on a scale that owed no national allegiance, that benefited from "international hermaphroditism"[40] and cared not whether they were buying or supplying de Wendels or von Wendels, whether they paid dividends to or shared the profits with Vickers-Armstrongs [Britain], Krupps [Germany], Bethlehem Steel [United States], Schneider-Creusot [France], Skoda [Austria-Hungary] or members of the Comite des Forges. War was a source of profit that benefited them all, and the longer it lasted, the greater that profit.

As the American Marine Corps General Smedley Butler later wrote in the light of the events he personally experienced:

> War is a racket. It always has been. It is possibly the oldest, easily the most profitable, surely the most vicious. It is the only one international in scope. It is the only one in which the profits are reckoned in dollars and the losses in lives. A racket is best described, I believe, as something that is not what it seems to the majority of the people. Only a small "inside" group knows what it is about. It is conducted for the benefit of the very few, at the expense of the very many. Out of war a few people make huge fortunes. In the World

> War a mere handful garnered the profits of the conflict. At least 21,000 new millionaires and billionaires were made in the United States during the World War. They mainly admitted their huge blood gains in their income tax returns. How many other millionaires falsified their tax returns, no one knows.[41]

21,000 new millionaires or billionaires have to be balanced against an estimate of 8,500,000 military deaths, with civilian casualties and civil wars and atrocities pushing that figure towards a number between 15-20,000,000 victims.[42]

And we must remember that this "racket" had an ultimate purpose beyond mere profit. The Secret Elite who had originated in Britain and were in the process of extending their base across the Atlantic, intended that Germany be crushed and the Anglo-Saxon domination of the world securely established.[43] They had no interest in a short war. Crushing Germany and removing the Teutonic threat to their position required a lengthy struggle. They were committed to the long-haul. Briey was simply a small part of the whole endeavor. Every action they took deliberately prolonged the war by feeding the enemy, providing them with means to continue fighting and rank profiteering.

Summary.

- The French army mobilized on 1 August, 1914 after their commander-in-chief, General Joffre sent an ultimatum to President Poincaré, that he would not take responsibility for the French Army if he delayed any further.
- Briey in the northeastern border with Germany was the center of iron ore and coal for France's own munitions production – a crucial strategic and economic asset.
- Four days later on 5 August, the Germans walked into the ore rich Briey basin without a shot being fired.
- Its control was absolutely essential to the German war effort. Without it the Germans could not have fought a prolonged war. The Leipzig newspaper Nueste Nachrichten reported in 1917 that had the French penetrated a mere twelve kilometers into Lorraine, the war would have been lost by Germany within six months.
- The French army though poised a mere three miles from the strategically vital Briey fields, was ordered not to take action.
- On 19 August, the French 3rd Army was brought together to retake Briey but did not move on the target. It was dissolved on the 25th without firing a shot.
- Proposals later in the war to bomb Briey to oblivion were dismissed without action.

- Claims were made in the French Chamber of Deputies that orders were given to military commanders not to bombard Briey and the blast furnaces and smelters.
- The Comite des Forges, a powerful group of French iron and steel producers, held enormous power over government departments and they were closely linked to major banks.
- Francoise de Wendel, president of the Comite des Forges, was elected to the National Assembly and worked closely with Edouard de Rothschild. His every action protected his vast mineral assets at and around Briey.
- High-level collusion between the French and German armaments owners safeguarded the factories and mines at the expense of prolonging the war.
- They colluded by protecting each other's supplies of ore and in so doing prolonged the war and enabled thousands of businessmen to become millionaires.

Chapter 4

The Myth Of The Great Blockade – Lies And Deception

The British naval blockade of Germany between 1914-1916 was a cruel charade that was designed to fail. It had to appear that a blockade was in operation because such action had been seen as an essential weapon of war long before its success in the Napoleonic wars. Britain had predicated its massive naval expenditure since the beginning of the twentieth century on its capacity to use such tactics. Britannia ruled the waves, did it not? The public would have held any failure to blockade Germany as a gross dereliction of duty.

A blockade by one nation against another has been a strategy of war throughout history. In other epochs different tactics have been employed to achieve similar ends; namely, defeat of the enemy by stopping its trade in essential goods, excluding it from the benefits of international exchange, starving the population and bringing about its ruin and defeat.[1] The physical capacity of the Royal Navy to cut off the sea trade routes between Germany and her markets throughout the world was unquestioned.[2] It was taken as an axiom by the British public that after war began, a blockade would seal Germany off, prevent food and war matériel from entering, and swiftly bring her to her knees. The public believed that an effective blockade had been put into effect. As the *Times* reported some seven months into the war, the nation retained "supreme and unquestioning confidence in the Royal Navy."[3] Given the huge percentage of gross domestic product spent on warships and dreadnoughts, anything other than full confidence in the fleet would have been extremely demoralizing.

On 23 August 1911 it had been evident to a small coterie of trusted ministers who attended a special meeting of the Committee for Imperial Defence, that the Royal Navy's plans for the coming war with Germany were ill-considered. Equally worrying was the fact that no strategic plan had been agreed upon between the army and the navy.[4] Part of the fall-out from that particularly disturbing meeting was the appointment of Winston Churchill as First Lord of the Admiralty. He brought the rigor of his own certainty to the position and, inspired largely by Admiral Lord John (Jacky) Fisher, the recently retired First Sea Lord, he introduced a more modern approach to that bastion of tradition. He did not, however, share Admiral Fisher's views on how and where to operate a naval blockade.

Fisher advocated an aggressive close blockade of the German coast by destroyers in order to bring matters quickly to a head. In addition to limiting Germany's importation of food and essential war matériel via the Atlantic trade routes, a close blockade would prevent imports by local coastal shipping from the Scandinavian countries or neutral Spain. In Fisher's plan, the British Grand Fleet of dreadnoughts and cruisers would always be on standby to protect the destroyers from German warships should the need arise. An additional benefit of a close blockade of ports on the Jade and Elbe estuaries was that the German fleet would be trapped in port, hence the threat of a German invasion of Britain, or the possibility of a German attack on British trade routes, would be removed.[5]

Faced with imminent maritime strangulation, the Imperial German Fleet might have been forced out of its safe harbors into action, but Fisher was adamant that it would then be crushed by the overwhelming power of the Royal Navy's capital ships. On the other hand, those who argued against a close blockade claimed that while the enemy's largest warships might well be hemmed in, Germany could use mines, torpedoes and submarines to destroy the blockading vessels. Fisher believed that this was a spurious argument because submarines would have insufficient depth of water in which to operate and, in any case, would not attempt to attack destroyers.[6]

Destroyers were specifically adapted to deal with the U-boat menace. They had the speed to intercept them, strengthened bows to ram them, and the fire power and torpedoes to sink them. They carried hydrophones for identifying them and depth charges to destroy them. Destroyers were perhaps the submariner's greatest fear. In any case, at the start of the war Germany had only 29 submarines to Britain's 73, and so a close blockade could deal with that relatively small number.

It has been suggested recently by Professor Hew Strachan that Fisher's close blockade "rested on an overestimation of the destroyer and an underestimation of the submarine" and would lead to a suicidal over-extension of naval resources. Britain, he stated "had fewer destroyers than did Germany: forty-two to eighty-eight in 1914." Hew Strachan also maintained that "the blockading destroyers would have to return to coal every three to four days. As the nearest British port was 280 miles from the German coast, the blockading fleet would require three reliefs – one on station, one in port, and one en-route – or twice as many destroyers as Britain possessed."[7] His statistics are wrong. In reality, by August 1914 the Royal Navy boasted some 221 destroyers.[8]

Admiral Fisher believed that a close blockade was of crucial importance to winning the war quickly. Had winning quickly been the true intention a great many more than 42 destroyers could have been allocated to the task. With regard to Strachan's assertion that two-thirds of the force would be absent at any given time to take on coal, it must be remembered that by 1914 a large number of Royal Navy destroyers were powered by oil. Fisher had introduced oil-fired boilers and steam turbines to all destroyers built after 1905, apart from a temporary reversion to coal in the Beagle class of 1908. In a written parliamentary reply in February 1914 about the numbers of naval ships of all classes which were "fitted or to be fitted" for oil fuel only, Winston Churchill cited 109 destroyers and 252 vessels in total.[9] Had oil-fired destroyers been used in a close blockade, coaling issues would have been irrelevant. In the event, such coaling problems gravely limited the efficiency of the antiquated British cruiser fleet sent to perform the distant "blockade" that was finally agreed upon.

As matters stood in early August 1914, had the short sharp defeat of Germany been genuinely desired, a close blockade of North Sea ports provided the very best chance of success. That was not what the Secret Elite intended. The utter destruction of Germany required much more than a quick victory and an armistice. The aim was not merely to destroy the German army and navy, but the country's entire financial commercial and industrial infrastructure. That would require a long war.

To that end the Secret Elite's men in the Admiralty and the Foreign Office decided on a distant blockade of the North Sea approaches from the Atlantic Ocean and a similar blockade of the Atlantic approaches south of Ireland. It gave Sir Edward Grey and his fellow Secret Elite members in the Foreign Office far more power to control how a "blockade" would be managed. To the general public it mattered not. They had been assured of a quick, successful and punitive war and initially paid little heed to how the blockade was being run. They trusted Churchill. He personally raised the level of confident expectation that an iron grip would be effectively placed on German sea trade which would slowly but surely strangle her economy and bring the war to a victorious conclusion. He addressed a meeting of bankers, financiers, politicians and senior military personnel at the Guildhall banquet on 9 November, 1914 in the company of Prime Minister Asquith and minister of war, Lord Kitchener. Churchill loved such high profile occasions and did not disappoint his audience, definitively assuring the nation that an effective naval blockade was in operation. In his accustomed stentorian manner he claimed:

> The punishment we inflict is very often not seen and even when seen cannot be measured. The economic stringency resulting from a naval blockade requires time to reach its full effectiveness. Now you are only looking at it at the third month. But wait a bit. Examine it at the sixth month, and the ninth month, and the twelfth month, and you will begin to see the results – results which will be gradually achieved and silently achieved, but which will spell the

> doom of Germany as surely as the approaching winter strikes the leaves from the trees.[10]

It was an empty promise full of sound and fury, and it signified deception. That there was no effective blockade in 1914 or 1915 was not down to a failure of the Royal Navy itself, but the masters in London who controlled it. Many British sailors braved the worst storms the North Atlantic could throw at them to try to implement a blockade, but were betrayed. While the people of Britain and the Empire believed as fact the lies and misleading claims about the enemy's growing enfeeblement and its lack of war materials and food, what difficulties Germany faced in the early years of the war were not caused by a blockade. Indeed, far from restricting German supplies, evidence presented in the 1920s proved that British commerce and trade continued to assist the German war effort to the extent that the war was prolonged "far beyond the limits of necessity."[11] Surely that could not be true?

Before August 1914, every act of preparation for war, every advantage that naturally accrued to Britain through her unparalleled maritime strength, argued in favor of a close blockade of Germany, but it did not materialize. The raw statistics remain breath-taking. At least one-half of the world's sea-carrying capacity sailed under the British flag. The British fleet dominated every sea-gate in Europe, the North Sea, the Atlantic, the narrow Gibraltar Straits passage to and from the Mediterranean Sea, and the Indian and Pacific Oceans. "The actual and physical power of the Fleets of England to cut off from the armies and inhabitants of the German Bloc all supplies whatever from oversea was undoubted."[12]

Germany was effectively barred from these seaways and, apart from the battle of Jutland, for most of the war the German High Seas Fleet remained in harbor behind their protective screens of mines. Ships of the Imperial German navy at sea when war was declared, were systematically hunted down and destroyed. The German light cruiser *Emden*, which independently raided across the Indian Ocean, sinking or capturing some thirty Allied ships, was engaged in battle on 9 November 1914 by the Australian navy cruiser *Sydney*. With a third of his crew killed in the engagement, Captain Muller ran the *Emden* aground on the Cocos Islands. On 8 December 1914 a large British squadron came out of Port Stanley in the Falkland Islands to engage and destroy the powerful German squadron of Vice Admiral Maximilian von Spee. Just one week earlier, von Spee had defeated a Royal Navy squadron off Coronel in Chile. The battle of the Falklands put an end to raids on Allied merchant shipping by German surface vessels, and international trade between Britain and the Americas successfully carried on until the advent of the German U-boat blockade later in the war.

Like Britain, international trade was vital to Germany's survival as a modern industrial nation. Her balance of trade deficit was largely caused by the importation of foodstuffs and raw materials.[13] Without sufficient imports of food, Germany would be starved into submission. When war was declared, over 600 German merchant ships took refuge in neutral ports. All German and Austrian vessels in British, French and Russian ports were immediately impounded, so that, by the end of August 1914, Germany's maritime trade ceased to operate, with the exception of the Black Sea and Baltic Sea.[14]

Almost a quarter of a million tons of German shipping was stranded in New York harbor, including the *Vaterland*, the largest passenger ship afloat, and three Norddeutschcher Lloyd liners, all capable of steaming at over 19 knots across the Atlantic. Another Hamburg-Amerika liner was laid up for the duration of the war at Boston. It was particularly important to Britain's maritime safety that these five powerful ships remained bottled up in American ports for fear they could be transformed into armed cruisers and cause havoc on the Atlantic passages. Although a Ship Registry Act that would have allowed these vessels to be transferred to the American flag was signed by President Woodrow Wilson on 18 August, it was not ratified by Congress and these great German liners were doomed to see out the war as prisoners in the safe haven of American harbors.[15] The *Vaterland* was later seized by the US government when America entered the war in April 1917, renamed SS *Leviathan*, and used as an American troop carrier.

With Germany's merchant fleet out of action, Churchill had boldly informed the Empire that a blockade by sea would quickly bring Germany and her allies to their knees. It did not. Why? The rules of naval blockade had long been an extremely contentious issue. For centuries privateers (privately owned, armed ships authorized by the Crown to attack and seize foreign merchant vessels during time of war) had been a means by which the Crown could mobilize armed ships and sailors at no cost to government. The plundered ships and their cargoes legally became Crown property, and their value assessed by an Admiralty "Prize Court." When a vessel and its cargo was sold, the prize money was shared between the captain, his crew and any individuals who had invested in the privateer.

Privateering was abolished by the Paris Declaration of 1856 (Respecting Maritime Law) which was ratified by fifty-five states. It was replaced with regulations on what constituted contraband of war and what was or was not liable to capture. The warships of a country at war were then entitled to stop and examine the cargo of any neutral merchant ship on the high seas. Neutral goods were exempted from seizure, but any material on the contraband list that might aid the enemy, such as weapons, gunpowder, cotton or army uniforms could legally be seized.

The Paris Declaration was not a treaty, nor was it signed by Britain or America, and so rules for stopping, searching and apprehending merchant vessels remained unclear. Discussions between the major maritime nations took place in London in 1908 and the consequent "Declaration of London" on "The Laws of Naval War" was issued on 26 February 1909. The British Foreign Office had been instrumental in organizing the conference, and Foreign Secretary Sir Edward Grey put great personal store in the declaration. It recommended the establishment of an International Prize Court, laid out guidelines on contraband and issued directives on how neutral countries should be allowed to trade with combatant nations.

Cargo that should be considered contraband was defined in two levels: a) Absolute contraband which included weapons of all kinds and their distinctive component parts. Projectiles, charges, and cartridges of all kinds, and their distinctive component parts. Powder and explosives specially prepared for use in war. Gun-mountings, limber boxes, limbers, military wagons, field forges, and their distinctive component parts. Clothing and equipment of a distinctively military character. b) Conditional contraband which included foodstuffs. Forage and grain suitable for feeding animals. Barbed wire. Clothing. Fabrics for clothing and boots and shoes suitable for use in war. Fuel, lubricants and explosives. In the event of war the contraband list had to be declared to the governments of enemy Powers, with a notification to all neutral powers after the outbreak of hostilities.

The Declaration of London ruled that the following would not be declared contraband and therefore not subject to seizure in a blockade: a) Raw cotton, wool, silk, jute, flax, hemp, and other raw materials of the textile industries, and yarns of the same. b) Oil seeds, nuts and copra (the dried kernel of coconut used to extract oil). c) Rubber, resins and gums. d) Raw hides, horns, bones, and ivory. e) Natural and artificial manures, including nitrates and phosphates for agricultural purposes. f)Metallic ores.[16]

Sir Edward Grey and the Secret Elite were pleased with the outcome of their conference, though it proved highly contentious in Britain. What sense did it make that the British government agreed to contraband regulations that would allow Germany in time of war to import cotton for her explosives manufacture, oil for her nitroglycerin and dynamite, jute for her sand bags, iron, copper tungsten and other ores for production of her guns, rifles, bayonets, and shells, rubber for tires and wool for military uniforms?[17] Little wonder that detractors dubbed it a "sea-law made in Germany."[18]

Many observers, especially those associated with the Royal Navy, were outraged at the stupidity of the greatest sea-power on earth agreeing to clauses and conditions that could only serve to strengthen its foes.

Serious tension developed between the Admiralty and the Foreign Office and 120 "Admirals" signed a written objection which was circulated to all members of the House of Commons.[19] Opposition was fierce and although the Declaration of London was approved by the House of Commons, it was summarily thrown out by the House of Lords in December 1911.[20] Since it failed to be ratified by the British government, it failed to have any legal standing within Britain or the Empire or indeed the United States, where it was also rejected.[21] From March 1911 until it produced a secret report in February 1913, the Committee for Imperial Defence had a sub-group examine the implications of trading with the enemy in war time.[22] This secret sub-committee comprised high-level civil servants from various government departments, and included both the Director of Naval Intelligence and the Chief of the War Staff at the Admiralty.

Lord Esher and Maurice Hankey, attended as "advisor" and secretary respectively. Esher warned the group on the impact of public opinion and expectations of the general public which would assume that the navy would blockade every avenue of approach to Germany. [23] He advised that it was likely that Germany would be "hermetically sealed" by the priorities of waging war. With an effective blockade of the North Sea ports, sea-borne trade in Europe would be "so danger-swept as to be practically closed to commerce." Lord Esher thus concluded that there was no need for parliamentary legislation. It could, he said, be taken for granted that in the event of war, trade of any kind between Britain and Germany would be so limited as to be negligible. All that would be required was a proclamation at the outbreak of war warning British subjects of their responsibilities and liabilities.[24] In other words, everyone expected a blockade, everyone knew not to trade with the enemy, so parliament need not be troubled. As we shall see, the reality was that the Secret Elite left a door ajar through which Germany was able to trade and access essential foodstuffs and war matériel. Esher and Hankey were adamant that there was no need for legislation to make cotton and other important war matériel absolute contraband because the law was already in place.

At a meeting of that secret sub-committee on 20 January 1912, Rear-Admiral Ernest Troubridge, chief of the war staff at the Admiralty, lashed out. As far as the navy, and indeed the army, was concerned, it was outrageous to assume that while the armed forces would be focused on crushing the enemy, neutrals would be allowed to supply Germany with the necessary resources to maintain her fighting forces and weapons production. He stressed the view that every possible obstacle should be placed on trade with Germany to stifle economic life, and make them so desperate that they would take dangerous risks that would lead to defeat.[25] No-one would openly refute such an obvious statement of fact. It would have been tantamount to treason. But agencies were afoot, even two years before war was declared, to thwart the best intentions of the Admiralty to mount an effective blockade that would bring war to a quick and successful conclusion. The navy may have assumed that it would be in control of any blockade, and the secret sub-committee may have assumed that its recommendations on goods to be prohibited would be fully absorbed into war policy, but powers greater than they exerted came into effect.

Despite Esher and Hankey's exhortations, the sub-committee's most important proposal was that British ships should be banned from carrying cargoes of cotton from America to neutral ports without clear and absolute proof that it was not destined for Germany. Cotton was crucial. It was the essential element in gun-cotton, the first high-explosive requirement for artillery shells, projectiles, machine guns and rifles. It was such an important element for armaments and ammunition that it headed the sub-committee's proposed list of prohibited exports.[26]

Without cotton, the great howitzers would have been unable to rain down their massive destruction on fortifications, towns and trenches. The front-line troops, huddled in their muddied trenches would have been spared the merciless bombardments and millions of lives would have been spared. Cotton, turned by science into gun-cotton, was a priceless element and both Britain and Germany depended on its importation, mainly from America.

Implementation of the proposal from the sub-committee on Trading With The Enemy to stop British ships from carrying American cotton across the Atlantic to neutral ports (from where it was anticipated they would be sold on to Germany) would have given Britain a powerful advantage and seriously limited Germany's capacity to manufacture shells and bullets. Yet, from the bowels of the Secret Elite lair in the Foreign Office, moves were afoot to abort this very straightforward and potentially effective embargo.

The sub-committee did not fall into line with the Secret Elite wishes, and the first salvo across the bows of those members who wanted a ban on cotton trade was fired by the legal assistant-advisor to the Foreign Office, Sir Cecil Hurst. Though relatively unknown at that juncture, Hurst, (he was knighted in 1913) was later identified by Professor Quigley as a close associate of Alfred Milner and the Secret Elite's Round Table group.[27] His argument ran as follows; the United States had a relatively small merchant marine fleet and depended on British ships to carry its cotton exports to Europe. Germany was a substantial importer of cotton and a blanket ban would ruin the southern U.S. planters. If such trade was closed to British merchant ships, and the fair assumption was made that the German flag would disappear from Atlantic voyages, there would be insufficient neutral tonnage to carry cotton exports. Freight prices would rise and British ship owners would be tempted to transfer their vessels to the American flag in order to take advantage of the grossly inflated profits available under such conditions.

In other words the American cotton manufacturers' desire to maintain their markets and make a substantial profit from the demand for cotton in wartime, linked to the unrestrained greed of British ship-owners to take advantage of the situation, would ensure the transfer of many British vessels to American owners. Loyalty to the cause? Obligation to the state or the crown? Forget it. Raw capitalism was stronger than any bond of blood or race, and raw cotton was worth more than its weight in diamonds to war profiteers.

Note the connection between the parliamentary rejection of the Declaration of London by the House of Lords in December 1911 and the Foreign Office appendix to the sub-committee on Trading With The Enemy presented by their legal advisor Cecil Hurst in 1912. When their Lordships threw out the ratification of the Declaration of London, they threw out the immunity for cotton as contraband. When Hurst presented his paper to the sub-committee, he, as a Secret Elite agent, placed it secretly back on the agenda. Basically the message was that Parliament could reject whatever it liked, but behind its back, the Foreign Office had every intention of proceeding as Sir Edward Grey and the Secret Elite ordained. And they did. They knew exactly what they were doing when they undermined the Committee of Imperial Defence plans to ban cotton exports to Germany immediately after war began.

Questioned by *New York Times* journalists in August 1915 on why cotton had not been declared contraband Lord Alfred Milner, the central figure at the heart of the Secret Elite, could only reply, "I do not suppose it was realized by the government or their advisers in the early months of the war that a vast demand for cotton for military purposes would arise."[28] Such spurious nonsense beggars belief. The British government knew all there was to know about the military need for cotton. Their own advisory committee had advised that it be the very first item on the contraband list. Without cotton, Germany could not have continued to rain down murderous shells on the beleaguered Allied troops on the Western Front. Without cotton Germany could not have continued in the war beyond 1915. Milner lied.

On 4 August 1914 a Royal Proclamation on trading with the enemy was issued. Goods were divided into three categories: absolute contraband, which covered articles for military purposes only; conditional contraband, or articles for either military or civilian use; and a free list, which included food. Only the first could be seized by a belligerent who declared a blockade. The second could be seized only if enemy destination was proved, and the third not at all. To the disgust of many, the free list included raw cotton, oil and rubber. Germany would be prevented from importing guns and explosives, but would be allowed to import the raw materials necessary for making them and much of it would come from America via neutral countries. The Admiralty protested vehemently. What use, they inquired, was it to deny freedom of the seas to the enemy if neutrals were to be allowed to supply him with all his needs?[29]

Next day, a second Proclamation was issued to prevent British shipping carrying contraband to any port in Northern Europe. British coal merchants were *asked* by the Admiralty not to supply bunker coal to any merchant vessel suspected of trading on the enemy's behalf. On 20 August an Order in Council was issued which stated that it was the government's intention to adopt the provisions of the Declaration of London "so far as may be practicable."[30] The Declaration favored the neutrals' rights to trade as against the belligerent's right to blockade. Despite the vociferous public and naval opposition to it, and the fact that Parliament had rejected it, the Foreign Office decided that the navy would abide by it. Neither the democratic process of decision-making nor public opinion ever stood in the way of the Secret Elite. As oft times before, they paid lip service to government and implemented their own policies.

Having summarily dismissed Admiral Fisher's call for a close blockade, allegedly because of the threat of mines and U-boats, the Royal Navy was tasked with an immensely difficult distant blockade. There were two sea routes by which goods might reach Germany by way of the Scandinavian neutrals; through the Straits of Dover or round the north of Scotland. A large minefield was laid in the Straits which compelled all vessels into a narrow passageway between the Goodwin sands and the coast of Kent, and every ship that passed through to or from Dutch or Scandinavian ports could be readily stopped and searched. Such a procedure was impossible in the northern route which stretched 450 miles from the north of Scotland to Iceland, and then a further 160 miles to Greenland. The Northern patrol was given the hugely difficult task of covering this 610 mile line of storm-tossed North Atlantic seas.[31]

On the high seas, two blockading squadrons were assembled. The Southern Squadron had the straightforward task of policing the English Channel, while the challenge for the Northern blockade was much more formidable. This task fell to the 10th Cruiser Squadron which, unlike the grand fleet, had been dispersed after the naval review at Spithead in the latter half of July. "How strange that every naval preparation by the Admiralty had been perfectly pre-planned, save for the vital blockading squadrons which could shorten the war." The 10th Cruiser Squadron was recalled and had to assemble, piecemeal, at Scapa Flow in Orkney. Headed by a tremendously capable leader, Rear Admiral Sir Dudley de Chair, what had previously been a Training Squadron was turned into the principle instrument of the British naval blockade. Eight of the oldest small cruisers in the British navy, ships of around 7,000 tons, all built between 1891-2, were dispatched north to stop and examine neutral vessels exiting or entering the Atlantic via the North Sea approaches.[32] Given that it was responsible for patrolling the North Sea from the Shetlands to Iceland and beyond, the aging, virtually obsolete coal-fired force was totally inadequate for the job. At best only six of the eight ships were available for action at any one time, the others having to return to port for coal in close sequence. When engines failed or unexpected damage was caused by the raging North Atlantic seas, even fewer were available for action. By November the storms had battered these craft into near submission.

They crawled through mountainous seas putting duty first, risking life and limb to stop neutral vessels and send search parties in small open boats to check their cargoes for contraband. By December 1914, it was finally acknowledged that the enormous task was beyond these gallant little ships.[33] Considering the years of planning that Churchill, Admiral John Jellicoe and the Admiralty staff had spent to master a proposed blockade, it seems ridiculous that the first blockade squadron was so antiquated and unfit for purpose.

To make matters even more difficult, the captains and crews became increasingly disheartened. Not by the state of their antiquated cruisers but by the ultimate fate of most of the neutral ships they boarded, caught with contraband, and sent to the contraband control base at Kirkwall. The legal framework in which the navy believed they were working, assumed that any neutral vessel suspected of carrying contraband to Germany could be detained and taken before a judicial board or Prize Court with the powers to confiscate the cargo and impound the vessel. This was fine in theory but rarely happened in practice.

As the American Ambassador to Britain, Walter Page explained, Britain would "go to any length to keep our friendship and good will. And she has not confiscated a single one of our cargoes even unconditional contraband. She has stopped some of them and bought them herself, but confiscated not one."[34] Time and again the crews put their lives at risk in wild seas only to receive orders from London to release the captive ships and let them proceed. This despite the fact that they knew the cargo was destined for Germany.

These brave men became increasingly disheartened and could not fathom why such cargoes were allowed through the blockade after the immense effort that had been put into stopping them. Walter Page, a very close friend of Sir Edward Grey, knew that the blockade was a sham. American ship-owners, traders, suppliers of foodstuffs, raw materials and all of the matériel of war, and the bankers and financiers who underwrote their businesses and financed the international trade were free to supply Germany and make huge profits.

And Winston Churchill stood on the Guildhall platform and promised the nation that an effective blockade was in place, the results from which would bear fruit in six to nine months. The public believed that Germany was being blockaded but knew nothing of the complex work of the men and ships that formed the blockading squadron. What actually happened was shielded from view by the convenience of official secrecy. The inference was that any detail of the squadron's work would have assisted the enemy, though as Admiral de Chair later acknowledged, "the Germans knew more about the squadron than did our own people."[35] The men of the 10th squadron knew that Churchill was misleading the public. They knew that the blockade was a mirage, a charade, a nonsense, and they deeply resented the tokenism in which they were involved.[36]

Despite the blockade, and the absence of a German merchant fleet, food and raw materials of every conceivable kind were exported to Germany from North and South America in British, American and other neutral vessels. Since the cargoes could not be carried directly into Germany, they were conveyed to neutral Scandinavian ports, then re-routed. That in itself was contrary to the international laws of blockade, since the doctrine of "Continuous Voyage" meant that, even if the ships were docking and unloading in neutral Scandinavian ports, it was the *ultimate* destination of the cargo that was the test of contraband. Massive quantities of food and essential war materials were sent to Scandinavia after August 1914. Though fully aware that much of it was immediately being transferred onto trains bound for Germany, the Foreign Office allowed this scandal to go unchecked.

The British government's lame excuse was that it dared not interfere with the transatlantic trade between neutral states because it would risk losing the support of America, Holland, Denmark and Sweden. In reality, there was never any likelihood of that happening. Official trade statistics proved that direct trade between the United States and Germany declined from $169 million in 1914 to $1 million in 1916,[37] but the figure was deliberately massaged to mislead. America certainly lost direct access to the German markets, but regained much more by trading indirectly with Germany through neutrals. Desperate German importers were willing to pay high prices, and ruthless American, Scandinavian and even British traders were willing to abandon any sense of propriety or patriotism to take advantage of the rich pickings. In addition, between 1914-1916, American trade with the Allies rose from $824 million to $3 billion.[38]

American industry produced whatever goods the Allies wanted and their business boomed. Financial credit was duly arranged through Wall Street banks linked to the Secret Elite, and the United States became "the larder, arsenal and bank"[39] for Britain and France. The United States thus acquired a direct interest in an Allied victory, and any other outcome would have spelled disaster for them. The British government's perennial excuse that they could not implement a strict blockade for fear of losing American support has been perpetuated by mainstream war historians. One quotation will suffice:

> The blockade would have achieved much more had the government enforced it more rigorously. But fearful of embittering neutral opinion and driving the neutrals, especially the United States, into Germany's arms, they often released neutral ships containing meat, wheat, wool etcetera that the Navy had, sometimes at considerable risk, sent into port for examination.[40]

The suggestion that the United States might ally itself with Germany was ludicrous in the extreme. That possibility was never considered in the corridors of power in Washington. "Neutral" America invested heavily in an Allied victory, fully supported Britain and France and, irrespective of the blockade, business thrived. Thousands of new millionaires were created year on year through war profiteering. The United States quickly professed her neutrality, but with equal alacrity accrued a vested interest in the Allied cause with a myriad of financial loans and munitions supplies that were initiated, and we cannot over-emphasize this fact, through Secret Elite links with the J.P. Morgan financial empire on Wall Street.

President Woodrow Wilson made the obligatory protests about Britain's interference with American trade. That was yet another charade played out on both sides of the Atlantic. Wilson's election in 1912 had been facilitated by the Wall Street bankers and big business who were themselves closely associated with the Secret Elite in London.[41] Not only had these financiers put their man in the White House, they gave him a minder, Edward Mandell House. The American historian and journalist Webster Tarpley described Mandell House as a "British-trained political operative."[42]

Woodrow Wilson was indeed President of the United States of America, but this shadowy figure, with his own suite of rooms in the White House, stood by his side "advising" his every move.[43] At every turn, Mandell House liaised and co-operated with the Secret Elite in London to ensure that, no matter the protests, they were always acting in concert. London knew that there was never any fear of losing American support. President Wilson played his part by issuing a series of protest notes which lent credence to the spurious notion that Britain should not implement a proper blockade for fear of alienating America.

For example, on 3 November 1914, the British Admiralty issued a proclamation to maritime shipping that a blockade was in operation in the North Sea and all ships were warned that they entered it at their peril. Scandinavian countries objected, but the United States government initially refused to join their protest. When American exporters and shipping companies complained to the State Department, a protest note was eventually sent to London on 26 December, but it was couched in very conciliatory language. Furthermore, prior to the note being sent, Mandell House discussed it with the British Ambassador, Sir Cecil Spring-Rice, so that any phrases that might upset British susceptibilities could be removed.[44]

Had a strict and proper blockade been in place, the impact on American traders would only have temporarily stopped their exports to Scandinavia. In consequence, the war would have been over by 1915 and the disruption short-lived. In addition, the Americans would never have risked breaking the blockade at the cost of a consequent ban from the huge British, French and Russian markets. Likewise, fears that neutral Scandinavia would side with Germany if Britain implemented a strict blockade were rootless. Sweden alone showed some pro-German sympathies, but there was a strong and vocal movement there which had enjoyed 100 years of peace. Neutrality was the only option. Sweden had long stood by its non-interventionist policy and its trade dependence on both Britain and Germany laced any other position with poisonous danger. On 3 August 1914 the Swedish government proclaimed the country neutral and the majority of Swedes supported that policy. Some in the upper classes were pro-German, but "there was a difference between admiring Germany, or identifying with German culture, and being prepared to side with Germany in war."[45] The so-called risk of driving the Scandinavian countries into Germany's arms was likewise a charade to justify Foreign Office policy.

Rear-Admiral Montagu Consett, the British Naval Attaché in Scandinavia from 1912 to 1918, dismissed the suggestion that these small neutral states might have sided with Germany. A staunch English patriot, Consett spoke with considerable knowledge of Scandinavian opinion:

> It was the universal belief that, should England become involved in a European war, Scandinavia would have to be prepared to make sacrifices. That all supplies from England would be cut off was not expected, but it was felt certain that bare requirements of domestic consumption would in no case be exceeded.... The prestige of this country never stood at so high a level. The name of England was ... mentioned with real respect. When war broke out the stream [of food and war materials] that poured into Scandinavia, amazed the Scandinavians.[46]

The Scandinavians admired and respected Britain and were prepared to make sacrifices to support her in the war. The suggestion put about by the British government that Norway, Sweden and Denmark would support Germany if they applied a strict blockade was a scurrilous lie.

As Rear Admiral Consett stated, "It is certain Germany was neither prepared nor equipped for a struggle of four years duration." The impact of a blockade which leaked like a sieve meant that the war "was prolonged far beyond the limits of necessity."[47] If a proper blockade had been enforced, knowledgeable contemporaries estimated that war on continental Europe would have been effectively over within 6-8 months.[48]

In their efforts to render the blockade ineffective, the Secret Elite faced two major obstacles, the Royal Navy and the Prize Courts. The officers and men of the blockading forces were absolutely determined to stop any supplies getting through to Germany, and risked life and limb to do so. "From August 1914 to the end of 1917, the 10th Cruiser Squadron intercepted 8,905 ships, sent 1,816 into port under armed guard and boarded 4,520 fishing craft."[49] Over the years of the blockade very few transatlantic steamers, merchant ships or fishing boats escaped their attention. The North Atlantic blockading force ordered thousands of vessels to heave to, no matter the mountainous seas or freezing temperatures, and sent crews in small open boats to examine the cargoes, inspect their permits and papers and ascertain their destinations. It was dangerous work. There was "a perilous interlude when engines had to be stopped before lowering away or picking up the boat with its boarding party; and these moments when the cruiser lay rolling in the swell were more than enough for a U-boat's captain to send his torpedo straight for the cruiser's side."

As early as 15 October 1914, *HMS Hawke* of the 10th Cruiser squadron was torpedoed by a U-Boat in the North Sea, turned over and sank with the loss of 525 lives.[50] These men were the unsung heroes of war, living on the knife-edge of uncertainty in a daily battle to deny solace to the enemy. The 10th Cruiser Squadron was permanently on the alert but was constrained both by its outdated ships and unbelievable decisions made deep in the heart of the Foreign Office.

Out at sea, suspicious cargoes were immediately seized by the boarding party and taken for inspection to the Orkney or Shetland islands. The integrity of British Prize Courts had never been questioned and if "cargoes were proved to be of enemy destination or origin, they would be condemned by the Prize Court and there would be no appeal except to the Judicial Committee of the Privy Council."[51] On paper this system was flawless and fair. Given the acknowledged zeal and professionalism of the Royal Navy's blockading fleet, very little contraband should have reached Germany from August 1914 onwards. That is what the public, the press and parliament in general believed. Winston Churchill had promised that the blockade would bring Germany to her knees. Not a word of dissent was voiced, yet powers greater than government ensured that the Prize Courts were neutered.

Behind the backs of the British people, in blatant defiance of the will of the British Parliament and widely accepted international law, the Prize Courts were sidelined and a more sinister authority was created to exercise the real power over the blockade. As the former Admiralty lawyer George Bowles wrote in sheer exasperation in 1926, "The process of stopping ships that were carrying contraband, bringing them before the Prize-Court judiciary so that international law could be applied and stripping them of illegal cargoes, was completely undermined by influences inside the British Foreign Office through an invention called the Contraband Committee." Bowles believed that lawful processes, "from first to last were checked, tripped up, manipulated and prevented from working by a deliberate and considered removal of the whole essential conduct of the war at sea from the Fleets and Prize Courts to the Foreign Office."[52] Look at the language Bowles used. There was no question of error or misunderstanding. Lawful process was hi-jacked and deliberately sabotaged.

Conjured by the Foreign Office, a small, carefully selected Contraband Committee was assembled in secret as a barrier between the Navy and the Prize Courts. While the Royal Navy stopped and searched every merchant ship in the North Sea and sent all suspicious cargoes into Kirkwall, the Contraband Committee ensured that very few of these were ever taken before a Prize Court. Under the guise of "freeing neutral shipping from all avoidable delay and inconvenience," the Contraband Committee made the final decision on virtually every ship stopped by the blockading squadron. This compact group of five or six shadowy figures decided what they considered contraband or not, and determined which cargoes should be allowed to proceed to their given destinations.[53] Their decisions were not arbitrary. They consistently rejected the Royal Navy's actions and released millions of tons of vital supplies that were ultimately bound for the German war effort.

The fate of the American oil tanker, the SS *Llama*, provided a typical example. With some difficulty the 10th Cruiser Squadron chased and captured the fully loaded tanker and an armed guard escorted her into Kirkwall. "But by a mysterious mentality someone in authority had ordered her release and allowed her to proceed on her way to Germany. She duly arrived at Swinemunde, where her most welcome cargo fetched a high price." Admiral de Chair thought it "incredible that after a year's war experience we should deliberately allow supplies to reach the enemy after the carrying-ships had been intercepted."[54] The *Llama* was at that time owned by Standard Oil of New Jersey and was part of J.D. Rockefeller's fleet. Rockefeller himself was closely linked to the Secret Elite in London and Wall Street.[55] When the *Llama* repeated the voyage she was again stopped by the 10th Cruiser Squadron and sent to Kirkwall. Ironically, and thankfully this time she hit a reef and sank.

Commander George Bowles's angry broadside summed up his view on the Foreign Office's illegal Contraband Committee: "This hitherto unheard of jurisdiction consisted, not, of course, in any form of open Court, but in a strange and suddenly invented Committee of persons nominated for the purpose by the officials concerned.... It acted, deliberated, and decided in secret. It was in continuous touch with Foreign Office opinion. It was bound by no law, custom, precedent, treaty, rules of evidence, rules of procedure, or legal restraint. It maintained upon the seas, against the rule of the Law of Nations, the rule of the Department; and it was used by that Department to ensure the prompt execution of its wishes in cases in which the Prize Courts of England could not be trusted to carry them out."[56]

Commander Bowles's assessment of the deliberate disruption of the blockade was perfectly valid, but he had no knowledge of the Secret Elite or their control of the politicians and mandarins within the Foreign Office. The secret cabal had assumed absolute control of the Foreign Office in 1905 when Sir Edward Grey was installed as foreign secretary. His minders, Sir Eyre Crowe, Sir Charles Hardinge and Sir Arthur Nicolson were proven establishment men closely associated with the Secret Elite.

These were the powerful individuals who actually ran the department while Sir Edward Grey fronted and deflected questions in Parliament.[57] They sat in Whitehall offices by day, and dined in their private London clubs of an evening. They and the Contraband Committee made a mockery of the tireless efforts of the brave men of the 10th Squadron out on the cruel, unforgiving seas of the freezing North Atlantic.

The prolific maritime writer, Commander Edward Keble Chatterton, concluded that the end result,

> allowed cargoes obviously intended for Germany to continue to their destination, whereas the blockaders had no sort of doubt, and the Prize Courts would certainly have condemned such cargoes... Today (he was writing in 1932) we know all too well how this misguided rule of allowing supplies to reach the enemy had the effect of prolonging the war.[58]

In December 1914 the worn-out warships of the 10th cruiser squadron were replaced by a mixed fleet of twenty-four armed merchant ships ranging from 2,876 to 21,040 tons. Some were passenger ships from the major shipping lines, others were cargo vessels, and several had been used in the banana trade. All of their captains had been hand-picked by Admiral de Chair. The executive officer and gunner on each ship also came from the Royal Navy, but the remainder of the officers and crews largely comprised merchant seamen. De Chair spoke of the outrageous conditions in which his men struggled to keep the nation safe. They faced blizzards of snow and hail and towering waves which made rest or sleep impossible. His praise for them was absolute. "It brought out the highest qualities of seamanship and navigation on the parts of the Captains, officers and seamen and there was no denying the remarkable discipline, devotion to duty, and firm resolve on the part of everyone."[59]

On 2 January 1915 two sailors from the blockading fleet were lost while attempting to rescue the crew of a Norwegian barque foundering in mountainous seas in a force 9 gale. A month later, on 3 February, *Clan MacNaughton* went down with her entire 284 officers and men. In those dangerous raging seas the cruisers of the Northern Patrol intercepted dozens of vessels every week. Between March 1915 and December 1916 an average of 286 ships per month were stopped.[60] Ten ships per day; every day. All the while, despite their heroic attempts to prevent vital supplies reaching the enemy, Secret Elite agents in the Foreign Office and Contraband Committee continually released ships with cargoes bound for Germany which brave men had risked their lives to impound.

Was it any wonder that the blockaders were indignant? And how did Commander Chatterton later see it? They were allowing supplies through to the enemy and so prolonging the war. Bear that in mind, please. They were prolonging the war.

The United States shipped 3,353,638 one-hundred pound bales of cotton to Scandinavia and Holland during the first five months of 1915 while previous shipments to these countries had averaged only 200,000 bales. The vast bulk of the excess was forwarded to Germany. British businessmen were quick to take advantage of the bonanza and made large profits by boosting the cotton trade to neutral countries which bordered Germany. Huge amounts of American cotton were also imported into Britain for munitions manufacture, but between January and May 1915, cotton dealers in England re-exported 504,000 one-hundred pound bales of that cotton to Scandinavia. This was around fifteen times higher than a previous five month period. For example, between April and May 1915, Sweden imported 17,331 tons of cotton (pre-war imports for the same time-period averaged 3,900 tons) of which 1,500 tons came directly from Britain. Holland virtually doubled her cotton imports during the month of April to 16,217 tons, of which 5,352 tons were exported from Britain. At the same time British re-exports to countries which did not border Germany were considerably reduced.[61] It was a scandal. Before any finger is pointed at others who profiteered from the war, the first and most disgusting culprits came from Britain herself.

Though Britain generously contributed to German cotton imports by ensuring its re-export through Scandinavia, most of the produce came from America where the right to sell cotton to any buyer was steadfastly defended. Cotton millionaires prospered as never before. The British Government had been offered the option to buy up much of the 1914 crop from the United States at a comparatively low price, but the offer was refused.[62] Asquith's government made no attempt to challenge the Cotton lobby in America. Indeed Lord Robert Cecil, under-secretary for foreign affairs in the coalition government insisted in Parliament on 12 July 1915 that Britain had a responsibility "to respect the legitimate rights of neutrals" and take into consideration the needs of both America and the Scandinavian countries.[63] His excuse was that if the cotton supply to neutrals was cut off it "would land us in international difficulties." Members of parliament "could not understand this cowardly policy in keeping cotton out of the contraband list."[64] No-one could. The British public was outraged and feeling was so strong that Lord Cecil was called a "murderer of his own countrymen."[65]

Commander Keble Chatterton of the Royal Navy could not hide his disgust that the government continued to ignore the loud demands that cotton supplies to Germany be stopped. He thought it pathetic that Germany had obtained practically all she wanted of the last American cotton crop via neutral countries, though Britain "could have stopped almost the whole lot.... So long as the Blockading Fleet was left alone to do its persistent duties, Germany was doomed.... She had gambled on a short, quick victory – and lost. Nothing could now save her from eventual collapse except some further folly that might issue from Whitehall."[66]

Germany should have been doomed. The blockading squadrons were doing their duty but were repeatedly obstructed by Foreign Office intervention. And, of course, there were further "follies," but what transpired was much more sinister than mere folly. In late June 1915, British delegates were sent to an Anglo-Swedish conference on cotton in Stockholm, and the result was that Britain permitted Sweden to import even more cotton. Despite all of the clamor raised against cotton exports, the Secret Elite continued to have their way.

The Foreign Office historian Archibald Bell recorded that, in complete contrast, the government in France consistently urged that cotton should be declared contraband. The French were astonished to learn through their ambassador that Sir Edward Grey had actually recommended that the British cabinet relax the blockade. The American ambassador at London, Walter Hines Page, a man "on intimate terms" with Sir Edward Grey, reported to Washington in mid-July, "that the government will make a vigorous effort to resist the agitation to make cotton contraband, with what result I cannot predict."[67]

Such was the wide-ranging clamor against cotton being exempt from contraband that the *Times* published a letter on 20 July 1915 from "A Neutral" which raised the issue to a higher level. It hit a chord with public anguish by reporting that, "the mothers of French soldiers think it inconceivable that you should continue supplying the enemy with the means of killing the sons of your allies." French people are continually asking, "What is the English fleet doing to allow cotton to go into Germany?"[68] Next day the *Times* responded through its editorial pages and raised the question of exportation of cotton and rubber to Germany, and of the "inadequacy of the steps so far taken by the British government to prevent these vitally important products from reaching an enemy destination," which was arousing serious anxiety both at home and abroad.

A further alarming point was raised by the Consulting Chemist to the Crown, Bertram Blount, that "there can be no doubt that if cotton had been made absolute contraband from the start the Russians would not now be retreating. If the proper steps had been taken at the beginning of the war to prevent Germany from obtaining supplies of cotton, the British and French troops would now be operating on German soil."[69] Here, from the pen of a government scientist was evidence that the allies had been denied a quick victory. He had no notion that the war was being deliberately prolonged.

Despite the widespread disgust in Britain, the government held out against the swell of public opinion and attempted to justify their inaction. Figures were later produced to make it appear that the cotton exports were not as great as had been widely reported. Lord Lansdowne told the House of Lords:

> Take the import of cotton to Scandinavia and Holland. The figure for 1913 is 73,000 tons. The figure for 1915 is 310,000 tons. That is a very alarming figure – an increase nearly fourfold. But if you make the comparison that I conceive ought to be made, and compare the year, not as a whole, but month by month, you will find – I put it this way for convenience sake – that in the last six months of 1913 the amount was 49,000 tons and for the last six months of 1915 was 52,000 tons.[70]

This was supposed to demonstrate an important turning point to the advantage of the Allies, but Rear-Admiral Consett worked through the statistics properly. He proved that while it could be argued that the last six month comparison showed only a 3,000 ton increase, the growth in the first six months of the year was from 24,000 tons in 1913 to a stunning 258,000 tons in 1915.[71] Lansdowne omitted to point out that the availability of cotton depended on the harvest. It took place in the autumn and through the latter part of the year, and consequently was only ready for exportation in the early months of the following year. There was always going to be a massive difference between statistics at different points in the cycle, but the government manipulated the facts to falsely indicate an improving situation.

Other factors intervened. The implications for maintaining the status quo were staggering. The men in the trenches, the families of those already sacrificed, the ordinary people in Britain and France would not have allowed the government to continue their ludicrous policy. Feelings ran high. It was all very well for the leader of the Secret Elite, Alfred Milner, to instruct his supporters to "disregard the screamers"[72] during the Boer War, but in an era of total war such high-handed disregard for public opinion was critically dangerous. In 1914 it had been simple to neutralize opposition to the war. One year on, the climate had changed. When MPs like the Liberal Sir Henry Dalziel refused to be muzzled on the cotton scandal no matter the implication for his career,[73] the writing was on the wall. The Secret Elite urgently needed an exit strategy. Their solution was to announce that the Americans no longer objected to cotton as a contraband.

Suddenly the claim was made that the munition contracts placed in America by Britain and France had increased their domestic consumption of cotton to the extent that loss of the German market would hardly be felt by big business. Sir Cecil Spring-Rice, British ambassador at Washington reported that President Wilson was "quite satisfied" that cotton should now be placed on the contraband list.[74] It reeked of an "old pal's act."

Summary

- The British Naval Blockade of Germany between 1914-1916 was a cruel charade which was designed to fail.
- The Foreign Office and the Admiralty decided to adopt a distant blockade rather than a close blockade on German ports.
- Churchill promised the British nation that within a year the blockade would bring the German nation to its knees. That was a lie.
- The so-called rules of naval war were determined by the Declaration of London of 1909, but these were never ratified by the British parliament.
- The Secret Elite's Lord Esher concluded that there was no need for legislation to close any gaps in the rules of blockade, in particular, the exemption of cotton from the list of contraband.
- The 10th Cruiser Squadron was cobbled together after war had been declared to guard the vast and wild expanse of the North Sea. Eight of the oldest small cruisers built in 1891-2 were sent to undertake the impossible task of blockading the North Sea from Scotland to the Arctic.
- Traffic to Germany was routed from America through the neutral Scandinavian countries Denmark, Sweden and Norway.
- The pretense that a full blockade would have had the disastrous effect of alienating America from the Allied cause was nonsense. The American commitment to the Allies was sealed in loans, in massive profits and mutual self-interest.
- A secret Contraband Committee inside the Foreign Office acted as a hidden barrier between an effective cruiser squadron empowered to stop supplies and resources reaching Germany.
- Almost every cargo ship caught on the high seas and sent to Kirkwall in the Orkney Islands by the blockading squadron was subsequently permitted to continue its journey to Scandinavia and then to its final destination, Germany.
- Naval experts accused the Admiralty of prolonging the war by allowing such volumes of produce to reach Germany.
- The outcry against the export of Cotton for use in shells and munitions grew so loud that by mid-1915 complaints by the press and in parliament caused a turnabout in policy, and it with high cotton sales guaranteed by Britain and France, President Wilson announced that he was 'quite satisfied' that cotton should be placed on the contraband list.

Chapter 5

The Myth Of The Great Blockade – Shameful Profits

From the very first days of war, merchants and importers in Stockholm, Oslo, Copenhagen, Helsingborg and Malmo found themselves inundated with orders from Germany to supply thousands of tons of animal feed, foodstuffs, ores, cotton and coal. Purchased from the Americas, North, Central and South, from Britain and the British Empire, from other neutral countries world-wide these imports literally bounced from the quay-sides and dockyards to the goods trains and canal boats that ferried them to their final destination. Germany.

Scandinavian merchants made profits beyond their wildest dreams because Germany was willing to pay grossly inflated prices to guarantee these vital supplies.[1] Denmark, and Holland too, became Germany's sea-based importers while Sweden served additionally as her workshop. In an international game of charades, neutral ships were moderately inconvenienced in the North Sea gateways to and from the Atlantic, but the loss of time was more than compensated by the immense profits that were made in America, in Scandinavia, and, we must not forget, in Britain

The volume of trade that was permitted to pass across the North Sea exceeded all previous quantities. British trade with Scandinavia was justified by the government on the grounds that guarantees were in place

The might of the Royal Navy.

to ensure that Germany would not benefit by these exports. The given pledges were worthless. Government departments knew precisely what was happening. The evidence was presented to them, but to no avail. As the British Naval attaché in Scandinavia stated: "All representations ... authentic statements of facts, supported by trustworthy analysis [presented to the British government] were disregarded."[2]

In addition to its naval supremacy, Britain boasted another strategic advantage. She held vast reserves of the next most important weapon for waging war – coal. Scandinavia had little or none. Germany had stockpiles sufficient to cover only a limited period and their shortage of coal soon gave cause for grave concern. Some was available from outside her borders. None of the Belgian coal mines had been destroyed by their retreating army, and Germany was "able to extricate herself from a very difficult position with Belgian coal."[3] But that in itself was insufficient.

The hot summer of 1914 had resulted in a surplus of British coal available for export and initially no national embargo was placed on it. Coal merchants were asked not to supply ships suspected of trading on the enemy's behalf, but no direct restrictions were placed on them before May 1915. An appeal to patriotism, to do the decent "British" thing, was considered sufficient, but the moral compass of the profiteer does not point to such a sentiment.

British coal was always in high demand. It was recognized across the world as a high quality product, especially for the purpose of generating steam power. The boilers in warships were designed for burning Welsh coal, and railway locomotives for English coal. Admiral Consett recorded that in Denmark alone, state railways, gas works, electrical light and power stations, even breweries, were dependent almost entirely on British coal.[4] Coal was power. And it was a power that the British government could well have used to good effect if its export to Scandinavia had been immediately curtailed. Consett wrote of: "Special fast trains packed with fish, the staple diet of many of the Danes, carried it to Germany, when fish was unprocurable in Denmark; incidentally, be it mentioned, the trains were run on British coal, and the fishing tackle was supplied by Great Britain."[5]

Most of the merchantmen in the Atlantic depended on British coal, and bunkering stations were scattered widely around the world to provide the necessary supply to the fleets of the Empire. An effective and instant blockade could have been introduced in August 1914 simply by denying coal to any ship suspected of trading directly or indirectly with the enemy. The Scandinavians expected that British coal supplies would be restricted or perhaps even entirely cut off on the outbreak of war, and feared that industrial disorganization would rapidly ensue. The curtailment of coal supplies at the very start of the war would have had the most profound effect. No coal meant no power, limited transport, no heat, no factory production. It spelled disaster for Germany.

Swedish factories and manufacturers were in the main working for Germany, yet no effort was made in Britain to control or limit the supply of coal, which continued to be exported to them until the end of 1915. Indeed, British coal fueled the transport of Sweden's invaluable iron ore to Germany, yet it was not until the spring of 1918 that any serious attempt was made to compel Sweden to reduce her exports to Germany. The Germans continued to purchase all the necessary imports for weapons' production until the end of the war "through the prodigal supplies of coal from her foolish and gullible enemy."[6] And all the while the government was exhorting British coal miners to do their patriotic duty and work harder digging coal for the British war effort.

Rear-Admiral Consett had no idea that it was not foolishness and gullibility that led to this, but a very deliberate policy of the British government. He noted that throughout the war, and particularly during the first two years, large numbers of German railway trucks were to be seen in all Scandinavian countries which were hauled to and from Germany with British coal. According to newspaper reports the state railways handled so much traffic that local requirements were frequently neglected. "Not only were we actively assisting German trade in Scandinavia, but we were performing valuable transport services for the enemy."[7]

There was another side to this raw profiteering. The loss of coal to exports impacted on the ordinary people of Britain. In 1915, Walter Runciman, President of the Board of Trade, was alarmed at the exorbitant coal prices that were crushing the poor in the great cities of Britain, especially London. In February of that year the *Times* reported that coal bought at 21 shillings per ton at the pit mouth sold in London for 32 shillings per ton with further rises anticipated.[8] Concerned MPs talked of the privileged class of colliery owners who, even with fixed prices at the pit head, had become millionaires.[9] Unquestionably coal owners controlled the price and the London Coal Exchange coal-ring ensured that prices remained excessive.[10] While tens of thousands of miners, around twenty per cent of the workforce, volunteered for Kitchener's army, the families they left behind were faced with coal-price increases of a criminal nature.

The poor were at the mercy of coal merchants and hawkers who went round the streets selling small quantities at exorbitant prices. Living hand to mouth, and having to make critical decisions between food or fuel, the poor city dweller bore the brunt of the mercenaries' callous profiteering.[11] On the other hand, as was pointed out by MP Sir E. Markham, the rich could easily buy however much coal they needed from Harrods (acting as the middleman) because they could afford the price.[12] Yet the politicians would have it that "we were all in this together." *We* were not. As ever it was the poor who bore the brunt.

Despite the desperate need at home, British coal continued to be exported to neutral countries. In September 1914, Sweden alone received 633,000 tons, a seventh of her whole yearly requirement. Scandinavian ships, using British bunkers, began to pour millions of tons of re-exports into Germany through Scandinavian ports.[13] The total amount of British coal exported to Scandinavia, from the outbreak of war up to the end of 1917, was 21,632,180 tons.[14] How many innocents froze to death in slums and hovels in the poorer quarters of British cities, or in remote and isolated villages during those awful war winters, victims too of the mercenary instincts of the coal profiteer?

That is another point which has been long neglected. Britain's success in the bitter struggle against Germany depended on man-power and the blockade. In other words the country had both to use its own working capacity to the utmost for war purposes, and reduce the enemy's productivity and resources by means of the blockade. Britain's policy on the export of coal conflicted with both of these conditions. The argument could be made that our man-power was being employed indirectly for the benefit of the enemy. Hard working miners, struggling against the odds to increase output with a much decreased labor force, were, in effect, helping to maintain the enemy's productivity because much of their coal ended up in Germany.[15] Had the miners known that they were digging for the "Hun," the government would have fallen. The scandal of cotton was matched only by that of coal. Indeed, a powerful case could be argued that those who permitted it betrayed their nation and were guilty of a vile form of treason. It did not stop there.

Germany produced only a fraction of the resources needed for the complex manufacture of her munitions industry, dominated as it was by the Krupp company. Nickel, manganese, aluminum, copper, wool and flax, and all of its requirements in rubber, oil, saltpeter and jute had to be sourced from abroad and imported at considerable cost. A survey by the German navy in 1913 confirmed that on average, munitions companies held only sufficient resources for three months production, though some might have lasted longer. Their calculations indicated that, due to the lack of raw materials, the production of the weapons of war in Germany would slump after that point. But no such collapse took place. According to Oxford historian Professor Sir Hew Strachan, "Germany's most significant import for military purposes, iron ore, seemed relatively impervious to maritime intervention."[16] *Seemed relatively impervious?* What a meaningless phrase. Was there some mystery? None at all. The undisputed fact is that for at least the first two years of the war, Germany was allowed to import the raw materials for her war industries despite Britain's clear ability to stop it.

The earlier chapter on the non-defense of Briey explained how, throughout the war, the French gifted Germany much of her vital iron ore from the Briey basin on the Franco-German border. She also obtained vast quantities of ore from Sweden, supplies which the Allies were perfectly capable of stopping. High quality ore was one of Sweden's natural resources and the top-grade steel it produced was used in ship-building, and in particular, U-boats. Germany's iron imports increased immediately after war broke out, and Rear-Admiral Consett warned the Admiralty that this must be stopped. What outraged Consett most was that "the haulage of ore from the mines to the coast was carried out to a large extent by the Swedish railways with British coal; its further transport by steamer across the Baltic was also (certainly for the first two years) effected by British coal."[17]

Much of the Swedish ore was carried to Germany by Danish ships which served effectively as a replacement for the German merchant fleet bottled up in ports on both sides of the Atlantic. Such loyal service came with an added bonus. Not a single vessel belonging to the Danish owned East Asiatic line was sunk by German submarines during the war, and the company was able to pay a 30% dividend to its shareholders in 1916.[18] Fired by British coal they shipped between four and five million tons of Swedish ore into Germany each year. Consett stated bluntly, "Nothing would have hastened the end of the war more effectively than the sinking of ships trading in ore between Sweden and Germany, or by economic pressure brought to bear on the Swedish ore industry."[19]

Sweden sent other valuable ores and metals across the Baltic to Germany including copper, which was required for every phase of naval and military warfare. Although there was no indigenous production of copper in Sweden, she increased her imports on the outbreak of war, then re-exported to Germany more than three times the amount she had formerly purchased from abroad. The authorities in London were aware of this, but rather than banning British exports of copper to Sweden, they permitted them to be doubled from 517 tons in 1913 to 1,085 tons in 1915. Throughout that same period, Sweden's exports of copper to Germany increased well beyond her normal peacetime levels.[20] Two years into the war, supplies of these commodities were still pouring from the Baltic into Germany. [21] Two years of desperate struggle on the Western Front against the explosive power of German howitzers was literally sustained on the back of these unchallenged imports to Scandinavia. Copper was carried into Britain from America and elsewhere across the world in British ships burning British coal. Considerable quantities of it were then exported to Sweden in British ships using British coal. Much of that copper was then sent on to Germany in ships which were, once again, powered by British coal. It was the worst of human nature.

The British government argued that it dared not halt exports to Sweden lest the Swedes retaliate by banning exports of her own products essential to Britain and the war effort. This was but one more sham excuse that collapsed under investigation. A shortage of materials like pit-props or paper could be sourced either from home or the Empire. Sweden offered nothing that could not be found elsewhere by the Allies. Britain was not dependent on Sweden. Quite the reverse. Sweden was dependent on Britain and neutral nations for a wide range of imports including coal, cereals, lubricants, petroleum, fodder and fertilizers.[22] Had it wanted to, the British government could have exerted tremendous pressure on Sweden to stop all exports to Germany, but took no definitive action until very late in the war. If Sweden had appealed to the international courts about her loss of trade, it would have been perfectly feasible for Britain and her allies to allay such fears and purchase everything that was bound for Germany. It was not to be.

Sweden also exported zinc, steel and other essential metals to Germany, in addition to wire, machinery, timber and large quantities of food. As if that was not sufficient, Britain sent Sweden more than twice her pre-war imports of the most valuable of all ingredients for strengthened steel, nickel. In 1915, of Sweden's total imports of 504 tons of nickel, 65 per cent came from Britain and her Empire. Of this, 70 tons were sent directly to Germany. The remainder was used in Sweden to manufacture war materials for Germany. The furious British naval attaché reported that "We sent Sweden twelve times the amount of nickel in 1915 that we did in 1913,"[23] and all of it to the benefit of the enemy.

There was a further scandal that the government tried desperately to keep from public knowledge. Crucial supplies of nickel were regularly exported to Germany from Norway. Nickel is a very hard metal essential for the manufacture of strengthened steel for guns, ships and armaments of various type. A small amount of nickel, 2 per cent to 4 per cent, was all that was required to harden the metals, so the ore itself was very valuable, and few countries had good natural supplies.[24] Most known deposits of nickel were already in Allied hands through the Mond Nickel Company in Canada and the great deposits in the French Dependency of New Caledonia in the Pacific. Germany's stock of nickel in 1914 was meager. She had sufficient only for a short war and, apart from the nickel supplied by Britain through Sweden, Germany had to rely on Norway as her sole supplier. There was only one factory in Norway capable of producing the amount Germany needed, the Kristiansand Nikkel Raffineringswerk, known as the K.N.R, which smelted about 60 tons of nickel per month, almost all of which went to Germany.

The British government agreed to a contract with K.N.R by which they paid the company £1 million to limit their export of nickel to Germany to 80 tons per month.[25] While the tactic of trying to restrict German imports of nickel was understandable, the deal itself was fraudulent. The agreed 80 ton limit was greater than the company's total output, so Germany continued to import her full quota, and Britain received no benefit from the deal. Basically, K.N.R was handed £1 million for a contract that did not interfere with its exports to Germany.[26] Consett angrily claimed that by applying appropriate pressure, Britain "could have prevented the export of the larger part of the nickel to Germany, or could have stopped the production of the nickel itself." His official and repeated representations to the Admiralty to have the nickel traffic stopped were to no avail.[27]

If the British government was unwilling to take action, others, closer to hand, were. Norwegian ships had been sunk by German U-boats using torpedoes made from steel hardened with Norwegian nickel, and there was a deep and bitter enmity towards Germany. Norwegian patriots took matters into their own hands and blew up the works in May 1917.[28] Though hardly worth a mention in the British press, this act of defiance was a serious blow to German shell production and a major rebuilding program was quickly undertaken. Then the K.N.R scandal deepened. Newspapers in Canada revealed a connection between the British Government, the British American Nickel Corporation and K.N.R. The accusation was that, though nominally Norwegian, K.N.R was in fact controlled by a German company in Frankfurt.[29] The claims were entirely justified. But it went even deeper than was realized. The murky world of international armaments and munitions reeked of scandal and collusions which linked compliant governments with powerful agencies and cartels often referred to as the "merchants of death."

It is absolutely unquestionable that the quantity of essential war materials that were exported from Britain, her Empire and elsewhere, through Scandinavia to Germany was vast, almost unmeasurable. There is no conclusion to be drawn other than the horrifying realization that millions were needlessly sacrificed and the war knowingly prolonged.

From 18 February 1915, Germany began a blockade of the British Isles. They considered it an act of retaliation. Foodstuffs and fodder had been added by the British government to the list of conditional contraband on 29 October 1914 as a reaction to the German decision to assume national control for all grain and flour in the country. The argument ran that no distinction could be placed between the military and civilian population, so all imports of foodstuffs had to be considered contraband.[30] The German Admiralty had been angered by the British decision that the whole North Sea be treated as a military area since November 1914, and interpreted the embargo on foodstuffs as a declaration of unlimited economic war.[31]

The German Admiral Hugo von Pohl duly warned neutrals that their merchant ships would be targeted if they tried to break the blockade. Almost immediately U-boats struck with punishing precision. An average of two British-bound cargo ships were sunk each day and many brave merchant seamen lost their lives in the cold Atlantic or North Sea approaches, but the size of the British merchant fleet and the sheer scale of the imports it carried from across the world ensured that the German blockade had little immediate effect on life on the home front. Germany continued to import ever increasing quantities of food. Had the British naval blockade been properly enforced at the start of the war, before sufficient U Boats had been built, Germany would have been brought to her knees by the end of 1915.

This was the backdrop to Germany's survival. A nation has to eat to survive, and the collapse of agriculture and food production in Germany meant that her capacity to fight beyond 1915 was critically threatened, not by guns and bullets, but by the lack of bread and potatoes. The *einkreisung* (encirclement) of Germany by Britain, France and Russia had given the Allies a distinct advantage in starving Germany into submission, but they did not take it. The opportunity to enforce a short, sharp economic war was deliberately thrown away. Victory alone was not the objective. The Secret Elite had always demanded that Germany be crushed.

Rear-Admiral Consett's book, *The Triumph of Unarmed Forces,*[32] written in 1923, detailed the facts, figures and information which proved beyond doubt that the Foreign Office enabled the German army to be fed and provisioned through Scandinavia for over three years. Denmark's home-grown supplies of food, if properly rationed, were sufficient for its own population, and an effective blockade, in combination with an embargo on British exports to Denmark in 1915, would have brought about Germany's collapse. But no. British coal and British agricultural machinery was sent to Denmark and in some cases was unloaded from the merchantmen's holds straight into railway trucks for transit to Germany.[33] "It was well known to Britain's Allies and to the Americans in Scandinavia that Britain was actually competing with neutrals in supplying the enemy. Had the supplies been withheld it would have sounded Germany's death knell at an early date."[34]

The facts are overwhelming. In 1913 Britain exported 370 tons of tea to Denmark, but by 1915 it had risen to 4,528 tons. In March 1916, Consett found the Copenhagen wharves choked with cases of tea, "a large part of which was from our colonies en route to Germany." Coffee was likewise re-exported to Germany. In 1913 Britain exported 1,493 tons to Sweden, Norway and Denmark, and this fully met their demands. In 1915, however, British exports of coffee to Scandinavia had risen dramatically by 500 per cent to 7,315 tons.[35] In addition, oil cake and vegetable and animal oils and fats poured into Germany from Britain via Scandinavia. Used normally for food, soap, candles, lubricants and fuels, in wartime the glycerin was extracted for explosives. Consett explained that: "the importance of these raw materials was based on their suitability for meeting the ultimate requirements of Germany for explosives. For three years Germany and her neutral neighbors succeeded in realizing their wishes. Denmark was supplied with oils and fats and oil cake from the British Empire far in excess of the quantities she had obtained from us in peace time."[36]

What a chilling observation. British merchants were actively competing to supply the enemy with much needed produce and material, while their own young men were being slaughtered in Flanders. The home comforts of tea and more particularly coffee, gave succor and sustenance to the German army, and the profits flowed back to Britain and the Empire.

Lord Sydenham, a former British army officer and Colonial administrator, fiercely attacked the government's decision to sign a trade agreement with Denmark which many considered to be a worthless sham. He berated them in the House of Lords on 20 December 1915: "There is no doubt whatever that Denmark has been doing an enormous trade with Germany and Austria during the last seventeen months, and the prosperity of all here is too apparent.… You [the government] have helped in this, and your new Agreement will help much more than ever for Germany to be fed, the war prolonged, and your blockade made a joke. This Agreement is very wrong and should be canceled, and you should wake up and stir up your officials or dismiss them."[37]

Strong language indeed. He lashed out at the blockade as a "joke." And here again, as many before and after claimed, was the stark accusation that the British government prolonged the war. Sydenham exposed where the intransigence lay. Unfortunately, his exhortation that the government should "stir up" or indeed dismiss the officials in charge, missed the crucial point. Foreign office committees were stacked with the chosen appointees prepared to do the bidding of the Elite. These men were anonymous.

Fish, beef, pork, fats, butter and other dairy produce had been flooding into Germany from Denmark since August 1914 despite the indisputable fact that Britain could easily have stopped it. Trade Agreements with neutral countries like Denmark were sound in principle but weak in practice and the foodstuffs flowed through Scandinavia in ever greater quantities, such that Germany was able to stem the tide of starvation in difficult years. The Scandinavian farming and fishing industries sustained Germany, but those industries were themselves supported by imports of fuel and fertilizers often directly from Britain. During the last six months of 1914, Denmark sold 68,000 horses to Germany and thousands of live cattle were exported every week. These animals provided more than just meat. Britain allowed Denmark to import raw hides, boots and shoes through the blockade, thus enabling her to export the horses and cattle which would otherwise have been required for her own leather industry.[38] Did no-one see the connection?

Danish farmers were selling to Germany at huge profit. In the first seven months of 1916 agricultural exports amounted to 117,000 tons. The meat-export alone during this period was 62,561 tons, sufficient to provide a million meat rations per day for the German army, yet Danish meat and dairy produce exports to Britain dropped by 25 per cent.[39] Britain provided the basic fodder and fertilizers to boost Denmark's agricultural output, and the vast bulk of the produce was sold to feed the German people and their army.

During the first two years of the war, not only was fish vital for the German army, but it provided much needed glycerin for explosives production. Rear-Admiral Consett exposed how the Norwegian fishing industry, by far the largest and most important in Northern Europe, depended upon British or British-controlled supplies. He believed that "the moment and circumstances immediately following the outbreak of war could not have been more favorable for Britain purchasing the Norwegian catch in return for a guaranteed supply of all fishing accessories." The opportunity was ignored.

From his offices in Christiana (Oslo), Consett watched in horror as mountains of exports were piled onto the quayside in Scandinavian ports and re-routed to Germany in plain daylight. This was not a secret operation. Open trade was conducted in contempt of whatever loose agreements Scandinavian merchants had signed with Britain to keep their ships off an official black list. Consett was adamant that the blockade could have been enforced and Germany ruined, but for the open trade that was conducted through Scandinavia. By 1917, "we we're reaping what we sowed in 1915 and 1916 when we were building up great food industries and establishing them at the gates of Germany."[40]

The magnitude of the traffic going to Germany was scandalous. To his great credit, Consett reported every detail of these infringements and blatant abuses. He sent indignant reports and letters to the Foreign Office, the Admiralty and eventually, tired of being ignored, to anyone in Britain he thought might listen. With questions in Parliament and critical newspaper articles in the press, something had to be done to nullify his scathing exposé.

In late 1915, the Foreign Office sent Sir Alexander Henderson (later elevated to the Peerage as Lord Faringdon) to visit Scandinavia and Holland in order to make "independent" inquiries on trading practices. Henderson, a member of parliament and deputy chairman of the Shipping Control Committee,[41] was linked through financial interests to members of the Secret Elite like Ernest Cassel and Lord Revelstoke. He was in insider and was tasked to investigate the allegations that foodstuffs and vital supplies were hemorrhaging through Scandinavia to Germany. Consett was "exhilarated." At last a member of government had the opportunity to see for himself the extent of the Scandinavian abuse. He fully expected immediate action. The result was a secret report that the government refused to release. Sir Edward Grey called it "very satisfactory," in that it showed that "the amount of leakage in the trade passing from overseas through these neutral countries to the enemy is ... much less than might have been supposed." To emphasize that all was well with the blockade, Grey claimed that "the general tendency of the report is to show that the maximum which can be done is being done."[42] This was no investigation; it was a whitewash.

As before, Sir Edward Grey reprimanded parliament for forgetting the rights of neutrals to supplies for their own consumption. "You have no right to make neutrals suffer" was one admonition, and he maintained that "no ships are going through to German ports at all." Fair enough, if you constrain the analysis to German ports. The Foreign Secretary's claim concluded that "we are stopping the trade coming out, and we are also stopping the imports; more than that you cannot do."[43] But Grey was deliberately dealing in semantics. It was not Germany that Henderson (Lord Faringdon) had visited; it was Scandinavia.

Sir Edward Grey chose not to differentiate between direct trade (through German ports) and indirect trade (through Scandinavia) where a veritable armada of merchant shipping, coal transporters, oil tankers, fishing boats, coastal traders and the like, was transporting the life-blood for Germany's survival as a fighting nation.

Skeptical MPs like Sir Henry Dalziel asked to see the report. Sir Edward Grey refused. And would not budge. Not for the first time, nor the last, Edward Grey lied to parliament. When asked how long Lord Faringdon had spent in Copenhagen and which other Danish ports he had visited, Grey did not "consider such answers necessary" and stressed that Lord Faringdon was "quite capable of judging the value or amount of information at his disposal."[44] Such a patronizing performance was worthy of a Secret Elite agent. Lesser mortals had no need to know what was going on, or why.

Consett was bitterly disillusioned. He knew exactly what Faringdon had witnessed and could scarcely contain his anger at the deception. He bluntly countered that the report "on which the future and especially 1916 so much hinged, did not represent the facts as reported to Lord Faringdon by myself, or as reported by me officially through the British legation to the Foreign Office; or as disclosed by official statistics published after the war: all of which showed that the Scandinavian trade with Germany at the time of Lord Faringdon's visit was on an unprecedented scale."[45]

Faringdon colluded in a whitewash. Consett noted scathingly that, "Sir Alexander Henderson came, saw and reported, and became Lord Faringdon."[46] And he was right. Immediately on his return, Alexander Henderson was raised to peerage as Baron Faringdon of Buscot Park – his 3,500 acre estate, this the "just" reward for a monumental cover-up. Faringdon's fawning claim was that "the government were to be congratulated on the way they had dealt with many difficulties, and they deserved encouraging support." Enough said.

Despite the literal slap on the face from London, Consett kept up a barrage of complaints. He was relentless. In the summer of 1916, Commander Leverton Harris, Director of the Restriction of Enemy Supplies Department at the Foreign Office, and later parliamentary secretary to the Ministry of Blockade, was sent to Scandinavia to investigate the situation once more. Leverton Harris was Lord Robert Cecil's right-hand man. Consett warned him about two burning issues; the huge tonnage of fish going to Germany and the need to stop supplies of petrol to the Scandinavian fishing fleets. He explained: "Truth is certainly stranger than fiction. That we should be supplying the Danish fishermen with all necessities; that the fishermen should be sending practically the whole of their catch to Germany ... and be able to obtain unlimited quantities of petrol without hindrance from the British authorities who could kill the industry ... was both strange and true."[47] His claim was indisputable, but nothing changed until later in the war. In 1916 there was just sufficient food and munitions for Germany to continue the struggle, but there was no margin for error, even though she had an additional food source from Belgium.[48] An effective blockade in combination with an embargo on British exports to Scandinavia in 1915 and 1916 would have guaranteed Germany's collapse. But the war continued.

In 1916 a sea change took place in Britain. Early public expectation of a quick decisive victory predicated on naval supremacy and a successful blockade had been shattered by its abject failure. Profound disappointment, indeed a sense of disenchantment, followed. The pliant and supportive British press of 1914 began by 1916 to look for reasons victory seemed as far away as ever. Their focus turned to the naval blockade. Stories of vessels being released to neutral nations with cargoes of cotton, oil, ores, fish, meat, flour, lard and much more bound for Germany, drew an angry response. The *Daily Mail* campaigned against the "Sham Blockade" and the *Morning Post* criticized the "Make Believe Blockade." They carried rumors that Cabinet Ministers would be impeached and Sir Edward Grey was forced to deny the accusations in Parliament.[49]

For as long as the instigators of war held office, they continually lied to parliament about the blockade, its apparent limitations and its effectiveness. Winston Churchill had raised the level of expectation in November 1914 by insisting that Germany would be doomed within a year; that the blockade would absolutely bring Germany to her knees. He lied. He lied too in Cabinet on 3 March 1915, claiming that the blockade was "in every sense effective: no instance is known to the Admiralty of any vessel, the stopping of which has been authorized by the Foreign Office, passing them unchallenged. It is not a case of a paper blockade, but of a blockade as real and as effective as any that has ever been established."[50] False but clever semantics. The Foreign Office was in the business of ordering the release of these vessels before they were impounded. Churchill deliberately glossed over what had actually transpired.

The farce of the blockade was described in Parliament by Sir Henry Dalziel, on 27 March 1917 in the following term:

> For the first eighteen month of the war, the Admiralty were in a state of despair with regard to the actions of the Foreign Office. They were bringing in, day after day, ships which were admittedly carrying cargo to the benefit of the enemy. What happened? A telegram was sent to London to the Foreign Office, and in reply, often in the course of a few hours, a telegram came informing them that they ought to let the ships go through … which tended to make our sailors absolutely depressed and in despair.… The whole thing was treated as a farce, though ship after ship, to the knowledge of the officers, carried goods for Germany.[51]

Britain effectively fed and supplied Germany, effectively prolonged the war. Heads should have rolled. Guilty men ought to have been mercilessly exposed.

Several strong-minded members of parliament pursued the issue relentlessly, even when threats were made to silence them.[52] Sir Henry Dalziel raised the question of cotton supplies to Germany despite being "threatened if I raised the question tonight that I would be counted out." Dalziel would not be silenced. He railed that Britain still allowed cotton, "the most essential factor in the making of high explosives to go to our enemy, and we are assisting them to make munitions that kill our soldiers.… Without the cotton.… Germany would have been practically unable to continue the war up to the present time."[53]

In February 1916, when the failure of an effective blockade was lambasted by an outraged Press, Lord Charles Beresford, a former First Sea Lord and highly respected Admiral, stood in the House of Lords and bluntly stated that had a full blockade been put in place, rather than the ambiguous and colander-like Treaty of London, "the war would now have been over."[54]

The bitter anger against those responsible for the sham blockade became very personal. At the end of the war Brigadier-General Henry Page Croft, MP for Christchurch, who fought at the Somme with noted bravery, accused government ministers of lying about "the indefensible export of essential and vital foodstuffs during 1915 and the first half of 1916."[55] Having witnessed the selflessness and bravery of men at the front, he became intolerant of the opportunism of politicians at home whom he held responsible.[56] Croft wanted blood. He wanted names. He wanted the public to know who had made these decisions. The answer he was given was that no minister was responsible. Croft responded with warranted sarcasm, "We fed Germans because no minister was responsible." His patience snapped. "No minister was responsible during this time, and yet we find millions of tons of produce and raw materials left this country – ore for shells to blow our men to bits in the trenches, cotton to provide explosives for these shells, and food to feed the Germans who fired those shells."[57] Read these words aloud and feel the anger. The Brigadier-General suggested that Foreign Secretary Sir Edward Grey, Prime Minister Herbert Asquith and president of the Board of Trade Walter Runciman be impeached. One can only imagine the consternation amongst the Secret Elite and their agents. But nothing substantial happened. As ever they deflected accusations, camouflaged the guilty and ignored the questions.

Without a doubt, the most important, detailed and accurate information about the failures of the blockade that had been meticulously recorded and forwarded to the government came from the British naval attaché in Scandinavia, Captain (later Rear-Admiral) Consett. His damning exposé showed page by page, statistical column by statistical column, that Britain had effectively allowed Germany to be fed and supplied with metals for armaments production through Denmark, Sweden and Norway and in so doing had prolonged the war. In response, Sir Edward Grey criticized "reckless statements" and painted an entirely false picture. What nailed Grey's lies was a military analysis prepared in 1916 for the senior staff conference between the British and French commanders. Their top-secret "Note on the Blockade of the North Sea" was sent to the Committee of Imperial Defence in March 1916:[58] "Germany has been able to continue to export merchandise and securities, and thus obtain money and credits from neutrals. She has even been able to import, at a high price it is true, the provisions and goods of which she stood most urgently in need ... the economic struggle has not yet been undertaken; it is of urgent importance, however, that the Governments concerned should adopt the necessary measures without delay." The adoption of these measures ... "would certainly have the effect of diminishing the enemy's power of resistance, and therefore of shortening the war."[59]

So there it was, twenty months into the war and the blockade was not effective. Indeed the Allied military staff went so far as to say that the economic measures which would have shortened the war had "not yet been undertaken." Their assessment stood in stark contrast to the lies which were routinely spouted by Grey and other government ministers.

The facts spoke for themselves. The real blockade had yet to be put in place. The outcry became unstoppable. Time and again contemporary writers, parliamentarians and senior military and naval personnel, repeated the mantra that war could have been won within eighteen months had there been a real blockade. George Bowles, Conservative M.P. and Admiralty Lawyer, claimed that the conflict would have been over within four-and-a-half months.[60] Others like Lords Sydenham and Beresford estimated that war would have been over in the last months of 1915. But the war was prolonged. Millions of men were sacrificed. Profits grew ever higher. The anguished voices of reason were eventually carried by the Press and forced change. From 1917 until 1919 a very different blockade came into effect.

So how did the Secret Elite reconcile history once the war was ended? How did they justify the sham of the blockade? Their normal tactic was to ignore criticism and remove it from official records. Pretend it never happened. Keep it from the public eye and deny it. Most of the official records of the Admiralty, Foreign Office and Board of Trade were removed, presumed destroyed. Some, a century later, might still be locked away in the secret British government archives at Hanslope Park in Buckinghamshire.[61] Interestingly, even in 2005, The Imperial War Museum's Book of The War At Sea, 1914-1918, made no reference whatsoever to the Blockade.[62] Apparently the heroics of 10th Cruiser Squadron out on the Atlantic Ocean and the North Sea, their hardships, sacrifice and losses, their honourable and magnificent contribution, had no part to play in the history of the war at sea.

Those who sought to deny the scandal of the blockade were, however, thwarted by the publication of Rear-Admiral Consett's damning book *The Triumph of Unarmed Forces,* published in 1923 and subject of the most extraordinary debate in the House of Lords.[63] Sir Edward Grey, the man at the very heart of the sham blockade and by then, Viscount Fallodon, attended the debate. He claimed to know nothing about the details revealed in the book save what he had heard that day, but proceeded to argue that the zealous man on the spot knew only one part of a whole picture, while at the center "some mind which can take in much more" knew all the consequences. Grey stated that if the government had taken the action advocated at that time by Admiral Consett, "we should certainly have lost the war."[64]

This was an utterly incredible statement and without doubt an act of deliberate obfuscation. His defense was that had a blockade been fully implemented in the early stages of the war, "Britain would have had such trouble with the United States that it would have been futile to the future of the Allies." He reiterated the old canard that, had Britain upset America in the early years of the war, "it would have been absolutely fatal."[65] Fatal to whom? This is nonsense. There were no conditions under which America would have stopped trading with Britain, or taken sides against her. It might have caused some localized trading difficulty in 1914 but a strict blockade would have ended the war very quickly. Had he forgotten too about the Lusitania, sunk in May 1915 by a U-Boat? What chance then of America siding with Germany? None.

But the charade went on. It prolonged the war and extended the profits. But darker actions lay ahead to which we will come in due course.

A different blockade, a total and merciless blockade was unnecessarily and comprehensively implemented and extended after the signing of the armistice in 1918. It ensured that Germany was crushed. Not just beaten, crushed. After the guns fell silent, hundreds of thousands more men women and children would die of starvation in Germany before the later blockade was finally lifted.[66]

Summary

- Scandinavian merchants, British re-exporters, American suppliers, neutral grain-growers, international merchant shippers, financiers, insurers and bankers all made fortunes from prolonging the war in Europe.
- The volume of trade with Scandinavian countries exceeded all previous records during the first world war.
- British coal was considered the world's best for powering steamships, railway engines, factories and heating homes. Scandinavians expected that it would stop completely.
- The complete curtailment of coal exports from the first day of the war would have had a profound effect on its duration. That did not happen.
- While profiteering in exported coal had never been greater, coal prices in Britain rose so high that the poor could hardly afford to keep their homes warm.
- Danish ships replaced the German fleet in the Baltic which had been stranded in foreign ports since the start of the war. No ship belonging to the Danish East Asiatic line was sunk by a U-Boat and the company paid a 30% dividend to its shareholders in 1916 alone.
- The ores and metals vital to munitions productions in Germany, flowed through Sweden.
- British merchants actively competed with their rivals in America and the Empire to supply the enemy with vital produce.
- Eventually the Foreign Office sent Sir Alexander Henderson (later Lord Faringdon) to investigate the evidence of excessive trade and corruption sent by Captain M W Consett, Naval Attaché in Christiana (Oslo) but his findings were kept secret. Parliament was informed that "the maximum which can be done is being done." It was a whitewash.
- By the end of 1915, the so-called blockade was attacked in the House of Lords as a joke which had prolonged the war.
- Despite being mocked as a farce, and growing evidence that a full blockade would have ended the war, certainly by 1916, Sir Edward Grey defended the Foreign Office policy even though a report from senior British and French Commanders in March 1916 concluded that the economic struggle had not been undertaken and that if put into effect would shorten the war.

Chapter 6

The Ottoman Enigma – Saving Constantinople

For centuries Britain had opposed Russian expansion towards Constantinople and feared her intentions in Persia, Afghanistan and India. This had to be put aside in the Empire's interest. In 1908 Russia was duped by an astonishing but empty, promise. Britain secretly agreed that she would no longer object to her seizing Constantinople, capital city of the Ottoman Empire and the "Holy Grail" of Czarist foreign policy.[1] The French had also given clear assurances in 1908 that they would support Russian policy in the Bosporus and the Dardanelles.[2] It was a golden carrot. From the time of Catherine the Great, Russia's obsession with a warm-water port on the Black Sea, with unrestricted year-round access to the Mediterranean, was predicated on seizing Constantinople. Historians have claimed that Russia went to war in 1914 in support of Serbia, but there was little genuine Russian concern for the Serbs. That was an excuse. In truth, they harbored a "widespread obsession, bordering on panic" about gaining Constantinople and the Straits.[3]

While Constantinople was seen as the glittering prize, other choice pickings would be on offer after the Ottoman Empire was purposefully driven into an alliance with Germany and then destroyed. The Russians believed that the sacrifice of millions of men in a war against Germany and Turkey would be rewarded not merely with Constantinople, but with a share of the spoils in oil-rich Persia and Iraq. They were sadly deluded. Britain "had no mind to share anything."[4] While it was a promise the Secret Elite never intended to keep, every aspect of their plan for war depended on Russia remaining certain that Constantinople would be hers. As Kaiser Wilhelm correctly advised his cousin Czar Nicholas, Britain was not to be trusted and was using Russia as a "cats-paw."[5] He was right.

Britain and France had long been deeply involved with the Ottoman Empire and bled it dry. Indebted to them for massive loans, Sultan Abdul Hamid II had granted extraordinary concessions and permitted them to gain a stranglehold on the financial and economic life of the nation by the grossest form of corruption. In 1908 an uprising of Turkish army officers rocked the Empire. The dramatic and virtually bloodless success of these Young Turks ended the 33-year autocracy of Abdul Hamid, and introduced constitutional rule. A number of them had been educated in

Western European universities and were staunch admirers of French and English institutions.

Over the next five years their political fortunes fluctuated, but on 26 January 1913 the Young Turks assumed complete control of the Ottoman Empire through a brutal coup d'etat. A triumvirate of Pashas (a high rank similar to a British peerage or knighthood), named Ismail Enver, Mehmed Taalat and Ahmed Djamal, pledged reforms, but did not hesitate to employ the odious tactics of the old regime.[6] Their liberal dream withered into dictatorship. Financially, the new government remained bankrupt; morally it reverted to Abdul Hamid's old system of coercion and corruption.[7]

Foreign specialists were appointed to modernize their outdated and incompetent army, navy and police forces. British Admiral Sir Arthur Limpus arrived in Constantinople in 1912 to take charge of the Ottoman Navy. He persuaded the Turks to refurbish and upgrade their decaying port and naval facilities. Contracts were promptly awarded to British armaments giants, Armstrong-Whitworth, and Vickers, in which the Secret Elite had huge vested interests. When Britain and France declined to enroll Turkish officers in their military academies, the Young Turks turned to Berlin.[8]

In 1913 German General, Liman von Sanders, was invited to reorganize the Turkish army which had been soundly defeated the previous year by the Balkan League forces. Since the French had been asked to take charge of the Turkish gendarmerie, the three most senior military and civilian commanders were drawn from the European powers. Von Sanders' appointment was not a specific demonstration of pro-German sympathies as some suggest. A German had been chosen as Inspector General of the army, but the Young Turks made it clear "all else, in finance, administration, navy, and reforms" would be under English guidance.[9]

The Young Turks steadfastly wished to remain on good terms with their traditional allies, the British. They generally disliked the Germans and their growing influence,[10] and made three separate attempts to sign an alliance with Britain, but were rebuffed on each occasion.[11] In July 1914, Djamal pleaded with the French Foreign Minister to accept the Ottoman government into the Triple Entente,[12] "and at the same time protect us against Russia."[13] Poor fools. A crucial feature of the Entente was the alliance with Russia at the expense of the Turks, not an alliance with the Turks to protect them from Russia. Despite trying to find common ground with France and Britain, and even with their old enemy, Russia, every overture made by the Young Turks to these allies, was dismissed.

The American historian Ron Bobroff concluded that a formal agreement with Turkey would have greatly improved the Triple Entente's capacity to contain Germany.[14] That was not the point. Britain and France had exclusive plans for the future disposal of the Ottoman Empire, though these had yet to be fully agreed, and Russia remained deluded by the promise of Constantinople. This scenario could only take place once the old empire was destroyed along with Germany, and for that very reason the Young Turks were deliberately pushed into the German camp.

War fever and the prospect of taking Constantinople consumed St. Petersburg. In February 1914, six full months before the First World War began, the Russian high command planned to seize the city with an amphibious landing of 127,500 troops and heavy artillery from Odessa. Unfortunately for the Russians, one monumental problem lay ahead. The Russian Navy was terrified at the prospect of the arrival in Constantinople of two modern battleships currently being built in Britain for the Turkish Navy. These state-of-the-art dreadnoughts would prevent Russian landings and, even worse, leave the entire Russian Black Sea fleet at their mercy.[15] Russia was preparing for war in 1914 in the clear understanding that Constantinople would be hers, yet Britain was about to deliver two new warships to Turkey which would undermine the Russian ambitions. What was going on?

Russia made several unsuccessful requests to Foreign Secretary Sir Edward Grey in May and June 1914 to have the Turkish contract canceled. By late July over 500 Turkish sailors had arrived on the river Tyne in north-east England to take the first of the mighty warships back to Constantinople. The *Sultan Osman I* and her sister ship, *Reshadieh* had been bought in part by generous subscriptions from the ordinary Turkish people. Naval regattas and street parties were planned and widespread public excitement anticipated their arrival.

By 30 July the matter became extremely urgent. The Russian foreign secretary, Sergei Sazonov, warned Britain that it was a matter of "the highest degree of importance" that the Turkish ships stayed in England.[16] His thinly veiled threat implied that, if the ships were released, the Czar would not be willing to go to war. He was not to be double-crossed over Constantinople. Indeed.

Swift action was required. First Lord of the Admiralty, Winston Churchill, ordered armed troops in Newcastle to prevent Turkish sailors boarding *Sultan Osman I,* and specifically instructed that the Turkish flag should not be raised over the ship. The Turks were outraged. Churchill insisted that the warships were vital to Britain, and "with a margin of only seven dreadnoughts we could not afford to do without these two fine ships,"[17] but the truth ran much deeper. The Turkish warships were retained at the eleventh hour for fear of a Russian reaction and last-minute refusal to go to war.

The Secret Elite achieved two important objectives by commandeering the Turkish warships. It kept the Czar on track and it steered the angry Turks towards the enemy camp. As late as July 1914 the majority of the Turkish cabinet had been "friendly disposed" towards Britain,[18] but the British government's seizure of the two dreadnoughts drove them to distraction. As an essay in provocation, it was breathtaking.[19] "If Britain wanted deliberately to incense the Turks and drive them into the Kaiser's arms she could not have chosen more effective means."[20]

That was not the problem. Without the two Turkish dreadnoughts, what was to stop the Russians sailing into Constantinople when the opportunity presented itself? The answer was already cruising in the Mediterranean.

On 31 July, the day after Sazonov's demands, the British Cabinet accepted that the warships should be retained by the Royal Navy. British sailors boarded *Sultan Osman 1* that same day and the Ottoman ambassador was informed that the warship was being detained for the time being.[21] Buoyed by their seizure and confirmation from France that the government there was in "hearty high spirits" and "firmly decided on war,"[22] Russia continued full speed with the general mobilization of her armies on Germany's eastern border. At 4PM on 1 August, the French also ordered general mobilization. There was no turning back. It meant war.[23] Over the previous two days the Kaiser had repeatedly pleaded in vain with the Czar to withdraw his armies as Germany would be left with no option but to retaliate. Faced with invasion from both east and west, the Kaiser was the last to order general mobilization. As the Secret Elite had planned, Germany was provoked into a retaliatory war. In St. Petersburg at 6PM on 1 August the German ambassador Count Pourtales handed over Germany's declaration of war on Russia and broke down in tears.[24] Unlike the French, he was most definitely not in "hearty high spirits" at the prospect.

In Constantinople that same day, 1 August, Enver Pasha, Minister of War, informed the other Young Turks to their bitter disappointment that their two warships had been seized by the British.[25] Within 24 hours a "secret" alliance was signed between Turkey and Germany. Directed against Russia, it did not commit Turkey to war.[26] Despite the bitter disappointment and provocation caused by the seizure of their ships, the Grand Vizier and a majority of the Young Turks hoped that Turkey would not be dragged into the conflict. Article 4 of the treaty stated: "Germany obligates itself, by force of arms if need be, to defend Ottoman territory in case it should be threatened." The Ottoman Empire in turn undertook to observe strict neutrality in the European conflict.[27] Germany committed itself to defend Turkey from a Russian attack, though Turkey still remained nominally neutral. Despite the treaty, her involvement in the war was not yet certain.

It is no exaggeration to state that Enver Pasha was the driving force behind the Turkish alliance with Germany. He signed the secret pact without the knowledge, permission or approval of the majority of his own cabinet. Sir Louis Mallet, British Ambassador at Constantinople, stated that Enver was "dominated by a quasi-Napoleonic ideal," while "the Sultan, the Heir Apparent, the Grand Vizier, Djavid Bey, a majority of the Ministry, and a considerable section of the ruling political party were opposed to war with the Allies."[28] Enver was headstrong and bold. He ordered the general mobilization of the Turkish army and the immediate closure and mining of the southern end of the Dardanelles, though a small passage in both the Bosporus and Dardanelles was kept open to admit friendly vessels.[29] Reeling from Britain's seizure of her two warships, and acutely aware of the threat that Russia's Black Sea fleet posed to the defenseless Constantinople, an alternative proposal was put forward. According to the dispatch sent to Berlin on 2 August 1914 by the German Ambassador at Constantinople, Baron von Wangenheim, Enver Pasha formally asked Germany to send her two Mediterranean warships to Constantinople.[30] Germany agreed.[31] It was a like-for-like replacement; for the British-built *Sultan Osman* and *Reshadieh*, read the German fleet's *Goeben* and *Breslau*.

The Black Sea and Mediterranean

Map by Gordon Smith, please acknowledge www.naval-history.net

The battle-cruiser *Goeben* and its close escort, the light cruiser *Breslau,* had been in the Mediterranean since 1912, and, from October 1913, sailed under the command of the energetic and imaginative Rear-Admiral Wilhelm Souchon. Goodwill visits were regularly made to cities and ports throughout the Mediterranean and Aegean, including Constantinople. The Royal Navy kept them under close watch and continually updated the Admiralty in London as to their whereabouts.

Goeben, a powerful and impressive battle-cruiser, had been commissioned in 1912. She was slightly smaller than a battleship with a displacement of 22,640 tons, and ten 11-inch guns. The *Breslau* was much smaller at 4,570 tons, and armed with 4.1-inch guns. *Goeben* had a nominal full speed of 26-27 knots, but was plagued with problems. Faults in her coal-fired boilers caused a power-loss and she spent July in dock at Pola, the Austrian naval base at the head of the Adriatic. The boiler re-fit was incomplete when war broke out and, though unable to achieve more than 18 knots, she took to sea.[32] This should be borne in mind.

On the declaration of war *Goeben* and *Breslau* were ordered to the coast of Algeria to disrupt the embarkation of the French X1X Corps bound for Marseilles and onward to deployment on the Western Front.[33] It would be no easy task. A combined British and French fleet of seventy-three warships was ranged against the only two enemy craft in the Mediterranean, for the Austrian navy remained in port. France had sixteen battleships, (one of which was a modern dreadnought) six armored cruisers and twenty-four destroyers. The British fleet, based in Malta, comprised three battle cruisers, four armored cruisers, four light cruisers, and sixteen destroyers.[34] The three battle cruisers displaced 18,000 tons, were capable of around 23 knots, and carried an armament of eight 12-inch guns. It was David against Goliath's army. Two warships, one wounded, versus a veritable armada.

The British fleet was divided into two squadrons. The first, under Admiral Sir Berkeley Milne, comprised the three powerful battle-cruisers. The second, with eight smaller cruisers and sixteen destroyers, was commanded by Rear-Admiral Sir Ernest Troubridge. Admiral Milne, Commander-in-Chief of the Mediterranean fleet "was an officer of inferior caliber, utterly lacking in vigor and imagination," and his appointment had been largely due to "Court influence."[35] Previously posted as Flag Officer, Royal Yachts, Milne was a close friend of the royal family and former groom-in-waiting to King Edward VII. When Churchill appointed him to the post, Admiral John Fisher, First-Sea-Lord, was outraged. He labeled Milne "an utterly useless" commander, a "backstairs cad" and a "serpent of the lowest type."[36] Was this the template for everyone who commanded at Gallipoli?

The fate of the *Goeben* and *Breslau* in their mad-cap dash across the Mediterranean to the safety of the Dardanelles has become part of the folklore of the First World War. The escape was astonishing; the consequences staggering. Mainstream historians claim that from the German perspective it was a blessing that verged on a miracle; for the British it was a great embarrassment. Churchill ranted that it was a "curse."[37] The truth is somewhat different. The British Foreign Office and the Admiralty knew precisely where the German warships were in the Mediterranean and, crucially, where they were headed. Far from attempting to destroy the *Goeben* and *Breslau,* the Secret Elite in London took active steps to keep them from harm and ensured their safe passage to Constantinople.

Had the sinking of the German cruisers been the real objective, neither the *Goeben* nor *Breslau* would have survived.

Having bombarded the French embarkation ports on the Algerian coast at around 6 AM on 4 August 1914, the German cruisers set off, as ordered, on a 1200-mile race across the Mediterranean and Aegean Seas to Constantinople. Every opportunity the Royal Navy had to catch and destroy them was apparently bungled in a series of incredible errors that were later put down to incompetence. Barbara Tuchman, the Pulitzer Prize-Winner wrote, "No other single exploit of the war cast so long a shadow upon the world as the voyage accomplished by their commander during the next seven days."[38] As eminent a seafarer as he was, Admiral Souchon could not have escaped the clutches of the British unless aided and abetted by powers he did not comprehend.

Consider the facts. Souchon's original order was to attack and destroy French troop-transport ships plying between the North African and French coasts. The bombardment of two embarkation ports in French Algeria, Bone and Phillipsville was a very public announcement of their presence, yet the French navy did not give chase. *Goeben* and *Breslau* set off east for Messina, completely unmolested by the large French fleet which was on its way south from Toulon, and fast approaching that very spot. The question remains, why did the French fleet not wipe out the German cruisers, which were the only threat to their transport ships in the Mediterranean?

Around 9.30AM while heading east, Admiral Souchon was doubtless expressing incredulity that his cruisers had not been attacked, when two British heavy cruisers appeared on the horizon. They were heading at full speed directly towards him. The *Indefatigable* and *Indomitable,* which had been steaming west all night to intercept the German cruisers, encountered them off Bone. Their precise co-ordinates were immediately telegraphed to the Admiralty in London but the crucial information regarding the direction in which the German cruisers were headed, was not passed on. Churchill, allegedly, "assumed they were heading west with further evil intent upon the French."[39] That was utter nonsense. Churchill and the Admiralty knew full well that the German ships were heading east, and that their ultimate destination was Constantinople.

Every British naval action that followed literally channeled the *Goeben* and *Breslau* towards the Dardanelles. *Indomitable* and *Indefatigable* held fire on sighting their "prey." Churchill had telegraphed a caution to all British warships: "The British ultimatum to Germany will expire at midnight GMT, 4 August.[40] No acts of war should be committed before that hour ..."[41] That being the case, *Indomitable* and *Indefatigable* passed within close range of *Goeben* and *Breslau,* the Admirals eyeing each other from their bridges.[42] The British cruisers swept round and followed closely in their wake. They were later joined by the light cruiser, HMS *Dublin*. Given her defective boilers, the three predators were clearly faster than the *Goeben* and should easily have been able to stay on her tail. Admiral Milne, Commander-in-Chief of the Mediterranean fleet, was reminded by London that "the speed of your Squadrons is sufficient to enable you to choose your moment,"[43] and with their 12-inch guns could have sent her to the bottom.[44]

Goeben remained just ahead of the British pack throughout the entire day. In the mid-summer heat of the Mediterranean, many of her stokers collapsed, and four died, horrifically scalded by steam blasting from faulty boiler tubes. Let there be no doubt that the *Goeben* toiled to survive ahead of a formidable pack. At the 11PM deadline, Churchill ordered the Admiralty to signal all ships, "Commence hostilities at once with Germany ..." Prior to the given order, the gap between *Goeben* and the pursuers widened and she disappeared into the night. The official excuse later proffered was that the British warships had been unable to maintain their course due to a shortage of stokers.[45] What rotten luck ... and bad timing.

Having defied the odds to reach Messina in north-east Sicily, Admiral Souchon was given 24 hours by the neutral Italians to load coal and clear out. German merchant ships, which had previously been ordered to rendezvous with *Goeben* at Messina, had their decks ripped open and railings torn away to enable the transfer of coal. Every crew-member was pressed into action. By noon on 6 August 1,500 tons had been manually transferred. Men fainted with exhaustion in the summer heat and "blackened and sweat-soaked bodies lay all over the ship like so many corpses."[46] 1,500 tons of coal was sufficient to reach the Aegean Sea, where Souchon had arranged, through the Greek government, to meet another merchant collier.

With *Goeben* and *Breslau* at Messina it was a relatively simple task for Admiral Milne to bottle them in. He had a large fleet at his disposal, including three battle-cruisers together with four heavy cruisers from Admiral Troubridge's squadron, and a further four light cruisers and sixteen destroyers. Souchon knew his ships were sitting ducks at Messina. The massed British fleet could either move in and force their surrender, or wait for them to emerge and blow them out the water. Trapped in the tight channel between Sicily and the toe of Italy, there was only one narrow exit north from Messina leading to the western Mediterranean, and one narrow exit to the east. On 5 August the German authorities asked the Austro-Hungarian fleet to leave its base in the Adriatic and head south to assist the German ships, break-out of the Messina Strait, but the naval commander, Anton Haus, declined. The mobilization of his fleet had not been completed. Furthermore, the Austrian foreign ministry had instructed him to avoid the British or French fleet and so he remained in port.[47] In truth, it would have been a fool-hardy act since Austria was not yet at war with Britain.[48]

British warships were specifically ordered not to enter neutral Italian waters or approach within six miles of the Italian coast. How odd. Here were the Germans caught in *flagrante*. Technically, Souchon was abusing Italian neutrality by coaling within her waters, but we are asked to believe that the combative, blood-roused Churchill was suddenly overcome by diplomatic nicety.

Having allowed his men five hours of rest, the German Admiral ordered steam. Aware of the overwhelming forces ranged against him, he ran the gauntlet at 5pm. All day excited Sicilians crowded the quays selling postcards and souvenirs to "those about to die." Extra editions of the local papers were headlined "In the Claws of Death."[49] *Goeben* and *Breslau* headed down through the eastern outlet of the Messina Strait with an all-pervading sense of doom. But where was the British fleet? Logic dictated that Milne put sufficient warships at both exits from the Messina Strait to render escape impossible but incredibly, he had posted only one light cruiser to cover the eastern escape route – a route the Admiralty knew he would take since he was sailing towards Constantinople. Milne had not been fully informed. His heavy cruiser squadron was stationed to the west of Sicily, and in consequence, could do nothing as Souchon escaped to the east. Meantime, Admiral Troubridge with his four armored cruisers, lay close to Kephalonia some 150 miles away to prevent Goeben entering the Adriatic.

Weighing only 4,800 tons and carrying 2 six-inch guns against the might of the *Goeben*, HMS *Gloucester*, under Captain Howard Kelly, watched the German cruisers exit the Messina Strait, and immediately telegraphed their position to Milne. Other than that he could do nothing but stay out of harms way. Souchon made a feint to the north as if heading for the Adriatic, but once darkness fell changed course to the east for the Aegean. Troubridge took his four cruisers south from Kephalonia to intercept *Goeben*, but soon turned back. He had been ordered by Churchill not to engage a "superior force," and he deemed *Goeben* superior to his four armored cruisers and their accompanying eight destroyers.[50] The fox had bolted and had been channeled inexorably towards the Dardanelles and Constantinople.

Each segment in the charade of the *Goeben* and *Breslau's* "escape" becomes harder to swallow. That two large squadrons of the mighty British navy failed to prevent a couple of German cruisers, escape was explained as a fiasco of tragic blunders attributable to the "listless and fumbling" conduct of Sir Ernest Troubridge and Sir Archibald Berkeley Milne.[51] Oxford historian, Sir Hew Strachan claimed that the escape rendered the actions of every British naval commander in the Mediterranean, with the distinguished exception of Captain Kelly of HMS *Gloucester*, "incompetent."[52] So there you have it. The *Goeben's* great escape to the Dardanelles was entirely down to listless, fumbling incompetence; oh, and too few stokers. No-one appears to have considered how very convenient it was that these German warships would be able to replace the confiscated Turkish ships and protect Constantinople against the Russians. The truth of the matter was, the "escape" proved a triumph of British manipulation which protected their real interests.

The true story of *Goeben's* escape is very different from that presented by the mainstream. Historians blandly state that Churchill and the British government knew nothing of the secret agreement that Turkey signed with Germany on 2 August, or that the German warships were heading towards Constantinople. Apparently no-one even considered the possibility that *Goeben* and *Breslau* were engaged in a political mission that would profoundly affect and prolong the course of the war.[53] In fact, British Intelligence had for some considerable time been intercepting messages between the German embassy in Constantinople and Berlin, and it is quite astonishing that while the treaty between Turkey and Germany was being kept secret from most of the Turkish cabinet, British and French Intelligence knew of it almost at once.[54]

On 3 August the Kaiser advised King Constantine I of Greece by telegram that the Turks had thrown in their lot with Germany and that the two German warships presently in the Mediterranean would proceed to Constantinople. The strongly pro-British Greek Prime Minister, Elephtherios Venizelos, passed this information to the British charge d'affaires who in turn cabled the news to London.[55] Lest there be any doubt that the authorities in Britain knew from the outset where *Goeben* and *Breslau* where headed, King Constantine also shared the information with Admiral Kerr of the British naval mission in Athens. [56] Thus key officials in both the Foreign Office and the Admiralty knew about Admiral Souchon's orders before Britain had declared war on Germany.

Indeed it is perfectly possible that the plans approved by Berlin were known in London before Souchon had sight of them on board the *Goeben*. Public Records Office files reveal that naval intelligence had decrypted the encoded radio-message sent from Berlin to Souchon on 4 August. The brief instruction read; "Alliance concluded with Turkey, *Goeben* and *Breslau* proceed at once to Constantinople." The intelligence passed from Greece on 3 August was instantly confirmed by the decoded radio message on the 4th. London knew that Souchon had been instructed to set course immediately for the Dardanelles.[57] There was no ambiguity.

There was another source which constantly monitored all that was happening in and around Constantinople. By 1914 Russia's intelligence on Turkey was uniformly good and manifestly better than that of Britain or France. As Souchon headed across the Mediterranean, "the Russians knew perfectly well where he was going and why."[58] Russian Foreign Secretary Sazonov had informants inside the Ottoman cabinet and Mikhail Girs, the Russian Ambassador at Constantinople, was exceptionally well informed.[59] Given the dire consequences for Russia if the Goeben and Breslau sailed unmolested into Constantinople, and the fact that they had no warships of their own in the Mediterranean to stop them, it is inconceivable that the Russian Foreign Ministry would not have immediately passed the crucial information to British Intelligence. Indeed Sazonov was in ready contact with Sir Edward Grey at the Foreign Office, demanding that the German cruisers be sunk. Herein lay the dichotomy. Russian imperial ambition required the immediate removal of the menace, but to further Britain's own geopolitical strategy, the Secret Elite had to ensure that *Goeben* and *Breslau* reached their destination safely.

The crucial information about Souchon's destination was withheld from the Royal Navy squadrons in the Mediterranean, and most of the information they received from London "was either useless or inaccurate."[60] Rear-Admiral Milne apparently labored under the impression that Souchon intended to turn back west after coaling at Messina. Had false intelligence to that effect been relayed to him from London, or was Milne party to the conspiracy to allow the German ships to escape? Either option would certainly explain some of the bizarre events in this strange tale. If Milne had been fully briefed on the latter it would account for the fact that the three cruisers which closely shadowed the *Goeben*, handicapped by her defective boilers, "lost" their prey just a few hours before the 11PM declaration of war. It would explain why he positioned the cruiser squadrons to the west of Sicily, and by the island of Kephalonia, while placing only one totally inadequate warship to guard Souchon's escape route towards Constantinople. Had it been sent by semaphore, Milne's message to Souchon could hardly have been clearer; "We are not preventing your passage to the Dardanelles." Witness the geographic position of the hunters and the hunted. The Germans were prevented from sailing west into the Mediterranean, or north to the Adriatic. The reasonable conclusion such tactics warranted was that Souchon was purposefully shepherded towards Constantinople. The suggestion that Admiral Milne could have been part of the conspiracy is not as outrageous as it might first appear. He was a favorite of the British monarchy and had been close to the late King Edward VII, a man who was himself closely linked to the inner core of the Secret Elite.[61]

When *Goeben* and *Breslau* left Messina on 6 August, the proverbial fly in the Admiralty's ointment was Captain Howard Kelly in HMS *Gloucester*. Although comprehensively out gunned by *Goeben*, Kelly stubbornly trailed the German cruisers. Milne signaled Kelly to give up the chase.

Why? Was it to protect the *Gloucester* or to allow the German ships to disappear into the safety of the eastern Mediterranean? Whichever, Kelly defied the Admiral's instructions and continued his pursuit. Souchon was forced to order *Breslau* to turn back and confront the small British cruiser, but the defiant *Gloucester* opened fire. Eventually all three warships engaged in the fight, but in the late afternoon, when *Goeben* entered the Aegean Sea, the fearless Kelly finally gave up. At the end of the day he was the only British naval officer to emerge with any credit. Interestingly, rather being court-martialed for disobeying an order from the Admiral, Kelly was created Companion of the Bath by the King and went on to enjoy a glittering naval career.

Early on 7 August Admiral Milne informed the Admiralty that as soon as his three battle-cruisers completed coaling at Malta he would follow *Goeben* and *Breslau* into the Eastern Mediterranean. He received no response. Despite all the precise intelligence that the Admiralty held on *Goeben's* plans and whereabouts, Milne allegedly remained 'entirely without information' as to its whereabouts and intentions. Later that afternoon, at 5:40, the Admiralty received another signal from Milne repeating his intentions. At this point the saga became even murkier. Evidence "unfortunately disappeared" from the Admiralty file on this exchange.[62] Despite two reliable reports from different sources that *Goeben* had been seen at the Aegean island of Syra and had formally requested permission to coal, these were filed away without comment and the information was not passed to Milne. The only report he received was that *Goeben* had passed Cape Matapan on the 7th, intelligence that he had previously sent himself to London.[63]

Desperate for coal, and confirmation that he could sail into the Straits, Admiral Souchon lingered in the Greek archipelago for approximately sixty hours, during which "the British Mediterranean fleet had ample time to make up for all previous errors and catch up with their prey."[64] And herein lies another conundrum. After his escape from Messina, Souchon requested permission from the Greek government to take on much-needed coal when he reached the Aegean. Had they denied him fuel, or procrastinated long enough for the Mediterranean fleets to catch him, the flight might well have ended there. Instead, Prime Minister Venizelos "agreed at once" to release 800 tons from the sequestered stock of German coal at Piraeus. The British Foreign Office later suggested that the staunchly pro-British Venizelos, a friend of Lloyd George, had simply "acted out of a desire to be fair to all sides."[65] What rubbish. British intelligence knew well in advance where Souchon was headed, and that he would need coal in order to reach Constantinople. They opened the doors; they approved the fueling; they ensured that the German ships continued in comparative safety. Most importantly, they hid all this from the Russians.

Venizelos had immediately informed Rear-Admiral Mark Kerr in Athens that *Goeben* would be rendezvousing with a coal ship at Denusa in the days ahead. Kerr, a staunch British patriot, had been seconded from Britain to head the Greek navy. We are asked to believe that he did not pass on the information about *Goeben's* whereabouts to London. Incredible. Considered from another angle, Kerr, like the Admiralty, knew that the German ships had been ordered to Constantinople. King Constantine had personally shown him the telegram of 3 August from the Kaiser authorizing this.[66] That he kept it to himself, or lingered long before eventually telling the Admiralty, is fanciful. It was part of the smoke-screen, part of the post-event blame-game which deflected any focus away from the Admiralty or Foreign Office. Above all else, under no circumstances could Russia be made aware of the depth of British complicity in this charade.

While Souchon was more or less marooned in the south Aegean Sea awaiting coal, Admiral Milne took his three heavy cruisers and a light cruiser east towards the Aegean in a direction that would have led him to the German ships. En-route, he received a message from London warning that Austria had declared war on Britain. In accordance with long-standing, explicit orders detailing what he should do in that event, Milne turned north for the Adriatic to blockade the Austrian fleet. He was later informed that the report was false and back-tracked east, but 24 hours had been lost. Thus historians could record that Souchon "might well have been searched out and destroyed had not the Admiralty sent Milne on August 8th the false report..."[67] According to Winston Churchill, the misinformation was rooted in simple error. "The fates moved a blameless, punctilious Admiralty clerk to declare war upon Austria."[68] Oh, dear; how calamitous. A "blameless" clerk just happened to send Admiral Milne, and Milne alone, an erroneous message to the effect that Britain was now at war with Austria. Consequently, secret orders immediately took effect and changed, not just Admiral Milne's course, but the course of history. Are you prepared to accept that? It is a wonder that the Russians did.

Against overwhelming odds, and thanks to the Secret Elite, *Goeben* and *Breslau* entered the Dardanelles at 5PM on 10 August and arrived unscathed at Constantinople the next day. According to the All Souls and Oxford historian Charles Crutwell, they carried with them "graver destinies than any other vessels in modern history."[69] They immediately rendered Russia's aging Black Sea fleet strategically useless. Sir Louis Mallet, British ambassador to the Ottoman Empire, later admitted that the presence of these warships acted in British interests because they protected the Straits against Russia.[70] Russian Foreign Secretary Sergei Sazonov was furious. In a telegram to London, he raged that Souchon's success was all the more regrettable because Britain could have prevented it.[71] Had he learned that far from preventing the "escape," Britain had deliberately facilitated it, Russian involvement in the First World War would have been terminated.

The Ottoman ambassador in Berlin telegraphed home: "Considering the displeasure and complications which a Russian attack on Constantinople would produce in England, the British navy having enabled the German ships to take cover in the Sea of Marmora, has, with the Machiavellianism characteristic of the Foreign Office, foiled any possibility of action by the Russian Black Sea Fleet."[72] And he was absolutely correct.

Summary

- The prime reason for Russia's commitment to war was the understanding that her reward for victory over Germany would be Constantinople, the Bosporus and a warm water port on the Black Sea
- Britain, France and Germany had a variety of interests in the decaying Ottoman Empire based on Constantinople.
- In 1908, a coterie of young Turkish army officers - The Young Turks- engaged in a take-over which introduced a more constitutional government. In 1913 a brutal coup d'etat organized by the Young Turks gave them complete control of the Ottoman Empire.
- Modernization of the army, navy and police forces took place under British, German and French influence.
- The Young Turks wanted to be part of the Entente but were rebutted because the long term aim of dismantling the Ottoman Empire was predicated on their being defeated along with Germany.
- Britain's arbitrary decision to commandeer two dreadnought-type battleships which had been built for the Turkish navy shocked the Turks and delighted the Russians.
- Within 24 hours Turkey signed a secret alliance with Germany though remained neutral in terms of the war between Britain, France, Russia and Germany.
- Having stripped Turkey of her naval defenses the British Admiralty ensured she had a replacement. The German battle-cruiser *Goeben* and the smaller *Breslau* were literally shepherded into the Dardanelles by the Royal Navy and having reached Constantinople, were gifted to the Turkish navy by a very astute German government.
- The charade in the Mediterranean was orchestrated to ensure that Russia could not simply sail into an unprotected Bosporus and capture Constantinople.

Chapter 7

The Ottoman Enigma – Neutral Till It Suits

No-one at the time appeared to consider that the *Goeben* and *Breslau's* escape to Constantinople had been carefully orchestrated by the Foreign Office in conjunction with the Admiralty to stop Russia seizing the city,[1] but that was certainly the immediate effect. It also demonstrated the over-reaching power exercised by Enver Pasha in granting permission to the German warships to make their spectacular entry into the Bosporus without consulting either the Grand Vizier or any other member of the Turkish government. Anchored in the Golden Horn, the cruisers were never asylum seekers. They were game-changing defenders of the Ottoman Empire, though they posed an awkward question in terms of international law. Since Turkey remained neutral (her secret agreement with Germany of 2 August did not commit her to war) why did she provide a safe haven for the German warships? As has been noted, Enver Pasha had asked the German Ambassador to send both cruisers through the Dardanelles to replace the dreadnoughts which Britain had so deviously commandeered.[2] In order to maintain Ottoman neutrality, the warships were hastily incorporated into the Sultan's navy.[3] The famous names of *Goeben* and *Breslau* were replaced by *Sultan Jawuz Selim,* and *Midilli.* The German crews exchanged their floppy dark-blue sailors' caps for red fezzes and raised the Turkish flag, but nothing else changed. They were German ships, controlled by a German Admiral and crewed by German sailors who took their orders from Berlin.

Churchill appeared enraged in public since it reflected so badly on the Royal Navy. The British fleet received orders to proceed immediately to blockade the entrance to the Dardanelles.[4] According to Herbert Asquith, Churchill wanted to send a torpedo flotilla through the Dardanelles "to sink the *Goeben* and her consort,"[5] but it was all posturing. Britain asked that the German crews be removed, but "were reluctant to pressure the Turks to send the German vessels away."[6] Reluctant? Indeed, they were more than reluctant. Having gone to extraordinary lengths to shepherd them into the pen, Churchill and the Foreign Office had no intention of driving them out.

Their safe arrival rendered a Russian amphibious operation against Constantinople well-nigh impossible.[7] Although Sazonov protested furiously, London attempted to rationalize the situation. It was better, they suggested, to have the warships in the Sea of Marmara as part of the Turkish navy than in the Mediterranean as German combatants. Russia had been kept out of Constantinople, but the Secret Elite faced the considerable problem of keeping her focused on the eastern front. How enthusiastic would the Russians be to continue the war if they failed to gain the great prize of Constantinople? It required a delicate balance of assurances and timing, and in this the elites were magnificently served by a most trusted agent, Sir Louis Mallet, Ambassador at Constantinople. Mallet's critical role at the start of the war was to keep Turkey neutral until it suited Britain to shunt her into the war on Germany's side.

Described by the Turkish Minister, Ahmed Djamal Pasha, as "a particularly fine man, thoroughly honest and very kind,"[8] Mallet's appointment in 1913 raised eyebrows in diplomatic circles. He had been head of the Eastern Department in the Foreign Office since 1907, not a court diplomat, and trusted completely by Foreign Secretary Sir Edward Grey and Sir Arthur Nicolson, his permanent secretary. Mallet was close to the inner circle of the Secret Elite and had worked for years on the development of British policies in Egypt, Persia, and India. He understood the geopolitics of the Middle East, and was totally conversant with British interests and long term aims in the region. Louis Mallet was sent to Constantinople as the embodiment of British sympathy for the Young Turks who considered his appointment an act of friendship. His role was to keep the Porte (Constantinople) neutral in order to buy time for the British Empire in the troubled early months of the war. Mallet was well able to match the Ottomans at their own game of flawless duplicity.

Louis Mallet absented himself from Turkey in the summer of 1914, and was "on leave" when Enver Pasha signed the secret alliance with Germany on 2 August. It is hard to imagine that during these days of unprecedented international crisis Mallet was, as suggested by mainstream historians, simply on vacation. At the very moment when the Foreign Office and the Admiralty were deciding the fate of the Turkish dreadnoughts, when Sazonov and the Russians were ranting about the need to keep these massive warships from the Turks, when the *Goeben* and *Breslau* were making good their escape, it is inconceivable that the British ambassador was not deeply involved, giving advice and making recommendations. Mallet was one of the most knowledgeable men in the Empire on Ottoman matters, yet we are asked to accept that he was on leave and consequently not involved. Absence was the perfect excuse to distance him from all that transpired. He was out of the firing line when the Turkish warships were seized. How fortuitous.

Mallet became the main instrument in the charm offensive devised to soothe the anxious Turks. He returned to Constantinople on 16 August with promises to make good the financial loss incurred by the loss of the dreadnoughts, and pursued a determined line that Ottoman neutrality was in the best interests of everyone. Asquith noted his satisfaction on 19 August, "Happily, Louis Mallet is back in Constantinople," and relationships "will be further improved if we offer to return their two seized battleships at the end of the war."[9] The Foreign Office's only stipulation was that the German crews had to be sent home, a condition they knew could never be met. Note what was specifically implied here. Britain was not asking Turkey to surrender the warships, or promise not to use them. Keep the warships; defend Constantinople, but remove the Germans. It was as well that Asquith's letters did not reach Sazonov.

Mallet and the British Foreign Office knew about the "secret" Turkish alliance with Germany long before his return to Constantinople. The British Ambassador could literally watch the *Goeben* and *Breslau* from his residence at Therapia as they sailed past every other day, their guns ready for action.[10] He knew exactly what was going on behind the scenes but pretended ignorance. Neither Mallet nor the London conspirators were fooled by soft words or vague promises, but they played the game of duplicity in order to keep Turkey neutral for as long as possible.

There were two imperatives. The first was to keep Russia in the war. The second was to keep the Muslim world on-side; to prepare India and Arabia for the certainty that if war broke out with Turkey, the Holy Places would be protected. Since 1517 the Ottoman Sultan had been recognized as a Caliph, the religious and political successor to the Prophet Muhammad. The Ottoman Caliph was held to be the leader of the worldwide Muslim community and defender of the holy cities of Medina and Mecca. Muslims might forgive Britain for going to war against the only significant independent Islamic power, but not the disruption of pilgrimages to the Holy Places of Arabia.[11]

In those early days of the Secret Elite's war, the Foreign Office and the War Office had to ensure that everything was in place to deal with any religious uprising when the Ottomans entered the war. Kitchener and Prime Minister Asquith agreed that, "…in the interests of the Muslims in India and Egypt," Britain must not do anything which could be interpreted as taking the initiative in a war against the Ottomans. Turkey ought to "be compelled to strike the first blow…"[12] Two weeks earlier they had "compelled" Germany "to strike the first blow," in Europe then heaped the blame on her for starting the war. It was the mantra repeated so often before Britain went to war. Sir Edward Grey later reminded Ambassador Mallet that "I do not see how war can be avoided, but we shall not take the first step."[13] That said it all. Perfidious Albion dressed herself in apparent innocence before "being compelled" to go to war. It was an oft repeated hypocrisy.[14]

Once Admiral Souchon and his warships were assimilated into the Turkish navy, British Rear-Admiral Sir Arthur Limpus, who had been the naval advisor to the Turkish government for two years, was withdrawn by Churchill on 9 September 1914. Limpus knew the precise details of all the Dardanelles defenses and had a prodigious knowledge of every aspect of Turkish naval planning.[15] Logically, he was the prime candidate in every sense to replace Milne as Commander-in-Chief of the Mediterranean fleet. Instead he was relegated to the desk-bound job of superintendent of the Malta dockyards while Vice-Admiral Sackville Carden, who had spent the past two years in this relative backwater, was given command. It was a strange decision by any standard. Sackville-Carden was considered slow and ineffective,[16] but the arrangement was apparently based on the need to reassure the Turks that Britain, as their natural friend, would not take advantages of Limpus's invaluable knowledge.[17] While that argument held little credibility in September 1914, it became absolute nonsense when Britain declared war on Turkey in late October. Incredibly, Limpus's unique and detailed knowledge of the Dardanelles was ignored by the Admiralty in the Royal Navy's subsequent foray into those waters. Or perhaps they chose not to listen to his advice.

On August 15 Churchill sent a personal telegram to Enver Pasha warning him that Turkey must remain neutral.[18] Indeed, Churchill sent several communications of a private and personal nature directly to Enver, which raises justifiable questions about their relationship; questions that have never been answered. He reminded Enver that the Allies held overwhelming naval power and could transport troops in almost unlimited numbers to Constantinople. However, if Turkey maintained strict neutrality, he promised that her territorial integrity would be respected at the end of the war.[19] It was part of a calculated tactical maneuver. The Secret Elite had no wish to see the Ottoman Empire remain neutral, nor the slightest intention of genuinely guaranteeing its integrity. In truth, Britain made no significant concession.[20] It was all about buying time before they pushed the Turks into the German camp.

Russia too was playing for time. Foreign Secretary Sazonov instructed his ambassador at Constantinople to be firm but cautious regarding *Goeben* and *Breslau*, but not to press too hard or "drive affairs to a rupture."[21] His goal was also to delay Turkish entry into the war for as long as possible so that they would not be over-extended on two fronts. On 5 August Enver Pasha made a surprising proposal. Just 3 days after the secret Ottoman treaty with Germany had been signed, and before the *Goeben* arrived, he suggested an alliance with Russia for a period of 5 or 10 years. Turkey, he insisted, was not bound to Germany, had no aggressive intentions against Russia, and had only mobilized her forces for her own safety. Enver claimed that Turkey would provide Russia with military assistance in the war if Russia supported Turkish interests to regain the Aegean islands lost to Greece, and territory in western Thrace lost to Bulgaria in the Balkan wars.[22]

Was this a game of bluff with all sides playing for time to get their armies into position or was Enver prepared to double-cross the Germans and make a genuine attempt to realign his country with Russia and the Entente? If so, he was never given a chance to succeed. Sazonov said the Turks would need to demobilize their armies as a sign of good faith, but such action would have left Turkey defenseless to a Russian double-cross and they could not possibly comply.[23] Enver's proposal was rejected on 9 August.[24] The Young Turks later admitted that they too had remained neutral with the sole object of gaining time to complete their mobilisation.[25] It was all smoke and mirrors. Russia attempted to trick the Turks who in turn tried to deceive the Russians. Neither realized that Britain was hoodwinking them both.

By September, the stakes in this dangerous charade had risen to alarming heights. Louis Mallet was given authority to determine when the Embassy staff, together with British officials working in the service of the Ottoman government, British residents in Turkey and shipping agents should be instructed to leave.[26] Though his posting was almost over, he had been able to send invaluable information to London; information that was to be outrageously ignored in the months ahead. He advised his bosses that the defense systems along the Dardanelles had been "rapidly fortified" and were manned by Germans.[27] He reported that over 2,000 cases of shells for the *Goeben* and the Dardanelles forts had been delivered from Germany, and that new shipments of mines had been transported down the Danube. "Neutral" Turkey was armed by Germany, and the Foreign Office knew all the facts and figures.[28] That in itself was sufficient reason for Britain to declare war, but Sir Edward Grey refused to take that step in order to make it appear that "we had done everything to avoid war and that Turkey had forced it."[29]

Despite appearances to the contrary, Britain continued to goad the Turks. On the morning that Admiral Limpus departed from Constantinople, every member of the Ottoman Cabinet was warned that Turkish ships would be treated as enemy vessels if they stepped outside the protective waters of the Dardanelles.[30] The Grand Vizier asked the Royal Navy to pull their fleet back from the mouth of the waterway, but Churchill refused. Although Turkish mines had been laid across the Narrows, Allied merchantmen had been allowed to use a safe channel through. This consideration was brought to an end on 26 September when a Turkish torpedo boat attempted to exit the Straits but was ordered to heave to under threat by the Royal Navy and sent back. There was no justification for this high-handed action [31] other than to raise the stakes. In response, the Turks extinguished the lighthouses and closed the strategic waterway to all vessels. If they weren't allowed out, then no-one would be allowed in. In responding this way the Ottoman authorities violated their obligation under international law to keep the Straits open, but "once again they appeared to have been provoked to do so by the actions of Winston Churchill."[32] Indeed, it was as tactless as the confiscation of the two Turkish battleships.[33] The closure of the Dardanelles on 27 September cut Russia off from almost all of her international trade. Sazonov was apoplectic. The time was fast approaching for Russia to "settle accounts" with her ancient enemy and resolve the question of the Straits for good.[34]

On 11 October Enver Pasha informed the Germans that he would authorize *Goeben* and *Breslau* to attack Russia as soon as Germany deposited two million Turkish pounds in gold in Constantinople to support the Ottoman military forces. Time for neutrality had run its course. On 29 October, eight days after the last shipment of gold arrived by rail, the Turkish fleet under Admiral Souchon fired the first salvo in Turkey's unannounced declaration of war. At 3.30 am the Black Sea ports of Odessa and Sebastopol were bombarded, though the Russian fleet remained virtually unscathed. Enver Pasha had authorized the provocative attack without regard to his Cabinet colleagues. They in turn, immediately insisted on offering an apology to the Russians. Isolated but unrepentant, Enver reaped what he had sown.[35]

Responding before the Turkish apology was even drafted, Sir Edward Grey ordered the British Ambassador to deliver an ultimatum which demanded the dismissal of the German military and naval missions, and the removal of all German personnel from the former *Goeben* and *Breslau* within twelve hours. If the Turks failed to comply, the Ambassador and Embassy staff were instructed to ask for their passports and leave.[36] From the outset, it was a patently impossible request,[37] but by late October the time was right for Britain. She was now ready for war in the Middle East. Plans had been hatched, warships were in place in the Arabian gulf, propaganda about the safety of Holy Places was already in circulation and the Pan-Arab movement was being quietly encouraged. Mallet had been instrumental in buying three valuable months for Grey and Kitchener,[38] and the Turks were shocked when, within a week of war being declared, the British army was encamped in Kuwait, and an expeditionary force from India was headed to Baghdad.[39]

Britain broke off diplomatic relations with Turkey on 30 October and the following day a "cock-a-hoop" Churchill ordered the British warships to bombard the Dardanelles.[40] He gave the order to "commence hostilities with Turkey" without informing the Cabinet or formally declaring war.[41] Typical. Put Churchill aside for the moment and ponder the behavior of Enver Pasha. Enver had agreed to the secret pact with Germany on 2 August. Enver had asked them to send the *Goeben* and *Breslau* to Constantinople. Enver instructed Souchon to attack the Russian Black Sea ports. Enver had made the first move. Enver had delivered the condition for war. Enver, Churchill's personal and confidential friend, had given the Secret Elite exactly the excuse they needed. Inside Asquith's Cabinet, Churchill declared, "it was the best thing since the outbreak of war."[42] You might be forgiven for considering Enver an agent of the Secret Elite.

On 2 November, Russia declared war on the Ottoman Empire, and Britain and France followed suit. Russia could now focus attention on her most treasured war aim; to take control of the Straits and Constantinople. After centuries of yearning, her great dream stood on the verge of realisation.[43] Every member of the Council of Ministers in Petrograd was agreed; Turkey must be dismembered. The only point of dispute was over which precise parts of the Ottoman Empire would be incorporated into Russia.[44] In his official declaration of war against the Turks, Czar Nicholas stated, "It is with complete serenity ... that Russia takes on the appearance of this new enemy ... the present conflict will only accelerate her submission to fate and open up Russia's path towards the realization of the historic task of her ancestors along the shores of the Black Sea."[45] Russia's date with destiny had apparently arrived, but the Secret Elite dictated a very different agenda.

Summary.

- The British Ambassador at Constantinople, Louis Mallet, was close to the inner-core members of the Secret Elite and matched the Turks in their own game of flawless duplicity.
- Britain wanted to keep Turkey officially neutral for as long as was feasible. They had to keep Russia in the war and the Muslim world on-side.
- Winston Churchill was frequently in direct contact with the most important of the Young Turks, Enver Pasha
- Both sides seemed to be engaged in a game of promise and counter-promise to buy time.
- On 27 September, the Dardanelles were closed by order of the Turkish government.
- On 29 October, having received two million Turkish pounds in gold from Germany, Enver Pasha authorized a naval attack on the Russian fleet at Odessa and Sebastopol.
- By late October the British strategy for the Middle East was in place. Warships were in the Gulf of Arabia, propaganda about the safety of the Holy Places was being promoted and a Pan-Arab movement, quietly encouraged.
- Russia declared war on the Ottoman Empire on 2 November 1914. Britain and France followed suit.

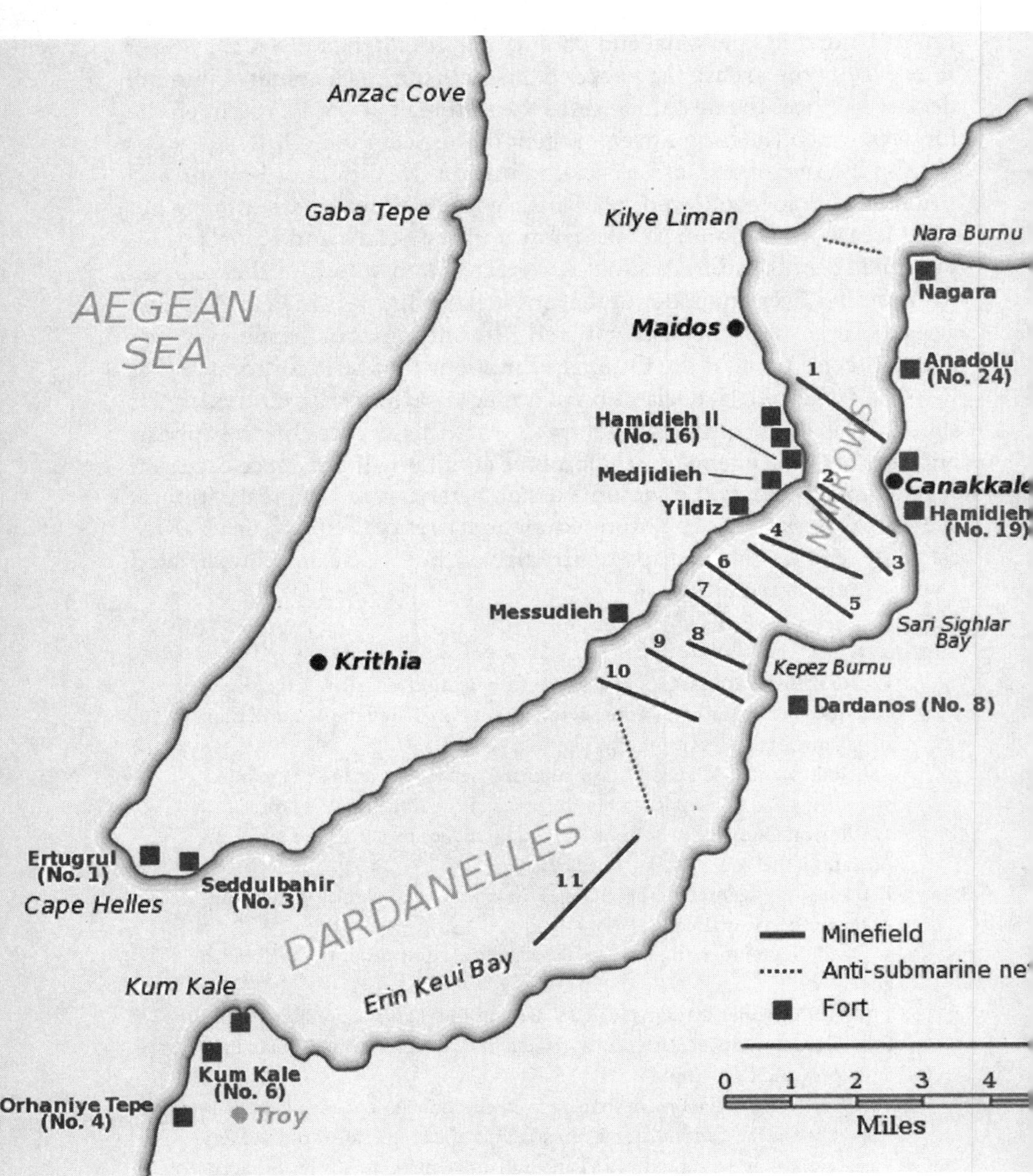

Turkish forts and minefields which made the Dardanelles impenetrable.

Chapter 8

DARDANELLES – THE RUSSIAN DREAM

Once the immediate German threat to Paris had passed, and the Western Front stuck fast in the mud of a four year-long stalemate of miserable trench warfare, London was faced with a serious problem. The Russians had been badly beaten on the Eastern Front. They had invaded Germany's eastern borders but were driven back by the German defensive-offensive at the Battle of Tannenberg and the first Battle of the Masurian Lakes. Despite outnumbering the German Eighth Army under Paul von Hindenberg and Erich Ludendorff by almost two to one, the Russians had lost some 300,000 men by the middle of September 1914. Rather than face the wrath of the Czar, General Alexander Samsonov shot himself.

Russian morale plummeted. Such heavy and unexpected losses only six weeks into the war drained their enthusiasm and with the way to Constantinople blocked by the *Goeben,* some of the Czar's advisors began to consider an armistice with Germany.[1] If Russia threw in the towel, Britain and France faced imminent disaster. This was the grand strategy envisaged by the Secret Elite at that point in the war. The possibility of a victorious German army switching all available forces from the Eastern to the Western Front sent shivers down the spine of Whitehall. London became preoccupied with the need to encourage an increasingly reluctant Russia to hold fast.

Make no mistake, Russia was prepared to sacrifice her young men for one reason, the acquisition of Constantinople and the Straits. How were the Secret Elite to deal with this? Russia's ambitions clashed with British and French post-war imperial intentions for the Ottoman Empire and could never be countenanced. Indeed, two centuries of relentless insistence that Russia had to be kept out of Constantinople underpinned the fact that in truth, "the Allies would try anything to stop Russia gaining Istanbul (Constantinople) and the Bosporus."[2] The French wanted Syria; Britain wanted Persia and just about everywhere to its west, while the little known Zionists talked about "returning" to Palestine. Several schemes took shape in the corridors of power in London and Paris which were bound to be obstructed if Constantinople was in Russian hands.

French fears were later expressed by President Poincaré in a letter to his Ambassador in Petrograd: "Possession of Constantinople … would introduce her… into the concert of western nations and this would give her the chance to become a great naval power. Everything would thus be changed in the European equilibrium.…" Poincaré's great fear was that once Germany had been defeated, Russia would have little reason to adhere to the Franco-Russian Alliance, and as a result, her naval expansion would undermine French interests.[3]

The annual Guildhall Banquet which the City of London lavished on its political leaders on Monday 9 November reached truly iconic status in terms of British duplicity. Churchill promised that a blockade would bring Germany to her knees in six, nine or twelve months, and promptly failed to take the action required. Kitchener announced that "the men are responding splendidly … but I shall want more." Prime Minister Asquith told the greatest lie. He claimed that, despite all his government's efforts to safeguard Turkish neutrality, "it is they and not we who have wrung the death-knell of Ottoman dominion.… The Turkish Empire has committed suicide and dug its grave with its own hand."[4] No Russian Imperialist could have said it better. The Ottoman empire was scheduled for demolition.[5] It was to be torn apart under the guise of suicide.

In November 1914 Sazonov notified Count Alexander Benckendorff, his Ambassador in London, that Russian troops operating against Turkey would be compelled to violate Persian neutrality. Foreign Secretary Sir Edward Grey immediately issued a "hands off" dictum stating that a Russian incursion into the neutral Moslem country would provoke anti-Entente ferment among the Mohammedans of the East. Just two days later Britain landed her own troops at the head of the Persian Gulf. They occupied the oilfields near Ahwaz, and advanced on the Turkish town of Basra, capturing it on 22 November.[6] Apparently a Russian invasion of Persia would excite religious tensions among Muslims, but a British attack was perfectly acceptable. The hypocrisy was stunning.

Benckendorff cabled the Czar that his cousin, King George V had said that "as concerns Constantinople, it is clear that it must be yours." The deception worked perfectly. The Secret Elite never intended that Constantinople would fall to the Russians, but Nicholas II was elated by the news.[7] Sazonov abandoned his designs on Persia. He had the King-Emperor's word.[8] The British government immediately pursued its interests further and announced that they intended to annex Egypt, still nominally inside the Ottoman Empire, and replace the pro-Turkish Khedive with a sympathetic figure-head. The Russians agreed in the belief that this was a step towards their inevitable march to Constantinople. Czar Nicholas thought it "excellent."[9] In terms of grand geopolitical scheming and diplomatic double-dealing the Czar was utterly naïve.

Sazonov was not so readily reassured. He felt that the time had finally come to resolve the question of the Straits. It was now or never. Like many others in Petrograd he was unwilling to wait until the end of the war for complete Russian control of Constantinople, including both sides of the Bosporus and the Sea of Marmara.[10] The great dream was to take both European and Asian banks of the Dardanelles, which would be the springboard to even greater imperial acquisitions. This and this alone justified the terrible sacrifices which were being made on the Eastern Front.

On 21 December Sazonov wrote to his Chief of Staff, General Nikolai Yanushkevich, that it was imperative that Russia took the Straits, and that it could "not be achieved by diplomatic action alone." He demanded to know "what military operations had been decided upon for the actual penetration and seizure of the Narrows and their environs." The answer was not what he wanted. The Black Sea Fleet, short of dreadnoughts, fast mine-layers and modern submarines, was barely on a par with the Turkish Navy, and the loss of one or two vessels would upset the precarious balance. Above all, the Russian generals were bound by long-standing agreement to concentrate efforts on the Eastern Front. Yanushkevich answered Sazonov on 25 December: "In the present circumstances … the question of allocating special forces for taking possession of the Straits cannot be raised until we have achieved a decisive success over our Western enemies."[11]

Sazonov was faced with the stark reality; Russia was currently unable to take Constantinople. His expectations had been totally unrealistic, but the Secret Elite were, as ever, much better informed. The British Military Attache at Petrograd, Colonel Alfred Knox, was an astute observer and by December 1914 his reports worried Kitchener. While the Grand Duke Nikolay Nikolayevich, Commander-in-Chief of the Russian army and the Minister of War, remained outwardly confident (Churchill described it as blind or guilty optimism)[12] Knox spoke of the criticisms he heard from Russian commanders. They believed that the delayed French offensive was caused by the "diabolical cunning" of the other Allied governments who wanted Russia to "waste her strength so that she may not emerge too strong from the war."[13] Lack of guns and ammunition and disorganized communication left the Russian army incapable of a serious offensive.[14] and the 6th Army at Petrograd trained new recruits with only one rifle to three men.[15] There was an almost suicidal culture in Russian military circles of representing situations in a falsely favorable light, but increasingly the need to make peace with the Germans was voiced by high-ranking Generals.[16] Accusations were made that the burden of the war was being borne unequally by Russia; that Britain was not committing sufficient men to the front.[17]

The British government began to have "grave forebodings" that the Russian armies, paralyzed by the lack of munitions, might collapse entirely and "be forced into a separate peace." Churchill believed that such a disaster could be averted if Britain and France encouraged Russia "to dwell upon the prizes of victory."[18] He knew, as did every member of the Secret Elite, that the "prizes of victory," namely control of Constantinople and the Straits, were prizes Russia could never be allowed to win.

The Secret Elite had to conjure an initiative which gave the illusion of support and promised glittering success so that Russia would continue the struggle. Russia had to be reassured; had to be kept in the war but kept out of the Straits. Russia's focus was fixed on Constantinople, but Sazonov knew that it would be exceedingly difficult if not impossible for the Czar's forces alone to take either the city or the Straits. Emotionally it was their Achille's heel, an issue so sensitive that the Secret Elite began to deliberate how they could use it to keep Russia from defection. What best to do? The man tasked by the Secret Elite to solve the conundrum was Lieutenant-Colonel Maurice Hankey, Secretary of the War Council, and a trusted inner-circle member of the secret cabal.[19] He was a strategist to whom they listened carefully. Hankey spent the whole of Christmas Day considering options they might take. His report became known as the "Boxing Day Memo."[20] It proposed an operation against the Dardanelles and suggested that Britain should move three army corps to participate with Greece and other Balkan states in a combined naval and military attack.[21] Note the date; Boxing Day 1914. It was an idea that needed to be carefully considered in view of Russian sensitivities. From it would arise the Gallipoli disaster of 1915.

Sir Edward Grey was concerned that Russia "might well change sides in the war,"[22] which clearly demonstrated how critical and dangerous the whole issue of Constantinople had become. Serious though it would be if Russia signed a peace treaty with the enemy, Grey feared that she might thereafter actually join Germany against Britain and France. It was a potential disaster that sharpened their minds. Arthur Balfour, the sole conservative politician on the War Council and a senior member of the Secret Elite's inner-core,[23] immediately pointed to "the menacing question of Constantinople" and who would own the city.[24] This was the nub of the problem; Britain, despite her promises, would never allow Russia to take Constantinople, while the Russians would not countenance anyone else "owning" it. Would they stay in the war if tricked into believing that Britain intended capturing the Dardanelles and Constantinople on their behalf? The best chance of their falling for the ruse was if they believed that it was their idea in the first place.

The Secret Elite had the very man in place in Petrograd to subtly influence them, the Military Attache, Brigadier-General Sir John Hanbury-Williams. He had served in South Africa under the Secret Elite's leader, Lord Milner, with whom he kept in regular contact,[25] and with Earl Grey, a member of the Secret Elite's inner core.[26] Hanbury-Williams was identified by Professor Carroll Quigley as one of Milner's Kindergarten, the men at the very heart of the Secret Elite.[27] His ancestor, Sir Charles Hanbury-Williams had been ambassador at the court of Catherine the Great, which gave him access to the Russian Imperial family. He was considered a "sincere friend" by Czar Nicholas II.[28]

On 30 December 1914, Hanbury-Williams met with Grand Duke Nikolayevich, Commander-in-Chief of the Russian army, and used the opportunity to plant the idea of a British intervention against Turkey in his mind. "I asked him, in the event of it being possible, whether he thought a naval demonstration [against Turkey] would be of any use. He jumped at it gladly."[29] How clever. Just days after Hankey and his Secret Elite compatriots had considered how they would carefully advance their strategy for keeping Russia in the war, Hanbury-Williams "just happened" to mention to the Grand Duke the possibility of Britain attacking Turkey. With a growing anti-war element, civil unrest and revolution was a realistic fear in the minds of the Russian leaders. The Commander-In-Chief's thoughts were focused on Russia's fragile domestic morale, and he had not even raised the subject of Constantinople or the Dardanelles with Hanbury-Williams.[30] The latter's suggestion was subtly transformed into an appeal for help from the Grand Duke. Hanbury-Williams noted in his diary that "this conversation was really the origin of what eventually developed into the Dardanelles operation."[31] Absolutely so, but the seed was sown by the Secret Elite, not by the Grand Duke.

Late on 1 January 1915, Sir George Buchanan, the British Ambassador at Petrograd, and one of the Secret Elite's diplomatic enforcers,[32] sent a telegram to London stating that Grand Duke Nikolayevich had asked Britain for help to relieve pressure on his army in the Caucasus. Before a response was possible, the problem solved itself. The Ottomans attacked the Russians in the Caucasus at Sarikamish on 29 December, and lost 30,000 men to a Russian counter-attack. Enver Pasha, the questionable Turkish Minister of War, ordered his troops to abandon their greatcoats and packs before struggling over 10,000-foot mountain passes in atrocious winter conditions. Tens of thousands froze to death; less than 18,000 Turkish soldiers survived. It was an absolute disaster. As with many of his decisions, Enver's judgment was either profoundly stupid or served some other purpose. In this instance his actions changed the political picture. Within days the Turkish threat against the Russian army had been crushed, and "any plan to force the Dardanelles ... ought to have died a fairly quick death."[33] In truth, there was never any need for a British "demonstration" in Turkey to help the Russians. Buchanan's telegram and all that followed was part of the Secret Elite's game-plan.

Kitchener discussed the next step with Churchill. He pointed out that there were no troops available for another front.[34] If there was to be an intervention it would have to be naval.[35] That same day, Kitchener sent a telegram to Petrograd, "Please assure the Grand Duke that steps will be taken to make a demonstration against the Turks." Churchill later recalled, "It was the least that could have been said in answer to a request of a hard-pressed Ally."[36] This was a typical example of Churchill's clever dissembling which concealed the true reason for Gallipoli, a falsehood that mainstream historians have repeated ever since. Churchill ignored the fact that the "hard-pressed Ally" had already crushed the Turkish army in the Caucasus.

On 3 January First Sea Lord, Admiral Fisher, sent a note to Churchill saying that an attack on the Dardanelles by the navy could not succeed. He advocated a joint naval and military campaign with warships forcing the Dardanelles while large numbers of troops were landed on both the Asian and European shores.[37] Admiral Frederick Tudor, Third Sea Lord, also advised Churchill that the navy could not do this on its own.[38] He sought other opinions, including those of Admiral Jackson, who thought that he would be "mad to try and get into the Sea of Marmora without having the Gallipoli peninsula held by our own troops or every gun on both sides of the Straits destroyed." Churchill was very careful not to show this to his colleagues in the War Council.[39] There was no going back.

Summary.

- Russian defeats and losses on the Eastern Front drained their enthusiasm for the war they had started.
- Russia wanted Constantinople and the Straits to give them year round access to the Mediterranean but this clashed with British and French ambitions. France wanted Syria; Britain wanted Persia and as much as could be grasped on the route towards India. Neither would contemplate Russian ownership of Constantinople, no matter what they said in public.
- The Russian foreign secretary, Sergei Sazonov doubted the intentions of the other allies, and there was a growing belief in Petrograd that Russia was bearing an unequal burden in the war.
- The Secret Elite had to conjure the illusion of support for Russian designs so they would stay in the war, but at the same time keep them out of Constantinople.
- Maurice Hankey produced a 'Boxing-Day Memo' on 26 December proposing an operation against the Dardanelles.
- In Petrograd, the British Military Attache, Hanbury-Williams planted the idea of a British intervention against Turkey in the mind of Grand Duke Nicholas, the Russian Commander-in-Chief.
- This was then translated into an appeal by the Grand Duke for action to relieve pressure on the Russian army in the Caucasus.
- Churchill took up the cause and proposed a naval attack on the Dardanelles which virtually every senior Admiral thought impossible. He always needed to be in the limelight of war.

Chapter 9

The Dardanelles – Impossible Quest

The Secret Elite knew an attack on the Dardanelles could not succeed and did not want it to succeed. The last thing on their minds was to capture the Straits – and hence Constantinople – for Russia. It merely had to be a demonstration to the Russians that Britain was *trying* to take it for them. The Admirals knew nothing of the geopolitical machinations behind the decision to attack the Dardanelles. Some strategy had to be found to side-step their objections to it. Determined to find a naval figure who would agree, Churchill worked his way through the Admiralty ranks. He telegraphed Vice-Admiral Sackville Carden, Commander of the Mediterranean Squadron. Was the forcing of the Dardanelles by sea a practicable operation? This time he added a point which was intended to influence the response: "Importance of the results would justify severe loss." The callous disregard for human life was typical of Churchill and his type.

Eager to please, Carden replied cautiously on 5 January: "I do not think that the Dardanelles can be rushed, but they might be forced by extended operations with a large number of ships." Churchill had at last found a semblance of naval support. Next day he assured the Vice-Admiral that, "high authorities here concur in your opinion" and asked what number of ships he would need. The Vice-Admiral assumed that the "high authorities" included the Admiralty representatives on the War Council, Admirals Fisher and Sir Arthur Wilson.[1] Churchill had duped him into the response he wanted. No "high authorities" had agreed with his opinion. Not one of them. Both First Sea Lord Fisher and Admiral Frederick Tudor had bluntly stated that the navy could not take the Dardanelles. Admiral Sir Arthur Wilson, brought back from retirement as Churchill's "strategic adviser," was neither asked for, nor proffered, an opinion because Churchill knew he would never agree to the madness of a naval attack on the heavily mined Straits.

If everything was above board, as mainstream historians would have us believe, surely Churchill would have turned to the Admiralty's expert on the Dardanelles, Rear-Admiral Arthur Limpus. As the former head of the British naval mission in Constantinople, he was the man who "knew the Turks and the Dardanelles' defenses intimately,"[2] and "all their secrets."[3] Yet Churchill shunned him. Why? The stark truth was he knew that Limpus, like Admirals Fisher, Tudor and Jackson, was opposed to his plan.[4] Limpus believed that the first stage of any attack on the Dardanelles would have to be an amphibious landing.[5] It could not be undertaken by the navy alone.

This was not the first time that such views had been clearly expressed. In 1906 the Admiralty considered a naval assault on the Dardanelles too risky, concluding that it would "have to be undertaken by a joint naval and military expedition."[6] Churchill had himself agreed in 1911 that it was "no longer possible to force the Dardanelles."[7] Four years later it had become so imperative for wider political and geo-strategic reasons that he canvassed opinion across the higher echelons of the navy until he found the answer he wanted. Vice-Admiral Carden was not told about the wide consensus of opposition to a purely naval assault on the Dardanelles. He had been reassured that "people in high authority" agreed with his assessment. Poor Carden. The man asked to prepare a naval attack on the Dardanelles was the one with least knowledge. He was denied access to the vast quantity of intelligence which had been gathered on the Dardanelles defenses by Admiral Limpus, Ambassador Mallet and others. Carden was set up to be the perfect patsy when the plan failed, for fail it must.

On 6 January 1915 Winston Churchill sent a telegraph to Sackville Carden asking how many ships he needed to break through the Dardanelles and how he would go about it? In his response five days later Carden suggested a force of 12 battleships, three battle-cruisers, three light cruisers, 16 destroyers, six submarines, four seaplanes and 12 minesweepers. In addition, he would require a dozen support vessels. Surely but subtly, responsibility for the operation that could never succeed was passed to Carden.

His response was not so much a plan as the order in which the ships might attack the Dardanelles forts,[8] but from that moment on Churchill presented Carden's list as if it was a carefully considered strategic proposal. The old Vice-Admiral imagined that battleships would first bombard the outer forts guarding the entrance to the Dardanelles from a long distance. Minesweepers would then clear a passage for the battleships to progressively bombard the defenses as they advanced. Kept in ignorance, Carden believed that naval gunnery could do the job. He had never been given sight of the vast amount of credible naval intelligence which agreed that the only way to disable the Dardanelles forts was the landing of troops in considerable numbers.

At a meeting of the War Council on 13 January, Churchill unveiled the Carden "plan." There was little discussion. Crucially important issues were ignored. Kitchener, who still refused to allocate troops for a joint attack, thought it "worth trying" and there were no dissenting voices.[9]

Senior military and naval figures were not asked for their opinions nor did they volunteer them. They disagreed with Churchill and Kitchener but "loyally" put obedience to service etiquette first.[10] Their expertise was rendered irrelevant. Sir Edward Grey saw "great political prospects." Arthur Balfour said it was difficult to imagine a more useful operation.[11] What "expert" would risk his career questioning the Secret Elite?

Churchill pushed ahead, but in an astonishing minute to Asquith, Grey and Kitchener on 14 January he stated that unless "adequate military force is forthcoming to storm and hold the forts after the bombardment, there are no means of producing good results." This was a crucial admission that he knew the Dardanelles' forts could not be destroyed without adequate military assistance. The political threat from Russia became so immediate that he was prepared to sanction an attack and ignore the critical issue that it could not succeed.[12]

Expert opinion at the Admiralty remained unanimous. Admiral Sir Henry Jackson advised Churchill that the first stage of Carden's "plan" might succeed in destroying the outer forts but warned that the Turks had at least 200 Krupp guns of 6-inch and above and that all of them would need to be silenced. These great cannons were mobile, well concealed and protected from direct naval gunfire. They could only be destroyed by troops on the ground.[13] Experts on the War Council tried to tell Churchill that guns mounted on warships were much less accurate than shore-based batteries, but "he so bewitched them, they were reduced to supine or servile acquiescence in a scheme which they knew was based upon a series of monstrous technical fallacies."[14] It was not Turkish military competence that worried the Admirals, but the insanity of what they were being asked to achieve.[15] Knowing it would fail, the Secret Elite-dominated War Council approved Carden's "plan." He was ordered to prepare a naval task force in February "to bombard and take the Gallipoli Peninsula with Constantinople as its objective." The notion that ships could take a peninsula, any peninsula, was utterly absurd.

The plans were set without Russia's knowledge. How would they respond? Despite Hanbury-Williams' influence, the Foreign Office anticipated that the Russians might suspect British intentions. On 16 January, Sir Edward Grey warned, "we must say something to Russia, not necessarily in detail, or she will think we are stealing a march to forestall her ambitions at Constantinople. The peg to hang our communication on would be the Grand Duke's appeal to us some days ago to make a diversion to prevent Turkish pressure in the Caucasus."[16] In other words the Foreign Office planned to use the Grand Duke's "appeal," the suggestion made to him by Hanbury-Williams, to justify their actions. The imputation was that "we are doing this for you" but as Grey spelled out, their intention was to forestall Russia's ambitions at Constantinople. Churchill wrote to the Grand Duke on 19 January saying that in response to his "request," Britain would make a serious effort to break down Turkish opposition.[17] Churchill generously suggested that Russian naval and military involvement would be valuable, knowing full well that they had no resources to spare. The Grand Duke welcomed the British operation, but confirmed that neither Russian naval nor military support was available.[18] Thus the Secret Elite's plan to thwart Russia was unwittingly given the stamp of Imperial approval by the Russian Commander-in-Chief.

Sergei Sazonov was not so gullible. He later recalled that when the British Ambassador informed him of the proposed expedition, "I intensely disliked the thought that the Straits and Constantinople might be taken by our Allies and not by Russian forces."[19] This indicated the extent of Sazonov's justified mistrust.[20] The Russian Foreign Secretary immediately asked the Czar's commanders if they could take part in the occupation of the Straits. Anticipating a negative answer he wondered "if it might not be better to request our Allies, in view of the change in our favor in the Caucasian situation, to delay the intended actions against the Dardanelles." He smelled a rat, but was reassured by his own military colleagues that the capture of the Straits by the Allied navy was almost impossible.[21]

In London, First Sea Lord Admiral Fisher had clearly been fed the lie that it was the Russian Commander-in-Chief who was insisting on the naval attack. He noted: "apparently the Grand Duke Nikolayevich has demanded this step, or I suppose he would make peace with Germany." Fisher added, "I just abominate the Dardanelles operation unless a great change is made and it is settled to be a military operation, with 200,000 men in conjunction with the Fleet." He wanted joint operations or no operation at all.[22] On 25 January, Fisher asked Churchill to circulate his views to members of the War Council but neither the Prime Minister nor any of the others had asked for his opinion or objections.[23] His views were ignored as were those of Victor Augagneur, former Minister for the French Navy. At a meeting in London on 26 January he informed Churchill that French Naval Intelligence believed a purely maritime operation was unlikely to achieve anything. French Intelligence officers insisted that the way must first be cleared by military operations. Augagneur, like Fisher, was wasting his breath. Although they lost ships and men in the campaign, all decisions on the Dardanelles-Gallipoli attack were taken without a French voice in strategy and tactics. They were merely kept informed.[24]

Despite overwhelming expert opinion that a naval attack on the Dardanelles must fail, the War Council decided to proceed on 28 January 1915. Warships and support vessels from across the world were ordered to head for Lemnos in the Aegean Sea. The Greek island had a large natural harbor at Mudros Bay, which lay just three hours by sea from the entrance to the Dardanelles. Apart from one modern, oil-fired dreadnought, HMS

Queen Elizabeth, the battleships allotted the task were slow and outdated; indeed they had been deemed unfit for battle in the North Sea.[25] Admiral Fisher's first concern was that the Grand Fleet remained at full strength, but Churchill was at pains to show that he could find sufficient ships to take on the Dardanelles without weakening the North Sea defenses.[26] No troops were to be involved, but Rear-Admiral James Oliver, Chief of the Admiralty War Staff, advised Churchill to send two battalions from the Royal Naval Division. They comprised some 2,000 men culled from ships and shore establishments, essentially sailors used as infantry. Oliver commented, "they are pretty rotten, but ought to be good enough for the inferior Turkish troops now at Gallipoli."[27] Unlike the tens of thousands of men who died facing those "inferior" troops, Rear-Admiral Oliver passed away peacefully in his bed at the age of 100.

Still bristling that his advice had been ignored, Admiral Fisher wrote to Churchill on 29 January: "It will be the wonder of the ages that no troops were sent to cooperate with the Fleet with half a million ... soldiers in England."[28] Fisher lost his fight within the War Council, and the Carden "plan," impossible and implausible though it was officially endorsed. A major campaign whose success depended on months of detailed joint military and naval planning, careful preparation and, above all, sufficient troops on the ground, went ahead without any of these prerequisites. The fleet "was to attempt, without the aid of a single soldier, an enterprise which in the early days of the war both the Admiralty and the War Office had regarded as a military task."[29] Admiral Lord Nelson's sage advice that no ship should ever attack a fort, advice supported by almost every admiral in the fleet, was studiously ignored.[30] Every aspect of the naval assault beggars far deeper research, but mainstream historians have simply accepted that the War Council followed Churchill's lead. He didn't carry sufficient influence on his own, but encouraged by Grey and the Foreign Office, Churchill championed the Secret Elite agenda and was allowed to proceed.

Mines, which had been carefully laid in multiple rows across the Straits, constituted the Turk's principle defense. The main role of the guns and fortifications was to protect the minefields. One hundred and eleven guns were stationed on the European side of the Straits and one hundred and twenty-one on the Asiatic side.[31] Twenty-four heavy mobile howitzers had also been brought in to support the Turkish artillery, and dummy placements which emitted smoke were constructed to draw the warships' fire.[32]Additionally, shore based torpedo tubes had been installed at various locations along the Dardanelles. By February 1915 the defenses were so formidable that Maurice Hankey reported, "From Lord Fisher downwards every naval officer in the Admiralty who is in [on] the secret believes that the Navy cannot take the Dardanelles without troops."[33] "Every naval officer" believed that it was impossible, but the Secret Elite already knew that.

Antagonism among senior naval officers grew steadily, and an impromptu meeting of the War Council was held on 16 February. Just before the meeting, Kitchener called one of his intelligence officers, Captain Wyndham Deedes, to his office. Deedes, who had been attached to the Turkish Army for several years and had closely studied the Dardanelles defenses, was asked for his opinion on a naval attack. His reply, that it was a fundamentally unsound proposition, angered Kitchener, who dismissed the well-informed officer, telling him that he didn't know what he was talking about.[34] Kitchener and the Secret Elite were faced with a difficult dilemma. They had agreed on a plan to keep Russia in the war and out of Constantinople, but members of the armed forces who had no knowledge of the secret cabal or its scheming, began to prove difficult.

At its 16 February meeting, the War Council attempted to stifle the criticism. Kitchener agreed that the 29th Division comprising 18,000 regular soldiers should be sent to Lemnos "within nine or ten days." The Division was currently in England, earmarked for the western front. In addition 34,000 Anzac troops, who were in Egypt awaiting transfer to France, were placed on stand-by "in case of necessity." This sudden about-turn did not mean that the addition of troops would convert the Carden "plan" into a combined operation. It was a cosmetic compromise. It would appear as if the attack was intended as a joint offensive to deflect criticism, but nothing tangible had changed. The naval attack, which was scheduled to begin on 19 February, was not postponed to await the arrival of troops, and "no thought had been given by the War Council as to what these troops were to do."[35] "Churchill and Kitchener were agreed that the Fleet should go through the Narrows before the troops need be used."[36]

On 18 February the French Government, having agreed to provide 20,000 troops, urged Britain to suspend the naval operations until their arrival at the Dardanelles. London replied that "naval operations having begun cannot be interrupted." That was a lie. Not a shot had been fired, but French views did not appear to matter in the Gallipoli campaign. To confuse matters further, Kitchener announced a complete reversal in military deployment. The following day, the very day that the naval bombardment of the Dardanelles began, he withdrew permission to release the 29th Division, and ordered the dispersal of transport ships already in place to take them to Lemnos. His given reason was that, in view of Russian setbacks, these men were needed in France. But his decision was not absolute. He kept the door open by adding that the 29th might be sent to the Dardanelles at some unspecified future date "if required."

In Kitchener's opinion the Australian and New Zealand Divisions already in Egypt would be "sufficient at first" for any attack on the Gallipoli Peninsula. Later, when asked by Prime Minister Asquith if the Anzacs were "good enough" for the task, Kitchener replied, "they were quite good enough if a cruise in the Sea of Marmora was all that was contemplated."[37] What was going on inside the War Minister's head? On the one hand, the Australians and New Zealanders were considered quite "sufficient" for an attack on Gallipoli, but with his next breath Kitchener was suggesting that they were fitted only for a cruise. What was his state of mind? Was he confused, deliberately devious or stark-raving mad?

Phase 1 of Vice-Admiral Carden's plan, the naval assault, began at 9.15 a.m. on 19 February 1915 with a slow, long-range bombardment of the permanent forts and outer Dardanelles defenses at Sedd-el-Bahr on the European side, and Kum Kale on the Asian. It continued all morning. In the afternoon Carden ordered his warships to close to within six thousand yards. The Turkish batteries failed to respond so several ships went even closer and bombarded the shore. With the light fading, and having drawn fire from only two of the smaller forts, Carden ordered the recall. It was evident that the Fleet would have to approach much closer to the shore and engage the Turkish guns individually.[38] Early signs of success from the long-range bombardment had proved deceptive, and the hope that heavy naval gunfire would devastate the targets on land, proved forlorn.[39] It was exactly as the experts had predicted. The weather broke that night and for five days rough seas, bitterly cold winds and sleet and snow, delayed the attack.

In London, after a War Council meeting on 24 February, Churchill telegraphed Carden to inform him that two Anzac Divisions, The Royal Naval Division and a French Division were being held ready to move within striking distance. "But it is not intended that they should be employed in present circumstance to assist the Naval operations which are independent and self-contained." In a further telegram that day, Churchill again warned Carden that major military operations were not to be embarked upon.[40] Was Churchill as mad as Kitchener? No, they were both working to the Secret Elite agenda. The intention was to dupe the Russians into believing that Gallipoli was a serious military campaign, designed for their benefit.

On 25 February, when the storm had blown itself out, Vice-Admiral John de Robeck led the attack to the mouth of the Straits. The Ottoman gunners withdrew under the heavy barrage, and by the end of the day the outer forts had been successfully silenced. Over the following days, parties of marines roamed at will across the tip of the Gallipoli peninsula blowing up abandoned guns and destroying emplacements. The door to Constantinople lay open. Had 70,000 troops been available to pour through, Gallipoli might just have fallen. But that had never been the objective.

By the following week it was too late. Realizing that this was not a major invasion, the defenders recovered their confidence and drove the marines off with heavy rifle fire. In total, the naval battalion suffered twenty-three killed, twenty-five wounded and four missing. It was little more than a skirmish in terms of what followed, but the Turkish troops gained a valuable boost to their morale. No further landings were attempted until 25 April, by which time the defenses had been rebuilt and considerably strengthened.

The Dardanelles were heavily defended. The Turks had placed 370 mines across the Straits in ten lines, plus an eleventh line of 26 mines parallel to the shore, a mile or so from the beach at Eren Keui Bay. Rather than powerful Royal Navy minesweepers as Admiral Carden had requested, the Admiralty supplied unarmed fishing trawlers manned by volunteers and commanded by a naval officer with no experience in minesweeping.[41] The trawlers faced serious problems, especially at night, when picked out by powerful searchlights and exposed to gunfire from mobile howitzers and field guns. It was a vicious circle. The make-shift minesweepers could not do their work until the guns had been silenced, and the battleships could not get close enough to silence the guns until the mines had been cleared. [42] The bombardments achieved little. Indeed, they "destroyed all hope of surprise, and were directly responsible for strengthening the enemy's defenses and increasing his power to resist a military landing."[43]

Meantime, on the political front, the pressure from Russia was raised another notch. Foreign Secretary Sir Edward Grey warned that they were asking for control of the Straits and wanted an immediate answer. Richard Haldane, former War Secretary and member of the War Council, stated that unless Britain made an explicit offer, Germany would seize the opportunity to conclude a peace with Russia.[44] Czar Nicholas informed the French ambassador that his people were making terrible sacrifices without reward and consequently they would only be satisfied once Constantinople became part of his empire.[45] Sazonov piled more pressure on the Allies by threatening to resign. He made it clear that he would immediately be replaced by Count Sergei Witte, a pro-German sympathizer who would likely seal a treaty with Germany.[46] The Russians continued to turn the screw, and the crucial need to stop them from wavering dictated the War Council's decisions.[47] The Czar's advisors knew that a naval assault on its own would fail. Kitchener's hand was forced. Something more had to be done to convince Russia that Britain was serious.

Responding to the pressure, on 10 March Kitchener decided that he would indeed send the 29th Division to Gallipoli to join the Anzac Corps of 34,100 men currently sitting in Egypt, and a French Division of 20,000. He had changed his mind yet again. After three weeks of this "shilly-shallying" the Division was finally allowed to sail for Gallipoli,[48] but the delay had momentous consequences. Churchill would later write, "Without 29th Division, the army could do nothing. They were the professionals who mattered, the sole regular division whose movements and arrival governed everything."[49] Yes indeed, the opportunity had gone, but if one person was to be blamed for not pushing for a joint attack, it was himself. An official Ottoman account related that up to 25 February "it would have been possible to effect a landing at any point on the peninsula and the capture of the Straits would have been comparatively easy."[50] But the opportunity had been completely lost when they attacked the Dardanelles forts without sufficient men on the ground to take and hold them. The naval attack was counter-productive. It only served to give the Turks ample warning to strengthen their defenses.

The War Council intervened. General William Birdwood had been sent out on 23 February "to assess the situation." His response was no different from that of the senior naval officers. The navy could not successfully force the Dardanelles. Large numbers of men were required. It had to be a combined operation.[51] Birdwood's advice, like that of everyone else who proffered the same opinion, was ignored. No-one in authority was prepared to publicly admit that the naval bombardment was hopeless. Poor Carden continued to do his best, but that could never be good enough. On 11 March a further naval incursion came under heavy fire and the minesweepers turned tail and fled. It was a ridiculous state of affairs. You could no more expect fishermen to successfully man minesweepers than you could expect an ordinary seaman to land a catch in the North Sea swells.

That same day Kitchener informed the War Office that he was sending General Sir Ian Hamilton to prepare a Mediterranean Expeditionary Force. Within twenty-four hours of his totally unexpected promotion and without requisite briefing or planning, Hamilton found himself speeding across France to Marseilles on a special train, then by the fast cruiser, *Phaeton,* to the eastern Mediterranean. He arrived at the island of Tenedos on 17 March to find Vice-Admiral Carden collapsed with exhaustion and anxiety. It was no surprise. In fairness to Carden, he was never fitted for the post, which should have been given to the exceptionally competent Admiral Limpus, former head of the naval mission to Turkey. No man knew more about the Dardanelles and its mined defenses.[52] Eliminating these was key to safe passage through the Straits. Whatever his faults, Carden knew this and felt completely undermined by the Admiralty's refusal to provide custom-built minesweepers. Fishing trawlers were not up to the task. Overall they made 17 attempts to sweep the mines, but only reached the main minefield twice. Out of a total of almost 400 mines only two were cleared.[53] Words cannot capture the enormity of that failure, but volunteer fishermen were not to blame.

On his arrival General Hamilton was surprised to find the Gallipoli shore-line so well defended, but his initial shock was as nothing compared to what he witnessed on the following day. On 18 March the serious business of attacking the Dardanelles began. With fine clear skies and a calm sea, the main force of battleships and battle-cruisers entered the Dardanelles in three divisions arranged four abreast. Cruisers, destroyers and the trawlers, which were now crewed by the Royal Navy, followed on. The front division, line "A," comprised four British battleships, including the new dreadnought *Queen Elizabeth*, with two others flanking the line. One mile astern came line "B" with four French battleships. Bringing up the rear, line "C" were another four British battleships.[54] In a tremendous spectacle of naval might they went in with all guns blazing.

The plan was to knock out the forts at the Narrows and the batteries protecting the minefields. Minesweepers were to follow that night to clear a channel. Next morning at first light, the Fleet would destroy any remaining forts at close range while the last of the mines were swept. All being well, the Fleet was scheduled to reach the Sea of Marmara within two days.[55] It all sounded so straightforward but, as Robert Burns warned, "the best-laid schemes o' Mice an Men gang aft agley."[56] Vice-Admiral de Robeck was aware of the problems faced by the trawlers, and the fact that the minefields remained intact. Yet he failed to have them swept. Eight powerful destroyers which could have easily been fitted with sweeps remained idle that fateful day while the officers sat playing cards.[57]

The battle began at 11:30 AM and grew in intensity as one line of ships after another opened fire on the forts. An hour later, about six miles inside the Straits, many of the shore batteries maintained their barrage. The French battleship *Gaulois* was holed below the waterline and had to be beached. HMS *Inflexible* was forced to retire to extinguish fires and repair damage. *Lord Nelson, Agamemnon, Charlemagne* and *Albion* were hit, but carried on firing. The French battleship *Bouvet* struck a mine, heeled over and vanished with most of her crew. A second mine crippled *Inflexible* and she began listing. *Irrestible* and *Suffren* were badly damaged. *Ocean* suffered an internal explosion and sank several hours later. The trawlers were urged on to sweep ahead, but ran into a rain of howitzer shells and even though manned by sailors, fled in disorder. Three battleships had been sunk with the loss of over 700 men, and three crippled. It was a rout. The fleet had not even reached the Narrows when the attack was called off. On the Turkish side, two 14-inch guns and several smaller ones had been put out of action, but none of those guarding the minefield was damaged. The minefield itself was untouched.[58] It was, as so many knew it would be, a disaster.

Throughout the campaign, warships never again ventured into the Straits. The major task for the navy would henceforth be limited to ferrying soldiers to the beaches. Maurice Hankey told General Haig that the operation had been run "like an American cinema show" in that every step had been widely advertised long before it was carried out.[59] Of course it was. And it was so blatant that we have to believe this was their intention; to completely remove any possibility of surprise. Why would any military strategist do that, unless ... well, unless they did not want to succeed. The Naval operation had been set up to fail and it did. In five short weeks it would be the army's turn.

Summary.

- The Dardanelles campaign began as a demonstration to the Russians that Britain was trying to capture the Straits - and hence Constantinople - for them.
- Churchill sought Admiralty approval for the impending folly, but only one Vice-Admiral, Sackville Carden, was cautiously supportive. Churchill immediately adopted him rather than senior naval figures with years of experience.
- Suddenly there was the 'Carden' plan which Churchill unveiled at a War Council meeting on 13 January 1914.
- Kitchener was adamant that he would not waste his army on a plan which could never work.
- With the exception of one dreadnought, *HMS Queen Elizabeth*, a battle fleet of warships and support vessels, slow, outdated and unfit for battle on the North Sea was sent to the Mediterranean to attack the Dardanelles' forts.
- The first attack on 19 February had little effect. Long-range bombardment proved ineffectual and a serious storm delayed the second assault four days.
- The Dardanelles was heavily defended. One hundred and eleven guns were stationed on the European side of the Straits and one hundred and twenty-one on the Asiatic side. 370 mines had been placed across the Straits in 11 lines.
- The "minesweepers" sent by the Admiralty were merely trawlers crewed by fishermen who had no previous experience in such work.
- The Russians knew that a naval attack on its own was mere dressing and Kitchener was obliged to send the 29th Division along with the Australian/ New Zealand (Anzac) corps of 34,100 men. This was augmented by a force of 20,000 French troops.
- When the serious attack began on Gallipoli on 18 March, naval losses were embarrassing. Three battleships were sunk with the combined loss of 700 men and three were crippled.
- Surprised? No-one in real authority was. Maurice Hankey described it as like an American cinema show in that every step was widely advertised before it was carried out.

Anzac bravely rescuing wounded comrade

Chapter 10

Gallipoli – Prepare To Fail

Organization of the military campaign to attack the Gallipoli peninsula was every bit as shambolic as the seaborne assault. As the Australian author Les Carlyon succinctly put it, "Instead of being planned for months in London, down to the last artillery shell and the last bandage, this venture was being cobbled up on the spot, and only after another enterprise, the naval attack, had failed."[1] The only other war-time action of similar stature lay thirty years ahead on the beaches of Normandy, and the planning for that amphibious landing took not two weeks, but nearly two years.[2] Ellis Ashmead-Bartlett, British war correspondent at Gallipoli, wrote that no country other than Great Britain would have attacked the peninsula without months of reflection and preparation by a highly trained general staff composed of the best brains of the army. He added, "Never have I known such a collection of unsuitable people to whom to entrust a great campaign.... Their muddles, mismanagement, and ignorance of the strategy and tactics of modern war brought about the greatest disaster in English history."[3] Ashmead-Bartlett had, of course, no inkling that the mismanagement, muddles and chaos were orchestrated; no idea that third-rate commanders had been deliberately chosen to ensure that the campaign would not succeed.

Military leadership was barely functional.[4] The War Council had considered neither tactics nor logistics for an amphibious assault on the peninsula, and until 12 March 1915 had not even chosen a commander. General Sir Ian Hamilton, like Vice-Admiral Carden before him, was selected while eminently more suitable officers were overlooked. The genial Scot, then in the twilight of his career, had been Kitchener's chief of staff during the last months of the Boer War. He was hamstrung by his long-subservient relationship to Kitchener[5] and never once did he challenge his authority. Hamilton was scared of Kitchener and the depth of his fear can be gauged from a comment made in his diary after requesting more troops, "Really, it is like going up to a tiger and asking for a small slice of venison."[6]

He was stunned when Kitchener appointed him:

> Opening the door I bade him good morning and walked up to his desk where he went on writing like a graven image. After a moment he looked up and said in a matter of fact tone, 'We are sending a

> military force to support the fleet now in the Dardanelles and you are to have command." At that moment K wished me to bow, leave the room and make a start.... But my knowledge of the Dardanelles was nil, of the Turk nil, of the strength of my forces next to nil.... K, went on writing. At last he looked up again with, "Well?"[7]

Hamilton was informed he would be leaving next day because "time was of the essence,"[8] but neither Kitchener nor anyone else had any clear idea what Hamilton was to do. General Charles Callwell, Director of Military Operations, was called to the office. He advised that the Greek General Staff had recently studied the possibility of an amphibious landing on the Gallipoli peninsula and estimated that 150,000 men were *essential* if it was to stand any chance of success. Kitchener dismissed this as nonsense, telling Hamilton that half that number would do him handsomely.[9] Strange indeed, because just two days earlier at a War Council meeting Kitchener himself had stated that a force of 130,000 would be required.[10] Admiral Jacky Fisher, who correctly forecast disaster, had insisted that it would need 200,000 men.[11] Initially, only 75,000 were sent. That might have been enough men "for garrison duty around Constantinople and for raiding parties on the way there, but Hamilton didn't have the numbers to make opposed landings against six Turkish divisions."[12] The number of troops needed was predicated on the fleet getting through to Constantinople, not on the numbers required for a successful amphibious attack after the navy had failed.

Kitchener was surely aware that 75,000 men would not be enough, but he assured Hamilton that if a British submarine "popped up" opposite the town of Gallipoli and waved a Union Jack, "the whole Turkish garrison on the peninsula will take to their heels..."[13] How typical of the arrogance and inbred racism of the British imperialist. Like the deferential schoolboy anxious not to provoke the wrath of an authoritarian headmaster, Hamilton didn't ask for more men lest he upset Kitchener.[14]

He wasn't the only officer taken aback by the proposed campaign. General Wolfe Murray, Chief of the Imperial General Staff (CIGS), and General Archibald Murray, (Depute CIGS) were then called into Kitchener's office, together with Major-General Walter Braithwaite who had just been appointed as Hamilton's Chief-of-Staff against Hamilton's wishes.[15] Incredibly, none of these Staff Officers had heard of the Gallipoli scheme and "the Murray's were so taken aback that neither of them ventured to comment."[16] They had been kept entirely in the dark. The plan was cobbled together on the hoof and so disorganized that even the Chief of the Imperial General Staff knew nothing of it. Why? How could such a massive strategic initiative come as a surprise to officers at that level? Quite reasonably, Braithwaite "begged" that the expedition be given a contingent of up-to-date airplanes, experienced pilots and observers, but Kitchener turned on him,"Not one!"

The spotter planes that were provided were old and so heavy that "the damned things could barely rise off the water."[17]

Look at the common factors here. Just as Churchill had placed an old subservient Admiral in charge of an aging fleet, so Kitchener appointed a similarly pliable General to take command of the military force. Both were inadequate, unfit for the task and instructed to operate with insufficient men and decrepit equipment. Once again, experienced officers who disagreed were either ignored or said nothing publicly.

Next morning, General Hamilton returned to the War Office for his first and only briefing. Kitchener had penned three different sets of instructions, none of which helped Hamilton understand the enemy, the politics or the country. He was left to his own devices. Thirteen officers had been hurriedly assembled to serve on his staff. Only one had seen active service in the war and one or two, according to Hamilton, put on a uniform for the first time in their lives with "Leggings awry, spurs upside down, belts over shoulder straps!" He knew none of them.[18]

Hamilton sought up-to-date information about Gallipoli from Military Intelligence, but all he was given were two small tourist guidebooks on western Turkey, an out of date and inaccurate map that was not intended for military use, and a 1905 textbook on the Turkish Army. The Intelligence officers were unable to assist with any information on weather patterns in the region, and nobody had given thought to the sea currents that would cause major problems during the landings. They did not know how many enemy troops manned the peninsula, or the names of the Turkish or German commanders.[19]

Hamilton was given nothing of value, yet the Foreign Office, the War Office and the Admiralty held volumes of up-to-the-minute intelligence on Gallipoli and Constantinople gathered from missions, ambassadors and military and naval sources. Between 1911 and 1914, successive military attaches at Constantinople and vice consuls posted to the Dardanelles had sent detailed intelligence reports on the defenses to the War Office. These were never disclosed to Hamilton or his staff. Lieutenant-Colonel Charles Cunliffe-Owen, the British military attaché at Constantinople had conducted a detailed survey of the area and on 6 September 1914, sent accurate, current reports and assessments to General Callwell, at the War Office.[20] They included information on gun sites, minefields and the topography of the peninsula. Hamilton was clearly desperate for facts and figures about Gallipoli and the Dardanelles, yet the Director of Military Operations withheld the most up-to-date reports from the area. He was the most senior officer who had studied the Dardanelles in the intelligence department before the outbreak of war,[21] and had access to all of the information gathered from a range of military personnel stationed there previously, yet kept it from Hamilton.[22]

Why did the War Office leave Hamilton to scavenge for crucial military intelligence in tourist guides and outdated maps? Why did General Callwell remain silent? There can be no rational reason other than he was ordered to. His silence would otherwise have equated to treason. Had the War Office furnished Hamilton with expert advice and local knowledge, Admiral Limpus's reports would have been brought from the Admiralty; Ambassador Mallet could have advised him in person. Had they wanted him to have the benefit of detailed military intelligence, Cunliffe-Owen would have been included among his staff officers. He was one of very few who had seen Gallipoli on the ground. Why was this wealth of knowledge and experience unwelcome?

Before Hamilton set off for the eastern Mediterranean on 13 March, on the ironically named HMS *Foresight*, he went to say goodbye to his former chief, but Kitchener did not even wish him good luck.[23] Hamilton was equipped with little more than enthusiasm and wishful thinking. No attempt had been made to co-ordinate intelligence about the defenses at Gallipoli, not even at strategic level, and he had been given no indication of Government policy, priorities or plans.[24] According to the principles laid down in Field Service Regulations, he should have been given an outline plan of the operations he had been tasked to undertake. This was the clear responsibility of General Wolfe Murray, Chief of the Imperial General Staff, and General Callwell, Director of Military Intelligence. No plan was produced and all detailed up-to-date intelligence was withheld.

Ian Hamilton was chosen to command the operation for the following reasons: (A) He was considered incapable of performing the task. (B) He knew nothing of Gallipoli or its defenses. (C) He would never challenge Kitchener's orders, no matter how outrageous. (D) Like Admiral Carden, he made the perfect patsy when the Gallipoli campaign failed. It has been suggested that, from the outset, Hamilton was the victim of gross dereliction of duty on the part of the General Staff,[25] but it was much more than that. Make no mistake, this was no act of stupidity, dereliction of duty, or "cock-up." Hamilton did not at this point know it, but without a combined operation with the navy and at least 150,000 well-equipped troops, he could never have succeeded. He was not appointed to succeed. Consider this; "At a moment's notice he had been given an impossible task to perform, and somehow or other he must perform it. It wasn't bricks without straw – it was bricks without clay, straw, kiln, hod, or anything else."[26]

On 17 March 1915, just five days after his surprise appointment, General Hamilton landed at Lemnos. At first light the following morning, the day appointed for the big naval attack, he inspected the shore facilities at Mudros Bay and found them "gravely wanting." The Royal Navy cruiser *Phaeton* took him along the west coast of the Gallipoli peninsula to make a preliminary reconnaissance of possible landing sights. With the element of surprise gone, the Turks had been "furiously digging in"[27] and every part of the coastline even remotely suitable for amphibious landings was defended by trenches and barbed wire.[28] Hamilton had a ringside seat on *Phaeton's* bridge and observed the naval disaster unfold. He informed Kitchener by telegraph that Vice-Admiral de Robeck was willing to "have another go," but he [Hamilton] personally considered it unlikely that the Dardanelles could be forced by battleships alone. A combined attack was essential, with a "deliberate and progressive military operation carried out at full strength" to open a passage for the Navy. Kitchener replied that he should go ahead.[29]

This then was the situation on 21 March. Despite his losses, the naval commander was prepared to try again without help from the army, but the military commander was convinced that he could not succeed. On 22 March De Robeck took the *Queen Elizabeth* over to Lemnos for a conference with Hamilton. The Vice-Admiral had changed his mind and agreed that the fleet could not prevail without military support. "There was no discussion" Hamilton reported, "and we at once turned our faces to the land scheme."[30] De Robeck informed the Admiralty that he too now considered a combined operation essential, but that no further action could be taken until the military force scattered across the Mediterranean was ready for action.[31]

Following the abortive naval operation, the War Council in London never reconvened to consider a military landing; it was approved by default. "There was no discussion, no plan, and no political authorization," and "this was in fact a worse situation than preceded the naval operation."[32] It certainly was, but historians and academics failed to appreciate that major decisions about Gallipoli were made not by the War Council, but by a cabal of Secret Elite agents. Churchill, Kitchener, Balfour, Grey, Hankey, Asquith, Haldane and others closely linked to the Secret Elite held regular meetings to decide the course of action. It would have been virtually impossible otherwise to set the Gallipoli campaign up to fail. All that mattered for the present was that the Czar and Sazonov believed they were trying to take Constantinople and the Straits for Russia. The crucial decisions were taken before the War Council met and naval and military "advisers" kept their counsel; their attendance was cursory.

The chaos which plagued the naval attack, overwhelmed the military operation. It was just as Churchill, Kitchener and Balfour intended. As General Hamilton noted in exasperation, "the Dardanelles and the Bosporus might be in the moon for all the military information I have got to go upon…"[33] Lack of detailed information was not the only problem. The late Robert Rhodes James wrote; "Never, in fact, was a gallant army so miserably mishandled by its chiefs as were the British and Dominion soldiers on Gallipoli. Never was a higher price paid for such a complete misunderstanding of a strategical situation."[34] Absolutely, but he never questioned why those incompetent "chiefs" were chosen in the first place. Second- or third-rate senior officers had been selected not because outstanding men were unavailable, but because lack of ability and incompetence was exactly what was required to ensure failure.

Disheartened by the naval fiasco and the topography and defenses on the peninsula, General Hamilton crossed to Egypt on 24 March. His task was to prepare a disparate force of mainly untried and untested recruits to take on the most difficult military operation in the field of warfare: landing an army from the sea in the face of an entrenched and well-armed enemy. All the evidence of history demonstrated the advantage which defenders enjoyed unless the assault was accompanied by overwhelming force supported by an adequate artillery bombardment.[35] Hamilton had neither. His preparations were additionally handicapped by the absence of his personal and logistics staff, who had not even left England.[36]

It went from bad to worse. The Allied forces were scattered in confusion over much of the Mediterranean, and some battalion commanders could not trace their companies. Such was the lack of preparation that even the simplest questions could not be answered. Was there drinking water on Gallipoli? What roads existed? Were troops expected to fight in trenches or the open? What sort of weapons were required? What was the depth of water off the beaches? Were there strong currents? What sort of boats were needed to get the men, the guns and stores ashore? What casualties were to be expected, and how were they to be transferred to the hospital ships?[37]

Hamilton's spirits sank under the pressure of ridiculous expectation. His diary entry for 5 April revealed a nearly broken man: "Time presses: K. prods us from the rear: the Admiral from the front. To their eyes we seem to be dallying amidst the fleshpots of Egypt whereas, really, we are struggling like drowning mariners in a sea of chaos; chaos in the offices; chaos on the ships; chaos in the camps; chaos along the wharves."[38]

Hamilton's administrative staff did not arrive in Egypt until 11 April. In Alexandria they began their task in a dilapidated former brothel without drainage, light or water.[39] A period of hectic improvisation began. Men were sent into the bazaars of Alexandria and Cairo to buy skins, oil drums, kerosene tins – anything that would hold water. There was also a shortage of guns, ammunition, aircraft and men. Hamilton would later write that the War Office had sent them into battle with "museum pieces."[40] In theory the British Divisions should have had 304 guns, but had only 118. Ammunition supplies were minimal. There were no periscopes for trench fighting, no hand grenades or trench mortars. Material to build piers and jetties was non-existent. In the absence of maps, staff officers scoured the shops for guide-books. Hamilton sent a series of messages to Kitchener asking for reinforcements, artillery and shells, but was met either with terse refusals or no reply at all.[41] He noted in his diary: "Special craft are being built back home for possible landings on the Baltic coast. Each lighter can carry 500 men and has bullet-proof bulwarks. They call them 'beetles.' Landing from these would be child's play.… I've asked K for the beetles myself." He was curtly refused.[42]

Hamilton's divisional commanders were far from enthusiastic. A surprise attack was clearly impossible. One officer stated, "To land would be difficult enough if surprise were possible but hazardous in the extreme under present conditions."[43] Secrecy was non-existent. The Egyptian press reported the arrivals of Allied forces and their proposed destination.[44] General Albert d'Amade, commander of the French contingent, gave an interview in which he discussed the invasion plans at great length.[45] Indeed, he presented the enemy with a blueprint for the landings.[46] Allied activity in Egypt was closely observed by Turkish and German agents who were able to "deliver a complete Allied order of battle to the head of intelligence in Constantinople by the middle of March."[47] Sixty-five days elapsed between the first naval attack and the amphibious landings on 25 April, during which time the Turkish defenses were transformed. It was, strategically, a ridiculous state of affairs.

The Greek government had suggested that 200,000 men would be required, and in January Kitchener had estimated 150,000,[48] but Hamilton could only count on half that number. They included 18,000 well-trained regulars (the 29th Division,) 34,100 physically fit but raw Anzac troops, a ragbag Naval division of 11,000, and a French division of 20,000. Many of these soldiers had barely completed basic training and collectively they had never worked together. Most of the senior commanders were inexperienced and their staff had little practical knowledge of the appalling problems that would face them on a daily basis. "This was a disaster waiting to happen."[49] Marshall Joffre, the French C-in-C, was profoundly opposed to the whole operation and initially refused to provide troops, but political expediency forced his hand.[50] A French army officer, Colonel Alain Maucorps, who had spent years in Turkey, also opposed the attack; but like everyone with intimate knowledge of the subject, his protests were dismissed and his intelligence reports, ignored.[51]

After much dithering, Kitchener had finally agreed to release the 29th Division from England. Its commander, Major-General F. Shaw, had served with distinction at Mons and was considered a highly competent and "impressively professional soldier." Two days before embarkation, however, when continuity was all-important, Kitchener inexplicably replaced Shaw with Major-General Aylmer Hunter-Weston, a snobbish boor. He refused to travel in the ship he was allocated because it lacked first-class accommodation, and demanded to be transferred to the luxury liner *Andania*.[52] Major-General Shaw suffered the same fate as Admiral Limpus. A highly competent and knowledgeable officer was rejected in favor of the laughing-stock of the British Army.[53] It was as if the esprit de corps of the 29th Division had been neutered. Spectacularly incompetent, Hunter-Weston was considered one of the most brutal commanders of the First World War.[54]

Preparations blundered on. Ships arrived from Britain without specific destinations.[55] Supplies were packed in the wrong order and chaos ensued.[56] Hamilton had no choice but to order some supply ships back 700 miles to Egypt to be unloaded and properly repacked.[57] Reorganization of the equipment took more than a month, and partly explains why the Army was unable to land on Gallipoli soon after the naval disaster of 18 March. The blame for most of this chaos rested with Graeme Thomson, Director of Transport at the Admiralty. Churchill had personally appointed him despite protests by senior officers. Admiral Oliver stated that Thomson knew all about the City but nothing of warfare. Had the far abler Vice-Admiral Edmond Slade been given the job, as recommended by Admiralty insiders, "the transports for the Dardanelles would have been properly loaded and arrived in the proper order."[58] Yet again, an incompetent was deliberately appointed over a man fitted for the task.

The long delays made it impossible for Hamilton to co-ordinate a joint attack. While there was only one Turkish division based on Gallipoli during the naval assault, General Liman Von Sanders, the German military advisor, increased the defensive strength to six divisions over the following months.[59] The Peninsula might have been taken by a combined operation in March, but the failure of the naval bombardments only served to warn the Turks that the Dardanelles had become a pressing target for the allies. Consequently, they reinforced the defenses and held the upper hand. As widely advertised across the western Mediterranean, a horror-show was on its way to Gallipoli.

Summary.

- Gallipoli was a disaster. The planning veered between non-existent and totally shambolic.
- The quality of the High Command was exceptionally poor. General Sir Ian Hamilton knew nothing of the land, the enemy, the targets, the supplies or even his own staff.
- Military Intelligence provided him with two small tourist guide-books while the War Office, the Foreign Office and the Admiralty offered no information. Indeed they hid up-to-date intelligence from him.
- As the Allied forces gathered, the Turks, aided by German officers, dug-in and every part of the coast-line that might have been suitable for a landing was defended by trenches and barbed wire.
- Secrecy was impossible. The Egyptian press announced the arrivals of Allied forces and their proposed destination.

• Sixty-five days elapsed between the first naval attack and the amphibious landing on 25 April by which times the Turkish defenses were nearly impregnable.
• Though the 29th Division was ordered to Gallipoli, its highly competent commander, Major-General Shaw was inexplicably replaced by a snobbish boor and laughing stock of the British army, Major-General Hunter-Weston.
• The peninsula might have been taken in a joint assault in March against a single Turkish division, but by late April they faced a hugely reinforced enemy with highly competent German advisors.
• It became a widely advertised horror-show.

British field hospital at Gallipoli

Chapter 11

Gallipoli – What Did They Care?

The docks at Alexandria were crammed with vessels of every type from Ocean liners to Thames tugs. Emptying and repacking badly loaded ships went on round the clock. Once ensconced in the Metropole Hotel, General Hamilton and his staff considered their options, and decided to take the southern part of the Gallipoli Peninsula in a *coup de main*. That is, an attack that relies on speed and surprise to attain its objectives. It was a sick joke. The element of "surprise" had long gone. The Turks had been given five weeks, warning and a considerable amount of detailed information on Hamilton's plan through unrestricted articles in newspapers like the *Egyptian Gazette*.[1]

Serving under Ian Hamilton as divisional commanders were Lieutenant-General Sir William Birdwood, an English officer who had overseen Anzac training alongside the pyramids in Egypt, Hunter-Weston of the 29th Division and Sir Archibald Paris of the Royal Naval Division. All three disliked Hamilton's scheme. Birdwood's chief-of-staff, Brigadier-General Harold Walker, was absolutely "appalled" by it. His military instincts were first class. General d'Amade, the man who divulged Gallipoli plans to the press and hence to the Turks, was Divisional commander of the 20,000 French troops.

Before leaving Alexandria for Lemnos on 8 April, Hamilton wrote to Kitchener that his commanders could now see all the difficulties with "extraordinary perspicacity" and "would each apparently a thousand times sooner do anything else except what we are going to do." He later added, "The truth is, every one of these fellows agrees in his heart … that the landing is impossible."[2] Despite this, Hamilton and his divisional commanders proceeded as instructed. It was "impossible," but they did not insist it should be canceled. Nor did Kitchener. As ever, what good sense these men possessed lost out to their obsequious obedience to the ruling-class masters.

By 20 April more than 200 ships were crammed into Mudros harbor. Many of the troops were to be taken in transport ships to within 3 kilometers of the peninsula. Then, in complete silence and total darkness, descend wooden ladders into rowing boats roped together in chains of four. Each chain would then be towed by a launch to within fifty to a hundred meters of the shore, cast off, and rowed by naval personnel as close to the beach as possible. The first heavily laden troops were timed to land just as dawn broke.

British troops were destined for five different beaches, labeled through S to X, around the toe of the peninsula at Helles. Additionally at V Beach an old coal boat, the SS *River Clyde*, which had been adapted to carry 2,000 troops, would be run straight up onto the beach in front of the ancient fort at Sedd-el-Bahr. The modern-day Trojan horse had been modified to disgorge troops rapidly through sally-ports cut in the hull. Some 25 kilometers further along the western shore at Z Beach near Ari Burnu, the Anzacs were scheduled to land from rowing boats. Across the Dardanelles, at Besika Bay and Kum Kale, the French division would make a diversionary feint in an attempt to confuse the Turks. That was the plan. As they passed those nerve-jangling days on Lemnos, the majority of the invading force lived on the transport vessels, but constantly trained ashore or rehearsed rapid, silent transfers down the sides of the ships into rowing boats. The landing was scheduled for 23 April when the moon would wane leaving a pitch black night, but bad weather intervened.[3]

Between 23 and 24 April, 62,442 troops were transported to the Gallipoli Peninsula on 67 transport ships supported by an armada of warships, destroyers, and associated smaller craft. It was, as anticipated, carnage. On V Beach at Helles at 06:22 on 25 April, the *River Clyde* nosed in and grounded herself. The sally-port doors swung open and "in seconds the gangways were blocked with dead and wounded whose blood stained red the water around the ship."[4] Turkish infantry commanded the entire beach from the front and both sides. A few of what Hamilton referred to as "the forlorn hope" from the River Clyde made it to the shore and found shelter under a small ridge, but as men kept running from the ship the Turks kept killing them. About 1,000 stayed aboard, safe but impotent until darkness fell. British battleships bombarded the shore defenses, but achieved little. Their agony was prolonged

The first to come in on tows at V Beach were the Dublin Fusiliers, commanded by Brigadier-General Henry Napier. Officers on the *River Clyde* screamed at him to go back, but Napier carried on and he and his staff died before they reached the shore. "The beach was the scene of sustained butchery, and only forty or fifty men managed to get to the low cliffs and dig themselves in."[5] Few survived the first minute. "Most did not even leave the boats, which drifted helplessly away with every man in them killed."[6] Air Commodore Samson flew over V Beach that morning and later reported that the calm blue sea was "absolutely red with blood" for a distance of some fifty yards from the shore. In a scene reminiscent of the Western Front, bodies lay entangled in the impenetrable barbed wire.

When the 29th Division was counting its dead in thousands, someone commented to Hunter-Weston about the causalities. "Casualties?" he snapped, "What do I care for casualties?"[7] All three brigade commanders at Cape Helles died in action, and the two colonels who replaced them were killed instantly. With no senior officer or tactical headquarters onshore, the men struggled through bewildering chaos.

General Hamilton had ordered a landing at an isolated spot four miles along the coast at Y Beach to attack the Turks from the rear and 2,000 men from the Plymouth Battalion and the King's Own Scottish Borderers landed there unopposed. They could have headed south at will and encircled the enemy position at Sedd-el-Bahr and Teke-Burnu, where, less than an hour's march away, their comrades were being slaughtered. Two Colonels headed the main force at Y Beach but were unsure which of them was in charge. For eleven undisturbed hours these troops sat on the cliffs at Y Beach awaiting instructions, without digging in. The Turks arrived in force and by the following morning there were over 700 casualties. The navy evacuated the survivors,[8] without the permission of an incensed General Hamilton. He was shocked to witness "loose groups" of "aimless dawdlers" on the shore and could not understand why, having dug themselves in, they had failed to establish a bridgehead.[9] Incredibly, they had not been ordered to "dig themselves in" and suffered the consequence.

W Beach was a death trap of land mines, sea mines and wire entanglements concealed under the surface. Further entanglements stretched along the length of the beach close to the water's edge. Machine guns were concealed in holes cut in the cliff face, with pom-poms and more machine guns further back. Further north at Z Beach, the Anzacs faced similar horrors. In the darkness a strong current had swept the boats about a mile north of the intended landing-place, and some of the attackers faced steep cliffs rather than the low sandbanks they had expected. Most were put ashore at a small cove south of Ari Burnu, which would later be known as Anzac Cove. Heavy Turkish rifle and machine-gun fire broke out as the boats carrying the first wave of 15,000 troops were about thirty yards from the shore. Some died as they sat, others drowned under the weight of their packs when they slipped in the water and couldn't recover.[10] As more waves of men landed in the face of heavy fire, the beach became "a crowded shambles, so littered with lines of wounded that it was difficult to pick a way to the sea."[11] Against all the odds it appeared that the Anzacs might break through, but Turkish reserves poured into the heights above and pushed them back. Birdwood went ashore that evening and held a meeting with two divisional generals who urged an immediate evacuation. When a message to this effect reached Hamilton in the middle of the night, he refused permission to withdraw, and urged them to "dig, dig, dig, until you are safe."[12]

Over 2,000 Anzacs were killed that day, with many more wounded. Only two hospital ships had been provided to cover all the landings and were immediately overwhelmed. When wounded men were eventually taken off the beaches, it was to filthy and overcrowded ships with insufficient doctors or medical orderlies. They then faced a voyage of six- or seven-hundred miles without adequate treatment. "The wounded suffered dreadful privations and many who might have survived succumbed to the effects of gangrene or suppurating wounds before they got to a proper hospital in Egypt."[13]

The disastrous attack on the Gallipoli peninsula began as predicted. Youthful expectation was sacrificed without compunction. What did Hunter-Weston care about casualties? Nothing. What did the Secret Elite care about the terrible losses? That was never their concern. The truth of the matter, which has never been honestly addressed by historians, is that the attack was ordered in the expectation of certain defeat. In reality, the thousands slain on that first day alone died, not for civilization or justice, but for the Machiavellian plans of rich and powerful men at the heart of the British Empire.

The Allies managed to land 30,000 men on the Gallipoli Peninsula, but suffered 20,000 casualties in the heroic effort. They gained a foothold, but were unable to push forward more than a mile. Ellis Ashmead-Bartlett, a journalist embedded with the British military noted: "At Anzac any further advance is out of the question.… No army has ever found itself dumped in a more impossible or ludicrous position, shut in on all sides by hills, and having no point from which it can debouch for an attack, except by climbing up them." At Helles, the 29th Division had lost half its number, and Bartlett's concluded "we are barely holding our own on the Peninsula, there is absolutely no question of an advance…"[14]

By 29 April food, water and ammunition were running low, and the initial impetus had spent itself. "As the days dragged by and the heat of the sun increased, the position became as stalemated as it was in the trenches of France and Flanders."[15] After less than one week, Gallipoli could at best be described as a bloody stalemate. Every capable strategist had repeatedly said that only a joint military and naval operation could succeed, and Commodore Roger Keyes, Admiral de Robeck's Chief of Staff, felt strongly that the navy should help the exhausted army by making another attempt to break through the Narrows. Keyes had resolved the minesweeping problem by adapting destroyers for the purpose and replacement battleships had arrived.

De Robeck asked London to approve a combined attack, but permission was denied. Indeed, on 12 May the First Sea Lord, Admiral Fisher, ordered the *Queen Elizabeth* back home. There would be no joint operation. Fisher wanted to end the Dardanelles expedition immediately and, two days later at the War Council, he resigned.[16] Churchill's future hung in the balance. On 17 May, in the Prime Minister's room in the House of Commons, a confrontation with Asquith marked the end of Churchill's career as First Lord of the Admiralty.[17] On 25 May a new coalition government was formed. Churchill was replaced by Arthur Balfour, former conservative Prime Minister, and member of the inner core of the Secret Elite.[18] Names changed, but the secret cabal's control of policy remained unaffected.

Fighting continued throughout the summer. As the death toll rapidly mounted, the incompetence, stupidity and inhumanity of the senior officers defied explanation. Ashmead-Barlett wrote, "We carry on at this hopeless game, ignoring all the strategical possibilities … by persisting in these murderous frontal attacks on impregnable positions, losing tens of thousands of our best and bravest men without achieving any result …"[19] Orders issued to the 29th Division were seldom intelligible, and frequently had to be changed, modified or ignored. The fate of the fallen was horrendous. Thousands of soldiers were left to perish between the lines after attacks had failed, tormented by the intense heat, flies, and thirst, until death came as a merciful relief. The Turks regularly agreed to a temporary armistice to collect wounded men, and actually asked for one at Hellles, but British commanders refused. Nothing could have been more demoralizing for the ordinary soldier than knowing that hundreds of his brothers-in-arms lay mutilated and unattended only a few yards away in the baking heat, suffering the agonies of the damned in a long, lingering death.[20]

Casualties were of no importance to Hunter-Weston, provided the objective was met,[21] but he sacrificed the lives of thousands in the 29th Division without meeting any objective. Under his command, the equivalent of three British divisions were lost in front of Achi Baba without a single salient position being won.[22] His over-optimistic reports played an important part in misleading Sir Ian Hamilton.[23] Hunter-Weston developed dysentery in July 1915 and was promptly ordered home, abandoning thousands of his men whom he left in a much worse condition.

John Hargrave, who served at Gallipoli with the Royal Army Medical Corps, described the appalling physical state of the troops just ten days before the Allied offensive in August. Shortly after their arrival at Lemnos the newcomers developed dysentery so severe, that some died. They "were already an army of sick men" and instead of becoming acclimatized they were steadily devitalized.[24] They visibly struggled. Many were still unwell as a consequence of recent cholera inoculations. The suffocating heat, the rapid dehydration, the alien foliation which stank in their nostrils, diarrhea, disorientation, fatigue and heatstroke broke the healthiest of heroes. Could no-one see this? Even on the island of Imbros, where troops had been disembarked in preparation for the attack, water was so scarce that armed guards had to be detailed for water-carts. Instead of training for the assault, they spent hours rushing to the latrines "dozens of times a day."[25]

Yet the August offensive went ahead. Despite their wretched condition, troops were "packed like herrings in the beetles and destroyers, silent and listless."[26] Many had been on their feet since early dawn on 5 August, sweltering under heavy uniforms completely inappropriate for the climate. That evening men stood crushed together on the decks of the transports, some for as long as seventeen hours.[27] Conditions were akin to eighteenth-century slave-ships. On embarkation, each man had a pint and a half in his water bottle and was solemnly warned not to drink it until absolutely necessary. It was utterly surreal. These troops were condemned to debilitating medical deterioration, depressed, desperate to relieve their bowels, tormented by unquenchable thirst and disoriented in their lethargy and confusion. Confidence and esprit de corps oozed away. They should have been sent to hospital, not battle.

The great Allied offensive began at Helles on the afternoon of 6 August with a naval bombardment. Once again, a terrible slaughter ensued. Desperate hand-to-hand fighting followed the brutally effective Turkish machine-gun fire and the communication trenches were choked with dead and wounded. The 88th Brigade lost nearly two-thirds of its officers and men. The following morning, 7 August, three brigades of VIII Corps lost nearly 3,500 officers and men, and gained nothing.[28]

That same morning an amphibious landing of 20,000 sick and debilitated soldiers took place at Suvla Bay. Hamilton had asked for experienced corps commanders to be sent out from Britain to lead the attack – men like Sir Henry Rawlinson who were battled hardened on the Western front, but Kitchener saddled him "with the most abject collection of generals ever congregated in one spot."[29] Command of the IX Corps was given to probably the worst of them all, 61 year-old Lieutenant-General Sir Frederick Stopford. He had been retired for five years, barely seen active service and had never commanded troops in battle.[30] Physically, Stopford was so feeble and unwell that he was unable to lift his own dispatch case onto the train when he set off for Gallipoli, yet he was sent to a climate which taxed the fittest of men. Despite the fact that Hamilton knew Stopford's limitations, he gave him free rein to plan and control the Suvla operations; "it was like giving a blank, signed check to a bankrupt."[31] During the landings, Stopford remained aboard HMS *Jonquil* and slept on deck. No officer was sent ashore to assess the situation. His chain of command broke down completely.[32]

What many historians have failed to record is that the most deadly factor at Suvla Bay was not Turkish machine-guns but an absolute failure to protect the Allied forces from dehydration. Some parched men emptied their water-bottles before, or soon after, landing.[33] Only 2 of 5 supply-boats carrying water arrived on 7 August and both grounded on a sandbank, too far for the water to be piped to the shore. "No water was available for use from them until the morning of the 8th."[34] Effectively, already dehydrated soldiers were left to survive on one and a half pints of water over two days or more in scorching heat.

The numbers who died of dehydration at Suvla Bay remain a mystery. Hundreds? Thousands? We will never know, for the establishment had a vested interest in suppressing the truth. Imagine the public outrage if it was discovered that their loved ones had died not from wounds, but from dehydration in the searing temperature; died because the military high command failed to provide even the basics for survival. On 5 August, Hamilton had informed Kitchener of the "sickness of the Australians, indeed, all the troops here,"[35] but his concern did not matter. On 12 August Kitchener responded to the news that the operation had ground to a halt by urging Hamilton to "ginger up" the men. Safe in the privileged world of ruling-class England, Kitchener urged greater "energy and dash" from emaciated, dying soldiers. Like any decent human being, Hamilton was sickened by this response.[36]

Summary.

- Hamilton informed Kitchener that all his commanders were appalled by the impossibility of a successful landing.
- The assault was, as anticipated, carnage. With thousands of dead, the casualties mounted. The two hospital ships were overwhelmed.
- 30,000 men were landed on the Gallipoli Peninsula, but suffered 20,000 casualties in the heroic effort.
- Far from approving a joint military and naval attack, the Admiralty ordered the single dreadnought, *Queen Elizabeth,* home lest she was damaged by submarine attack.
- In London, the Liberal government lead by Prime Minister Asquith was replaced by a coalition. Churchill was dismissed and replaced by Arthur Balfour.
- Throughout the summer of 1915 the death toll rapidly mounted thanks to incompetence, stupidity, scorching heat, flies, thirst and disease.
- It became in effect an army of sick men, yet another offensive began in August. If anything, the losses were even more inhumane. We will never know the true numbers who died from dehydration alone.

SS River Clyde, Gallipoli 25 April 1915

Chapter 12

Gallipoli – The Cover-Up

Most of the critical mistakes made in the original landings on Gallipoli in April were repeated in the August offensive.[1] Thousand of men were again sacrificed to no purpose and the commanding heights of the peninsula remained in the hands of the Turkish defenders. The attack at Lone Pine alone cost the Australian force 2,000 dead. General William Birdwood had taken command of the Anzacs in December 1914, but his confidence was not backed by military success. Like other contemporary senior commanders, Birdwood failed to understand the debilitating effect of dysentery and other illnesses on his Anzac troops[2] and as a consequence lost more than 10,000 men. Thousands of wounded were left for days under a scorching sun without water.[3] Bloated and rotting corpses lay everywhere and the stench of death sickened the living.

When it seemed that the horrors of Gallipoli couldn't possibly get any worse, hundreds of wounded men on the slopes of Scimitar Hill were condemned to an agonizing death, unable to escape the flames of a raging grass fire. Ashmead-Bartlett wrote, "When the fire passed on, little mounds of scorched khaki alone marked the spot where another mismanaged soldier of the King had returned to mother earth."[4] These lads were denied the glorious, noble death for civilization concocted to justify the slaughter. Sick, wounded and abandoned, betrayed by hapless commanders, they were sacrificed without remorse.

Throughout August the surviving troops continued to suffer from dysentery or a virulent form of paratyphoid. Hardly anyone escaped. Eventually, more than a thousand sick and dying men were evacuated on a daily basis.[5] The Anzacs, who had arrived in peak physical condition, shrank before their commanders' eyes, thin and gaunt with sunken cheeks. The Australian and New Zealand Army Corps was "melting away through disease at the appalling rate of 10 per cent per week," and nearly 80 per cent of the Allied troops on the peninsula suffered from debilitating sickness. When GHQ offered advice on steps to be taken to avoid the infestation of flies, an embittered Australian doctor responded that he "might as well have spat on a bushfire."[6] At the end of August, Allied casualties totaled 89,000 and Turkish morale had risen.[7]

Maurice Hankey, Secretary to the War Council, was sent out to Gallipoli to gather "first hand information." He held the rank of Lieutenant-Colonel and was given a "very unusual" directive from the Prime Minister to go wherever he wanted and be at liberty to report directly to Downing Street. Before Hankey left London, Kitchener reassured him that he did not intend to allow the army to advance on Constantinople even if they were victorious on the peninsula.[8] It was a stunning admission, a clear indication of the true nature of the campaign of which Hankey was, of course, aware. From the outset the stated objective had allegedly been to take control of the Straits and seize Constantinople on behalf of the Russians. It was not. Constantinople was never to be handed to Russia. Tens of thousands of men had been, and continued to be, sacrificed for a lie. All that mattered was that the Russians believed it.

Hankey arrived at Lemnos on 25 July and spent three weeks on conducted tours. He watched the disaster of Suvla Bay unfold much as Nero watched Rome burn. On 14 August he telegrammed the Prime Minister and Kitchener that the "surprise" attack had "definitely failed.… Already enemy is entrenching within 3,000 yards of Suvla Bay."[9] Were these coded messages? There could have been no surprise attacks. The Turks were well entrenched, dug-in deep like the Germans on the Western Front. Every piece of evidence that Hankey had to hand stated explicitly that only a joint naval and military attack with legions of men, had any chance of success. Even his phraseology, "definitely failed" carried no element of disappointment or surprise. It was exactly as expected.

While hovering around the Gallipoli shores, observing and recording the ongoing tragedy for a very select audience, Hankey made contact with a number of old acquaintances. Foremost amongst these was Major Guy Dawnay, a member of Hamilton's general staff at Gallipoli. Dawnay had spent three years working with Hankey on the Committee of Imperial Defence and served in the War Office from September 1914 until March 1915.[10] With such close and direct association with both Hankey and Kitchener, it seems fair to speculate that Dawnay had been sent to keep a careful watch on Sir Ian Hamilton on their behalf.

Poor Hamilton was more than naive in his assessment of Maurice Hankey, whom he welcomed into his headquarters "as a real help." Hamilton believed that the Secretary to the War Council and close confidant of the Prime Minister would set the record straight. "From my personal standpoint, it will be worth anything to us if, amidst the flood of false gossip pouring out by this very mail to our Dardanelles Committee, to the Press, to Egypt and to London Drawing Rooms, we have sticking up out of it, even one little rock in the shape of an eye-witness."[11] He was to be sorely disappointed.

When Hankey returned on 28 August he had sufficient first-hand evidence to recommend that a pretext be found for a withdrawal from Gallipoli. The chances of "a reasonable prospect of achieving success" depended on a heavy investment in men and equipment, exactly as Sir Ian Hamilton

Dead, dying and wounded transported away from the beaches.

had repeatedly requested, but Kitchener refused. In a "very secret" part of his report he wrote, "The Government may well ask themselves whether they are justified in continuing a campaign which makes so tremendous a toll on the country in human life and material resources."[12] Other options were completely unpalatable; there could be no repeat of the naval attack or an embarrassing diplomatic arrangement with Turkey and Russia.[13]

Maurice Hankey, who had originally brought the idea of an attack on the Dardanelles to the War Council in order to deceive the Russians and keep them in the war, knew by the end of August 1915 that the ploy had worked. Four Russian Officers had witnessed the Sulva Bay landings and informed Hamilton that his actions had saved the whole Army of the Caucuses, "and the Grand Duke knew it." They added that the Czar "bitterly regretted" that lack of supplies had prevented his army corps from "standing by to help."[14] Russia remained committed to the war in the belief that Britain had sacrificed tens of thousands of men in a gallant effort to capture Constantinople on her behalf. Doubtless they were impressed by a useless slaughter akin to any Russian defeat on the Eastern Front. The job was done. The next step was to arrange a strategic withdrawal, and ensure that a sacrificial scapegoat was prepared.

The man responsible for creating that scapegoat was, again, Maurice Hankey, though he was careful to conceal his role from the public domain. As ever, the Secret Elite used others to do their dirty work. Shortly after speaking with Hankey, Major Guy Dawnay left Gallipoli for London. General Hamilton harbored a misplaced trust in Dawnay who had convinced him that someone had to go and put the case for reinforcements directly to the government. Kitchener had remained deaf to Hamilton's pleas and rumors of exaggerated military success were proving counter-productive. Dawnay was the true viper in Hamilton's nest. A friend of the royal family and Prime Minister Asquith, Major Dawnay had access usually restricted to high-ranking members of the Secret Elite. On his arrival in London he told his story of Gallipoli incompetence to the King, and was permitted to present an unexpurgated analysis to the Cabinet. It was, as the Oxford Dictionary of National Biography recorded, "exceptional for a young staff officer to advise ministers to overrule his own Commander-in-Chief."[15] His audience included Asquith, Lloyd George, Bonar Law, Curzon and "just about everybody else with influence."[16] Sir Ian Hamilton was set up to take the blame for the failure of the Gallipoli Campaign and as the case against him gathered pace in London, one final twist of the knife was to come from an unexpected source which would deflect attention from the secret cabal.

Popular wisdom and official histories would have us believe that Sir Ian Hamilton's career and the Dardanelles offensive were brought to an end by an unknown junior Australian journalist, Keith Murdoch.[17] In Australia, his role has been given iconic status amongst the myths surrounding Gallipoli, but the decision to remove Hamilton had already been taken on the recommendation of Maurice Hankey, aided and abetted by Major Guy Dawnay. The Murdoch's intervention made it appear that the truth about the Gallipoli disaster was exposed by a tenacious young journalist. As Alan Moorehead observed in his masterly history, Murdoch's "entry into the explosive scene is one of the oddest incidents in the Gallipoli campaign."[18]

Who was Keith Murdoch and how was he able to gain access to the British Establishment and the very heart of the Secret Elite? A Son of the Manse, his father was a Scottish Presbyterian Minister who had emigrated to Melbourne in 1884. Murdoch sought a career in journalism but was handicapped by a serious speech defect. He went to London in 1908 in an attempt to break into Fleet Street and have his debilitating stammer cured, but unlike any other young aspirant newspaperman he had "a sheaf of introductions" from the Australian Prime Minister, Alfred Deakin.[19] One year earlier, Deakin had attended the Colonial Conference in London and was befriended by Alfred Milner with whom he formed a close bond.[20] Milner was the most influential spokesman on Imperial affairs. Given his own journalistic connections, Alfred Milner was a natural contact to advance the young Murdoch's career. On his return to Australia in November 1909, Murdoch became Commonwealth parliamentary reporter for the *Sydney Evening Sun* and was soon in close contact with Deakin's successor as Prime Minister, Andrew Fisher, and other leading Labour Party Ministers. He helped found the Australian Journalists' Association (AJA) in 1910 and was totally sympathetic to the developing ideas of Milner and his Round Table associates.[21]

Murdoch had sought the position of Australian Press War Correspondent but was beaten into second place by Charles Bean, who later became the official Australian War Historian. Disappointed by this failure, Murdoch sought new horizons, and was "told privately" that a job associated with the *Times* in London was his if he wanted it.[22] The 29 year-old left Melbourne again on 13 July 1915 to become editor of the United Cable Service at the *Times* offices in London.

Official accounts relate that he was asked by the Australian government to break his journey at Egypt in order to inquire into complaints about delays in soldiers' mail. It was strange indeed that for such a mundane task, Murdoch carried letters of introduction from both the Australian Prime Minister (Andrew Fisher) and Minister of Defence (George Pearce). The Prime Minister's letter specifically stated that "Mr. Murdoch is also undertaking certain inquires for the Government of the Commonwealth in the Mediterranean theatre of war."[23] How peculiar. A journalist had been asked to conduct an investigation on behalf of his government rather than his employers. There were many Australians at Gallipoli who could have undertaken such an inquiry, which begs the question of Murdoch's real purpose. What was he sent out to do? What were his private instructions from the Australian government?

On arriving at Cairo in mid-August, he wrote to Sir Ian Hamilton and was duly given permission to visit Gallipoli to speak to the Australian troops. Hamilton wrote in his diary that Murdoch "seems a sensible man,"[24] but wondered why his duty to Australia could be better executed with a pen than with a rifle.[25] Keith Murdoch spent four days at Gallipoli and met Charles Bean and two other Australian Journalists. Given that there were at least three other independent Australian journalists already in place, why was Murdoch there at all?

More pertinent to all that followed, he held confidential meetings with Ellis Ashmead-Bartlett, the British war correspondent. According to Murdoch's biographer, Ashmead-Bartlett was disgusted by Hamilton's handling of the campaign and asked Murdoch if he would take a sealed letter addressed to Prime Minister Asquith and post it when he arrived in London.[26] Ashmead-Bartlett, on the other hand, related a different story. According to his recollections, Murdoch, fearful of the impact on Australian morale of a winter campaign, "begged" him to write a letter to the authorities which he would carry uncensored to London. Ashmead-Bartlett allegedly coached Murdoch on what to say when he reached England, but Murdoch insisted on having something signed personally by the British war correspondent.[27]

On 8 September Ashmead-Bartlett agreed to write a letter to Asquith informing him of the true state of affairs at Gallipoli: Men had been sacrificed in impossible conditions; the Army was in a deplorable condition and the men thoroughly dispirited; mismanagement was rampant and the Army was incapable of a further offensive. Ashmead-Bartlett concluded that

> ... we have not yet gained a single acre of ground of any strategical value.[28] This was not news to the British Cabinet or War Office, for Hankey and Dawnay had already revealed the full extent of the disaster.

According to official accounts, when Murdoch reached Marseilles, he was met by a British intelligence officer with an escort of British troops and French gendarmes and ordered to hand over Ashmead-Bartlett's letter.[29] It has been suggested that another journalist, Henry Nevison, had been eaves-dropping on Murdoch and Ashmead-Bartlett during the private conversation at Gallipoli and betrayed them to the authorities. To this day no convincing evidence has been produced to explain how British Intelligence learned of the letter or, indeed, if the incident at Marseilles ever took place.

Murdoch arrived in London on 21 September and made his way directly to the offices of the *Times,* described by Professor Carroll Quigley as the mouthpiece of the Secret Elite. He began typing up a report for his own prime minster which was highly critical of Sir Ian Hamilton.[30] His first contact just happened to be the *Times* editor, Geoffrey Dawson, a man at the inner-core of the Secret Elite.[31] As the Australian author, Les Carlyon, shrewdly observed. Murdoch "might just as well have been walking around with the sign 'Pawn' on his back. Powerful men who wanted Britain out of the Dardanelles, would push him all around the board."[32] They did. The job was done.

Over the following days this young journalistic nobody met with individuals who had been responsible for initiating the Gallipoli disaster, including Prime Minister Asquith, Foreign Secretary Sir Edward Grey, minister of war, Lord Kitchener, Sir Edward Carson and Winston Churchill. Murdoch criticized Hamilton and the General Staff for "disastrous underestimations and stubbornly resisting in the face of hopeless schemes" and "gross wrongdoings."[33] No mention was made of Hamilton's lack of the men and munitions needed to successfully undertake the campaign or his countless requests that Kitchener studiously ignored. Without checking the accuracy of Murdoch's accusations, or giving Hamilton a chance to respond, Asquith had them printed on Committee of Imperial Defence stationary and distributed to the Cabinet.[34] Consider the implications. Members of the Cabinet were formally issued with Murdoch's unsubstantiated report as if it was an official British Government document. Hamilton's reputation was traduced while, from 1915 onwards, Murdoch became intimately linked to the most powerful men in the British Empire; men who greatly valued his contribution to their cause.

Meanwhile, Ashmead-Bartlett had been ordered home by General Hamilton, and on his arrival in London immediately met with Lord Northcliffe, owner of the *Times.*[35] "The snowball was now gathering momentum."[36] The witch-hunter-general took charge. Northcliffe told Ashmead-Bartlett that a great responsibility rested on his shoulders to inform the government, and the country, of the true state of affairs at Gallipoli.[37] It was time to get out.

Three days later in the House of Lords, Lord Alfred Milner gave his blessing to a withdrawal from Gallipoli: "To speak quite frankly, I should have thought that whatever evils had resulted from the disastrous developments in the Balkans there was at least this advantage, that it might have given us an opportunity which may never recur of withdrawing from an enterprise the successful completion of which is now hopeless."[38] Milner had spoken. Of course it was hopeless. The whole charade had been designed to be hopeless. That very night the Dardanelles Committee decided to recall General Hamilton because "he had lost the confidence of his troops,"[39] Hands reached down to push him under the water[40] and "Kitchener was asked to do the drowning,"[41] an unfortunate turn of phrase, as it turned out.

On 17 October the chief scapegoat boarded HMS *Chatham* to begin the long journey home. He was replaced by General Sir Charles Monro who almost immediately recommended evacuation. When Hamilton returned to England he received a very cold reception and people "cut" him and his wife in the street.[42] The Secret Elite made a spectacular gesture in recalling Hamilton and ensuring through their pawns, Murdoch and Ashmead-Bartlett, that his career was over. He was dubbed the man responsible for the disaster; responsible for the deaths of tens of thousands of men. In truth, no one could have succeeded at Gallipoli under the conditions that Kitchener imposed. But remember, the plan was set to fail. Constantinople could not be given to the Russians.

In the event, the nightmare on the peninsula was not yet over. Kitchener went in person to Gallipoli in early November and saw for the first time the impossibility of the task. He advised General Birdwood that "quietly and secretly" a scheme should be devised to withdraw the Allied forces.[43] On 23 November the War Committee officially decided to evacuate on military grounds. Three days later the troops, who were still without winter kit, were faced with hurricane force winds and the heaviest rainfall and blizzards to hit the Dardanelles in forty years. Sentries froze to death still clutching their rifles, and five-thousand men suffered frostbite. Flood water ran down into the Allied trenches carrying the rotting corpses of Turkish soldiers washed out from their shallow graves. Two hundred

British troops drowned. "Survivors could think of nothing but getting away from that accursed place."[44] On 12 December the men at Suvla and Anzac were told for the first time that they were being taken off. By 9 January the last man stepped safely onto a boat at Helles. Questions remain unanswered about how the massive withdrawal was completed under the noses of the Turkish army without a single Allied casualty.

In 1916, when the British government set up the Dardanelles Commission, they turned first to the most important member of the Secret Elite, Viscount Alfred Milner. Prime Minister Asquith and conservative leader, Bonar Law, both asked him to be its chairman,[45] but Milner turned the offer down in favor of more immediate work with Lord Robert Cecil at the Foreign Office.[46] Anyone could supervise a whitewash. Alfred Milner's influence went well beyond that of a commission chairman. They turned to another associate of the Secret Elite, Evelyn Baring, Lord Cromer, who accepted the position knowing full well that "it will kill me."[47] And kill him it did. He died in January 1917 and was replaced by Sir William Pickford.

Others volunteered willingly. The position of Secretary to the Commission was taken by barrister Edward Grimwood Mears, who agreed to the post if they gave him a knighthood.[48] He had previously served on the Bryce Committee, which falsified reports and generated volumes of lies about German atrocities in Belgium. Mears was trusted as a reliable placeman. Maurice Hankey, Cabinet Secretary "organized" the evidence which politicians presented to the Commission. He rehearsed Lord Fisher's evidence with him, and coached Sir Edward Grey, Herbert Asquith and Lord Haldane.[49] Asquith insisted that War Council minutes be withheld and thus managed to cover up his own support for the campaign. Churchill and Sir Ian Hamilton, who both stood to be cast as villains, collaborated on their evidence and planned to blame the disaster on Lord Kitchener.[50] Unfortunately for them, that strategy sank in the cold North Sea when Kitchener was drowned off the coast of Orkney in 1916, and was henceforth confirmed for all time as a great national hero; an untouchable.

Churchill informed the Commission that Vice-Admiral Sackville-Carden's telegram (in which he set out a "plan" for a naval attack) was the most crucial document of all,[51] but there is no acknowledgment in the Commission's findings that Churchill had duped Carden into producing a "plan" or had lied when telling him that his plan had the overwhelming support of "people in high authority."[52] In the final report, delayed until the peace of 1919, criticism was again polite, bland and vague. "The authorities in London had not grasped the true nature of the conflict" and "the plan for the August offensive was impractical."[53] Stopford received a mild reprimand. Major-General Henry "Beau" De Lisle suggested that politicians were trying to pin the blame on the soldiers. The Commission ostensibly investigated the campaign's failings, but effectively suppressed criticism and concealed the truth.

Far more important than covering up individual culpability, the greatest fear was that should the report reveal the truth, it would irrevocably damage imperial unity. Gallipoli had served to lock Australia more firmly into the British Imperial embrace. Before the final report was published, General Hamilton warned Churchill that it had the potential to break up the Empire if it "does anything to shatter the belief still confidently clung to in the Antipodes, that the expedition was worth while.... If the people of Australia and New Zealand feel their sacrifices went for nothing, then never expect them again to have any sort of truck with our superior direction in preparations for future wars."[54]

This was the crux of the matter, even in 1919. The truth would threaten the unity of the Empire, run contrary to the Anzac mythology and expose the fact that official histories were complicit in presenting falsehood and lies as the truth. Prior to the final report, Hamilton wrote again to Churchill that the Commission's chairman, Sir William Pickford should "put all his weight on the side of toning down any reflections which may have been made."[55] In other words, it had to be a whitewash. The warning was heeded. The following year, Pickford was raised to the peerage as Baron Sterndale. Mears eventually received a knighthood and everyone, apart from the hundreds of thousands who died or were badly maimed at Gallipoli, was rewarded. It was ever thus for those who served the Secret Elite.

The British, French and Anzac troops who perished at Gallipoli have been portrayed by mainstream historians as heroes who died fighting to protect democracy and freedom, not as ordinary young men duped and abused by a great lie. Barely mentioned are the quarter-million dead or maimed Ottoman soldiers who defended Gallipoli and the sovereignty and freedom of their homeland against aggressive, foreign invaders.

The myths and lies that saturate the Gallipoli campaign remain prevalent in the Antipodes. "No-one could pass through the Australian education system without becoming aware of Gallipoli, but few students realize that the Anzacs were the invaders. Even after all these years, the Anzac legend, like all legends, is highly selective in what it presents as history."[56] It is that well preserved and highly inaccurate account that is fed to impressionable schoolchildren in Australia, New Zealand and elsewhere. The myth has been rebranded to mask the pain of the awful truth of Gallipoli. The emaciated, dehydrated victims have been turned into the bronzed heroes of Greek mythology who *proved* their loyalty to the British Empire.

Gallipoli was a lie within the lie that was the First World War. Don't be fooled. Those young men died at Gallipoli not for "freedom" or "civilisation," but for the greater empowerment of the bankers and wealthy manipulators who controlled the British Empire. They died horribly, deceived, expendable, and in the eyes of the power-brokers, the detritus of strategic necessity. There was no objective other than to convince the Russians that the Allies intended to capture Constantinople for the Czar's benefit. That was imperative. They had to keep Russia believing in the war and their dream of Constantinople – to prolong the agony with a low-cost, under-resourced, ill-planned assault that would fail.

Summary.

- Sick, wounded, abandoned, betrayed by hapless commanders, the flower of Australian and New Zealand youth was sacrificed for nothing.
- Maurice Hankey was sent out to report personally to the Prime Minister. Naively, Ian Hamilton thought that Hankey's visit would "set the record straight" and justify his command. He was to be sorely disappointed.
- The Russians sent four high-level observers to witness the attacks in August and they were impressed by the sheer loss of life. To them, it reflected a genuine commitment from the British and French. The ploy had worked. Russia believed the lie that the Allies were undertaking the offensive on their behalf.
- Behind his back, Sir Ian Hamilton was set up to take the blame for the failure.
- The Australian Prime Minister sent a little known journalist to find out what was really happening under the guise of investigating failure in the mail service for Australian troops. His name was Keith Murdoch.
- Murdoch met with other journalists and reputedly carried a secret message back to London for the Prime Minister's (Asquith's) eyes. Allegedly this letter was intercepted by British Intelligence in Marseilles.
- In London he was employed by the *Times* and his typed report was read by the editor, Geoffrey Dawson of the Secret Elite's inner circle. Consequently Murdoch was invited to give evidence in front of the British Cabinet.
- With Alfred Milner's approval, the consensus was that the troops should be withdrawn from a hopeless situation.
- Hamilton was blamed for the "failure" of an exercise that was designed to fail.
- A Dardanelles Commission was established to whitewash the instigators and blame Hamilton and the hapless Vice-Admiral Sackville-Carden in particular.
- The final report was delayed until 1919. It was a whitewash. Had the truth emerged it would have broken apart the British Empire.
- The mythology of the Anzac legend created at Gallipoli remains part of Australian folklore even today because historians have ignored the true purpose of one of the most disgusting charades in British history.

Chapter 13

LUSITANIA – LOST IN A FOG OF LIES

On 5 August 1914, Churchill's Admiralty landed the first intelligence blow of the war.[1] In the early hours of the morning, while most of Europe was still abed, and few across the Empire even knew that Britain had declared war on Germany, a decision that had been taken by the Committee of Imperial Defence in 1912 was quietly effected. The British Cable Ship *Alert* ripped out the first of five German Trans-Atlantic cables which ran from Emden on the Dutch border through the English Channel and on to Spain, Africa and the Americas.[2] It was the first step in Britain's dominance of propaganda from 1914 onwards[3] and at the same time, it set the stage for a secret coup known to very few, even in the highest echelons of the British Cabinet.

The impact on German transmissions to and from its colonies, its embassies and consulates, and with press agencies in neutral countries, was instant. Cut off from this vital link, Berlin immediately became reliant on wireless communications which the Admiralty in London had already begun to monitor on Saturday 1 August, three days *before* the fateful declaration of war. Rear Admiral Sir Douglas Brownrigg had been drafted into the Admiralty as chief censor of radio telegraphy to scrutinize radio messages from all over the world and keep tabs on the movement of both British merchant ships and "hostile' vessels."[4]

By far the most important cog in the intelligence wheel was established inside the Admiralty in a small, private room about which even insiders knew nothing. German warships and merchantmen constantly sent coded wireless transmissions to each other or to their naval headquarters which, when decoded, provided priceless information. Intercepts from the post office and the Marconi Company initially overwhelmed the Naval Intelligence Department. Its director, Captain Reginald "Blinker" Hall, used Room 40 at the Admiralty as the base for a small team of code-breakers. They were to become a secret weapon whose importance to the outcome of the First World War was as vital as that of Blechley Park in the Second. Room 40 was a secret hidden inside the dark passageways of the Admiralty, know to only a select few such as Churchill and Admiral Fisher; and knowledge is power.

The German navy started the war with three highly complex sets of codes and cyphers to protect their messages from prying eyes or ears. Within four months, the Admiralty was in physical possession of these three codes books and had access to all wireless traffic emanating from the Imperial German Fleet.

On 11 August, barely one week into the war, the first code, the Handeloverkehrbuch (HVB), was captured from a German-Austrian steamboat, *Hobart.* She was stopped and searched off Melbourne by a boarding party purporting to be a quarantine inspection group. Led by Captain J.T. Richardson of the Royal Australian Navy, disguised in civilian clothes, the German captain was caught attempting to destroy confidential papers. Trapped at gun-point with the vital codes in his hand, he surrendered the HVB to the Australians, who did not fully realize that these were the precious codes used by the German Admiralty and their high seas fleet to communicate with their merchant ships. The British Admiralty in Whitehall did not hear about the fortuitous capture until 9 September, and by the time the documents had reached them in London at the end of October, an even more remarkable stroke of good fortune had blessed their ventures.

What happened had all the hallmarks of a bible story; miraculous, truly incredible, so utterly blessed with divine intervention that you can but shake your head in disbelief. The story should have been written by John Buchan, but he was creating his own fictional heroes at the time.[5] British historians have since described these events as pure chance,[6] a remarkable windfall,[7] or indeed, more accurately, if you wish to accept convenient co-incidences,[8] two windfalls, one after another.[9]

On 26 August the German light cruiser, *Magdeburg* ran aground in fog off the Gulf of Finland. Before the vessel could be scuttled, two Russian cruisers appeared from the mists and opened fire. In the confusion, the captain and fifty-seven German sailors were taken prisoner and confidential papers removed. These included the SKM (Signalbuch der Kaiserlichen Marine), the most secret and valuable German naval code, which was only used in major operations. Official German accounts stated that the secret papers, including the signal books, were thrown overboard. They clearly believed that was the case, for they continued using the codes. Yet the Russians produced a copy of the signal book which British Grand Fleet records show were delivered by Commander Smirnoff of the Imperial Russian Navy on 10 October and swiftly rushed to London. A different version was voiced by Count Constantine Benckendorff, son of the Russian Ambassador at London, who claimed in his autobiography that the Russians found a treasure-trove of secret information in the *Magdeburg's* charthouse. The haul included the code, its key and war diary. Benckendorff claimed that he brought a copy to the Admiralty himself, landing at Hull in a Russian Volunteer Navy ship.[10]

And there is a third version. Churchill's recollection was much more dramatic, but improbable. According to him, after the *Magdeburg* was wrecked in the Baltic, "the body of a drowned German under-officer was picked up by the Russians ... and clasped in his bosom by arms rigid in death, were the cypher and signal books of the German Navy and the minutely squared maps of the North Sea and the Heligoland Bight."[11] The flaw that ruined Churchill's dramatic version was that the code, Copy number 151 of the SKM, which remains in the National Archives at Kew,[12] bears no sign of ever having been immersed in salt water. But Winston always liked to paint a dramatic picture, even if he wasn't the principal character. There is a suggestion that the *Magdeburg* carried three copies of SKM, numbers 145, 974 and 151,[13] but why on earth would one light cruiser have three sets of codes, and why do all these different explanations ring false?

Putting aside for the moment the great fortune which linked the first two discoveries, the deliverance of the third code, the Verkehrsbuch (VB) was truly miraculous. Following the sinking of four old German destroyers near the Dutch island of Texel on 17 October, a British trawler allegedly dragged up a lead-lined chest from that same spot some six weeks later. The chest included the priceless Verkehrsbuch, used primarily by Flag Officers to communicate with the German army. When they took possession of the last piece in this wondrous jig-saw, the decoders in Room 40 referred to it as "The Miraculous Draught of Fishes."[14] How a British trawler, fishing off the coast of Holland had, by chance, managed to capture a lead-lined document-filled chest from one of four sunken destroyers remains more than a mystery. It was simply not possible. Consider these stories; a mock-quarantine patrol in Australia, a drowned German officer dragged from the sea in rigor mortis and a one-in-a-multi-million chance-catch by a passing trawler just off the coast of Holland gave the Admiralty access to more enemy information than any other military command had ever possessed. This is the stuff of *The Boy's Own* magazine.

Churchill appointed Captain Reginald Hall to take charge of Room 40 in October 1914, and "Blinker" as he was known, expanded the work of his team to examine commercial, diplomatic and military traffic of every kind. Hall's leadership was approved and appreciated by Prime Minister Asquith and a joint War Trade Intelligence Department was established to enlarge the scope of surveillance. Understandably Churchill wanted to guard his precious secret rigorously. It became a tiny magic circle[15] the like of which perfectly suited the covert operations sanctioned by the Secret Elite.

The fact remains that by the fifth month of the war, virtually every wireless signal sent by the German Navy could be intercepted. It was an overwhelming intelligence disaster for the Germans,[16] but its effectiveness was diluted by the limitations placed on its use by those few who knew of its existence. The captured SKM codes and their use in the decryption of intercepted orders to submarines brought about a fresh focus on German naval communications. This was a gift from the gods. Room 40 could follow the movements of the German fleet and knew the positions of the U- Boats which were active at sea, and which lay in port or had failed to return.[17]

Keep that fact in mind. It is of crucial importance in understanding the fate of the *Lusitania.*

When the *Lusitania* was torpedoed on 7 May 1915, a veritable avalanche of accusations, half truths and obfuscations filled newspapers across the globe. On the face of it, a trans-Atlantic passenger liner had been deliberately targeted and sunk by a German U-Boat with the tragic loss of 1,195 civilians, including 124 neutral Americans. It was a propaganda disaster for the Germans and a coup for the Allied cause. Unfortunately, the truth remains mired in the disinformation and lies that grew through the tragic loss into a massive cover-up. Admiralty telegrams and wireless communications have gone missing. The claims and counter claims made against the Cunard Captain are still the subject of debate. Some of the more blatant lies have been uncovered in recent years, but still the *Lusitania* rests uneasily on the Atlantic bed, near the south coast of Ireland, an underwater monument to those that the Secret Elite willingly sacrificed in their war.

The *Lusitania* was not an innocent trans-Atlantic liner, nor was she built to be. An agreement had been signed on 30 July 1903 between the Admiralty and the Cunard Steamship Company whereby the Treasury agreed to provide a loan of £2,000,000 for two ships[18] at a much reduced level of interest, (2.75% rather than 4.00%) so that, in time of war they could be used by the Admiralty to "command the Atlantic" and use their speed to carry supplies from America to Britain.[19] Crammed into an all-night sitting of the House of Commons on 2 August 1904, a much-shortened debate on the issue saw the Liberal opposition speak out against an agreement which they deemed very much in Cunard's favor. The political posing meant nothing for, one year later, when the Liberals formed a government, the men who spoke out against the Cunard deal, Sir Edward Grey, Winston Churchill and David Lloyd George made no attempt to cancel the agreement. Indeed the loan was extended to £2,6000,000 (around £245 million in today's terms) and the company received an annual operating subsidy of £75,000 per ship, and a mail contract worth £68,000 per annum. This secret pact had at its core an agreement that the ships would be built to Admiralty specifications so that they could become auxiliary cruisers in time of war.[20] The two vessels, one built at John Brown's yard on the Clyde, and the other by Swan Hunter on the Tyne, were RMS *Lusitania* and RMS *Mauretania.*

There is no argument. The Lusitania was specifically built as an auxiliary cruiser to support the Royal Navy in wartime. During construction, secret compartments were added to carry munitions,[21] and immediately war was declared both the *Lusitania* and the *Mauritania* were requisitioned as Armed Merchant Cruisers.[22] Though it was denied in public and in parliament, the *Lusitania* doubled as an Admiralty transport ship carrying pas-

Lusitania sank within 18 minutes

sengers as part of her cover when she crossed from America to Liverpool. Desperate to counter German claims that *Lusitania* was regularly transporting munitions across the Atlantic, the British government accepted that the ill-fated ship was carrying "a number of cases of cartridges" and that "this ammunition was entered in the manifest," on its last journey in May 1915. In other words, they were prepared to concede that some ammunition was on board the liner, but in quantities that were so negligible as to be of minor significance.[23] The detailed manifest for the *Lusitania's* final voyage as given by the company, and reported by the *New York Times,* confirmed that claim.[24] It was clearly fraudulent, part of the screed of lies and half truths woven into official histories which have continued for a century.[25]

By May 1915 there was a serious Allied crisis in munitions; a crisis which Secret Elite associate J.P. Morgan in New York was being well paid to alleviate. Munitions' supplies had been ingloriously mismanaged by the War Office, Lord Kitchener and the British Cabinet. The scandals of insufficient munitions and lack of high explosive shells were literally dynamite. On the Western front, the duration and weight of the British bombardment was deemed inadequate to destroy the German defenses or wipe out the front-line machine-guns because high-explosive shells were not available. Furthermore, British artillery equipment was in poor condition through over-use and faulty manufacture. None-the-less, the slaughter continued unabated.

In common with other Cunard liners, *Lusitania* regularly carried munitions, principally ordered from the J.P. Morgan-controlled Bethlehem Steel Corporation on every eastbound voyage. According to a telegram sent by the Cunard General Manager in New York to his counterpart in Liverpool, dated 29 June 1915, these were stowed in a trunk-way on the lower deck beneath the bridge, just forward of the foremost bulkhead.[26] The somewhat crude inference here was that the *Lusitania* had little room for large volumes of munitions. It was a lie. Previous consignments carried by the *Lusitania* included filled shrapnel shells and fuses which consisted of the highly sensitive fulminate of mercury and were consigned to the Royal Arsenal at Woolwich. The former German Colonial Secretary, Dr Bernhard Dernburg, the Kaiser's spokesman in the United States, accused Cunard of using the *Lusitania* to carry 260,000 pounds of brass, 60 pounds of copper, 189 cases of military goods and 1,271 cases of ammunition. Brass, copper and military goods were officially classified as contraband of war.[27]

In 2012 the *Lusitania's* 27-page supplementary manifest for its fateful voyage, never previously mentioned in any document, report or newspaper, nor referred to at Lord Mersey's later inquiry, was unearthed in the Franklin D. Roosevelt Presidential Archives in the United States. It's discovery was due entirely to the persistence and determination of researcher Mitch Peeke.[28] Listed on page 2 of the supplementary manifest[29] are 1250 cases of shrapnel – not cartridges – shrapnel sent from Bethlehem Steel to the Woolwich Arsenal,[30] together with 90 tons of lard destined for the Royal Navy Weapons Testing Establishment in Essex. Taking even the boxes of cartridges from Remington and Union Munitions Company alone, 4,200 cases weighing over 125 tons were consigned to the Royal Arsenal at Woolwich. In addition, large quantities of aluminum, nickel, copper, brass and rubber were stowed inside the cargo hold. Bernhard Dernberg's original claim was, if anything, an underestimate.

One of the consignments of wool (Sheet 4, receipt 86) was destined for Erskine Childers, the man who had organized the pre-war gun-running for the Irish Volunteers.[31] How strange. Childers had been called to the Admiralty Intelligence Department when the war broke out, and questions remain unanswered about which side he was truly on. How likely is it that this was some random import of wool? Could it have been highly volatile gun-cotton? Were there other imports destined for Admiralty personnel? Why too was the original copy of the *Lusitania's* manifest hidden in the vaults of President F. D. Roosevelt's archives? While we are unlikely to be able to answer this question, Mitch Peeke's investigative work has destroyed the myth that the *Lusitania* was simply a Trans-Atlantic passenger liner.

The *New York Times* reported a visit by the German Ambassador, Count Johann Bernstorff, to President Wilson in early June 1915 at which he quoted directly from Bethlehem Steel's shipping records. These showed that the shipment carried by the *Lusitania* included 5,000 filled shrapnel shells weighing 103,828 pounds, which was completely at odds with the official custom's records in New York. Dudley Field Malone, Collector of Customs for the Port of New York had been appointed in 1913 through the patronage of President Wilson, whose election he had helped organize. Malone was a pliable lawyer; a political placement whom the President's advisors used to their own advantage. He wrote to the manager of the Cunard operations in New York that no "cargo was loaded [in the *Lusitania*] in violation of American shipping law, particularly as regards passenger steamers. It was a lie, but presented as truth at the formal inquiry later in London."[32] Whatever the extent of the joint cover-up on both sides of the Atlantic, there can be no doubt that the *Lusitania* carried a large consignment of war matériel, including gun-cotton, when she was sent to the bottom of the Atlantic.[33]

At Prime Minister Asquith's Cabinet meeting on 11 May, his concern about the fate of the *Lusitania* was not a caring reflection on the sad loss of life or pity for the victims and their families, but a caustic analysis that betrayed his real priority. "The one thing to fear and avoid is that they [the Americans] should be provoked, in order to save their traveling millionaires from the risk of being torpedoed, to prohibit the export of munitions of war to us: which would be almost fatal."[34] So it was true. The traveling millionaires acted unwittingly as a screen behind which Britain was secretly importing munitions from America. Dr Dernburg's statement to the *New York Times* proves that Germans knew this as fact. Despite all of the denials, the mockery of a whitewashed inquiry, the indignant Cunard Company statements and the virulent anti-German propaganda that the sinking was a war crime, the willful murder of unarmed civilians,[35] the British government knew that the *Lusitania* was authorized to carry much needed munitions and contraband of war from the eastern seaboard of America to Liverpool. The munitions had been ordered by the War Office on behalf of the Royal Arsenal. Kitchener, Lloyd George, Asquith and Churchill were all complicit in the act. Little wonder they wanted to focus blame elsewhere.

In the first six months of the war the German submarine fleet was mainly used on reconnaissance missions and attacks on warships. In total over that period, the U-boat fleet sank only ten British merchant ships. The first was the steamer *Glitra* on 20 October 1914 off the Norwegian coast. Having been ordered to heave-to, the ship's company was given time to lower their life-boats and no lives were lost.[36] According to the recognized practice of international law, a submarine commander had to ascertain the identity of the target and make adequate provisions for the safety of crew and passengers before attacking an enemy merchant or passenger ship. Since it was impossible for the cramped submarines to take on board the numbers present on large ships, the best they could do was stop the ship and give the crew a chance to take to the lifeboats.[37] Initially, this was common practice. By early 1915 British merchant shipping still operated on a virtual peacetime basis without any reliance on a convoy system. Admiralty Intelligence assessed that the German Imperial Fleet had no more than 25 submarines capable of blockading the British Isles, and since these had to operate in three reliefs, no more than eight were likely to be active simultaneously.[38]

Although international law was generally recognized by U-boat captains in the first months of the war, changes in British anti-submarine tactics led them to re-assess the risks they faced when surfacing near merchant vessels to give the crew the opportunity to abandon ship. At the outbreak of war, thirty-nine large British merchantmen had been fitted with 4.7-inch deck guns and increasingly more were armed with such weapons. Whereas ships could generally survive several hits, a submarine which had surfaced was very vulnerable to attack and a single hit might make it impossible for her to dive. First Lord of the Admiralty, Winston Churchill took an even more aggressive stance against submarine warfare by ordering merchant ships to attempt to ram U-boats on the surface.

In addition, the introduction of armed decoy tramp steamers (later named Q ships) greatly increased the risk to submarines operating from a surface position. With guns carefully concealed as deck-structure, the decoy would suddenly drop the disguised or camouflaged boards which concealed their weapons and open fire. This tactic was immediately successful but caused U-boat captains to rethink their strategy. The rules of engagement had been torn up and U-boats remained submerged for their own safety. Now, there would be no warning. The first and only indication a merchant crew might get was a fast, steady stream of tell-tale bubbles heading towards them. Submarine warfare entered a new phase of silent approach and unheralded torpedo attack. In the bitterness of war the struggle for command of the seas brought ever-increasing danger to maritime traffic.

On 1 February 1915 the German Chancellor approved a submarine campaign against sea-borne commerce in retaliation for the British blockade of Germany and the illegal tactics used by British merchant ships flying false "neutral" flags.[39] The objective, to cut Britain's sea communications and starve her into submission, was totally unrealistic given the paucity of U-boats and the huge volume of international trade. Nevertheless, the campaign was endorsed three days later by the Kaiser. A designated war zone was created around the coast of Britain and out into the Atlantic. Germany claimed the right to dispense with the customary preliminaries of visit and search before taking action against merchant vessels. They warned that belligerent merchantmen were to be sunk and it was no longer possible to avoid the danger to crews and passengers. Neutral shipping was advised to stay out of the zone from 18 February onwards or face due consequence. There was an immediate outcry. The *Times* portrayed the German tactic as a "war on neutrals" and dismissed the Kaiser's proclamation as a "new piracy."[40]

Initially the American press dismissed the declaration as "bluff." The *Public Ledger* (Philadelphia) dismissed it as an "intimidation calculated to raise insurance rates and instill fear in shipping circles."[41] On the other hand, international lawyer Frederic Coudert fumed that it was an "absolutely unprecedented stroke of barbarism" that was "not in any way justified by law or morality." In reality, analysis of the German War Zone decree showed it to be very similar to the earlier British "blockade" on Germany, and government officials in the American State Department realized that the Germans had executed a clever counter-diplomatic stroke.[42] Winston Churchill remained adamant that, "no appreciable effect would in fact be produced upon our trade, provided always that our ships continued boldly to put to sea. On the other hand, we were sure that the German declaration and the inevitable accidents to neutrals arising out of it would offend and perhaps embroil the United States."[43]

Despite the initial hysteria, the German blockade of the British Isles began as promised on 18 February. That same day a British merchant ship was torpedoed in the English Channel, and by the end of the first week eleven British ships had been attacked and seven sunk. But put this into perspective. In the same period no less than 1,381 merchant vessels had safely arrived in, or sailed from, British ports. Trade continued unabated. In April 1915 twenty-three ships were sunk out of over 6,000 arrivals and departures. Six of these were neutrals. At least four U-boats were destroyed in the same period.[44] This was not Armageddon.

Given that the total number of U-boats which operated around British shores at any given time was strictly limited, the secret codebreakers in Room 40 had, by February 1915, the capacity to track their wireless messages and follow their direction as they moved from area to area. Though not yet an exact science, the information was priceless. On 15 February 1915, three days before the German War Zone took effect, Churchill wrote a secret memo to the President of the Board of Trade, Walter Runciman, outlining an opportunity which the German tactic presented. It was the kernel of an idea which appealed to both him and the inner-core agents of the Secret Elite:

"It is of the utmost importance to attract neutral shipping to our shores, in the hope of especially embroiling the U.S. with Germany. The German formal announcement of indiscriminate submarining has been made to the United States to produce a deterrent effect on traffic. For our part, we want the traffic – the more the better; and if some of it gets into trouble, better still."[45] The Secret Elite in London plotted to use the German submarine campaign to provide their American partners with a means to counter the strong anti-war sentiments prevalent in the United States and bring her into the war. Room 40 became a secret weapon on its own with Churchill, a key Secret Elite operative, as its master and commander.

He did not supervise the day-to-day operations, that was the duty of Captain "Blinker" Hall, but all were answerable to him. Arguments have been constructed around the climate of absolute secrecy inside the Admiralty which insist that Churchill did not know all the circumstances surrounding the *Lusitania's* voyage. What nonsense. He was obsessed by control; obsessed by his own image; obsessed by the public perception that he *was* the Admiralty. Of course he knew.

Consider the information available to Churchill. In Room 40 the cryptographers knew precisely which U-boats were at sea and actively hunting down merchant shipping. They could follow radio messages from area to area and plot their location. The Admiralty Intelligence Division understood how the German submarines operated and the conditions they required for a successful hit. They were aware of almost every German vessel's position. The Admiralty Trade Division knew which merchant ships and passenger liners were approaching British waters and which were scheduled to leave. No-one had instant access to these departments, save Churchill, the First Sea Lord, Jackie Fisher and Admiral Henry Oliver, chief of Admiralty war staff.

To have such detailed information put Churchill in a position few leaders have ever enjoyed. He had quickly determined that the information could be used to "embroil the U.S. with Germany." How had he expressed it to Runciman? The greater the traffic, the greater the opportunity for German U-Boats to sink a neutral ship, and "better still" if some American traffic got "into trouble." This wasn't a chance remark. It was a statement of intent.

The Secret Elite intended to engineer a crisis that would swing public opinion in the United States towards war. The plan which took shape was not discussed in Cabinet, nor recorded in official papers, but Churchill's letter demonstrated clearly that the idea of an American ship getting "into trouble" was considered secretly at the highest level. The fall-out from a U-Boat torpedo sinking a trans-Atlantic liner carrying American passengers was not only discussed with the Prime Minister, foreign secretary, Sir Edward Grey and even the King, but the means to enable such a traumatic incident had been agreed. The Secret Elite intended to facilitate an international incident to Britain's advantage using German submarines to their own end. Had it not been the *Lusitania,* another such ship would have served the same purpose, but the *Lusitania* was the perfect target. She regularly transported the richest of Americans across the Atlantic. The endangerment of a thousand migrants or working class souls has long been of less concern that an international millionaire banker or icon from high society. If only the Admiralty could isolate a target, channel it towards a prowling U-boat and leave the rest to the fates …?

The German authorities made it plain that they considered the *Lusitania* a legitimate target. She was. Notices to that effect were published in all major American newspapers on 30 April 1915, specifically warning that the German Government considered any vessel flying the British flag as "liable to destruction" and that travelers did so "at their own risk."[46] Like many other papers, the *Washington Times* splashed a warning from the German

Ambassador to the United States, Count Bernstorff, across their front page with an account of "scores of prominent passengers receiving anonymous telegrams" warning that the *Lusitania* would be sunk.[47] The State Department responded that Germany would be held strictly accountable for any action which affected American citizens.[48] It read like a wild-west standoff. Many passengers considered it a bluff.

As Captain William Turner steered *Lusitania* from Pier 54 with 1,266 passengers and 696 crew aboard in New York, he was fully aware of these dire warnings, but confident that he could outrun any pursuing U-Boats. He received his instructions from Cunard's General Manager in Liverpool, but, like all merchant captains, was subject to Admiralty control under the rules of the Liverpool and London War Risks Association. This understanding obligated all merchant ships to follow Admiralty instructions. Failure to do so meant that ship owners forfeited their rights to insurance indemnity.[49] Cunard prized Captain Turner as among their very best. He was a company man and no risk-taker. At 11:00AM on 7 May, after six relatively uneventful days at sea steaming through thick fog, *Lusitania* broke into a crystal clear day off the Old Head of Kinsale in Southern Ireland.

His nemesis, Captain Walther Schwieger, lay close by. Schwieger and the U-20 had been actively hunting unsuspecting victims in and around that area for several days. On 5 May he sank the schooner, *The Earl of Latham*, but not before permitting the 5-man crew to take to their lifeboat. On landing safely near Kinsale, news of the U-Boat activity was transmitted to Queenstown and on to the Admiralty. U-20 then chased but failed to sink the *Cayo Romano*, a British steamer flying a Cuban flag. She docked safely and immediately reported the U-boat attack. The crucial point here was that both the naval authorities at Queenstown (now Cobh in Ireland) and the Admiralty in London, knew that U-20 was within 20 miles of the Irish coast and prowling the main shipping lanes for Atlantic victims. Schwieger's submarine was closely monitored by the decoders in Room 40. They knew the precise areas which were threatened and had identified the specific submarines involved.[50]

The officer in overall charge of naval intelligence, Rear-Admiral Henry Oliver, was a taciturn workaholic who had a thorough knowledge and understanding of U-boat movements. Indeed, Room 40 had been monitoring U-20's every move in precise detail since September 1914. But initial procedures were changed. For some unexplained reason, the previous policy of reporting U-boat locations was not followed in early May 1915, nor were the practices that had been set up to protect major shipping targets. It was as if the Admiralty had revised its operational procedures just as the *Lusitania* steamed into a highly dangerous shipping lane.

It is important to consider how the *Lusitania* was treated on her previous voyage from New York in early March. Rear-Admiral Oliver ordered two destroyers out to sea to escort her, and the first Q-ship, HMS *Lyon*[51] was sent to cruise Liverpool Bay.[52] In other words *Lusitania* was given high priority, even though on that occasion the destroyer captains failed to make contact with her because they had not been given the appropriate maritime code. On 7 May matters were entirely different. There were no destroyers or decoy ships sent to escort her safely to Liverpool.

There was, however, an identified U-boat which was running amok in the crucial sea lane. U-20 was rampant. The day before (6 May) she chased and sank the SS *Candidate* after ordering the crew to abandon ship. By 3:40 P.M. they had been rescued and their predicament relayed to London. Schwieger missed the opportunity to sink the 14,000 ton White Star liner *Arabic*, but in the afternoon sank the SS *Centurion* which took an hour and twenty minutes to go down.[53] News was sent to Queenstown and the Admiralty before 9 o'clock that morning, though the decoders in Room 40 had already read the message from U-20 on the day before. Whether or not either of these Harrison Line steamers, *Centurion* and *Candidate*, or indeed any of the patrol boats reported the incidents by wireless remains uncertain, because all of the relevant records were "lost." Between 5 and 7 May at least five official radio messages were received and acknowledged by the *Lusitania*. Copies of these were later sent by the Post Office, which operated the wireless stations, to the Admiralty wherein the documents disappeared for ever, a recurring theme when the official version of the *Lusitania's* demise was challenged.

What can be established with absolute certainty is that Rear-Admiral Oliver knew by midday on 7 May 1915 that U-20 was in the vicinity of the advancing *Lusitania*. So too did other key players. Cunard Chairman Alfred Booth, who worked in Liverpool, heard about the sinking of the *Candidate* and *Centurion*, but for some inexplicable reason was not allowed to warn his own ship because that was an Admiralty duty. He was determined to have a warning transmitted to Captain Turner and went in person to encourage Admiral Harry Stileman, the senior Admiralty representative in Liverpool, to send one. Stileman promised to do what he could,[54] but no direct warning was ever sent to Turner. Nor was there to be an escort to protect her.

Two days earlier the cruiser *Juno* had been ordered to abandon her mission to accompany the *Lusitania* through the war zone. Why? The Admiralty war diary offers no explanation. Apparently no-one knew who took that decision, but of one thing we can be certain; no-one would have dared give such an order without the explicit approval of Churchill or Fisher.[55] *Lusitania* was left isolated while destroyers *Legion, Lucifer, Laveroc* and *Linnet*, in company with Q-Ships *Baralong* and *Lyons* remained tied up in Milford Haven. Captain Turner was not informed that he had no escort as he closed on the waiting U-20.

On that same morning two very strange conversations took place in London, both with men closely associated with the Secret Elite. Sir Edward Grey asked President Wilson's personal minder Edward Mandell House, who was allegedly engaged on a peace mission, about the probability of an ocean liner being sunk by a U-boat. Mandell House believed that the outrage would bring "such a sweep of indignation across America" that she was bound to join in the war. House was a British-trained political operative who held great influence over the American president.[56] One hour later, in an audience with George V at Buckingham Palace, the King asked him: "suppose they should sink the *Lusitania* with American passengers on board?"[57] How odd. Unless the King had access to a crystal ball, he demonstrated amazingly accurate prior knowledge. That these men should have queried the topic at precisely the time the *Lusitania* was sailing towards her doom, raised the question of precisely what they knew?

At 2:10 PM U-20 fired a single torpedo at the Lusitania from 700 metres which struck the starboard side. Within seconds of the torpedo's explosion, a separate, very distinct and massive internal explosion tore the ship apart. The liner quickly sank with the loss of 1,195 passengers and crew, of whom 140 were American. With one blow tentative talks of a US-brokered peace ended. America's relationship with Germany soured immediately, and the British propaganda machine moved into hyper-drive. But from the moment the first survivors reached Queenstown, the Admiralty lost control of the script as a coterie of able journalists met survivors and reported their unfolding story. This was not as the Secret Elite had planned.

Queenstown became the center of uncensored information. Next morning, 8 May, newspaper columns across the globe reported that local people had been well aware of the submarine activity. *The Scotsman* carried the news that the *Earl of Letham*, had been sunk on Wednesday evening in the same area as the *Lusitania* and "earlier in the day the same submarine discharged a torpedo at the British merchantman, *Cayo Romano* near Fastnet and missed her stern by a few feet."[58] While dwelling on the outrage and speculating on American reaction (first reports claimed that eighty percent of the passengers were American) editors were soon fed Admiralty disinformation. In anticipation of accusations to come, the *Times* bluntly stated that the *Lusitania* "was not built for cargo."[59] Strange that from the outset her cargo should be deemed an issue worthy of denial. More worryingly for Churchill and the Secret Elite, the *Times* gave early notice that questions would be raised whether the Admiralty took special measures to protect the vessel, "in view of the threat and of the known presence in the waters she had to traverse of German submarines."[60]

Matters raced forward at an unanticipated pace. Before a Board of Trade Inquiry could be announced, a Coroner's Inquiry opened at Kinsale on the afternoon of Saturday 8 May. This turn of events caught London completely off guard. John J. Horgan, a local lawyer who doubled as the Kinsale Coroner, traveled to Queenstown, and gathered together a jury of local tradesmen, shopkeepers and fishermen. He served notice on Captain Turner and had concluded his investigations before the Crown Solicitor arrived to stop the Inquest.[61] Horgan was an active member of Sinn Fein from County Cork and may have been inspired by devilment, but his quick action temporarily blew a hole in the Secret Elite cover-up.

Horgan's key witness was the *Lusitania's* Captain, William Turner, who had been rescued by the small steamer *Bluebell* after three hours in the water.[62] Though the liner had literally sunk under his feet, he had not left his post till the end and his bravery shone through the fog which the Admiralty sought to close around the tragedy. Turner chose to appear before the Coroner even though he could have justifiably claimed to be exhausted and disoriented by his near-death experience.

Under oath, Captain Turner made it clear that he was fully aware of the German threats made in New York before the *Lusitania's* departure. According to a detailed report carried in *The Scotsman* on Tuesday 11 May, the Captain denied that he received any warning message about the ships sunk off the Old Head of Kinsale. Perhaps he was confused because the *Lusitania* had been sent a general warning the previous evening about U-boat activity south of Ireland. Critically, in all that was to transpire, Captain Turner stated that immediately after the first explosion caused by the torpedo, there was a second explosion "that might possibly have been internal." He confirmed that no warships had escorted the liner and "none were reported to me as having been sent." Fair man that he was, Turner added that he had not asked the Admiralty for an escort "since that was their business, not his."[63] The Coroner ended his inquiry with unstinting praise for Captain Turner, and the jury unanimously charged the U-20s officers, the Kaiser and the government of Germany with willful and wholesale murder.

Alarm bells rang around all who had prior knowledge of the *Lusitania's* possible fate. Captain Turner had not gone down with his ship. His evidence clearly indicated that the *Lusitania* had not been informed of the U-boat activity off Kinsale and, most damningly, he was of the opinion that the second explosion was internal. All of this was documented before witnesses could be bound by the sub-judice rules of silence of an official Board of Inquiry. The stricture that nothing could be said lest it prejudiced the formal findings had not applied to the Coroner's Inquest. The truth was laid bare.

Churchill's enemies in Parliament gathered their indignation and wrapped it in very pointed and embarrassing questions. Like many of the Secret Elite before him, Churchill was "out of town" when the dirty deed was done. His convenient absence on other "secret duties" during the critical period has been wrongly used by some historians to deny Churchill's involvement in the *Lusitania's* demise. From 6-8 May he took up privileged residence in the Ritz Hotel in Paris on the basis of his attendance at a conference on the naval aspects of Italy's participation in the war.[64] His presence there was met with a mixture of amusement and scorn by the French,[65] who treated him with ill-disguised contempt. Gallipoli was falling apart, his relationship with Lord Fisher at the Admiralty deteriorated by the day, and the *Lusitania's* fate was accompanied by serious accusations of incompetence. His dalliance in France, where he chose to spend two additional days visiting Sir John French, was derided in Parliament.[66] Churchill seemed to have no appreciation of how low his stock had fallen. Even King George V made comment on "Winston's joy-rides."[67] This was not his finest hour.

The Board of Trade Inquiry began at Central Buildings, Westminster on 14 June, 1915 under the Wreck Commissioner, Lord Mersey. In the short time between the dinner party in May thrown by Ambassador Page on behalf of President Wilson's so-called peace emissary, the political landscape in Britain had changed. Asquith had reshuffled his Cabinet. A few well-known figures had been discarded. Churchill was removed from the Admiralty because the Tory Party leaders demanded that he go. His like-for-like replacement was the Secret Elite's Arthur Balfour. Lloyd George was switched from the Exchequer and given the highest-profile new post, minister for munitions. Sir Edward Carson was appointed attorney general, the most senior legal advisor to the government, and Mr F.E. Smith was promoted to solicitor general, the second most senior legal advisor in England. Sir Edward Grey stayed at his post in the Foreign Office. What few realized was that more political agents associated with the Secret Elite had begun to move into government. This coalition or National Government had as its most immediate priority to find a solution to the alleged munitions shortage which had been turned into a public scandal.[68]

Asquith's new government could ill afford any more public criticism, and Lord Mersey's Inquiry had to focus on two highly contentious issues; the role of the Admiralty, and the fact that would be denied for nearly a century, namely that the passenger liner was carrying much needed munitions.[69] Sadly for Captain Turner, a coalition of vested interests, all Secret Elite controlled, set out to make him the scapegoat.

Lord Mersey was privately instructed on the outcome that the Admiralty sought in a note passed to him inside official papers before the Inquiry began. It simply said that it was "politically expedient that Captain Turner, Master of the *Lusitania,* be most prominently blamed for the disaster."[70] The Secrete Elite intended to ruin Captain William Turner. Witnesses were carefully selected. Every surviving member of the crew gave evidence in sworn statements to the Board of Trade, but inexplicably only 13 of those 289 depositions were ever made available for public scrutiny. All begin with the identical opening sentence and all incorrectly claim that the ship was hit by more than one torpedo. Furthermore, even the illiterate seamen who signed their statements with the letter X wrongly placed the point of the torpedo's impact in midship or well-aft. The Board of Trade had stated that passengers who wished to submit evidence to the inquiry should do so. One hundred and thirty-five "proofs" were submitted by passengers who wished to testify, but only five were invited to appear before the court. Not one passenger who referred to an explosion further forward than amidships, appeared.[71]

Contrary evidence was unwelcome. The architect, Oliver Bernard was on deck when the U-20's torpedo struck. His famous eye-witness drawings of the liner as she sank were printed in the *Illustrated London News*.[72] Commissioned in 1916, Bernard became a Captain in the Royal Engineers, and winner of a Military Cross. He was adamant that only one torpedo hit the Lusitania, and therefore, was not called to give evidence.[73] The American consul in Queenstown obtained sworn testaments from the American survivors and these were sent onwards to the State Department in Washington and copied to the Board of Trade. Neither organization used them at their respective inquiries, and currently there remains no trace of the copies sent to the British Board of Trade.[74]

The reader may begin to sense a theme. Today we have access to the full proceedings of Lord Mersey's Inquiry on the Internet[75] and over the five days 14-18 June, 1915, it is clear that Captain Turner was subjected to a concerted legal attack from the British establishment. The Admiralty had concocted its highly prejudicial "evidence" in the form of a memorandum from Captain Richard Webb, Director of the Admiralty's Trade Division; a memorandum which was seen by Lord Mersey before the sitting began.[76] This secret document shaped the lines of inquiry and directed the assault on Captain Turner, deflecting questions about the cargo and concealing the truth about the telegrams sent (and not sent) to the *Lusitania*. It was the script approved by the Secret Elite, but it was, by their standards, seriously flawed.

Sir Edward Carson used his persuasive and carefully rehearsed inquisition to undermine William Turner on the first day of the Inquiry. With the public removed from the hall, Carson attempted to belittle Turner's seamanship, implying that he was sailing too close to the coast in contravention of Admiralty instructions. Turner would have none of it. He did not navigate a great liner by approximations and guesswork.[77] More devious tactics were required. Carson began to paint a picture of the Irish Sea "infested" by German submarines, and repeatedly pressurized Turner to admit that he had disobeyed a clear Admiralty directive by failing to steer the Lusitania in a zig-zag manner. Lord Mersey asked Carson to reread the Admiralty advice on zig-zagging which drew some confusion from Captain Turner. He couldn't quite remember the precise wording; "it seems different language," he complained. And he was right. The instructions which were read out in court had not been given final approval by Winston Churchill until 25 April, and their widespread distribution did not begin until 13 May, five days after the disaster.[78] Turner was deliberately misled, confused by Carson's determined assertion that he had received orders from the Admiralty about zig-zagging which he had allegedly flouted. These orders had never been sent. The Court of Inquiry was deliberately lied to by the Attorney General. Surely an astonishing turn of events in any democracy?

In its mockery of justice, the Crown treated the inquiry as a trial, and selected its evidence to that end. The single member of naval or Admiralty staff called as a witness, Captain Anderson, was asked only about the merits of traveling at top speed and adopting a zig-zag pattern to reduce any chance of submarine attack. No question was asked about the Admiralty's plan to protect the *Lusitania*. Indeed, all questions to be put to the inquiry had been carefully preselected. Churchill had written on the infamous Webb memorandum that "Turner be pursued without check,"[79] and even though he was no longer at the Admiralty in June 1915, his replacement, the Secret Elite's Arthur Balfour, maintained that course.

But the case, biased, even as it was, collapsed at the last hurdle when Lord Mersey discovered that the evidence with which he had been presented was not the same as that being used by the Solicitor General, Mr F.E. Smith. Confusion broke out over the alleged telegrams which had been sent to the *Lusitania*. Though both the Commissioner (Lord Mersey) and the Solicitor General were apparently working from documents headed *Lusitania*, a memorandum prepared by officials of the Board of the Admiralty, they were not identical. Someone had fouled up. In addition, Lord Mersey realized that having seen the questions to be asked at his inquiry in a previous draft, these had been altered in order to avoid any references to messages received by the *Lusitania*.[80] This fiasco forced the court to end Captain Turner's torture.

The Secret Elite made one final bid to change Lord Mersey's mind. Clearly Sir Edward Carson and Mr F.E. Smith had failed to strip William Turner of his dignity, so they brought forward the heavy artillery. From the Foreign Office, Sir Arthur Nicolson and Lord Crewe let it be known that if Turner was censured, there would be no objection to that being made public. They insisted that the new first Lord, Arthur Balfour, agreed with their view and would gladly speak with Lord Mersey "at some convenient time." Lord Mersey was too long in the tooth to be bullied. Disgusted by what he had been made party to, he wrote to Prime Minister Asquith and resigned from any further government appointment. He is reputed to have told his children that the case of the *Lusitania* was "a damned dirty business."[81]

His findings still amounted to an absolute whitewash. The whole blame for the catastrophe was allotted to "those who plotted and committed the crime," Germany. Praise was heaped on 18 year-old Leslie Morton, the look-out who spotted that two torpedoes hit the ship, before saving nearly 100 lives assisted by his mate, Perry. Seriously, this is recorded in the Inquiry findings, not the *Boy's Own Annual.* So, *two* torpedoes, then, from the U-Boat that fired only one. Not so. Lord Mersey found that a third torpedo had been fired at the port side, and thus "proved" that there was indeed more than one submarine. Mersey directed that no explosives had been on board save about 5,000 cartridges as entered in the manifest. German accusations about the *Lusitania's* cargo were deemed "baseless inventions."

Incredibly, even amidst this litany of nonsense, Lord Mersey was able to praise the Admiralty which he claimed had "diligently collected all available information likely to affect the voyage of the *Lusitania.*" He saluted the manner in which they "did their work." No warnings for Captain Turner, no escort or convoy, no clear information about the whereabouts of U-Boat 20, yet they did their work diligently? Amazing. And for Captain Turner there was praise of sorts and not the damning condemnation which the Secret Elite had wanted. Mersey concluded that Turner was "fully advised" of the Admiralty's advice on how to avoid the perils of submarine warfare but had "exercised his judgment for the best." But finally it was, as ever, the fault of the Germans.[82]

It was indeed a damned dirty business, compounded by lies and a legion of "lost" reports, memoranda, documents and telegrams. And what of those who served the aspirations of the Secret Elite? Lord Mersey was raised to the rank of Viscount. Captain Webb, author of the falsified memorandum, was rewarded with promotion to Admiral. Sir Edward Carson was elevated to Lord Carson and was given a state funeral. F.E. Smith became 1st Earl of Birkenhead and was Secretary of State for India between 1924-28. Such rich pickings from one valuable whitewash.

Captain William Turner never forgave the Admiralty. When in 1923, Winston Churchill published the first volume of his memoirs of the First World War under the title *World Crisis,* his criticism of Turner's actions reopened old wounds.[83] He reiterated the fallacious claims that Captain Turner had disobeyed Admiralty instructions, that U-20 had fired two torpedoes at mid-ship and aft and that the *Lusitania's* cargo contained only a small consignment of rifle ammunition and shrapnel shells.[84] Churchill's lies have been repeated in history books and taught in our schools and universities for generations.

Summary.

- The Imperial German Navy started the war with three highly complex sets of secret transmission codes and cyphers; within four months the Admiralty possessed copies of them all, and had access to all wireless communications to and from the German fleet.
- The codes, and the deciphering of these messages, took place in the Admiralty, where a very secret unit in Room 40 was set up under Admiral "Blinker" Hall.

- RMS *Lusitania* of the Cunard Steamship Company was built on the Clyde and launched in 1906. The government paid Cunard handsomely to build the ship to Admiralty specifications so that it could become an auxiliary cruiser in time of war.
- When war was declared, *Lusitania* regularly transported munitions across the Atlantic as part of the trade in desperately needed munitions, ordered and provided through the J.P. Morgan banking organization.
- The Kaiser's spokesman in America, Bernhard Dernberg repeatedly claimed that the Cunard ships carried munitions. When in 2012 the *Lusitania's* 27-page supplementary manifest was discovered in the Franklin D Roosevelt Presidential Archives, the truth about the large volume of armaments carried on board was proved correct.
- President Wilson was given chapter-and-verse evidence of the complicity of Bethlehem Steel, J.P. Morgan and Cunard in enabling these exports but took no action to stop it.
- Evidence from the private correspondence of the British Prime Minister showed that the inner circle of power knew that *Lusitania* regularly brought armaments to Britain. Asquith's main concern after the *Lusitania* had been sunk, was that the supply of munitions would suffer.
- Warnings were issued in America that the German submarine campaign which began on 18th February 1915, meant that ships like the *Lusitania* would be prime targets.
- Knowing that the intercepts from Room 40 meant that all U-Boats could be monitored, the Secret Elite engineered a crisis which would swing public opinion in America towards war.
- Whereas in her previous voyage from America, *Lusitania* had been allocated an escort on her final journey, no destroyers were allocated to safeguard her passage through danger zones.
- Shortly before the U-Boat attack, President Wilson's personal assistant (and minder) was asked by Sir Edward Grey and King George V, independently, what impact the sinking of a liner form America would have.
- The *Lusitania* was sunk by the U-20 after she was hit by a single torpedo. A further explosion followed quickly afterwards, and the Admiralty claimed that she had been struck by two or three torpedoes.
- 1,195 passengers and crew, including 140 Americans, were lost.
- At the coroner's inquest held immediately at Kinsale in Ireland, Captain Turner of the *Lusitania* denied that he had been warned about U-Boat attacks in the area, had not been met with a destroyer escort and that there was second explosion which may have been internal.
- A formal Board of Trade inquiry, headed by Lord Mersey, attempted to lay the blame on Captain Turner for disobeying instructions. He was attacked by the British legal establishment, was faced by a highly prejudicial memorandum from the Admiralty, was 'accused' of malpractice, faced highly selective "witnesses," but this mockery of justice collapsed.
- Lord Mersey is reputed to have told his children that it was a 'damned dirty business.'

Lusitania propaganda poster

Chapter 14

Lusitania – Protecting The Guilty

It has taken a century of investigation to prise open the fragile remains of the evidence that was buried at that time. The very credible proof presented by writers and historians Colin Simpson, Diana Preston, Patrick Beesly, and Mitch Peeke in particular, has destroyed the myths and lies with which the Secret Elite covered their crimes. Like every expendable soldier and sailor, the *Lusitania* was sacrificed to prolong the war to crush Germany. It was turned into a propaganda coup to bolster Britain's standing in the United States. But it had been a risky business. Had the truth been known in the days and weeks afterwards, both the American and British governments would have been in crisis. For nearly a century, court historians held fast to the lie which protected them.

The Anglo-American Establishment, the expanding Secret Elite so effectively identified by Professor Carrol Quigley,[1] placed power and influence into hands chosen by friendship and loyalty to their cause, rather than merit, and have thus controlled politics, banking, the press and much else in Britain and the United States for the past century. Sometimes referred to obliquely as the "Deep State," the "money-power," the "hidden power" or "the men behind the curtain," these utterly ruthless individuals amassed vast profits for their companies, banks and industries through the war against Germany.[2] Their complicity in the sinking of the *Lusitania* and its cover-up demonstrated just how far their influence extended inside both Whitehall and the White House.

The influential diplomat and historian, Lewis Einstein, captured the Secret Elite's sense of inter-dependence and mutually assured future perfectly in an article published in 1913 in the London edition of the *National Review*.[3] He argued cogently that the United State's share in the world power system meant that America would have to ensure that Britain was not defeated in a war with Germany, and would have to intervene in any future major European war if that was threatened.[4] Such views were shared by the Anglophile American historian and correspondent for the Secret Elite's *Round Table* journal, George Louis Beer,[5] the U.S. Ambassador at London, Walter Hines Page, President Wilson's personal mentor, Edward Mandell House, the U.S. Ambassador at Berlin, James Gerard and, most importantly in terms of the American involvement with the *Lusitania*, the up-and-coming presidential advisor, Robert Lansing.[6] Woodrow Wilson was a political puppet of the Secret Elite, and the men surrounding and representing him were entrenched

Anglophiles who staunchly believed in the ultimate victory of the English-speaking race. Ordinary Americans may have thought their President and their country neutral, but in the corridors of real power in Washington, neutrality was a sham.

One prominent politician who attempted to ensure U.S. neutrality was Secretary of State William Jennings Bryan. In August 1914 he advised President Wilson not to allow the Rothschild-backed bankers, J.P. Morgan and Co. to raise loans and credits for the allies,[7] but the bankers soon retaliated through their favored trade advisor to the President, Robert Lansing. Despite Secretary Bryan's repeated objections, Lansing and the State Department sided with the bankers and munitions manufacturers to alter the rules on credit and trade. They insisted that an embargo on arms sales by private companies was unconstitutional and enabled the U.S. to become the supply base for Britain and France despite the so-called neutrality.[8]

The Germans knew from their spy network that the "secret" British purchases of munitions and matériel of war was constant and extensive. J.P. Morgan Jr. was intimately linked to the Rothschild Dynasty and through them, the Secret Elite. His banking empire was at the core of the conspiracy to arm the Allies. In January 1915, he signed a contract appointing him sole purchasing agent for Britain as well as the Treasury's primary financial agent.[9] Morgan's associate, E.C. Grenfell, a director of the Bank of England, personally acted as a go-between with Washington and London. Britain's munitions procurer, George Macauley Booth, (of the Shipping company, Alfred Booth) readily gave his support to Morgan. In addition to his pre-eminence in U.S. banking, Morgan controlled a vast tonnage of shipping through his International Mercantile Marine Co. George Booth was well aware that an alliance with Morgan meant that both his ships and Cunard's would benefit greatly from the huge upsurge in Atlantic trade.[10] Vast profits were made. From the start of the war until they entered in April 1917, quite apart from weapons, the United States sent the Allies more than a million tons of cordite, gun-cotton, nitrocellulose, fulminate of mercury and other explosive substances. British servicemen in civilian clothes were employed in the scheme and customs at both ends turned a blind eye to the illicit trade underwritten by the merchants of death. Unfortunate passengers on the liners which carried the munitions knew nothing of the dangers that lurked in their holds.

On the dock-side in New York, cargoes were inspected by the British Admiralty forwarding agent, and the more urgently needed exports were allocated to faster ships. Cargo manifests were a charade of false names and supposed destinations. Security was tight, but munitions are difficult to disguise, even if the cargo list claimed that raw or gun cotton was "furs," or that weapons of war appeared as "sewing machines." It was standard British practice to sail on the basis of a false manifest with the tacit blessing of the Collector of Customs, Dudley Field Malone, another of the President's place-men.[11]

A friend and protégé of President Woodrow Wilson, Malone had known and supported him since the beginning of his political career. In November 1913, after a brief period at the State Department, Malone was appointed to the post of Collector of the Port of New York. It was a political sinecure, paying $12,000 a year for supervising the collection of import duties.[12] That being the case, it was mere child's play to have the manifest stamped with the approval of Messrs Wood, Niebuhr and Co., Customs Brokers of Whitehall Street, New York.[13] The Admiralty in London was advised in advance which ships carried what cargo, and of their destination and estimated date of arrival. Such was the understanding between governments that British Consul-General Sir Courtney Bennet, who directed British counter-intelligence operations in New York, had his own desk in the Cunard general manager's office.[14] The export of munitions from America to Britain in "passenger liners" was so blatant that it should embarrass every historian who denies the practice or claims that the *Lusitania* was simply a passenger ship.

The sinking posed a problem for President Wilson's administration. On 9 May 1915 an official statement from the German government stated that the *Lusitania* was "naturally armed with guns ... and she had a large cargo of war material."[15] Alarmed by possible ramifications, Wilson telephoned Robert Lansing demanding to know precisely what the *Lusitania* had been carrying. Lansing had a detailed report from Malone on the President's desk by noon stating that "practically all of her cargo was contraband of some kind" with lists denoting great quantities of munitions. This was political dynamite of the most damning kind. Lansing and Wilson realized that if the public learned that over a hundred Americans had lost their lives because of their abuse of neutrality by allowing passenger ships to carry munitions and explosives, they would not survive the inevitable backlash.[16] Consequently, the official statement from the Collector of the Port of New York stated that the initial "Report is not correct. The *Lusitania* was inspected before sailing as customary. No guns were found."[17] The denial was given full coverage by the international press and became the mantra of court historians from that time onward. The real manifest was consigned to obscurity and may never have seen the light of day had Franklin Delano Roosevelt, at that time Assistant Secretary at the Navy, not saved it for posterity,[18] and Mitch Peeke and his team not traced it to the FDR Presidential Archives.[19]

The text and terms of the American Note of protest to Germany of 11 May 1915 was a historic and deliberately abrasive document. Omitting the customary diplomatic civilities, Wilson protested that American citizens had the right to sail the seas in any ship they wished even if it was a belligerent and armed merchantman. His words were "unanimously approved and commended by the financial community" where a group of leading bankers and financiers vowed to help finance the Allies in memory of the capitalist, Cornelius Vanderbilt, who went down with the ship.[20] The official German reply from their Foreign Office regretted that "Americans felt more inclined to trust English promises rather than pay attention to the warnings from the German side."[21] Germany deeply regretted the loss of American lives and offered compensation, but complained that British merchant vessels had been instructed by Winston Churchill to ram and destroy German submarines. It meant that no submarine commander could safely surface, give warning, and allow passengers and crew to take to the boats before torpedoes were fired. They refused to concede that the sinking of the *Lusitania* was an illegal act, and repeated, correctly, that she was a vessel in the British Navy's merchant fleet auxiliary service and had been carrying munitions and contraband of war.

The final, irrefutable proof that the *Lusitania* had been used contrary to international law came with the resignation of President Wilson's Secretary of State, William Jennings Bryan on 8 June 1915. His resignation statement was clear and unambiguous, though he posed his distaste as a rhetorical question. "Why should American citizens travel on belligerent ships with cargoes of ammunition?" He believed that it was the government's duty to go as far as it could to stop Americans traveling on such ships and thus putting themselves, and by default, the American nation, at risk. His parting shot clarified what had happened on the *Lusitania*. "I think too that American passenger ships should be prevented from carrying ammunition. The lives of passengers should not be endangered by cargoes of ammunition whether that danger comes from possible explosions within or from possible explosions without. Passengers and ammunition should not travel together."[22] He might just as well have said, "it matters not whether the *Lusitania* was sunk by a torpedo or an internal explosion from munitions in the hold. The truth is she was carrying munitions." To his credit, Bryan would have nothing more to do with the Wilson Administration. He was replaced by the Wall Street champion, Robert Lansing, whose connivance in favor of both the money-power and the Allies in Europe, and his lies about the *Lusitania*, had established his credentials.

Despite Bryan's brave stand, suppression of evidence continued unabated. Wesley Frost, the American Consul in Queenstown, had obtained affidavits from every American survivor and forwarded them to the State Department in Washington and the Board of Trade in London, yet not one of the thirty-five statements was ever used in British or American inquiries. Nor is there any trace of the copies sent to London save the acknowledgment of their receipt.[23] Why? We can only speculate that they did not corroborate the lie that more than one torpedo had been fired. Charles Lauriat, Jr., for instance, a Boston bookseller, survived the ordeal, and on his safe return to London, met Ambassador Page. Surely his independent testimony would have been very valuable? He was convinced that there had been a single torpedo. Lauriat was also angry about the manner in which survivors were threatened by the British authorities at Queenstown.[24] He was not called.

And what of that powerfully influential coterie of American Anglophiles who gathered at Ambassador Walter Page's residence on the evening of 7 May? What did they really know? Just five days before the sinking, Page had written a letter to his son Arthur forecasting "the blowing up of a liner with American passengers." On the same day he wrote "if a British liner full of American passengers be blown up, what will Uncle Sam do?" Note that the question concerned a ship being blown up, not sunk. He then added "That's what's is going to happen."[25] What too of Mandell House's discussions on 7 May both with Sir Edward Grey and King George V? They questioned him directly about the impact on America of a passenger liner being torpedoed,[26] yet House found nothing suspicious in their foreknowledge. They knew that a disaster was about to happen, because they had been complicit in its organization and preparation. On both sides of the Atlantic evil men pursued greater profit from human loss.

The official American reaction to the sinking of the *Lusitania* contained so many lies and went to such a depth to conceal government complicity, that there can be no doubt they were complicit and shared guilt for the dreadful incident. American authorities, bankers, financiers and politicians close to the Secret Elite were obliged to hide the truth that they were supplying Britain and France with much-needed munitions in contravention of international law. In addition, they allowed unwitting American citizens to be exposed to grave danger. Yes, Captain Schwieger of U-20 fired the fateful torpedo, but the great liner had deliberately been set up as an easy target, or, as the cold, scheming Churchill called it, "livebait."[27]

Outraged newspaper editors denounced the sinking as the mass murder of innocent American citizens. The *New York Times* likened the Germans to "savages drunk with blood"[28] and *The Nation* declaimed that "the torpedo that sank the Lusitania also sank Germany in the opinion of mankind."[29] These New York publications had been galvanised by the powerful Eastern Establishment and Anglo-American interests whose profits were already mounting in millions by the day. But the further one traveled through the Mid-West to the Pacific coast, the sinking of the Cunarder excited less and less attention. The British Ambassador at Washington regretfully informed the Foreign Office that the United States was still a long way from war with anybody, while his counterpart at Paris described the Americans as "a rotten lot of psalm-singing, profit mongering humbugs."[30] Changing opinion requires patience and the constant reiteration of propaganda. The successful cover-up by two complicit governments played an important role in bringing about an eventual sea-change in public opinion across America, two governments which were complicit in the sinking of the great liner and the murder of 1,195 men, women and children.

Consider these dismissive words from the Imperial War Museum's own history, *War At Sea*. "Conspiracy theorists have flourished ever since, centered on a plot to allow the Lusitania to be torpedoed to bring America in to the war. Like so many conspiracy theories based on a fantasy world of ignorance and naivety, this one does not stand up."[31]

Make up your own mind.

Summary.

- The Secret Elite on both sides of the Atlantic closed ranks quickly to protect the guilty parties involved with the *Lusitania* debacle.
- The JP Morgan banking empire was at the core of a conspiracy to arm the Allies while America protested neutrality.
- His control over the International Mercantile Marine Company gave him immense power over shipping during the war years, and its British owners knew that an alliance with Morgan was good for Cunard business.
- On the New York dock-side, President Wilson's placeman and Controller of Customs, Dudley Field Malone, literally stamped the American government's approval on all illicit cargoes to Europe destined for Allied nations.
- Every government department and agency in America denied the German claims that the *Lusitania* was carrying munitions.
- President Wilson's Secretary of State, William Jennings Bryan resigned on 8 June 1915. His letter of resignation stated that American passenger ships should be prevented from carrying ammunition, a clear confession that this practice was widespread at the time.
- Suppression of evidence from the American side included the loss or dismissal of affidavits from every American survivor, independent testimonies taken then ignored, and categoric denials of claims which later proved to be true.
- The successful cover-up by both governments which were complicit in the sinking of the great liner and the murder of 1,195 men, women and children, played an important role in bringing about an eventual sea-change in public opinion across America.

Chapter 15

The Relief Of Belgium – The Great Humanitarian

WARNING: Any narrative about the Commission for Relief in Belgium based on official documents, such as journals or diaries written by members of the Commission or their friends, must be treated as suspect.[1] In classic Secret Elite mode, the central characters involved in one of the world's greatest swindles wrote their own version of history and removed or destroyed all contrary evidence. It may seem unbelievable, but the real story of Belgian Relief has never been taught in schools or universities in Belgium. We were stunned to discover at a conference in Brussels on 6 November 2014,[2] that the subject of Belgian Relief is still not covered in Belgian colleges today. Generations of Belgians remain ignorant of the machinations of the bankers and financiers, politicians and governments (and here we include the Belgian, British and American governments) and ordinary citizens, who abused what purported to be a charitable venture in order to prolong the war and make obscene profits. If the Commission for Relief of Belgium was so vital to the nations' survival, why is it not given pride of place in Belgian history?

As the Belgian academics, Michael Amara and Hubert Roland made clear "To this day a dark shadow hangs over the history of Belgian Relief. For many, the story of food provision has been raised to a myth created after the war."[3] What is this dark shadow? What is this myth? Why does a sense of embarrassment hang over the work of "American Relief," as it became known, like a dirty family secret ? The Musee Royal de L'Armee et d'Histoire Militaire in Brussels put together a special centenary exhibition in 2014 about the city during the First World War. It featured an "American Relief" shop with crates of Columbia River salmon, fancy apricots from San Francisco and other relatively exotic produce. The background narrative to the exhibition was bland and made no effort to explain the central purpose of an organization which helped Belgian citizens survive and, at the same time, supplied the German army with much-needed foodstuffs. It is yet another example of unpalatable history which governments still seek to hide from their own people.

Little wonder the facts of the story remain so sketchy. All of the pertinent primary evidence about this "relief" organization was removed from Europe after the war on the instruction of its director, Herbert Hoover, and taken to America. What Hoover could not control, including adverse reports in newspapers, official court judgments or published company returns, he tried to suppress. Furthermore, those who dared make claims about the illegal nature of his dealings were quashed, threatened or otherwise marginalized.

The Commission for Relief in Belgium (CRB) between 1914-1917 was an organization that hailed itself as "the greatest humanitarian undertaking that the world had ever seen."[4] Indeed, by the time the Commission closed its doors and rendered what passed as public accounts in 1920,[5] it claimed to have spent over $13,000,000,000 on relief for the people of Belgium. (In current monetary values that would be approximately $154,000,000,000)[6] According to one official history, "A chapter was written in the history of the Great War that will be read with the deepest interest for hundreds of years to come."[7] It will not. Not if those who control history continue to have their way.

Few histories of the First World War even make mention of the CRB. It has slipped inexplicably under the radar of most academic historians. Additionally, the war memoirs of Lloyd George (Prime Minister 1916-1922) and Sir Edward Grey (Foreign Secretary 1906-1916)[8] two of the senior British cabinet members with whom this organization had direct contact, failed to mention Belgian Relief. Likewise, there is no reference to this "humanitarian" work in the otherwise verbose letters from Herbert Asquith (Prime Minister 1908-1916) to his secret love, Venetia Stanley.[9] It feels like an act of denial, as if they were trying to say "it had nothing to do with us." It most certainly did.

Belgian Relief was reputedly organized to feed the poor and needy in Belgium and Northern France. It was but in addition, it provided cover for the fraud that lay behind the scam. Through this initiative, the Secret Elite deliberately supplied the German army with much needed foodstuffs, without which the Germans could not have continued to fight. The food sent to Belgium by the relief organization enabled much of the home grown produce to be directed to Germany. Little known, but strongly denied, the men directly involved, especially the bankers, made fortunes through it. The humanitarian aspect was a vital and effective cover for a clandestine organization that benefited the 'money-power' and quite deliberately prolonged the war.

A number of key individuals were central to the creation, continuation and promotion of the two main agencies which supplied food to Belgium during the German occupation. Namely (1) the Commission for Relief in Belgium (CRB) and (2) the Comite Nationale des Secours et Alimentation in Brussels (CNSA). Both were linked by profession, business or diplomatic status. A combination of American, German and Belgian bankers, businessmen and diplomats, approved and advised by the Secret Elite in

London and Washington, were entrusted with the responsibility of managing what in normal circumstances of war would be termed, "feeding the enemy." Under the guise of saving the starving populations in Belgium and Northern (occupied) France, this became a bold, well-planned organization which involved a prodigious propaganda campaign supported by national governments. Ultimately, Belgian Relief was accountable to no-one.

It spent hundreds of millions of dollars in procuring food and other war supplies, largely, but not exclusively, in America and Argentina. The organizations shipped millions of tons of produce through the neutral port of Rotterdam to the mouth of the Rhine where it was allegedly handed to the Belgian Comite National for local distribution. Rotterdam was the gateway to Germany, more so than Belgium; a glance of any map of Europe will confirm this. By agreement of both neutrals and belligerents, the sole port of entry for all the food and materials sent to Belgium was literally sited at the head of Germany's arterial river. All exits from Rotterdam and Holland passed through Germany or German-occupied territory. Dutch neutrality guaranteed nothing. The whole of the Belgian Relief program depended on German willingness to countenance these imports. They did, but behind this veneer of international humanitarianism, a cruel confidence trick was played out on the world stage.

Between 1914-1919, hundreds of thousands of hungry and sometimes desperate Belgian and French communities were supported by 4,500 local committees comprising workers' groups, Catholic and Protestant benevolent societies and other local agencies in ten Belgian provinces and six French districts. These good people worked tirelessly to save their fellow countrymen from hunger. Of that there is ample evidence.[10] Many desperate and needy Belgian mothers, children and families in poverty were indeed supported through the barren war years by the relief organizations, but they provided a front, a public focus, behind which Germany was enabled to sustain its armies so that war dragged on well beyond 1915 – the point at which it could have ended. Some of the Belgian Relief food went directly to the German army on the Western Front, and it enabled home-grown Belgian produce to be sent across Europe to German cities and towns. Not by chance, but by design; not in a haphazard occasional manner, but methodically, with clear channels of communication that provided regular supplies.

This Secret Elite-inspired solution to Germany's critical food problem was an affront to the concept of humanitarianism. It required a trusted and ruthless manager with a proven track record of greed and loyalty to the British Establishment. He had to appear to act independently yet have access to political and financial power in Britain, Europe and America. He required the services of international banks to handle vast sums of money and had to have connections with world-wide shipping companies to facilitate very complex transportation logistics. He needed to be a neutral citizen, to understand the power of positive propaganda, and have access to newspapers on both sides of the Atlantic. One candidate with proven experience, who could be trusted not to flinch in the face of a moral dilemma, was known to and favored by the Secret Elite.

His name was Herbert Clark Hoover, later the 31st President of the United States.

In Herbert Hoover the Secret Elite found the perfect man to lead the great Belgian "relief" deception. His entire career had been built on the back of dubious mining investments and through a cruel, ruthless exploitation of the workers he made fortunes for his employers and for himself. One example of this centered on his exploitation of the Sons of Gwalia Mine in Australia at the turn of the twentieth century. Here, his cost-saving reduction in the number of safety props led to the injury or death of many miners. He fed the newspapers with stories that the mine was producing $140 worth of gold to the ton when in fact it had barely reached $20. Consequently the company he represented, Bewick-Moreing of London, profited by over $120 million on the mine's flotation. Such was Hoover's constant modus operandi.[11]

The American–born mining engineer lived in London for years and was a business colleague of the Rothschilds. He was a friend of Alfred Milner, leader of the Secret Elite, and had provided the slave labor to man the Transvaals gold mines, so important to their control of South Africa at the end of the Boer War. He was a confidence trickster and crook who, in 1901, cheated the Chinese out of their rightful ownership of the massive Kaiping Coal fields and put them in the hands of British and Belgian bankers.[12] In addition to the illicit fortunes he made for himself and his backers, Hoover provided the British navy with much needed coaling facilities in the Far East and in doing so, gained the trust and gratitude of the Foreign Office in London.

A deeper analysis of Hoover's activities in defrauding the Chinese of their coal mines, reveals an association with Belgian bankers, industrialists and diplomats, including Emile Francqui, which would prove entirely pertinent to his eventual role in the Commission for Relief in Belgium some thirteen years later. In raising the necessary capital to swindle the Chinese officials out of their mines in 1901, Hoover turned to Belgian backers. In turn, they persuaded the Banque d'Outremer of Brussels to invest £100,000 in exchange for a large allocation of stock in an organization called the Oriental Syndicate. When he returned to China to finalize the fraudulent deal, Hoover was accompanied by Chevalier Emmanuel de Wouters representing the Belgian bankers.[13] De Wouters later became a member of the Chinese Ministry of Foreign Affairs and Vice President of the Banque Belge pour L'Etranger, to which we will return.

Accusations of malpractice and the total disregard for "binding agreements" with the Chinese authorities brought matters to a head.[14] On 18

January 1905 the Chinese Engineering and Mining Company of Tientsin, in the person of Chang Yen Moa, Director of Mines, took legal action at the High Court in London against Hoover, De Wouters and the British mining company of Bewick, Moreing and Co. Amongst an impressive array of expensive defense lawyers, Hoover and the company was defended by two powerful Liberal MPs, Rufus Isaacs and Alfred Milner's loyal friend and Secret Elite member, Richard Haldane. Both held the senior legal post of King's Counsel. Hoover was questioned in the witness box for two days and was obliged to admit that statements he had previously made were untrue.

On 1 March, the judge, Mr Justice Joyce came to the conclusion that the British company had acted in bad faith. Interestingly, Richard Haldane made a special plea to the court on behalf of the Foreign Office claiming that Mr Justice Joyce's decision might have far-reaching diplomatic implications.[15] In reporting the court decision next day, The *Times* hailed Chang's success as proof of British impartiality and concluded that the court's findings "will be useful to British capital and enterprise in the struggle now going on against formidable commercial rivals."[16] It was nothing less than a classic spin which ended by praising fair British legal practices in a world threatened by "formidable commercial rivals." Neither Herbert Hoover nor the Foreign Office was mentioned by name. Despite a court ruling to the contrary, Hoover remained on the board of the discredited British-based Chinese Engineering Mining Company until 1911, abetted in this defiance by the Foreign Office which considered coal for the navy more defensible than contempt of court.

A clear picture begins to emerge of Herbert Hoover's connections with the hidden power controlling British and American politics. He had assisted Alfred Milner in South Africa. He held shares in the Rothschilds' Rio Tinto Company and was associated with the same all-powerful Rothschild dynasty which invested in his Zinc Corporation. He had aided the South African mining millionaires Abe Bailey and Alfred Beit; all of whom operated at the innermost core of the Secret Elite.[17] He was defended in court by Richard Haldane and was well acquainted with several high-profile members of the British cabinet.[18] We know for certain that his acquaintance with Foreign Secretary Sir Edward Grey in the pre-war days was sufficiently close for Grey to ask Hoover if he might borrow his motor-car for a Sunday afternoon drive.[19] Even today you would have to be a close friend of anyone whose car you wished to borrow for an afternoon's drive. One hundred years ago, it surely indicated a very confident acquaintanceship. Lord Eustace Percy at the Foreign Office was Hoover's strong and loyal supporter, [20] as was Lord Crewe, the Leader of the House of Lords.[21] Hoover's association with all of these important Secret Elite politicians and financiers is a matter of record. In addition, he had close links to Belgian bankers like Emmanuel de Wouters and Emile Francqui, and institutions like the Banque d'Outremer and the Banque Belge pour l'Etranger. As the narrative unfolds, please keep all of these connections in mind. Herbert Hoover knew, and was known by, all the "right" people.

Hoover was a rabid opportunist. He had served the masters of international finance and spent his engineering career ruthlessly exploiting the underdeveloped resources of China, Australia, Burma, Russia and South Africa. His dealings mixed human traffic with raw materials, and ensured that he had the confidence of important Secret Elite backers who knew he was the right man to front their new enterprise in Belgium in 1914. Herbert Hoover had gravitated to London, the center of finance for worldwide mining. By August 1914 he had been based there for more than a decade. He held stock in zinc and gold mines in Australia, a fabulous zinc-lead-silver mine in Burma, copper mines and smelters in Russia, vast untapped mineral deposits in Siberia and the re-constituted oil fields in California.[22] Though not yet 40 when war broke out, he was very wealthy with a personal fortune estimated somewhere between three to four million dollars, lived in style in a magnificent Kensington villa, and worked from prestigious offices at no.1 London Wall buildings.[23]

Hoover's biographer would have us believe that in 1914 he experienced a "Road to Damascus" moment whereby his former Quaker background induced a complete change of character such that the mercenary engineer was transformed into a caring humanitarian. No matter how diligently his acolytes have striven to paint Hoover as a noble human being motivated entirely by good works for others, even the few official records made available to the public demonstrate a man who bullied, lied, cheated, manipulated and rewrote events to his own advantage. These were the qualities so admired by the Secrete Elite, for they knew that he would do their bidding, protected always by their global influence.

Herbert Hoover cast aside the mantle of the pitiless profit-seeking, opportunist engineer and had himself re-branded as a humanitarian savior just as the first wave of war refugees spilled into London in August 1914. They were Americans, stranded on the wrong side of the Atlantic by the unexpected outbreak of war in Europe. Most were tourists, school teachers with students, businessmen and the like. Four different support groups had been organized to help distressed Americans get home safely, but Hoover was not initially involved with any of them. The first American Citizens Committee was led by Fred I. Kent, vice-president of the Banker's Trust Co.[24] and the diplomat, Oscar Straus. Its Headquarters were sited in London's Savoy Hotel.[25] At the American embassy, the recently appointed U. S. Consul, Robert Skinner, could barely cope with inquires and angry demands for instant repatriation in the early chaos of those August days.

Step forward Herbert Clark Hoover. Watch carefully how he operated. Hoover let nothing stand in his way to gain control of a situation from which he could make money. He manipulated officials, lied about his circumstances, invented credentials, leaned heavily on government contacts in America and Britain and emerged triumphant. This was how Hoover did business.

Fred Kent and his American Citizens Committee had prompted the U.S. Ambassador, Walter Page, to seek funds from Washington to enable their stranded citizens to return quickly to the United States. Congress instantly approved an advance of $2,500,000 in gold on 5 August and sent it across the Atlantic on the USS *Tennessee* that same day.[26] Hoover smelled an opportunity and pushed his way to the fore. He claimed that Robert Skinner telephoned him in person and asked for his help. Skinner's version was that Hoover appeared out of the blue and offered his assistance.

Hoover next telephoned an associate in America, Lindon W. Bates, and asked him to approach the Wilson administration in Washington to appoint him as a special commissioner to handle the return of stranded Americans.[27] He convened a meeting of fellow mining engineers and trusted associates and had himself appointed chairman of a "Committee of American Residents in London for Assistance of American Travellers." He called Bates again on 6 August to announce that he had "today been elected President of a Relief Committee established in London by American residents to look after the 40,000 stranded Americans."[28] He did not mention that it was his own, self-styled, unauthorized committee.

Hoover meant business. Within 24 hours he printed stationary with the new committee's logo on the masthead. Like the proverbial cuckoo he moved in on Kent and the original American Citizen's Committee and pushed them out of the nest, claiming with his customary disregard for fact that his rescue group was organized under the "official auspices" of U.S. Ambassador Walter Page whom, he alleged, had agreed to be honorary chairman.[29] The Ambassador had not been consulted. Indeed on 9 August, Ambassador Page pointedly did not invite Hoover to join a committee empowered to distribute $300,000 in advance of the arrival of the USS *Tennessee*. Instead, he appointed Fred Kent.

Relationships deteriorated. When the Congressional money arrived in London on 16th August in the care of the U.S. under-secretary of war, Henry Breckinridge, Hoover magnanimously proposed that they join forces, but was rebuffed in no uncertain manner both by the under-secretary and the ambassador.[30] Why would they have surrendered a huge sum of public money to the care of an unknown American mining engineer resident in London?

Despite the clear antipathy expressed by both the American ambassador and the under-secretary for war, a seismic change in their opinion occurred, literally, overnight. It was as if there had been divine intervention. The situation was completely turned on its head. By the evening of 17 August, Hoover and his Resident's Committee had been formally invited by the Ambassador to take over and manage the entire distribution of the funds. Why? How? Neither Page nor Breckinridge knew or had worked with Hoover, so who instructed them that he should be entrusted not just with the money, but in his own words, "take over the entire distribution?"[31] Given that Kent had impeccable credentials in the United States as a high-profile banker from the J.P. Morgan stables and Straus was a government-favored diplomat, what more could Herbert Hoover have to offer? He too was associated with the Morgan empire in New York, but Hoover's connections traversed the Atlantic. He alone had Secret Elite backing from British politicians and business. That was the difference.

Hoover's victory was absolute. He was given undivided management of the congressional funds. Page also authorized Hoover to use the money to reimburse any costs which had already been incurred by the Resident's Committee. A "most opportune" subsidy, as he later described it.[32] This was not a change of heart; radical surgery had been involved.

In a private letter to President Wilson dated 23 August 1914, the ambassador reported that "the organization and measures for helping our stranded people were energetic and right..." thanks to the "Americans of ability who conducted the American Relief Committee."[33] Did he mean Hoover? What pressures were exerted on Page and Breckinridge to bring about such a complete about-turn? Who, within the darker recesses of Washington politics, could have authorized a decision so much at variance with the initial instincts of both the ambassador and the under-secretary? This is a very important question, and one which will be asked over and again. Who was behind Herbert Hoover? Unquestionably Hoover had many friends in, and associated with, the Wilson Administration in Washington and, as we have shown, in London.

When President Wilson approached Walter Page in 1912 with a view to his appointment as Ambassador to Great Britain, Page was reluctant to accept the position because he did not think that he could support himself in the necessary style, give lavish dinners and mix with the wealthy upper-class society of London.[34] Wilson arranged for his personal banker, Cleveland H. Dodge of the National City Bank of New York, to add $25,000 per annum to Page's account[35] to sweeten the burden of office. Cleveland Dodge was the financial powerhouse behind Woodrow Wilson.[36]

Thus Britain was gifted an American Ambassador financed by a major stock-holder of the National City Bank, who also happened to be one of America's munitions magnates[37] and financial collaborator with J.P. Morgan. Hoover's connections in Washington linked him to President Wilson's right-hand-man, Colonel Edward Mandell House and the Morgan banking empire. Strangely, while House's semi-autobiography, *The Intimate Papers of Colonel House,* contains no reference to Herbert Hoover, a volume of correspondence about Hoover and his work in Belgium, sent between House and the President, can be found in Woodrow Wilson's private papers.[38] What was House determined to hide?

Hoover allegedly "forsook his private pursuits" and entered the "slippery road of public life"[39] for the greater good of humanity. Events as they unfolded proved just how great a lie that was. He did not forsake his private pursuits. In fact, in order to take advantage of the excessive profits offered by the war, Hoover defied the international embargoes and Acts of Parliament by which the British government forbade trading with the enemy and bought cyanide from Germany for use in his mines in October 1914. At precisely the same time as he was thrusting himself forward at the Foreign Office as the one man who could save the starving in Belgium, he purchased a valuable shipment of the chemical from Germany through a Swiss agent. His cargo was carried down the Rhine to Rotterdam and paid for by the Swiss agent so that the cash transfer could not be traced back to him. Since both Holland and America were neutral countries, the transaction was untouchable. Once his cyanide was safely in Rotterdam it could be forwarded to almost any port in the world.

Hoover understood how business manipulated legal barriers, tax liability and contractual obligations. To deceive the British Censor, Hoover instructed his agent to use the word "stock" rather than "cyanide" when he cabled London.[40] His business "ethics" did not include loyalty. If the Germans could supply a product at a lower cost, he bought from Germans; war or no war. The Secret Elite understood.

Indeed, contrary to the impression that he abandoned his predatory capitalist instincts in favor of charitable humanitarianism, Hoover continued to promote his own business interests from 1 London Wall Buildings. His Russian investments (sold at profit quite miraculously before the Revolution of 1917) still earned him a sound return as did his holdings at Lake View and Oroya in Australia.[41] His Zinc Corporation, which he formed while in partnership with Bewick, Moreing & Co (of Kaiping infamy), flourished.[42] Though he did not attend the 1914 Annual General Meeting of the Burma Corporation in person due to his "duties connected with his position as President of the American Belgian Relief commission," his brother, Theodore, was present as a Board member.[43] Hoover wrote the Chairman's Report. It promised great wealth to investors, claimed that the company owned one of the ten most important mining discoveries since the turn of the century, and promised that the Burma Corporation would have "an important bearing on the future course of the world's production of lead, zinc and silver." With costs of extraction at £3 per ton and selling price a variable between £11- £18 per ton, expectations were high.[44] His prediction was no idle boast. Share prices later rose tenfold between August and December 1915.[45] Of course, as in any war, all sides paid high prices for the ores from which to manufacture death. Herbert Hoover was no humanitarian.

Shortly after the German invasion of Belgium, hundreds of thousands of refugees trudged westwards to France, across the channel to England and northeast to Holland, leaving behind a shocked and disoriented population. Estimates of the number of refugees vary widely from the CRB's conservative guess of approximately 600,000[46] to around 1.5 million.[47] The much lower number suited the CRB's more grandiose claims that around 9.5 million "otherwise inevitably starving people" who remained behind had to be fed.[48] Despite the destruction caused by the invaders, there was at first no shortage of food supplies.[49] However, some areas of the country were particularly badly affected by the German advance, and a number of different local committees set up organizations to provide food, clothing and even accommodation for those in distress. In a very short time, these groups had been amalgamated into an enormous supply chain which none of the belligerents "dared or cared" to stop.[50]

A number of important assumptions still exist which have helped conceal the clever sleight of hand behind the organized system that supplied food to both the civilians in Belgium and the German army on the Western Front. The first and most concerning is the extent to which the illusion of starvation or impending starvation in Belgium was created. Belgium was highly industrialized but at least 60 per cent of the country comprised rich agricultural land which was intensively cultivated. During the war years the general conditions of farming were sound, though modest.[51] When war broke out Belgium found herself in a very favorable position with regard to food stocks. The new cereal crop had been exceptionally good and, despite the presence of an invading army, there was at first no shortage of food and prices hardly rose.[52]

So from what evidence did the myth of a starving nation emerge? Haunting images exist of starving Boer children in South Africa, of starving German families and children in 1919, of the atrocities visited on the starving holocaust victims in 1945, of pitiful Biafran innocents in the 1960s, but not from Belgium in 1914. The immaculately staged images, published by the Hoover Institute, of Belgian children show large numbers[53] of adequately clothed youngsters with suppliant begging-bowls, presumably hungry. There is, however, a world of difference between hunger and starvation. There was need, no-one would deny that. But there was no evidence of a starving nation. There are no memorials to victims of starvation in Belgium during the First World War, as there are say, in Ireland to the millions who died in the great famine. Why has this myth been accepted as fact?

A second assumption spread by journalists and historians who have unquestioningly accepted the claims made by Herbert Hoover and his associates, was that the supply of emergency foodstuffs was undertaken by a single organization called the Commission for the Relief of Belgium, or as many preferred, the American Relief Committee. It was not. Two or-

Belgian Relief propaganda

ganizations were in operation, one from New York and London, the other from Brussels, but they rarely acted as, nor considered themselves to be one body. The third assumption is that these organizations were entirely charitable; indeed "benevolence" was their favored term.[54] Again, this is not true. Much of the food was sold and the profits allegedly flowed back to the relief fund to purchase more. How much this amounted to, we will never know. But this is the essential problem with Belgian relief in all of its guises; it has been successfully covered up and re-branded, and what is recorded, lends itself to myth.

The groups which emerged by the end of 1914 to provide food to Belgium (and later Northern France) gathered immense power and their prestige grew through a combination of bankers, financiers, racketeers, lawyers and politicians. They were unaccountable to any democratic chamber and wrote their own history. Though not all were motivated by self interest and greed, the system that operated favored the powerful banks. Indeed, with both the King and the Belgian government in exile, by November 1914 the Brussels Comite Nationale was regarded by many Belgians as the provisional government.[55]

Consider the initial response to a serious situation. The provision of adequate food for citizens caught up directly in the consequences of the German advance through Belgium towards Paris had caused an immediate problem. Many villages were totally destroyed and towns like Louvain, Dinant and Aerschot razed to the ground as the might of the German army pushed its way westward. Around twenty per cent of the population may have fled the country and the capital, Brussels, sheltered around 200,000 refugees.[56] Factories closed and civil servants and local government employees went unpaid. A "private charitable organization" was formed in

Brussels to counter the growing crisis by raising money to buy food and distribute it to the needy, unemployed or destitute in and around the city.

It described itself as a triumph of good organization and careful preparation which coordinated the disbursement through local volunteer relief agencies, distribution centers and uniform rationing. But food was not supplied free of charge. Only the "verifiably poor" received free rations and those who could, had to pay.[57] In Brussels the organizing group called itself the Comite Centrale and its most unusual feature was that it comprised virtually every senior banker in the land. Banks rarely involved themselves directly in charitable works unless, of course, there was an underlying benefit.

As the history of the Rothschilds has proved, certain banks are always first to know what is about to happen.[58] In 1912, two years before the cataclysm of world war, a series of events took place which anticipated what was to come to pass; events which made a mockery of Belgian "neutrality." King Albert convened a secret meeting of the Belgian parliament and disclosed that he had evidence that Belgium was in dire and imminent danger. Two crucial moves followed. Firstly, the strength of the Belgian army was raised by 340,000 men, an enormous expansion given the "neutral" status of a small nation.[59] Secondly, the National Bank of Belgium began preparations to cope with the financial emergency that war would bring. In utmost secrecy, they printed 5-Franc notes to replace silver coins and planned the transfer of their reserves of gold and note-making plates to vaults in the Bank of England in London.[60] Not only had the Belgian banks prepared for a war that no-one allegedly knew was coming, they had chosen sides. So much for neutral Belgium.

While this chapter focuses on the lesser known and often denied malpractices from which key players made fortunes, there can be no doubt that thousands of volunteers and civic administrators worked ceaselessly to feed and safeguard the ordinary citizen, man soup-kitchens, issue daily rations, provide milk and other suitable food for mothers and babies and shelter the destitute. The infant mortality rate in Belgium fell from 151 per 1,000 live births in 1914 to 119 by 1918[61] which would surely have been impossible in a nation wracked by starvation. In addition to food, a central warehouse was opened in Brussels in September 1914 to collect, restore, distribute and sell second-hand clothes.[62] This is a history of immense kindness on the part of many, and despicable exploitation by the few.

The task of sourcing foodstuffs from both inside Belgium and from neutral countries was initiated by the Comite Centrale in Brussels in September 1914. Dannie Heineman, an American-born electrical engineer who had spent most of his life in Germany, apparently suggested to the Comite Centrale that diplomatic channels might be opened with American and Spanish approval to purchase food abroad. Subsequently, the Comite authorized him to contact the German authorities. The official

CRB histories describe Heineman as an American businessman, resident in Brussels,[63] but this is entirely misleading. He was taken to Germany by his widowed mother when he was eight years old and was educated there, graduating from the Technical College of Hanover in 1895. His first post was in Berlin with a company directly associated with the American giant General Electric. In 1905, he headed a small three-man Belgian-German company which specialized in electric power and transport. Established by Belgian bankers, the Societe Financiere de Transports et d'Enterprises Industrielles (SOFINA) became a powerful player in the nascent energy industry. It grew into an international company employing 40,000 workers and owned tramway and electrical power systems throughout the world.[64] How could Heineman possibly have raised the finance to achieve such success? Who was backing him?

Dannie Heineman, the moving spirit,6[5] played a particularly important, though often underrated role in what followed because he was trusted by the Germans. Not everyone approved of him. The head of the American Legation at Brussels, Brand Whitlock, had reservations about Heinemann. He noted in his diary on 14 October 1914: "A call from Heineman towards noon. He has been discussing with his German friends the revictualing of the city and also the affairs of the banks. Heineman, invaluable, clever little Jew, eyes like a rat. Very strong with the Germans."[66] Quite apart from the despicable anti-semitic pejoratives, consider the implications here. Dannie Heinemann was first and foremost a friend of the Germans.

Time and again over the following three years, the chief role in negotiations with the German Governor-General "fell naturally" to Heineman.[67] By October 1914 he had been elevated to vice-chairman of the CRB and director of the Brussels office. Why? It is our contention that this man, who was closely linked to Germany was placed in a key operational role because it gave him ample scope to divert supplies to the occupying forces. Surely the British authorities were aware of this? It stood to reason that, no matter their assurances, the occupiers would abuse the proposed system. Were these not the same "heartless" Prussians lambasted for almost a decade by the British press for their inhumanity? Why would the Germans have agreed to allow the importation of foodstuffs into their area of occupation unless there were substantial benefits to their own war effort? And where does Heineman and "the affairs of the banks" fit into this jig-saw puzzle? The answer is at the very core of all that the Secret Elite constructed around the facade of humanitarian relief.

Heineman discussed the proposals with the German civil administration, which in turn approached the military authority to obtain the requisite permission to purchase food for Belgian citizens. Assurances that imported food would not be requisitioned by the German army were given to the American Legation. Further, promises were made that the Germans would not tax, seize or requisition any supplies imported by the Comite Centrale for the needs of the civilian population in Belgium. On the face of it, if the British government was prepared to allow the Americans to feed Belgian civilians; then the responsibility for doing so passed from the German occupiers. It was a win-win solution from their point of view. If Belgians were fed with imported food, it would make some of the food actually produced in Belgium available to the Germans to sustain their armies. From the start the German civil administration reserved the right to decide how and where flour and wheat were to be distributed.[68] The Comite would not have absolute control over distribution even though they pretended otherwise.

Dannie Heineman's close confidante, Millard Shaler, a mining engineer whose background, like that of Emile Francqui, lay in Belgium's cruel and ruthless exploitation of the Congo, was chosen to make representation to the British government. He duly made his way to London with a credit note for £20,000, and instructions from the Comite Centrale to buy foodstuffs on their behalf. Critically, he also carried the written assurance from the German Governor-General that they would not seize any of the food imported to feed the civil population.[69] Shaler was also instructed to meet a representative of the Banque Belge pour l'Etranger in London to organize, in co-operation with the Belgian Minister resident there, a sub-committee to raise funds and purchase food on their behalf.[70] The important point to recognize is that in these early days this was an all-Belgian affair, organized in conjunction with the Belgian government in exile in association with Belgian banks. Funding and purchasing was to be channeled through the largest Belgian private bank, the Société Générale de Belgique, a vitally important cog in all that was to transpire. Its London affiliate, the Banque Belge pour l'Etranger was the British connection. In what the bank's own history terms a "providentia" move, a direct link between the main Belgian bank's headquarters in Brussels and the London branch had been established in 1913. Amazing. What lay behind this providence?

The early success of the Brussels committee attracted the attention of a number of mayors and community representatives in other cities and districts who appealed to them for help, and the Comite Centrale's scope was widened to encompass most of occupied Belgium. Under the Presidency of Ernest Solvay, head of the international Solvay Chemical companies, and the patronage of the Spanish and American "Ambassadors"[71] as well as the Dutch Minister at Le Havre, the Comite Centrale expanded into a more important and influential organization called the Comite National de Secours et Alimentation. (CNSA)

It is no exaggeration to say that the Belgian people saw the CNSA as a symbol of opposition to German occupation. It had 125,000 agents operating in the cities and provinces, a visible sign of Belgian solidarity.[72] The ordinary people were doing their best to help others. They had no notion whatsoever that the CNSA was working in harmony with the German occupiers. Two vitally important factors should be made clear at this stage. Firstly, the CNSA was a Belgian affair. Secondly it's controllers were mostly creatures of finance and banking.

So how did Belgian Relief, which originated with the Comite Centrale in Brussels, mutate in the minds of most of the world into The Commission for Relief in Belgium and, by default, American Relief?

By September 1914 there was a proliferation of funding groups and organizations in Britain and America to support Belgium and Belgian refugees, and a considerable amount of money had been raised. Channelling food and basic essentials through war zones required the agreement of both neutral and belligerent governments; no easy task. The American Legation in Brussels willingly represented British subjects and British interests in occupied Belgium and maintained a proper but friendly relationship with the German civil administration. It was the obvious conduit for negotiations on food imports.

The first U.S. diplomat involved was Hugh Gibson, secretary to the American legation in Belgium. He arrived in London carrying messages of support for the Belgian Comite Centrale to Walter Page, the American Ambassador to Britain. By 6 October the diplomatic wheels were beginning to turn. Although the British government agreed that supplies of foodstuffs might be sent to Brussels through the good auspices of the American legation, approval for such an immense responsibility had not been granted by Washington. Indeed, the U.S. Secretary of State had yet to have it confirmed from Berlin that the German authorities would give their approval.[73] It was all very well for the German and Belgian authorities to agree on a local understanding, but its delivery demanded inter-government approval at the highest level. The proposal hung in the balance, tempting providence. While it would undoubtedly bring rich pickings, that was never the prime reason for Belgian Relief. Nor was it why the British government agreed to the deal. Every decision approved by the Secret Elite had a very clear objective; to prolong the war and crush Germany.

Take care not to fall into the habit of believing all that is written in official histories. They generally slip into convenient plausibility. In this instance, the notion that Herbert Hoover just happened to be available to give his time and effort for the good of the Belgian people, is fantasy. Hoover had never visited Belgium, but he had a long history connecting him to Belgian banks and Belgian investors in the Far East. In raising the necessary capital to facilitate the fraudulent take-over of the Kaiping mines in 1901, Hoover had turned to Belgian bankers and persuaded them to invest heavily. When he returned to China to finalize the fraud it was in the company of the Belgian aristocrat, Chevalier de Wouters.[74] Though they were both criticized for acting in bad faith by Mr Justice Joyce at the High

Court of Justice in 1905,[75] they continued to thrive in malpractice and manipulation. Hoover had also been associated with Emile Francqui, one of the richest men in Belgium, in the corrupt Chinese venture and was intrinsically connected by him to Belgian banks and investments. Hoover's interest in Belgium was not chance.

What is the truth behind Herbert Hoover's take-over of Belgian Relief? According to Tracy Kittredge's history (which Hoover later ordered destroyed) Millard Shaler, an American engineer residing in Brussels, traveled to London and approached Hoover on 26 September requesting his help.[76] However, according to Shaler's own account in his book "Development of the Relief Movement," it was a British Committee interested in the Belgian refugees which first approached Hoover for his assistance.[77] Now who could that have been? Who was involved with the "British Committee" which approached Herbert Hoover? Shaler's revelation is exceedingly important because it links Hoover and his consequent take-over of Belgian Relief with an unidentified interest group in Britain; a group whose standing empowered Herbert Hoover to move forward with their support and blessing.

Why Hoover? He was the perfect fit. Unscrupulous, greedy, a ruthless exploiter of men and opportunities, he was utterly devoid of humanitarian sympathies. Knowing as he did, that the scam would prolong the war and all of the misery that followed, Hoover had the complete confidence of the Secret Elite. He should have been neutral but his whole history was that of a rampant Anglophile who had built his success inside the British Empire and been richly rewarded. Hoover had lived so long in London "that he had fairly intimate relations with many men close to the British Government."[78] He knew the top men in Britain, and he knew how to railroad an organization and turn it into his own. His life's work had been built on such bully-boy tactics, whether the victims were farmers in the mid-west of the United States, miners in Australia, Chinese officials in Kaiping, Chinese "coolies" sold into slavery in the gold mines of South Africa,[79] or fellow Americans in London who had already organized relief for their stranded compatriots.[80] He used the same lies, the same half-truths, the same access to media exposure and the same patronage to get his way. The generally accepted story of how he achieved this "acquisition," and that is the most accurate term to describe his take-over of Belgian Relief, has been drawn from official documents as recorded by his great friends Hugh Gibson, Millard Shaler and Edgar Rickard, former editor of the Mining Engineer, men whose later success was bound to Hoover's coat tails.

Chosen for this task by the London elites who deliberately caused the war, Hoover visited Ambassador Walter Page on 10 October to seek diplomatic support for providing food for Belgium.[81] Please remember that virtually all of the "evidence" comes from Hoover, his close associates, and approved members of the Commission for the Relief of Belgium when he was unquestionably in charge of it. Two years later, when the Americans were attempting to rewrite the record and claim precedence over the original Belgian Comite Nationale, Edgar Rickard stated that Hoover had conferred with Ambassador Page in London as early as 4 October. Not so. Time and again, records relating to Herbert Hoover were altered or "lost," always to the benefit of the American "humanitarian."

Even Hoover's official biographer, George Nash, concluded that any claim that Hoover was involved prior to 6 October is at best un-corroborated.[82] Everyone agreed that Hoover was responsible for driving forward the Belgian Relief plans, whatever that actually meant, in October 1914. Not so. No one man could ever have managed such a gargantuan task. The Secret Elite ensured that he controlled their venture, its organization and its finance, but he operated through their trans-Atlantic tentacles, their banks, their shipping, their businesses. In 1916, Ambassador Page put in writing to Hoover that the Belgian Relief effort came "around you and at your suggestion."[83] Did he believe that, or did he just want to ensure that should the truth ever be revealed the blame could not be attached to himself? Whatever, it was not Hoover's suggestion.

An odd alliance developed between Hoover and Hugh Gibson, his man in the Brussels Legation, and Walter Page, the Ambassador in London. Basically, the diplomats colluded with Hoover in altering documents, writing and then rewriting their own history and using adulterated and fabricated reports to establish their accounts as the truth and justify their claims. A prime example of this tactic can be found in Hoover's manipulation of the American Press to sway opinion so that a sense of burning urgency lent pubic support to government decisions in Washington that would otherwise have been widely criticized. When the U.S. state department stalled over their involvement in Belgian Relief in October 1914, Hoover turned to his media allies. He was an "adroit manipulator of the levers of publicity"[84] and had cultivated a number of friends in the London press corps. These included a fellow alumnus of Stanford University, the "strategically placed" Ben S. Allen of Associated Press and Philip Patchin of the *Tribune*.

The initial announcement of an American organization for relief in Belgium appeared in a Press Association dispatch on 15 October 1914, in which Hoover outlined the plan. Firstly, he claimed that it was absolutely necessary that all funds collected for Belgian relief outside Britain should be centralized in his committee. Allegedly he wanted to avoid the problem of overlapping waste and intended to establish a single commission to absorb all the workers and committees already set up in London and Belgium.[85] In truth, this was the Secret Elite ensuring their absolute control. He also suggested that the best way to aid Belgian refugees would be to repatriate them, a task which could only be undertaken by an American organization in agreement with all the appropriate governments.[86] This strange and ridiculous suggestion was ignored by the Allies. Perhaps his success with the "repatriation" of Americans stranded in Europe had clouded his judgment. It was nonsense, but demonstrated Hoover's incapacity to grasp the reality of the situation. Repatriation in war-time would have been an act of gross inhumanity by the great "humanitarian."

From that early point Hoover's press releases were relentless. He wrote to state governors with appeals to state pride in being the "first" to fund a "Kansas" ship or a "Chicago" cargo. He organized personal appeals from King Albert of Belgium.[87] He learned to dramatize events so that every press release screamed of an immediate crisis. He made bold and deliberately vague claims that "the American commission for relief in Belgium ... was the only channel through which food can be introduced into Belgium, and by its association with a committee in Belgium, has the only effective agency for the distribution of food within that country."

So much for the leading role played by the Comite Nationale in Brussels. His press release also claimed that 80 per cent of the country was unemployed and the relief agencies needed $2,500,000 per month or the consequences would be dire. Laughably, he assured America that "every dollar represents actual food."[88] Headlines in major newspapers across the Allied countries screamed "America must feed Belgium this winter. There never was a famine emergency so great."[89] There was no famine. There was need, but his lies were deliberately set to alarm. They were intended to create the impression of crisis which would force governments and individuals to back the so-called Herbert Hoover initiative.

One of the main problems with which Hoover and his Commission for Relief in Belgium (CRB) had to contend was the proliferation of relief funds and war charities. Collections for Armenia, for the American Red Cross, for Jews suffering through the war, for prisoners of war, for the French wounded were among the many that sprang up like mushrooms in the United States.[90] Hoover had no time for other groups competing for charitable donations. His major concern was the Rockefeller Foundation which was independently organizing food and supplies for Belgium. To make matters worse, a well-respected New York philanthropist, Robert de Forest, formed yet another independent Belgian Relief Committee in America just days before the CRB was established. Keeping control of such organizations in the United States was much more problematic than holding a monopoly in Europe.

Hoover was concerned that the Rockefeller Foundation intended to establish an independent relief channel into Belgium which would supplant his own,[91] an intolerable situation given that it would undermine the Secret Elite plan to supply Germany. There was a financial consideration too. Had the Rockefeller Foundation won the day, they would have operated through

Rockefeller banks rather than the Morgan Guaranty Trust Bank through which future funds were to be channeled to Hoover. A counterattack was launched through the same channels Hoover had used to grab control of the American Citizens' Committee in London. He lied and misrepresented his status in precisely the same manner, and called on his powerful political connections to enable him to have his way.

Ambassador Page dutifully dispatched a blunt cable to the Rockefeller Foundation which, in all probability, was ghost-written by Hoover himself.[92] The telegram insisted that the CRB was the "only organization" recognized by both belligerents in the war, and the only one capable of co-ordinating support from all parts of the world. Hoover was absolutely insistent that shipping be organized by the CRB and wanted guarantees that the Rockefeller Foundation would restrict itself to the purchase and collection of food.[93] He would deal with the funds or, rather, Secret Elite associate J.P. Morgan Jr. would through his Guaranty Trust Bank of New York.

As part of his orchestrated move against the Rockefeller Foundation, Hoover had asked his friend and long term business associate, Lindon Bates, to open a branch office in New York to handle all shipping and transportation in the United States. While Hoover sought to give the CRB the appearance of inclusion by offering both the Rockefeller Foundation and de Forest representation on his Commission, he had no intention of sharing control with them. He informed Bates in a private letter that he did not "propose to be dictated to by any little hole in the corner organization in New York."[94] Hoover sent the Rockefeller Foundation a cable declaring that he had received a loan from the Belgian bankers which was absolutely conditional on his complete control of shipping and transportation.[95] Lie after lie. Dishonesty and deceit. Does this read like a humanitarian venture?

Hoover's close ties to the Anglo-American establishment had given him access to the sympathetic American Ambassadors, Walter Page in London and Brand Whitlock in Brussels. They stirred every issue to the advantage of the CRB, portraying a sense of immediate urgency either to the U.S. government or the press. In October Whitlock sent an alarming message to President Wilson advising that "in two weeks the civil population of Belgium will face starvation." He sought urgent support "to provide foods for the hungry ones in the dark days of the terrible winter that is coming on."[96] It all made good copy and Hoover's backers won the day.

To permit the smooth running of the CRB, agreements were co-ordinated through diplomatic channels that operated well above the scope and level of access to which any ordinary citizen was normally accustomed. At Hoover's request, Ambassador Page asked the British Foreign Office to designate a sufficiently important link with the Commission to obviate the red tape which constantly slowed down effective decision making. His personal friend, Sir Edward Grey, duly appointed Lord Eustace Percy. A member of the British establishment and the Secret Elite's Grillion's Club,[97] Percy fully co-operated with Hoover and enabled CRB members to go directly to senior government officials rather than wait for diplomatic permission.[98]

The Foreign Office liaised with the Belgians to rubber-stamp agreements between German military authorities and the neutral representatives, namely the American and Spanish Ambassadors in Belgium. The Spanish Ambassador, the formidable Marquis de Villalobar, an old-school aristocrat, "mad and touchy," according to Brand Whitlock,[99] was considered "ornamental" by Hoover[100] but that was both unfair and typical of Hoover's dismissive nature. The Spanish Ambassador proved to be exceptionally hard working on a day-to-day basis, and had no fear whatsoever of Prussian arrogance. That, he could equal.[101] He threw himself into the work, believing it to be a grand humanitarian effort and we have found no evidence to connect him to the Secret Elite.

The conditions under which the relief for Belgian civilians were permitted to operate were set in October 1914 and explained in a letter to Ambassador Page from the Foreign Office: "Sir Edward Grey has written to Baron Henri Lambert [a leading Belgian banker in the Comite National and related by marriage to the Rothschilds] telling him that we are not stopping any food supplies going to Rotterdam – from neutral countries in neutral ships – which we are satisfied are not for the use of the German Government or Army, and we shall not therefore interfere with the food supplies for the civil population of Belgium unless we have reason to suppose that the assurance given by Marshal von der Goltz to the American and Spanish Ministers is not being carried out."[102]

The Foreign Office, the Secret Elite's strongest arm in government, thus made it plain that Hoover's organization had their blessing. But Grey's letter was deliberately vague. As far as the British public were concerned, the Commission for Relief in Belgium was only permitted to operate under a series of strict and binding guarantees. The Germans guaranteed that they would not requisition supplies destined for the civil population.[103] Neutral governments, in this case America, Spain and Holland, agreed to monitor the relief agency, and the Belgian government in exile was required to approve the whole process. Neutral ships would carry the produce to a neutral port where the Comite Centrale (later the Comite National) would deal with its distribution. Ambassadors and heads of legations in Washington, Madrid, London, Berlin and Brussels were directly involved in a flurry of permits and promises.

A group of American students drawn from Oxford University, Rhodes scholars, were employed as neutral observers. They were supposed to check the imported produce, where it went and how it was disbursed so that the CRB could prove that the international conditions were met. In truth, if all twenty-five of them concentrated on a single ship-load, there was no certainty that they had the necessary skills to understand what was happening.

At no stage was the task of the Commission for Relief in Belgium (CRB) easy or straightforward. Despite all of the advantages of his connections both with the Secret Elite and the American and Belgian diplomatic corps, Hoover had to fight hard to establish his absolute control. He had then to ensure that it, and it alone, had a monopoly of foodstuffs supplied through Rotterdam to Belgium, and, most importantly of all, to Germany. That was the unspoken part of this complicated equation. Readers will find no reference in the official histories of supplies being directed to Germany, but they certainly were.

By the end of the first six months of the war, the structure was more or less in place. The CRB's headquarters in London was controlled absolutely by Hoover at no. 3 London Wall Buildings in the heart of the financial district. What grace of fortune kissed his venture and granted him rent-free premises two doors away from his own company offices in the very same prestigious London Wall Buildings?[104] Even more fortuitously, the firm which signed off on the final accounts covering October 1914 to September 1920, Deloitte, Plender, Griffiths & Co., were registered at 5 London Wall Buildings. Amazing. A century later these premises remain part of the J.P. Morgan empire in London.[105]

In many ways the organization that Hoover led was utterly unique. The CRB was unincorporated, had no legal status in commercial law, was unanswerable to any shareholders, had no prospectus or annual general meetings, no business plan or set targets, yet it signed up to international agreements, engaged in worldwide transactions and spent huge sums of money for which successful international banks willingly co-operated. It ran its own fleet of ships with its own flag. It made claim to be American but that, as we shall demonstrate, was also a flag of convenience. What Hoover constructed was described as "a piratical state organized for benevolence."[106]

More appropriately we would describe it as a piratical state organized for and by unaccountable men who masked the immense benefits they reaped for themselves behind the good works of others. They also masked their true objective – a war of sufficient length to crush Germany's economic prowess and remove her as a threat to Anglo-Saxon pre-eminence across the globe. All that was required was the money to pay for it.

Summary.

- A dark shadow still hangs over the history of Belgian Relief, like a dirty family secret which cannot be mentioned.
- All of the primary evidence about this "relief organization" was removed after the war on the instruction of its director, Herbert Hoover, and taken to America.

- What Hoover could not control, he tried to suppress. Those who dared make claims about the illegal nature of his dealings were quashed, threatened or otherwise marginalized.
- The Commission for Relief in Belgium (CRB) between 1914-1917 was called "the greatest humanitarian undertaking the world had ever seen" by its own historians and diarists.
- Belgian Relief was reputedly organized to feed the poor and needy in Belgium and northern France. In fact, through Belgian Relief, the German army was fed with much-needed supplies without which the war would have ended.
- The two main agencies involved were the Commission (CRB) in New York and London and the Comite Nationale des Secours et Alimentation (CNSA) in Brussels. Both were linked by profession, business or diplomatic status.
- Hoover was known to the Secret Elite, a business colleague of the Rothschilds, a friend of Alfred Milner, an ally to the Foreign Office and a disreputable fraudster and opportunist.
- He took charge of the relief committee for stranded Americans in August 1914 and although both Ambassador Page and the U.S. under-secretary of war tried to block his involvement, pressure was brought to bear to allow his control of funds sent from the United States.
- He retained his many mining-stockholdings and made a vast profit from them during the war.
- The first relief agency in Brussels was headed by a consortium of bankers, politicians and lawyers. Many had made their fortunes in the rape and exploitation of the Belgian Congo.
- The early success of the Brussels committee led to the cry for a national committee to provide for all of Belgium.
- According to Hoover, he was approached by a group of British interests to take control of the relief for Belgium.
- He was well connected with the international press and used his many contacts to push scare-stories about the absolute urgency of the impending starvation of the Belgian people.
- He effectively strangled all competition for relief so that he could control it all under his banner and funding was organized through the J.P. Morgan Guaranty Trust Bank of New York.
- A group of young Americans at Oxford, Rhodes Scholars, were recruited to act as neutral supervisors for the relief project. They were hopelessly ill-suited to the task.
- Hoover's CRB had no legal status in commercial law, had no shareholders to whom it was accountable, ran its own fleet of ships and flew its own flag.
- It was a piratical state organized for and by unaccountable men who hid their profiteering behind the good works of others.

Chapter 16

The Relief Of Belgium: A Generosity Of Bankers

Perhaps the cleverest aspect of the whole Commission for Relief in Belgium (CRB) business was that it dealt mainly in money and kept its own books, accountable to no-one. It sought more from all possible sources with unbridled avarice. Appeals for Belgian relief were initiated across the English-speaking world from 1914 onwards, and it has been assumed that the generous giving from ordinary people sustained the international program. This was simply untrue. Although the word American was literally stamped across all that was imported (it was generally called "American Relief" even in Belgium), most of the food for the people of Belgium and Northern France was financed by the Allied governments. So too, were the supplies that sustained Germany and the German army on the Western Front. The volume of funds required was enormous, and well beyond the scope of charity. Banks, and in particular banks that had international connections, were absolutely central to the control and abuse of Belgian relief.

As early as November 1914, a loan of $3,000,000 had been advanced from the immensely wealthy Belgian Bankers associated with the Comite Nationale for the purchase of food for Belgium. It was a loan, not a gift. However, Herbert Hoover unilaterally announced that these funds had been granted to his organization to be used for transportation. As previously explained, that was a lie aimed at undermining a rival organization under the Rockefeller banner. No such restriction had been laid down by the Belgians.[1] Indeed, at exactly the same time he was dictating that the loan from the Comite Nationale was for transport, Hoover was negotiating with American suppliers for free transportation of grain across the United States.[2] Hoover was absolutely determined to be the sole controller of money, food-purchase and transport and to crush any parallel charitable organization. Over the next three years he brooked no rival and successfully negotiated with national governments and international banks for loans totaling multiple millions of dollars ... and how and where it was spent. Such was the power he assumed that an independent observer might have believed it was Hoover's money.

Belgian banks formed a formidable and influential power-base at the core of European and international finance in the last decades of the nineteenth century and grew rich on the exploitation of the Congo, China and South America. The principal independent Belgian bank, the Société Générale de Belge stood above them all. From 1902 it launched a number of foreign expansions and in 1913, its most significant move was to make the Banque Sino-Belge an official subsidiary of the Société Générale under the title of the Banque-Belge pour L'Etranger.[3] To all intents this appeared to be a benign decision based on natural expansion, but its branch office in London served as the headquarters of the Société Générale outside occupied Belgium during the First World War. The connection was absolutely critical to the dealings of the Comite National.

A second important connection stemmed from the Banque d'Outremer, an international company for commerce and industry. Formed in 1899, its shares were owned by an interesting combination of Rothschild banks, Belgian financiers enriched by the rape of the Congo, and British investors close to the Secret Elite. The Société Générale was the largest subscriber closely followed by Rothschild's Banque de Paris et des Pays Bas, Banque Leon Lambert and Cassel & Cie. Both Sir Ernest Cassel, King Edward VII's banker[4] and Sir Vincent Caillard, of Vickers, friend of Lloyd George and Basil Zaharoff, were shareholders. Coincidentally, its specialty was mining and metallurgy and Banque d'Outremer bought large shareholdings in companies across the globe.[5]

A further "co-incidence" was that Emile Francqui, the President of the executive committee of the Comite Nationale de Secours et Alimentation, (CNSA) was a director of both banks, the Outremer from 1905-11 and the Société Générale from 1911 onwards. In 1915, when the Chairman of Outremer, Albert Thys, died suddenly, Francqui took control of both it and the Société Générale.[6] When one considers the financial and banking power held by these individuals alone and their direct association with the Secret Elite, it is little wonder that the phrase "money-power" became common parlance; the House of Rothschild, both in London and Paris; Ernest Cassel, Nathan Rothschild's financial associate in creating the armament's giant Vickers; Baron Leon Lambert, his son-in-law, who ran his own family bank; Emile Francqui had been King Leopold's man in the Congo. He was associated with Herbert Hoover in China and South Africa, controller of two of the most important banks in Belgium and President of the executive committee of the CNSA. All these men were all linked by blood or money. But that was only the tip of the financial imperium.

Almost every important Belgian banking houses was represented in the CNSA. Josse Allard, formerly a director of the Belgian mint, headed the Banque Allard et Cie, which in turn was affiliated to the Banque Josse Allard in Brussels and an associate of the Dreschner Bank in Germany.[7] But the links crossed the Atlantic too. Franz Philippson, head of the Banque Philippson, which was formed to finance loans for the independent state of Congo in 1888, joined with prominent American-German bankers Kuhn, Loeb and Co. in New York and their Hamburg banking colleagues, the Warburgs, to form a Portfolio company to specialize in selling U.S. securities in Europe. Because these banks were integral to the structure of the commercial life of Belgium and aided the Germans by guaranteeing payments to the occupying force, their foreign investments were not subject to interference. It proved a convenient understanding.

The Banque National de Belge, the National Bank of Belgium, (NBB) its central bank, had formerly printed all of the bank notes for the nation, but as punishment for transferring its gold reserves and "a large number of State bonds" to the Bank of England in August 1914[8] the Germans chose to operate through Francqui's Société Générale, thus giving it even more international kudos. The Banque Nationals' auditors had included Baron Leon Lambert of Rothschilds and intriguingly, Edward Bunge, the Antwerp banker and grain importer.

Edward Bunge's family connections reached into Argentina, where his brother Ernest and his brother-in-law, George Born, emigrated from Antwerp and by 1909 their grain exporting company, Bunge and Born owned Argentina's largest and most profitable flour mills, grain silos and harbor installations. They were the exporting arm in the joint business. Edward owned Bunge and Co. as the independent European outlet for the massive grain importing business and the operating hub for these companies was Antwerp.[9] Like many other rich entrepreneurs, Bunge and Co. had been involved in King Leopold's notorious exploitation in the Congo and administered the affairs of the company which was given rights over the 12,000 square miles of the Mongalla district by the Belgian monarch.[10] Trusted by the Belgian royal family, Edward Bunge was in a perfect position to both assist Hoover in purchasing grain and benefit spectacularly from the venture.

While Hoover and the Commission later produced a chart showing membership of the CNSA, the banking connections were hidden in a forest of names. While Hoover and the Commission later produced a chart showing membership details of the CNSA, the banking concerns were hidden in a forest of names. The president was President Ernest Solvay, the wealthiest industrialist in Europe. Solvay's firms were spread across the world and major plants and factories could be found in Germany, Austria, France, Belgium and America. The executive committee, the select group which was charged with day-to-day decision-making was chaired by Emile Francqui, director of the Société Générale and the single most powerful banker in Belgium. By the end of the war he was a man whom even wealthy bankers feared. Francqui was supported by men who held high office in the Société Générale or Solvay's companies, including Chevalier de Wouters d'Oplinter, the same co-accused who stood side by side with Herbert Hoover in the infamous London court case of 1905.[11]

They were ably assisted in full committee by Baron Leon Lambert, head of Banque Lambert, the second biggest private bank in Belgium. Both Lambert and Francqui had previously enjoyed direct involvement with the rabid Belgian exploitation of the Congo despite the atrocities that happened there.[12] Francqui had negotiated loans with the U.S. financier Pierpont Morgan on behalf of King Leopold II and on return to Belgium had invested his fortune in banking.[13] Dannie Heineman, an engineer of German descent, though born in America, was head of the international SOFINA Group and his associate, William Hulse, also of SOFINA were pro-German. SOFINA was founded in 1898 as a German company which held vital tram and electricity concessions in Spain, Argentina, Italy, the Austro-Hungarian Empire, France and Turkey.

Thus, the Comite Nationale was headed by the most important and influential industrialists and bankers in Belgium, whose assets crossed national boundaries. But the interconnections ran much deeper. They had holdings in minerals and ores essential for the war, chemicals that offered new ways of spreading death and foodstuffs located in neutral countries that could provide bread to the warring factions. They could make loans, underwrite borrowings and discount bills of exchange. Everything they did made a profit. This was surely one of the oddest collections of humanitarians in history. When the full committee met together there was also a coterie of King Albert's representatives, some high-placed lawyers and genuine politicians representing the complete spectrum of Belgian society, the Workers, the Catholics and the Conservatives, whose aim was to serve a needy people. But these were in a minority, kept away from the power-base executive which made the real decisions and reaped the eventual rewards.

More powerful than the barons of medieval England, the Comite Nationale dictated its own charter on 31 October 1914 and had it rubber-stamped by all of the delegates from across Belgium who depended on it. They announced that two new organizations had been created, one the Commission for Relief in Belgium, by this time, Hoover's CRB, and a second, the Provincial Committees whose work would be supervised by the delegates appointed by the Comite Nationale. They declared that the Comite Nationale would "maintain intimate co-operation" with the CRB through its offices in Brussels. However, the chief feature of this declaration of virtual self-government was the agreement that "the Comite National would centralize the accounts, fix the price of merchandise and look after the payment of supplies sold to the provincial committees."[14] Through this system, provincial committees paid the CNSA for the foodstuffs it received, and resold to consumers at fixed prices so that they could earn "a small profit." The local committees were also obliged to pay an insurance premium to cover any damage or misfortune that might befall their supplies.[15]

Furthermore, each provincial committee had to maintain an account with the Société Générale with sufficient funds to cover at least one month's shipments of food. This was not charitable humanitarianism; it was monopolistic control. The Comite National fixed the price of the food and clothing, whether donated or bought by Allied funds. Putting aside food allocated for the destitute, everything was sold for cash at a profit with payment guaranteed and the Société Générale as the central banker. Francqui and his banking associates literally set up a system where they could dictate ever rising prices, allocate the scarce resources and make ever-increasing profit. Even the cash flows ran through his all-powerful bank. And they called it benevolence. What impertinence.

Certainly Hoover had the backing of the financial power-houses of New York and London, but the Belgian banks boasted international muscle that challenged even his authority from time to time. The reader might wonder why, with so much wealth, the Belgian banks did not risk their assets to relieve their fellow-countrymen? What? They were banks, for goodness sake; banks don't operate charities, do they? Yet they would like you to believe that they played a major role in this relief scheme. That's what their records claim.

In August 1914, the Banque National de Belge transferred its gold reserves and "a large number of State bonds" to the Bank of England and despite protestations from the Germans that these assets should be returned, they remained safely in London vaults along with the printing blocks for official Belgian currency.[16] This arrangement had been previously agreed between the two countries, and though several members of the board of the National Bank of Belgium were sent to London by the Germans in February 1915 to "recover" bonds and gold, the mission was little more than tokenism. There were no circumstances under which gold would have been returned. Which raises the question of what was it all about?

The critical issue for bankers in early 1915 was the circulation of money, which was becoming an ever increasing problem for both the CRB and the occupying forces. A solution had to be found. Without money, commerce would shudder to a halt. Herbert Hoover journeyed to Berlin in February 1915 to meet, among others, the German Minister of Finance.[17] The Reichsbank offered to solve the impasse by raising a $50,000,000 loan in America, guaranteed by Germany, but to be repaid by Belgium. They suggested the construction of a "relief bank" but the proposal had to be rejected. No matter how important he considered himself, Hoover did not have the power to impose a $50,000,000 debt on the Belgian government.[18]

Another proposition demonstrated just how much the "Relief" business was worth to international bankers. According to Hoover's memorandum of the meeting on 4 February, 1915, the Germans suggested that the CRB might use "friends of the German Government in New York City" to discount their bills of exchange through Max Warburg in Hamburg and the New York banking firm of Kuhn, Loeb and Co. International trade worked effectively through this system whereby one party, say, a German importer pays for American grain by giving the American exporter a bill, much like a check, to be paid in three months time. If the exporter needs the cash early he can take the bill of exchange to a merchant bank, which will discount it. That means the bank will instantly pay him a sum of cash at less than the bill's value. The bank can afford to wait three months and take the full amount. It has always been big business. In wartime it was huge business.

The Warburg brothers, Max and Paul, were key players in international finance. Like the J.P. Morgan empire, both Warburgs had strong Rothschild connections.[19] Paul had been instrumental in the creation of the Federal Reserve System in America, and basically both these men were deeply involved in the business deals which were wrapped around Belgian Relief. How convenient was this for the Secret Elite? Max Warburg offered to take over the market in discounting South American grain bills[20] which would divert the profits from London.

Later that same evening, Warburg met with Hoover at Berlin's Adlon hotel and talked about his great success in discounting bills for cotton shipments from America to Germany through Kuhn, Loeb in New York. He believed that his firm could offer a better return for discounting the grain bills.[21] Next day, Hoover held talks with Albert Ballin, head of the Hamburg-America shipping line, and a frequent visitor to London before the war.

Indeed Ballin's connections in Britain gave him access to Secret Elite controlled politicians and, days before the final declaration of war, he went to London "ostensibly on business." Here he met Sir Edward Grey, Richard Haldane and Winston Churchill but we do not know what transpired.[22] Official histories limit their discussions to assurances given to Ballin that Britain would remain neutral, but was that all? Barely one week later, Albert Ballin and Max Warburg had been put in charge of the Zentraleinkaufsgesellschaft, (ZEG) the state-owned organization charged with purchasing food for Germany from foreign countries.[23]

The Hoover memorandum stated that Ballin was keen to have his impounded Hamburg-American merchant ships released for use by the CRB,[24] but Hoover knew that it would not have been acceptable to the British public for German ships to carry goods freely across the Atlantic. Having taken a cargo to Rotterdam, it would have been comparatively easy for Ballin's ships to slip into German waters. It was a bridge too far even for the Secret Elite. However there was another consideration. Both men were rivals for the scarce commodity, food.

Hoover had the great advantage of access to the world market, while Ballin was restricted to the Romanian grain harvest and what could be imported from America through the mock blockade. Ballin would also have known about the vast quantities of CRB imports flowing through Rotterdam, and precisely how much was being diverted to Germany. Given that Albert Ballin was in charge of German food procurement, and Herbert Hoover headed the Commission for the Relief of Belgium, how likely is it that their talks were limited to shipping and finance? Are we to believe that Hoover and Ballin failed to talk about food importation? Be mindful that Hoover's memorandum is the only known record of their discussions.

Hoover's visit continued with a meeting with the financial advisor to the Imperial government in the company of Max Warburg who repeated "two or three times" that his brother's influence with the Federal Reserve System would be financially beneficial to the CRB.[25] The Warburgs were desperate to muscle into the markets for discounting bills of exchange, and the claim that they had influence over the Federal Reserve in New York was no mean boast. Unfortunately for them, so too did J.P. Morgan. Both sides had to find a solution to the tricky problem of money. Without money workers couldn't be paid, pensioners would go penniless and trade would stutter to a standstill. Faced with that reality-check, both the Belgian government in exile and the German government of occupation accepted a solution which was mutually beneficial.

Emile Francqui's Société Générale was appointed to act as the national bank in Belgium, and was granted the exclusive right to issue banknotes until 20 November, 1918.[26] Instructed by the German authorities, these notes did not carry any national emblem or picture of the Belgian royal family or indeed anything that symbolized patriotic loyalty.[27] By this point Emile Francqui had become the "national mediator"[28] and little wonder, given the power that was devolved to his bank. Naturally, banks charged for their services, and the Société Générale had much to gain. More pertinently, this arrangement suited all parties, belligerent and neutral, and helped prolong the war.

When Herbert Hoover negotiated the massive loans for Belgian Relief from Allied governments he used the J.P. Morgan organizations in America, co-ordinated through Morgan Guaranty Trust of New York which, in turn, made the requisite transfer to London. Part of the "money" was then transferred on paper to Banque Belge pour L'Etranger in London to pay for civil servants, pensioners, schoolteachers and many other Belgian government workers. From there, the money was transferred to the Société Générale in Brussels.

Though this was managed on ledger accounts, like all paper currencies, if accepted in exchange, the system worked. The Société Générale had, under German authorization, printed acceptable banknotes estimated at 1,600,000,000 Fr which circulated through the economy and underscored trade and commerce. Franqui's bank was permitted to issue bills to the value of three times its holdings in gold, in foreign currency, in Reichsmarks and in credits on foreign banks.[29] The Société Générale's role was, therefore, absolute. Francqui was the bankers' banker. At this point, with an acceptable currency in circulation and used by both the public and by international banks, the German government imposed a 40,000,000 Fr (£1,600,000) tax per month on Belgium. This equates to £114,500,000 per month at today's values. There was muted outrage, but little else. The bankers protested, but paid up rather than risk their personal fortunes. The Germans had agreed on an important trade off. They did not interfere with overseas investments held by Belgian Banks. Perhaps that is why their protests amounted to a mere whimper.

There was an additional problem with the lack of money in circulation. Belgians were by nature cautious and inclined to save their spare income. In any case there were very few luxuries available outside the American Relief shops in Brussels and Antwerp. However, in September 1916, the occupying force took stringent measures to annex the public savings accounts in both the Banque National de Belge and the Société Générale. They demanded that the funds held in Reichsbank notes be transferred back to German control or the banks would be sequestered. Whether or not the threat was real, $120,000,000 was collected for the German treasury and transferred to Berlin.[30] Germany first imposed a tax and carried off about one quarter of the money which the American loans had guaranteed, and then annexed savings. This money boosted the Reichsbank's holdings and was used by the German government to buy foreign goods. So the war was effectively prolonged because Belgian Relief provided Germany with food to sustain her armies and funds to pay for her war effort.

The popular belief was that the funds used for Belgian relief came from public charity, mostly of American origin. Not so. Though Hoover embarked on many fund-raising initiatives and made constant appeals to individuals, national groups, even Pope Benedict XV, whose Papal message to America in early December 1916 was strategically timed to coincide with Christmas gift-giving,[31] the major source of income came from official government loans organized through J.P. Morgan's American consortium. In early 1915, Hoover had negotiated an Anglo-French-Belgian subsidy of $5,000,000 per month and in 1916 this was increased by 50% to $7,500,000 per month.[32] In 1917, The *New York Times* ran an article which implied that Hoover was being "shamed" by the paucity of charitable funds sent from the USA, a mere $9,000,000 (under 4%) of the total

$250,000,000 spent by the end of 1916, even though "fat profits had been made in America from the sale of supplies for Belgium."[33] It was a clever ploy, targeted at American public conscience, for Hoover did not care where his funds came from. Nor do his figures make sense. Thousands of committees had been formed to collect funds. The *Literary Digest* alone donated over $300,000 and numerous institutions, magazines and newspapers in America "gave till it hurt."[34] We will never know the true extent of the fraud.

Once America declared war in April 1917, Hoover was able to access even greater funds from the U.S. government, which agreed to contribute directly. In May 1917, $75,000,000 was appropriated for his use. The incredible fact is that these sums were credited to the French, British and Belgian Governments, but spent, as in all cases by the CRB. The money from the American Government was advanced in installments of $12,500,000 per month, of which $7,500,000 went to Belgium and $5,000,000 to France, whether or not the aforementioned had asked for it.[35] These were awesome figures and the language used signaled Hoover's primacy in deciding how funds were to be spent. His agencies decided what would be bought from suppliers all over the globe, which shipping agencies would carry the cargoes, which distributors would be employed. Fortunes were made.

Hoover was fearless in overspending other people's money. By mid-1916 the commission's expenditure in Belgium exceeded its income by $2,000,000 a month,[36] but Hoover knew that he would be able to source the funding for the simple reason that it was planned. The political will was there; it simply had to find reasons. Financial muscle was never far from his center of power. The Morgan/Rothschild axis was wrapped around the entire project; but they were not the givers, they were not donating funds; they acted as suppliers of funds ... at a price. They were bankers.

Summary.

- Banks, and loans from America, not generosity, sustained the relief work in Belgium, and by default, aided the supply to Germany.
- Powerful Belgian banks were dominated by the Society Generale de Belge, headed by Hoover's former colleague and friend, Emile Francqui.
- Almost every Belgian bank was involved in the CNSA. It centralized its accounts, fixed prices for the merchandise received they received through the relief program and resold it at a profit. Local committees were even obliged to pay an insurance premium to cover any loss.
- The National Bank of Belgium had transferred all of its gold reserves, bonds and printing presses for notes to London in August 1914.
- Hoover did have competitors for the market in foodstuffs. The Warburgs in Germany, with their direct links to Kuhn Loeb in New York, wanted to muscle into the markets which Hoover dominated on behalf of

the J.P. Morgan banks. Warburg claimed that his family had influence over the Federal Reserve in New York and it would be beneficial to the CRB to discount bills through him.

- Paper money proved to be a problem. The Society Generale was appointed issuer of bank notes by the German occupiers in Germany.
- The flow of money was co-ordinated through Morgan Guaranty in New York to London, transferred to Banque Belge pour L'Etranger in London and thence transferred to the Societe Generle in Brussels. Here money was printed for use.
- The Germans taxed the Belgians and carried off about one quarter of the money which American loans guaranteed. They then annexed savings.
- When America joined the war in 1917, the sums multiplied. The CRB spending exceeded $2,000,000 per month.

Chapter 17

The Relief Of Belgium – Pirates At War

Because the official histories of the First World War omit the Commission for Relief in Belgium, the extent of the deception has gone unnoticed. How could the flow of foodstuffs be maintained in such quantities that the Belgian need was more or less met and at the same time the German people and army were able to benefit from the great volume of supplies that became available? Did no-one see this? Were there no complaints? Surely, with such massive sums of money flowing between New York and London, and the volume of trade between America, Rotterdam and Brussels so obvious, that malpractice could not be hidden from public scrutiny. The answer is remarkably straight-forward. It was. There was no scrutiny.

We know that the Germans gave the necessary formal assurances in a letter to the American Legation headed by Brand Whitlock, on 14 November 1914. They promised faithfully that any imported supplies would be scrupulously respected, free from seizure or requisition and their possession, control and disposition would be entirely in the hands of the Comite Nationale de Secours et Alimentation (CNSA).[1] All went well until Hoover's claims of imminent disaster were unmasked by an article published in the *New York Times* on 22 November 1914. The personal adjutant to the military governor at Antwerp mocked the claim that the Belgian people were on the brink of starvation. He boasted that "an inter-communal commission had been organised at our suggestion and that all districts are being supplied." The adjutant[2] claimed that "if America has not been so soft-hearted as to send foodstuffs ... we should certainly have considered it our duty to bring food from Germany, for ... it is our duty to see that the people do not starve."[3] He was of course, absolutely correct, but this was precisely the message which could have destroyed the CRB before it was fully established. Hoover and the commission stamped on it immediately. When he threatened to close down American Relief, the German Government quickly denied the claim and thanked the Americans for their vital work in helping avoid starvation.[4] Apparently, it was a misunderstanding made worse through poor translation. Not so. It was the very truth that everyone involved feared might spoil one of the world's greatest con jobs.

Caution became the by-word. Great care had to be taken to avoid alerting detractors to the scheme. In London, the British cabinet was split over the issue of supplying food to Belgium. Indeed the impression given in October 1914 was that cabinet ministers thought they were discussing whether or not to approve the entry of food into Holland under the guarantee of the Spanish and American Ministers, to be used solely for refugee Belgians[5] rather than the entire civilian population. Kitchener, Churchill and Lloyd George voiced concerns that the Germans would use these supplies and take advantage of Belgian produce, but Grey, Haldane and Asquith were in favor and despite objections, the "relief" went ahead. How unusual. The ministers for war and the Admiralty, the voices of the army and navy, were strongly set against the importation of food to Belgium, as was a majority in cabinet, yet it went ahead.

As early as December 1914, when Hoover was thwarted by the slow progress in obtaining the necessary funds to kick-start the CRB, he received a prudent note from Lord Eustace Percy at the Foreign Office. Knowing who and what he represented, Hoover expected doors to open and government approval given automatically at every turn, but the Secret Elite could not deliver instant success. As ever, the ordinary person's opinion remained vital to public support for the war. Matters had to be agreed in secret.

Churchill's department was positively obstructive. The Admiralty Trade Division took independent action to dissuade shipowners carrying cargoes of food to Dutch ports, [6] stating unequivocally that "the Admiralty considers it most undesirable that any British vessels should be employed in adding to the already very large supplies of grain etc., which are flowing into Holland." Such interference had to be stopped and Lord Percy leapt to Hoover's support stating that he would "push the matter with all the force I can."

What Lord Percy promised was unequivocal. His actions confirmed that a coterie inside the Cabinet was fully committed to support the CRB, even though, from time to time, newspapers complained that the Germans were siphoning off the food supplies. Percy calmed the turbulence by assuring Hoover that:

> ...you must not let the momentary difficulties created by the action of overworked officials at the Admiralty or elsewhere dishearten you. Neither must you feel hurt if I put to you from time to time the unfounded rumours we hear about what is happening in Belgium. I want to nail the lies as they come up, but you mustn't take any such enquiry as indicating that our sympathy with you in your work is slackening in any way. Whatever appearances may be, please accept my word of honour that we only desire to help, not interfere.[7]

"Unfounded rumours ... nail the lies ... my word of honour ... we only desire to help." This was a letter of affirmation, a promise to Hoover that the Foreign Office was right behind him, even though from time to time, it may have to appear to take a different public stance. Games would be played. Warring sides would have to appear to be at cross purposes. But "our sympathy with you in your work" will not slacken. It was a promissory note. And Lord Eustace Percy, on behalf of the Secret Elite, was as good as his word.

Hoover was not. He was prepared to make any promise, give any assurance and fabricate any answer to promote his venture and mask the real picture. In this he was greatly helped by Chancellor Lloyd George's dramatic conversion from Cabinet skeptic to Treasury enthusiast. Hoover wrote a memorandum of a meeting on 21 January 1915 with Lloyd George, Lord Emmott,[8] Lord Eustace Percy and the Attorney General Sir John Simon, a personal friend of Secret Elite leader Alfred Milner and valued member of the cabal.[9] At the start of the meeting Lloyd George made it plain that he would veto Hoover's proposals about the international exchange of money to facilitate the CRB 's work because Belgian Relief was assisting the enemy. By the end he had apparently undergone a personal epiphany to the extent that he gave his instant approval to Hoover's proposals.[10] Yet again a key player changed his stance to fall in line with the Secret Elite. How could Lloyd George switch from his conviction at the start of the meeting that Belgian Relief was aiding the enemy and thus prolonging the war, to an absolute about-turn which gave it his full support?

When asked by Lloyd George in February 1915 to put the needs of the civilian population of Belgium on paper, Hoover produced a memorandum which began: "Except for the bread stuffs imported by this Commission there is not one ounce of bread in Belgium today."[11] He must have been aware that there were a large number of civilians in Belgium and Holland who knew better. There were spy rings and information flowed regularly across the English Channel.[12] Every alleged fact he produced could be checked out, but it was grist-to-the-mill of the propaganda machine. Although Hoover continued his bombast, he was prepared to concede that "foodstuffs are sold at a small profit in order to compel the more well-to-do population to assist in the support of the destitute." What arrant nonsense. Food prices in Belgium were continuously raised by the CNSA and the profits never satisfactorily recorded.

Herbert Hoover stated categorically that "there has never been any interference (by the German government) with the foodstuffs introduced by us. We can account to the satisfaction of any auditor for every sack of wheat from the time it leaves Rotterdam until it reaches the Belgian civil consumer."[13] This lie was to be unmasked later, but in February 1915 Hoover raised the stakes with a more extreme threat: "Unless foodstuffs are introduced into Belgium from foreign sources, the decimation of this population will begin in thirty days."[14] Threat of the ultimate starvation of the Belgian nation was to become a constant theme in newspaper articles and appeals voiced by members of the CRB. There was never any evidence of "ultimate starvation." Yet the myth remained unchallenged even in Belgium. Strange.

In early March 1915, Hoover complained to Ambassador Whitlock, "I have had a severe drilling this week from the English Government with regard to our whole organization in Belgium."[15] He was upset that they were investigating the claims he had formerly made due to "the constant lying reports which appear in the English press as regards to our food-stuffs being taken by the Germans or devoted to their requisitions in the operations zone." Hoover knew that there was what he called "the military party," which included Churchill and Kitchener, ever ready to find fault. He had to be careful. Complaints had been lodged that there were not enough independent Americans employed to oversee the distribution: "I told them we had about fifty Americans at work, which was deemed insufficient." Later in the same letter, Hoover admitted that he had lied to the British Government: "I am assured that if the knowledge came to them that our staff had been limited to twenty-five members, they would at once say that this is absolutely inadequate."[16] It was a sure sign of complicity that he confided so intimately with the ambassador. CRB was not going to comply with the official demands. It didn't have to. Lord Percy had explained; no matter how it might be made to look, "please accept my word of honor that we only desire to help."[17]

This particular passage completely undermined Hoover's claim that every sack of flour was accounted for. It also laid bare the naked lie that sufficient independent American observers were employed to ensure that the Germans fulfilled the conditions of non-interference. Given the thousands of kilometers of canals and rivers in Belgium, the broken roads and railways, where dangerous passage had to be negotiated carefully and by-roads and diversions abounded, how could twenty-five American Rhodes scholars plucked from Oxford undertake this task properly?[18] These well-meaning undergraduate students may have had a smattering of French, but were ignorant of Flemish or the Walloon dialect, and were accompanied everywhere by Germans who dictated what they saw and where they saw it.[19] Although they had been warned to expect personal hardship, the "observers" had "luxuries thrust upon them, chateaux in which to live, automobiles in which to ride, and appointed offices in which to work."[20]

To add insult to injury, the American Legation staff in Brussels quickly came to the conclusion that the Rhodes scholars lacked maturity and discretion and had a conceit of themselves which made relationships difficult. One volunteer from Oxford told Brand Whitlock that God had called him to go to Belgium. Whitlock was determined to obtain "through

Hoover's intercession" a call for him to go back.[21] The Germans ensured that these American students found it impossible to keep a close scrutiny on the importation and delivery of foreign foodstuffs. The Rhodes scholars served the Secret Elite purpose as a mere fop to the pretense that the food was destined for Belgian mouths only.

Hoover lied without compunction. Indeed his communications with the German Governor, General Moritz von Bissing, proved that at exactly the same time as he was vying for Lloyd George's financial commitment, Hoover warned the Germans that the English Government strongly objected to the introduction of foodstuffs into Belgium on the grounds that it absolved Germany from the duty of feeding the Belgians ... "which was a great military advantage to the Germans and a great military disadvantage to the English."[22] And finally he touched on the truth, "We feel that while our service is personally beneficial to the Belgian civil population, it is nevertheless of the utmost importance to the Germans from every point of view."[23]

While Hoover had approached his appeal to Lloyd George from the standpoint that Britain had a responsibility to save the Belgians from starvation, his position with General von Bissing was that this whole organization worked to the utmost benefit of the Imperial German Army "from every point of view." The subtext clearly warned von Bissing that if the CRB withdrew, the consequences for the German war effort would be disastrous.

The Germans could be very difficult about the number of passes granted to American observers, and when the novelty of chaperoning the Rhodes scholars wore off, they treated some of them with contempt. The American Under-Secretary Hugh Gibson squared up to Baron Oscar von der Lanken, who headed the German political department, in November 1915 and submitted a memorable note of the meeting. Gibson complained bitterly that while German authorities in occupied Belgium placed all kinds of obstacles in the way of CRB, the military authorities in the North of France "evidently understood the vital importance of the work." He warned the Baron that if the Americans withdrew, the British Government would not entertain any other neutrals taking over. Von der Lancken retorted petulantly that Germany "has plenty of food now [late 1915] coming from the Balkans and that the Belgians would not starve."[24]

Gibson's reply was very instructive. In sarcastic mode he regretted that the Germans had not informed the CRB of this at an earlier meeting. He pointed out that the relief agency continued the work "only because we thought it was needed by the German Government as well as by other belligerents." Consider that statement. Gibson acknowledged that the CRB continued its work because it thought the importation of foodstuffs "was needed by the German Government...." The Commission was working for Germany too. Von der Lancken of course knew this and apologized profusely.[25]

In fact the exchange between Gibson and von der Lancken was a double-bluff which added more to the charade which surrounded the importation of supplies, than the reality of what was actually happening. Both knew that the German army was desperate for the supplies of food that flowed through the port of Rotterdam. Oscar von der Lanken spoke with the forked tongue we have long associated with senior members of diplomatic corps. His official reports to Berlin told a very different story. He and members of his department met with the CNSA on a daily basis and, as he saw it, constantly thwarted the CNSA's attempts to lay down the law in Belgium.[26] The Germans were also sensitive to their vulnerability to spying and took measures "to make espionage and the transmission of illicit information to Britain, as was practiced by some members of the CNSA, impossible."[27] The comment was written in August 1915.

Germany's very survival depended on the continuation of the Belgian Relief agencies. When the British Foreign Office laid down conditions and demands in response to revelations in the London press that Germany was requisitioning Belgian produce, these could not be ignored. Von der Lancken wrote in his report to Berlin in August 1916 that the whole question of wheat imports was so critical to survival, that the British government should be given no excuse to suspend the CNSA's activities. In his 1916 reports he acknowledged that the continuation of food supplies to Belgium and the North of France was of "major self-interest to the Reich"[28] Interestingly, when the German authorities backed down from wholesale removal of the Belgian harvest, von der Lancken noted that German soldiers could still buy produce from Belgians for their personal use with the approval of the British government.[29] One can but wonder what the Allied troops confined to the filthy strictures of trench warfare would have made of that fact?

As his official reports between 1915 and 1918 demonstrated, von der Lancken took pride in Germany's success in using the CRB to its own benefit. He mocked the ineffective checks made by the Rhodes students writing:

"In spite of this supervision, we have, once again, successfully routed an appreciable quantity of foodstuffs to the [western] front or to Germany, and ... made use of local products for the occupying force ... by means of the clauses which were kept voluntarily elastic or thanks to arrangements contracted secretly with the neutral committee or again with their unspoken tolerance."[30] This was a breathtaking admission which blew apart all other claims that Germany did not interfere with the food for Belgium.

Von der Lancken's reports indicated collusion and collaboration. He clearly admitted that the German authorities were secretly re-routing appreciable quantities of relief food both to the army at the front and to the civilian population in Germany. Furthermore he explained how it was done. The elasticity of the regulations which were supposed to ensure that the foodstuffs went only to the needy Belgian population made a nonsense of such claims. In another official report he scorned the agreements within which the German army of occupation was supposed to operate as "deliberately woolly and vague," claiming that the advantages that Germany gained from the work of the CRB continued to grow apace.[31] Sadly, no mainstream historian appears to have spoken out against this scandal.

Let there be no doubt. The German army and its subsequent capacity to continue the war depended on the continued success of The Commission for Relief in Belgium. How much plainer can we be? The CRB played its part in deliberately prolonging the war.

Despite the backing of the most powerful and influential men in Britain, France and America, the Commission for Relief in Belgium (CRB) frequently ran into both international and local squabbles which threatened to undermine its prime objective; to prolong the war by feeding both Belgium and the German army. Personal relationships, human frailty, including jealousy, and the lure of making even more from the rich pickings, motivated a greed which could well have back-fired in many different ways.

Rumblings at Westminster tended to be muted in the early stages of the war, but by 1916 more and more MPs voiced their concerns about the relief program. They asked questions about the total value in Belgium of the foodstuffs imported by the Neutral Relief Commission (another name for the CRB) and the amount of contributions made by the United States, by other neutrals, by the British Empire and by other Allied governments.[32] Critics quickly became swamped by an avalanche of disinformation that included the tonnage of foodstuffs, including bacon and lard exported to Belgium. Lard was of particular interest because glycerin for high explosives could be extracted from it.[33] Parliamentary suspicions were entirely justified. Food certainly flowed into the German ranks, whether by the requisition of home-grown products or resale of imports by unscrupulous Belgians, but overwhelmingly it was sanctioned by secret agreement between the CRB/CNSA and the German government. Baron von der Lancken's official reports proved that.[34]

On 21 January 1916 Lord Eustace Percy wrote a worrying letter to Herbert Hoover about the volume of rice which had been stockpiled in Belgium by the CRB. He was "much disturbed" to find that large quantities had been re-exported to Germany through Holland and been sold to the Germans "by the Relief Committee in Belgium."[35] Emile Francqui assured Hoover that the matter had been investigated and that the "information" from Lord Percy was exaggerated. Apparently it was the fault of a private German company which bought the food from a Belgian dealer who purchased the rice from "consumers." Hoover's problem was that while he had Foreign Office approval to import 5,000 tons of rice per month, between September and November around 34,000 tons had been landed, much more than double the agreed amount. Percy threatened to ban the import of rice until the Germans handed over an equivalent amount from their own stock. Hoover's response was firstly to rebut the statistics used by the Foreign Office and added that "some of the local committees, finding the fabulous price at which they could sell rice, have done so entirely in innocence of heart and have invested the money in potatoes...."[36] There was no innocence of heart in black-marketeers.

In March 1916 Lord Percy wrote another concerned letter to Hoover. He had received reports from an "unusually trustworthy" source that as much as half of the food imported by the Commission to the district of Ghent was going directly to the German army or being redirected to Breslau in Germany. Between November 1915 and January 1916, British sources claimed that seven boatloads of coffee, rice, beans, flour and oil nuts, some 4,200 tons in total had reached Germany through Holland. Lord Percy named one particular mill owner in Brussels who was extracting oil from the milling process and selling it to the Germans "for munitions purposes."[37] Hoover's standard reply was to insist that the total leakage was very small but that the smuggling of overseas material through Holland was much greater than previously believed.[38] Deny, deflect and deceive were his watchwords, but constant complaints that the concession to the CRB was indeed feeding the enemy, gathered volume.

There was a further dimension that appeared to be scrupulously ignored. Belgians knew that the system was being abused by their own countrymen. At first the Comite Nationale made little effort to monitor the day-to-day workings of the provincial committees but by December 1915 they had to acknowledge the "innumerable breakages of their instructions" were leading to serious abuses which had caused adverse comment abroad. The CNSA conceded in their report on general operations in 1915 that imported foodstuffs were not being exclusively sold in their appointed shops or being distinctively identified as relief produce,[39] which had been part of the basic agreement. In other words, the focus was limited to Belgians who were ignoring the rules and selling or reselling food to the Germans. By so doing, attention was drawn away from the greater scandal – Hoover's Faustian pact with the German government.

In Parliament, honorable members sharpened their questions when the German government of occupation began to use food provision as an inducement to encourage unemployed Belgians to work for them.[40] Lord Robert Cecil, Under Secretary for Foreign Affairs dismissed the claims: "I cannot agree that the alleged facts are admitted." The Foreign Office simply closed down discussion.[41] MPs were also rightly anxious about the volume of maize and other foodstuffs imported into Holland (the inference being that such product was then re-exported to Germany.) Cecil assured them that "according to the Dutch statistics, only two tons of vegetable or animal oils" had been exported to Germany that year.[42] Two tons. Ridiculous. Time after time valid questions were answered with weak assurances or avoidance. Eventually, in August 1916, two years into the war, the blunt question was put:

> Is his Majesty's Government satisfied that the funds of the National Committee for Relief in Belgium are in fact devoted to the relief of loyal Belgians in the occupied territories, and not to that of Germans or of Belgians working for the German Army?[43]

Lord Robert Cecil's reply was hardly convincing. He blustered on about "satisfactory guarantees covering all domestic foodstuffs" but was obliged to concede that "violations of these guarantees by the Germans still arise" although the "United States, Spanish and Netherlands representatives at Brussels are taking energetic steps, [to stop this] and the Germans are well aware that a continuance of such violations will endanger the whole work." Was that a serious intention? Did assurances mean anything? He insisted that "His Majesty's Government are satisfied that the foodstuffs imported by the Relief Commission run no risk of appropriation by the enemy."[44] Satisfied? He knew what was happening. The Foreign Office had evidence of the German appropriations, of railway trucks rolling from Holland to Germany, of the disappearance of food stocks, but of course admitted nothing. How could it, given the complicity of the Secret Elite?

There was a stock reply. "His Majesty's Government have assisted the relief work in response to the wishes of the Allies, including the Belgian Government, and in the interests of the whole population."[45] If necessary, when challenged about the volume of imports into Belgium, the answer was tantamount to, "our figures very often do not agree with those published elsewhere."[46] The policy was being pursued despite loudly voiced complaints and problematic questions. And the Germans continued to feed their army and their civil population from the well-stocked nest that was occupied Belgium. In mid-November the CRB reported to the American Legation that "the Germans were shipping 3,000 head of cattle per week in to Germany, and much grease."[47] This was not a leakage, it was a torrent behind which a desperate struggle for power was waged.

Tensions between the CRB and the Comite Nationale in Brussels heightened in 1916. By that time the system had been more or less established and the Belgians felt that too much praise had been heaped on the Americans while their immense efforts often went unrecognized. They were jealous. A bitter battle of wills developed with Hoover and his right hand man, Hugh Gibson in one corner and Francqui and the Comite Nationale in the other. It never bodes well when thieves fall out. The Belgian government in exile at Le Havre agreed to recognize the CNSA, or "Francqui and Company" as Brand Whitlock sarcastically dubbed them, as its representative in Belgium, and in return Francqui "agreed to abdicate when the king returns."[48] In the eyes of the head of the American Legation, "Francqui assumed the power and rank of a dictator and has even told Hoover that the CNSA must be shown the respect due to a government."[49] While recognizing that Whitlock was partisan, his outburst when Francqui declared that Belgium wanted no more charity from America and that the Americans were "invaders," was classic. He found "the chicanery, the double-dealing, the black treachery of some participants" to be so loathsome that words failed him.[50] Yet the world assumed that the CRB and its Belgian arm, the CNSA, were as one, united to feed the needy and destitute of Belgium. It was no less than a global scandal.

The stakes were enormous. The CNSA bankers were well aware that it was Hoover's CRB which could cream off the profits from international transportation and trade in foodstuffs and gifts of clothing. They wanted their share.

Hoover had admitted to Whitlock in August 1916 that the CRB had accumulated a vast profit running into millions of dollars. He claimed to have suggested to Francqui that it should be used after the war to fund a scholarship for Belgian boys in American Universities and vice-versa.[51] The parallel with Cecil Rhodes and his Oxford University scholarships must have been music to Secret Elite ears. Perhaps it was suggested by them.

In private, the name-calling was slanderous. Hoover called Francqui a "financial pirate" and the CRB's head of the Department of Inspection, Joseph Green, accused Francqui of leading a corrupt financial ring in Brussels, claiming that his dubious reputation "was known in financial circles on three continents."[52] Note the clear emphasis on finance. When the squabbling was reduced to basics, it was all about money, power and control.

Hoover became further embroiled in a heated argument with the Belgian Government in exile when he presented them with an audited account for $65,000,000 which the CRB claimed to have spent to the end of 1915, money that had been channeled from the Allied borrowing in America to the Belgian government. Aloys van de Vyvere, the Belgian finance minister, said that he would not finally discharge the claim until the government in exile returned to Brussels and could verify the data. To have automatically approved Hoover's accounts without careful scrutiny would have been a dereliction of duty. Herbert Hoover was outraged. His organization was, in his view, answerable to no government and in a petulant memorandum to Walter Page, which he expected the ambassador to sign,[53] he asserted that he had no legal liability to the Belgian government and the charitable gifts given to his organization were his to dispose of as he saw fit.[54] Francqui and Hoover were both hewn from the same rotten elm. Their arrogance was unrestrained.

Both agencies, the CRB and the Comite Nationale behaved like mobsters, goading, name-calling and threatening dire consequences as they struggled to assert their domination over the same territory. But it was Hoover who had the protection of Big Brother. The Foreign Office laid down the law. Sir Edward Grey, recently ennobled as Lord Grey, ordained that the CRB must have undivided responsibility not just for the importation of food, but its distribution and use of the money raised from sales.[55] Lord Eustace Percy joined the attack by warning that British officials were of the opinion that the Comite Nationale was not fulfilling its duty of inspection to ensure that the Germans did not abuse the importation of food. He was right. The Comite's processes were corrupt and allowed widespread abuse.

Francqui ordered the Prosecuteurs du Roi to stop sending information to the CRB about charges brought against Belgian citizens for violating food regulations. Such reports had to be sent directly to his offices, and any request for information was to be routed through the CNSA. From August 1916 onwards, he entirely suppressed important cases and adjusted and amended official figures so that no-one could accurately measure the extent of Belgian malpractice in selling food to Germany.[56] By October, the CNSA had begun to replace American flags and billboards indicating "American Relief" with their own banners at distribution centers. It may seem petty but Ambassador Page in London was offended. He demanded that the message be clearly understood: "The Comite Nationale is not the pivot upon which relief work revolves in Belgium."[57]

Every ounce of Secret Elite muscle was brought to bear on Francqui's stance and by mid-December 1916 the Belgian government changed tack and agreed that the CRB should control the distribution of food in Belgium. Hoover won but Francqui was not cowed. He had to accept the British decision to back Hoover, but in doing so revealed his own ace card. He told the head of the American legation that he had written a 600-page history of Belgian Relief, and asked if Hoover "wished to risk being shown in his true colors in a book that will remain a standard history?"[58] According to Brand Whitlock, Francqui added that "there is even a chapter on the role of the protective ministers." Such an exposé would have blown away more than Herbert Hoover. Unfortunately, the promised book never saw the light of day. The quarrel was glossed over in a barely disguised standoff, but relationships remained strained. Thus the flow of food to Germany was protected, and the Secret Elite made clear their confidence in Herbert Hoover. Meanwhile, the real war continued its carnage.

One of the essential skills that the shrewd investor requires is the ability to recognize the moment to sell and move on. The really successful investor has an additional edge; insider information. Herbert Hoover was blessed with well-concealed contacts who advised and directed his career paths so that he was guided into safe waters from the storm that would surely follow the closure of the Commission for Relief in Belgium. Towards the end of 1916 Hoover wanted out. For nearly two and a half years he had fronted the international funding for the relief program and had accrued good impressions upon which he intended to build.

His New York office manager, William Honnold, told him confidentially that President Wilson intended to create a Relief organization in America to co-ordinate and collect funds. Hoover instantly saw this as an opportunity for a position within the Wilson government. He confided to an associate in November 1916, "I would like to get out of Europe and I would like to get out with dignity."[59]

Hoover tried to set up a new mode of finance for the CRB which would remove the burden from Britain and France, who were financing the Commission with loans from America. The solution was to raise an American loan rather than continuing to channel funds firstly to Britain and France which they then fed into the CRB. J.P. Morgan and his banking associates knew well that the Allies could not continue to support Belgium indefinitely and they advised Hoover to suggest a more direct approach.[60] In December 1916, he confidently reported that: "The bankers include Morgans, Guaranty Trust, and all other important groups, who are acting entirely out of good feeling" were prepared to support the loan. Bankers acting entirely out of good feeling ... an oxymoron surely? Hoover then proceeded to advise his men in Europe that the French and Belgian governments should settle the details with Morgan's bank in London.[61] Clearly it was impossible for J.P. Morgan to advocate a relief loan which his banks could fund through the Federal Reserve System, from which they would make considerable profit, but if the suggestion came from the head of the CRB, it had much more chance of being approved by Congress.

When Hoover set off for America on 13 January 1917 with the clear objective of refocusing his career, the omens for the CRB were not auspicious. The Miners' Battalion from New South Wales formally requested that their State Relief Fund Committee stop sending money to support Belgian Relief because they could see that the Germans were seizing the food supplies.[62] Apart from New Zealand, the people of New South Wales had contributed more money per head of the population than any other state in the world and this was publicly recognized by King Albert of the Belgians.[63] According to one report, Australian soldiers had seen so many instances of relief food going to the German troops that the CRB was asked to return $220,000 of as yet unspent money.[64] Several continents away, Hoover's men ignored the Australians' well-founded allegations and produced a "barrage" of positive, fawning articles in the *New York Times* in recognition of their leader's achievements.[65]

Herbert Hoover always appeared to be in the right place at the right time. He had been in London at the outbreak of war in 1914, in Berlin with Arthur Zimmermann and the banker Max Warburg in 1915.[66] He had returned to Washington on 31 January 1917; he met with President Wilson on the same evening that Germany announced the commencement of its unrestricted submarine warfare.[67] Within three days two CRB ships, the Euphrates and the Lars Cruse carrying 2,300 tons of maize had been sunk.[68] All Relief shipping was suspended. In the ensuing rush to safe harbor two CRB ships made it to Rotterdam, a further two were torpedoed, and the remainder sought refuge in British ports.

The British government declared that it would be "a crime on their part" to allow cargoes of foodstuffs, which were needed immediately in Britain, to be put at risk from German torpedoes and duly ordered that the food be unloaded.[69] Twenty-five thousand tons of merchandise purchased in Britain was instantly held back. Forty-five thousand tons of foodstuffs was "unavoidably" detained and a further forty thousand tons already on the high seas destined for Belgium was ordered into British ports.[70] Allegedly the food was to be held in storage, though not indefinitely, until the Germans gave cast-iron guarantees of their safe transportation.[71] At a stroke, one-hundred thousand tons of food was lost to Belgium and sold to, or requisitioned by Britain.[72]

Hoover was faced with an immediate personal dilemma. What would be the consequences for him if he disbanded the CRB? His distrust of Francqui and the CNSA was profound. He sent an urgent cable to London: "I wish to make it absolutely clear: the CRB must be liquidated and disappear," except as a purely benevolent soliciting agency in the USA. "The whole of the files must be transferred to New York."[73] He insisted that a definitive break had to be made if relief was to continue, that the separation had to involve the complete "dissolution" of the original CRB, and that he would "positively refuse" to surrender its money, its organization or its ships, on any other terms.[74] Who did he think he was? On his instruction alone, the international relief program was to be liquidated. All the files had to be gathered together and sent to New York. What motivated Herbert Hoover was self-preservation. To hell with Belgian Relief; so much for the starving poor. This was the action of an endangered dictator whose first thought was to close down the operation and remove all evidence of wrong-doing. What caused this panic? Did he suddenly realize that if someone else took charge, the CRB's true purpose would be unmasked?

That same evening he attended a special dinner in the Astor Hotel in New York as chief guest of five hundred of the State's most prominent citizens. Though not an official Pilgrims Society meeting, it boasted all the trappings of the elite. In the full knowledge of his absolute instructions to London, the speech he apparently improvised was cynically disingenuous: "If we must retire ... then other neutrals must take up this work. The world cannot stand by and witness the starvation of the Belgian people and the Belgian children ... the obligation of the American people towards Belgium continues." He stood on the platform of the Astor Hotel and delivered these words, having just ordered that the whole program be liquidated. His gall knew no bounds. In justifying what had taken place he declared that "the German army has never eaten one tenth of one per cent of the food provided. The Allied governments would never have supplied us with $200,000,000 if we were supplying the German army."[75] The assembled elite audience swallowed every syllable of the lie.

We do not know what pressure was brought to bear on him, but next morning Hoover sent a second urgent cable to London to stop the liquidation. Everyone was instructed to stay at their posts. Hoover had erred. The "great humanitarian" had over-reached himself. He was answerable to a higher authority. The Secret Elite would decide if and when the CRB and the feeding of Germany would come to an end.

Herbert Hoover found it difficult to stomach the fact that the CRB was not his to dissolve. In Brussels, Brand Whitlock wanted to leave the relief program intact under the control of the Spanish and Belgian agencies. Hoover, who passionately disliked and distrusted Francqui and the CNSA, advocated a Dutch takeover. The confusion continued with a flurry of instructions to Brand Whitlock and the CRB office in Brussels, but on 5 March 1917 Hoover wrote a long and confidential letter to Vernon Kellogg in Belgium which betrayed his real objective. A full month before America declared war on Germany, Hoover primed his key men in Belgium for the eventuality. They were instructed to "do nothing to create the impression that he [Hoover] was running away from the Relief." He had clearly been briefed by the Secret Elite to adopt their basic tactic of making sure that the blame would be pinned on Germany, or the state department, if it ordered the Americans to leave. If the CRB was "compelled to abandon its mission," Hoover instructed that it was to be "absolutely" liquidated as a business and released from all financial obligations.[76]

When this instruction reached Brussels, Whitlock believed that "Hoover must be losing his head."[77] He raged that though Hoover was three thousand miles away, he thought that he knew better than the men on the ground in Belgium, and "was able to impose his brutal will on the [state] department."[78] To an extent he was. Hoover had cultivated his friendship with the President's Advisor, Edward Mandel House, another Secret Elite agent close to the Morgan banking influence. Furthermore, Hugh Gibson, (whose own story will appear in the next few chapters) had been dispatched from the American Embassy in London to the state department in Washington. Once again his trusted right-hand man was employed where Hoover wanted him; at the heart of American foreign policy.

And so it came to pass as they ordained. On 23 March, three CRB ships were sunk, and the U.S. State Department ordered Brand Whitlock and all American members of the CRB to withdraw from Belgium.[79] When the diplomatic staff departed on 2 April, Prentiss Grey and three CRB accountants were left behind "to close the books" and train up their successors.[80] Hoover himself dealt with the business end of his London office. Euphemistically, his purpose was to wrap up the loose ends. The wrap-up became a full-blown disposal of incriminating evidence.

On 6 April, 1917, America declared war on Germany.

A solution was found for the CRB, one which Hoover could still control yet took him out of the direct firing line. He (more probably his Anglo-American patrons) proposed the establishment of a "Comite Neutre de Protection et Secours" under the high patronage of the King of Spain and the Queen of Holland, and the immediate patronage of the Ambassadors and ministers of Spain and Holland. They were to provide the guarantees formerly undertaken by the Americans. The Commission for Relief in Belgium proposed to continue its financial control over the purchasing and shipping of food and the supplies would be turned over to the CNSA in Belgium and Comite Francais in the north of France.[81] Hoover, again reversing all that he had originally proposed, decided to remain as overall chairman of the Commission.

Make no mistake, the provisioning of Germany continued. In his half-yearly report to Berlin from February to July, 1917, Baron von der Lancken wrote: "we have continued successfully to export to Germany, or distribute to our troops, appreciable quantities of food. Certain parts of the agreement have been voluntarily exploited [by the Belgians]. The advantages which Germany accrues through the relief work continues to grow."[82]

In May 1917, America agreed to appropriate $75,000,000 to support the revised Commission. Although credited to the British and French governments, the funds were to be spent, as before, by the CRB. The only matter to which Congress would not give its approval was a $2,000,000 gift which Hoover requested to cover his administrative expenses.[83] He knew no shame. In formally withdrawing his request, Hoover cited the alternative solution to cover his costs. "As we have been compelled to resell a large quantity of foodstuffs bought but which we were unable to ship due to the suspension of our operations for a period at the outset of the submarine war, we have made a considerable profit on these goods against which we can debit the Commission's overhead costs..."[84] In other words, when Congress refused to pay for his administrative costs, he used the money from the sale of foodstuffs earmarked for the "starving poor" of Belgium. So much for charitable giving.

Herbert Hoover was appointed Food Commissioner for the United States by President Wilson in May 1917,[85] "fresh from his triumph on the Belgian Relief Committee."[86] It was but another step in his corrupt ascent to the 31st Presidency of the United States of America.

Herbert Hoover's reputation could not have survived the war years without protection from his Secret Elite masters. Once he had been presented as the humanitarian face of the so-called relief program, and his status transformed from unscrupulous and crooked mining-engineer to quasi-diplomat, he had access to the inner chambers of the American, British and German governments. Commission for Relief in Belgium (CRB) records show that between 1914-1916 he had discussions with Foreign Secretary Sir Edward Grey,[87] Prime Minister Henry Asquith,[88] and chancellor Lloyd George,[89] yet interestingly they blanked him entirely from their official memoirs. Why? U.S. President Woodrow Wilson and various Secretaries of State discussed policy with Hoover, as did German Foreign Secretary Arthur Zimmerman[90] and Chancellor Bethmann-Hollweg.[91] The Kings of Spain and Belgium and countless senior diplomats across Europe knew Hoover personally, yet their reticence on the subject of Belgian Relief speaks volumes

Critics were silenced, rebutted or otherwise dissuaded in order to protect his reputation as the "great humanitarian." The greater Hoover's success at the CRB in prolonging the war, the stronger the Secret Elite's cordon of protection was drawn around him. Almost everyone who spoke out or questioned him was crushed or discredited, beaten into submission or forced to retract their claims in the face of violent threats and legal retribution. It was as if his past history had never happened. Officially.

Convinced that Belgian Relief was damaging the British war effort as early as April 1915, the Admiralty asked naval intelligence to investigate Hoover's background. Allegations were made that he was "untrustworthy, had sinister business connections with German mining corporations," and that "his foodstuffs had passed into German hands."[92] His activities were subjected to a formal investigation headed by Sir Sidney Rowlatt who duly whitewashed his findings and gave his formal stamp of approval to the Foreign Office. Loyal member of the British establishment, Rowlatt was later responsible for the repressive Rowlatt Act in India which led to serious unrest in the Punjab and the shocking Amritsar Massacre in 1919.[93]

Hoover steadfastly lied about his business connections. Initially, he claimed to have resigned from his mining company directorships because the relief program left him no time for private business.[94] He is famously quoted as saying, "let the fortune go to hell,"[95] yet records from *Skinner's Mining Manual* show that he served on thirteen boards of directors in 1914 and on sixteen in 1915. By 1916 he not only remained on thirteen boards but was chairman of one and joint manager of both the Burma Corporation and Zinc Corporation.[96] His companies returned immense dividends during the war largely through the unprecedented increase in demand for metals and munitions. When rumors of his impropriety in the dealings of the Zinc Corporation surfaced in 1916, law suits followed. He approached the Foreign Office to directly intervene on his behalf, on the grounds that his work with the CRB was too important to the war effort. At his behest, the Ambassadors from Belgium and France confirmed Hoover's vital role in Belgian Relief. The Foreign Office advised Hoover's solicitor that, if "The Court" sought their opinion about the importance of his work, they would willingly reply. The British establishment knew how to protect its assets.

In legal proceedings taken against his Burma Corporation, he attempted to pervert the course of justice by claiming to have previously resigned from the company. His "resignation" was a sham, a temporary convenience to avoid court proceedings. Back on the Board of the Burma Corporation, Hoover brokered a deal in December 1917 with the head of the CRB office in New York and Ernest Oppenheimer to develop gold mines in the Rand. He organised the finance chiefly through the CRB's bankers, J.P. Morgan & Company and Morgan's Guaranty Trust Company of New York. Thus the Anglo-American Corporation of South Africa was born, a mining giant in its field from day one.[97]

Consider these connections. Hoover used the CRB banking agencies[98] to broker a deal that rewarded him with a huge shareholding (plus options) which reaped him yet another fortune. Who was greasing whose palm? Hoover's access to "insider-knowledge" brought him an enormous stroke of "good fortune." Like Lord Rothschild some time before, he liquidated almost all of his direct Russian holdings in late 1916, just in time to avoid the consequent take-overs obligated by the Russian Revolution. Every one of his former Russian enterprises was confiscated,[99] and other unfortunates had to bear the consequent loss. Lies and evasion, deceit and malpractice were laced into Hoover's mentality. Yet his illegal business practices were successfully covered up by his Secret Elite minders.

At the end of the war Herbert Hoover was given one final task in Europe by the Secret Elite. It was almost a reprise of his role with the Commission for Relief in Belgium; but there were even more sinister undertones. We will address this scandal in due course.

Summary.

- Hoover's early claims in October - November 1914 that Belgium was on the brink of imminent disaster were downright lies. The German military governor in Antwerp mocked his claim, but when Hoover threatened to close down the relief program, the German government stepped in to apologize. It was apparently a problem caused by translation.
- With Kitchener, Churchill and Lloyd George apparently set against sending food to Belgium you might expect that the idea would have been abandoned. Not so. Despite their objections, others prevailed.
- Hoover's friends in the Foreign Office protected the venture. Lord Eustace Percy sent him a note promising that 'we only desire to help'.
- He lied about the state of the population, the control of the exports, the massive leakage to Germany, the number of Rhodes Scholars who supervised the distribution and was in effect prolonging the war by ensuring that German troops had enough food to continue the fight.
- Deny, deflect and deceive were his watchwords.
- Tensions between Hoover's CRB and Francqui's CNSA in Belgium grew bitter. The CRB was in a position to cream off profits on an international scale. The CNSA felt that its contribution was belittled by Hoover's people.
- Hoover called Francqui a 'financial pirate'. His backers in London closed ranks to ensure that Hoover won the battle with Francqui, but not before the Belgian banker warned the Americans that he had written a 600 page exposure of the CRB.
- Unfortunately the book never materialized and the rupture was glossed over.
- In 1917, Hoover wanted out. Complaints were growing. He instructed that the CRB be liquidated and disappear.
- When America declared war in April 1917, the work of supplying food to Belgium and Germany did not stop.
- Hoover requested $2,000,000 gift to cover his administrative expenses, but Congress refused.
- He was appointed Food Commissioner for the United States by Woodrow Wilson.
- Critics who questioned the truth of his "great humanitarian" work were silenced or rebutted.

Chapter 18

The Martyrdom Of Edith Cavell

Edith Cavell was the most celebrated British heroine of the First World War. The distinguished head of a Belgian nursing school, the Berkendael Institute in Brussels, was executed by order of a German military court on October 12, 1915. She admitted aiding over two-hundred Allied soldiers to escape from occupied Belgium and return safely to their regiments in France or Britain, in direct contravention of German military code. According to a BBC Radio 4 program in September 2015, Dame Stella Rimington, formerly director of MI5, said it was more likely to have been nine-hundred.[1]

She died a patriot and was transformed into a martyr of iconic status in England and Belgium. The truth of what happened to her has been mired in false claims, officially concocted reports and hagiographies that exaggerated her virtues into sainthood. Despite this, Edith Cavell was undoubtedly a courageous patriot who put the health and security of her charges before her own safety.

Executed in secret, her exploits were immediately championed by the British propaganda machine and transformed into a rallying call to men and women alike, proof positive of the evil Hun and his disregard for the sanctity of womanhood.[2] Her death boosted recruitment to the British army, and was almost as valuable in terms of propaganda as the sinking of the *Lusitania*.[3] It spawned posters, articles, pamphlets, commemorative medals and statues. Streets, hospitals, schools, gardens, parks and even a mountain bears her name, yet the circumstances of her conviction and death do not sit easily with the official history as originally pronounced by the American Legation in Brussels and the British Foreign Office.

Edith Cavell was born in 1865 at Swardeston in Norfolk. The eldest child of four, her upbringing as the daughter of the local vicar was strictly Christian. She worked as a children's governess for some years before deciding, at the age of thirty, to become a nurse. After four years at the London Hospital Nurses Training School, she moved to St. Pancras Infirmary as night supervisor. Her next move took her to Shoreditch as Assistant Matron at the Infirmary, but, at the age of forty-one, the straight-laced, devout Christian was appointed to a prestigious nursing post in Belgium.

Edith Cavell's work was recognized as pioneering. Well organised and demanding the highest of standards from her nursing staff, she was recruited in 1907 by the eminent Belgian surgeon, Dr. Antoine Depage, to be the Matron of his newly established nursing school. The L'Ecole Belge d'Infirmieres Diplomees grew steadily under her progressive direction and by the outbreak of War she was training nurses for three hospitals and thirteen kindergartens.[4] The project had been part-funded by the eminent Belgian industrialist and philanthropist, Ernest Solvay to the tune of 300,000 francs.[5] He was an exceptionally important businessman and later President of the initial relief commission for Belgium, the Comite National de Secours et Alimentation. (CNSA). Edith's arrival in Brussels did not please everyone for she effectively challenged the monopoly previously held by the Sisters of Charity, Catholic nuns who by custom and habit, "had there own way of doing things."[6] She also branched out into journalism and had sufficient self-confidence to publish the professional magazine, *L'Infirmiere,* from 1910 onwards.[7]

At the outbreak of war, Edith was at home in England visiting her mother and might easily have stayed there in relative safety. Instead, she chose to return at once to Brussels, where the Depage clinics and nursing school were given over to the Belgian Red Cross. She immediately involved herself in the preparations for emergency hospitals and relief stations for the wounded.[8] Her biographers depict Matron Cavell attending to the war-wounded Belgian, French, British and to a much lesser extent, German troops, and there can be no doubt that she did so with magnificent grace.[9] But that was not her only contribution.

Edith Cavell had become a very senior figure in Belgian nursing circles not least because of her association with Antoine Depage and his wife Marie. Antoine was the founder and chairman of the Belgian Red Cross and the Surgeon Royal, personal physician to King Albert, with whom he served in exile. Antoine had also founded the Boy Scout movement in Belgium in association with several figures from the upper echelons of Belgian society like Ernest Solvay, whose vast multinational chemical company had spread across all of central Europe. [10] Marie Depage, always active in the Belgian Red Cross, stayed behind in Brussels for the first two months of the German occupation but later joined her husband in exile with the King at La Panne. She agreed to go to the United States in 1915 to tour on behalf of the Belgian Red Cross and was magnificently successful in fund-raising across the continent of America before returning home on board the ill-fated *Lusitania.*[11] Marie Depage was drowned, her body recovered, taken to Ireland and reclaimed by a grieving husband, a victim of war like those for whom she gallantly campaigned.

Edith Cavell took charge of the clinics and hospital in Belgium in the full knowledge that she had access to all of the circles of influence and power that remained there. She was associated with the aristocratic De Croy family, the Depages, churchmen and diplomats at the American legation. Her work brought her into contact with increasing numbers of soldiers, many wounded, some lost or displaced from their regiments in the chaos of war, all striving to escape from the Germans and the certainty of imprisonment or worse if they were caught. German military law made it a capital offence to harbor enemy soldiers, and public notices warned of the dire punishments for any such infringement.[12]

Stranded soldiers were brought secretly to Brussels by members of an underground group with whom Edith collaborated. The official record of Nurse Cavell's valor leaves the impression that she was the sole figure in a dangerous wartime activity, whereas she was in reality a member of a highly organised and well-connected network comprising more than thirty equally courageous Belgian patriots working tirelessly to repatriate and save Allied soldiers.[13]

As autumn 1914 passed into winter, the Western Front began to settle into a series of entrenched defenses paralleling great stretches of no-man's land across western Belgium and south across France. Stalemated defense systems and battlefield confusions made it difficult to determine precise boundaries. The first great battle at Mons, which began on 24 August 1914, resulted in men from both sides being isolated from their comrades in strange and unaccustomed terrain. Underground organizations were quickly set up in Belgium to assist displaced Allied soldiers. These men also served to pass messages and information to London to disrupt and unsettle the German forces of occupation. Spy networks abounded[14] and Brussels had long been a hub of intelligence activity.[15] While an essential part of this work was to assist Allied soldiers trapped behind enemy lines, wounded or otherwise, gathering information about the German army was also of great importance.

News of troop dispositions, the location of armament dumps and other supplies, railway timetables and information about enemy morale were equally valuable. The underground networks also carried mail and family messages to and fro between Brussels and London and aided in the distribution of anti-German news-sheets like *Private World* and *Free Belgium.*[16] All of this was extremely dangerous work and marked anyone involved as a spy. The British Secret Service was the principle source and provider of funds for the activity, and regular reports on the German occupiers were channeled via Brussels and Holland to London and the War Office.[17] British Military Intelligence knew about the organization which successfully repatriated hundreds of soldiers, as did the Foreign Office, important players in what was to become a highly suspect game of denial.

The underground network in which Edith Cavell played a key role, operated from the Franco-Belgian border between Bellignes, Mons and Maubeuge, through Brussels and on to Antwerp and various points on the Dutch border. It was a very reputable organization headed by Prince Reginald de Croy, the Belgian aristocrat and diplomat, and included his sister, Princess Marie de Croy, whose war memoirs provided a unique insight into the events surrounding the arrest and trial of the entire network in 1915. The de Croys belonged to one of the most prestigious families in Europe, whose family ties crossed geographic boundaries.

The de Croy network included men and women from across the social spectrum. War is often a great leveler. The grand chateaux of the de Croys at Bellignes housed many escaped Allied soldiers, especially after the battle of Mons, who, once suitably recovered, were routed to safety through Edith Cavell in Brussels where they were kept hidden in safe houses.[18] Noblewomen, including the Princess de Croy and the Countess de Bellevilles, worked with servants and townsfolk to help transfer literally hundreds of desperate soldiers across dangerous forests, minor roads and little-used paths to the border. The Catholic clergy and religious houses were involved in what they saw as a work of mercy, and all along the route, ordinary citizens risked their lives to aid and abet these harried and often starving escapees. Food, clothing, false documentation and money were provided for them, though it often took weeks to organize. The Belgians did this without reward and without regard for their personal safety. There is, however, no doubt that Edith Cavell ran the Brussels-based hub of the de Croy network.[19]

It is important at this juncture to explain the international connections enjoyed by the House of de Croy. Reginald, Prince de Croy was a Belgian diplomat, who doubled as a messenger and conduit for the Resistance. Prior to the war, he spent ten years in the Belgian Embassy in London and risked arrest constantly as he ferried to and fro across the Franco-Belgian-Dutch borders.[20] His sister Marie explained in her memoirs that "He was entrusted with various messages from the French to the Commission of Relief for Belgium (CRB). He carried these to Brussels where the Committee sat, and also to the American Embassy [Legation], as several concerned breaches of our rules of war. Of course it was useless to complain of abuses."[21]

What kind of breaches of the rules of war would concern the Commission of Relief for Belgium (CRB)? In what breaches would the American Legation in Brussels be interested? The Americans claimed to be neutral; the Commission was allegedly only involved in the provision of food and clothing for the starving Belgians and French in occupied zones. The "abuses" must therefore have referred to an abuse of the food supply, and the most likely scenario is that the Resistance could see that the food was going, not just to the Belgian population, but to front-line German soldiers. Indeed by 1915 such allegations were known within the highest levels of the Foreign Office in London, and had caused adverse comment in what Herbert Hover referred to as the "constant lying reports which appear in the English press."[22]

Reginald's brother Leopold served in the bitter fighting around Ypres in Belgium, and such was his level of importance to the British war effort that when he returned through London he "called at the War Office, wherein he was able to catch up with news from 'home' from a dozen men recently come back from Bellignes"[23] Both brothers were frequent visitors to London where the troops who had escaped through the de Croy network were debriefed. British Intelligence was aware of what was happening in that part of Belgium from all manner of sources. They knew of de Croy's valuable network, and the role of Edith Cavell, that is certain, but were they simply passive recipients of occasional information, or actively managing a high-level spy network?

One amazing security lapse almost unmasked the entire network. Marie wrote that her brother Reginald, "after calling at the War Office" was on his way to catch a boat back to Holland when his attention was drawn to a newspaper article which all but identified the underground network headed by the de Croy family. Reginald "rushed to a telephone and called an official, with whom he had been in touch, begging anxiously, that unless they wanted us all shot, this sort of publication should cease."[24] Thereafter the censors stepped in. Unfortunately they failed to stop some of the rescued soldiers from sending Edith Cavell postcards to express their gratitude and let her know that they had successfully returned home.

Marie de Croy stated that "Reggie" was well aware of Edith Cavell's personal investment in the safety of these Allied soldiers. She had spent all of her own savings on clothes and food "which had to be paid for in ready money, and Reginald was determined to try and obtain subsidies from the army, especially for Miss Cavell."[25] Edith operated within a high-profile network, known to the British Government, the American Legation, the Belgian Government in exile, the Comite National de Secours et Alimentation in Brussels and the CRB. It actively liaised between them, was aided by them and sought funding from them as necessary.

Like many of her generation, Edith Cavell was an avid letter writer. She served on the editorial board which launched Belgium's first nursing magazine, *L'Infirmiere*, in 1910, and wrote occasional articles for the weekly *Nursing Mirror and Midwives Journal* in Britain. Edith cared passionately about nursing, about nursing techniques and good practice, and understood the value of promoting educational articles. When war broke out she wrote to the editor of the *Times* on 12 August 1914,[26] launching an appeal for subscriptions from the British public to support her preparations to deal with "several hundreds" of wounded soldiers anticipated to arrive shortly in Brussels, signing herself as "Directrice of the Berkendael Medical Institute."

Once war had been declared, Edith contacted the editor of the *Nursing Mirror and Midwives Journal* and wrote an article headed "Nursing in

War Time" which was published on 22 August 1914. In March 1915, she repeated the process, and sent both a covering letter to the Editor and an article about Brussels under German rule. This in itself contravened German military law. She did not identify herself by name but signed the missive "from your Nurse Correspondent."[27]

The Editor was at great pains to explain to the readers of *Nursing Mirror* that the package sent from Brussels had been "torn open on both sides" and that the letter arrived at his desk "resealed by the General Post Office in London." It had originally been dated 24 March, but the date-stamp on the envelope was 15 April. The most likely reason for this was that Edith had given the letter to some trusted person or someone from within the American Legation for onward transfer to England. It had been opened, presumably in London, by a government official. We do not know what else was in the package. Had other material been removed? Who, inside the War Office, Foreign Office, or the intelligence services, had a primary interest in Edith Cavell's correspondence?

Questions have to be asked about the letters and postcards Edith received from soldiers whom she had helped escape from Brussels. Though it might seem ridiculous to us today, grateful soldiers did send messages back to Matron Cavell to announce their successful return to England. One such incriminating postcard was presented as evidence at her trial. Since she received mail from England it had to be sent via trusted contacts or the American Legation, and since the latter only accepted mail from British government departments, it had to have passed through official channels. This means that Edith Cavell was a known and trusted contact for officers in the British intelligence services.

Edith sent news to England, and not just to the *Nursing Mirror*. She maintained a steady flow of correspondence to her family and friends. She wrote a cautious letter to her mother on 15 September 1914, in which she claimed that "life goes on as usual" and to her sister, Florence, three days later, in which she expressed concern about the homeless and the misery that might follow a bad winter in Belgium.[28] In these instances her mail was routed through Vecht and later, Bergen op Zoom in Holland, but Edith's letters home became progressively incautious. In a reply to her cousin Eddy, dated 11 March 1915, she explained that she received his missive through the American Consul and enclosed a list of soldiers about whose safe return to England she had concern. Unwittingly, Edith Cavell became indiscreet. She told her mother on 14 March that she could "tell you many things but must save them till later."[29] Ten days later she sent her epistle to the editor of the *Nursing Mirror*.

The international mail system had been subject to all kinds of restrictions and was virtually closed to unofficial correspondence, but Edith Cavell had diplomatic contacts which gave her a sense of confidence. On 14 June 1915 she confirmed to her mother that "if anything very serious should happen to me you could probably send me a message through the American Ambassador in London (not a letter)."[30] Clearly this was a privilege which she greatly valued, but had to keep secret. That point was reinforced by her request to the editor of the *Nursing Mirror* not to try to forward a copy of the paper to Brussels. She had no wish to make public her contacts with London.[31]

Edith's second article in the *Nursing Mirror* reads at first as a calm and considered account of daily life in Brussels. Indeed it was so non-controversial that the reader would wonder the value of printing it at all. The point of the article appeared to contradict the prevailing message from the Commission for the Relief of Belgium that the country was in crisis. She took the reader through the hoped-for success in the early days of August "when we were full of enthusiasm for the war and confidence in the allies," to the arrival of the Germans with much "pomp and circumstance." However, in stark contrast to the widespread impression that Belgium was being systematically raped by the advancing German army, Cavell's article painted a widely different picture:

> On August 21st many more troops came through ... some were too weary to eat and slept on the street. We were divided between pity for these poor fellows, far from their country and their people ... and hate of a cruel and vindictive foe bringing ruin and desolation on hundreds of happy homes and to a prosperous and peaceful land. Some of the Belgians spoke to the invaders in German and found they were very vague as to their whereabouts, and imagined they were already in Paris; they were surprised to be speaking to Belgians and could not imagine what quarrel they had with them. I saw several of the men pick up little children and give them chocolate or seat them on their horses and some had tears in their eyes at the recollection of the little ones at home.[32]

This image does not sit easily with that of the propagandist. No rape, no pillage, no starving children, no shootings or other such hideous maltreatment? Goodness, the Bryce Report was due for publication in May, and the story in the *Nursing Mirror* was completely at odds with the horror stories and anti-German allegations contained in that shameful instrument of propaganda and hate. Edith's portrayal of Brussels is an almost silent one without cars or bicycles in the street; no sense of bustle, no newspapers except German-sponsored editions, nothing permitted from England; no telephone contacts and movement by train was greatly restricted. In her final paragraph, she depicts the Belgian attitude to the invader as one of quiet but studied rejection: "The people have grown thin and silent with the fearful strain. They walk about the city shoulder to shoulder with the foe and never see them or make a sign; only they leave the cafés they frequent and turn their backs to them, and live a long way off and apart."[33]

Life in occupied Brussels was quiet, and the spirit of the people remained defiant. But what about the picture of national destitution put about by the Commission for Relief in Belgium? What of the starving population that had become the international concern of Herbert Hoover? Perhaps these unfortunate people were in the countryside? Yet in Belgium, a mainly rural and agricultural nation, you would expect to find the starving populous in the great cities, like ... well, like Brussels. Of course there was need and poverty. Such was the fate of the poor everywhere. Those with nothing are always the first to suffer. It was as true in Glasgow and London as it was in Bruges and Brussels. But this was not the focus of Edith's attention. She wrote about the strain of the people, not the hunger. Something does not ring true here. It is not possible to have both sets of circumstance. And Edith had no axe to grind. Her agenda was to save lives and repatriate Allied soldiers.

The German authorities forbade Edith and other British nurses to deal with their wounded. She found herself disbarred from her professional duties. Most of the wounded German troops were "sent straight back home, as far as possible," and Allied wounded "do not come." A few wounded men, too seriously damaged to be able to fight again, were nursed at the King's Palace in Brussels which served as a military hospital. But they were "nursed by Belgians under their own doctors."[34] Edith found herself isolated from her calling, left more like the head of a religious order than a nursing school. She was not involved in ministering to the injured and dying from either side as the legend would have it, but instead, rendered unemployed, or at best, hugely underemployed. This explains why she had the time to be so actively involved in the underground movement.

An interesting piece of corroboration of life in occupied Belgium comes from Harry Beaumont, one of the Allied soldiers whom Edith Cavell helped to escape. Harry was injured in the retreat from Mons on 24th August 1914 and saved from capture by a Belgian family called Neussy. His escape route included Brussels, Louvain and the Monastery of Averabode, where the monks looked after a group of wounded British soldiers with immense care.[35]

Harry stated that Edith Cavell was "running" the escape route and their Belgian courier "promised to report our position to Nurse Cavell." His story is not one of hardship and austerity. He made no mention of starving children and desperate queues for food. The very opposite is true. Harry wrote of one safe house in glowing terms; "our hostess was a very wealthy woman. Her house was stocked with everything of the best and for eight days, we lived like Lords."[36] Indeed Harry Beaumont admitted that such was the generosity of the people that even when Belgian citizens were issued with ration cards, he and his fellow escapees received far more than they would have been entitled to had they depended solely on rations. There were shortages of meat and flour, but vegetable and eggs were plentiful and the local fraternity provided extras.[37]

He also, quite innocently, demonstrated the complicity of the Commission for Relief in Belgium, which clearly knew all about the de Croy network. When one of the Belgian agents in Antwerp demanded cash payment for hiding him from the authorities, Harry and his companion, at that point an Irishman, went to the headquarters of the "American" Commission for Relief in Belgium. They told of their escape and their need for funds. The money was forthcoming. Furthermore, the Americans took control and subsidized Harry's relatively prolonged stay in Antwerp. He was given an allowance of sixteen francs a day and placed in a safe-house of their choice. Eventually, several weeks later, on 16 May 1915, having cracked open a bottle of celebratory champagne, he boarded a tram to the outskirts of the city and eventually reached Holland safety. His guide was provided by the CRB.[38] Does anyone imagine that the Americans in Brussels were not fully informed of what was happening by their compatriots in Antwerp? Of course they were. They were actively and secretly complicit.

Harry's account gives us some clear pointers. The network for escapees was organised in Brussels through Edith Cavell. The soldiers were well fed and well treated. There was no awareness of the alleged widespread hunger and want. The Americans knew about their network, and supported it, albeit in a clandestine manner. They knew about Edith's correspondence, and most probably knew precisely what she was reporting to London. Spying on one's allies is not a recent phenomenon. When she was arrested in her office by the Germans on Thursday 5 August, the police found a letter sent from London; it bore the seal of the American Consulate in Brussels.[39]

Thus Edith was a major figure in Brussels medical circles whose work was highly valued by her employer, the King's personal surgeon. She was acknowledged as one of the leading nursing practitioners in the land, but forbidden to practice by the occupying forces. Edith was active inside an underground and espionage network which, among other work, repatriated soldiers stranded behind enemy lines. Her correspondence was widespread and fearless. We know that she wrote to her family, to the British press and the *Nursing Mirror*. She wrote about the conditions of the people as she experienced it, and hinted strongly of wrong-doing. Edith Cavell was sufficiently important to the authorities in London and Brussels that her correspondence was transmitted through the American Legation. They had just delivered a letter to her from London when she was arrested.

Yet the Americans at the Legation and in the Commission for Relief in Belgium apparently knew nothing about her arrest … or so they were to claim.

Summary.

- Edith Cavell was the most celebrated British heroine of the First World War. Head of the Berkendael Institute in Brussels, she was recruited by the King of Belgium's personal surgeon.
- She was an eminent nursing teacher, founded a professional magazine, *L' Infirmiere,* contributed to the *Nursing Mirror and Midwives Journal* in Britain and wrote letters to *The Times*. Edith was a multi-talented correspondent on several levels.
- At the start of the war she was in England visiting her mother, but chose to return to Brussels immediately. After the chaos of the Battle of Mons in August 1914, hundreds, if not thousands of British and French troops were stranded behind enemy lines and Edith became part of a network organised to save and repatriate these men.
- Her work as a member of the underground network, organised by the Belgian aristocratic de Croy family, was integral to its success.
- Evidence clearly shows that the network was linked to the War Office in London. Edith operated within a high-profile network known to the British Government, the American Legation, the Belgian Government in exile, the Comite National de Secours et Alimentation in Brussels and the CRB. It actively liaised between them, was aided by them and sought funding from them as necessary.
- She used the American Legation in Brussels as a conduit for her letters to England. She wrote to her mother in March 1915 that she had information which could not be trusted to the post, but would be saved till later.
- Her communications in the Nursing Mirror were at odds with the British propaganda about the German atrocities in Belgium.
- Her role in the escape network, and the fact that the Americans were complicit in supporting the network was recorded in an account by a British soldier of his escape from occupied Belgium. Harry Beaumont's story, *Old Contemptible,* remains both a terrific read and indisputable proof of Edith's endeavors on his part.

Chapter 19

Cavell? Seemingly No-One Knew

The German secret police became increasingly suspicious of the de Croy organization and the whole network realized that they were being watched. As 1915 wore on, it was evident that the police were watching them and had identified their safe houses. In April of that year Marie de Croy and Edith Cavell met secretly in Ghent. Following this, both suffered the indignity of having their homes searched and realized the great danger they were facing. Marie wanted to close down the network, but Edith would not take her advice, insisting that "if one of these men got caught and shot, it would be our fault."[1] A compromise was agreed whereby no more Allied soldiers would be sent to her clinic, but Edith could continue to organize and direct the guides who ran the escape routes to Holland. It was too late.

Inevitably, traps were set and, betrayed by a collaborator, Gaston Quien, most of the members of the network were apprehended. In all, the secret police arrested 70 suspects in a wide sweep around Brussels and the surrounding area.[2] The first to be apprehended were Phillipe Baucq and Louise Thuliez. Baucq was an architect and committed patriot who printed and disseminated free newspapers which carried anti-German stories. His clandestine news sheet, *La Libre Belgique,* incensed the German Governor-General with its sarcasm and jibes, many of which were directed at him.[3] Indeed von Bissing took great personal umbrage at being lampooned.[4] Louise Thuliez , a school teacher, was one of the principal guides who ferried lost soldiers across Belgium to safety in Holland.

Thuliez was originally condemned to death, by German court marshal, but her sentence was commuted to life imprisonment. On return from captivity in Germany in 1918 she penned a long report on what she termed "The Cavell Organization" in which she admitted that, while working with Edith Cavell, she had actively sought out military intelligence about a supply dump at Cambrai in German-occupied territory in northeast France.[5] This evidence clearly indicated that Edith was operating inside a Belgian spy ring. But it ran deeper. Matron Cavell, she claimed, "was closely connected to Britain's intelligence services."[6]

Henry Baron, a British agent in France, was "working with the Cavell Organization."[7] When he later learned that his former contact, Louise Thuliez, was about to publish a booklet "on the Cavell affair," Baron reported his fears to British Intelligence. Her revelation not only implicated

Edith Cavell in spying but also "speaks about the participation of members of the agency in the Cambria spy affair."[8] Such explosive information had to be suppressed. Knowing that proof of Edith's involvement in espionage would ruin the official British narrative, publication was forbidden. Baron was instructed that the British military authorities considered it highly undesirable that anything that implicated Edith Cavell in "matters of espionage" should be published until after the Versailles Treaty had been finalised.[9] It never was.

Yet another source of incriminating evidence was recently unearthed from private archives in the Royal Museum of the Army and History of War in Brussels.[10] Herman Capiau was part of the de Croy/Cavell underground network in 1915, and like Louise Thuliez was arrested, tried and condemned to death, but his sentence was commuted to 15 years hard labour.[11]

Before his arrest, Capiau wrote a secret report in which he identified another agent linked to the underground network's spying activities and yet again, Edith Cavell knew and approved. He stated: "... In agreement with Miss Cavell and Mademoiselle Thuliez, I sent the French government, through the intelligence agent Paul Godefroy, a request for material assistance for large-scale organization of an evacuation service for young French recruits. ..." Thus not only were British intelligence services supporting Edith's work in Brussels, but the French government was directly approached for support and aid. This was likely to be financial since repatriation was an expensive business. Although the majority of Belgian citizens willingly helped the underground network without personal gain, some looked for payment.[12]

But Capiau's report revealed that the network's activities went beyond helping stranded soldiers to escape: "... whenever it was possible to send interesting intelligence on military operations, this information was forwarded to the English intelligence service punctually and rapidly."[13] Spying was not an occasional activity. Capiau admitted that at every opportunity, information about German military activity was passed to British Intelligence, "punctually and rapidly." By May 1915, precise information on trench formations, vehicle and troop movements, arms caches and aircraft maneuverer around Valenciennes was sewn into the clothes of soldiers who were being repatriated.[14]

Herman Capiau cited Paul Godefroy as his link with the secret services, but unfortunately Godefroy died in the Rheinbach prison in 1916.[15] After the war, the prison was occupied temporarily by British military units and his files disappeared. Why? Herman Capiau also left a handwritten note, currently in the archives in Brussels under the title, "L'Affaire Cavell" which names Edith, Louise Thuliez, Paul Godefroy and himself as members of the "organization" with a further list of names attached.[16] In addition to its work on behalf of displaced soldiers this was a clandestine organization which was spying on German troops.

Capiau's lists also placed Edith as the prime link in the Brussels hub of the network whose "grand chef," literally "big chief" was "Dr Bull, War Office." Doctor Tellemache (or Telemachus) Bull was, according to the Whitlock family archives, King Albert's personal dentist, and a relation by marriage to Brand Whitlock.[17] He appears to have remained inexplicably airbrushed from the Edith Cavell story until relatively recently, when a BBC Radio 4 program, *Secrets and Spies*[18] identified Bull as a British Secret Service operator who ran a number of networks from Belgium. He was arrested by the German secret police, charged firstly with treason and tried in Antwerp on May 19, 1916. He received an extremely light sentence of three months imprisonment and a five thousand mark fine.[19] No matter how distant, his family connections with the Whitlocks seems remarkably coincident. The head of the American Legation was preparing to throw a party to celebrate Dr. Bull's release in July when he discovered that Bull was to face a second trial directly related to his involvement with Edith Cavell.[20] This took place on 16 October 1916, with a representative from the American legation present. Bull and sixteen others were charged with conspiring to help Edith Cavell in "aiding young men to cross the frontier," and of supplying her with funds to assist them. He was sentenced to six years imprisonment.[21]

Apart from any further and as yet unknown connections, Bull's direct involvement means that Edith's activities were part of an ongoing War Office and Secret Service clandestine operation. Edith Cavell was deeply involved in more than nursing the wounded and the Brussels she wrote home about must have been on a planet far distant from that portrayed by Herbert Hoover.

The very survival of Hoover's CRB was at risk in the first quarter of 1915. Continued support was threatened by the bad press it was receiving in Britain and the awkward questions raised in the House of Commons about the foodstuff "taken" by the German army. Herbert Hoover was certainly suspicious that his organization was being undermined by individuals inside Belgium. In a letter to Brand Whitlock dated 6 March 1915, he complained that he had been severely grilled about the amount of food which was requisitioned by the German army of occupation and was alarmed that the London government intended to follow up claims which had originated in Belgium. He berated the "constant lying reports which appear in the English press with regard to our foodstuffs being taken by the Germans or devoted to their requisitions in the operation zone..."[22]

Who in Belgium had the contacts and confidence to make such damning allegations? Who would be so morally outraged that, if the government appeared to be doing nothing, could write directly to their contacts in the British press? These allegations were not "constant lying reports," but the products of good intelligence.

Hoover was himself a consummate liar and master of press manipulation. Lies were his stock-in-trade. The CRB's propaganda campaigns were immediately stepped up. A special meeting in Carnegie Hall in New York, called in support of the Allies by American fund-raisers, heard a message from Brand Whitlock stating: "Supply of food now in Belgium is sufficient only to last through this month, and that after April 1st, the need of food and clothing would be as pressing as ever, and that the entire Belgian population must continue to depend for subsistence on the generosity of the American People."[23]

The entire Belgian population? What nonsense; but a terrific soundbite.

Yet the *Nursing Mirror* reported in April 1915 that in Edith Cavell's Brussels, the cafés were open and cigars were still being smoked.[24] What Cavell's article demonstrated was at complete odds with Hoover's alarmist reports. Can you imagine how angry the vested interests in the CRB were when they were made aware of this? The woman was dangerous. What would she write next? Given her intelligence contacts all over Belgium, what else did she know? What else had she already reported? If the network was indeed the Cavell Organization, as Herman Capiau suggested, rather than the more aristocratic "de Croy organization," then Edith's role must have been more proactive. To whom was she reporting?

In June 1915, Hoover left the comfort of his London home to go to Belgium in person to meet with Baron von der Lanken, head of the German political department in Brussels, and a key German figure in the international liaison of the CRB. It is important to remember that the leading members of the CRB and the Belgian Comite National de Secours and Alimentation (CNSA) moved naturally within the highest circles of the German administration in Belgium. Hoover was present to negotiate the fate of the coming harvest, a role he assumed, though the CNSA strongly objected to his presence.[25] He was well aware that London wanted the press stories about German abuse of the relief organization, squashed. So too did the Germans. Their war effort had become dependent on the food supplies they accessed through Belgium.

In view of the strong links between the underground network for which Edith worked and its direct connections with London, facilitated by the de Croys, she was in a prime position to provide regular information to British intelligence agencies. We know she wrote directly to the *Nursing Mirror*, and to the editor of the *Times*,[26] but given the evidence of Edith's complicity in espionage, the British secret service would have known that and much more. She reported to them. Such knowledge would also be the concern of the CRB and the American Legation, for those were prime conduits for the transfer of information to London. Had Edith become a potentially dangerous thorn in the side of the CRB and the Secret Elite? Matron Cavell was a well-known professional figure who carried weight in the British press. Her word could poison their whole venture.

Remember, Edith Cavell was arrested in her office at the Berkendael Institute in Brussels on Thursday 5 August 1915.[27]

In his self-serving memoirs, Hugh Gibson, first secretary to the American legation in Brussels and close friend of Herbert Hoover, claimed that Edith was "quietly arrested" and that "it was some time" before the news reached the legation.[28] That is simply untrue. Edith was escorted from her office by Otto Mayer, head of the German Secret Police, and her distraught nursing staff witnessed the deed. She had expected to be arrested. Her associates in the underground network, Louise Thuliez and Philippe Baucq, had been taken into custody on Saturday 31 July and news of their fate spread fast. Realizing that the whole network had been compromised, Reginald de Croy rushed to Brussels to warn Edith, and other members of the group to destroy all evidence. This was no quiet affair. For a start, Edith was just one of seventy initially imprisoned, of whom thirty-five were charged with harboring soldiers and conducting them back to the enemy.[29] Marie de Croy's arrest followed soon afterwards, but to the chagrin of the German authorities her brother Reginald, Prince de Croy, escaped their clutches. To claim that the arrest and imprisonment of such distinguished people went unnoticed by members of the CRB is utterly ridiculous.

Edith was first held in a communal women's cell in Brussels' main police station at the Kommandantur, opposite the Royal Park, and held there for two days until she was transferred across the city to the harsher quarters of St Gilles prison. Hugh Gibson's claim that he did not know about Edith Cavell's arrest becomes even more preposterous when weighed against the fact that she was initially incarcerated barely one street away from Hoover's headquarters. At the end of December 1914, Herbert Hoover had moved his commission's offices from 48, Rue de Naples to take possession of three floors of the magnificent Société Générale building at 66, Rues de Colonies.[30] It had formerly served as the headquarters of the Banque Belge pour L' Etranger and comprised a glorious sweep of imperial grandeur on the hill leading to the Kommandantur. They were virtually neighbors, barely 200 yards apart.

From the very beginning, everyone officially associated with the Commission for Relief in Belgium (CRB) denied knowledge of what was happening. Given that the de Croy's network had close ties to the Americans,[31] that when arrested, Edith had in her possession a letter sent through the American Legation[32] and the general stir caused by the flurry of arrests, it is simply incredible that Hugh Gibson and his colleagues did not know what was happening around them. But that was their claim; a claim accepted without demur by the British government. It formed the basis of their justification for being unable to take steps with sufficient speed to save Edith Cavell.

What unfolded was no less that a macabre pantomime in which all of the key players who might have influenced the Germans, managed to delay their intervention sufficiently long enough to ensure that Edith could not be saved from her fate. The American Legation had accepted international responsibility for all British citizens in Belgium after the German occupation and thus had a legal duty of care for Edith Cavell. The senior diplomat responsible for her safety, Brand Whitlock, "was ill in his bed at this time."[33] His role was assumed by Hoover's loyal agent, the aforementioned Hugh Gibson. He had been a member of the CRB in Brussels from October 1914.

A formal letter from Maitre Gaston de Leval, the Belgian legal advisor who worked for the Americans for many years, was sent to Brand Whitlock on 12 October 1915, the day Edith was executed. It claimed: "As soon as the Legation received an intimation that Miss Cavell was arrested, your letter of August 31st was sent to Baron von der Lancken"[34] (who was in charge of the German political department in Brussels.) De Leval clearly felt it necessary to send a formal letter to his friend and employer, Whitlock, to have it appear on the record that the American legation did not hear of Edith's arrest until more than three weeks after the event. The immediate American reaction to her execution was to cover their own tracks. The letter served to excuse, retrospectively, their studied inaction.

Others immediately tried to have Edith released. The loyal nurses who witnessed her arrest rushed to the Kommandantur but were subjected to ridicule by the guards. On 10 August they learned that Edith had been transferred to the prison at St Gilles and turned to the one friend "in whom we could confide or from whom we could ask information," Maitre van Alteren. He was the lawyer who represented the governors of the Nursing School and he agreed to plead her cause with the military authorities. Van Alteren was promptly arrested and imprisoned.[35] The medical fraternity in Brussels knew of Edith's arrest, as did the governors of the Nursing School, but de Leval alleged that the American Legation knew nothing for almost a month.

Consider the implication of the timing of these events. Edith Cavell had been arrested on 5 August in plain daylight, yet the Legation, itself fully aware of the de Croy network, claimed not to have known for 26 days. This is not just unlikely, it is impossible. Networks by their very essence, connect, and breaks in the connection become immediately apparent. Edith's own family in England were notified by a Dutch source that she had been imprisoned. They even knew that the date of her arrest was

5 August. Having heard no more than that, her brother-in-law, Dr Longworth Wainwright wrote directly to Sir Edward Grey at the Foreign Office on 24 August. The British Foreign Secretary formally asked Walter Page, the American Ambassador in London to investigate what had happened in Brussels.[36] Page cabled Brand Whitlock on 27 August, yet the official record later released by the Foreign Office and published in great detail in the *Times*[37] would have us believe that it was 31 August before the American legation knew about the arrest and contacted the German authorities. Hugh Gibson's published journal clearly claimed that was the case. Again, it was an outrageous lie.

It borders on the absurd to claim that the legation waited a further ten days before their lawyer, Maitre de Leval, officially requested permission to visit Edith Cavell in prison. Two days later, according to him, the German authorities refused.[38] Edith's legal representation was an orchestrated farce. De Leval neither met with her nor represented her, though "history" was to claim otherwise. As ever, when the Secret Elite bury their involvement, facts and circumstances become mired in confusion. So it was with Edith's legal representation. While it was the duty of the American legation to represent British citizens in Belgium, for some unfathomable reason in Edith's case that duty was assumed by Emile Francqui's Comite Nationale de Secours et Alimentation (CNSA). One of its senior committee members, Eugene Hanssens, agreed to defend her.[39]

However, since he was a constitutional lawyer, Hanssens had no accreditation to plead before a military tribunal. He in turn chose as his substitute, Thomas Braun of the CNSA.[40] Braun hailed from a distinguished legal family and his father, himself an eminent lawyer, had been appointed to represent Princess Marie de Croy. The crucial point to note is that Hanssens and Braun were senior members of the CNSA and can be identified in the Belgian war-time records of the Comite Nationale in session.[41] Despite the claims of ignorance made by the Americans and their paid counselor, the men from the CNSA with whom they met on a regular, often daily basis, had put together a legal team to represent the de Croy/Cavell network. The men with whom they shared responsibility for the daily disbursement of foodstuffs had stepped forward to protect the captive network ... including Edith Cavell.

Matters became mystifyingly convoluted. According to the documents and letters released by Brand Whitlock, when the legation wrote to Baron von der Lancken for clarification about Edith Cavell on 31 August,[42] it was informed that the legal representation for Miss Edith Cavell was in the hands of Advocate Braun, who "has already been in touch with the competent German authorities." This official reply from von der Lancken was written on 12 September,[43] but there was a fatal and worrying flaw to his claim. "Advocate" Braun had previously been removed from the case. Braun had received a letter from the German government of occupation dated 1 September, 1915 accusing him of improper behavior in defaming them in court, being incapable of objectivity and of using his position to his own political advantage.[44] As of 1 September, Thomas Braun was banned from representing anyone, by order of the German Military. Yet Whitlock could produce a letter from von der Lancken dated ten days later, which claimed that Edith's case was being represented by Braun, her appointed lawyer. Either one or both were lying.

Thus at a stroke, in a crucial twenty-four hour period between 31 August and 1 September, Edith Cavell was cut off from any representation associated directly with the Commission for Relief in Belgium. Once the American legation was obliged to admit that they knew of Edith's arrest, the Germans banned Thomas Braun from the case. Was this an act of collusion? These had been trying months for Hoover. His negotiations with London and Berlin to keep the funds flowing and the food pouring into Rotterdam, had been fraught with dangerous allegations in newspapers. We have already established Edith's links to both the press and the War Office in London. Furthermore, the threats she made in her letters that she had damning information which would one day be made public would have caused great concern, assuming that more than just her family read her mail. We have to ask whether the timing was chance or were the Germans asked to extricate the CRB from any responsibility for Edith's fate? Suddenly, no-one even loosely associated with Herbert Hoover was directly involved in attempting to save her.

Next in line for this poisoned chalice was an established member of the Brussels' Bar, Maitre Sadi Kirschen, who was approached by both Hanssens and Braun on 7 September.[45] Kirschen was not involved with the CNSA. Sadi Kirschen wrote to ask Edith if she would accept him as her defense replacement, but his letter never reached her. Furthermore, the Germans decided to deny Maitre Kirschen access to Edith immediately before the trial[46] and he was not given sight of the prosecution's evidence. Sadi Kirschen discussed the case with his legal colleagues, and the unanimous opinion was that the worst she might expect was five or so years in prison.[47]

In his later report, which was no better than a litany of excuses, Gaston de Leval made great play of his willingness to attend the trial in person and of being advised not to do so by Mr Kirschen lest the Germans be affronted by his presence. Apparently de Leval's attendance might have prejudiced Edith's case. What a bizarre excuse. Every sentence in de Leval's report was written to absolve himself, the Americans and key figures of the CRB from responsibility or complicity.[48]

Why did the Americans go to such lengths to protect themselves but not Edith? Their constant denials begin to grate. By wrapping themselves around their own supposedly legal statement, which was rapidly published by the British government, repeated in Gibson's diary and apparently "authenticated" by Brand Whitlock, these men wrote their own version of history; a version that goes uncontested, even though it is ridiculous.

In Brand Whitlock's second volume about his years in Belgium, written in 1919, he opened his account of Edith Cavell's tragic betrayal with the following words: "Early in August Brussels had heard, and all Belgium – or at least all that part of Belgium that lived in chateaux – had heard that Princess Marie de Croy and the Countess of Belleville had been arrested."[49] While concentrating on the Belgian noblewomen, he mentioned "Mademoiselle Thuliez, and certain others" and claimed that the Princess did not know what became of the Allied soldiers they were protecting "after they reached Brussels." Then with carefully chosen words, he stated: "One day in August it was learned at the legation that an English nurse named Edith Cavell had been arrested."[50] This was utter drivel, a blatant attempt to cover his own back.

By relegating his knowledge of her predicament until "One day in August" Whitlock sought to alter history so that he could acknowledge that "all Belgium" knew about the aristocrats and the demise of the underground network, yet distance himself from the responsibility he held for Edith Cavell. That it was the twenty-seventh day apparently slipped his mind. The lies simply became ever more ridiculous. His bold claim that Marie de Croy knew nothing about the fate of these soldiers once they reached Brussels is absurd. Princess Marie de Croy wrote a precisely detailed book when she returned from captivity, in which she detailed the underground work overseen by her brother Reginald. This included her visit to Edith and his admiration for her dedication.[51]

Recent evidence doggedly researched by Hugo Lueders and his associate in Brussels has unearthed proof that Edith Cavell and Marie de Croy met together in Ghent in April 1915 at La Ville D' Audenarde. Edith Cavell stayed several times at the guest-house, known to be an important hub for members of the Belgian and French resistance movements as well as profiteers associated with the relief movement.[52] Marie knew what she was talking about. Whitlock did not.

Marie de Croy's autobiographical account of her trial added yet another twist to the tale. She was represented by Alexander Braun whose services had been employed by her many influential friends in Brussels, but she specifically identified his son, Thomas Braun as part of the defense team for all the accused. He led the final defense summary "with a fine appeal" pleading that the Belgian defendants had been faced with the choice between helping their countrymen or denouncing them.[53] Thus Thomas had been removed from representing Edith, but retained as a leading player in the defense team. This astounding piece of evidence lends credence to the fact that the CRB wanted Edith's defense distanced from their associates.

Maitre Gaston Leval's report on the execution of Edith Cavell is currently being presented on the Internet by firstworldwar.com as a Primary Document for readers, schools and universities. It is little more than a bundle of misleading, self-serving assertions that do not stand up to scrutiny. It is part of the propaganda to which the British government was happy to accede in 1915. One hundred years later, it is still presented as the truth.

Of the 70 people initially arrested by the German secret police, 35 were tried together in the Senate House in Brussels on 7th and 8th October 1915. The 22 men and 13 women were charged with a variety of related crimes including, conveying soldiers to the enemy, assisting with their safe-keeping, circulating seditious pamphlets and illegally carrying letters and correspondence. [54] It was a closed trial, and neutral observers were not permitted to attend. The five German judges were unnamed, but the central prosecutor, Kriegsgerichtsrat Eduard Stoebar, had allegedly been "brought to Brussels especially for this case as he was known as a hanging judge."[55]

Edith pled guilty to the charge laid against her, namely aiding enemy soldiers to return to their homeland and was not questioned about her other activities. The precise nature of the charge under paragraph 68 of the German military penal code included "conducting soldiers to the enemy" which carried the death sentence,[56] though no-one apparently expected it to go that far. We know that she was a prolific correspondent, and the Germans had in their possession a letter that had been recently delivered to her through the American legation, but though she was clearly in possession of illegal correspondence, Edith was not accused of illegally sending or receiving mail. What embarrassment would that letter have caused had it been produced in court? Yet no reference was made to it at all. Why? It has been suggested that in her plea of guilty, she took the opportunity "to conceal greater and more serious activities, including spying."[57]

While that is an interesting way of suggesting that Edith somehow set the parameters of the charges she faced, the responsibility for framing the trial lay entirely with the German court. The pertinent question would ask why she was not interrogated about the content of the letters she had sent or the frequency of such correspondence? She was known to be an honest, frank, God-fearing woman who would not have lied under oath. Had she been asked, would Edith have spoken out about the German use of the food imports facilitated through the CRB? Was this what she meant when she told her mother that she "could tell you many things, but must save them till later?"[58] Could the Germans or the Commission for Relief in Belgium have afforded to take that risk?

Summary.

- German suspicions of the de Croy organization, which they considered a spy-network, resulted in the arrest of 70 members in August 1915. Edith was arrested on 5 August in front of her nurses at the Institute.
- One of the members of the network who was arrested at the same time, later wrote a long report about 'The Cavell Organization' which she claimed was closely connected to the British intelligence services. It was suppressed by the military authorities.
- Further evidence has recently surfaced in the Royal Museum of the Army and History of the War in Belgium from Herman Capiau, another member of the network arrested together with Edith. His record, entitled *'L' Affaire Cavell'* described the spying activities they undertook and its links with the War Office in London.
- The very survival of Hoover's CRB was threatened in 1915 by leaks about supplies going to Germany reported in the London press.
- Hugh Gibson at the American Legation claimed that they knew nothing of Edith's arrest on 5 August. That is ridiculous. All Brussels was agog with stories of the multiple arrests.
- The lawyer sent by the Nursing Institute was himself arrested and imprisoned.
- Edith's legal representation was an orchestrated farce. Members of the CNSA tried valiantly to find an appropriate legal representative for Edith. Maitre Sadi Kirschen was the eventual choice.
- Nurse Cavell pled guilty to the charge of aiding enemy soldiers to return home. She was not accused of illegally sending or receiving mail. She was not accused of spying. Why?

"PRO PATRIA"

She was glad to die for her Country! *Her Spirit Endureth Ever!*

Chapter 20

Cavell – The Unedifying Circus

Edith was not the only non-Belgian, nor even the only English woman on trial. The highest profile female prisoner, Princess Marie de Croy, was born in London, a fact recorded on her charge sheet, and made known to the court.[1] If the purpose of the exercise was to frighten or subdue the population and stop the repatriation of refugee soldiers, then the execution of that noblewomen alone would have sufficed. She was both English and of Belgian aristocracy. Her brother was held to be the leader of the underground movement. But they spared Marie de Croy and executed the English nurse and one unlucky other, Philippe Baucq, the man responsible for *La Libre Belgique,* which had lampooned General von Bissing. The Spanish Ambassador, the King of Spain[2] and even Pope Benedict XV became involved in international pleas for mercy. The remaining members of the network who were condemned to death with Edith had their sentences remitted to imprisonment with hard labor. Only Edith and Philippe Baucq were summarily shot by firing squad on 12 October. Members of the CRB, the American Legation and the CNSA would have us believe that they did everything humanly possible to save Edith Cavell. Judge that for yourself, please.

Brand Whitlock was unwell and kept himself out of the action. He did however know about Edith Cavell's dire circumstances. In his journal, Whitlock casually recorded on 11 October, "I don't remember whether I mentioned her in my notes before of not. She was arrested weeks ago..."[3] He could not remember whether he had mentioned her before? Apart from the convenience of poor recall, Whitlock was admitting prior interest in Edith's fate, though nothing about her was included in his earlier diaries or journals. However, at the eleventh hour, he sprang into action. If the accounts from Hugh Gibson and Gaston de Leval are to be believed, and these are the sources from which historians have drawn their conclusions, the charade of last minute pleadings went as follows.

Whitlock records that he was brought news of Edith's death sentence at 9.00 pm on 11 October by his friend and confidante, de Leval who had "just heard from the nurses who were keeping him informed ... that the sentence of death had been pronounced on Miss Cavell at two o'clock that afternoon and that she was to be shot next morning."[4] In his later account, *Belgium Under German Occupation,* Whitlock altered the timing to read, "the sentence of death had been pronounced on Miss Cavell at half-past four in the afternoon and she was to be shot at two o'clock the next morning."[5]

Perhaps he just wanted to heighten the tension. There is a further point. No-one has ever explained how these nurses knew what was happening, yet the most influential men in the land apparently did not. But that is not all. With divine prescience or, more likely, in the expectation of such news, Brand Whitlock, on the advice of Maitre Gaston de Leval, had that very afternoon signed a plea for clemency to the Governor General (von Bissing) and a "letter of transmittal" to be given to the head of the German Political Department, Baron von der Lancken. Whitlock described it as a "premonition."[6] They claimed not to know about the court's verdict, but had prepared letters of appeal in advance. What amazing foresight.

As the circus gathered, key figures could not be found. General von Bissing was at his chateaux at Trois Fontaine, apparently playing bridge. Hugh Gibson and Gaston de Leval found the Spanish Ambassador, Marquis de Villalobar at Baron Lambert's house in the company of the most powerful banker in Belgium and the executive president of the CNSA, Emile Francqui. Happily the meal was not greatly ruined since they were already at coffee. All, save Francqui, rushed round to Baron von der Lancken's empty offices at Rue Lambermont, only to be told he was at "Le Bois Sacre," a seedy variety theatre.[7] Von der Lancken insisted on waiting until the end of the performance. He dismissed claims of Edith's impending execution as "impossible," but was prevailed upon to phone the prison. He claimed that it was only at that point that he learned Edith was indeed to be executed in the dark of night. Or so the story was written by the Americans. Let us recap here. Von der Lancken claimed not to have known about the decision to shoot Edith Cavell and Philippe Baucq. Von Bissing was at his chateaux playing cards. The most important figure in Belgian politics and finance, Emile Francqui chose to remain at his friend's house and finish his coffee while the others rushed about like headless chickens. At what point did coincidence collide with convenience and mutate into fiction?

While Hugh Gibson, de Leval and the Marquis de Villalobar apparently appealed for clemency or at worst, the postponement of the death sentence, a different round of buck-passing began. Baron von der Lancken claimed that von Bissing, though Governor-General, had no power to overrule the new Military Governor, General von Sauberzweig, on matters decided by a military court, and it was up to him to grant a stay of execution. Von Sauberzweig refused. He had been appointed only days before. Interestingly he later became quarter-master for the German army, which suggests that von Sauberzweig had more than a passing interest in the work of the CRB.

The token appeals for clemency were dismissed about midnight and, according to Hugh Gibson, two hours later Edith Cavell faced the firing squad.[8] The phrase "you couldn't make it up" summarizes Gibson's account. Edith was executed at dawn on 12 October 1915, in the company of another hero, Philippe Baucq. In her last hours with the British chaplain, the Reverend H. Stirling Gahan, she calmly reflected: "I have seen death so often that it is not strange or fearful to me."[9] She died as she lived, a heroine and a patriot … and a key member of a successful underground network spying on the German invaders.

Spies were regularly shot and it was not unknown for women spies to suffer the same fate. The French authorities had executed Marguerite Schmidt and Ottillie Voss for spying in March and in May 1915,[10] but Edith Cavell had not been charged with espionage. Though she was later referred to as the "Spy Cavell" by the German authorities, no-one appeared to have expected that the military court would pass the death sentence even though warnings about the consequences of harboring enemy soldiers had been widely posted across Brussels. Spies were shot, yes; smuggling soldiers across the border was cause for imprisonment. Not this time.

The German Under-Secretary for Foreign Affairs, Arthur Zimmermann, issued a formal press release from Berlin about Edith Cavell's execution. It stated: "no war court in the world could have given any other verdict, for it was not concerned with a single emotional need of one person, but a well thought out plot, with many far-reaching ramifications, which for nine months succeeded in doing valuable service to our enemies to the great detriment of our armies."[11]

But why did this not apply to all who were charged? He added that her execution was regrettable but necessary and just, because as a result of the underground activities, "countless Belgian, French and English soldiers are again fighting in the ranks of the allies" thanks to the group "whose head was the Cavell woman."[12] The German authorities in Belgium knew that Edith Cavell was not in charge of the network. Von Bissing wrote a letter to his cousin on 23 October 1915 in which he categorically stated that "the brother of the princess (Reginald de Croy) was the leader of the organization and, if arrested, would undoubtedly have been condemned to death."[13] Thus the Germans knew that Edith Cavell was directly involved but not the leader of the organization. Did the German Under-Secretary lie, or was he not party to all the facts?

Governor General von Bissing was not interested in clemency. Marie de Croy thought that she saw him sitting amongst other officers in the Royal Box in the Senate House during the first day of the trial, "but later it was announced that he was out of Brussels at the time."[14] What a strange denial. Why would the German authorities need to distance the General from the trial? Unless of course his complicity goes far deeper than historians have recorded. And of what were they so scared that they sentenced Edith to death in camera, and carried out the sentence almost immediately? These are questions on which we should ponder, for the consequence of Edith Cavell's execution was far reaching. It stirred violent emotion and the cycle of blame was rapidly twisted into a whirlwind of propaganda, lies, and contempt for Germany. Now, as then, there was a darker purpose. Edith's death deflected attention away from the CRB and its role in feeding the German army. A role which Belgian historians seem determined to suppress.

In his later account, Hugh Gibson made much of his remonstrations with Baron von der Lancken on the eve of Edith Cavell's execution, but Gibson, first and foremost a Hoover man, was merely going through the motions. The focus of Gibson's "evidence" centers on himself, Brand Whitlock, the Marquis of Villalobar and the Belgian lawyer, Maitre Gaston de Leval, but he knew that the most important and influential person in Belgium was Emile Francqui, the President of the executive committee of the CNSA. Francqui resented Hoover's interference in Belgian affairs on a personal level, but if any individual could have taken effective steps at the last minute to save Edith Cavell, it was him. He did not lift a finger to help. Why? You might well ask, did Edith Cavell's death suit the needs of the Commission for Relief in Belgium and the CNSA? Had she been identified as the source of critical articles in the British press? Was there detailed information about the German abuses of Belgian Relief inside the parcel which had been ripped open and examined before it reached the editor of the *Nursing Mirror*? Bear in mind that Hoover had demanded such leaks must stop.

What too of the inventive Maitre Gaston de Leval, wrongly described by the *New York Times* as "legal advisor to Edith Cavell"?[15] That very claim inferred that Edith had been given legal council, but she was never properly represented by those charged with her safety and did not speak with Leval at any point. He was a company man and played a major part in concocting the impression that Brand Whitlock and his American associates had tried every avenue to save her from the firing squad. Leval was invited to address a meeting of the Secret Elite's inner sanctum in New York, the Pilgrims of America, on 26 January 1916 at which Lord Bryce, author of the *Bryce Report on German Atrocities in Belgium*, was present.[16] Co-incidence? What fate brought together the author of the greatest single piece of anti-German propaganda and lies in the opening years of the war, and the man who claimed to represent Edith Cavell and whose false testament appeared to clear the Americans of any charge of complicity?

Feted in the United States, Gaston de Leval's story grew in the telling and he repeated his accusations against Edith's real lawyer, Sadi Kirschen. He claimed that Kirschen had deliberately kept him in the dark and had been mysteriously unavailable on the night that Edith was sentenced. True, Sadi Kirschen had left Brussels for the weekend having been assured that nothing would happen to the prisoners. As he grew bolder, De Leval's allegations became increasingly malicious. His nefarious slanders were circulated in the press. He alleged that Thomas Braun had asked to be replaced as Edith Cavell's lawyer and Kirschen was depicted as an Austrian and a spy. De Leval claimed that Edith had been abandoned in her hour of need and handed over to an enemy lawyer.[17]

Sadi Kirschen's reputation lay in tatters, and he literally took the matter into his own hands, confronted Leval in the Palais de Justice in Brussels on Christmas Eve 1918 and knocked him to the ground. Kirschen accused Leval of slander and in the resulting court case, the Brussels Bar Council adjudged that Leval had made no attempt to meet Kirschen between 8-11 October 1915. In other words it was Leval who had lied. *He* was guilty of slander. No matter; he had served the Americans well. He was a man without honor whose courtship with fame knew no bounds. Gaston de Leval presented himself as one of the chief mourners at Edith's later internment in England. He joined the official family group following her coffin into Westminster Abbey on 15 May, 1919.[18] He had never met, nor spoken to, nor represented her in court, but lived the lie that he had tried everything to save Edith. Despicable.

There was one further incident that is generally ignored by historians. When the Foreign Office decided to publicize the letters and reports from Leval and Brand Whitlock in the *Times*, the German authorities, and Baron von der Lancken in particular, were appalled. He summoned Whitlock to his office on Monday 25 October 1915, and demanded that the head of the American Legation retract his lies and make a formal apology. He was particularly enraged by Gaston de Leval's so-called "report," which as we have demonstrated, was laced with lies. Von der Lancken threatened to have the Belgian lawyer sent to a concentration camp in Germany.[19] He was visibly incensed by the totally inaccurate version released by Hugh Gibson and Whitlock and pointed to the lies contained in the reports. He told Brand Whitlock to his face that he, as head of the American legation, had *not* made frequent inquires about Edith Cavell's condition and representation,[20] and he insisted that the American Legation had never asked to be kept informed about the legal process.[21] Von der Lancken demanded that an immediate retraction be written. Notices were published in the streets of Brussels denying that Whitlock was kept ignorant that the death sentence had been pronounced, or that the German Authorities, by proceeding rapidly, had prevented him from intervening in favor of the accused.[22] Thus, the official version, published and approved by the Foreign Office, was lambasted as utterly false. Brand Whitlock never changed his story, but received permission from Washington to issue Gaston de Leval with an American passport to get him urgently out of Belgium. After all, they could hardly have allowed him to be interrogated by the secret police.

The fallout did not stop with de Leval's enforced departure. Hugh Gibson was not forgiven by the Germans for his jaundiced report of Edith Cavell's trial. He became persona non grata.[23] Though he lingered at the

Brussels legation, antagonism towards him steadily grew until on 7 February, 1916 Von der Lanken arrived at Brand Whitlock's door and demanded that Gibson leave "today or at the latest, tomorrow."[24] The reason noted by Whitlock was quite specific. "His [Gibson's] firm stand in the Edith Cavell affair, and his statements upon it afterwards, had now resulted in a crisis. It was felt desirable to give him leave of absence."[25] It says much that Whitlock made no serious protest about the loss of his secretary. In this intricate web of complicity, Hugh Gibson, a young man-on-the-make of the type with whom Hoover surrounded himself, who had proved his loyalty to the CRB, found himself promoted to the American Embassy in London. Hoover arranged the prestigious appointment personally.[26]

And what of the British Government? In this amazing litany of Pontius Pilates, all lining up to distance themselves from the execution, the Foreign Office also played its part. It firstly claimed that it was powerless to intervene, but confidently trusted that the American legation in Brussels would see that Edith had a fair trial. Sir Horace Rowland at the Foreign Office "was afraid that it was likely to go hard with Miss Cavell." In documents that only saw the light of day in 2005, Lord Robert Cecil, wrote in words that paraphrased de Levall's excuse, that "any representation by us will do her more harm than good."[27] In other words, they did nothing. However, after Edith had been executed they took the unprecedented step of publishing all of the reports and letters received from the American Legation in Brussels. The Foreign Office used Reuters to guarantee a worldwide audience. The daily editorial and an entire page[28] inside the *Times* was given over to Brand Whitlock's false account. He, Gibson and de Leval were duly praised for their "chivalrous zeal" in trying to save "our countrywoman's life."[29] What shameless hypocrisy.

Once dead, Edith Cavell presented the British propaganda machine with the perfect cause celebre; the patriot-saint, a matron dressed in martyr's robes, transformed in death into a rallying call against the evil Hun. In the House of Lords, the public mood was caught by Lord Desart (from the Committee of Imperial Defence) in an outraged condemnation. "She was tried in cold blood; she was convicted in cold blood; she was executed in cold blood." Lord Lansdowne assured everyone "that the representatives of the United States and of Spain at Brussels up to the very last moment neglected no opportunity or effort in order to obtain a commutation of the death sentence passed on Miss Cavell, or even to obtain at least a period of suspense before that sentence was carried into effect."[30]

It was such a cleverly worded absolution – which inferred that the American and Spanish representatives had done everything they possibly could for Edith. We know now that they had moved so painfully slowly that any chance of assistance came too late. Edith's links with the de Croys, and her letters to the *Nursing Mirror* were carefully airbrushed from history and replaced with ridiculous stories and downright lies.[31] Most importantly, they deflected criticism from the CRB. Indeed, they removed the Commission's name from any association with Edith's death. Propaganda posters spawned myths, but their value for recruitment, for justification of war, and for the agitation of the American public was priceless.

For a century these sad lies have been allowed to persist, promoted by establishment historians. They are regurgitated now despite the fact that contemporary research has unmasked the fraudulent claims and deliberate obfuscations. We share the concerns of those who have asked, what was the real purpose behind Edith Cavell's "martyrdom?"

In 1919 Edith Cavell's body was disinterred from its unmarked grave in Brussels and given a formal memorial service in the Gard du Nord in the presence of the Allied Commanders. The coffin was loaded with all reverence onto a special train draped in black and covered with beautiful flowers. Her remains were met with great ceremony in England, and Queen Alexandra attended the military service at Westminster Abbey. Finally, Edith was laid to rest outside Norwich Cathedral with all the panoply of a grateful nation.[32] Let it be clearly understood that she was a patriot who willingly gave her life to save brave men. Her self-sacrifice is beyond doubt and worthy of high honor. They called her a martyr, and amid the sacred pomp and circumstance of the iconic cathedral, she was lauded in triumph.[33] In truth, Edith was knowingly and unrepentantly a key figure in a Belgian resistance network which was spying for the allies and sending military intelligence to London.[34] Furthermore, she had a tale to tell.

And the deliberate myth-making, the manipulation of her contribution, contrived to deflect criticism away from the Commission for the Relief of Belgium (CRB) and the Comite National de Secours et Alimentation (CNSA). More importantly, it camouflaged the fact that through these organizations the Allies were effectively feeding the German army. With the Cavell/de Croy organization broken, the flow of adverse criticism from Belgium was somewhat stemmed. There would be no more compromising letters from the Berkendael Institute. The supply of food available to the German army continued; so too did the fighting. The CRB's massive international organization comprising bankers and financiers, shipping magnates and grain exporters could breathe more easily. So too could the Belgian bankers. A whistle blower had been silenced.

In addition there was an ironic bonus for the Secret Elite. With her body buried in an unmarked Belgian grave in 1915, the monsters of propaganda twisted Edith Cavell's Christian values so that the protective Angel of Mercy was translated into an Avenging Angel of Death.[35] The Bishop of London pronounced that "the blood of this brave woman will be the seed of armed men."[36] Recruitment posters appeared with Edith's image set against an emboldened background which proclaimed "Murdered by the Hun." Sadly her example of selflessness was transformed into a rallying call for enlistment. Her life's purpose had been to save others but her image was rebranded and distorted to send tens of thousands to their graves on the Western Front. A recent estimate claims that 40,000 more men, or somewhere between two and three infantry divisions were formed on the strength of the Cavell propaganda.[37] It was such perfect timing, for the flow of volunteers to Kitchener's rallying call was fast drying up. Edith's sacrifice smoothed the path to conscription in 1916. And it was all based on vile propaganda.

The British War Cabinet set up a secret committee under the Attorney-General in November 1918 to "Inquire into the Breaches of the Laws of War" committed by the German army, and considered the case of Nurse Edith Cavell. In a report that was kept buried deep, the committee duly found that the court-martial (Feldgericht) was justified in finding that she had committed the offenses of which she was charged, and had the power in law to condemn her to death.[38] In the cooler reflection of a two-year old victory, the secret report of 26 February 1920 decided that; "it seems impossible to say that the tribunal which tried Miss Cavell, or the persons which carried out its sentence, were guilty of a war crime"[39] and there was "no prospect that the prosecution of any of the persons concerned in the trial of Miss Cavell would result in a conviction." Having buried the truth, the Secret Elite had no interest in any further debate. So much for Lord Desart's rhetoric of "tried in cold blood."[40] Edith was a patriot, but she was guilty of the charge the Germans chose not to bring against her. Espionage. Edith Cavell was certainly a victim of war, but whose victim?

Consider this "co-incidence." Herbert Hoover was present in Brussels during Edith Cavell's trial. He lunched with Brand Whitlock on 6 October and had discussions with Baron von der Lancken on the afternoon of 8 October. [41] The Chairman of the CRB left the city on 9 October, the very Saturday on which the German Judges sat in secret session to decide the sentences of the military court[42] and only three days before Edith Cavell's execution.

Every aspect of Edith Cavell's arrest, imprisonment and execution was framed by the CRB or its Belgian partner, the CNSA. All the received histories have built their accounts of Edith's fate on "evidence" presented by members of the American Legation who were associated with the CRB. Furthermore, this "evidence" is still accepted as fact. Thus the lies continue.

And they grew darker. The German military governor who ordered that Edith be shot at dawn on 12 October 1915, General Traugott Martin von Sauberzweig, was described as a burly, aggressive brute of a man who endorsed violence as a tactic.[43] His stay in Brussels was so comparatively short that one can but conclude that he was specifically sent there on a mission. Sauberzweig was allegedly unknown to Brand Whitlock, who claimed never to have met him. On the day before Edith's execution, Whitlock noted in his diary that von der Lancken "Finally telephoned the Military Governor, a new one, I must get his name…"[44] We are asked to believe that the Head of the American legation did not know the name of the recently appointed German military governor when so many Belgian citizens were being tried by a military court. Perhaps Whitlock's memory had simply failed him once again. By 2 November, Sauberzweig was reported to have been removed from office and replaced,[45] but that may have been wishful thinking. Other sources claim that he held on to his post until June 1916.[46] Whichever, it was likely that he was parachuted in as military governor to ensure that Edith Cavell was silenced.

How strange it all was, but no stranger than the later meeting that the cursed General apparently requested with Herbert Hoover and his CRB colleague, Vernon Kellogg, when they "happened to be in Berlin" in August 1916. According to Hoover, Sauberzweig, haunted by remorse, asked to speak with him and confessed that he had been responsible for having Edith Cavell shot before there was any time for an effective appeal. How convenient for Hoover and the CRB that Sauberzweig should accept full responsibility, referring to himself as "the murderer,"[47] exclusively to Hoover and Kellogg. Here for the historical record was their final "proof" that Cavell's death had nothing to do with the CRB.

In his account, Vernon Kellogg painted a different image of Sauberzweig's remorse. He was drunk, "on his nth whisky," and had just come from his son's hospital bed where the young man was lying blinded and disfigured. "And the sight of his son – and the memory of Miss Cavell made him remark that this was a horrible war."[48] He repeatedly referred to "Die Cavell; that 'The Cavell' was a thing that interfered with German control of Belgium. 'It had to be got rid of, so I had her shot.'"[49] Not much remorse there, no matter how you read it, but what did Sauberzweig mean by stating that Edith Cavell interfered with German control of Belgium? After his stay in Brussels, Sauberzweig was appointed Quartermaster-General at the Imperial German Supreme Headquarters.[50] Who better to understand the importance of the unfettered CRB supplies reaching his troops than the man responsible for feeding the German army?

No matter how it was dressed up in fraught meetings and bitter recriminations, the CRB's relationship with the German war effort could only be described as collaboration. Anyone who endangered the status quo was indeed interfering with the war effort, but not just Germany's. A sense of a multi-layered self-interest pervaded the Commission and its work. Decisions were taken at the highest levels of real power which embraced America, Britain, France and Germany. Had the CRB collapsed, the American economy would have been immediately damaged. So much had been invested through the Morgan – Rothschild axis, the Kuhn, Loeb and Co. banking house, through Bethlehem Steel and America's blossoming armaments industry, that any action which risked a sudden end to the war would have affected them all. Some writers have claimed that the decision to have Edith Cavell killed could be traced back to the British Head of the Secret Service in New York, Sir William Wiseman. Not so. Wiseman was recuperating in Britain from gas poisoning inflicted on him in Flanders earlier in 1915, and when he was posted to the United States in December, Edith Cavell had been dead for two months.[51] Nevertheless, the American connection was spread much further than Herbert Hoover and the Brussels' legation.

Nor should we imagine that British hands were clean. Though they never acknowledged Edith's role as a spy (no government would) we have shown that she worked for the Intelligence Services. One hundred years later the former Director-General of MI5, Stella Rimington, admitted so in public[52] Most of all, the Foreign Office in the personages of Sir Edward Grey and Lord Eustace Percy knew about the vast tonnage of food and thousands of livestock which were transferred into Germany while the CRB maintained its "humanitarian" front. They knew the pressure that Hoover's men were under to stop such information reaching London. This is a matter of record.[53] They were all in collusion.

On her way to prison in Germany, Princess Marie de Croy sat on her cases in a railway station and inadvertently summed up this whole episode with a single observation:

> The sergeant told me he was going on holiday and, like all the German soldiers whom I saw traveling, he was loaded with provisions to take home. Although a promise had been made to America that food should not be taken out of Belgium, which was the condition the United States had made for provisioning the population, this was certainly done.[54]

The Committee for Relief in Belgium was not supplying provisions for the sole use of the "starving" Belgian population. It was feeding Germany too; feeding the German army and sustaining the German population. In dissecting the myriad of lies which have been woven around Edith Cavell, the evidence that the German, American, Belgian and British authorities colluded in her murder is overwhelming. Had she lived to expose the truth behind the CRB, the consequences for the Secret Elite would have been catastrophic. Her death ensured that the agony of a miserable war was prolonged.

Summary.

- Edith Cavell was condemned to death by German court-martial and executed along with one other, Philippe Baucq.
- The American Legation in Brussels went to extreme measures to bury their complicity with Edith Cavell's execution. Their leader, Brand Whitlock was 'unwell' and removed himself from the action.
- The accepted sources for events in Brussels were taken from Hugh Gibson and the CRB lawyer Gaston de Level, both of whom were deeply involved in ensuring that Edith was not saved from her fate.
- A circus of a charade followed with everyone claiming either not to know where key officers were, whether an execution had been ordered or who had the power to rescind the verdict of the court.
- Though he never met Edith Cavell and at no point gave legal advice to her, Gaston de Level posed as the man who tried to save her. He was taken to America where he was feted and profited from his lectures which exonerated America from any responsibility.
- De Leval rashly accused Maitre Sadi Kirschen of failing to undertake his proper legal responsibilities, made scurrilous and entirely false claims, and was assaulted for his troubles. In the court case that followed it was proved that de Leval was the liar.
- The Germans in Belgium were outraged at De Level and Gibson by their false statements and accusations. Gibson was re-assigned to the American Embassy in London.
- Edith Cavell became the center of a twisted propaganda campaign which made a mockery of the patriotic work she willingly undertook.
- In 1918 a British War Cabinet committee secretly judged that the German court was justified in its conclusion and was empowered to sentence her to death.
- It was later discovered that Herbert Hoover had been physically present in Brussels during Edith's trial. He lunched with Brand Whitlock on 6 October, and met with Baron von der Lancken on 8 October. He left the city on the same day that the judges met in secret session to decide the sentences handed to Edith and her co-accused.
- The former Director General of M15 in Britain, Dame Stella Rimington confessed in a Radio program that Edith Cavell had been spying and sent her messages in tiny micro-writing sewn into the clothes of the repatriated soldiers she helped.

Chapter 21

Oil – The Uneven Playing Field

The Secret Elite intentionally prolonged the war beyond the Spring of 1915 by providing Germany with raw materials for armaments production and food for her army. There were various facets to the great deception. We have already described in detail how, from the outset, Germany's crucial source of iron ore from the Briey basin on the Franco-German border was deliberately left intact though it could have been destroyed. German commanders admitted that the war would have been over by the summer of 1915 had the Briey supplies been halted.[1] Britain simultaneously ran a sham naval blockade through which food, gun-cotton and desperately needed minerals, including zinc and copper, for armaments production were allowed to pour into Germany.[2] In conjunction with these actions, a great "humanitarian" deception under the guise of "Belgian Relief" was used as a cover for provisioning the German army. This allowed it to keep fighting and so prolonged the war.[3] Closure of just one of these spigots would have seriously damaged Germany's war effort. Closure of all three would, without a shadow of doubt, have ended the war by early 1915. That was never their intention.

The Secret Elite also prolonged the war by ensuring that Germany was able to maintain ample oil supplies. It was absolutely crucial to their war effort. There could be no effective modern war without sufficient supplies of oil and whoever controlled these supplies, controlled the war. In 1914 contemporary commentators spoke of the revolution in military strategy and the awesome power of destruction brought about by machines.[4] The internal combustion engine changed every dimension of warfare and the mobility of forces on land and sea and, now, in the air. The mechanical innovations included oil-fired ships and submarines, motorized divisions, airplanes and tanks. Virtually every new development depended on access to plentiful supplies of petroleum, and year by year oil increasingly lubricated the means of war. As the leading French politician Henry Berenger stated, "On the battlefield, on land, on the sea and in the air, a drop of petrol is equal to a drop of blood."[5] Since both Britain and France on one side, and Germany on the other, had no indigenous supplies, sourcing it was critical to the ability to keep fighting.

The Secret Elite, the power base that caused the first World War[6] either controlled oil production across the globe, or was intimately linked to those who did. It included the Rothschilds in Europe,[7] and J.D. Rockefeller's empire in America.[8] The Rothschild dynasty operated one step removed from the public eye and one step ahead of its competition. Their massive investment in banking and oil gave it a geo-political power that few could equal. The Secret Elite knew that long-term secure supplies of oil, not just for the allies, but for Germany, would be absolutely crucial as they maneuvered Europe into a protracted war. They ensured that the British Government, and the Foreign Office in particular, was conversant with the developing and potentially vital new oil discoveries in Burma, Sumatra, Mexico, Mesopotamia and the Gulf. Indeed, it was no accident of history that the British Government took ownership of the Anglo-Persian Oil Company through one of the final Acts of Parliament introduced just as the war began.[9]

Aware that war was coming, the Admiralty, Foreign Office and Board of Trade signed contracts with several oil companies in advance of the hostilities – yet it was claimed that Britain was "woefully unprepared" for war.[10] Lord Curzon, senior member of the Secret Elite, later summed up its absolute importance when he stated in 1918: "The Allied cause has floated to victory upon a wave of oil."[11]

The German government was no less aware of oil's strategic and economic importance, but struggled to ensure that supplies could be freely guaranteed. Pre-war opinion in Germany that its complete dependence on a foreign trust like J.D. Rockefeller's Standard Oil was absolutely intolerable, had crystallized into fear that in any future war, lack of oil could do more damage than the most powerful enemy.[12] Germany had emerged by 1914 as a leader in manufacture and export growth, and that "stuck in John Bull's craw."[13] Their dynamic pre-war economy was bristling with confidence and technological innovation, but despite attempts to be masters of their own destiny, the German government was dependent for oil on a small number of international producers, refiners and distributors. Even they were not fully aware of who actually owned these. Indeed, such was the labyrinthine nature of European banks and oil company ownership, that few individuals had any notion who really controlled the global oil supply.

Germany, like Britain, had solid supplies of coal, but no oil. With a stealth and determination that characterised much of the industry, Rockefeller's Standard Oil had in the pre-war years grasped a significant position in the supply to Germany. Standard's chosen technique was to acquire existing companies, but operate them under their original names in order to create the illusion that they remained German. It retained prominent German oil merchants as shareholders and this had the effect of diluting objections to its monopolistic growth. Behind the closed doors of corporate greed, such tactics shielded Standard from a public outcry against what had been described as an alien corporation.[14] Standard operated under the banner of the Deutsche Petroleum Verkaufgessellschaft which by 1912 controlled 91 per cent of all German oil sales. The Deutsche Bank was allowed to buy into the company but its stake accounted for little more than nine per cent of the total holdings. Devoid of an independent and secure source of supply, Germany had been locked tightly in the grip of Standard Oil.[15] The massive profits that accrued through this monopoly attracted European investors. It also attracted other companies to become major players capable of challenging Standard's grip on the oil market.

Standard Oil had created the global market game and learned to negotiate terms and reach settlements with a profusion of imperial, national, provincial and local governments.[16] But from 1910 to 1912, they found themselves in a bitter and protracted dispute with the Austro-Hungarian Empire in what Austria's leading newspaper called a "petroleum war."[17] It was not Standard Oil as such that had run into trouble, but its Austrian subsidiary, Vacuum Oil Company AG, Vienna.[18]

America remained the unrivaled global leader in oil with 60 per cent of total world production. But thanks to its Galician oil fields, Austria-Hungary could claim to be the third largest oil-producing country in the world behind the United States and Russia, and produced far in excess of its domestic requirements. Determined to hold on to its European monopoly, Standard (through its Vacuum Oil subsidiary) used underhand competitive tactics to undermine Austrian producers. The ensuing row embroiled the governments of both Austria-Hungary and America. The U.S. State Department became deeply involved and created an interesting precedent for twentieth century "globalization." It demonstrated clearly that businesses, even those as powerful as Standard Oil, relied on diplomatic support from their governments.[19] It had long been so. The British East India Company thrived on the back of diplomatic and military intervention on the Indian sub-continent in the eighteenth century, while the Opium Wars in the nineteenth century were an extension of the commercial/political ambitions shared between companies and their national governments.

The relevance of this "petroleum war," a minor dispute in the history of the global oil industry, is that even in the twentieth century, internationally powerful companies looked to their home base government for protection and support. Ironically, Galician oil production had peaked in 1909, though no-one at the time realized this. Nevertheless, the United States believed it had the right to intervene in a dispute between the Austrian government and a company incorporated inside Austria but owned by American shareholders; come what may, the Vacuum Oil Company was in a meaningful sense, American[20] – and how dare any foreign country in which it operated attempt to control it? Bear this in mind as we review the sources which supplied Germany during the First World War.

Theoretically, the German-Austro-Hungarian alliance faced a major obstacle in that their one indigenous oil source in Galicia lay in the hands of alien companies. By 1914 the number of large foreign joint-stock companies investing in Galician oil production, including Rockefeller's Vacuum, had grown dramatically. The major British player which emerged after its formation in 1910[21] was the Premier Oil and Pipe Line Company, which swallowed up numerous competitors, large and small. By the beginning of the war Premier Oil was the most important foreign company in Galicia. In 1912-13 it owned around 2,752 acres and produced over 262,000 tons of crude oil – almost a quarter of all Galician production. Though its British shareholders queried the legitimacy of its actions, and the company's relationship with German banks,[22] by the war's end its holdings encompassed twelve Austrian subsidiaries, 21,000 acres, 110 oil wells and four large refineries.[23] The phenomenal growth of this London-based company was derived from supplying the enemy with desperately needed oil throughout the war.

According to historian Alison Frank, the Galician wells provided approximately 60% of the Central Powers' needs.[24] The vast bulk was used by Austria-Hungary. However, the Galician oil supplies fell into decline at the precise moment when the outbreak of war brought the huge pressure of high demand. Although ownership rested in the hands of foreign companies including British, American, French and Belgian interests, they continued to provide oil and petroleum for the Austrian enemy. But what of Germany? Since Galicia was unable to satisfy her growing demand, from which sources could she draw her oil, surrounded as she was, by enemies?

In the decades before the outbreak of war the German government, companies and banks understood the vulnerability of the country's dependence on imported oil. Supplies from the rich Russian fields at Baku on the Caspian Sea were piped 450 miles overland to the port of Batum on the Black Sea, shipped by tanker to Romania, then taken in barges up the River Danube to Germany. Romania itself was fortunate to have major oilfields and since it was much closer to the industrial power-house of central and northern Germany, it became Germany's main supplier. Romanian oil was first registered in international statistics in 1857 when 250 tons were produced.[25]

Development was initially slow, but by the turn of the century international oil magnates, banks and investors descended like vultures and reaped rich pickings as it became the third largest oil producing country in the world. Its main commercial advantage lay in the fact that Romania was comparatively close to most European capitals and the river Danube offered a relatively straightforward route for transportation. The major fields at Ploesti and Campina, some 80 kilometers north of Bucharest, had their own refineries and storage installations. By 1900 production had risen to 250,000 tons, and by 1914 it stood at around 1.8 million tons. [26] Growth was spectacular. One might think that Romanian oil was controlled by the state. It was not. Ownership belonged to foreign investors who had their own agenda and profits flowed abroad rather than to the Romanian people.

One of the major Romanian fields, Steaua Romana, was bought over by German capital in 1903, and Germany thus appeared to have control of some 35 per cent of Romanian production. The Romano-Americana complex was gobbled up by Rockefeller's Standard Oil in 1904, and Astra Romana, the second largest, in 1910 by British investors in the Royal Dutch Shell company. By 1914, Romanian oil had been thoroughly internationalized [27] with British, Dutch, French and American interests controlling a majority of the wells.

Who actually owned the companies that controlled Romanian production and supplied Germany throughout the war? In 1913 Germany imported 125,000 tons of oil per year from Romania, approximately 10 per cent of its total production. The advent of war cut Germany off from her other suppliers and consequently she needed every barrel that could be squeezed from Romania. Apart from small and rapidly diminishing Galician supplies, Romania became the only major source of oil available to Germany.[28]

German investment gave them a nominal 35 per cent control of Romanian oil by 1914, but behind this bland fact lies the question: what precisely did German ownership mean? Was it the German government or German industrialists, merchant banks and investors? Or were there other *owners*? While Germany, through the Deutsche Bank and the Disconto Gesellschaft bank, appeared to have a considerable stake, Disconto Gesellschaft was in fact a Rothschild concern[29] and so under British and French influence rather than German. Disconto bought up three substantive Romanian companies, Concordia SA, which drilled for oil, Vega, which refined it and Creditul Petrolier which stored and transported it. In reality, Germany only controlled around 20 per cent of Romanian oil, far less than the statistics might suggest.

Who then were the decision-makers who permitted the commercial agreements and understandings that directed the supply of oil before and during the war? The dark and murky world of international business stood ready, as always to shed patriotism for profit and it is important to examine the historical facts. The greatest name in global oil in the nineteenth century and around the time of the First World War was J.D. Rockefeller. His Standard Oil Company had not only been vulnerable to the American anti-trust lobby which in 1911 demanded its dissolution into smaller parts,[30] but had been stalked by more dangerous predators, the Rothschilds. Before the turn of the century the Rothschilds had no intention of allowing Rockefeller to monopolize European oil fields, and they moved swiftly to take control of Russian oil at Baku on the Caspian Sea.

Oil had been discovered in the Baku district of Russia (now Azerbaijan) in the1850s. Such was the extent of these massive fields that in 1901 Russian production outranked American output, but that situation was rapidly reversed. The problem of limited investment in Baku was neatly summarized by Prince M. Golitsyn, Governor-General of the Caucasus: "The lack of free capital, the limited industrial infrastructure, the low level of agriculture, the lack of technical knowledge and weak business initiative of the resident population are long term obstacles to the economic growth of the region." They needed foreign inward-investors urgently;[31] amongst whom were the Nobel Brothers, Robert and Ludvig, as well as the ubiquitous Rothschilds.

The Nobels came originally from Sweden. Their rags to riches story involved the rather fanciful tale of Robert traveling through Russia in search of rare walnut timber for rifle stocks, and chancing upon Baku where he immediately grasped the commercial potential of the oil wells. The brothers founded the Branobel Oil company in 1876, purchased wells near Baku and constructed an eight-mile long pipeline to carry the oil to the Caspian Sea. They also built the world's first oil tanker, the Zoroaster, to transport the raw product for export. Within a few years the Nobels had built a railway system with hundreds of tank wagons and a network of storage depots. Branobel became a dominant company in the Russian oil market, and, remarkably, it managed to keep Standard Oil at arms length.[32] This systematic and expertly co-ordinated development was the complete antithesis of what was happening in Austrian Galicia. So, how did the Nobel brothers manage to fund such an awesomely expensive investment? They didn't. The Rothschilds did.

Reports filtered back to Standard Oil that the Nobels could not meet their obligations and were heavily in debt to the Paris Rothschilds.[33] The Rothschild Dynasty built much of its massive fortune by absorbing potentially successful companies and banks which had overstretched themselves. While the Nobel brothers appeared to control Russian oil in Baku, they operated as an important front for Rothschild interests. Their main advantage in Baku was their good relationship with the Czarist government.[34] The advantage that the Rothschilds had over Rockefeller and Standard Oil was that they served as official bankers to the Czar. In any event, by the turn of the century the Rothschilds had amassed vast and highly profitable investments in Baku, and there was little space left for Standard Oil.

At least that is how it seemed. While the Rothschilds and the Rockefellers were apparently engaged in the "oil wars" of the 1890s, grasping control over whatever oilfields and companies that could be drawn into their clutches, relationships were different behind the scenes. Certainly there were periods of "blistering competition"[35] but there was also a will to divide the spoils and share out the market.

In 1892, Baron Alphonse de Rothschild accepted Rockefeller's invitation to go to New York for secret talks behind the closed doors of Standard Oil's headquarters on Broadway. As Rockefeller's biographer saw matters: "Beneath the competitive veneer, the Rothschilds were keen to come to terms with Standard Oil."[36] No doubt the Rothschild version of events would reverse that order, for clearly both saw mutual benefit from monopolistic collusion. Standard Oil's chief spokesman, John Archbold, reported directly to Rockefeller that they had quickly reached a tentative agreement (without being sufficiently indiscreet to add its precise nature), but stressed that "it was thought desirable on both sides that the matter be kept confidential."[37] Indeed, Alphonse de Rothschild thought it desirable to keep the Nobel brothers out of the discussion and in the pre-war years, much of the great rivalry between Rothschild and Rockefeller was a convenient façade, though both would have the world believe otherwise.

These were the powers who dominated the oil industry and endlessly continued to grasp more and more of the global market; powers that were deeply involved in the close-knit Anglo-American cabal, the Secret Elite, who planned to crush Germany. Ironically, in order to do so they would provide her with oil. The Deutsche Bank's relationship with Romanian oil throws an interesting light on just how complex the matrix of oil ownership was. When a consortium led by Deutsche purchased the Steaua Romana Petroleum Company in Romanian in 1903, its major market lay in Germany. Steaua had access to substantial oil deposits lying south of the Carpathian Mountains, and owned barges on the Danube to transport it on to Germany from holding tanks at Regensburg in Austria.

It was alleged by those historians who saw imperialist ambitions as the driving force inside the Kaiser's empire, that Deutsche Bank yielded to pressure from the German government to take over Steaua. Not so. The impulse sprang from national economy, not national politics, though the two were often interwoven.[38] By 1914 Steaua had become the largest and most productive plant in Romania[39] and would play a significant role in supplying Germany during the war. Steaua's success, however, had only been achieved through sourcing vast sums of money, and much of that investment came from the Rothschilds.

In due course, Deutsche Bank appointed a friend and colleague of the Rothschilds, Emil von Stauss, to manage the Steaua Romana company. He was Managing Director of the Rothschild/Nobel/Deutsche Bank oil consortium, the Europaische Petroleum Union (EPU), which had originally been set up to counter the ever ambitious Standard Oil.[40] Thus, in the pre-war years, a strategy emerged to guarantee Germany's future oil supplies under the benign direction of the Rothschilds. With this vital link secured, the German Government was confident that economic growth would continue unabated, but in reality their source of oil was far from exclusively German. The Rothschilds, who were among the first to invest in the European oil markets, had their own agenda and no intention of sharing control with the German or any other government. They built a hugely profitable framework for the production of Romanian oil, and its distribution from Romania to Germany, but ensured that its control remained in their gift. In essence, while the major German bank, Deutsche Bank, played a significant role in Romanian oil, the Rothschilds played a significant part in Deutsche Bank. It was never exclusively "German" oil.

In addition, important Rothschild banks involved in the European oil industry, including Romania, were the Disconto Gesellschaft bank and its associated Bleichroder Bank. Established in 1851, the Disconto Bank grew steadily in size and importance through a series of amalgamations to become a leading player in German finance. It was generally considered to be a Rothschild front. In 1901 Disconto officially acquired the Rothschild Bank in Frankfurt, original seat of the Dynasty. The bank was allegedly sold on for two reasons; there was no male Rothschild heir in Frankfurt and it was deemed to be unprofitable. All staff members at the Rothschild Bank were transferred to Disconto and the Rothschild name was withdrawn.[41]

What conceivable reason would they have for doing this? Germany at that time was experiencing massive economic, industrial and technological growth. It was the emerging power-house of manufacturing in Europe.[42] Indeed from the viewpoint of the Secret Elite, Germany was the most dangerous threat to their wider ambitions.[43] Banks were booming. Selling an important asset, especially one in Frankfurt with sentimental and historic associations sits at odds with the Rothschild modus operandi of the previous two centuries. They were in the business of amassing assets, not liquidating them. The sale was undoubtedly a sham. Little had changed other than the bank's name. Disconto was nothing more than a front. The assets and the staff were simply transferred while the Rothschilds retained control behind the scenes.

The *New York Times*, reporting on the German stock market in 1902, identified "Disconto Gesellschaft and other concerns in the Rothschild Group" as the agents behind a massive one million crown loan adjustment to the Hungarian Government.[44] In 1909, Senator Nelson Aldrich presented a joint report to Congress in conjunction with Professor Reisser from the University of Berlin on the condition of European banks.[45] It concluded that "Disconto Gesellschaft, as a member of the Rothschild syndicate, participated in large numbers of Austro-Hungarian state, railroad and other transactions."[46] Clearly the Americans knew that Disconto was a Rothschild organization despite protestations that it had become an independent German entity. It was simply the way Rothschilds worked. They minimized public awareness of their role in the hundreds of banking, oil and industrial concerns they controlled, but maximized the impact they could wield on governments no matter on which side those governments fought in any given war.

The Bleichroder Bank was yet another Rothschild front.[47] "It maintained close contacts with the Rothschild Dynasty; the banking house of Gerson Bleichroder acted as a branch office of the Rothschild Bank in Berlin."[48] Bleichroder was known as Bismarck's banker. Thus, despite the removal of the Rothschild name from the front office of German banking, they retained all of their influence and control through the "back office" of their Disconto and Bleichroder banks, and their placements and stock interest in Deutsche Bank. In addition, the most crucial product over which that control extended, was oil. The Rothschilds controlled Germany's oil supply from Europe through these companies. They were to be found in every aspect of European oil, quietly amassing a monopoly. In 1904 they bought up Deutsche Petroleum AG as well as refineries in Galicia and elsewhere, and consolidated them into a company called OLEX.[49] One year later they also bought up and amalgamated a small but significant number of Romanian oil producers to form Allgeneine Petroleum Industrie (APAIG). Aware that a major global war was looming, it was very sound business.[50]

The Rothschild holdings diversified throughout Germany, reaping great rewards at every stage from the rapid economic expansion. It was Germany, not Britain that was surging ahead in economic growth in the first decades of the twentieth century. The new scientific and technological developments in Germany were feeding an emerging colossus, and success bred ambition to develop its industries further. [51]

The Rothschilds, behind a myriad of different company titles, constructed oil tank wagons for the railways, storage depots and refineries for the production of petrol and kerosene, and bartered with Government departments over concessions and favorable rail cargo fares. OLEX centralized its management at its Berlin subsidiary, OLEX – Petroleum – Gesellschaft, and thus identified itself as a German-based company operating from the heart of the capital, close to the political and military decision-makers. With OLEX secure in Berlin, another Rothschild concern, Deutsche Erdol Aktiengesellschaft (DEA) was created by Disconto. It took over APAIG in Romania and gained control of more north German refineries. Disconto, as DEA's major stockholder, directly administered the finances of these newly integrated oil enterprises.[52]

Behind this bewildering flurry of name changes, of company amalgamations, of buy-outs and stock holdings, of new donations and aggressive take-overs, the Rothschild Dynasty had control of supply, distribution and storage of Romanian oil throughout Germany. They produced much of the oil, transported it through railroad systems and oil wagons across Austria-Hungary and then Germany itself. They stored the oil in great purpose-built depots. They refined it into its marketable end products. In essence, they ensured that Germany and the Central Powers would have the supply of oil and infrastructure crucial for the long war planned by the British Secret Elites. And it looked like normal business practice.

In most of their business organization, they operated a complex and sophisticated network of interlocking front companies and trusts which concealed not just the true extent of their ownership of key industries, but their unrivaled power over nations. They had the finance; they ran the merchant banks that mattered; they controlled politicians and sometimes, governments. Most importantly, the Rothschilds had knowledge.[53] They had a first-rate intelligence gathering service stretching across the business and political world that enabled them to double and then redouble their capital with swift market operations that caught rivals off balance. They had more information at their finger tips than any secret service. They knew what was happening. Everywhere. More importantly, they knew what was about to happen. Their links to numerous governments were legendary, and they ensured that all within the dynasty shared crucial knowledge. Their agents knew more about local business developments, trade agreements, industrial unrest, treaties and concessions than any individual ministry or Foreign Office. They knew exactly what they were building up and facilitating in Central Europe. One cannot over-estimate the power and spread of influence that the House of Rothschild vested in Germany. In the knowledge that war with Germany was imminent they made it appear as if they had abandoned their financial, industrial and commercial interests there. Reality could not have been more different.

Summary.

- Having examined how the war was prolonged through the failure of the French to defend Briey, by the British through the failure of the sham blockade and the rampant deception which allowed the German army to be suitably fed by the Belgian Relief scam, we turn to the next scandal; ensuring that Germany had enough oil to fight a world war.
- The Rothschild Dynasty in Europe and the Rockefeller Empire in America controlled most go the world's production of oil.
- Having no natural source of oil in Britain at that time, the Foreign Office was well aware of the important potential of Burma, Sumatra, Mexico, Mesopotamia and the Gulf. It was no co-incidence that the British

government took ownership of the Anglo-Persian Oil Company just days before war was declared.

- The Germans were aware of their vulnerability to dependence on foreign oil. By 1912 Standard Oil held a monopoly of supply to Germany under the banner of a German company, Verkaufgessellschaft which controlled 91% of German oil sales.
- Oil in Galicia which lay along the Austro-Hungarian-Polish-Russian borders lay in the hands of foreign companies. Rockefeller owned the Vacuum Oil Company; Premier Oil and Pipeline Company was a British-owned concern which by the end of the war had made huge profits from supplying Germany with desperately needed oil.
- Unfortunately for Germany and Austria, Galician oil was in decline at the outbreak of the world war.
- Romanian oilfields, again owned by foreign investors, grew substantially at Ploesti and Campina near Bucharest, and had the immense benefit of a location close to the River Danube. This made transportation to the heart of Europe easier.
- German interest in Romanian oil was considerable, but the Discount Gesellschaft bank was in fact a Rothschild-owned concern.
- Rothschild also had control of the Baku oilfield on the Caspian Sea through the Nobel brothers, Robert and Ludvig.
- Although it appeared that Rockefeller and Rothschild were in blistering competition, they had since 1892 colluded to maintain prices to their mutual advantage.
- The Bleichroder Bank was yet another Rothschild front and acted as a branch office of the Rothschild Bank in Berlin.
- The Rothschild Dynasty controlled much of Europe's oil and had never abandoned their financial, commercial and industrial interests there.

Anglo-Persian oil well in 1914

Chapter 22

Oil – Britain First

Britain herself had no indigenous oil and in the late nineteenth century had been reliant on America, Russia or Mexico for supplies. This dependency on foreign companies was a cause for concern in times of peace but was completely unacceptable in the event of armed conflict.[1] The Secret Elite had to ensure that British companies rectified this deficiency before unleashing the dogs of war.

It should be appreciated that the starting point was not 1914. Long before that date, the strategic importance and economic necessity of securing oil supplies preoccupied minds inside the Secret Elite. We are told that the most outspoken and influential champions of oil, and indeed the development of an oil policy, were Winston Churchill as First Lord of the Admiralty, and Admiral Jackie Fisher, who chaired the Government's Royal Commission into Oil Fuels in 1912.[2] Unquestionably they were important figure-heads. Churchill was a personal family friend of Nathaniel Rothschild, whose advice he cherished. Churchill and Fisher were strongly supported by men with global ambitions for Britain, and ever-protective of its Empire. Thus political, financial, commercial, strategic and imperial interests were all interlocked in the drive to secure oil; a drive which was well underway, but given little publicity, in the first decade of the twentieth century.

British interests in Romanian oilfields included the Royal Dutch/Shell Company, an amalgamation in 1907 of the Royal Dutch Petroleum Company and the Shell Transport and Trading company, which in turn had close links to the Rothschilds. As companies began to grapple with the detailed requirements and long-term financial commitment that was a prerequisite for successful development, mergers and amalgamations became the order of the day to cut costs and increase profits. Extracting oil from often remote sources was dangerous, and required complex and technically advanced transport arrangements for the refined, highly volatile petroleum.

Marcus Samuel, founder of the Shell Transport and Trading Company, understood the need for purpose-built tankers that could be loaded, moved and unloaded in complete safety. He began by converting merchant ships to tankers that carried oil from Rothschild fields in Russia.[3]

In 1906 fields were acquired in Romania, and by way of further preparation in 1908, two new companies were created; Bataafsche Petroleum

Maatschappij in Holland and the Anglo-Saxon Petroleum Company in London. Shell Transport and Trading placed all its assets in these companies, which also held the assets of Royal Dutch/Shell.[4] Every possible competitor was bought up or absorbed. Between 1910–1914 fields were acquired in Russia (1910), Egypt (1911), Venezuela (1913) and Trinidad (1914). Henry Deterding, chairman of Royal Dutch/Shell,[5] later claimed that the group carefully cut the ground away from Germany's feet. This was achieved partly by getting into oil fields in which Germany hoped to establish herself, and partly by extending Royal Dutch/Shell influence in the German market, and in effect over German internal affairs.[6]

In Persia and the Arabian Gulf, geologists had determined that the region was a prime candidate for oil exploitation. There were, however, a small but important number of immediate problems. The land technically belonged to the Ottoman Turks and Persian rulers. To further complicate matters, Russia had long held designs on the same territory in order to establish a warm-water port. At the beginning of the twentieth century the Conservative Foreign Secretary, Lord Lansdowne, and his successor in the Liberal government, Sir Edward Grey, maintained identical policies approved by the Secret Elite. Quietly, and with no mention of the word oil, they extended British interests in the region and kept warships in the Gulf.

The Secret Elite, the Foreign Office and the Admiralty were, as always, inextricably linked with forward planning to meet the Empire's ambitions. Concessions were bought, officials were bribed, explorations were started and treaties established. It took more than two decades of painstaking preparation, but once everything was in place, a local champion was found to promote the purchase of a company that both offered reliable quantities of oil and necessitated a British presence on the direct route to India. William Knox D'Arcy, a wealthy gold mine director, became the front-man for British investment in Persian oil. Ultimately, however, the real power behind it was the unspoken ambitions of both the Admiralty and the Foreign Office, and the men behind them. They created a company which was "little known but intimately tied to the British Foreign Office and the secret intelligence services worldwide in the quest for control of future oil discoveries. The company was called the D'Arcy Exploitation Company."[7]

The Royal Dutch/Shell view of D'Arcy was disdainfully suspicious, and raised the specter of Secret Elite involvement.[8] "The only point that is still not clear is whether he [D'Arcy] undertook this extremely important affair entirely on his own initiative and at his own expense, or from the very outset, as a confidential agent of political circles representing British Imperialism."[9] The official History of the British Petroleum Company took a different view. D'Arcy's action "was simply a personal initiative for profit" and it dismissed as nonsense the "most Machiavellian of motives presumed to account for his investment."[10] Well, they would, wouldn't they?

Of course he was being used, and willingly so, for oil in Persia was supposed to make him an even greater fortune, and it brought him a credibility within the Secret Elite. In 1901 the Shah of Persia awarded D'Arcy a "firman," or royal concession with the rights to drill for oil for a period of sixty years provided the Shah received 16 per cent of the profits from whatever oil was discovered.[11] It was a transaction of historic importance, and the Shah's wasteful, extravagant lifestyle heralded the era of oil in the Middle East with a bribe. It would not be the last.

D'Arcy's venture in Persia was no instant success. By 1903, only a few traces of oil had been found, and he wanted out. Behind the scenes in London a frantic search was underway to find the right sort of dependable man to ensure that the concession was not abandoned. A British oil company which had been set up in Burma by a Scottish investment group was lured towards the Persian concession. Burmah Oil was entirely British in ownership and it merged with D'Arcy and Royal Dutch/Shell in 1908. It was a combine that required the word "British" stamped all over it to send out messages both to investors and to the international community. D'Arcy asked Lord Alfred Milner, leader of the Secret Elite, to take the post of chairman of this new company, but Milner was the puppet-master, not a marionette, and declined the offer.[12]

The published prospectus for the new company caused apoplexy in the corridors of power. It blandly stated that it was the Admiralty had suggested the development of Persia.[13] The company was immediately informed that if this became a matter of public comment, the Admiralty would deny the statement. What an amazing faux-pas. The carefully constructed secret plan for Persia, masked by commercial investment, was laid bare. And what is more revealing, the company was immediately warned that the government would not hesitate to lie about it if the story became public. They had, after all, "fought like a tiger" to take control of Persia's oil resources.[14]

The pre-war activity of the British oil industry was far more extensive than is generally acknowledged. Indeed, few official historians give space to the unprecedented lengths to which the British government went to discover and protect supplies. Certain individuals inside or closely related to the Secret Elite played crucial roles. The Rothschilds, in addition to supplying Germany, invested in oil fields across the world which would be invaluable to the Allies. Others such as Marcus Samuel and Lord Cowdray, with oil interests that ranged from Romania and Russia to Mexico and the Far East, were likewise linked to the Secret Elite and the British government. "New" men, loyal and dependable servants of the British Empire whose fortunes were based on success in Canada and Australia, were also encouraged to underwrite and champion the search for "British" oil.[15] Essentially, British interests grabbed control of as much of the world's oil as possible in the run up to war. At every turn they were aided and abetted by the Foreign Office and the Admiralty for military and strategic reasons that were kept closely under wraps.

Having spent a great deal of his personal fortune on exploration in Persia without any convincing returns, William Knox D'Arcy had had enough. The anticipated profit had not materialized and he transferred his holdings to Burmah Oil, recouped his outlay in full and made a profit of 170,000 Burmah shares, valued around £895,000, or just over £83,000,000 in 2016 values.[16] for himself and his associates.[17] It was clear to the Secret Elite that D'Arcy's personal fortune was more important to him than the future of the Empire and as a consequence he received no official honor for his "loyalty." Not even a knighthood. Then, lo and behold, the barren deserts spouted the priceless oil shortly after, in a district which had been identified as oil-bearing more than half a century before.[18] D'Arcy was either decidedly unlucky, or the victim of a calculated plan. In the summer of 1908, two tremendously profitable gushers were struck to the delight of his replacement, Lord Strathcona, a Scottish born Canadian financier, and other investors.

As Chairman of the Hudson Bay Company and Empire philanthropist,[19] Strathcona had all the international contacts necessary to lead from the front. From 1909 he played an active role as the Anglo-Persian Oil Company's first chairman, ably assisted by Charles Greenway, a British businessman. Greenway's ambitions reflected those of the Secret Elite; to obtain sufficient capital to transform Anglo-Persian into a major force in world oil, resist the early and unwelcome overtures from Royal Dutch/Shell, and gain the Admiralty contract to supply the Navy. In 1913 he offered them a twenty-year fuel contract that would both guarantee their supply by a "British" concern and, co-incidentally, rescue the company from financial straits. [20] Greenway shamelessly played on Marcus Samuel's "Jewishness" and Henry Deterding's "Dutchness" to better accentuate his own patriotic intent, arguing repeatedly that Anglo-Persian was a natural adjunct to British strategy and policy and was a significant national asset.[21]

Admiral Fisher, retired, but still highly influential at the Admiralty, was impressed by these arguments, and in May 1914 an agreement was signed with the British government. Much of Greenway's biased rhetoric was reiterated in Churchill's speech to Parliament on 17 June 1914, when he sought Parliamentary approval to purchase a majority shareholding of the Anglo-Persian Oil Company at a cost of £2.2 million.[22] Its importance, he stated, was that "over the whole of these enormous regions we obtain the power to regulate developments according to naval and national interests."[23] It was classic British Imperialism at its worst. "National interests" covered a multitude of sins.

Churchill's role was to front the signing of a deal that flew in the face of all previous Liberal Free Trade philosophy. To accusations of "Jew baiting" he steered the proposal through what could have been troublesome Parliamentary waters with commendable success. His intervention dressed the purchase of oil from Persia in naval uniform and wrapped it in the Red Ensign. It focused minds on the fleet, on the price of oil, on the manipulation of greedy multinational oil companies, and on German rivalries. It played on old bigotries and new-found fears. Though Sir Marcus Samuel and his colleagues at Royal Dutch/Shell were apoplectic at Churchill's sneers and misrepresentations,[24] they could not influence the government's intentions.

Quietly and effectively they planted the Union flag in the Persian Gulf. Some seven weeks before the outbreak of war the government bought a fifty-one per cent holding in the Anglo-Persian Oil Company, and at a stroke changed the rules of engagement. The claim to Persian oil was thus backed by the might of the British government, not some commercial company. Eleven days before the assassination of Archduke Ferdinand in Sarajevo, the proposal was presented to Parliament for its approval. Ramsay MacDonald, leader of the Labor opposition, warned that the contract "was far more political in its significance than economic" and, with considerable prescience added, "commercial concessions, especially when government money was in them, had an unhappy knack of becoming territorial acquisitions."[25]

Six days after war had been declared, the Bill received Royal consent.[26] The Secret Elite had played a master-stroke in what one of their leading players, Lord Curzon, described as "the game for the domination of the world."[27] Without the consent of any other government, and in full denial of such intent, the Foreign Office effectively created a new protectorate to sit beside Egypt, Sudan and the route to India. And it all began with the bribe which D'Arcy used to gain the concession from the Shah.[28]

Once the deal with Anglo-Persian was approved, Churchill quickly contacted Henry Deterding of Royal Dutch/Shell to negotiate a new agreement with them. Having trashed their reputation in public, he quietly secured their oil. Deterding promised that Britain "shan't want for oil or tankers in case of war." He was a practical man. He understood what had happened.[29] Despite Sir Edward Grey's denials, this was not primarily about the availability of oil, nor the price of oil. It was about a strategic and vital stretch of land in the Middle East. The decision had been driven not just by the Admiralty, whose technical imperatives demanded that Germany never got ahead in the Naval race, but, more importantly, by the Foreign Office. It both secured the future of Anglo-Persian as a "British" oil company and signaled the fact that this region was now firmly a British sphere of influence.

And where did the money come from? It had not been included in the Naval Estimates, so technically it could not be allocated from the Admiralty. Amazingly, money was found by the Chancellor of the Exchequer without any requirement for additional borrowing.[30] It was indeed fortunate that such a large sum, roughly £189 million at today's prices,[31] just happened to be available. The Treasury, Admiralty and the Foreign Offices were in cahoots. In a month of unparalleled domestic upheaval, the rights to a small piece of land in Persia were purchased for the nation by the triumvirate of Secret Elite agents inside the Cabinet without parliamentary discussion. This oil-bearing land had been acquired on the basis of supplying the navy. That was the public position. Inside the close-knit corridors of the Foreign Office, oil had been transformed into an instrument of national policy. It gave the government claim to own part of Persia.

Thus in the weeks immediately before the declaration of war, Britain established its ownership of a potentially invaluable future source of oil. Unlike Germany, which was dependent to a large extent on the monopolies she could not break, it was relatively straightforward for Britain to purchase and transport by sea, oil from America, Mexico, Trinidad, Borneo, Romania and beyond, to guarantee supplies for the Royal Navy. So there was no urgency, no immediate necessity to protect the navy's oil supplies even in time of war. The deal that was rushed through the British parliament had future ambition written large behind its front cover. The Anglo-Persian field would require more time to prove economically effective and it did not disappoint in the long run.[32] But as Britain entered the mammoth struggle with Germany, it had established a claim on the disintegrating Ottoman region around Persia and the Gulf.

And even if the decision to acquire a majority stake in Anglo-Persian had been only an economic consideration, if it was simply the supply of oil for the navy that was of concern, surely that was sufficiently important to beg another question. Given that the politicians and planners knew how critical the supply of oil would be in time of war, why did the Allies not move immediately to deny Germany and the Central Powers access to oil at the outbreak of war? No-one can claim that the British government was unaware of this. Churchill spoke about the impact of such an embargo in the House of Commons when he argued that, "if he [the enemy] were able to stop oil ships and enforce his doctrine of contraband, he could also stop the grain ships, the meat ships, and the ships bringing cotton and all the other varieties of raw material to this country and, of course, he could very quickly bring the war to an end by that means."[33] He was absolutely correct. It therefore follows that had Britain stopped the supply of oil and other commodities to Germany from the outbreak of war, it would very quickly have been brought to an end.

And let us not forget another point which Churchill correctly identified. Control of oil throughout the world was in the hands of a relatively few very powerful oil companies. These were essentially Standard Oil (American) and Royal Dutch/Shell (Dutch/British), with Mexican Eagle (British) and the nascent Anglo-Persian Oil Company (British) running far behind those two giants. Even though Germany had some influence through Deutsche Bank holdings, most of the shareholdings in Romanian and Russian oil lay with the Rothschild Dynasty and had by 1914 been amalgamated into the Royal Dutch/Shell giant.[34] Such a comprehensive stranglehold on the supply of oil should surely have spelled disaster for Germany after stalemate on the Western Front prolonged the First World War beyond the expectation of most observers. It did not.

Perhaps the most searching question is why, on the outbreak of war, the British government did not force home-based multi-national oil companies, such as those owned by the Rothschilds or Marcus Samuel, to use their influence to stop supplying Germany. There can be no excuse that the government did not realize what was happening. Its close scrutiny of the oil industry in the run up to the war meant that key members of senior departments and the cabinet understood the precise nature and structure of the global oil industry.[35]

Churchill defined the prevailing situation to Parliament one year before war broke out: "Our power to obtain additional supplies of oil fuel in time of war depends on our command of the sea," and spoke of "Two gigantic corporations.... In the New World there is Standard Oil; In the Old World the great combination of Shell and Royal Dutch with all their subsidiary and ancillary branches has practically covered the whole ground and has even reached out into the New World."[36] The British government had analyzed and itemized the world supply of oil in fine detail in order to assure itself of reliable supplies. It knew exactly where the oil was, who owned it and precisely how Germany obtained her oil.

On the outbreak of war, Germany should have been unable to source oil supplies directly from America. However, oil was not initially included in the definition of contraband, and as a result she could still legally import oil from the USA and other neutral countries.[37] That situation was supposed to have been changed in November 1914 when the House of Commons was informed: "His Majesty's Government have reliable information that in the present circumstances any oil, copper, and certain other substances that may be imported into Germany or Austria will certainly be used exclusively for warlike purposes, and ... have for this reason felt justified in adding those items to the list of absolute contraband. Every possible care is being taken to ensure that oil and copper intended for neutral countries should not be interfered with."[38]

Examine Prime Minister Asquith's words. His government acknowledged that any oil allowed into Germany would "be used exclusively for warlike purposes." Despite this, parliament was informed that oil intended for neutral countries should not be interfered with. It was classic double-speak. The government was well aware that much of the oil and other goods allowed through the naval blockade to neutral Scandinavian countries was being transferred on to Germany. Placing oil on the absolute contraband list was a sham. It changed nothing. Germany was still allowed to purchase oil from her neighbors in vast quantities.

Enticements were breathtaking. In 1915 Germany offered 1,800 marks (£90) per barrel of oil whose market value in neighboring Denmark was 125 kroner (about £7) Lubricants were always in short supply in Germany, but most especially in 1915 and 1916.[39] By December 1915 the American Ambassador in Berlin, James W. Gerard, recorded in his war diary that "probably the greatest need of Germany is lubricating oil for machines."[40] General Erich Ludendorff, Deputy Chief of Staff, wrote later: "As Austria could not supply us with oil, and as all of our efforts to increase production were unavailing, Romanian oil was of decisive importance to us. But even with deliveries of Romanian oil, the question of oil supplies still remained very serious, and caused us great difficulty, not only for the conduct of the war, but for the life of the country."[41] Two points should be considered here. Yet again, the German High Command acknowledged that without oil the war could not have continued. General Ludendorff also considered Romanian oil crucial. Who owned the "decisively important" Romanian oil fields? International conglomerates closely linked to the Secret Elite.

German imports of American oil through Scandinavia were well known to the British authorities from an early stage in the war. Rear-Admiral Consett repeatedly sent detailed and urgent alerts about this from his office in Copenhagen to the Admiralty, but nothing was done. Such large-scale abuse of the contraband restrictions became a scandal. In Copenhagen, German ships were openly berthing alongside tankers from America, transferring the oil, and trans-shipping every drop to Germany. Likewise in Sweden, virtually every consignment of oil imported through Stockholm was re-exported to Germany.[42] Profits for the Americans and the Scandinavians were enormous, but what did it profit the British government to turn such a biblical blind eye?

Summary.

- Britain's political, financial, commercial, strategic and imperial interests were all interlocked in the drive to secure oil; a drive which was well underway, but given little publicity, in the first decade of the twentieth century.
- Royal Dutch / Shell bought up a prodigious number of their competitors in Russia, Egypt, Venezuela and Trinidad.
- Geologists knew that the Arabian Gulf was a prime candidate for oil exploitation, but was owned by either the Ottomans (Turks) or Persians.

- With that certain knowledge the British government and the Foreign Office looked around for pliant British oilmen to take charge of potential sites.
- William Knox D'Arcy undertook to front the British interests in Persia but gave up in 1908. He transferred his holdings to the Burmah Oil Company (British) and in 1909, having become the Anglo-Persian Oil Company, a Scottish-born Canadian and Empire philanthropist, Lord Strahcona took charge.
- Soon after, two tremendously profitable gushers were found and oil was firmly established in Persia.
- The Admiralty and the Foreign Office colluded in rushing a bill through parliament seven weeks before the outbreak of war in Europe by which Britain purchased 51% of the Anglo-Persian shares.
- It was signed into law by King George V six days after the war had begun. The British flag was firmly planted in the sands of Persia.
- Given the fact that control and ownership of oil rested in the hands of a very few powerful companies, why did the government not insist that they used their influence to stop British companies supplying Germany with oil?
- German importation of American oil through Scandinavia was known to the Admiralty and the Foreign Office but they did not block the trade, despite oil being declared as contraband.

German U-Boat Deutschland, Baltimore 1916

Chapter 23

Oil - Prolonging The War Again

Though government departments protested they were doing their utmost to prevent oil reaching Germany, their actions made a mockery of the valiant efforts of the Royal Navy in the dangerous, storm- tossed waters of the North Sea.[1] When American vessels had been sunk by German U-boats, outrage followed from both sides of the Atlantic,[2] yet American companies continued to provide the oil which fueled those very U-Boats. It was not all they provided.

On 9 July 1916 the large German merchant submarine *Deutschland* sailed into Baltimore harbor after a 16-day journey from Bremerhaven. She was welcomed with a cacophony of siren blasts, and an official dinner was hosted by the Mayor of Baltimore.[3] Her cargo of chemical dyes, gemstones and medicinal products was unloaded and when she left for Germany on 2 August she carried 341 tons of nickel, a mineral essential for hardening steel for weapons production, 93 tons of tin and 348 tons of rubber. On a return journey in November 1916 to Connecticut she sailed home with a full cargo which included 6.5 tons of silver bullion.[4] America not only provided Germany with oil and the means to produce heavy weapons, she also helped fund her war effort. The hypocrisy was breathtaking. While the U.S. President apparently urged peace on Europe, *American money enabled both sides to continue the war.*

The hypocrisy was by no means confined to America. In exactly the same manner as raw materials such as silver, nickel, tin and rubber, and essential supplies of foodstuffs were deliberately allowed through the British naval blockade, critical supplies of oil poured into Germany from British-owned companies in the first two years of the war. In the House of Commons in July 1916, Walter Runciman, President of the Board of Trade was asked: "Whether he can ascertain what sales and deliveries ... of petrol, benzine, kerosene or other petroleum products have been made to enemy countries ... and which of the companies under the control of the Shell Trading and Transport Company, or any of their associated companies, have done this, other than the Astra Romana Company?" Runciman did not reply in person, but sent his deputy, Lewis Harcourt, a long-time associate of the Secret Elite[5] to provide a typically cryptic non-answer: "I have no reason to think that any such sales or deliveries of petroleum products have been made, and the Shell Transport and Trading company inform me that they have not."[6]

The MP who put forward the question, Major Rowland Hunt, was well aware that the British company's field at Astra Romana was selling to Germany. In effect he was not wanting to know if they were supplying oil to it, but how much. The answer was stunning in its conceit. Harcourt, as the government's spokesman "had no reason to think that any sales or deliveries" had been made. Shell said they had not, so that was the end of the matter. No further discussion, no independent investigation was required on this crucial matter. The government appeared to accept without question the word of a multinational company that multiplied its profits by supplying the enemy.

It was, however, not a matter of naivety that shaped the official answer. It was a cover up. The war was deliberately being prolonged by oil companies partly owned by British shareholders supplying the enemy, and the top echelons of power in Britain colluded with them.

Much to the fury of British naval officers and ratings of the blockade fleet who had risked life and limb to prevent American oil getting through to Germany between 1914-1916, faceless men in the highest echelons of the British government gave orders that apprehended ships be released and allowed to continue their journey.[7]

Germany was certainly aided by quantities of oil which had been inexplicably allowed through the naval blockade, but the vast bulk of her supplies throughout the war came from Romania, by way of the river Danube. Romania remained neutral for the first two years of the war; thus its government was free, by international law, to supply anyone it wished. However, the oil fields were neither owned by the Romanian government nor Romanians, but by individuals closely linked to the Secret Elite. Romania's neutrality was convenient but immaterial.

Had there been the will to turn off the Romanian oil wells owned by Rothschild and Rockefeller, and bring Germany's only major supply to a standstill, it would have happened. Royal Dutch/Shell could perfectly reasonably have claimed to be British, but instead played the neutral card held by Holland. Rockefeller's Standard Oil followed suit, using its Austrian connections. French banks controlled the Aquila Franco-Romana field, and Rothschild banks and companies centered on Rue Lafitte in Paris, owned and supplied most of the Kaiser's oil. While Germany's Deutsche Bank held considerable shares in the Romanian Steaua oil field, they did not own these fields wholesale. Unquestionably, a shut down would have come at a huge cost in terms of profit to the investors and the banks, though they were already making massive profits by supplying the Allies. A concerted Allied attempt to isolate Germany from Romanian oil was never attempted. Indeed the very opposite took place. Barriers to supplies were mysteriously removed and thousands of Danube barges constantly sailed back and forth with oil for Germany without the slightest obstruction. Criticism inside Parliament became vociferous and increasing pressure was put on Asquith's government to take action.[8]

By 1916, with the rapid and massive developments in mechanical warfare, sufficient oil was critical for Germany's survival.[9] Without oil, defeat was certain. How fortunate then for the warmongers and oil barons that in August that year the Allies enticed Romania into the war with lavish promises of increased territory from Hungarian spoils once victory was finally assured.[10] On the face of it, this might have appeared as a master-stroke to increase the Allied forces and relieve pressure on the Western Front. Furthermore, once Romania declared war on Germany and Austria, their vital supplies of oil and grain would cease. Effectively the war could be brought to an end within a few months. But this was never the intention.

The Romanian army of 650,000 men in 23 divisions quickly routed Austro-Hungarian forces in Transylvania, but German troops under General Erich von Falkenhayn entered the fray and overwhelmed them.[11] By Christmas 1916, the German army had conquered most of the country and occupied Bucharest. Before reaching the capital, they had captured the oil fields at Ploiesti, and so the same oilfields and wheat fields that had provided much of her needs through 1914-16, continued to serve the German war effort. It was a disaster. According to Lloyd George, "it was a blunder of the most inexplicable character."[12]

"Inexplicable"? Not so. The Allies knew that the Romanian army had no heavy guns or adequate supplies of ammunition. Lloyd George went so far as to write: "our military advisers must have known that if the Germans chose to withdraw from the attack on Verdun and send a few of their reserve divisions to Romania, the Romanian forces would be quite unequal in the face of such an attack."[13]

Allegedly no-one considered the possibility that Germany, faced with the loss of vital resources, would react. Consignments of ammunition bound for Romania from Western Europe were deliberately sidetracked on Russian railways[14] and it was only after the German attack had advanced into a near defenseless Romania "that the Allies improvised hurried expeditions to rescue [her] from her doom."[15] Lloyd George accepted that if Germany conquered Romania, "the Germans" stores, much depleted, will be stocked with great quantities of oil and corn, which will place the Central Powers above any anxiety in these two important respects – and yet no one seems to have thought it his particular duty to prepare a plan, which would avert a "possible disaster of the first magnitude to their cause."[16]

No one seems to have thought of it? How likely was that? In reality, Romania was hung out to dry; deliberately sacrificed. Why would anyone approve a strategy that would so clearly enable the enemy to fight on, unless that was the intention all along? And this from the pen of Lloyd George. Under the cover of Allied incompetence and blunder, the oil companies could continue to supply Germany without any criticism from inquisitive parliamentarians.

A story was put about in Britain that the Romanian oil fields had been utterly destroyed,[17] and the country's wheat stores despoiled so that the Central Powers gained little from the capitulation of Romania. It was a fantastic story; the stuff of legends.[18] A British Lieutenant-Colonel and member of parliament, Norton Griffiths MP, had, according to reports placed in newspapers, single-handedly sabotaged the Romanian oil fields, which were spread over several hundred square kilometers, minutes before the German troops marched in. He had, allegedly, destroyed the oil wells together with 70 refineries and 800,000 tons of crude oil.[19] The plumes of smoke over Bucharest some 60 kilometers away were reported to have blocked out the sky, such was the devastation Griffiths was said to have caused. It was as though Indiana Jones had taken on the might of the German army and thwarted their designs on Romanian oil. Unfortunately Norton Griffiths was a legend in his own mind, a maverick self-publicist with a history of "incredible" adventures. John Buchan could not have penned a more daring tale for Richard Hannay. It made great copy for the propaganda machine but in reality the greater part of Romania including its wheat and oil, "lay under the heel of the invader."[20]

There was some damage and disruption to production, but before the end of the war over one million tons of oil had been transported from the Ploiesti fields to the Central Powers, mainly Germany. Had it been otherwise, the German war machine would have ground to a halt. This is not some lame theory. After the collapse of Bulgaria on 3 October 1918, the German General Staff asked the question:

"If to-day Romania falls away, how long can we last out with petrol? Will the collapse of Romania compel us at once to abandon hostilities?" The stark truth was that "aircraft can maintain their full activity for roughly two months (one month's service at the front, one month's service at home). Then they will have to cut down to half service. Lubricating oil is available for six months. Then all machines will be brought to a standstill. ... the illuminating oil industry (i.e. provision of petroleum for the civil population and agriculture) will collapse in one to two months ..."[21]

In a session led by the Reich Chancellor on 1 October 1918, the Minister of War explained that Germany could only carry on fighting for a month and a half if Romania was not at their disposal. Lloyd George wrote in his memoirs that if the Allies had taken steps to secure the Balkans, and thus control of Romanian oil in 1915, "as we ought to have done ... the failure of oil supplies would have shortened the war by at least two years."[22] Make no mistake, the Germans knew that the war would have been over within six weeks without access to Romanian oil. Lloyd George as British Prime Minister later agreed that war would not have lasted beyond 1916. Hindsight lends itself to wise conclusions, but if the British government knew this before war was declared, which they most assuredly did, why was appropriate action not taken in 1914-15 to halt supplies to Germany?

And that oil continued to be supplied by Royal Dutch/Shell and all of the other Allied companies, including Standard Oil once America entered the war in 1917. Money has no loyalty; it is the currency through which greed may be measured. The oil companies amassed vast wealth in the war years, serving whichever master paid the asking price. Between 1914 and 1919 Anglo-Persian declared consolidated current assets that rose from £266,297 to £4,352,083, or roughly eighteen-fold.[23] Their group financial performance rose from £62,258 in 1914/15 to £2,651,931 in 1918/19 or just over forty-fold. This allowed an annual return on investment of 30.1% and a dividend rate of 10%.[24]

The story at Royal Dutch/Shell was equally awesome. At the end of the war, Sir Marcus Samuel announced to a stockholders meeting in London that cash resources amounted then to £24,000,000 and the Shell company fleet had risen from 255,965 tons before the war to 263,746 tons in 1919. Investors might well have expected a serious decline in shipping tonnage, given the U-Boat menace and its impact over the last two years of warfare. The *New York Times* reported that profits and dividends were outstanding. "Despite the cutting off of the Romanian and Prussian (Galician) oil fields, while war was on, the Shell company continued to pay large dividends."[25]

In truth, the Romanian oil fields had never at any time been "cut off" from Germany. From 1913 to 1918 the annual disbursement to share owners amounted to 35%. In 1918 a 60% stock dividend was paid. Sir Marcus assured bankers who were interested in a 1919 Wall Street share issue, that the cut in excess profit tax from 80% to 40% in Britain, meant that the company could look forward to increased profits.[26] Truly enormous profits were made by the share-holding classes; but at what a cost to the men in the trenches or on the High Seas?

Matters would have been so different if oil had been blockaded from the Central Powers from 1914. The senior executives of all the great oil monopolies, trusts and merchant banks were close to their governments and moved inside the circles of influence. Rothschilds in London and Paris acted as agents for Allied loans, Marcus Samuel and Henry Deterding (Royal Dutch/Shell) met with Sir Edward Grey, Winston Churchill and senior cabinet ministers. Rockefeller and J.P. Morgan had instant access to Mandell House and President Wilson; they were already in his gift. The political, financial and business worlds operated with mutual co-operation. Why then did they fail to take concerted action to sever Germany and the Central Powers from oil? Is greed a sufficient answer? No. Primarily, the Secret Elite was determined to destroy Germany in a prolonged and exhausting war, not defeat her in a manner which left the primacy of British domination undecided. The accumulation of massive profit margins was a welcome but subsidiary bonus. Hypocrisy abounded.

Summary.

- Critical supplies of oil poured into Germany from British-owned companies from 1914-1916.
- Shell Oil (Shell Trading and Transport Company) sold its oil from the Astra Romana field to Germany, and when questioned by MPs, told the government that they had not.
- The government did not question this multi-national company which multiplied its profits for British shareholders.
- A concentrated Allied effort to isolate Germany from Romanian oil was never attempted.
- When Romania entered the war on the side of the Allies in 1916, the German army under General Falkenhayn overwhelmed them.
- It was a disaster because occupied Romania continued to supply both grain and oil to Germany.
- The story was put about that a British agent and MP, Norton Griffiths, had almost single-handedly destroyed the Romanian fields and 70 refineries. Unfortunately Norton Griffiths was a legend in his own mind.
- Before the end of the war one million tons of oil had been transported from the Ploiesti fields to Germany and her allies.
- Lloyd George admitted in his *Memoirs* that had the Allies secured the Balkans in 1915, the war would have been shortened by two years.
- The oil companies amassed vast wealth in the war years, serving whichever master paid the asking price. Between 1914 and 1919 Anglo-Persian declared consolidated current assets that rose from £266,297 to £4,352,083, or roughly eighteen-fold.
- Royal Dutch/Shell was equally profitable. At the end of the war, cash resources amounted to £24,000,000 and the Shell company fleet had risen from 255,965 tons before the war to 263,746 tons in 1919 despite the U-Boat menace.

Chapter 24

Lloyd George – Open For Business

Despite all the advantages which private British armaments companies enjoyed, the supply of guns, shells and ammunition was hindered by the infighting, lack of co-ordination and traditional red-tape that haunted the War Office when war broke out. Richard Haldane's reforms from 1906 onwards had created the small, well-armed British Expeditionary Force, but leadership of the army was controlled absolutely through the "Roberts Academy,"[1] which remained wedded to the primacy of cavalry regiments and was rooted not in the coming war, but in the Boer War. Britain's reserves of shells in 1914 were reckoned to be two and a half times greater than they had been in 1899.[2] The requirements had been based on guess-work and assumptions, covering a notional supply for four major battles of three days duration each over the first two months.[3] No-one suggested otherwise in August 1914.

While the volunteers pressed themselves through recruiting stations in the vain expectation that they would see off the Germans before Christmas, little thought had been given to the fact that there were insufficient rifles, cannon, machine guns, mortars, uniforms or basic equipment on hand for the eager young men who signed in droves. Cabinet members anticipated around 100,000 volunteers when Kitchener's campaign began in 1914, but the swell of public enthusiasm obliged them to raise the

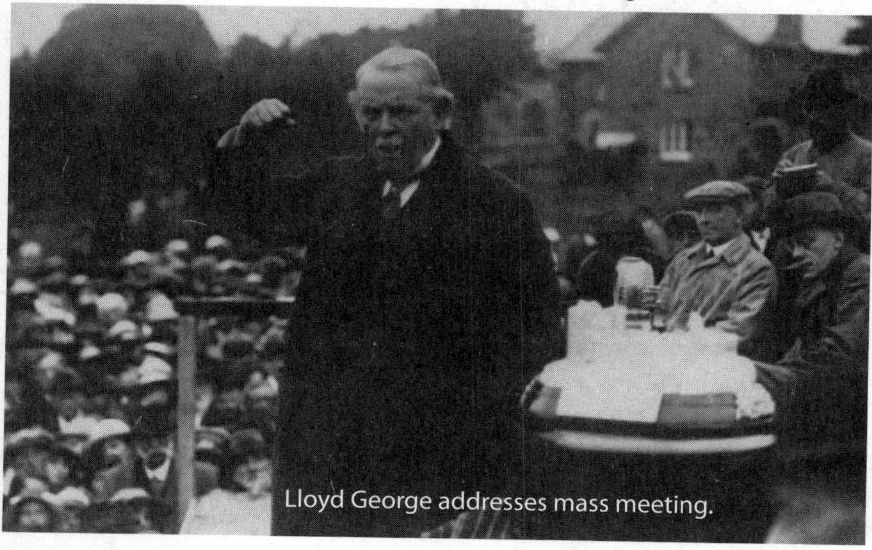

Lloyd George addresses mass meeting.

limit to 500,000 and then beyond. Of volunteers there was no scarcity. But what use was this, even had they been given competent leadership from their Generals, when they did not have explosive shells, sufficient machine guns, aircraft or artillery? There were horses; 25,000 in 1914 and over half a million had been used by the end of the war. When horses and men faced explosive shells and machine-gun enfilades, the result was inevitable. The Roberts Academy had prepared for the wrong war.

The national arsenals, (they were called Royal Arsenals) at Woolwich, Enfield Lock and Waltham Abbey had been in decline since the end of the Boer War and much of their machinery was run down.[4] The private munitions companies had largely specialized in ship-building and naval contracts but Vickers at Newcastle, Armstrong, Whitworth at Elswick and the Birmingham Small Arms Company also diversified into other engineering ventures including motorbikes, cars and airplanes. On the one hand the potential for increased production existed in theory, but the practice turned into a nightmare of red tape, tradition, pig-headedness, self-interest and greed.

War Office procedures choked under the volume of newly placed orders. The Ordnance Department had only ever dealt with a small circle of approved contractors and was reluctant to expand its suppliers. The years of underinvestment in the Royal Arsenals reaped an embarrassing dividend. They were not fit for purpose. Privately, many of the recognized contractors accepted orders that they could not complete within the required timescale and, at the same time, committed themselves to undertake massive additional orders from the Russian government. Greed is a powerful master, and these men were in a position to maximize the benefits for themselves, so the armaments' ring talked of the risk of over-expansion. What would happen to them if they built new factories and the war was indeed over by Christmas?

The Western Front was a completely different battleground. It quickly became a stalemate. The high-explosive shell, used to such shattering effect by the German howitzers, had not been part of the original strategic thinking.[5] Mobility and speed of action dominated the Roberts Academy pre-war plan. Shrapnel was the undisputed shell of choice and in consequence, the demand for high explosives was originally relegated to around 30% of total orders. Ironically, despite years of careful preparation, the British Army was not as well equipped for the war that lay before it, as had been presumed. In August 1914, all of the British Army's 13- and 18-pounder guns were soley supplied only with shrapnel.[6]

And it only got worse. Shrapnel had no effect whatsoever on well-constructed parapets, deep trenches with blockhouses, on machine-gun posts or barbed wire defenses. By the first week in September the General Headquarters in France was requesting supplies of high-explosive shells, which simply did not exist. Repeated pleas for increasing numbers of this ordnance were specifically made on 15th and 21st September, 1914. The army claimed that they desperately needed 50% of their shells to be high explosive but the War Office treated their requests as if the men in the field were over excitable schoolboys. The grounds on which the Ordnance Department based this attitude was that "the nature of these operations may change as they have done in the past."[7] But just how far was munitions shortage a reality?

In one critical area there was never a shortage; indeed, there was constantly an oversupply. When shell shortage was proclaimed a national "crisis" in 1915, a focus manufactured by the Northcliffe press to damage the Asquith government and deflect attention from military failures, historians and journalists followed this explanation unquestioningly. Truth to tell, there was an abundance of shells – for Dreadnoughts and battleships.[8] The navy claimed its long-assumed priority over shells and the cordite required to fire these immense projectiles over five to nine miles. Early in 1914, the Admiralty agreed to raise the number of rounds from 80 to 100 per gun on battleships and to 110 per gun on battle cruisers.

In fact, by 1916, 8-gun battle cruisers were stocked with fifty per cent more ammunition than they were designed to carry.[9] Churchill was obliged to recognize the navy's over-provision in October 1914 by permitting the transfer of 1,000 tons of cordite to the army.[10] Yet over-supply to the navy was not meaningfully reduced. The armaments companies continued to produce their heavy caliber shells despite the fact that there were very few naval engagements which would have consumed the ammunition. The navy continued to have priority over the army with the private producers and while there were perceived shortages on the western front, stocks hoarded by the Admiralty were "bountiful."[11] Clearly heavy caliber explosives were being produced in great quantities, but not for the army, for whom the word "shortage" had become a mantra.

High explosives were deemed to be the technological panacea,[12] and the lack of these became the ready excuse for failure. It also became an integral part of the problem. If the only solution to stalemate on the western front was even more extravagant use of heavy artillery, then the more these great guns blasted, often aimlessly, the more they accentuated the shortage. With governments ever willing to throw increased expenditure at the perceived "solution," the armaments trusts could only reap untold profits. Kitchener believed that the shortage was exaggerated, but his generals in the field became fixated by this god-given "reason" which rationalized their failures and justified their strategies. At every turn they wanted more.

There was an impasse. Kitchener's War Office wanted to retain full control of munitions. They were suspicious of offers from American companies or orders placed in America by British government agents. Likewise they had no faith in dozens of smaller engineering companies across

Britain which offered to switch production under license. Kitchener's stubborn Master General of Ordnance, who had to approve all orders, Sir Stanley von Donop, insisted that only firms experienced in the delicate operation of arms manufacture, firms that had a skilled workforce capable of safely producing the guns and shells, should be used.

The men who controlled the private armaments firms, their supply, manufacture and price, effectively a sub-set of the Secret Elite, were determined to secure their stranglehold by taking control away from the War Office. But how? Lloyd George found a way. Despite Kitchener's objections, the government set up a Cabinet Committee in October 1914 to examine the issues of munitions supply. Absolute control did not immediately pass from the War Office, but within eight months Kitchener was sidelined.

When Lloyd George, as Chancellor of the Exchequer, met on 13 October with the major representatives from Armstrong, Vickers, the Coventry Ordnance Works and Beardmore, he offered them a blank check. Incredibly, the nation had been held hostage. Lloyd George promised that the British taxpayer would cover whatever the cost of extending production lines, building new factories or investing in new machinery, irrespective of how long the war lasted. He committed the government to compensate them and any of their sub-contractors for any subsequent loss. The War Office protocols to protect the public purse were torn to shreds.

Not surprisingly, the open checkbook had a miraculous effect. The merchants of death immediately promised to increase output by every possible means. For example, artillery gun production, which was doubled from 878 to 1,606, was to be completed no later than August 1915.[13] These great firms, owned and run by self-serving capitalists who boasted their patriotism in parliament, pulpit and the press, were literally subsidized by the government to increase production and make outrageous profits. The Secret Elite removed the impasse. What price patriotism?

Lloyd George assumed a proprietary interest in munitions. His work as chancellor of the exchequer ought to have kept him occupied in monetary and fiscal matters, raising war loans and extending credit, but his voice as a Secret Elite agent in Asquith's cabinet repeatedly brought him into conflict with Kitchener. He interfered with War Office orders, placed twenty-million pounds at the disposal of the Master-General of the Ordnance and virtually freed the Ordnance Department from Treasury control.[14] He also looked for assistance from America.

The Anglo-American establishment closed ranks behind its British associates, and the U.S. State Department, which had previously blocked a request from the J.P. Morgan banking dynasty to make loans to the allies, issued a press release on 15 October 1914, declaring that, on reflection, it had "no authority to interfere with the purchase of goods by belligerents, even of munitions, and it would be highly unneutral for it to do so." Pressure had been exerted on the Woodrow Wilson's government "to permit the belligerent nations to buy goods and raw materials in America."[15] That pressure emanated directly from the J.P. Morgan group, with its Rothschild connection, the powerful Pilgrims Society, which included a select "collective of the wealthiest figures of both Britain and the United States who were deeply involved with the Secret Elite,"[16] and the presidential advisor, Robert Lansing.[17] Though professing an absolutely neutral stance, the door to American finance had been opened for the allies by President Wilson's administration from October 1914.

The British Cabinet Committee meeting on 21 October agreed to contact the War Office agent in America with a request for 400,000 rifles and three days later sent their representative, Captain Bernard Cecil Smyth-Pigott to New York. They did not know that Lloyd George, whom the Secret Elite had determined would have ultimate control, had already acted independently. He had sent his most able Treasury expert, Basil Blackett, to America to evaluate the logjam that had built up in military procurement. His first reports insisted that the War Office and the Admiralty had to start co-ordinating their purchasing strategies because suppliers were raising prices and playing one off against the other.[18]

In November 1914, the chancellor of the exchequer contacted his acquaintance, Edward Charles Grenfell, senior partner of Morgan-Grenfell & Co., and director of the Bank of England, to discuss whether rifle production in the United States could be increased and engineering production switched to munitions manufacture. The line of contact started in the Treasury with Lloyd-George, through Grenfell to J.P. Morgan & Co., the largest investment banking firm in America. Morgan immediately promised to liaise with two armaments firms, Remington and Winchester, "friends" of his group, and an understanding was reached.[19] Delivery would however take eleven months.[20] Trusted Secret Elite agents had created a very pro-British accord which would benefit them all in a prolonged war.

But Kitchener would not have it. He contacted J.P. Morgan directly, demanding that the order be canceled. In his view, munition supply was War Office business and no-one else's. Lloyd George was furious; Edward Grenfell, outraged. The carefully planned Trans-Atlantic accord appeared to have been smothered by Kitchener's intervention, but the Chancellor had powerful friends on both sides of the Atlantic. Grenfell complained bitterly that "the manner in which the War Office have dealt with the proposed rifles contract with Morgan, Grenfell and Co, will have a detrimental effect on Public opinion in America."[21] It was always a good line to take. American public opinion mattered to the British government. That same day Lloyd George smoothed Edward Grenfell's ruffled feathers by assuring him that Kitchener's communication to Morgan was based on a regrettable "misapprehension" and asked for Morgan's cooperation.[22] Subsequent orders were placed with Morgan's chosen men without interference.

The British Embassy in Washington had reported that a large number of purchasing agents were abusing their position and accepting ridiculously high prices for goods bought in America, so George Macaulay Booth of the shipping company, Alfred Booth and Co. was dispatched to the United States to assess the extent of the problem. Here he found that British buyers were paying thirty-seven shillings for coats that could have been procured for twenty-four shillings. Though Kitchener hated interference from any outsider in War Office business, he had a high regard for Booth's hard working efficiency. Lloyd George was less convinced but retained his rosy view of business entrepreneurs.[23]

The British Ambassador, Spring Rice, recommended that J.P. Morgan be appointed sole purchaser to protect British interests, and Booth returned in mid-November to report that there was an over-riding need for a sole purchaser ... and that it should be Morgan. Booth was well aware that in addition to his dominant position in American banking, Morgan controlled a vast shipping tonnage in International Maritime Marine, and an alliance with him would guarantee the use of Booth's company in the Allied interest. Apparently historians have concluded that it is not exactly clear "just which cabinet minister formally asked which British or American Morgan partner to take on responsibility, [for munitions] or when."[24] It was clearly Lloyd George. He had the confidence of the Secret Elite, and they had facilitated the arrangement.

As a result, a purchasing contract was signed in January 1915 between J.P. Morgan and the British Treasury, appointing the New York firm as its sole purchaser in the United States. It should hardly be a surprise. Morgan was intimately linked to the Secret Elite,[25] had offices in London (Morgan-Grenfell and Co,), Paris (Morgan, Harjes & Co.) and New York, (J.P. Morgan and Co.) and E.C. Grenfell personally acted as the go-between. This was not the usual order of business. Under normal circumstances the British Embassy in Washington would have been the point of liaison. What emerged was unprecedented. Control over the spending of thousands of millions of British tax-payers' pounds was placed in the hands of an American plutocrat and his British agent in London.

Each morning, Edward Grenfell called at the Bank of England with the latest pound-to-dollar exchange quotations from America. He would discuss this with the joint-permanent secretaries at the Treasury before walking back to his office in Old Broad Street. There, he had the orders of the day encoded and sent by secret cable directly to New York. And here again we find that Secret Elite agents operated above the law of the land, without the knowledge of the cabinet, in contravention of the Defence of the Realm Act and over the head of the official censor. Lloyd George permitted Edward Grenfell in London access to an unrestricted direct cable to J.P. Morgan in New York so that its messages were more secure and absolutely secret.[26]

Ponder for a moment on this unique arrangement. Unrestricted coded cables were sent on a daily basis to a New York banking company agreeing purchasing orders, banking instructions and exchange rates. Taking this line of argument one step further: the men who created and ran the Federal Reserve System were in cahoots with the British central bank to secretly agree the values of their respective currencies without the scrutiny of any political or democratic agency. The Secret Elite, as embodied in the whole Anglo-American Establishment, was absolutely in control. It could be argued that the British economy was being run from J.P. Morgan's offices in New York. Is there any clearer example of what was called "the Money Power"? Questions were asked in Parliament when rumors of the government's agreement were leaked to the press. Morgan was known to favor his own or associated companies to the exclusion of others, a practice which ran contrary to public policy and could adversely affect British manufacturing interests. The MP for Newry, John Mooney, alleged that Morgan companies were buying up goods and selling them on to the British government at higher prices.[27] But to no avail.

If we take one step back and look at these arrangements in the cold light of reflection, Lloyd George's interference in armaments and munitions dated from September 1914, when he informed the War Office that he, as chancellor, had set aside £20 million to finance extensions to factories for the production of armaments. His consequent disgust at their intransigence in contacting the armaments "trade," as he called it, to push forward additional supplies of "guns, rifles and ammunition" has been well documented.[28] That he was the first to register serious concerns about the likelihood of a severe shortage of munitions,[29] arguing vehemently against Kitchener in Cabinet meetings that War Office practice was outdated, is in itself interesting. His informants were "prominent industrialists" from "all over the country."[30] In other words, Lloyd George was the armament trust's voice in Cabinet. His confidence was such that he could initiate orders and organize processes, sanction agreements and by-pass War Office restrictions in the knowledge that he would be supported. Little wonder Kitchener felt undermined.

Lloyd George was also in a unique position compared to other Cabinet ministers. He knew of the frequent requests from Sir John French for more shells for his howitzers; requests that became the theme of "almost daily telegrams" from the front.[31] While Kitchener was concerned about the unprecedented rate at which shells were being "expended," urging Sir John French to economize, Lloyd George met with representatives of

Vickers, Armstrongs, Beardmore and the Coventry Ordnance to promise them that the government would find the money to increase their capital expenditure on munitions.[32] That money would come from America. Much of that money would be spent in America on armaments and component parts and be paid for, eventually, by the British tax-payer.

Alfred Milner and his associates held a barely disguised contempt for democracy and party politics.[33] The Secret Elite knew well that the greater their control, the more easily they could lead the Empire towards their vision of a one-world government and that vital control was strengthened by the passing of a second Defence of the Realm Act in March 1915.[34] With many individual freedoms already curtailed through the initial Defence of the Realm Act,[35] Lloyd George boldly extended the government's powers over production and manufacture in Britain, claiming that he was forced to take such action because of the indolence and drunkenness of the working man.

Behind a rallying call to mobilize the vital work inside the munitions industries, Lloyd George's Bill gave the government power to take over works and factories which were capable of being adapted to war production. In a dramatic if not drastic step, any manufacturer could be ordered to produce goods that the government wanted. Without any prior warning or discussion, the Liberal economic policy of "laissez-faire" was cast aside. Any work in any factory could be directed and changed by order of the Admiralty or the Army Councils,[36] plant could be summarily removed, land requisitioned, and armaments production exempted from previous protections under the Factory and Workshop Act.[37] Control over the movement of population was also extended so that workers in key industries could not gravitate to areas where wages were higher. On sober reflection, only Lloyd George could have convinced the workers' representatives that this had to be done in the national interest. That was his absolute value to the Secret Elite. He, and he alone amongst parliamentarians, could convince the working classes that they could put their trust in him.

As a result of a series of conferences between 17 March and 27 March, Trade Union Representatives signed a Treasury Agreement by which they agreed to recommend an end to restrictive practices for the duration of the war, on the clear understanding that private employers did not make additional profits. Unions felt that the proposed package demonstrated that employers and labor were both surrendering their rights for the worthy cause of winning the war. How naïve. The international munitions industry bent its knee to no government and the idea that they would hand over the management of their business to an executive committee was entirely notional. The only substantial element in "taking over the industry" was the limitation later put on their profits.[38] Lloyd George intended to oversee the organization of munitions production in Britain, boosting the profits of his friends in business on the basis that the crisis in shell production was far greater than the general public imagined – and had to be solved.

There is no doubt that the level of shell wastage had been extensive. The German diarist, Rudolf Binding, wrote in late October, 1914 of the "regular evening blessings of shrapnel and heavy explosive shells" which always accounted for "some victims." He disparagingly commented on the French batteries after Passchendaele opening fire on a single horseman.[39] How much of the alleged shortage covered military inadequacies? When the failure of British troops at the Battle of Neuve Chapelle in March 1915 was analyzed, the lack of high-explosive shells was deemed to have been critical. On 15 March, Kitchener expressed his concern in the House of Lords, admitting publicly that a very large number of orders had not been completed on time. But whose fault was that? The War Office? The armaments and munitions rings? No, the official reason was the failure of the ordinary working man. He claimed that:

> ... while the workmen generally ... have worked loyally and well there have, I regret to say, been instances where absence, irregular time-keeping, and slack work have led to a marked diminution in the output of our factories... It has been brought to my notice on more than one occasion that the restrictions of trade unions have undoubtedly added to our difficulties, not so much in obtaining sufficient labor as in making the best use of that labor.[40]

Shortage of labor began to make itself felt across the country, from agriculture and farming to heavy industry and armaments. Labor shortages in skilled work was a problem for the munitions industries despite attempts by the Board of Trade to restrict the recruitment of engineers and other highly experienced workers to the army. Kitchener's insistence that any man who wished to enlist should be allowed to do so held true for the first eight months of war, and it was not until March 1915 that he accepted the obvious principle that it was of greater advantage to keep a skilled worker in the workshop than to allow him to join the army and abandon his trade. While he maintained that commanders like Sir John French wasted ammunition by sheer extravagance, Kitchener added the callous comment "it isn't the men I mind. I can replace the men at once; but I can't replace shells so easily."[41]

Such was the pressure of public opinion that all able-bodied men should enlist, that badges were issued to workers in armaments firms to save them from abuse in the streets. Trade Union reaction to the limits placed on their legal rights and the admission of semi-skilled, unskilled or female labor into factories and occupations that had previously been restricted to skilled men, was understandably negative. The sudden price rise in early 1915 made matters worse and added to the acute shortage of skilled men in workplaces contracted to supply government orders. The unrest was followed by major strikes. Lloyd George's answer was greater control over these workmen and workplaces, but that required a resolve that others in the Liberal government simply did not have.

Asquith was in denial that there was any real problem at all. In a speech at Newcastle on 20 April, he claimed that the allies had not been crippled by "our failure to provide the necessary ammunition. There is not a word of truth in that statement … which is calculated to dishearten our troops, discourage our allies and stimulate the hopes and activities of our enemies."[42] Kitchener had assured the Prime Minister that the British army would have as much ammunition "as his troops will be able to use on the next forward movement."[43] The confusions continued.

In an atmosphere of conflicting opinion, Lloyd George brought special government proposals before the House of Commons on 29 March. He wanted drastic action to curb drink amongst the munitions factory workers. He painted a lurid picture of laborers and unskilled workers on the Clyde and Tyne, "loafing in public houses instead of doing their honest day's work."[44] Stories were cited of one street in Scotland with thirty pubs within a half-mile of the yards, of one big bar in Scotland where on a Saturday night a hundred bottles of whiskey were filled in the expectation that all would be sold between 9.30 p.m. and closing time.[45] Lloyd George complained that congestion at the docks occurred because men could earn enough money in two or three working days to keep them in drink for the rest of the week. The fault, he claimed, lay with weak-willed working class and the demon drink. He proposed to use the Defence of the Realm Act to grasp the power to close any public house deemed prejudicial to the output in munitions work and increase the duty on spirits and wine through a heavy surtax. These were draconian powers, but served his purpose well. As a tactic to raise much-needed government income and to deflect criticism away from the government and the armaments industry, his proposals were typically shrewd.

Sir Richard Cooper, the Liberal MP For Walsall, challenged the Chancellor's attempt to focus the blame on others and declared that, "this resolution is nothing more than an attempt to saddle upon the working people of this country the responsibility for the delays in the production of munitions for war." James O'Grady, Labour MP for Leeds East, ripped Lloyd George's statistics apart; pointing out that the men in shipyards had only just survived vile working conditions during the worst winter for years and that materials were often unavailable. He stated that large numbers of orders had been exported abroad included munitions. More importantly, O'Grady explained that the level of physical exhaustion and illness was legitimately high because men were working a 53-hour minimum week; a

45 hour minimum if on permanent night-shift. Many were working even longer hours. He quoted two Sheffield steelworkers, both union branch secretaries, both teetotalers, who for the first time in ten years were unable to work because of exhaustion. Finally, he pointedly turned to the claims made at Newcastle by Asquith that "we had sufficient munitions for war and the workmen were working 67-69 hours per week."[46]

An independent report by Harry J. Wilson, a Glasgow Inspector of Factories, on 3 April 1915 also demolished much of the apocryphal nature of Lloyd George's accusations. He interviewed shipbuilders, engineers and the Chief Constable of Govan to determine the extent of the problem caused by drink. Wilson reported that there had been no noticeable change in drinking habits since the war began and in a yard employing 10,000 men, it was unusual to find more than 3 in one night who were intoxicated. 0.003% of the workforce hardly constituted an epidemic. Harry Wilson found that due to the shortage of skilled men who had volunteered in 1914, some who kept bad timekeeping were tolerated. His conclusion was that the problem was caused by a small minority of men in important shipbuilding yards and workers across the country resented the implication that they all had to be punished.[47]

But Lloyd George prevailed. He successfully switched the public spotlight from the government to the ordinary working class. He was backed by King George V, who wrote to offer his support by personally abstaining from alcohol, "if it is deemed advisable" and banning it from the royal household so that "no difference shall be made ... between the rich and the poor."[48] There it was. Drink and loafing were to blame, and the King himself would surrender at least the first of these to do his bit for the war effort. "Squiffy" Asquith made no such generous offer.

The Northcliffe-dominated press, in particular the *Times* and the *Daily Mail*, began a very personal attack on Lord Kitchener after the ill-fated offensive at Aubers Ridge on 9 May.[49] Aubers was an unmitigated disaster for the British army. No ground was won and no tactical advantage gained. On that single day, 9 May 1915, 11,000 British casualties were sustained and it took three days to process the wounded through the Field Ambulances.[50] German losses were reported to be under 1,000.

This dreadful failure has been blamed on Kitchener's alleged inability to provide high explosive shells. Prior to the attack, Sir John French, Commander-in-Chief in France, had assured the War Office that he had sufficient ammunition[51] and had written a letter to Kitchener on 2 May stating; "the ammunition will be all right."[52] After the disaster Sir John French deflected attention from his own poor leadership by telling the *Times* correspondent, whom he had personally invited to witness what he anticipated as "one of he greatest battles the world has ever seen,"[53] that it had failed because of a shortage of shells.[54] This wasn't just disloyalty; it was a lie. The attack at Aubers was preceded by an intense and prolonged artillery barrage which those present thought heralded "the complete destruction of the enemy's lines."[55] It did not.

The Secret Elite supported the attack on Kitchener. His attitude to munitions, his inability to be a team player and the whispering of the commanders whom they trusted, like General Sir Henry Wilson, undermined him. Geoffrey Dawson, editor of the *Times,* shared the plan with Lord Milner, their undisputed leader,[56] who was equally determined to bring down Asquith's liberal government. This deeply contrived "shell shortage" added to the problems the government was facing over Gallipoli and riots in the streets after the sinking of the *Lusitania.* Milner told his close friend, and member of the Secret Elite's inner core, Sir Harry Birchenough[57] that the "chickens are indeed, coming home to roost."[58] But there was a major stumbling block. The conditions imposed through the Defence of the Realm Act meant that before any news from the front was published, it had to be given formal approval by the censor. On 11 May, Charles Repington, the *Times* war correspondent, sent a private letter to Geoffrey Dawson with the curious message that his report would be stamped "passed by the censor," though he (the censor) would not have seen it.[59] In other words an un-named source was about to fabricate official permission from the censor so that the *Times* could print Sir John French's lie. It was a criminal act dressed as a duty to expose the "truth" in order to undermine Kitchener and Asquith.

On 14 May, 1915, headlines in the *Times* screamed of "Need for Shells and Lack of High Explosives." Northcliffe maintained the pressure on Kitchener through his *Daily Mail,* which wrote of the folly of using shrapnel against the powerful German earthworks and wire entanglements, claiming that it was as effective as a peashooter.[60] On 21 May Northcliffe threw all caution to the wind and wrote the editorial for the *Daily Mail* with the headline, "Kitchener's Fatal Blunder." He pulled no punches; "Lord Kitchener has starved the army in France of high explosive shells. The admitted fact is that Lord Kitchener ... persisted in sending shrapnel – a useless weapon in trench warfare. He was warned repeatedly that the kind of shell required was a violently explosive bomb which would dynamite its way through the German trenches and entanglements and enable our brave men to advance in safety."[61]

At the front, soldiers were "raised to a pitch of fury" by the "perfectly monstrous" attack on Kitchener. Major General Sir Henry Rawlinson lambasted the "diabolical plot" to focus attention on high explosive shells stating that: "the true cause of our failures is that our tactics have been faulty, and that we have misconceived the strength and resisting power of the enemy. To turn round and say that the casualties have been due to the want of H.E. shells for the 18-pounders is a perversion of the truth."[62] In the trenches, soldiers were likewise disgusted by the press attack at a time when everyone should have been working against the enemy.

Instead of stirring public outrage against Kitchener, Northcliffe's tirade provoked a torrent of loathing against himself and his newspapers. "It shocked the public, shook Whitehall and threw Northcliffe's critics into paroxysms of rage."[63] Reaction was swift. The Services Clubs in Pall Mall barred the *Times* and *Daily Mail* from their doors. Subscriptions were canceled; advertising slumped. Copies of the *Daily Mail* and the *Times* were burned on the floors of the London Stock Exchange, the Liverpool Provision Exchange, the Baltic Exchange in London and the Cardiff Coal and Shipping Exchange. Though the *Westminster Gazette* praised "the manly and honorable impulse" of the stockbrokers who cheered for Kitchener and booed Northcliffe,[64] there was more than just a whiff of payback about this allegedly impulsive demonstration.

Three years earlier, the city editor of the *Daily Mail*, Charles Duguid, had become so concerned about the high cost of dealing in shares on the London Stock Exchange, that he decided, with Northcliffe's blessing, to launch the *Daily Mail's* own cut-price share service. Demand was so heavy that Duguid had to establish a small bureau to handle the administrative burdens of running a do-it-yourself stock market. When the London Stock Exchange closed its doors to trading on 31 July 1914, the *Daily Mail Exchange* took out half-page adverts in the *Financial Times* and the *Financial News* declaring it was open for business.[65] The Stockbrokers did not burn Northcliffe's papers out of patriotism. Theirs was an act of spiteful revenge. But it caught the popular mood. Kitchener was an untouchable; a national icon whom the masses still revered. Sales of the *Daily Mail* on the morning of the attack on Kitchener topped 1,386,000 copies and overnight slumped to 238,000.[66] This was not the effect that Northcliffe expected, but he did not desist or retract.

What makes this turn of events even more significant was that, in rejecting Northcliffe's claims, the public refused to treat shell shortage as a "crisis," though the supply of armaments remained a high priority. Official historians later adopted Northcliffe's line and consequently the concept of a "crisis" took root. There were however, important consequences. Herbert Asquith was unable to hold together a government that had been elected in 1910 with no experience of managing a war. Had they been forced to hold a general election, Liberals feared that the Conservatives would be swept into power, and Asquith surrendered to a multitude of pressures from outside parliament to agree a swift and dramatic coalition;[67] but the Secret Elite were reminded that public opinion had to be carefully manipulated to achieve major change. It could not be taken for granted. They did have one outstanding success. Overall control of munitions was taken away from the still popular Lord Kitchener.

A Ministry of Munitions was created as a discrete department inside the coalition government of 1915, and it was headed by their worthy agent, David Lloyd George. It may have looked like a side-ways step for the Chancellor of the Exchequer, but it was not. In many ways it was the most important post he could have held. The Secret Elite sought complete control of all war production to maximize their profits under the guise of sustaining the war effort. Lloyd George had proved his worth.[68] Once a committed pacifist who had preached arms-control, the popular Welsh MP was the one man who could have led a successful concerted opposition to war in August 1914, but sold-out to the "Money Power."

His access went beyond the political realm and his association with businessmen and financiers in Britain and America gave him power and status greater even than the Prime Minister. Lloyd George had developed close relationships with men who should have been political enemies. He regularly consulted Arthur Balfour, the former conservative party leader and Prime Minister, and through him had the confidence of Bonar Law who fronted the opposition party in 1915. Alfred Milner, consumed by the certainty that national conscription was the only way forward, considered Lloyd George the most able man in the government.[69] Knowing full well how to manipulate the Welshman, Milner noted; "if properly handled, [he] will end up going for it (conscription) and he is the only man who could carry it, if he could be induced to try."[70]

The Ministry of Munitions Act, which received Royal assent on 9 June 1915, was followed by an Order in Council which transferred the main functions of the War Office in ordinance contracts, supply and inspection to a discrete department of government headed by the man who wanted it most, David Lloyd George. The Defence of the Realm Act of 1915 (No. 2 March 1915) also allowed his ministry to take over any factory and its labor force to prioritize war production. Keen to be remembered as the man who saved the day by rescuing munitions from its "crisis," the egocentric Lloyd George described his task as politically: "A wilderness of risks with no oasis in sight."[71] In reality, he had the full backing of the powers that operated behind the scenes on both sides of the Atlantic. In the process of advancing his political career, the once-principled Welshman comprehensively sold his soul and proved himself devoid of all moral qualities.[72] Let there be no doubt, Lloyd George was in the political ascendancy and through him, the Secret Elite expanded their stranglehold on output and production. The one-time pacifist was indecently eager to give them the chance to make huge profits providing they gave him the shells.[73]

In moving from his stewardship of the nation's finances to master of munitions, Lloyd George entered a world where he was free to spend unlimited amounts of money on provisions of war which were never subject to targets or upper limits. The public perception was that more shells equaled certain victory, and any voice contrary risked accusations of treachery. He is reputed to have estimated the shell requirement by the following proposition: "Take Kitchener's maximum; square it, multiply that by two; and when you are in sight of that, double it for good luck."[74] What he did went well beyond the wildest dreams of the armament's trusts. He once again cast himself in the role of the friend of big business and the industrial-financial elite whose favor he had curried at the Board of Trade in 1906.[75]

Lloyd George gathered round him men from business and industry, including Sir Hubert Llewellyn Smith, a Ruskin adherent and old Oxford University acquaintance of Secret Elite leader Alfred Milner. Smith had been responsible for the system of war-risk insurance to protect shipping company owners, and in 1915 played a crucial role in wresting munitions supply policy from the War Office. He later developed Lloyd George's wartime manpower policy[76] into a shape approved by Milner. Sir Percy Giraud, managing director of the Elswick Works of armaments giant Armstrong, Whitworth, became director-general of munition supply, and was succeeded by Sir Frederick Black, Director of Naval Contracts. It was to Black that George Macaulay Booth had reported when he advised that J.P. Morgan should be appointed sole purchaser for Britain in the American market.[77] While so many names may at first be overwhelming, they demonstrate the links between influential businessmen, American bankers, trusted high ranking civil servants and Secret Elite agents who pervaded Lloyd George's munitions department.

His supporters in the national press, especially Northcliffe's, hailed Lloyd George's appointment as a decision that would "satisfy the country,"[78] and the owner of the *Times* sent him a personal note dramatically claiming that he (Lloyd George) had taken on the "heaviest responsibility that has fallen on any Briton for 100 years."[79] The general perception was, "War Office, bad; Ministry of Munitions, good," but the legend that Lloyd George saved the day in 1915 and the early months of 1916 is preposterous.[80] Raw statistics appeared to justify this self-proclaimed achievement. He took up office on Whit-Monday [May 24] 1915 and by 31 December shell deliveries totaled 16,460,501, the vast majority of which arrived late in the year. In fact 13,746,433 of these had been ordered beforehand,[81] and had nothing to do with the rush to "rescue the situation" as painted by Lloyd George's sponsors. In truth, these impressive statistics were the result of the steady conversion and expansion of war industry since August 1914,[82] an expansion that was primarily set in place by Lord Kitchener.

Unquestionably Lloyd George appointed some able organizers. Sir Eric Geddes, who epitomized his "man for the job" approach, became Deputy Director of Munitions Supply, responsible for rifles, machine guns, field guns, motor lorries, field kitchens, and innumerable other items. As head of the Gun Ammunition Department he earned undying gratitude for improving shell output in time for the opening of the Somme offensive.[83] The additional supplies of heavy artillery enabled the generals to continue their awesome wastage, and ironically, it was Lloyd George's radical drive which allowed them to continue with their orthodox military policies.[84] Over six days almost two million shells were fired at German positions at the Somme before the doomed infantry attack. You might even believe that it was a striking victory if viewed in terms of the profligate use of munitions rather than the awful carnage and wasteful sacrifice of mutilated armies.

Lloyd George promoted the Secret Elite desire to replace politicians and traditional career civil-servants with businessmen who, in his own words, "had touched the industrial life of the country and of the Empire at every point."[85] The War Office caution was cast aside in favor of business managers and innovators. The Ministry of Munitions conducted a national survey of engineering resources, divided the country into manageable regions and local boards of management which issued local contracts. While Lloyd George appeared to nationalize the munitions industry, he did nothing of the sort. A number of state factories were established with considerable fanfare, but most of the local boards opted for a system of contracts placed under the management of the major arms firms.[86] This was a clever move because the ministry's relationship with the armaments trusts remained mutually positive and productive. In many cases the national factories were integrated with or attached to existing firms, and prices remained excessively high.

The Secret Elite's need to control went deeper and further than the issue of armaments. Powerful trades unions had to be brought into line. Lloyd George began a campaign to convince the country that war work was second only to that of the fighting forces of the Empire. Brooking no objections and fearing no-one, he set out on a crusade to tame industrial unrest, backed as ever by Northcliffe's newspapers. The *Times* naturally supported his call for a relaxation of trades union practices and the employment of women in munitions.[87] Lloyd George's repeated warnings that he had powers under the Defence of the Realm Act that he might be forced to use, presaged the action he intended to take. A special conference was convened in private on 10 June with 75 representatives from 22 major workplace unions at the new ministry, and on 16 June a second conference at the Board of Trade was held with over 40 representatives from trade union associations. Lloyd George had the courage to make it personal, to meet the workers and their leaders and, in his own words, "tell you the truth."[88] The truth and Lloyd George had long been distant bedfellows, but his rhetoric appealed to the masses and thrilled the employers.

He went to Cardiff to set up a national munitions factory in South Wales and, though he always found room to warn about the necessity of compulsory powers, Lloyd George urged his audience to "plant the flag on your workshop; every lathe you have, recruit it."[89] In Bristol the exhortation was to let the men in the trenches "hear the ringing in the forges of Great Britain, of the hammer on the anvil…"[90] A deputation of workers from Wm. Beardmore and Co. and the Dalmuir shipyards on the Clyde had been sent to France to visit front-line troops and returned urging "more shells, and more high explosive shells."[91] Let it be clearly understood; Lloyd George was the only national politician who could have carried off the most all-encompassing restrictions planned on personal freedom and choice in Britain since Oliver Cromwell, without a revolt. He was an invaluable operator for the Secret Elite.

The Munitions of War Act (2 July, 1915) stamped an unprecedented control over the British worker. Despite its innocuous title, the new law introduced draconian limitations on the rights of the working man and woman. Arbitration in disputes about wages, hours and conditions of work became compulsory. Factories could be deemed "Controlled Establishments" whose profits were to be limited by a munitions levy or tax and no wage increases were allowed without the consent of Lloyd George's ministry. While apologists hailed this move as evidence of a fair-minded approach,[92] the notion that profits were henceforth restricted to just 20% more than the average of the last two years of peace missed the point that pre-war profits were already exorbitant and the orders were now so vast that enormous gains continued to be made. However, on the face of it, the law appeared to demand an equal sacrifice from capitalist and labor,[93] and that was his message.

Strikes and Lockouts were prohibited. Workers could no longer move from one part of the country to another without explicit permission, and anyone attempting to relocate had to have a "leaving certificate." The Minister himself could organize war munitions volunteers, demand the removal of labor from non-munitions work and issue or withdraw badges identifying men who should remain in armaments production rather than volunteer. Workers were obliged to take certain jobs and work overtime, paid or unpaid. Fundamentally, workers in the munitions industries remained civilians bound by quas-military restrictions on their personal rights.

Towards the end of 1915 the Glasgow Rent Strike erupted into a popular protest against greedy landlords who abused the housing shortage by raising rents in seriously sub-standard tenements whilst the family breadwinners were fighting and dying on the Western Front. That landlords and their factors could treat the suffering poor with such heartless war-profiteering and widespread evictions, stirred resentment to action. Protests were widely supported by left-wing groups in and around Glasgow and Clydeside including the Labour Party and trade unions, but mainly women left to protect their own.[94] Forced by the impact the protest was having on the great armaments workshops, engineering factories and ship-yards arrayed along the banks of the Clyde, where imminent disruption to production was threatened in favor of the women's resistance, the government passed a Rent Restriction Act.[95] This once-liberal government was moved not by social justice, but by the threat to war production.

Problems of labor dilution by which less skilled workers were permitted to take on more skilled work, and their consequent loss of status, was a serious concern throughout the engineering industry. But the Minister of Munitions was determined to drive forward his plans for 80,000 new workers in "state-owned, state-erected, state-controlled, state equipped factories with no profits for any capitalists."[96] What arrant nonsense, but it sounded good. His public profile was such that he outshone everyone else in the government, including Kitchener, and his stock rose even further with the Secret Elite. It certainly propelled him from offices in Whitehall Gardens to Downing Street.

David Lloyd George had a special friend in the armaments business about whom he was publicly in denial.[97] In the murky world through which the Welshman had built his political career and abandoned the principles which he once held precious, none is stranger than his relationship with the international arms dealer, Basil Zaharoff. Neither Churchill, Sir Edward Grey, Asquith or Lloyd George mentioned him by name in their biographical histories, though we should always remember that the censor intervened to ensure that details which the state wanted to remain secret were ruthlessly expunged before publication. But Zaharoff lurked in the shadows of Whitehall, dealing and double-dealing mainly through the offices of Lloyd George whether minister of munitions or Prime Minister.

Who was this shadowy figure from whom the public record shrank after the war?

Basil Zaharoff was born into a middle-class home in Mugla, Anatolia in 1849 and died on 27 November 1936 in the height of luxury at the Hotel de Paris in Monte Carlo. His family were Greeks living in Turkish Asia Minor where persecution of Greek Orthodox Christians threatened genocide. They fled to Odessa in Russia, but did not stay long, returning to the Greek quarter of Constantinople when the political upheavals had settled.[98] Zaharoff had all the records and diaries which pertained to his life, destroyed. His biographer, Robert Neumann was exasperated by the lack of historical documentation:

> You ask for his birth certificate. Alas! A fire burned all the church records. You ask for a document concerning him in the archives of the Vienna War Office; the folder is there but the document has vanished.... You obtain permission to inspect the papers in a law case ... but no-one in the office can find them.[99]

So successfully was he airbrushed from the accepted establishment history that no mention is made of him by Lloyd George in his *War Memoirs*, and Zaharoff was ignored by almost every one George's biographers.[100] The *Times* newspaper has in its accessible archives no reference to Basil Zaharoff between 11 May 1914, when he donated £20,000 to the French National Committee of Sports and 6 July 1918, when he made a ten guineas donation to a Concert on behalf of Belgium.[101] What does that tell us about his ability to remain anonymous during the war, for Zaharoff was deeply involved in munitions and international politics during those years. Crucially, and perhaps most importantly, he was a Rothschild man.

On the eve of the First World War Zaharoff had taken up residence in Paris. He represented Vickers on the Board of Societe Francaise des Torpilles Whitehead, and when Albert Vickers retired from the Board of the French "Le Nickel" company in the spring of 1913 he was replaced by Zaharoff on account of his "great expert knowledge and powerful industrial connections."[102] Le Nickel had originally been an Australian company based on the French-owned Pacific island of New Caledonia, but was bought into by the Rothschilds who had acquired most of the nickel refineries in Europe. The discovery of nickel reserves in Canada forced them into a market-sharing agreement with the American-Canadian International Nickel Company,[103] and nickel remained an invaluable asset as part of the steel-making process. The Rothschild-backed company operated two nickel plants in Britain and the cartel arrangement between Le Nickel and British nickel-steel manufacture ensured that prices were kept artificially high.[104] Thus by 1914 Basil Zaharoff, an adopted son of France, sat on the Boards of Vickers and Le Nickel, both Rothschild-financed and influenced.

Two events took place in Paris on 31 July 1914 that epitomized the chasm between good and evil. The ancient grudge of the warmonger wiped out any lingering hope by assassinating the peace-maker, while the wicked procurer was raised onto a public platform and promoted to the rank of Commander in the Legion of Honor by the French President.[105] At 9:20 PM the charismatic French Socialist leader Jean Jaures was in the Café Croissant at Montmartre in Paris discussing the critical situation in Europe with the editors of his publication, *L'Humanite*. He was shot twice in the back of the head at point-blank range. History has recorded the assassination as the work of Raul Villain, a 29 year-old right-wing student, but no serious attempt was made to discover "whether any other motive power directed the assassin's arm."[106] Villain was later acquitted of murder.

Days before, Jaures stood on a political platform in Lyon-Vaise and urged his International Socialist brothers in France, Britain, Germany, Russia and Italy "to come together, united, to turn away from the nightmare" which faced Europe. He raged against war and the makers of war, and his message carried great weight.[107] Jaures was in Brussels with the

Scottish socialist leader James Keir Hardie on 29 July thanking the German Social Democrats for their splendid demonstrations for peace. With impassioned eloquence he urged workers throughout Europe to rescue civilization from a disastrous war.[108] He returned to Paris after an emergency meeting with Rosa Luxemburg and was deep in conversation about how war could be averted when his life was taken.

Shock and consternation filled the streets of Montmartre, and the Paris police reacted by throwing a cordon around the palatial home of Basil Zaharoff at 41 Avenue Hoche.[109] It may seem an odd reaction, but in July 1914, Zaharoff the arms dealer was invaluable to the French government's war preparation, and that very day President Poincaré had announced his elevation to Commander of the Legion of Honor. The irony is odious. Jaures, the peace-maker, murdered in cold blood; Zaharoff, the merchant of death, hailed as an outstanding Frenchman. In fact, Parisians were too traumatized to turn their wrath against Zaharoff, and were dragged into war so quickly that the moment for instant retribution passed without incident.

As an arms dealer Zaharoff was pre-eminent in his time but he was much more than simply a multi-millionaire international salesman whose stock-holdings crossed every important munitions company in Europe. Rarely have there been so many uncorroborated stories about someone who was later dubbed "the mystery man of Europe" by Walter Guinness in the UK Parliament. This unfortunate name-tag added mystique to Zaharoff's clandestine activities. His association with Lloyd George has been immersed in a legend that distracts from an alliance which was intrinsically linked through the Secret Elite to the war effort. Allegedly, Lloyd George had enjoyed an extra-marital liaison with Zaharoff's English wife, Emily Ann Burrows,[110] and this purportedly gave him some kind of hold on the Minister of Munitions. It was not an allegation that was ever proved. There was more than this to their unholy relationship.

What was absolutely critical was his dominance of the world of international armaments sales. The First World War represented the peak of his career and influence, and he was described as "virtually the minister of munitions for all the allies."[111] Wild claims continue to circulate that every Allied government consulted him before making plans for their grand attacks during the war. More convincing is the allegation that it was he who ensured that governments refrained throughout the war from attacking and destroying mines, factories, blast furnaces and armaments production sites, like Briey and Thornville in which he had an interest.[112]

When Lloyd George took over at 10 Downing Street in December 1916, he used Zaharoff as it suited him, if not as a pawn, certainly as a player in a game of deadly chess. The old arms dealer proved his worth in opening back-channels which Lloyd George used to influence politicians in the Balkans. Zaharoff was sent on a clandestine mission to Switzerland in 1917, carried secret promises from the British government to the Ottomans, and was even used to mislead the Turkish government about the future of Mesopotamia and Palestine. Of all the charges leveled against him, perhaps the worst is that he continually sought to prolong the war for his own ends. Zaharoff boasted to the Greek Prime Minister in 1916 that Germany was very vulnerable and that "only incredible stupidity on the part of the allies could give her victory." He added, "I could have shown the Allies three points at which, had they struck, the enemy's armament potential could have been utterly destroyed. But that would have ruined the business built up over more than a century..."[113]

As was discussed in the chapter on Briey, Zaharoff was absolutely correct in stating that German armaments production could easily have been wiped out. He was very wrong, however, in insinuating that only he knew this. Secret Elite agents in London and Paris were well aware that German armaments production could have been wiped out by the summer of 1915. They had the means to do it, including the destruction of Briey and the blockading of German imports of materials essential to their armaments industry, but chose to prolong the war.

When Zaharoff's advice was sought in 1917 about the advisability of bringing peace to Europe he is reputed to have insisted that the war had to be seen through, right to the end.[114] That of course had always been the Secret Elite objective; the absolute destruction of Germany. So much selfishness; so much misery. Like the vast majority of rich old men who had deliberately caused this war in which tens of millions of young men were slaughtered or badly maimed, Zaharoff died peacefully in his bed. His final years were spent as a recluse in Balincourt (France) protected by body-guards day and night. His records and memoirs were destroyed on his orders. He went to extreme lengths to safeguard his anonymity, including the buying up of every postcard printed of his private castle in Balincourt. Inquisitive journalists and private detectives "disappeared."[115] One can only hope that his obsessive fear of assassination was predicated on the realization of the depth of the evil for which he had been responsible. Probably not. Meanwhile, Lloyd George was, as always, open for business.

Summary.

- First problem caused by Lord Kitchener's outstanding recruitment appeal in 1914 was that there were insufficient rifles, cannon, machine guns, mortars, uniforms or basic equipment on hand for the eager young men who signed up in droves.
- There were however plenty horses. Given that the High Command was drawn mainly from the cavalry classes, it is fair to say that the Roberts Academy had prepared for the wrong war.

• Shrapnel was the undisputed shell of choice and in consequence, the demand for high explosives was originally relegated to around 30% of total orders

• In all of the wrangling about shells and munitions, it should be remembered that the Navy had for years claimed a long-accepted priority.

• Kitchener's War Office wanted to retain full control of munitions. They were suspicious of offers from American companies or orders placed in America by British government agents.

• The government set up a Cabinet Committee in October 1914 to examine the issues of munitions' supply. Absolute control did not immediately pass from the War Office, but within eight months Kitchener was sidelined.

• Lloyd George, then Chancellor of the Exchequer, offered munitions firms a blank check which covered them and their subsidiaries from loss. He also acted independently from the Cabinet Committee in liaising with Charles Grenfell, senior partner of Morgan-Grenfell and director of the Bank of England.

• JP Morgan was appointed as sole purchaser of British requirements in January 1915. Control over the spending of thousands of millions of British tax-payers' pounds was placed in the hands of an American plutocrat and his British agent in London.

• Lloyd George permitted Edward Grenfell access to an unrestricted secret direct cable to J.P. Morgan in New York. Unrestricted coded cables were sent on a daily basis to a New York banking company agreeing purchasing orders, banking instructions and exchange rates.

• A Factory and Workshop Act allowed control over the movement of population and was extended to workers in key industries

• The real problem was not so much shell shortage as shell wastage. So too was labor shortages in skilled work because so many skilled men had volunteered for war.

• The newspapers and some senior military figures blamed Kitchener for the lack of sufficient munitions but the attempt rebounded on them because Kitchener was such a universally admired military leader.

• Asquith was obliged to form a new government, a national government in May 1915. Lloyd George was moved to head a new department, The Ministry of Munitions. He was seen by the general public as the man who got things done. Links between influential businessmen, American bankers, trusted and approved high-ranking civil servants and Secret Elite agents were strengthened.

• He was able to persuade the trade unions and working class representatives to surrender their rights and accept major restrictions on their personal freedom through the Munitions of War Act in July 1915.

• His secret links with Basil Zaharoff the shadowy manipulator of the munitions and armaments industries have been in part air-brushed and in part lost in the murky double-speak of approved histories.

Chapter 25

The Fate Of A Field Marshal

Kitchener was not a man who relished being sidelined. Despite this, he remained in office after his role as Secretary of State for War was deliberately subverted by his enemies and detractors in 1915. For example, when he visited Gallipoli to assess the situation on the government's behalf, decisions were taken behind his back. As the *Times* noted, "in the absence of Lord Kitchener" a small War Committee was set up to co-ordinate the government's organization for war.[1] It comprised, Asquith, A.J. Balfour, Lloyd George, Bonar Law and Reginald McKenna, with Sir Edward Grey on-call, as was Kitchener when he returned from Gallipoli and the Near East.[2] By late 1915, he knew exactly what he was up against. In terms of armaments, Lloyd George had grasped control of the War Office Ordnance remit and subsumed it into a new department, the Ministry of Munitions.[3] Sir William Robertson was appointed Chief of the General Staff on 21 December, effectively taking charge of strategy on the Western Front. Robertson's focus was in line with the ultimate aim of the Secret Elite. He advocated the concentration of war in Europe in order to bring Germany down. While lack of success on the Western Front and the failure at Gallipoli reduced Kitchener's standing inside the Cabinet, his popularity with the mass of the populace did not waver. In stripping Kitchener of major responsibility for strategy, Asquith was sufficiently astute to retain him in office.

Maurice Hankey,[4] the Secret Elite's central cog inside 10 Downing Street, was the most knowledgeable and experienced strategist in the country. In his diary for 8 December 1915, he noted that Asquith wanted to be rid of Kitchener who, "darkens his counsel and is a really bad administrator, and he evidently wants to find some way of fitting K. [Kitchener] into his scheme so that the Government can still use his great name and authority as a popular idol.... Personally I can see no way of fitting him in without making him a cipher in every sense."[5]

This was the problem. How could the high priests remove the people's idol without losing their credibility? The only answer was to find him marginal tasks to keep him distanced from the center of power.

But Kitchener had always been his own man. He cared naught for politicians and cast doubt on their capacity to act wisely. He expressed these concerns to Sir William Robertson with honest clarity: "I have no fear as to our final victory, but many fears as to our making a good peace."[6]

Such intentions shook the Secret Elite and especially Alfred Milner. Alarm bells rang in the memory of those who served with Lord Milner in South Africa. Kitchener had interfered then, at the end of the Boer War, to bring about *his* peace. It had taken all of Milner's considerable influence to stop Kitchener agreeing a date for the restoration of Boer self-government.[7] Milner had gone to war against the Boers to break the mold and recast the country, not negotiate a political peace. Peace terms implied compromise. Milner had admitted to his acolytes that there was no room for compromise in South Africa. But Kitchener "paralyzed" Milner, and in his view, betrayed the peace.[8] Consider again the main objective of the Secret Elite. They wanted to break the mold of Germany and recast the country and its colonies so that it would never again pose as a threat to the British ascendancy. Surely Kitchener was not thinking about interfering in a European peace – in 1916?

Kitchener saw himself as the arbiter of a good peace, and his intentions were corroborated by Lord Derby,[9] who later reflected on Herbert Kitchener's state of mind in his diaries.[10] Had he attempted to publish these facts in the years immediately after the war, the official censor would have edited, withdrawn or destroyed the information. Derby's diaries would have been buried. But by good fortune, Lord Derby did not publish his book until 1938, by which time censorship was much less rigorous. Kitchener held very strong views that he intended to push to the fore when peace was eventually negotiated. Kitchener confided his philosophy to Lord Derby over dinner some three or four days before he sailed on his final fateful journey. Derby took notes immediately afterwards so that he did not have to rely on memory. He recorded Kitchener's absolute belief that "whatever happened," at the end of the war, the peace negotiators should not "take away one country's territory and give it to another." The fate of Alsace and Lorraine was included in his statement: "I think if you take Alsace and Lorraine away from Germany and give them to France there will be a war of revenge." He was insistent that Germany's colonies should not be taken from her on the basis that "if they have colonies they would go there peacefully and not want to engage in war for new territory."[11] His sense of a "good peace" had nothing in common with the complete destruction of Germany.

Kitchener's sentiments were anathema to all that the Secret Elite had worked towards. Leave Alsace and Lorraine as part of Germany? Let them keep their colonies? Good grief, would he next advocate the restoration of the Ottoman Empire? He still held influence in these eastern parts, and the British government had great ambitions for Persia after the war. Surely not. Kitchener spoke heresy. Such sentiments stood to undo the war against Germany which the Secret Elite had so carefully planned.[12]

Kitchener had also confided in Sir Douglas Haig[13] that only a decisive victory against Germany followed by a fair peace treaty, would prevent further wars in Europe. He had come to the conclusion that the war should not be about the conquest of Germany. [14] In the eyes of the Secret Elite, he had completely lost focus. Imagine if the concept of a "fair peace" had been leaked to the men in the trenches. That the great man himself was thinking ahead towards peace, had implications for the murderous continuation of war. And not just peace, but a fair peace? To the powers behind the government it was unthinkable. Unimaginable. Kitchener had become more than just a liability. He was a danger to the Secret Elite's ambitions. His future intentions put everything at risk.

Matters were exceptionally sensitive in 1916. There was talk of peace and peace conferences. Most of it originated from America where President Wilson had an election to win and "peace" was a vote-catcher. The war had reached a point of deadlock; victory was only likely to be achieved by the "guerre d'usure," the war of exhaustion. Certainly, Sir Edward Grey was in regular touch with Wilson through the controlling offices of his White House minder, Edward Mandell House,[15] but peace was not an issue that any of the warring nations could be seen to contemplate. Yet, a possible deal took shape. Mandell House and Grey jointly drafted a confidential memorandum on 22 February 1916 which was confirmed by the President. It proposed the restoration of Belgium, the surrender of Alsace and Lorraine to France, the acquisition of an outlet to the sea for Russia, and compensation to Germany in territories outside Europe. If Britain and France thought the time was right, President Wilson would propose that a "Conference should be summoned to put an end to the war. Should the Allies accept this proposal and Germany refuse it, the United States would probably enter the war against Germany."[16] Sir Edward Grey had actually worked with E.M. House to construct a memorandum which by definition was a basis for a negotiated peace.[17] By the end of the year Grey had been replaced.

But what to do with Kitchener? He was an enigma indeed. In June 1916, Asquith accused him behind his back of abdicating his responsibilities and lying. Undoubtedly it suited the Prime Minister's purpose to deflect criticism away from himself. He derided Kitchener's tortuous speech and his repetitive presentations,[18] but was obliged to defend him in Parliament in a brief but brilliant oration which was cheered from all sides.[19] Kitchener, for his part, kept faith in Asquith. Lord Derby wrote in his diary that Kitchener was devoted to the Prime Minister and liked him very much, which may partly explain why he stayed at his post. [20] As Asquith sat down in Parliament on 1 June, the conservative leader Bonar Law leaned forward and whispered; "That was a great speech, but how after it shall we ever get rid of him?"[21]

Inner-core members of the Secret Elite were very concerned. They had erred in their judgment about Kitchener. Lord Milner, especially so.

Yes, he had pushed him into the post of Secretary of State for War in August 1914 expecting an entirely different approach from that of the Boer War and in most respects he had been correct. Had Milner been misled by Kitchener's reassurance that the war would take three years or more? He had been the first to predict a long war, but by 1916 Kitchener saw himself as one of the "English delegates when Peace was made."[22] There were no circumstances in which this could be allowed. The Secret Elite intended to recast Germany and re-affirm the primacy of the British Empire. Kitchener's whispered ambition put all of that, and more, at risk. He had become a very serious liability.

Lord Kitchener knew that the government wanted him out of the way,[23] which naturally made him wary of any ploy which involved his leaving the country. At the end of April 1916, Asquith first suggested a political mission to Russia to discuss munitions and stiffen the Czar's resolve to stand firm against Germany. Originally, he nominated Lloyd George to head the visit and it was suggested that Maurice Hankey might accompany him.[24] That same day Hankey claimed to have heard that Kitchener wanted to go to Russia[25] and began lobbying to that effect. He wrote in his diary that "K[itchener] likely to accept and likely to ask me [to accompany him] – but I shan't go."[26] Hankey stood his ground and refused; but at the same time he actively lobbied for Kitchener's inclusion inside the War Committee. Remember that theoretically Hankey was just the secretary to the committee. We now know that he was a key figure inside the Secret Elite,[27] whose influence grew by the day. Consider the sequence of events. A mission which began as a putative political visit to Russia by the Secret Elite's men, Lloyd George and Maurice Hankey, was dramatically altered to substitute Lord Kitchener at its head. According to his biographers, Kitchener "suddenly announced that he would like to head the mission."[28]

Strange forces were at work and not one of them was sudden. The Secret Elite's man in Petrograd, Sir John Hanbury-Williams,[29] took steps to encourage Kitchener to travel to Russia. He wrote directly to the Secretary of State for War on 12 May to underline the Czar's "pleasure" on hearing that Kitchener might come to Russia,[30] precisely two weeks before the War Committee approved the mission. King George V was the surprised recipient of an upbeat telegram from the Czar on 14 May, describing Lord Kitchener's visit to Russia as "most useful and important." Someone had acted improperly. The King demanded clarification. Twelve days passed before the decision to send Kitchener was ratified. In the meantime, it was suggested that the Russian Ambassador, having heard that Kitchener *might* visit Russia, had presented the rumor as fact to the Czar's court in Petrograd.[31] By all accounts, written after the fact, and written to suggest that the Germans knew that Kitchener was destined for Petrograd, his impending visit was common knowledge by the third week in May.[32]

Interesting. In fact, no firm decision had been taken by the War Committee in London. When it was, the arrangements were substantially different. Firstly, Lloyd George was removed from the equation. Out of the blue, Asquith decided that he needed Lloyd George to go to Ireland to settle the aftermath of the Easter Rising.[33] He wrote a very brief note to him in secret on 22 May urging him to "take up Ireland: at any rate for a short time."[34] How strange. Lloyd George had never been involved in Irish matters before ... and for a short time? As he put it: "Much against my own inclination, I decided that I could not refuse Mr Asquith's request (to switch his priority from Russia to Ireland)."[35] Lloyd George never did anything that was not in his own best interest. Thus, by 26 May, it had been decided that Kitchener would go accompanied by his personal staff.[36] No senior politicians were to be included; no member of the Secret Elite.

Allegedly, the visit was common knowledge in Petrograd. Evidence suggests otherwise.

Final authorization for Kitchener's mission to Russia was approved on 26 May. One day later, Hanbury-Williams was given notice that Lord Kitchener and his staff (including three servants) would set sail for the Russian port of Archangel.[37] Kitchener was clearly keen to meet the Czar but was suspicious of the government's intentions once he was out of the country. He left Lord Derby with a private code by which he could be informed of any further changes which might take place while he was away.[38] He had every right to suspect dirty play. Alerted in early June to the possibility that his proposed visit to Russia might have to be put back several weeks to accommodate the Russian Finance Minister, Herbert Kitchener almost abandoned the mission. He wrote to Hanbury-Williams warning that "owing to the military situation" he could not spare time later in the year and if the visit was postponed, it would have to be abandoned altogether.[39]

He knew the timing of the proposed summer offensive in France and was determined to be back at his desk in the War Office before the action began. Here was an unexpected twist. Kitchener was prepared to abandon the mission unless it remained set in its allotted time frame. Hanbury-Williams moved fast. He immediately assured Kitchener that he had spoken to the Czar who "repeated twice that he wished you to come" and thought "your visit one of importance and would be of benefit to both countries."[40] The Secret Elite desperately wanted Kitchener to go to Russia. But why? If Kitchener was in position to call off the visit to Russia as late as 3 June 1916,[41] it could hardly have been vitally important.

Consider this. The political mission by Lloyd George and Hankey had been transformed into a personal visit to the Czar by the Field Marshal and Earl, Kitchener. The mission was represented as the Czar's wish. On 26 May Kitchener informed the Russian Ambassador that the War

Council had agreed that he should accept the Czar's invitation to Russia.[42] How clever. At a stroke, should anyone ask awkward questions about the purpose of Kitchener's visit, the answer was that he had been personally invited by Czar Nicholas II.[43]

Herbert Kitchener left for his visit to Russian in good spirits. Critics of his performance as Secretary of State for War had been quashed in a failed censure motion in parliament on 31 May[44] and on 1 June he met with over 200 MPs to give them the opportunity to hear his views on the war to date. He answered their questions openly and the parliamentarians responded with warm and prolonged applause.[45] That evening he had a farewell audience with King George V and went from Buckingham Palace to Downing Street for a lengthy meeting with Prime Minister Asquith. With hindsight it had the feel of a farewell tour.

At that very moment, out in the North Sea, near Denmark's Jutland Peninsula, the only full-scale clash between the British Grand Fleet and the German Imperial Fleet erupted. Both sides claimed victory, though the British suffered heavy losses including six cruisers and eight destroyers.[46] Almost immediately afterwards Admiral Sir John Jellicoe ordered an inquiry into the loss of so many cruisers[47] and as the fleet returned to Scapa Flow, bruised and damaged, the blame game began. While the loss of 6,097 men was a serious blow to Admiralty prestige, the German Fleet, which suffered 2,557 losses,[48] was afterwards more or less confined to port for the duration of the war. Both sides claimed victory, but Jellicoe's reputation never recovered. He was already under great strain, physically and mentally. [49]

And in the immediate aftermath off this naval trauma, the most iconic soldier in the Empire arrived at Scapa Flow. Kitchener and his staff had made the 700-mile journey north to Scotland overnight by train on a special coach from King's Cross station. Next day, Monday 5 June 1916, he arrived at the port of Scrabster near Thurso and made the rough two hour crossing to Orkney on the destroyer, HMS *Oak*. What is pertinent to all that transpired thereafter was that the Secretary of State for War was entirely in the hands of the Admiralty, and the Admiralty was in the hands of the Secret Elite's Arthur Balfour.[50] It was Admiral Jellicoe who allocated the old coal-fired armored cruiser HMS *Hampshire* to carry their precious passenger to Archangel in Russia even though she was reported to have sustained light damage at Jutland. It was Jellicoe who issued the initial orders on 4 June to the *Hampshire's* Captain, Herbert Savill, who had sailed the Orkney passages for over a year. Crucially, it was Jellicoe who changed these instructions at the last moment, directing the cruiser up the western coasts of the Orkney islands, allegedly a safer, more protected route. There was no protection from a cyclonic storm around Orkney save the stout safety of Scapa Flow harbor.

Kitchener at Scapa Flow, Orkney

The weather was foul. In fact it was about as bad as it could be in June. According to the local newspaper, the "Orcadian," a force-9 gale, the wildest summer storm Orkney had experienced for years, raged over the island. Alexander McAdie, Professor of Meteorology at Harvard University later destroyed the claim that Jellicoe and his staff could not have anticipated the raging gale which circulated around Orkney that day. A clearly identified cyclone was passing from the Atlantic to the North Sea and was on the point of recurve before heading into the Arctic regions. He stated that "the forecaster in London would have warned against starting under such conditions ... the counsel of the weather wise would have been to wait and follow the depression rather than try to precede it."[51] Apologists for the Admiralty and Jellicoe blamed "bad judgment and complacency."[52] In 1923, McAdie destroyed such a notion by claiming that "the lack of definite knowledge of the storm's position seems inexcusable."[53]

We are talking here about the Admiralty, with its centuries of experience in weather and seamanship. The Admiralty was responsible for the detailed planning of Kitchener's journey by sea. Jellicoe was the Commander-in-Chief of the Fleet. He knew Scapa Flow and its cyclonic storms and gales. He was in regular contact with London. Indeed Jellicoe telegraphed the Admiralty to seek permission to permit HMS *Hampshire* to remain at Archangel for the duration of Kitchener's visit and received approval at 6.08 p.m. on 5 June, once the *Hampshire* was underway.[54] Surely, as Commander-in-Chief of the Grand Fleet, Jellicoe could have made such a decision on his own. Why did London have to approve it? Undeniably communications were exchanged between the Orkneys and London that concerned the *Hampshire* before it was blown apart. It is therefore impossible to sustain an argument based on "confusion and poor communications" between the Admiralty and Jellicoe in Scapa Flow. There was no confusion.

Questions were soon raised about the choice of HMS *Hampshire* to carry Kitchener on the Arctic route to Archangel. An angry Portsmouth vicar wrote to the *Times* on 9 June: "Is no explanation to be given to us why the most valuable life the nation possessed was risked in an old ship like HMS *Hampshire,* unattended by any escort?"[55] This is a valid question. The *Hampshire* was a thirteen-year old Devonshire armored cruiser which might well have been scrapped. In February 1914, Winston Churchill, then First Lord of the Admiralty, supplied a written Commons answer to a parliamentary inquiry which listed two-hundred and fifty-two vessels, ranging from Battleships to Torpedo Boat Destroyers which were oil-fired, soon to be oil-fired or partially fitted for both power sources. HMS *Hampshire* was not included.[56] Yet the old coal-fired, four-funneled cruiser was Jellicoe's choice. She would hardly have been inconspicuous when steaming at full speed.

Thus, HMS *Hampshire* slipped her moorings in the relative safety of Scapa Flow at 4:45 PM on 5 June 1916 and headed west then north into the teeth of a storm. She was escorted by two destroyers, *Unity* and *Victor,*[57] neither of which had the capacity to cope in the vicious head-on gale. They joined the *Hampshire* at 5:45 PM and went through the motions of providing initial support for the cruiser. For thirty-five minutes *Unity* struggled against the odds to stay close, but even with Captain Savill's speed reduced twice, it was a forlorn hope in the mountainous swell. She was ordered to return to Scapa at 6:20. *Victor* lasted a further ten minutes in the severe gale, then turned back. By 6:30 PM, the *Hampshire* was plunging a lonely slow furrow, her decks battened down save for the hatch to 14 mess, like a floating coffin with a single air-vent. Channeled down Jellicoe's chosen route, past Hoy Sound, tossed and battered by the merciless storm, the official account would have us accept that "unconnected co-incidences"[58] drew the ill-fated ship into an unknown German mine-field, laid by *U-75* just off Marwick Head. Only twelve men survived. Kitchener was not one of them.

That an "unknown" German mine-field lay to the west coast of the Orkney Islands demands examination. Evidence now available demonstrates that vital messages about submarine activity on the precise route that Jellicoe had ordained the *Hampshire* must take, had arrived at the Naval Headquarters at Longhope on the Orkney island of South Wallis on the afternoon of 5 June. Apparently no-one paid attention.[59] The most prestigious passenger ever landed at Scapa Flow was already at the base and no-one had given instructions to update the commander-in-chief,

Admiral Jellicoe, or his senior staff, about submarine activity on the chosen route? This is unbelievable. Submarine activity in the proximity of Scapa Flow was always given the highest priority. Few places in the world were more conscious of the danger posed by a submarine. Given the vulnerability of the Grand Fleet after the Battle of Jutland, the disposition of U-Boats was of absolute importance. Failure to immediately alert the senior officers of the fleet to U-Boat dangers was a dereliction of duty which would have merited court martial. No-one was taken to task.

The Admiralty had possession of the three major codes used by the Imperial German Navy to transmit information to their ships and submarines before the war was four months old.[60] The decoders in Room 40 were able to decipher every naval wireless transmission and from these, plot German ship movements and build up detailed profiles on U-Boat commanders.[61] As the German preparations for what would be known as the Battle of Jutland took shape, three ocean-going submarine minelayers were sent to the sea lanes off the Firth of Forth, the Moray Firth and Orkney.

The commander of *U-75*, Kurt Beitzen, duly laid his mines in five groups of four across the sea-bed on the precise route which Jellicoe selected for the *Hampshire*. In Room 40, *U-75*'s course, and that of its two sister ships, had been detected and decoded. Take *stock* of this statement. When Kitchener's journey was being planned and approved at the Admiralty they knew of the risks caused by submarine activity. So too did Jellicoe. Two intercepts from 31 May and 1 June placed the new ocean-going minelaying *U-75* west of Orkney. On 3 June, *U-75*'s movements were transmitted to the Longhope station, and Admiralty records show that three messages logged on 5 June, all timed and dated from the Cape Wrath station, identified a submarine, *U-75*, at 2:40 PM, 5:15 PM and 7:15 PM.[62] *Hampshire* had put to sea at 4:45 PM, but was in radio contact with Longhope. Undeniably, Jellicoe had instructed HMS *Hampshire* to sail into a section known to have been occupied by a mine-laying U-Boat.[63] These were not the errors of some raw recruit or the hapless mistakes of an inexperienced trainee. Each of these decisions was dictated by Admiral Sir John Jellicoe, Commander-in-Chief of the Grand Fleet. It is claimed that Kitchener had been keen to press on with his journey despite the weather, and consequently the *Hampshire's* departure was not delayed. Really?

Are we to believe that had Admiral Jellicoe taken time to explain the debilitating effect of a force-9 storm, Kitchener would have over-ruled his advice? In fact, there was no such discussion. Jellicoe later wrote that, in his opinion, "I did not consider the delay necessary as I should not have hesitated, if need had arisen, to take the Grand Fleet to sea on the same night and on the same route...."[64] Of course Kitchener wanted to get underway, but was sufficiently astute to understand the adage "more haste less speed." He was a poor sailor. Claims that blame lay with Kitchener's blind determination to sail through the cyclonic storm ring hollow. The same might be said of the choice of HMS *Hampshire*. Of all the options available to Jellicoe, the old armored cruiser was the least-cost option. Her coal-burning boilers generated both power and steam and had she made Petrograd safely, how many submarine packs might have lain in wait for the return voyage?

In the weeks and months that followed, a great deal of heat was generated by allegations and conjecture about who, outside Britain, may or may not have known about Kitchener's proposed visit to Russia; as if that had bearing on the outcome. One factor, and one alone, did. Whoever knew about the *U-75* and its minelaying activity around Orkney, knew that the passage to Marwick Head was a death-trap. Whoever instructed Captain Savill to take the route, must bear some responsibility. But did Jellicoe act alone? How far does the trail of complicity stretch? At the Admiralty there was one man in the inner circle of the Secret Elite whose authority over-rode all else. That was the First Lord, Arthur J. Balfour.

On 5 June 1916, at 7:45 PM GMT, an urgent telegraph was sent from Birsay Post Office to Kirkwall and Stromness. It read "Battle cruiser seems in distress between Marwick Head and the Brough of Birsay." Twenty minutes later the words "vessel down" followed.[65] The cruiser was about a mile and a half from shore in tempestuous swells but clearly visible to the naval watching-post on land. Marwick Head is a jagged coastal fortress of cliffs and unwelcoming rocks. If there is such a place as the perfect ambush point for a ship such that the chances of survival are minimal, it is Marwick Head. The escort vessels, having failed to keep pace with the faster cruiser in the impossible weather, had been ordered back to Scapa Flow.[66] There were witnesses. Joe Angus, a gunner in the Orkney Territorial Forces shore patrol [67] saw a great cloud of smoke and flame bursting up behind the bridge of the *Hampshire*, and it was he who set off the alarm.[68] Having been alerted, Corporal Drever, who manned the naval watching post, raced to the post office.[69] What followed was, literally, diabolic.

EXAMINE THE TIME-SCALE: 5 JUNE, 1916, 7:45 [GMT] PM[70]

The *Hampshire* had been set on a course north, thirty degrees east.[71] It struck a mine which exploded just behind the bridge.[72] but did not sink immediately. In the ensuing mayhem only twelve out of around seven hundred men[73] survived both the floundering ship, the wrath of the angry North Sea gale and the cruel rocks. Of these, nine survivors specifically reported that a single explosion ripped the ship apart. William Bennet, officer on watch in the engine room, thought there were two or even three. They had to overcome the poisonous smoke and suffocating fumes to reach the deck. Estimates of the time between explosion and sinking, ranged from ten to twenty minutes. Confusion added to the howling wind and booming seas. Lifeboats could not be launched because the ship's power had been lost. Boats cut free were dashed to pieces in the cold, debilitating waters. Men with life belts jumped in desperation. Only the Carley safety floats offered any chance of survival.[74]

Time: 5 June, 1916, 8.00 [GMT] pm onwards

Stoker Walter Farnden was one of an estimated forty men who clung to No. 3 raft with its cork-reinforced edges and rope handles. One by one they disappeared into the deep, frozen, exhausted, unable to steer towards anyone still holding onto life amongst the debris. Stoker Farnden later described the torture he and his comrades endured: "An hour passed, two hours, and nearer and nearer to land the storm hurled us. Men were still dying in the agony of it all until there were but four of us alive."[75] Hundreds of men died in the wild seas because no-one was on hand to help. This human tragedy unfolded one and a half miles from the coast, witnessed and reported to the authorities at Scapa Flow within minutes, yet these despairing souls were left to die; abandoned outside the largest natural anchorage in the British Empire. Why?

At the moment when possibly dozens of men might have been rescued by a prompt response to the emergency call, the navy failed its own. Later a pathetic excuse was offered blaming the initial telegram for inaccurate detail. That ceased to have any relevance when the 8:20 message read "Vessel down." By 8:35 a third despairing message read: "Four funnel cruiser sunk 20 minutes ago. No assistance arrived yet. Send ships to pick up bodies." Men had been in the water for almost an hour. Still the Admiralty dithered.

Vice-Admiral Osmond Brock at the Longhope station on Orkney was informed that a vessel was down. Despite all that he knew, Brock did not immediately order out a rescue flotilla. Time was wasted confirming the telegrams. Brock had been one of the guests at the special lunch hosted in Kitchener's honor by Admiral Jellicoe that day. Brock knew of the late change to the *Hampshire's* course. He knew about Kitchener's mission to Russia. His failure to take immediate action remains incomprehensible. There was only one warship on that exclusive route. He knew that the stricken ship was HMS *Hampshire*.[76] His delay undoubtedly cost the lives of many dozens of possible survivors. Had Kitchener been in the water, he too would have been lost. Osmond Brock ended his career as Admiral of the Fleet.[77]

Orcadians who witnessed the tragedy could see that there were survivors amongst the bloated bodies, but the cliffs were a natural bulwark between the desperate sailors and safety. Unless there were secret orders in place, what followed remains a tale of incompetence, panic and bewilderment on a scale that fails to make any sense. At every point the reader must remember that the sinking took place just one and a half miles from the Orkney coast – an area bristling with naval activity – the home of the Grand Fleet itself.

In Stromness, news of the cruiser's loss was quickly relayed to the Royal National Lifeboat Institute, whose secretary G.L. Thomson rushed to alert the naval authorities and launch the lifeboat. He was stunned when told not to even try to do so. He demanded to speak with the senior officer only to be told that it was "none of his bloody business," and warned very clearly and very specifically that he would be charged with mutiny if he attempted to launch the lifeboat. Matters got so heated that he and his crew were threatened with arrest.[78] Lifeboats exist to assist those in peril on the seas. Their purpose is to save lives. Their history around the coasts of Britain is of great self-sacrifice and valor. That the navy should order the grounding of a lifeboat makes no sense. Had the Admiralty ordained that there should be no survivors?

In Birsay, the few locals who knew about the disaster wanted to help, but in some cases "were forcibly prevented [from trying to get to survivors] under dire threats" and even ordered to stay away from the shore or they would be fired upon. The local people were certain that had they been allowed to take immediate action, fifty more lives might have been saved.[79] Ponder that awful fact.

Time: 5 June, 1916, 9.45 [GMT] pm to midnight

It took over two hours for a tug and two trawlers to make their way out of Stromness, and then at 10 pm four more destroyers followed. Observers on the island of Birsay recalled that none of these reached the scene of the disaster before midnight. At around 1 pm, one of the Carley rafts washed up on the rocks of a small creek half a mile north of Skaill Bay. It carried around 40 men when it left the stricken *Hampshire*, picked up another 30 from the chilling seas, but only 6 survived the debilitating exposure when it smashed into the rocky cliffs. Fifteen minutes later a second life-raft reached the shore just north of the first with four living men amongst the 40-50 bodies. Can you imagine their physical and mental exhaustion? And none was yet safe. They faced the black cliffs with no-one in sight to offer assistance, throw down ropes or guide their hands as they climbed blindly upwards. One or two men reached a farm house, exhausted and barely alive.

Time: 6 June 1916, 10:30 am [GMT]

Initially, the authorities were unaware of survivors, and the following official statement was issued to the press at 1.40 pm on 6 June: "The secretary of the Admiralty has received the following telegram from the Admiral Commander in Chief of the Grand Fleet [Jellicoe] at 10.30 am this morning":

> I have to report with deep regret that HMS *Hampshire* (Capt. Robert J Savill, R.N.) with Lord Kitchener and staff on board was sunk last night about 8 p.m. to the west of the Orkneys, either by mine or torpedo. Four boats were seen by observer on shore to leave the ship. The wind was N.N.W. and heavy seas were running. Patrol boats and destroyers at once proceeded to the spot and a party was sent along the coast to search but only some bodies and a capsized boat have been found up to present. As the whole shore has been searched, I fear there is little hope of there being any survivors. No report has yet been received from the search party on shore. The *Hampshire* was on her way to Russia.[80]

The cover-up had begun. The Empire had been informed that "there is little hope of survivors' and the instant histories, like *War Illustrated* bluntly stated that 'Lord Kitchener … on board HMS *Hampshire,* had been drowned together with his staff and the whole complement of that cruiser."[81] The *Times* carried news from a special correspondent which inferred immediate assistance was sent. "Vessels which were instantly summoned to make a search found no trace of the sunken warship, or even, for a time, of any floating bodies."[82] The first announcements were false. Incredibly, there were survivors. However, no vessels had been "instantly summoned." Rear Admiral Brock had seen to that.

The Aberdeen trawler *Effort* passed the spot where the *Hampshire* sank two hours after the disaster. In the opinion of the crew, the sea was not so rough as to prevent small boats being launched, but nothing was seen of the wreck. By that time the weather had moderated. Strangely, the report from Aberdeen added that "the only craft observed was a Dutch vessel, which was steaming very closely."[83] Where did that come from? This mystery ship has never been identified.

Over the next days Orcadians reported seeing two lorry-loads of bodies arriving at Stromness Pier, barely covered, the lifeless crew piled high in open view, some almost naked as they were shunted down onto a waiting tug and taken for burial.[84]

No ships were sent to find survivors until hours later. The log books from HMS *Unity* and HMS *Victor,* the two destroyers originally sent back from escorting the *Hampshire,* show that they put to sea again at 9:10 PM[85] and took an hour and a half to reach the area of wreckage.[86] Critically, and some might say, criminally, Vice Admiral Brock, who knew every detail of the *Hampshire's* course, chose not to take immediate action to send assistance.

The Admiralty reject a public inquiry into the loss of the *Hampshire* despite the accepted protocol that whenever a ship was lost at sea, a public court-martial should be held to ascertain precisely why. Lord Kitchener's death commanded huge public interest and concern but no public inquiry was held.

Members of Parliament pointed out that in refusing to answer questions, the evasive Admiralty only added to wild speculation. They would not confirm whether the sea lane used by HMS *Hampshire* had been swept for mines. We know it had not. Jellicoe admitted this in his own history of the Grand Fleet.[87] There was no credible answer to questions raised about the announcement of Lord Kitchener's death. The formal communique about the loss of the *Hampshire* was issued in London at 2 P.M. on 6 June 1916, and that evening, the details of Kitchener's memorial service at St Paul's were announced before the War Office could reasonably assume that he had not survived.[88]

The bodies picked out of the sea or caught smashed against the jagged rocks were collected and quickly buried. There was no coroner's inquest, or, since the jurisdiction was in Scotland, "fatal accident inquiry."[89] It was as if the evidence had to be removed from the scene of the crime. To make matters worse, the Admiralty slapped a formal restriction on anyone going to or from the Orkneys on 7 June. Why did they want to keep journalists away from the island? At every turn officials behaved as if there was something to hide.

The Admiralty published their official statement on Saturday 10 June.[90] The narrative was brief and succinct to the point of mere repetition of what had already been published in the newspapers. It focused on the weather, the unexpected mine and the dignity of Lord Kitchener as he bravely faced death. How fortunate that one of the witnesses, Petty Officer Wilfred Wesson,[91] was able to confirm that Lord Kitchener was last seen on deck before the ship went down. Many years later in a newspaper article[92] Wesson's story offered food for thought. Despite the fact that the noise of storm and confusion was deafening, 'there were orders being shouted. They were mostly being caught in the gale and lost ... the wind howled ... immeasurable banks of waves burst in shivering cascades ... and then Lord Kitchener came on deck. An officer shouted: "'Make way for Lord Kitchener.' The captain had called to him to come up to the fore bridge ... that was the last I saw of Lord Kitchener."[93] Putting aside journalistic license, we might well wonder how Petty Officer Wesson actually heard what he claimed to in the raging storm? However, what was important to the Admiralty was that they produced a witness who could confirm that Herbert Kitchener made it onto the deck, and so must have been lost with the captain and other senior officers.

During the House of Commons exchanges on 6 July 1916, the parliamentary secretary to the Admiralty, Dr. Thomas McNamara, insisted that "a full and careful Court of Inquiry" had been held and "a full summary of the report published" covering the evidence from each survivor.[94] It would appear from subsequent evidence that questions were limited to "do you think the *Hampshire* hit a mine" and "did you see Lord Kitchener?" Why? Did they have reason to doubt that HMS *Hampshire* hit a mine? Were they concerned that some story of an internal explosion might raise other issues? And what did it matter if the Secretary of State for War was or was not seen on deck? The witnesses were asked leading questions.

The naval authorities did not consider it worthwhile to open an investigation on the allegations from the crew of the Aberdeen trawler, *Effort,* that the seas were much calmer when they passed the signs of wreckage or search for information from the Dutch trawler reported to have been around the scene of the sinking.[95] Commander Carlyon Bellairs suggested that "one of the reasons why the Admiralty of late have taken a dislike to courts-martial is that ... they have been known to bring in verdicts blaming the Admiralty." He made a startling statement: "Recently there has been a column in the newspapers about HMS *Hampshire* and the Battle of Jutland: some of us know that the *Hampshire* was never in the Battle of Jutland."[96] What? Commander Bellairs, a retired Royal Naval officer and Member of Parliament was recognized as a naval expert.

The official order of battle would disagree – but Bellairs was the naval correspondent to *War Illustrated,* and had many connections inside the Admiralty. Surely he was wrong – or was this yet another alteration made after the event by Lord Jellicoe when he was promoted to First Sea Lord?[97] The more one learns of the Admiralty's complicity in hiding the truth, the more one wonders what that truth really was.

Yet there was a full official report. It was kept secret. When asked in Parliament where the official inquiry had been held and who conducted it, the evasive answer given was "at a naval base under the presidency of a captain of the Royal Navy."[98] No names, dates or places. Little wonder suspicion of a cover-up began within a few days of Kitchener's death. Rumors ran rife. All of these muddied the waters with suggestions of foul play which ranged from an internal explosion masterminded by Sinn Fein in reprisal for the Easter Rising, to slack talk in Russia which had alerted the Germans to send a submarine to sink the Hampshire. Another suggestion was that he had committed suicide rather than face exposure to proof of his homosexuality. Such claims diverted attention from the most certain of facts.

The Admiralty was at fault to the extent that we have every right to suggest complicity. Ten years after Kitchener's death his friend and biographer, Sir George Arthur, had suffered so many queries about the "truth" surrounding the sinking of the *Hampshire* that he wrote a public letter to the *Times*[99] in which he exposed the Admiralty's duplicity: "... early in 1920 the First Lord of the Admiralty (the late Lord Long) invited me to read the secret , or unpublished, report on the sinking of the *Hampshire,* on the understanding that I would not divulge a word of it to anybody. I declined to read the document under these conditions,... [and]I told the First Lord that I should submit in my book that neglect, or at any rate carelessness, must be charged to the Admiralty, or the Commander of the Grand Fleet, in the arrangements made for Lord Kitchener's voyage." The reply of the First

Lord was, "I do not think you could say otherwise."[100] The impact of this revelation hit the Admiralty like an unexpected broadside. There had been a secret report. There were "versions" of the tragedy. "Neglect" or "carelessness" had been covered up. George Arthur forced the issue. The Admiralty was obligated to print the official narrative of the sinking of the *Hampshire* in the form of a White Paper[101] which could be bought for sixpence in August 1926. It added little to the information which had dripped into the public domain save repeating statements already published.

There is another, important but contentious fact. According to naval records, HM Drifter *Laurel Crown* was one of eight boats in a flotilla crossing the site of the *Hampshire's* sinking, when she was struck by one of the *U-75*'s mines on 22 June 1916, some seventeen days after the tragedy. There were no survivors. No-one to tell the tale. A number of concerns emerged. The first was how a small 81-ton drifter, literally a fishing boat pressed into minesweeping service, could hit a carefully located mine placed some seven meters from the surface?[102] One of the most important factors that apparently explained HMS *Hampshire's* fate was that her weight and displacement on the surging seas combined to take the ship to sufficient depth to cause the collision of mine and cruiser. In theory the German trap laid by *U-75* was set to catch much bigger fish than even the *Hampshire*. Yet a tiny drifter hit one of these mines? How bizarre.

Secondly, there is a clear difference in official records concerning the date of the *Laurel Crown's* demise. In the document, *Navy Losses, 1914-1918,* published in 1919, the hired drifter *Laurel Crown* was recorded "Sunk by mine west of Orkneys on 2.6.16."[103] The official German naval history,[104] described the *U-75*'s voyage in May 1916 and recorded that "on June 2nd the drifter *Laurel Crown* ran into one of *U-75*'s mines and was sunk." Thus both official records from the major combatants clearly stated that the *Laurel Crown* was sunk on 2 June, 1916.[105] Given that these official records corroborate each other, the Admiralty must have known of *U-75*'s mine barrier. It would have been abundantly clear to the authorities at Scapa Flow that there was a minefield sewn across the path of HMS *Hampshire*. Can we accept that in the confusion after the Battle of Jutland, reports of the trawler's sinking were delayed, ignored, or otherwise unknown to the senior staff in Scapa Flow? That would be ridiculous.

However, records from the Commonwealth War Graves Commission for the crewmen of *Laurel Crown* records their date of death as Thursday 22 June 1916. That is the same date given by the Court of Inquiry held in Kirkwall a week later. [106] Have these too been adjusted to suit the Admiralty's cover-up? The sinking of *Laurel Crown* was not included in the official British naval history, *Naval Operations, Volume IV* written by Henry Newbolt and published in 1928.[107] How odd. Official dates, altered dates, strange omissions. For reasons that have never been challenged, the sinking of the *Laurel Crown* has been relegated to confused claims and counter-claims about the date of its demise.

If, as is surely the case, the official records in Britain and in Germany are correct, Lord Kitchener, his party, and around 700 seamen were sacrificed to ensure that he was lost at sea. Do not be dissuaded by the enormity of the cost. Barely one month later on the killing fields of the Somme, hundreds of thousands more brave men were needlessly sacrificed in the name of civilization. Crushing Germany was all that mattered. One more ship was easily lost in the fog of Jutland's confusion.

The first reaction to the news of Kitchener's death was in its own right, suspicious. Lloyd George claimed that he heard the "startling" news on his way to a War Council in Downing Street on 6 June. When he entered the Cabinet Room he describe "the Prime Minister, Sir Edward Grey, Mr Balfour and Sir Maurice Hankey sitting at a table all looking stunned." This was indeed an inner circle of powerful men who understood what had happened, yet they were unable to talk about the consequences? Remarkably, given the enormity of what had just taken place, "Sir Maurice and I quite forgot for the moment that had it not been for the Irish negotiations, we would have shared the same fate."[108] That was untrue. From the outset Hankey said he would not go.[109] Apparently, Lloyd George and Hankey "quite forgot" that they should have been on that same ill-fated ship?[110] How many people could have reacted with such sang-froid? It defied human nature.

Indeed, without breaking step or pausing for a moment to contemplate the many contributions of the now-deceased Secretary of State for war, Lloyd George knew that "the passing of Lord Kitchener left an empty place at the War Office. I realized that this place might be offered to me."[111] This man of many plots, of endless carping behind the backs of others, who briefed the press, especially Northcliffe, against Kitchener, displayed a callous cynicism. Lloyd George did indeed accept that office on 4 July, but not before ensuring that all the powers that had been systematically stripped from Kitchener were re-invested in his replacement.

On hearing of Kitchener's death, Northcliffe is reported to have burst into his sister's drawing room declaring, "Providence is on the side of the British Empire."[112] Fawning tributes dripped from the mouths of the guilty. Admiral Jellicoe solemnly declared that the navy's grief for "a soldier" whose loss "we deplore so deeply. It was our privilege to see him last; he died with many of our comrades."[113] No mention was made of the unswept channel or blatant Admiralty culpability.

Look again at the depth of that culpability. HMS *Hampshire* was barely fit for service and its loss added little to the Navy's post-Jutland woes. Jellicoe and his masters at the Admiralty approved the ship's route into a known minefield. Naval intelligence at Room 40 had carefully monitored all U-Boat activity. References to the minefield and the sinking of the trawler, *Laurel Rose* were removed or altered to suit the cover-up "explanation" when difficult questions were raised about the fate of the *Hampshire*. The official report was kept secret. Key documents have still never seen the light of day.

The consequences of Herbert Kitchener's death were many-fold because his mission to Russia concerned more than just munitions. He hoped to establish closer relations and genuine friendship between the two empires. It was also understood that he would put an end to the intrigues in which George Buchanan, the British Ambassador to Russia, was involved. No matter whether the leading statesmen in Britain were or were not in sympathy with the Czarist regime in Russia, it was unpardonable to give support to radical elements of the opposition in the Duma and undermine Russian political unity. The Russians had hoped that Kitchener's presence in St Petersburg would paralyze the internal intrigues and give their government the moral support which it so badly needed.[114] This is not what the Secret Elite intended. Kitchener's death also denied a platform to the voice of reason during the armistice period in 1918-19. He would have demanded a just peace. It was not to be.

Kitchener's murder was covered with dripping platitudes and cynically penned obituaries. In the House of Lords, Lansdowne proclaimed that Kitchener's death "was a great and dignified exit from the stage upon which he had played so prominent a part during the long years of his life."[115] The two-faced Asquith lamented "his career has been cut short while still in the full tide of unexhausted powers and possibilities."[116] The Secret Elite's John Buchan ordained that "in a sense his work was finished" and "his death was a fitting conclusion to the drama of his life."[117] "Bollocks" may not be a recognized historical assessment, but "bollocks" it remains. They peddled lies as fraudsters do. The full panoply of State and Church gathered at St Paul's Cathedral on 13 June to hold a service of remembrance for Lord Kitchener and his staff. The service ended with all three verses of *God Save the King*.[118] Thus, with a great sense of theatre, his memory was consigned to the annals of received history. How quintessentially British. No-one has ever been held to account for the murder of Lord Herbert Horatio Kitchener and over 700 other men.

Summary.

- Kitchener's powers at the War Office were effectively reduced in Asquith's national government. A small War Committee was established to co-ordinate the government's strategy. Kitchener was not a standing member.
- He remained extremely popular with the public and the ordinary soldier, and could not be summarily dismissed. Kitchener simply lost his overall control of the military.

- Kitchener began to talk about his own concerns; that the government was not capable of 'making a good peace'. He told Lord Derby that if the Allies took away Alsace and Lorraine from Germany, there would be a war of revenge. His concept of a good peace had nothing in common with the Secret Elite's determination to crush Germany.
- He confided in Sir Douglas Haig that only a fair peace could prevent further wars in Europe.
- It was dangerous talk at a difficult time. President Wilson was seeking re-election in America and peace was a vote-catcher. The British government leaders wanted rid of Kitchener.
- A mission to Russia to stiffen the Czar's resolve was mooted and originally Lloyd George and Maurice Hankey were to be delegates.
- This was changed. Both men were withdrawn and Kitchener was substituted to head the mission.
- Talk of a delay almost resulted in Kitchener calling the mission off, but all obstacles were cleared. The Secret Elite desperately wanted Kitchener to go to Russia. Why?
- Kitchener's journey from Scapa Flow in Orkney, Scotland was entirely the responsibility of the Admiralty, and in particular Admiral Jellicoe. They allocated an old coal-fired armored cruiser, HMS Hampshire, to carry their precious passenger to Archangel in Russia.
- Jellicoe personally instructed the captain of HMS Hampshire to take the unusual western route from Orkney, despite the unmanageable cyclonic storm and the activity of German U-Boats in that area.
- The Hampshire allegedly struck a mine and sank one and a half miles from shore, in full view of observers on the cliffs. Messages were sent to Scapa Flow, but no action was taken for two hours. Four and a quarter hours passed before destroyers reached the area where Hampshire sank. It was midnight.
- The Admiralty rejected a public inquiry. There was no fatal accident inquiry. From 7 June 1916, journalists were banned from visiting the island. An official report for the Admiralty was kept secret until 1926, but it offered little additional information to that which had been dripped into the public domain over the preceding twelve years.
- No-one has ever been held to account for the murder of Lord Herbert Kitchener and over 700 others.

Lord Alfred Milner; undisputed leader of the Secret Elite.

Chapter 26

The Great British Coup 1916

Britain had been railroaded into war by a government which was neither capable of running it nor elected to do so. The belief that her naval and economic power was sufficient to defeat the Germans was one of the fundamental premises which underpinned the widely held assumption in Britain that it would be "business as usual."[1] Amongst a range of disinformation put about to assuage a gullible public was that the navy would protect Britain from invasion, strangle the German economy and win a low-cost war, safe behind a decade of naval investment. There was no invasion. Never at any stage in the proceedings did Germany plan for an invasion. A much-vaunted blockade was secretly reduced to tokenism. It was not "business as usual." Be of no doubt that the war could have been over by the Spring/Summer of 1915 had that been the prime objective. It was not due to incompetence, though the generals in the field merited that tag, miscalculation, or that the conflict was mismanaged, but by very carefully executed strategies to supply the enemy and prolong the war.[2]

In fact, the Secret Elite's men in government did a very capable job in prolonging the war. Asquith's dithering, his failure to change the nature of decision making in the Cabinet proved to be a stranglehold on progress. Lloyd George acted under the supervision of the banking and financial sectors on both sides of the Atlantic and used their backing to obtain loans and munitions through the exclusive J.P. Morgan/Rothschild portal.[3] Sir Edward Grey's men in the Foreign Office bent double to accommodate American interests and completely nullify the brave and tireless efforts of the navy to run an effective blockade. They rubber-stamped the secretive and illusionary "Belgian Relief" program run by Herbert Hoover to supply Germany with much-needed food.[4]

Victory in the field was not the objective unless it was predicated upon the complete destruction of Germany as an economic rival, and that would take time and absolute commitment. Two very different approaches were underway. Most of the Liberal Cabinet set out on a loosely sketched journey believing that a short war would be won at sea, and a small army would suffice for the continental struggle; the Secret Elite's men embarked on a long debilitating war which protected their interests, guaranteed great profits, and was backed by vast resources from the United States.

Even though the Liberal majority in Asquith's Cabinet were reluctant to abandon their laissez-faire principles, Lloyd George recognized that control of the railway network and guarantees for the shipping insurance business were absolutely necessary to the survival of social order.[5] In other words, government in times of modern warfare required direct intervention. Tellingly, Lloyd George's first actions had been to protect the banks, the money markets and the business of war. He took credit for saving the City after embracing advice from Nathaniel Rothschild and "a section of the business and financial world."[6] Of course he did. He was their man.

Prolonging the war was of course very profitable to them, but winning the war was everything. By 1915, the Secret Elite realized that Asquith's approach to war management was failing. He and his ministers were no longer dealing with the political issues for which they had been elected and could not be trusted with the unequivocal drive to crush Germany. The Secret Elite required a government focused on the destruction of Germany and these men were not up to it. Hundreds of thousands of young men had already been sacrificed. Prolonging the war required men with cold, hard hearts devoid of compassion, committed to the Secret Elite's cause. How had Milner expressed the steel required to see war through to the ultimate destruction of the enemy? His chilling advice to Richard Haldane during the Boer War was to "disregard the screamers."[7] It takes a special kind of "strength" to ignore humanitarian issues, ignore the utter chaos caused by the sacrifice of so many and yet be willing to sacrifice many more. Milner had such cold steel in his core. To the Secret Elite, Milner's deep-rooted fears were completely vindicated. Democratic liberalism, watered down as it had been since the death of Campbell-Bannerman,[8] denied Britain a co-ordinated agency to direct the war effort. In Asquith's cabinet, only Lloyd George, increasingly the sole candidate for Secret Elite support, grasped the need to shake up the traditional approach to government. Even a pretense of democracy would not deliver ultimate victory. It was poisoning their cause.

Change was required. In May 1915, the Conservative leader, Andrew Bonar Law sent a letter to Herbert Asquith stating: "In our opinion things cannot go on as they are, and some change in the constitution of the Government seems to us inevitable if it is to retain a sufficient measure of public confidence to conduct the War to a successful conclusion."[9]

He surreptitiously sent a copy of the same letter to Lloyd George. They were clearly in cahoots.[10] Lloyd George and Bonar Law claimed a personal friendship, "on terms of greater cordiality than is usual" according to the Chancellor himself.[11] In fact, Lloyd George was in agreement with the major issues raised by Bonar Law because the proposed coalition government was no threat to his own career. Subsequent events were more stage-managed than genuine. With astonishing speed, Asquith accepted the offer to form a coalition. Lloyd George played the role of marriage broker and physically took Bonar Law into the Cabinet Room in 10 Downing Street to talk through the conditions under which the Conservatives would join forces with the government. It took only fifteen minutes to bring to an end the last purely Liberal government in British history. Thus the deed was done. Or so we have been told.

But surely the offer was the wrong way round? To have had credence, to merit the sense of a government striving to do its best for the Empire, surely Asquith should have taken the first steps? Be mindful that a Prime Minister may appear to be in charge, but is always subject to the power-brokers above him/her.

Instead, a gun was put to his political head and he did not hesitate to capitulate. Why? Who had spoken to him? Hours later he told King George V that "the Government must be reconstructed on a broad and non-party basis."[12] Two days later the Prime Minister announced in the House of Commons "that steps are in contemplation which involve the reconstruction of the Government on a broader, personal and political basis." He clarified three points, inferring that all of this was of his own doing. He and Sir Edward Grey would definitely remain in post; the prosecution of the war would continue "with every possible energy and by means of every available resource." Finally, "any reconstruction that may be made will be for the purposes of the war alone..."[13]

The first steps in the Secret Elite takeover of every aspect of war government was underway, but it had a slow-burning fuse. Political niceties had to be followed. The main condition for "unity" placed on the table by Bonar Law was the immediate demise of Winston Churchill. The Conservatives would not countenance his continuation at the Admiralty after Lord Fisher's walk out and his insistence on the attack on the Dardanelles; the Ulster Unionists would never forgive nor forget his pre-war threats to their cause and, well, had he not abandoned both his class and his party by crossing over to the Liberals in 1904. Asquith also failed to stand by one of his best friends, Richard Haldane. It was a stain on his character that he dismissed Haldane, the man who created the BEF, whom he sent to the War Office on 4 August to initiate mobilization, and abandoned in May 1915 "after one of the most discreditable smear campaigns in British history."[14] Newspapers had claimed the Haldane was a secret German-sympathizer.

You might well ask why the Secret Elite were prepared to countenance the loss of two of their agents who had taken Britain into war; in this instance Churchill and Haldane? Basically, they were replaceable. All political agents no matter what their supposed allegiance, were replaceable. They still are. Ever in the know, Alfred Milner did not join Asquith's cabinet. Milner was of course a member of the House of Lords and an outspoken advocate for conscription rather than voluntary recruitment to the army. In truth, keeping unity among the coalition government was always going to test Asquith's skills, and he would have feared Milner's direct influence over so many in this Cabinet. Alfred Milner stood ready, but waited patiently for the turning tide.

British newspapers hailed the new non-party Cabinet for its inclusive strength, but John Redmond, leader of the Irish Home Rule Party, would not accept Asquith's offer of a minor post. He had little option given the prominent inclusion of leading figures from the Ulster campaign to oppose Home Rule from 1912-14. The men who had openly threatened a breakaway government in Belfast were back in power at Westminster. How ironic that British justice was placed in the hands of those who had been openly prepared to defy that rule of law in July 1914,[15] by raising and arming an illegal private army in Ulster[16] and conveniently taking Britain to the brink of what looked like civil war.

Lloyd George was paid his asking price. His disloyalty was bought off with the creation of a Ministry of Munitions in which he was given supreme authority.[17] He knew that the burning issue of the moment was the alleged lack of munitions and heavy artillery. He was aware of the clamor from the Military High Command for better shells; he knew that the exaggerated shortage of weaponry would gather public voice and turn to outrage if not addressed. He believed that this was a job that he alone could do, and that his backers in Britain and in America would support him all the way. He was correct.

Lloyd George received a remarkable letter dated 1 June 1915 from Theodore Roosevelt, former President of the United States, a Pilgrim[18] and close associate of the J.P. Morgan associates. Roosevelt was an enthusiastic advocate for the spread of the English-speaking, Anglo-Saxon expansion across the world[19] and as such was an agent of the Secret Elite. His letter read:

> I wish to congratulate you upon the action you have taken in getting a coalition cabinet, and especially your part therein. More than all I wish to congratulate you upon what you have done in connection with this war ... the prime business for you to do is to save your country.[20]

The former U.S. president gave the newly appointed Minster of Munitions his full approval for "what you have done." It was an apostolic blessing from the other side of the Atlantic. Lloyd George was congratulated for his action, not Asquith or Bonar Law, because Roosevelt knew that Lloyd George had masterminded this coalition and was the one man who understood what action to take. He was their man. That letter confirmed their approval.

The Secrete Elite's man at the hub of the war effort, Maurice Hankey,[21] remained exactly where he had always been, at the very heart of the decision making. In every reorganization, every shifting of seats or consolidation of power, in every alteration or formation of committee or council that had power and influence, that involved the inner cabinet, the real decision makers, Hankey remained quietly in the background as secretary or minute-taker. His was the ever-present hand that recorded the meeting and increasingly advised the members.[22] He, above all, was in the know.

But Asquith remained to the fore and so too did most of the problems. Getting rid of elected officials is always fraught with some danger, and there was a feeling that this national government would lack the competence to pull the nation together. When analyzed critically, the deckchairs had been shuffled but, with the exception of Lloyd George's new role, little else changed.

Asquith's coalition government of May 1915 altered little in terms of Britain's war management. It was hardly likely to, given that it was a basic reshuffle of old faces and older politics. Alfred Milner was well aware that this would be the case, and as such, it suited the Secret Elite to bide their time before catapulting their leader into front-line politics. Milner was initially stirred into action over Asquith's inability to make clear decisions, and criticized the "contradictions and inconsistencies which have characterized our action as a nation."[23] He began to turn the screw on the Prime Minister in the House of Lords early in 1916 and Sir Edward Carson did likewise in the Commons.[24] Carson had originally been the protégé of Alfred Balfour, and was a fellow member of the Secret Elite. It did not take long for the unnatural coalition of conservatives and liberals to unravel inside the Cabinet.

Maurice Hankey feared the generals were "bleeding us to death."[25] He warned Lloyd George that the British Army was led by "the most conservative class in the world, forming the most powerful trades union in the world."[26] It was an astute observation. The Staff "ring" (and these were *his* words) which had been brought together under the pre-war influence of Milner's great ally and former head of the Army, Lord Roberts,[27] was indeed a closed union of former cavalry officers, so self-satisfied and complacent that they ignored the views of others.[28] Whatever the obscene consequences of their mistakes, they continued to repeat them with the arrogance of those who are convinced that they know better.

Confirmed in their view that the democratic process had failed to provide the leadership and organization needed to win the war on their terms, Milner and the Secret Elite began the process of completely undermining the government and replacing it with their own agents. In January 1916 a small group of Milner's closest friends and disciples formed a very distinctive and secret cabal to prepare the nation for a change so radical, that it was nothing less than a coup; a planned take-over of government by men who sought to impose their own rule rather than seek a mandate from the general public.[29] Having ensured that the war was prolonged, they now sought to ensure that it would be waged to the utter destruction of Germany.

The men behind the carefully constructed conspiracy were Alfred Milner, Leo Amery, Sir Edward Carson, Geoffrey Dawson, editor of the *Times*, F. S. Oliver, the influential writer who believed that war was a necessity,[30] and Waldorf Astor, the owner of the *Observer*. They met regularly on Monday evenings to formulate their alternative plans for war-management over dinner. These men were drawn from the inner circle of Milner's most trusted associates.[31] Others who were invited to join them included Lloyd George, Sir Henry Wilson, (at that point a corps commander on the Western Front) Philip Kerr, another of Milner's protégés from his days in South Africa, and Sir Leander Starr Jameson, the man who almost brought down the British government in 1896 in the wake of his abortive raid on the Transvaal.[32] Could anyone have anticipated that Jameson would re-emerge in London inside a very powerful conspiracy some twenty years after he had almost blown Cecil Rhodes' dream apart?[33] But then he was always the servant of the mighty South African arm of the Secret Elite.

On the rare occasions that this clique has been mentioned by historians, it is usually referred to as a "Ginger Group." Yet another veneer of deception. Their objective was not to spice up the opposition to Herbert Asquith but to rule in his place. It was, as Alfred Milner's biographer put it, a very powerful fellowship devoid of party hacks and faceless civil servants.[34] Carson, still the hero of Ulster Unionists, was the foremost of his Tory critics in the House of Commons; Dawson at the *Times* was the most influential journalist in the Empire and had the full backing of its owner, Lord Northcliffe; Astor's *Observer* added hugely valuable weight to Milner's battalions in the press; Oliver was fanatical in his disdain of groveling peacemakers. He proposed that the whole nation rather than the armed forces must be conscripted.[35]

Alfred Milner was the undisputed leader of this "Monday Night Cabal."[36] The agenda notes for one of the meetings in February demonstrated clearly that they planned to demolish the widely held notion that there was no alternative to a combination of Asquith and Bonar Law. Their solution was to repeat "in season and out of season" that the current coalition was having a paralytic effect on the conduct of the war and it was absurd to believe that there was no alternative.[37] They were the alternative.

Here we find one of the few examples of precisely how the Secret Elite worked to influence and dominate British politics. The cabal comprised the key players at the core of the opposition to Asquith. They instructed their supporters and agents to lobby both inside and outside parliament for the policies that were determined over their private dinners. The rank and file were never invited to these exclusive gatherings, which remained the preserve of the select.[38] A second assaul route was driven by the press, whose influential leaders were also at the heart of the Monday Night Cabal. Public opinion had to be turned against the Asquith coalition. One of the most successful influences which the Secret Elite still wield is the power to make the public believe that they want the changes expounded by a corrupted press.

Geoffrey Dawson led the attack from his lofty office at the *Times*. Instructed in the Milnerite catechism of Coalition failure, his editorials began the campaign to catapult Alfred Milner into high office without the niceties of a political mandate. On 14 April his leading article was the first salvo in that offensive:

> Let there be no mistake about it. What the country want is leaders who are not afraid to go to all lengths or undergo all sacrifices, party or personal, in order to win the war.... We believe that in Lord Milner they possess yet another leader whose courage and character are needed in a national crisis. It is a most damning indictment of the coalition, and especially of those Unionist leaders who had a free hand to strengthen its composition, that such a man should be out of harness at such a time.[39]

The plot that had been carefully constructed over months of detailed planning was promoted in a series of newspaper editorials which advanced Milner's intentions. Their new mantra was that change was needed; change was vital to save the country from disaster. But not everyone would be sacrificed. No. Not at all. What was proposed was far more subtle. They proposed that the Secret Elite's chosen men in Cabinet (Balfour etc.) needed the support of a more organized system (behind them) and there was "no reason whatsoever why they should not continue...." However, those who had served their purpose, who "were encrusted in the old party habit, worn out ... by a period of office which has lasted continuously in some cases for more than a decade ... are a sheer danger to the State."[40] Translated into personalities, their targets were Herbert Asquith, Sir Edward Grey, Lord Lansdowne, Walter Runciman and the remnants of the original Liberal government.

Dawson rampaged against the "weak methods" and "weak men" who were failing the country. Unresolved problems of man-power, of food control and food production, of conflict over the output of aircraft and merchant ships were attributed to a system where, according to the clique, the country was being governed by a series of debating societies. He was disgusted that the War Committee had reverted back to the old habits of "interminable memoranda" and raged about the impossibility of heads of great departments having additional collective responsibility for correlating all of the work of a war government. Every design which the Monday Night Cabal had agreed on was promoted by Dawson at the *Times*.

Popular newspapers ensured that their message was unrelenting. Tom Clarke, then editor of the *Daily Mail,* wrote in his diaries that he was instructed by Northcliffe in December 1916 to undermine the Prime Minister. He was told to find a smiling picture of Lloyd George and underneath it put the caption, "Do it Now" and get the worst possible picture of Asquith and label it, "Wait and See".[41] It was to be billed as if it was Action-Man against the ditherer.

The major beneficiary of the conclusions of the Monday Night Cabal was David Lloyd George. Since the day he was given his first government post as President of the Board of Trade in 1905, Lloyd George had pursued his career with the singular intention of rising to the top. His firebrand oratory which made him a champion of the people masked his Machiavellian self-interest. While basking in the credit for providing pensions in old age, he befriended the leaders of industry, the bankers and financiers in the City, the money-men in New York and newspaper owners like Northcliffe and Max Aitken, (Lord Beaverbrook). The Secret Elite had identified Lloyd George many years before[42] as the man most likely to front popular appeal for their policies, but his negotiations with the conspirators in 1916 had to be carried out well away from prying eyes.

They chose Arthur Lee[43] as the facilitator. Many of the secret meetings between Lloyd George, Maurice Hankey, Alfred Milner and Geoffrey Dawson at Lee's house in the Abbey Garden at Westminster.[44] An opponent of Lloyd George in previous times, Lee had married into the New York financial elite and his wife Ruth inherited a substantial fortune. He was a close friend of Theodore Roosevelt, with whom he corresponded frequently.[45] Lee had apparently become increasingly frustrated with the conduct of the war by the Asquith government and sought out David Lloyd George as the one member of the government whom he considered had "sufficient courage and dynamic energy ... to insist upon things being done."[46] Note how Lee offered his services to Lloyd George, who invited him into the Ministry of Munitions as parliamentary military secretary. Later, in his *War Memoirs,* Lloyd George went out of his way to praise Lee's "untiring industry, great resource, and practical capacity,"[47] without mentioning his role as co-conspirator in Asquith's removal.

On Lloyd George's move to the War Office, Lee became his personal secretary. He was also a member of the Unionist war committee which acted as a focus of back-bench opposition to the Asquith coalition in 1916.[48] Whether he was aware of it or not, the Secret Elite ensured that Arthur

Lee was well placed to watch over Lloyd George in the critical months leading up to the coup. Safe from prying eyes, the conspirators drew an ever compliant Lloyd George to the center of their web. His closest aide ensured that they could contact him with ease without rousing the suspicion of mere mortals. They organized their policies, decided their tactics and picked their chosen men. The Secret Elite were poised to take over the governance of the war and run it along their lines, but the old order had to be removed. As ever with Alfred Milner, he required his opponent, in this instance, Asquith, to make the first unforgivable mistake.

As the Monday Night Cabal and Milner's wider circle of friends and associates continued their maneuvers through much of 1916, the issue which above all others fired their fears, was talk of peace. To the Secret Elite who had invested in the war, had funded and facilitated the war, this was a pivotal moment. Their aims and objectives were nowhere in sight. Indeed, cessation of the war would be a greater disaster than the huge loss of life if it continued.

The bloodletting across the Western Front was suitably reducing the masses who might be induced to rise against the plutocracies, but even in 1916 there was still a sense of denial about the human cost in the purified air of the upper echelons. In early February, Sir Edward Grey told President Wilson's emissary from America, Colonel House, that Britain had not been seriously hurt by the war, "since but few of her men had been killed and her territory had not been invaded."[49] Whether this was a stupid lie or callous disregard for the tragedies suffered in every part of the land we will never know, but in that same month the *Times* carried column after column of the lost legions of dead and missing every day.[50]

The cost of peace did not bear contemplation. Think of the massive and unprecedented loans that could only be repaid if there were spoils of

Lloyd George in typical pose

victory to plunder. Think of the manufacturers whose investments in new plants, new infrastructure and expanded capacity was predicated upon a long war. There were billions of pounds and dollars to be made from extortionate prices, but that only followed a period of sustained and costly investment. The profiteers had initially bought into procuring the loans and providing the munitions because they had been promised a long war. Such are the prerequisites of greed.

Nor would a negotiated peace safeguard the future of the Empire. Indeed it would have had the opposite effect. If Great Britain and the Empire and all of the Allies could not defeat the German/Austro-Hungarian/Ottoman powers, then the message would reverberate across the world that the old order had passed. Given the massive loss of life already inflicted on the troops from Canada, Australia, South Africa and New Zealand, the outcry against a feeble Mother country that had given up the struggle would grow to a clamor. Any notion of a commonwealth of nations would dissolve in cynical spasms of derision.[51] The real reasons for war, the elimination of Germany as a rival on the world stage, would not be addressed at all. Peace would be a calamity for the elite under such circumstances. To talk of it was sacrilege.

The flying of "Peace Kites," as Maurice Hankey described Colonel Houses' approaches, brought one benefit for Milner's intriguers. Those members of Asquith's coalition who were attracted to a negotiated peace exposed their lack of commitment to the ultimate goal. Reginald McKenna, then Chancellor of the Exchequer, felt that Britain would gain a "better peace now [January 1916] than later, when Germany is wholly on the defensive."[52] The Secret Elite watched and listened. Literally.

As Asquith's personal confidant and Secretary of the War Council,[53] Maurice Hankey was privy to many confidences but even he was shocked to learn that the Director of Naval Intelligence, Captain Blinker Hall,[54] had acquired American diplomatic codes and was monitoring the telegrams sent from "Colonel" House to President Wilson. The Americans claimed that they would broker "a reasonable peace"[55] and call a conference, whereafter, should Germany refuse to attend, the USA would *probably* enter the war on the side of the Allies.[56] Note that the promise was definitely not absolute. In late January, Hankey went to Hall at the Admiralty on another pretext[57] and discovered that Colonel House's visit was a "peace stunt." 1916 was, after all, a presidential election year, and President Wilson had to appear to be a serious peace broker. It was a sham. To his horror, Hankey discovered that Sir Edward Grey had given the Americans an assurance that he would trade Britain's blockade, euphemistically called the "freedom of the seas," against an end to German militarism.

Hall claimed that this priceless secret information had not been shared with Arthur Balfour, First Lord of the Admiralty, which begs the question, with whom was it shared? The Foreign Secretary had made promises behind the backs of his cabinet colleagues, and we are expected to believe that Captain Hall told no-one? Grey was clearly mentally exhausted. Fearful that he might miss an opportunity to "get a decent peace," if the war "went wrong" Sir Edward Grey brought the American proposals before the war committee in March 1916. They ignored it. When the Americans again pressed for a decision on the President's offer to intervene in May 1916, the Cabinet was split. Asquith, Grey, McKenna and Balfour were apparently in favor; Lloyd George and the Conservative leader Bonar Law, were against.

Alarm bells sounded. The Army Council, a body whose admiration for Alfred Milner could hardly have been stronger, threatened to resign if the War Council insisted on discussing "the peace question,"[58] but the threat had not passed. Asquith was prepared to accept that "the time has come where it was very desirable" to formulate clear ideas on proposals for peace and at the end of August suggested that individual members of his cabinet put their ideas on paper for circulation and discussion.[59] In September E.S. Montagu, then Minister for Munitions, advised that it was not safe to ignore the possibility of a sudden peace since no-one was more likely to "get out" when the fight was up, than the Germans.[60] He also asked what an unqualified victory might mean. The General Staff presented their own memorandum,[61] which erroneously claimed that the French Prime Minister, Briand, would likely have "very decided views worked out, under his direction, by very clever people who serve him and who do not appear on the surface of political life."

Foreign Office papers which were shared with the Cabinet in October 1916, showed that Germany was prepared to offer peace to Belgium irrespective of Britain's position. Herbert Hoover, who was running the scandalous Belgian Relief program,[62] warned the Foreign Office that the German government intended to negotiate with the Belgian government in exile. He had learned that the Germany was proposing to evacuate the country, guarantee complete economic and political liberty and pay an indemnity for reconstruction purposes. Furthermore, in order to end the conflict with France, they were prepared to cede the whole of the province of Lorraine under the condition that the French would promise to supply five-million tons of iron ore each year to Germany. Their "terms" also included independence for Poland and an unspecified "arrangement" in the Balkans.[63]

Hoover had no truck with such suggestions. When he next went to Brussels, the German-American member of the Belgian Comite Nationale, Danny Heinemann, approached him to try to find out what the British terms for peace might be. Hoover claimed that "he was not in the peace business." He most certainly was not. He was in the business of profiteering from war. The more circumspect Lord Lansdowne, a member of Asquith's coalition cabinet as Minister without Portfolio, asked a telling question on 13 November, 1916: "... what is our chance of winning [the war] in such a manner, and within such limits of time, as will enable us to beat our enemy to the ground and impose upon him the kind of terms we so freely discuss?" Lansdowne's immediate future in politics was decidedly limited.[64]

Kitchener's untimely and suspicious death in June 1916 brought to an end any chance of what he looked forward to as a just peace,[65] but for the Secret Elite, their immediate problem focused on politicians who clearly lacked the commitment to crush Germany. Asquith had run his course. His prevarications and capacity to "wait and see" had no place at a time when the Secret Elite needed decisive firmness to see it through. Although Asquith went to considerable lengths in Parliament in October 1916 to shun any notion of a settlement, it was too late. His pain was heartfelt[66] when he declared:

> The strain which the War imposes on ourselves and our Allies, the hardships which we freely admit it involves on some of those who are not directly concerned in the struggle, the upheaval of trade, the devastation of territory, the loss of irreplaceable lives – this long and sombre procession of cruelty and suffering, lighted up as it is by deathless examples of heroism and chivalry, cannot be allowed to end in some patched-up, precarious, dishonouring compromise, masquerading under the name of Peace. [67]

Less than two months later the men who had even considered defining peace terms had gone from government: Grey, Lansdowne, Montagu and McKenna were disposed of. They had committed sacrilege. Their unforgivable sin was the contemplation of peace. There would be no peace, yet.

Lloyd George, at that point Minister of War, nailed his colors to Lord Milner's flag from September 1916 onwards when, in the afterglow of the secret meetings held with representatives of the Monday Night Cabal, he reaffirmed the Secret Elite's policies for outright victory. First he gave a private interview to Roy Howard, President of the United Press of America and swept aside any talk of peace. His words were carried across the world. They were intended to warn that any step "by the United States, the Vatican, or any other neutral in the direction of peace would be construed by England as an unneutral, pro-German move." Here it was that he coined the promise that "the fight must be to a finish – to a knock out."[68]

Their design to reorganize the governing of the war, for which Lloyd George was ever ready to claim credit, began to be voiced by him at the war committee. Out of the blue, he proposed the creation of a "Shipping Dictator" to control all aspects of the shipping and ship-building industries on 10 November. Hankey considered this "an undigested and stupid waste of precious time."[69] Lo and behold, six weeks later "Lloyd George's" idea had been transformed into fact. He advocated a similar approach to address the problems with food supplies in a memo which promoted the central control of these vital commodities. What the others had yet to grasp was that the minister of war had begun to expound the basic principles of a complete reconstruction of government and its functions, principles underpinned by Milner's belief that success would only be achieved through organization on a national scale.[70]

Next, Lloyd George "adopted" the idea that the day-to-day conduct of the war should be placed in the hands of a select few in parliament who would concentrate on the focused leadership required for ultimate victory. According to his *Memoirs*, this idea stemmed from a discussion he had with Maurice Hankey when they were in Paris for a ministerial conference on 15 November 1916.

The given story, faithfully regurgitated by other historians,[71] has Hankey dramatically pausing alongside the Vendome Column before urging Lloyd George: "You ought to insist on a small war committee being set up for the day-to-day conduct of the war, with full powers. It must be independent of the cabinet. It must keep in touch with the P.M., but the committee ought to be in continuous session, and the P.M. as Head of the Government, could not manage that.... He is a bit tired too after all he has gone through in the last two and a half years."[72] Such a specific description of time and place, detailed and precise: unfortunately it was pure fiction. Lloyd George would have posterity believe that the strategy he unleashed on government originated from Asquith's trusted special and indispensable adviser, rather than the Monday Night Cabal and the secret dinners he had been holding with Alfred Milner, Edward Carson and Arthur Lee. He could hardly admit the truth.

Hankey remembered a *morning* stroll in Paris with Lloyd George "who was full of schemes..."[73] but made no specific reference to a new approach to government. Indeed, the Welshman was full of schemes, but what is of particular interest is the pivotal role given to Maurice Hankey. We know from Professor Quigley's work[74] that Hankey was in the inner circle of Milner's group inside the Secret Elite, though not the precise date of his inclusion. It later became evident that Lloyd George had talked about this inner-war committee with others before he went to Paris and had asked the newspaper owner, Max Aitken, to discuss the concept with the Conservative party leader, Bonar Law.[75] Given that revelation, why would Lloyd George try so hard to blame, or indeed credit Maurice Hankey for the suggestion? His source of inspiration was, clearly, Alfred Milner and the Monday Night Cabal. Was it simply part of his cover-up?

Lloyd George stabbed Asquith in an attack of Shakespearian cruelty as surely as Brutus stabbed Julius Caesar in the back. He presented Asquith with an ultimatum, threatening to resign unless a new, smaller war committee was appointed with himself as chairman and his political allies by his side. If he wished, Asquith would be allowed to continue to hold the post of Prime Minister without the means to lead the war effort. Lloyd George's friends in the Monday Night Cabal also unsheathed their knives. Geoffrey Dawson at the *Times* praised the minister for war in an editorial and, without a hint of embarrassment, added: "Mr Lloyd George, to the best of our knowledge, took his stand entirely alone so far as his colleagues in the cabinet are concerned, a fact which refutes the tales of intrigue."[76] What awesome deception. It was a ridiculous lie. The editor of the *Times* had been involved in the cabal to remove Asquith since its conception. He played a central part in the intrigue. Every detail of the trial of strength between Asquith and Lloyd George for the possession of 10 Downing Street appeared in Northcliffe's papers. Lloyd George protested that he was not the mole. No-one believed him then, and no-one should now. The coup was under way.

In the brinkmanship that followed, the key parliamentary conspirators, Lloyd George, Bonar Law and Sir Edward Carson resigned, removing Liberal, Conservative and Ulster Unionist support from Asquith. With an eye to posterity, Lloyd George ended his letter of resignation with the words: "Vigour and Vision are the supreme need at this hour."[77] His conceit was unbounded. Lloyd George imagined that he was talking about himself.

His coalition government torn apart, Asquith tendered his resignation to the King. Lloyd George had let it be known that he was willing to take up the mantle of leadership in his secret discussions with Alfred Milner and Geoffrey Dawson in September 1915, at which stage it was his open commitment to conscription which caught their attention. Lloyd George took every opportunity to strengthen his links with the conspiracy to replace the coalition government. One small but pertinent example of the extent to which these men tried to cover their traces can be gleaned from this particular meeting. "On 30 September, after a fair amount of scheming, a luncheon was arranged at Milner's house, 17 Great College Street. Dawson had first proposed that Milner and Lloyd George should meet at his home, but when the Minister [Lloyd George] learned that Reginald McKenna [the Chancellor of the Exchequer] lived opposite, he refused to go there."[78] Clearly Lloyd George had no intention of being caught on the doorstep of the editor of the *Times*.

Despite all of this well-documented intrigue, the official reason for Asquith's resignation given on the current Library of the House of Commons website, is, incredibly, "Hostile Press."[79] His government effectively destroyed from within, himself pushed from office by the secret intrigues of former political colleagues and opposition leaders who were backed by the awesome power of the Secret Elite, Asquith's fall from the highest office of government remains covered by a lie. No other Prime Ministerial resignation, retirement, or reason for leaving office is described this way. It is totally misleading and serves only to add obfuscation to an important incident in Britain's so-called democratic history that is regularly glossed over by historians. How Lloyd George would have laughed. Of course the British Establishment will never admit that Asquith was the victim of a bloodless coup.

By 5 December 1916 Asquith's coalition had been dissolved. That was followed by a purge of the old order of Liberal government dressed up as an administrative revolution.[80] There was no sense of military intervention in this putsch, but senior military commanders like Sir Henry Wilson rejoiced at the coup's progress. "Asquith is out. Hurrah," he wrote in his diary, "... I am confident myself that, if we manage things properly, we have Asquith dead."[81] He used the plural "we" to indicate his inclusion in the Monday Night Cabal which had planned the overthrow of government.[82] At the very least there was military collusion with the inner core of plotters.

Lloyd George immediately accepted the King's invitation to form a government on 7 December 1916. His own version of events dripped insincerity, giving the impression that the onerous task of leading the government was thrust upon him suddenly, as if by magic. "As soon as the King entrusted me with the task of forming an Administration in succession to the Ministry that had disappeared, I had to survey the tasks awaiting me..."[83] What arrant nonsense. "The ministry that had disappeared." This was not a Harry Potter film. Perhaps he was thinking more in terms of a mafia "disappearance." He would have been at home with the Mafioso.

One of Lloyd George's first moves was to summon Maurice Hankey to the War Office to "have a long talk about the personnel of the new Govt., the procedure of the select War Committee, and the future of the war."[84] He asked Hankey to write a memo giving his view on the state of the war and as early as 9 December, Hankey spent the whole day with the new war cabinet.[85] How more central could he have been to all of the discussions which finally approved Lloyd George's decisions?[86] Unlike many of his contemporaries, Maurice Hankey was not surprised to find that Alfred Milner had been appointed directly to the inner-sanctum of Britain's war planning. Unelected, unknown to many ordinary men and women, Milner appeared as if out of the ether to take his place among the political elite charged with managing the war to ultimate victory.[87] Lloyd George claimed, laughably, that "I neither sought nor desired the Premiership" and explained Milner's inclusion as representing the "Tory intelligentsia and Die-Hards."[88] What lies. Lloyd George had always exuded unbridled ambition and had been plotting the coup against Asquith with Milner's cabal for months. His premiership was conditional on their support. Lord Milner was to have pride of place by his side.

The myth of Lloyd George's "lightening rapidity" in assembling around him "all that is best in British Life" was coined by Lord Northcliffe in an article printed by the international press on 10 December.[89] Northcliffe had been highly influential in supporting Lloyd George, largely, but not exclusively, through his editor at the *Times*, Geoffrey Dawson. Although he thought nothing of telephoning the new Prime Minister in person,[90] the owner of the *Times* could not stop other influences obligating Lloyd George to retain what Northcliffe called "has-beens" in cabinet posts.[91] His *Daily Mail* and *Evening News* called for the removal of Arthur Balfour and his cousin, Lord Robert Cecil, to no avail. Did Northcliffe not know that both men were deeply entrenched inside the Secret Elite? Clearly not.

Let there be no doubt, the coup was devised and executed by members and agents of the Secret Elite. Once Asquith had been replaced, they permeated the new administration from top to bottom, and on all sides.[92] Let Lloyd George be the figurehead, but the Monday Night Cabal and their Secret Elite supporters were in charge of all of the major offices of state. Furthermore, Lloyd George was subtly but securely scrutinized at every turn. He would not be given free rein. Thus, their chosen men were placed in key positions, with a smattering of useful Conservative and Labour MPs given office in order to guarantee that the government could survive any parliamentary vote. On his return to London on 10 December, Hankey "had to see Lord Milner by appointment." He noted in his diary "I have always hated his [Lord Milner's] politics but found the man very attractive and possessed of personality and [we] got on like a house on fire."[93] Of course they did. Hankey would not have survived otherwise. He was well aware of Milner's power and influence.

Another myth still widely accepted is that Lloyd George's very special cabinet, which literally took control of every strand in the prosecution of the war, was assembled at break-neck speed by the Welsh genius. It had taken months of deliberation and consultation before appointments and tactics were finally agreed inside the closed ranks of the Monday Night Cabal. The final selection which bore Lloyd George's alleged stamp reflected the Secret Elite's approval of men in whom they had faith. The War Committee initially comprised Prime Minister Lloyd George, who had been in the Secret Elite's pocket since 1910,[94] Viscount Alfred Milner, the most important influence inside that secret movement,[95] George Curzon of All Souls and one time Viceroy of India,[96] Andrew Bonar Law, still the formal leader of the Tories and the Labour MP Arthur Henderson, an outspoken champion of the war effort.[97] This central core took charge. They held daily meetings to better manage the war. Sometimes two and three meetings took place in a single day. These five men alone were supposedly the supreme governors of the State.[98] But they were not in any sense, equals.

The old order of senior Liberal politicians was mercilessly purged. Out went Asquith despite his years of loyal service. Sir Edward Grey had forfeited his right to office when he began to consider possibilities of peace with the Americans. He was put out to pasture. Reginald McKenna, long a thorn in Lloyd George's side, was dismissed. Lord Crewe remained loyal to Asquith and was not considered. To his great disappointment, Winston Churchill was not deemed suitable. He had many enemies in the Tory party. One Liberal Party stalwart, Samuel Montagu, who took over at the Ministry of Munitions when Lloyd George moved to the War Office in July 1916, had to go in order to find room for other appointees, but his patience was to be rewarded some short months later when he was made Secretary of State for India.[99] This is precisely how the Secret Elite adjusts its favors and looks after its own. It still does.

The Secret Elite stamped their authority over every important level of government. With Sir Edward Carson at the Admiralty and Arthur Balfour at the Foreign Office, Lord Derby became Secretary of State for War and Lord Robert Cecil continued in his position as Minister of Blockade. Home Secretary, Sir George Cave took office barely months after he and F.E. Smith had successfully prosecuted Sir Roger Casement and refused his right to appeal to the House of Lords.[100] Secret Elite agents, every one.

Milner ensured that his close friends were given positions of influence and authority. Take for example the meteoric rise of Rowland Prothero. He claimed to know only two men "prominent in public life."[101] It transpired that these were Lords Milner and Curzon. In 1914 Prothero was first elected to parliament as one of Oxford University's MPs. In late 1915 he served on a Committee on Home Production of Food with Alfred Milner. In 1916, Milner's friend was given the cabinet post of President of the Board of Agriculture.[102] It took him a mere two-and-a-half years to move from new recruit to cabinet minister. In addition, Arthur Lee, who had accommodated many of the secret meetings which foreshadowed the coup, was appointed Director-General of food production. Other known members and supporters of the Secret Elite who shamelessly benefited from the coup included H.A.L. Fisher, President of the Board of Education,[103] Walter Long as Colonial Secretary and Sir Henry Birchenough at the Board of Trade.[104] They were everywhere ... and not just politicians.

Lloyd George had risen to high office through the unseen patronage of the Secret Elite. His performance at the Board of Trade[105] guaranteed him the benevolent approbation of leading figures in shipping and ship-building. As Chancellor he laid claim to saving the City;[106] took advice from Lord Rothschild, financiers and insurance brokers, linked the British economy to America through Morgan-Grenfell and met and socialized with the great mine-owners and manufacturers of the time. In December 1916 he revolutionized government control of production by bringing businessmen into political office. Unfortunately, the appointment of interested parties to posts from which their companies could reap great profit was not a success.

Sir Joseph Maclay was given charge of shipping. As a Scottish ship owner and manager, Maclay had been critical of the government's concessions to trade unions and he opposed the nationalization of shipping. The Admiralty treated Maclay with deep hostility, and opposed his idea of convoys after the onset of Germany's unrestricted submarine offensive in February 1917. Maclay was right,[107] though shipowners still reaped unconscionable fortunes.

The new Prime Minister made Lord Devonport food controller. Chairman of the Port of London Authority (1909-25), he broke the dockers' strike in 1912, causing great distress and hardship in East London. Imagining that his hard-man image equated to strength of character, Lloyd George appointed him Minister of Food Control.[108] Not so. Devonport protected his own grocery interests (he owned a chain of over 200 grocery stores) and resisted the introduction of rationing until May 1917.

Lord Rhondda, the Welsh coal magnate and industrialist, was entrusted with the Local Government Board and his popularity grew when he was asked to take over the role of the incompetent Devonport as minister of food control. He grasped the nettle, by fixing food prices and ensuring government purchases of basic supplies.[109] Compared to the others, he was a shining light. Weetman Pearson, later Viscount Cowdray, was placed in charge of the Air Board. Pearson had acquired oil concessions in Mexico through his questionable relationship with the Mexican dictator, Diaz.[110] His ownership of the Mexican Eagle Petroleum Company (which became part of Royal Dutch Shell in 1919) guaranteed Pearson vast profits throughout the war. Sir Alfred Mond, elevated by Lloyd George in 1916 to Commissioner of Works, was the managing director of the Mond Nickel Company and a director of the International Nickel Company of Canada. Nickel hardens armor and special steels. Basically it is a strategic material which came to the fore in the so-called naval race prior to 1914.[111]

The Mond companies made great profits during the prolonged war. In 1915 Britain sent twelve times the amount of nickel to Sweden than it had in 1913.[112] There, it was either manufactured into war materials and sold to Germany, or re-exported in its raw state. Incredibly, the Chairman of one of the Empire's most important metal processing and exporting businesses, which was directly and indirectly supplying Germany, was made Commissioner of Works. Questionable deals were subsequently negotiated between the British government and the British-American Nickel Corporation, which were strongly criticized in parliament,[113] but Alfred Mond ended his career as Lord Melchett of Landforth. It's too true to be believed.

In addition, Milner and his Secret Elite associates literally took over Lloyd George's private office. As early as 10 December Hankey realized that he was not to be the only member of the new Prime Minister's secretariat. At Milner's request, Leo Amery, his loyal lieutenant in South Africa, was unaccountably placed on the staff of the War Cabinet, but not as joint Secretary. Hankey remained secure in Lloyd George's trust – in charge of the War Cabinet organization.[114]

A curious new chapter in Downing Street's history was created outside the Prime Minister's residence. Physically. Temporary offices were constructed in the Downing Street garden to accommodate a select group of trusted administrators who monitored and directed all contact between Lloyd George and departments of government.[115] The man in charge throughout its existence was Professor W.G.S. Adams, an Oxford Professor, one of Milner's entourage,[116] and, according to Carroll Quigley, a member of the Secret Elite, who later became editor of War Cabinet Reports and Warden of All Souls at Oxford.[117] This appointment was swiftly followed by that of two former members of Milner's famous Kindergarten;[118] Philip Kerr became Lloyd George's private secretary and Lionel Curtis, another of Milner's loyal acolytes, was also drafted into service. It did not stop there. Waldorf Astor and Lord Northcliffe's younger brother, Cecil Harmsworth followed shortly afterwards.

To complete the pack, Milner insisted that Lloyd George reconsider appointing John Buchan (author of the Richard Hannay stories) to his staff after Haig's apologist had been turned down for a post. In a private letter, which has survived because it comes from the Lloyd George archives, rather than Milner's much-culled and carefully shredded papers, he wrote: "My Dear Prime Minister, Don't think me too insistent! I wish you would not turn down John Buchan, without seeing him yourself.... I am not satisfied to have him rejected on hear-say, & ill informed hear-say at that."[119] Buchan was appointed to the Prime Minister's staff as Director of Information. And historians would have us believe that these were Lloyd George's appointments.

It was as if the Monday Night Cabal had kidnapped the Prime Minister. Just as Alfred Milner had captured, then captivated, the nascent talent of young Imperialists from Oxford University at the turn of the century and taken them to South Africa to help him govern and renovate the post Boer-War Transvaal and Cape colonies, so now, the very same men "guided" Lloyd George and filtered the information which flowed to Downing Street. They were not Lloyd George's men ... they were Lord Milner's. He was in charge.

To the anguish of Asquith's political allies, this new bureaucracy had metamorphosed into an undemocratic monster fashioned by Alfred Milner. They could see it and railed against it. What we need to know is, why has this wholesale coup d'etat been studiously ignored by mainstream historians? Why do they continually write about Lloyd George's government and Lloyd George's secretariat when his very position was bound and controlled by Milner and his Garden Suburb minders? The radical journalist, H.W. Massingham published a vitriolic attack on Milner's organization in early 1917:

> ... A new double screen of bureaucrats is interposed between the War Directorate and the heads of [government] Departments, whose responsibility to Parliament has hitherto been direct.... The first is the Cabinet Secretariat ... the second is a little body of Illuminati, whose residence is in the Prime Minister's garden.... These gentlemen stand in no sense for a Civil Service Cabinet. They are rather a class of travelling empirics in Empire, who came in with Lord Milner.... The governing ideas are not those of Mr. Lloyd George ... but of Lord Milner ... Mr George has used Toryism to destroy Liberal ideas; but he has created a Monster which, for the moment, dominates both. This is the New Bureaucracy which threatens to master England ... [120]

It was indeed. This was the Secret Elite's most successful coup so far, accomplished by the critical silence and complicity of a compliant press. Elected parliamentary government had been purged. The Secret Elite spurned democracy because they ordained that democracy did not work. Their dictatorship was masked by Lloyd George, happy to pose and strut as the man who would win the war. Perhaps you were taught that he did? It is a self-serving myth. He operated inside a political straitjacket and fronted an undemocratic government.

The sacrifice of youth continued. And the profits of war grew ever larger.

Summary.

- Herbert Asquith, the Liberal Prime Minister since 1908, formed a wartime coalition government in May 1915 under joint pressure from David Lloyd George his Chancellor and the Conservative leader, Andrew Bonar Law.
- Lloyd George was paid his asking price. His disloyalty was rewarded by being made Minister of Munitions. But as an alliance of politicians, it soon began to unravel.
- Confirmed in their view that the democratic process had failed to provide the leadership, the organization and, crucially, the will to unnecessarily prolong the war, Milner and the Secret Elite began to undermine the government and replace it with their own agents.

- A group of conspirators led by Alfred Milner and his Secret Elite comrades formed a cabal which met regularly on a Monday night throughout 1916 to plot an end to political democracy in Britain.
- They were to promote themselves as the alternative government.
- Geoffrey Dawson of the *Times* was party to the cabal and he pushed their ideas in the editorial columns of that newspaper.
- Above all these men were determined to stave off any talk of peace. The war would have had no point if Germany was not crushed.
- In 1916, with President Wilson facing a difficult re-election, his advisor, Edward Mandel House was engaged in a round of peace "feelers" monitored by the British naval intelligence.
- Grey, Lansdowne, Montagu and McKenna were disposed of. Their unforgivable sin was the contemplation of peace.
- Lloyd George told the United Press that "the fight must be to the finish – to a knock out."
- The cabal ousted Asquith by proposing a small War Committee which would not include him. When he refused to agree, threats of resignation forced the issue.
- Lloyd George immediately accepted the King's invitation to form a government on 7 December 1916. He was the figurehead, but the Monday Night Cabal and their Secret Elite supporters were placed in charge of all of the major offices of state.
- He revolutionized government control of production by bringing businessmen into political office. Some like Sir Joseph Maclay made a success of his shipping remit; other like Lord Devenport who was appointed Minister of Food Control protected his own grocery interests.
- It was as if the Monday Night Cabal had kidnapped the Prime Minister. He was surrounded by Milner's young men who were appointed as his private secretaries to help inform policy and literally keep an eye on the shifty Welshman.
- This was the Secret Elite's most successful coup so far, accomplished by the critical silence and complicity of a compliant press. Elected parliamentary government had been purged.

I WANT YOU
FOR U.S. ARMY
NEAREST RECRUITING STATION

Chapter 27

American Mythology – He Kept Us Out Of War.

Woodrow Wilson's first term in office from 1912-1916 was predicated on an election victory subscribed to and underwritten by the "money-power" in New York.[1] He campaigned under the banner of "New Freedom" and opposition to big business and monopoly power,[2] yet like many presidents, before and after, his actions turned his promises to lies. However, the daunting task of defeating the incumbent Republican President William H. Taft, who had steadfastly attacked the powerful business combinations in the United States, seemed beyond any realistic expectation.

Taft was popular. The Supreme Court's legal actions against Standard Oil and the American Tobacco Company were decided in favor of his government.[3] In October 1911, Taft's Justice Department brought a suit against U.S. Steel and demanded that over a hundred of its subsidiaries be granted corporate independence. They named and shamed prominent executives and financiers as defendants. Big business was thoroughly shaken. William Taft earned many powerful enemies. Clear favorite to win a second term in office in 1912, Taft's chances of success were destroyed by a well-contrived split in the Republican vote. Financed by J.P. Morgan's associates, the former Republican, Theodore Roosevelt, created a third force from thin air, the "Progressive" Bull Moose Party and at the ballot box in November 1912, Wilson was elected President with 42 percent of the vote; Roosevelt gained 27 percent and Taft could only muster 23 percent. The split Republican voted totaled 7.5 million, while Wilson and the Democrats won with just 6.2 million.[4]

The year 1916 promised to offer better prospects for the Republican Party. The schism with Roosevelt and the Bull Moose was closing fast. Wilson's supposed neutrality was so transparently false that certain sectors of the American electorate were drawn to his opponent, the Republican, Charles E. Hughes, a former Supreme Court judge. German-Americans and Irish-Americans had been particularly annoyed by what they believed was President Wilson's partisan behavior and were expected to vote Republican. These groups came under sustained attack for what the President termed, "disloyalty." In his annual Message to Congress on 7 December 1915, Woodrow Wilson ranted against those born under foreign flags and welcomed "under our generous naturalization laws to the full freedom and opportunity of America, who have poured the poison of disloyalty into the very arteries of our national life ... who seek to make this proud country once more a hotbed of European passion."[5]

He expressed contempt for those who held fast to their original national identities because they did not put American interests first. These he termed "hyphenated Americans."[6] Wilson's attitude towards German-Americans was harsh but, in reality, those of German descent had watched from across the Atlantic as their former homeland was bounced into an exhausting war by a British Establishment financed and supplied by America.

By 1916, there were important and influential groups of "hyphenated Americans."

Table 1. 1910 Census of the United States: Total population 91,972,266 [7]

Defined by place of birth, by persons, both of whose parents were immigrants from that country or one of the parents was foreign born;

German - American	8,282,618
Austria - Hungarian - American	2,701,786
Irish - American	4,504,360
English - Scottish - Welsh - American	3,231,052
Russian - Finnish - American	2,752,675
Italian - American	2,098,360

Note: The U.S. Census of 1910 did not take into account renumbers of foreign-born grandparents or the huge numbers of immigrants from Europe who had settled in America over the previous two and a half centuries.

Social tensions diluted Democratic support among the American-Irish community. Though many Catholics were not Irish, and not all Irish were Catholic, there was a strong affinity between race and religion on the eastern seaboard states of America. In the aftermath of the 1916 Easter Rising in Dublin, Wilson made himself even more unpopular by refusing to endorse an appeal for clemency for Roger Casement.[8] The President's support for the anti-clerical President Carranza in Mexico gave rise to the claim that Wilson was anti-Catholic.[9] The New York weekly newspaper, the *Irish World*, accused his administration of "having done everything for England that an English Viceroy might do."[10] Quite a calculated insult by any standard. In truth racism and bigotry lay centimeters from the surface of American opportunity.

Little was said of another nascent power-block which was beginning to find its political feet; the hyphenated "Jewish-American." The spread of Zionism in America brought with it a fresh wind of political influence. Though still in comparative infancy by election day 1916, certain pro-Zionist Jewish-Americans, like Wilson's newly appointed Supreme Court Judge, Louis Brandeis, were held in high esteem inside the Jewish community. Though Brandeis, and by default, Wilson, who appointed him, were initially lambasted in the press.[11] It appeared to have little direct effect in November 1916. That would later change.[12]

Woodrow Wilson had one important advantage – the economy. At the outbreak of war in Europe, America was wallowing in a depression more serious than that of 1907-8, but the war trade brought phenomenal prosperity.[13] The very Trusts which Wilson had spoken against were profiteering on a scale hitherto unknown. Thanks to the massive order book from Britain and France, managed exclusively by the J.P. Morgan-Rothschild banks, the military-industrial complex thrived, as did the communities around them. There were more and better-paid jobs. On 21 August 1915 Secretary to the Treasury William McAdoo told President Wilson (his father-in-law) that "Great prosperity is coming. It is, in large measure, already here. It will be tremendously increased if we can extend reasonable credits to our customers."[14] The customers on whom he was focused were Britain and France. Wilson's America forged an economic solidarity with the Allies which made nonsense of neutrality, yet the tacit promise from the Democrats to the American nation in the 1916 election was that "He Kept Us out of War." That was true, as far as it went, but Wilson never claimed that he would continue this policy.

What matters in an American Presidential election is the Electoral College vote, and the 1916 election proved to be very close indeed. In 1912, there were 530 Electoral college votes, so the winner had to reach a minimum of 266.

When the first returns from the Eastern States were announced, Hughes appeared to have won by a landslide. By seven o'clock on 7 November it was certain that Wilson had lost New York and the other populous Northeastern States with their heavy votes in the Electoral College followed in swift succession; New Jersey, Connecticut, Rhode Island, Massachusetts, Illinois, Wisconsin and Delaware went Republican. It was a rout.[15]

Election extras were quickly on the streets bearing huge portraits of "The President Elect, Charles Evans Hughes." As night fell on Washington, strange forces spread across the United States. President Wilson's private secretary, Joseph Tumulty refused to concede. He was reported to have received a mysterious, anonymous telephone message warning him "in no way or by the slightest sign give up the fight."[16] Remarkably, the American historian and *New York Herald Tribune* journalist, Walter Millis wrote "Who it was he never knew; perhaps it was a miracle." Absurd. Ridiculous. Preposterous. Must we always be taken as fools? How many anonymous callers have the telephone number of the President's private secretary or could order him not to concede the election? Malpractice was afoot.

In London, the *Times* announced, "Mr Hughes Elected" in a Republican landslide. Its sober conclusion was that Mr. Wilson has been defeated not by, but in spite of his neutrality.[17] The *Kolnische Volkrientung* cheered that "German-Americans have defeated Wilson," while in Vienna, the *Neue Freie Presse* claimed that Hughes had been elected to bring an end to an era where "the Steel Trust and the Bethlehem works may still make further profits and that the price of munitions shares may be whipped up still further while Morgan further extends his financial kingdom."[18] The inference was that the people had turned against the military-industrial profiteers. But they were all running ahead of themselves.

At daybreak on 8 November, while the *New York Times* conceded Wilson's defeat, Tumulty remained unmoved. He was quietly informed that the rout had been stopped at Ohio by a margin of 60,000 votes. Colonel House ordered the Democratic Headquarters to put every county chairman in every doubtful state across America on high alert. They were urged to exercise their "utmost vigilance" on every ballot box.[19] How odd that such instructions should be issued on the day following the election. What did House know that others did not? Projections of a Hughes' victory shrank from certainty to doubt until the entire election result hung on the outcome from California. Secret Service agents and U.S. Marshals were drafted into the largest Californian counties to guard ballot boxes and supervise proceedings. California, with 13 Electoral College votes in 1916, was pivotal to determining the winner. On 8 November, the Electoral vote stood at 264 to Wilson and 254 to Hughes. Before the mystical, middle-of-the-night change of fortune, the Democrats had conceded California to the Republican challenger, but they declared their decision premature. After a two-day recount, Wilson was declared winner by a mere 3,420 out of a total of 990,250 Californian votes cast. Talk of election fraud and vote buying prompted the Republican party to file legal protests,[20] but nothing significant materialized. They were effectively too late. While scrutiny of the returns showed minor vote-tallying errors, and affected both sides, these appeared to be random. Nothing fraudulent could be proved.

An angry and suspicious Republican Party refused to concede the election. The final recount in California showed that Wilson had gained 46.65% of votes cast and Hughes 46.27%. The Republican candidate baulked at accusing his rival of fraud. His final statement acknowledged "in the absence of absolute proof of fraud, no such cry should be raised to becloud the title of the next President of the United States."[21] "Absolute proof" set a very high level of certainty. In New Hampshire the lead changed hands during the canvassing of returns and Wilson won the State by a mere 56 Votes.[22]

Vested interests jumped to close down the Republican options. In London, the *Times* could not believe that "the patriotic and shrewd men who manage the electioneering affairs of the Republican Party will attempt to impugn that decision [Wilson's claim to victory] without clear and conclusive evidence."[23] Consider the pressure that was heaped upon Charles Hughes. War in Europe raged on. A newly elected government in the United States would have brought about a complete change in all of the key cabinet posts with consequent dislocation of existing ties. Imagine the confusion if a President Hughes had to appoint new ambassadors, new consuls, new State Department staff, new White House staff and so forth.

Colonel House told the President that "Germany almost to a man is wishing for your defeat and that France and England are almost to a man wishing for your success."[24] They weren't wishing for his success, they were dependent on it. In the end, Wilson won more popular votes overall, (9,129,606 – 8,538,221) and no clear evidence of malpractice could be found. On 22 November Charles Hughes accepted the election result as it stood. His acquiescence did not go unrewarded. Charles Evans Hughes became United States Secretary of State between 1921 and 1925, a judge on the Court of International Justice between 1928 and 1930, and Chief Justice of the United States from 1930 to 1941. His son, Charles Evans Hughes junior, was appointed Solicitor General by Herbert Hoover.

Primed by his jubilant backers, Woodrow Wilson demonstrated an unexpectedly theatrical touch at the start of his second term in office. Not since George Washington had a president delivered his first formal presidential address to the Senate itself. Wilson did this on 22 January, 1917 in a barnstorming speech which created the impression of an enlightened, benevolent master-statesman to whom the world ought to listen. He called for "peace without victory" because:

> Victory would mean peace forced upon the loser, a victor's terms imposed upon the vanquished. It would be accepted in humiliation, under duress, at an intolerable sacrifice, and would leave a sting, a resentment, a bitter memory upon which terms of peace would rest, not permanently, but only as upon quicksand. Only a peace between equals can last.[25]

As rhetoric this was stout stuff and prophetic. As policy, it did not last for long. He claimed that his soaring vision for peace and the future was based on core American values unshackled by entangling alliances.[26] The shining centerpiece of his dazzling new utopia was to be a League of Nations which could enforce peace. The Senate sat mesmerized and many rose to salute him at the end of an impressive performance. Democrats waxed lyrical with claims that Wilson's speech "was the greatest message of the century ... the most momentous utterance that has a yet been made during this most extraordinary era ... simply magnificent ... the most wonderful document he has ever delivered."[27] His Republican rivals were more circumspect in their appraisal, describing it as "presumptuous" and "utterly impractical."

American newspapers split opinion in predictable fashion. The *New York World* saluted his principles of liberty and justice; the *Public Ledger* declared that Wilson's oration was inspired by lofty idealism and the *Washington Post* thought it constituted a shining ideal. The conservative *New York Sun* caustically remarked that having failed for four years to secure peace with Mexico, Wilson had no business lecturing the world on the terms for peace with Europe, while the *New York Herald* warned that "Mr Wilson's suggestion would lead to the hegemony of the Anglo-Saxon nations ... propaganda for which has been in evidence for a quarter of a century."[28]

In Europe reaction was naturally selfish. The British government refused to countenance his proposal first and foremost because he had added a passage on freedom of the seas which challenged their divine right to dominate the oceans. Rivers of blood shed on the fields of Flanders and beyond were not the only reasons the British elites were vehemently opposed to "peace without victory." The French novelist, Anatolia France, a Nobel Prizewinner for literature, likened peace without victory to "bread without yeast ... mushrooms without garlic ... love without quarrels ... camel without humps."[29]

But Wilson strode that world stage for darker reasons. Who, one wonders, whispered in his ear that all of his visionary pronouncements could not deliver a place at the high table of international settlement at the end of the war if America was not a participant? He could not logically take part in the final resolution of the conflict unless the United States was a full partner in absolute victory. Peace without victory was an empty promise, a misdirection to the jury of hope.

On 4 March 1917, President Woodrow Wilson gave his second inaugural address to Congress and proclaimed that America stood "firm in armed neutrality," but warned that "we may even be drawn on by circumstances ... to a more active assertion of our rights"[30] Twenty-nine days later, on 2 April, he again addressed a joint Session of Congress. This time his purpose was to seek their approval for war with Germany. In a lofty speech he revisited the same moral high ground with which the Secret Elite and their agents in Britain had previously gone to war. With claims about saving civilization it might have been penned by Sir Edward Grey:

"It is a fearful thing to lead this great peaceful people into war, into the most terrible and disastrous of all wars, civilization itself seeming to be in the balance. But the right is more precious than peace, and we shall fight for the things which we have always carried nearest our hearts-for democracy, for the right of those who submit to authority to have a voice in their own Governments, for the rights and liberties of small nations, for a universal dominion of right by such a concert of free peoples as shall bring peace and safety to all nations and make the world itself at last free."[31] America was encouraged to war in order to fight for democracy. The phrase has a familiar ring.

Four days later, America declared that war,[32] after the Senate approved the action by 82-6 and the House of Representatives by 373-50. In the Senate, a few voices were hopelessly raised against what was deemed "a great blunder." Opposition inside the House of Representatives pointed out that no invasion was threatened, no territory at risk, no sovereignty questioned, no national policy contested nor honor sacrificed.[33] Be assured of one important fact. There was no outcry for war among the ordinary American citizens. No excited crowds took to the streets. At Wellington House in London, the nerve center of British propaganda, they were concerned that the American press carried "no indications of enthusiasm except in a few Eastern papers."[34]

People were genuinely unsure why the United States was at war, but loyalty to the flag has always carried great weight in America. Enlistment statistics threw an interesting light on American society. Before 1917, the Eastern seaboard editors, lawyers, bankers and financiers, teachers and preachers, leaders of "society" in New York and Washington alike, had berated the Western states for their alleged unpatriotic attitude towards war. Recruiting figures showed that the response in the west was greater than their compatriots along the eastern seaboard.[35]

There was no instant Kitchener-effect in America. British propagandists watched this lack of enthusiasm with real concern. Woodrow Wilson set up the Committee on Public Information on 14 April to rouse the public to "righteous wrath."[36] Two and a half year's worth of Wellington House propaganda was at hand for regurgitation and dissemination. Even so, from 1 April until 16 May, total enlistment was a mere 73,000 men.[37] By June 117,974 men had joined the regular army, but the rate was falling. In July only 34,962 joined the ranks; in August it was 28,155; in September, 10,557.[38] A conscript army was required. On 18 May, 1917, the sixty-fifth Congress passed a military Act to enable the President to temporarily increase the strength of the army, and the "draft" became law.[39]

For all his talk of brokering peace between the waring factions in Europe, and many reported attempts at reconciliation, President Wilson led his country into war, provided the manpower to be sacrificed and stirred the hatred and propaganda necessary to popularize the slaughter on the Western Front. Why? Why within months of his re-election on the proud boast that he had kept America out of the war, was everything reversed; every assumed position revoked; every implied promise, broken? Some historians insist that Germany forced President Wilson into a declaration of war through two acts of blundering stupidity. Emphasis on such a focus has successfully deflected attention away from much more powerful interests which Wilson could not ignore.

On 17 January 1917, British code-breakers partially deciphered an astonishing message from the German Foreign Minister, Arthur Zimmermann, to his Ambassador in Washington. Though the analysts in Room 40 at the Admiralty could decipher some of the essential message, the new code which had been delivered to the German Embassy in Washington by the cargo U-boat Deutschland in November 1916, had not been fully broken. Senior British cryptographs were trying to reconstruct this particular code but had made only sufficient progress to form an incomplete text.[40] From their initial reconstruction it appeared that Zimmermann had requested the German ambassador to the United States, Count Johann von Bernstorff, to contact President Venustiano Carranza of Mexico through the German embassy in Mexico City and offer him a lucrative alliance. "Blinker" Hall, Director of Naval Intelligence, took personal control. His grasp of effective propaganda was second to none. Hall knew that once the full text was available it had to be carefully handled both to protect the anonymity of Room 40 and convince the Americans of its authenticity.

Room 40 focused on the ambassadorial messages between Berlin and the American continent and on 19 February the full text of Zimmermann's instructions to his Mexican ambassador was traced. It had been sent to Washington by a wireless channel which Wilson and House had previously allowed Germany to use for secret discussions on a possible peace initiative. This effrontery added insult to injury. Once Admiral Hall held the decoded and translated text in his hands, he knew that he had unearthed a propaganda coup of enormous importance. Zimmermann's telegram read as follows:

> Washington to Mexico 19 January 1917.
>
> We intend to begin on 1 February unrestricted submarine warfare. We shall endeavour in spite of this to keep the USA neutral. In the event of this not succeeding we make Mexico a proposal of alliance on the following terms:
> Make war together
> Make peace together
> Generous financial support and an undertaking on our part that Mexico is to reconquer the lost territory in Texas, New Mexico and Arizona. The settlement in detail is left to you.
> You will inform the President of the above most secretly as soon as

> the outbreak of war with the USA is certain, and add the suggestion that he should on his own initiative invite Japan to immediate adherence and at the same time mediate between Japan and ourselves. Please call the President's attention to the fact that the ruthless employment of our submarines now offers the prospect of compelling England in a few months to make peace. (signed) Zimmermann.[41]

After ensuring that they could conceal how they had obtained the telegram, the British Foreign Office released it to Walter Page, the American ambassador in London, who promptly sent it to the State Department in Washington. Woodrow Wilson received the transcript on 24 February 1917. He was stunned to discover that the Germans had abused the cable line which he had insisted they be allowed to access for peace negotiations.[42] It took President Wilson four days to release the telegram to the Associated Press and following expressions of disbelief, he authorized Senator Thomas Swann of Virginia to announce in the Senate on 1 March 1917, that the Zimmermann note to Mexico was textually correct. Robert Lansing made a similar pronouncement from the State Department. Clearly the American public was not easily convinced.

If the reader scans the infamous Zimmermann line by line, it quickly becomes apparent that it verges on lunacy. Alliances are not forged by telegram. Vague promises of generous financial support, of a detailed settlement being left in the hands of the Mexican government and the subsequent "reconquering" of vast tracts of America, did not make sense. Though the Mexicans gave no immediate response, the Japanese Ambassador authoritatively dismissed the proposition. And why did Zimmermann describe Germany's submarine tactics as "ruthless"? The whole incident seemed contrived.

One major American newspaper owner firmly rejected the Zimmermann story. William Randolph Hearst had kept his stable independent of the British censor. Just as he had refused to swallow wholesale war guilt, atrocity or war aims propaganda, Hearst cabled his editors that "in all probability" the Zimmermann note was an "absolute fake and forgery." He believed that the object was to frighten Congress into giving the President the powers he demanded. Hearst's anxiety was that "the whole people of this country, 90 percent of whom do not want war, may be projected into war because of these misrepresentations."[43] He also accused the president's advisor, Colonel House, of being a corporation lobbyist. Hearst was at Palm Beach in the weeks before America entered the war and his private telegrams to his editors and those of other newspapers, were later made public in an attempt to discredit him.[44]

Though publication of the telegram aroused some anger in the west and Midwest states, American newspapers generally chose to omit any reference to the fact that the proposed alliance would only take place after America had declared war against Germany.[45]

The original note had been passed to the American embassy in London in such secrecy that the State Department could not reveal its origins to inquiring journalists.[46] Indeed, the propaganda value was diluted by a suspicion that it was a forgery, as Hearst and his newspapers insisted, until, to the immense relief of British and American war-mongers, the naive Zimmermann acknowledged that he was the author. At a press conference on 2 March, Zimmermann was invited by the Hearst correspondent in Berlin, W.B. Hale, to deny the story. He chose instead to confirm that it was true.[47] In modern parlance, it was a wrong-way football goal. Some have said that the Zimmermann telegram incident was the "overt act" that brought the United States into the war. It was not. Woodrow Wilson did not ask Congress to declare war until 3 April 1917, fully six weeks after the British delivered the telegram to him.

Sympathetic historians were very clear as to the cause. German militarism. The diplomatic record left no room for doubt. "It was the German submarine warfare and nothing else that forced him [Wilson] to lead America into war."[48] Newton D. Baker, Secretary of War came to the same conclusion, but wrapped it carefully inside a moment of caution. He wrote that "the occasion" of America entering the war was the resumption of submarine warfare.[49] Don't confuse the words "cause" and "occasion." Indeed, consider that sentence again, but replace "occasion" with "excuse."

The German government had announced an unrestricted submarine campaign on 31 January, 1917. From that date U-boat commanders were ordered to sink all ships, neutral and belligerent, passenger or merchant, inside a delineated Atlantic and North Sea zone. Despite perfunctory American protests, the British blockade had begun to take its toll in Germany from late 1916. Hunger was to be a weapon of war which both sides could use to advantage. German strategists were aware that such a tactic was likely to bring America into the war, but had concluded that Britain could be starved out before America had time to raise an effective fighting force and bring it into the European theatre. As it stood, America could hardly offer the Allies much more assistance as a belligerent than it currently did as a neutral,[50] but one unforeseen consequence hit home quickly. American shipping was temporarily paralysed.[51] Great quantities of wheat and cotton began to pile up in warehouses. The American economy faced dangerous dislocation. American merchant shipping clung to the safety of their shoreline and trade stood still.

Look carefully at the twin "causes" of America's Declaration of War, the Zimmermann telegram and Germany's unrestricted submarine campaign and you will find flaws. The first was not a "casus belli." It was a propaganda coup to soften the American public's attitude to war, to stir indignation into resentment and add to the fear factor. No matter how ridiculous the notion that Mexican troops could invade Texas, New Mexico or Arizona, the very suggestion of an alliance through which three huge American states might be ceded to Mexico, placed Germany in a particularly bad light. Zimmermann admitted he was the author, but the clandestine nature by which the British secret service ensured that the information was passed to Washington, and the extent to which the Americans covered all traces of British involvement, leaves questions hanging in the air. Zimmermann was either having a cerebral meltdown or betraying Germany by handing this excuse to Wilson to enter the fray on a plate. Whatever, it was not the cause of war.

Greater weight may be placed on the general insistence that unrestricted submarine warfare brought about Wilson's fateful decision. Historians have thrown a vast array of statistics into the equation to prove the importance of this single factor. In the first month of the unrestricted warfare at sea 781,500 tons of merchant shipping was lost.[52] While it is true that after Woodrow Wilson's warning in February, ten American freighters, schooners or tankers were sunk, nine by submarines and one by a mine (laid originally by the Royal Navy), loss of American lives totaled 24 seamen. In total, 38,534 gross U.S. tonnage was sunk.[53] Was this sufficient to be a cause of war? The pro-war newspapers gave vent to their outrage when it was reported that three American ships, *Vigilancia, City of Memphis* and *Illinois* had been sunk on 18 March. The *New York World* screamed that "without a declaration of war, Germany is making war on America." The *New York Tribune* claimed that Germany was acting on the theory that already war existed; The *Public Ledger* demanded that Wilson's administration take immediate action, insisting its duty was to respond, while the *St. Louis Republic* was confident that the President and his advisors would act with wisdom.[54]

American newspaper editors and owners certainly played an important role in fomenting public opinion for war in 1917, similar to that of Lord Northcliffe in pre-war Britain. Indeed, control of the press in the United States was even more calculated and orchestrated than its British equivalent. Congressman Oscar Calloway of Texas exposed the machinations of the money power as it expanded its influence over the fourth estate in order to swing public opinion towards a "necessary" war. On 9 February 1917 he placed the following statement on the Congressional Record:

> In March 1915 J.P. Morgan interests, the steel, shipbuilding and powder interests and their subsidiary organizations got together 12 men high up in the newspaper world and employed them to select the most influential newspapermen in the United States and suffi-

> cient number of them to control generally the policy of the daily press of the United States.[55]

Congressman Calloway revealed that Morgan's twelve chosen men assessed the worth of over 170 newspapers across America and came to the conclusion that by purchasing twenty-five of the most famous titles, they could literally control the policies and direction of public opinion. An agreement was quietly reached whereby monthly payments were paid to them through the House of Morgan. A compliant editor was placed in each paper to supervise and edit the "news." Questions of American preparedness for war were raised in the context of alleged German aggression and Mexican duplicity. The governments' financial policy came under fire as did "other things of national and international nature considered vital to the interests of the purchasers."[56] Be certain; J.P. Morgan and his associates sat in the driving seat and carried American public opinion towards the slaughterhouse of a world war ... in order to protect their obscene profiteering. Taking America to war was not a forgone conclusion, even though the Germans had given up any hope of equal-handed neutrality. The people had to be manipulated.

The crucial factor lay at the heart of Wall Street where the money power decided that the time to abandon the illusion of neutrality had come. America had to go to war or their losses would have broken the back of the economy. Though fact, it has been vehemently denied ever since. Typical of this attitude is the claim from the American historian Charles Tansill: [57]

> There is not the slightest evidence that during the hundred days that preceded America's entry to the World War the President gave any heed to the demands from "big business" that America intervene in order to save investments that were threatened by possible Allied defeat.[58]

What nonsense. America's economy was inextricably linked to an Allied victory. Had the British and French been forced to come to terms with Germany after 1917, potential losses would have been catastrophic. And in April 1917 Wall Street was aware that the balance of forces in Europe had suddenly swung in favor of the Kaiser when his cousin the Czar was deposed. Thomas W. Lamont, of Morgan Bank, estimated that half a million Americans, many from the wealthy and influential east coast establishment, had invested in loans to the Allies.[59] Consider that statement; half a million wealthy influential people had a vested interest in an Allied victory. Do you imagine that they sat quietly waiting to see how their investment fared as Britain and France reeled from the shock of a slaughter-filled stalemate on the Western Front, which could only get worse when the Czar was deposed and Russia opted out of a hopeless war? This was but the tip of the iceberg of vested interest. Allegedly, Woodrow Wilson tried to the last to bring about peace but failed.

If President Wilson had hoped to convince the banks that they should stop extending credit to the warring nations to give him time to coax them towards peace, he was deluded. Too many financial opportunities presented themselves, which allowed New York to corner the market while competitors were crippled by war.[60] American banks had been building great stores of foreign securities as well as lending directly to London and Paris. National banks in America held around $15.6 million dollars of foreign securities in 1914. Within two years that sum had multiplied tenfold to $158.5. By September 1916 the total amount of foreign securities stood at almost $240 million, which naturally thrust Wall Street into a pre-eminent global position from where it could fund the massive increase in its domestic war industries.[61] With such a formidable war-chest to hand, could the money-power really contemplate anything other than war? No.

One immediate consequence of the German decision to embark on its unrestricted U-Boat campaign in 1917 was the panic it caused to traders along the busy eastern seaboard. American shipowners refused to send their vessels into the Atlantic war zone and goods purchased in the United States by the Morgan banks sat idle on the wharves. Profit was threatened; the American economy, intimidated. Morgan asserted his influence with the White House. Jack Morgan was shameless. On 4 April 1917 he wrote a letter to the President pledging his support and reminding Wilson of his connections:

> We are most heartily in accord with you as to the necessity of the United States assisting the allies in the matter of supplies of materials and of credits. To these matters we have been devoting our whole time and thought for the past two years. I write to assure you again that the knowledge we have gained in those two years of close association with the allies in these matters are entirely at the disposal of the United states government at any time ...[62]

He omitted to say that he had devoted his time and thought over the last two years to making a fortune from the war. His position of sole supplier and agent for the British government brought him immense wealth and prestige. This reminder could hardly have been better timed. It was almost as if he was saying to the President, "You know I can handle the money supply ... just get on with the war." Two days later, when war was declared, the House of Morgan held the reins of real monetary power in the United

States. Through his connections with Colonel Mandell House and President Wilson, J.P. Morgan took effective control of the major international loans emanating from the U.S. as all previous restrictions were removed.

On 24 April 1917, President Wilson signed a war finance bill which opened the Federal Reserve System's floodgates and removed any possible liability from Morgan's banks. Every which way was profit on the Midas scale. $200 million was loaned to Britain immediately. All formal banking technicalities were removed. The *New York Times* reported that in order to speed matters up the American Treasury would not even wait until British bonds arrived in New York. Subscribers were given four months to pay in installments as "had been suggested by banking interests and others to Treasury Secretary McAdoo with strong endorsement." Of course they gave Secretary McAdoo their full endorsement. It was their idea; Christmas and Thanksgiving rolled into one. What joy. As the *New York Times* added, "Little if any of the sum would be spent abroad. Virtually the entire loan to the Allies will be spent in this country for foodstuffs, munitions and supplies."[63] Subscriptions from American banks exceeded the initial sum of $200 million by 10 A.M. on the day of issue, and Secretary McAdoo increased the first limit to $250 million.

Consider what had happened. J.P. Morgan spent the first two years of the war using his banking and financial associates to sell British securities on the American market and spend the money on the weapons of war and all its accessories in America. His agents controlled the orders for steel and armaments, for cotton, wheat and meat, for the transportation of these goods across the Americas and the maritime fleets that crossed the oceans. A single example of what this actually meant can be gleaned from the post-war investigation set up under Congressional Investigation into the munitions industry in 1934. The du Pont company admitted that J.P. Morgan & Co. acted as agents, under sales contracts aggregating $351,259,813.28, which accounted for almost 72% of the total military business carried out for the British and French governments during the war. At a mere 1% commission, Morgan made a profit of $3,512,598, from that alone.[64]

Once America abandoned its sham neutrality, Morgan became the prime agent for Wilson's government at war. Loans which he had issued and underwritten on behalf of the Allies were guaranteed by the State. It was *now* impossible for his banks to lose money. The American economy continued to flourish. The British and French tax-payer would eventually be required to repay their debts. It was as if he was a Rothschild. Indeed. The reader might well ask: where were the Rothschilds?

Let the record show that the Rothschilds remained where they always were; at the center of the money-power, though not necessarily under their own name. J.P. Morgan's personal affiliation with the House of Rothschild dated back to 1899, from which point he represented Rothschild interests in the United States. [65] The first telegrams of the war sent to Morgan & Co. in New York, were from Rothschild Freres in Paris on 3 August 1914. The French government, anticipating some of the problems ahead, had approached both Rothschild and Morgan, Harjes & Co. (their French bank) for a loan of $10,000,000, but initially the Americans could not circumvent their own government's insistence that such a loan was "inconsistent with the true spirit of neutrality."[66] It was Lord Nathaniel Rothschild in London who personally advised Lloyd George as Chancellor of the Exchequer[67] before J.P. Morgan was chosen as the sole purchasing agent for Britain. While the financial autocrats pulled the strings behind the scenes, Woodrow Wilson was also driven by personal ambition. As America's Presdient, his place on the world stage had an immediacy which demanded he exercise power before his time had passed. He looked to the future in the belief that victory would place America at the center of a new world order and boost his chance of a third term in office.

The final word on the impact of the financial-industrial-munitions lobby which unquestionably pushed America into war should come from President Wilson's close friend and biographer, the Pulitzer Prize-winning journalist and historian, Ray Stannard Baker. He believed that the die was cast from the outset, observing "...by the end of 1914 the traffic in war matériel with the Allies had become deeply entrenched in America's economic organization and the possibility of keeping out of the war by the diplomacy of neutrality no matter how skilfully conducted, had reached vanishing point. By October, possibly earlier, our case was lost."[68] It was only a matter of time, of when America would go to war, not whether America would become actively involved. The occasion of war might well have been unrestricted submarine warfare, but the cause was closer to Wall Street. The American economy faced wipe-out if the Allies failed to win the terrible war of attrition. That could not be allowed.

Summary.

- President Wilson faced a difficult re-election vote in 1916. His supposed neutrality was so transparently false that certain sectors of the American electorate were drawn to his opponent, the Republican, Charles E. Hughes.
- Wilson's strategy was to attempt to undermine the hyphenated American vote, the German-Americans, the Irish-Americans , the English/Welsh/Scottish-Americans.
- His campaign was predicated on the slogan, "He Kept Us Out Of War."
- The Jewish-American power-block was in its infancy, but in 1916 had a champion in Supreme-Court Judge, Louis Brandeis, and strong and influential Zionist.

• The election itself was extremely close-run and first returns indicated that Charles Hughes and the Republicans had won handsomely.
• In the end all hinged on the result in California which the Democrats had at first conceded to the Republicans.
• Colonel House told President Wilson that all of Germany was supporting the Republicans while Britain and France supported his re-election.
• He gave a memorable Presidential Address in January 1917 in which he talked about "Peace without Victory," fine sounding words, but meaningless to those hell-bent on crushing Germany.
• By 2 April he stood before Congress and sought their approval for war against Germany. So much for Keeping America out of war.
• There was no great enthusiasm for war in the United States, so why did Wilson involve the USA? Was it the ludicrous "Zimmermann Telegram" unearthed by British Intelligence. In this the German Foreign Secretary apparently promised an alliance with Mexico in the event of war.
• Perhaps it was German submarine warfare which tipped the balance? Loss of American shipping was not high; nor was loss of life.
• The Congressional Record shows that J.P. Morgan interests had used the most influential newspapermen in the United States to influence and control American opinion towards war.
• The crucial factor lay at the heart of Wall Street where the money power decided that the time to abandon the illusion of neutrality had come. America had to go to war or their losses would have broken the back of the economy.
• Thomas W Lamont, of Morgan Bank, estimated that half a million Americans, many from the wealthy and influential east coast establishment, had invested in loans to the Allies.
• On 24 April 1917, President Wilson signed a war finance bill which opened the Federal Reserve System's floodgates and removed any possible liability from Morgan's banks. Every which way was profit on the Midas scale.
• The occasion of war might well have been unrestricted submarine warfare but the cause was to be found in Wall Street. The American economy faced wipe-out if the Allies failed to win the terrible war of attrition. That could not be allowed to happen.

Chapter 28

The Balfour Declaration – Mythistory

Possibly the most contentious centenary of the First World War, the Balfour Declaration of November 1917, has left in its wake so many controversies and is held to be the root of so much antagonism, that we have made every effort to focus on its history within the context of our narrative. But first an explanation.

The distinguished Israeli historian, Shlomo Sand[1] risked more than his reputation, when in 2008, he published his re-examination of Jewish history, to expose "the conventional lies about the past"[2] which, like all historical misrepresentations, served to justify the traditional narrative which the Elites have constructed to protect their primacy. He challenged the orthodox views from "the authorized agents of memory" who had steadfastly denied any deviation from the received version of Jewish history. What a wonderful phrase – the authorized agents of memory – the voice of those, and only those, whose research and writings are accepted as truth. Professor Sand has since been shunned by establishment Zionist historians and castigated because he refused to use terms like "The Jewish people," "ancestral land," "exile," "diaspora," "Eretz Israel," or "land of redemption," which were key terms in the mythology of Israel's national history. His refusal to employ them was held to be heretical. Shlomo Sand was not alone in such protests.

Those of us born into the Christian traditions were taught bible stories in school or at church – perhaps even from our parents. In the two-part theological litany of events (the Bible) as recorded by whom we will never know, the Old Testament was accepted as a history of the Jewish people despite a complete lack of evidence on which to base key assertions. Take for example the claim that the Jewish people were dispersed into exile by the Romans. Nowhere in the vast and well-documented records of the Roman Empire is there historical proof of a large refugee population around the borders of Judea after the three uprisings or wars in the first century CE; as there would have been if a mass flight had taken place.[3] Some Jews may have fled fearing for their lives, but the Roman conquerors did not enforce an exile. There was no Imperial edict.

Another Israeli historian, Adiyah Horon, insisted that there was no truth in the claim that an "exile" occurred after the destruction [of the

Temple] when the Emperors Titus and Hadrian supposedly expelled the Jews from Palestine. He too agreed that this idea, based on historical ignorance, derived from a hostile fabrication by the fathers of the Christian church who wanted to show that God punished the Jews for the crucifixion of Jesus.[4] The myth of uprooting and exile was fostered by the Christian legend, from which it flowed into Jewish tradition and grew to be the accepted "truth" engraved in history. [5] More recently, the Israeli historian Ilan Pappe [6] Professor at Exeter University, has attacked the "foundational mythologies" of Israeli history which insist that "Palestine was a land without people waiting on a people without land."[7] This isn't just bad history, it is patently wrong.

In 1976, Arthur Koestler, a Hungarian-born naturalized British citizen of Jewish parentage, demonstrated another misconception in his remarkable book, *The Thirteenth Tribe.* The ancient Ashkenazim Jews, who comprise most of the world's population of Jews today, sprang from barbarians living in the ancient empire of Khazaria between the Caspian and Black Seas.[8] In his masterpiece of world history, *The Silk Roads*, Peter Frankopan, Director of the Center for Byzantine Research at Oxford University, also explained the spread of Judaism in the ninth century when the Khazars chose to convert en masse,[9] which raised speculation that they might be one of the lost tribes of ancient Israel. Not so. Many of these Jewish converts migrated to what is today Poland and Russia, but the evidence of history demonstrates that they had no link to "the holy land" or "Palestine." A greater irony lies in the fact that significant numbers of Palestinians driven from their ancestral homelands over the past 100 years were likely to have been descendants of the original Jews of that land who converted to Islam following the Muslim conquest of the Levant in the first half of the 7th century.

Eran Elhaik, an Israeli geneticist, who served seven year in the Israeli Defense Force, and no critic of Israel, developed genome studies at John Hopkins University.[10] In tracing the geographical positioning of a number of Ashkenazim Jews, he found that their ancestral origins were not from the Middle East or indeed the Mediterranean but from a region that is now in northeast Turkey. This scientific evidence underscores the historical findings of Shlomo Sand and others that makes nonsense of the claims of an ancestral Jewish homeland and the diaspora. Don't be misled by the clamor raised against these brave professional historians and scientists against whom disparaging comments have been made, calling them "self-hating Jews."[11] To be pilloried by the establishment who seek to squash the truth, is a shameful consequence, but a typical one.

The reason we have introduced our sections on the Balfour Declaration in this manner is to enable the reader who is considering the impact of the First World War, to understand that several major pronouncements were made about Palestine, its contemporary status and its future stand-

A.J. Balfour

ing. Most educated people in Britain accepted the concept of the wandering Jews alienated from their biblical "homeland" after a "diaspora." The Christian tradition wallowed in such patronizing postulation. The terms were widely unquestioned across national boundaries.

At the end of the nineteenth century the concept of a Jewish "homeland" took on a life of its own with the advent of political Zionism, which increasingly expressed itself in "national" terms, as if it represented a nation-state. In the context of the Secret Elite's attitude towards Palestine and Zionist claims in 1917, the following chapters will demonstrate why one faction, the political Zionists, and another, the Secret Elite and the Allies, successfully used each other to help move forward their specific agendas. We have used terms like "Jewish homeland" and "diaspora" not because we are in agreement with them, or hold them to be true, but because they were part of the language of the time. Bear this in mind as the narrative unfolds.

LETTER FROM ARTHUR BALFOUR TO LORD WALTER ROTHSCHILD

Foreign Office
November 2 1917

> Dear Lord Rothschild, I have much pleasure in conveying to you on behalf of His Majesty's Government the following Declaration of sympathy with Jewish Zionist aspirations which have been submitted to and approved by the Cabinet:
>
> His Majesty's Government view with favour the establishment in Palestine of a national home for the Jewish people, and will use its best endeavours to facilitate the achievement of this object, it being clearly understood that nothing shall be done which may prejudice the civil and religious rights of existing non-Jewish communities in Palestine, or the rights and political status enjoyed by Jews in any other country. I should be grateful if you would bring this Declaration to the knowledge of the Zionist Federation.
>
> Yours sincerely,
> (signed) ARTHUR JAMES BALFOUR[12]

The above letter was released by the Foreign Office and printed in the *Times* on 9 November, 1917.

Why at this critical juncture did the British War Cabinet decide publicly to favor Palestine as a national home for Jews? Our instinct is to redefine that question to ask: where did this fit into the Secret Elite's strategy to crush Germany and advance its globalist ambition? How were these linked? How had it come about that a homeland for one specific religious group appeared on the war-time agenda as if it was a solution to an unspoken problem? Even if anyone believed the lie that the Allies were fighting for the rights of smaller nations, why had religious identity suddenly become an issue of nationhood? Had anyone considered giving Catholics such rights in Ireland or Muslims such rights in India? Was the world to be divided into exclusive religious territories? Of course not. To complicate matters further, one nation (Britain) solemnly promised a national home to what would become in time a second nation (the Jewish State of Israel) on the land which belonged to another people (Palestinian Arabs) while it was still an integral part of a fourth (the Ottoman/Turkish Empire).[13] In pandering to a small group of Zionists, the Balfour Declaration was bizarre, deceitful and a deliberate betrayal of the loyal Arabs fighting in the desert war against the Turks. Perfidious Albion had rarely plumbed such duplicitous depths. What power did these Zionists hold over the British government to ensure their unquestioned co-operation in the first steps towards a Zionist state at the expense of the rightful owners of Palestine?

The absolute destruction of Germany and her Ottoman allies promised to pave the way for a re-drawing of maps and spheres of influence which would advance the Secret Elite's overall strategy; namely the control of the English-speaking elect over the world. The strategic sands of Arabia and the oil-rich lands of Persia, Syria and Mesopotamia, had long been prime targets. These were the first in a number of prerequisites which would shape the Middle-East after 1919 to the advantage of Britain in particular. Critically, as a neutral, America had to be very careful about open intervention even after she had entered the war; and to an extent Britain acted as her proxy in putting markers down for a new world order. It is important to remember that when early discussions about the future of a Jewish homeland in Palestine were in progress, little mention was made of American involvement. The truth is otherwise. America was deeply involved in secret intrigues both directly and indirectly.

So too were small but influential groups of bankers, politicians and businessmen - English, American, French and Russian Jews spread across the world – that supported a growing movement to establish a Jewish state. They were called Zionists. Take care with this term. Initially it included a range of Jewish groups which held different views and aspirations. Some saw Zionism as a purely religious manifestation of "Jewishness", but a small, intensely vocal and subsequently powerful group fostered political ambitions. This latter form of Zionism included those determined to "reconstitute" a national home for their co-religionists. In the words of the former Viceroy of India, Lord Curzon, "a national home for the Jewish race or people" implied a place where the Jews could be reassembled as a nation, and where "they [would] enjoy the privileges of an independent national existence."[14] How do you reconstitute a nation? In truth, if the Ashkenazim Jews were to be "reassembled" it should have been along the Volga River in the true Khazarian "homeland," not along the Jordan river in Palestine.

There were a small number of suggested sites for the proposed new homeland, including one in Uganda, but in the first years of the twentieth century a more determined Zionist element began to focus their attention on the former land of Judea in the Middle East. They spoke of the creation in Palestine of an autonomous Jewish State, a political entity composed of Jews, governed by Jews and administered mainly in their interests. In other words, the recreation of a semi-mythical Jewish State as was claimed before the days of the so called "diaspora."[15] Few voices were raised to ask what that meant, on what evidence it was predicated or how it might be justified? It was an assumed biblical truth. Not every Jew was a Zionist; far from it, and that is an important factor to which we will in due course return.

Frequently historians write versions of history which imply that an event "just happened." In other words, they begin at a point which creates the impression that there was no essential preamble, no other influence which underwrote the central action. One example is the assassination of Archduke Ferdinand in Sarajevo on 28 June 1914. For generations, school pupils have been taught that this murder caused the First World War. As we have seen, such nonsense helped deflect attention away from the true culprits. Another example can be found in the usual interpretation of the Balfour Declaration, which has been described as the British Government's note of approval for the establishment of a national home for Jews, as if it turned up one day on the Foreign Secretary's desk and was signed like the other items in his out-tray. It has been downplayed; granted, as but a minor mention in the memoirs and diaries of the politicians who carefully orchestrated its single sentence. The Balfour Declaration was much more than a vague promise made by British politicians under the pressure of war's contingency. Such a simple interpretation has conveniently masked the international pressures which the hidden powers on both sides of the Atlantic asserted in favor of a monumental policy decision which opened the door to the eventual establishment of the State of Israel.

At the 261st meeting of the British War Cabinet on 31 October, 1917, with Prime Minister Lloyd George in the Chair, the membership comprised Lord Curzon, Lord Milner, Andrew Bonar Law, (Conservative leader) Sir Edward Carson, G.N. Barnes (Labour Party), the South African General Jan Smuts and Foreign Secretary Arthur Balfour. This was the inner circle formed mainly from the Secret Elite's political agents to run the war.[16] They remained behind the closed doors of 10 Downing Street after other war business had been completed. The military and naval representatives were dismissed before the War Cabinet's inner cabal proceeded to discuss the on-going issue of "The Zionist Movement." As always, Lloyd George's War Cabinet secretary, Sir Maurice Hankey, recorded the minutes. This coterie of British imperialists and Secret Elite members and associates, agreed unanimously that "from a purely diplomatic and political point of view, it was desirable that some declaration favorable to the aspirations of the Jewish nationalists should now be made."[17] To that end a carefully constructed form of words was tabled and the War Cabinet authorized Foreign Secretary Balfour "to take a suitable opportunity of making the following declaration of sympathy with the Zionist aspiration." It was no co-incidence that some five days previously the editor of the *Times* had urged them to make this statement.[18] The precise wording was as recorded at the beginning of this chapter[19] and unanimously approved by the War Cabinet.

While the seventy-eight words which comprise the core of the Balfour Declaration have had an explosive impact on the history of the world right up to the present day, in our time-frame we must concentrate on the period between 1917 and the end of the war. Who was actually involved in the secret machinations, how did they manipulate opportunities to their own advantage, and who financed and promoted the idea from its early origins to eventual realization?

Two days after the War Cabinet's decision a letter was sent from the Foreign Office to Lord Lionel Walter Rothschild (2nd Baron Rothschild) in London asking that he "bring this Declaration to the knowledge of the Zionist Federation." It was signed Arthur James Balfour, and henceforth was known as The Balfour Declaration, though it was the product of many more minds than solely that of the British foreign secretary.[20] Its precise wording was publicized across the Jewish communities who hailed the letter as the beginning of a new epoch in their history. Despite the apparent care with which the War Cabinet attempted to lay down conditions to protect non-Jewish communities, in particular the rights of the Palestinian Arabs to whom the country belonged, the event was celebrated by Zionists across the world as a "National Charter" for a Jewish homeland.[21] The genie was out of the bottle.

In truth, the letter was the product of years of careful lobbying in both Britain and America. It was neither a beginning nor an end-point. Though the communication was essentially between the British government and the Zionist Federation in Britain, it had an almost casual feel to it as if it was simply a letter between two members of the English gentry, Balfour and Rothschild. The Declaration was far from casual and much more contrived than a gentleman's agreement.

By all known processes of law and morality it was ridiculous. Consider the unprecedented nature of the proposal. Britain held no sovereign right whatsoever over Palestine or authority to dispose of the land.[22] As if this would not cause sufficient confusion, the British Foreign Office had already promised parts of Palestine to the French, to the Arabs who already owned the land, and finally, to the international Jewish community. Was there ever a better example of the wanton arrogance of the British imperialist ruling class? The very wording of the Balfour Declaration was ambiguous; the conditions set were impossible. What was meant by the phrase, "a national home"? It had no clearly defined meaning in international law. How could a foreign government promise to achieve world-wide approval for a national home for Jews in an Arab country without automatically prejudicing the rights of the Arabs whose ancestors had lived there for thousands of years?[23] Its very vagueness gave rise to interpretations and expectations which were certain to cause bitter dispute. What was going on?

The answer can be found by examining earlier versions of this controversial document and the extent to which Zionists on both sides of the Atlantic strove to nurture and protect it.

Far from any notion of their sudden conversion to Zionism, the political drive to establish a Jewish homeland in the sands of the desert, British politicians had been engaged in such discussions for several years. This fact had been conveniently omitted from official histories, memoirs and government statements.

A previous War Cabinet meeting on 4 October 1917 had considered an almost identical draft declaration from Lord Alfred Milner, the most influential leader of the inner circle of the Secret Elite. He included the words "favour the establishment of a National Home for the Jewish Race."[24] The capitalization of the term National Home was later altered, as was the very Milnerite phrase, "Jewish Race." Lord Milner was a very precise thinker. While the words National Home implied that Jews throughout the world should have a defined area to call their own, his version favored "the establishment" of such a place. It did not imply a return to a land over which they had assumed rights. Secondly, Alfred Milner held "Race" in great esteem. He defined himself with pride as a British "Race Patriot."[25] His wording was a mark of respect. Others feared that it was a dangerous phrase which might be interpreted aggressively. It clashed with the concept of Jewish assimilation, like Jewish-Americans, and hinted that as a faith group, Jews belonged to a specific race of peoples. Consequently, his version was toned down.

Secretly, the War Cabinet decided to seek the opinion on the final wording of the declaration from both representative Zionists (their phrase) and those of the Jewish faith opposed to the idea of a national homeland. It is crucial to clearly understand that inside the international

Jewish community there was a considerable difference of opinion in favor of, and against this idea of a Jewish "homeland." That these groups were apparently given equal standing suggested that the Jewish community in Britain was equally split on the issue. They were not. The number of active Zionists was relatively small, but very influential.

Furthermore, the War Cabinet sought the American President's opinion on the proposed Jewish homeland in Palestine.[26] The minutes of the 245th meeting of the War Cabinet in London revealed that Woodrow Wilson was directly involved in the final draft of the Declaration. So too was his minder, Colonel Edward Mandell House[27] and the United States, only Jewish Chief Justice, Louis Brandeis,[28] both of whom telegrammed different views to the British government.[29] On 10 September, Mandell House indicated that the President advised caution; on 27 September, Judge Brandeis cabled that the President was in entire sympathy with the declaration. Much can change in politics over two and a half weeks.

As each layer of the onion is slowly peeled away from the hidden inner core of the eponymous Declaration, it becomes apparent that the given story has glossed over key figures and critical issues. There are hidden depths to this episode that mainstream historians have kept from public view and participants have deliberately misrepresented or omitted from their memoirs.

The previous minutes of the War Cabinet Committee held on 3 September 1917, show that the earlier meeting had also been crammed with Secret Elite members and associates including Leo Amery, formerly Milner's acolyte in South Africa.[30] Item two on the agenda revealed that "considerable correspondence ... has been passed between the Secretary of State for Foreign Affairs (A.J. Balfour) and Lord Walter Rothschild ... on the question of the policy to be adopted towards the Zionist movement."[31] What? "Considerable correspondence" had been exchanged between Lord Rothschild and the Foreign Office; not a letter or inquiry, but considerable correspondence. A copy of one of these letters sent from the Rothschild mansion at 148 Piccadilly on 18 July 1917 has survived in the War Cabinet minutes. What it reveals shatters the illusion that the British government's promise of support for a Jewish national home in Palestine stemmed exclusively from the Foreign Office under the pen of Arthur Balfour. Lord Rothschild's letter began:

> Dear Mr. Balfour,
>
> At last I am able to send you the formula you asked me for. If his Majesty's Government will send me a message on the lines of this formula, if they and you approve of it, I will hand it on to Zionist Federations and also announce it at a meeting called for that purpose ...[32]

Rothschild enclosed his recommendation for a draft declaration. It comprised two sentences: (1) His Majesty's Government accepts the principle that Palestine should be reconstituted as the National Home of the Jewish people. (2) His Majesty's Government will use its best endeavors to secure the achievement of this object and will discuss the necessary methods and means with the Zionist Organizations.[33]

Balfour's reply "accepted the principle that Palestine should be reconstituted ... and will be ready to consider any suggestions on the subject which the Zionist Organization may desire to lay before them." What? How do you "reconstitute" a country? It might be interesting to consider the precedent that was being set. Could this mean that one day America might be reconstituted as a series of native Indian states or parts of England as Viking territory? Astonishingly, the Zionist movement was invited to dictate its designs for British foreign policy in Palestine.[34] This was not some form of loose involvement. It was complicity. Lloyd George's government, through the war cabinet, colluded with the Zionist Federation to concoct a statement of intent that met their (Zionist) approval. Furthermore, it was agreed that such an important issue, namely the future of Palestine, should be discussed with Britain's allies, and "more particularly with the United States."[35] This action had all the hallmarks of an international conspiracy.

How many lies have been woven around the design and origins of the Balfour Declaration? Lord Walter Rothschild was the chief intermediary between the British government and the Zionist Federation. In this capacity he had been involved in the process of creating and formulating a new and explosive British commitment to the foundation of a Zionist State in Palestine. More than that, Rothschild and his associates sought to control "the methods and means" by which it would be created. This mindset never wavered in the years that followed.

What influences had been activated to bring Lloyd George, in conjunction with Woodrow Wilson, to such a position by November 1917? Behind the scenes, who was pulling the strings? Who were these Zionists, and why were they given such immense support from the Secret Elite and, in particular, their British political agents? How could a minority group of no previous influence suddenly command such power on both sides of the Atlantic? An exceedingly small minority group of no previous political or religious influence, whose ideology had been dismissed by many leading Rabbis as contrary to true Jewish belief, emerged as if from nowhere to strut the world stage. This did not happen by chance.

The term Zionism was coined in the late nineteenth century to represent the movement for Jews to move to a so-called "historic homeland" in Palestine, though from the start the term was interpreted in different ways by different Jewish and non-Jewish communities. It grew from small beginnings in the second half of the nineteenth century. The First Zionist Congress was held in Basel between the 29th and 31st of August, 1897. Its aim was to have a recognized "and legally secured" home in Palestine.[36] Chaired by Theodore Herzl, an Austro-Hungarian journalist and keen Jewish activist, the meeting of around 200 participants created the World Zionist Organization. Who could have known that from such small beginnings a new State would eventually emerge? Small in number, these Zionists were zealots. Their stance was absolute. They accepted no criticism. They belittled as enemies those many Jews who believed in assimilation into the countries in which they lived, and who questioned Zionism's political aims. At the Second Basel Congress one year later it was clear that very few Jews were interested in the proposal. Consequently, their emphasis changed. Herzl recognized the need to galvanize Jewish communities, most of whom remained ignorant of, or completely disinterested in, or positively against the idea of Zionism.

In December 1901 a Jewish National Fund (JNF) was established in Britain to acquire land in Palestine as the "inalienable estate of the Jewish people."[37] It is entirely dubious whether any international law validated such an "inalienable" right, but what is important is that the JNF was part of the slow and unsuccessful process of encouraging Jewish settlers to go to Palestine. The focus on Palestine was one from which Zionists were not to be turned. We should not forget that the suffering and desperation of many Jews, especially in Russia, whose anti-Jewish pogroms were a barbarous indictment of the Romanov Empire, pressed heavily on the evolving Zionist movement. From their vantage point it was a crisis which no-one else was minded to solve.

Of the major world powers, Britain was the most progressively liberal in its Jewish assimilation. Wealthy Jews in banking, finance and business were increasingly included in what was known as "society." There were Jewish Members of Parliament; Jews ennobled and given membership of the House of Lords. Jewish refugees from the Russian pogroms settled in the slums in the East End of London and other major cities. Life was far from easy for the masses of impoverished immigrants, but Britain was a comparatively safe haven and more welcoming than France. The nascent cries for a "homeland" did not come from the ordinary Jewish refugee, but from the Zionist lobby which had begun to assert itself at the turn of the century.

A British offer of an autonomous homeland for Jewish settlers in East Africa[38] was considered at the Sixth Congress in 1903 and the Zionists agreed to send a delegation to examine the practicalities of a Jewish settlement in Uganda. They turned it down. Unsuitable. The Zionists had no intention of resettling in Uganda. Ever. It was not the "promised land." Another approach to the British government about the possible colonization of a strip of territory on the southern boundary of Palestine and Egypt called El Arish had been secretly conducted by Theodore Herzl, but was also found to be impractical.[39] What mattered was that British politicians appeared sympathetic to the aspirations of political Zionists.

Herzl died in 1904, and after a considerable struggle, Chaim Weizmann emerged as a charismatic and persuasive Zionist leader. He dominated the Eighth Congress in 1907 and managed to fuse together its political and the practical divisions into what was termed "Synthetic Zionism," which Weizmann built on common links between a variety of Zionist groups. Progress was slow. Numbers remained comparatively small, but Palestine was always the ultimate target.[40]

It seems strange that in his seminal work *The Anglo-American Establishment,* Professor Carroll Quigley made no mention of Chaim Weizmann's activities in Britain before or during the First World War. This is all the more puzzling when we unpick Weizmann's many and frequent associations with the key political forces inside the elite British Establishment. He penetrated the hidden web of political influence as no other previously had. Every possible door was opened to him and anything that might prove incriminating, that smelled of collusion, removed from the record.[41] Weizmann operated as the Zionist leader in Britain from 1904-5 onwards, meeting political sympathizers, using his contacts and building up a network of relationships which proved advantageous to his cause.

Weizmann initially met Arthur Balfour, formerly Conservative leader during the general election of 1906,[42] at a time when Lord Nathaniel Rothschild worked closely with the British Prime Minister.[43] Balfour wanted to know why the Zionists had turned down the British government's practical solution of a settlement in Uganda? Weizmann spelled out his philosophy with absolute clarity. He dwelt on the spiritual side of Zionism and his "deeply religious conviction" that only Palestine would do. In his eyes, any deflection from Palestine, was "a form of idolatry,"[44] an interesting form of words, rooted in religious abhorrence. He professed that Palestine had a magic and romantic appeal for the Jews; that no other homeland could energize the Jewish people to build up and make habitable, a wasteland. Palestine was not a wasteland nor was it uninhabited. In peddling this lie, Weizmann was very persuasive. His was not the policy advocated by the wealthy Jews who had made such important strides in British society. This was not an Englishman, proud to be English … and a Jew. Weizmann was not a privileged Rothschild or one of the many other rich upper-middle class Englishmen of Jewish faith who had been completely assimilated into British society. Weizmann was a Zionist zealot. Lord Nathaniel Rothschild was not.

Weizmann had one particularly influential mentor who knew precisely the names of the prime decision makers in Britain. He was Baron Edmond de Rothschild, head of the French branch of the banking dynasty. Edmond de Rothschild also believed passionately in Palestine. He had funded the establishment of Jewish settlements between 1880-95 and was later hailed as the father of Jewish colonization.[45] Although the initial months of the war looked bleak for France and her allies, Edmond de Rothschild was convinced of ultimate victory. His advice to Weizmann, whom he considered a capable leader, reflected the forward nature of Zionist thinking. This was the opportunity. That moment, in the first months of a murderous world war, was the time to act so "we might not be forgotten in the general settlement."[46] Consider that advice. Rothschild forewarned him that war would end in a settlement of conflicting claims, and the Zionists had to act immediately to ensure that theirs was successful. Chaim Weizmann's task was to influence British statesmen and politicians to support the Zionist cause in Palestine. It is inconceivable that Rothschild would have failed to identify the key personnel, the trusted agents and members of the Secret Elite whose support was vital to the Zionist ambition. When we analyze the list of men and women whom Weizmann targeted for support, there can be no other explanation, for they formed the core of the secret society that was revealed by Professor Quigley.[47] Weizmann may not have been fully aware of their one-world agenda but these were the people who could approve the transformation of Palestine from the unrequited holy grail to a Jewish state. They became his immediate targets.

Russian persecution also precipitated a wave of Jewish immigration from Eastern Europe to America in the first decade of the century,[48] but attempts to organize Zionist societies across the United States failed to ignite early enthusiasms. With two or three exceptions, the wealthy Jews in America would have nothing to do with Zionism in any shape or form.[49] The settled and prosperous upper class, mostly German Jews, believed in assimilation. Their wealth and social position proved to them that the melting pot analogy was working. Above all, they did not want anyone to question their loyalty to America or embrace an ideology that might rock their well-provisioned boat by advocating the creation of a foreign country specifically for Jews.[50] That might prove an uncomfortable transformation, especially if the argument focused on the theft of an already Arab country or the need for Jews to go and live there.

On the other hand it appeared that some poorer immigrants were becoming more vocal in their support, though it was not backed by an evident desire to move from the "Land of the Free" to the sands of Palestine. The Jewish leaders in America, Jacob Schiff and Rabbi I.M. Wise claimed that "America is our Zion."[51] The Jewish community in America was at best divided. There was no groundswell in the Zionists' favor and the State Department dismissed them as a minority political group without money, influence or social standing.[52] They were not listening. Slowly a generation of new Zionists began to assert itself among the aspiring middle classes of teachers, lawyers, businessmen and professors. They required a leader to champion their cause.

The flag-bearer for Zionism in the United States, Louis Brandeis, was a Boston lawyer hailed as a champion of the people. As early as 1890 he had created a legal storm with an article in the *Harvard Law Review*, a "Citizens Right to Privacy."[53] In 1905 he successfully challenged the J.P. Morgan banking and financial conglomerate over a proposed railroad merger, raged against the abuses of monopolies and championed women's working rights in a high-profile court case against the State of Oregon.[54] Brandeis was widely considered dangerous by his opponents because he couldn't be bought. Outrageous anti-Jewish rants were vented against him by magazines and journals owned or part-financed by the New Haven Railroad Company when he spoke out against their abuses.[55] Unbowed and unbroken Brandeis fought them and won.

Louis Brandeis was attracted to Zionism fairly late in his life. He first came into contact with Eastern European Jews among the New York garment workers whom he supported in the great strike of 1910. Burgeoning anti-Semitism in Boston and his own encounters with prejudice influenced his attraction to the Zionist cause and in an interview with the *Jewish Advocate* in 1910 he openly acknowledged his sympathy for Zionism.[56] Within two years it had become his life's purpose.

On 30 August, 1914, barely a month into the war, an extraordinary conference of American Zionists took place in New York at which Louis Brandeis, the Boston lawyer, was unanimously elected leader of the Provisional Executive Committee for General Zionist Affairs. This electrified the Jewish community. Here was a leader of national standing with the reputation of a fearless champion of the people.[57] He brought respect and authority to the post and under his direction a stream of other leaders in American Jewish life were attracted to the Zionist movement. He believed in a cultural pluralism in which ethnic groups retained their unique identity as did Americans of Scottish, Irish, German or any other nationality. His message was that there was no inconsistency between loyalty to America and loyalty to Jewry. Although some European Zionists viewed this as an anemic adaptation of their own passion,[58] Brandeis' approach to Zionism succeeded in encouraging far greater support in America for a "homeland" in Palestine. That did not, however, infer their intention to go and live there.[59] Ever.

Brandeis's magnetism in Jewish circles was further enhanced by President Wilson's surprise decision to appoint him to the vacant position on the Supreme Court on 28 January, 1916.[60] His many detractors gave vent to their anti-Jewish bile in a firestorm of protest. Newspapers called Louis Brandeis a red-hot radical; the *Sun* declared that it was the Senate's duty to "protect the Supreme Court from such an utterly and ridiculously unfit appointment." According to the press President Wilson had never made a worse mistake than his nomination of Brandeis. It added, "if he fails to withdraw it, the United States Senate should throw it out."[61] The Zionist leader had to endure six months of unrelenting abuse from opponents before winning Senate approval in June 1916.

The transformation of Mr Brandeis into Justice Brandeis should have reduced his active involvement in the Zionist movement. Not so. Louis Brandeis's influence and power increased a hundred-fold. Clearly his official involvement in overt Jewish matters should have been reduced to a minimum, but he held on to all the reins of influence.[62] He remained in daily communication by telephone, telegraph and conference with all the other leaders of the movement, and little escaped his attention. Brandeis was in the business of recruitment. He clearly understood the power that ordinary Jewish voters could wield at the ballot-box. But the struggle within American Jewry for control of their own community between the exceptionally wealthy few and the masses, descended into bitter accusation and counter-accusation.

Jacob Schiff, the New York financier, head of the great Kuhn Loeb banking firm was the foremost Jewish financier in the United States. His philanthropy towards Jewish causes was legendary. Nevertheless, in June 1916 he was shocked by the personal attacks leveled against him. He had originally held himself aloof from Theodor Herzl and overtly political Zionism and, in a speech at the Central Jewish Institute, he was reported to have said that Jews in Russia had brought many of their troubles upon themselves because they "kept apart as a separate people."[63] Schiff always claimed that he had been misrepresented by the pro-Zionist Jewish press; that he had been unfairly and improperly maligned. He told the *New York Times* that he had been warned that his opposition to the Jewish Congress movement would result in such an attack. Schiff revealed that the Zionists were determined to undermine Jewish confidence in him in a well orchestrated plan; that whatever he said, they would attack him. He was gravely hurt by the allegations and swore that Zionism, Jewish nationalism, the Congress Movement and Jewish politics in any form was thereafter a closed book.[64] Schiff's anger subsided later and he was persuaded to help the Jews in Palestine, provided the project could be presented to him as unrelated to Zionism.

The message was clear. Zionism was not to be crossed, even by the richest of its own co-religionists. There was an unsubtle message in this character assassination. No matter how rich, how influential, how generous, no-one would be allowed to criticize the Zionist agenda. No-one. Many others have suffered a similar fate since.

Louis Brandeis grew in stature. He had the President's ear. Precisely why remains a matter of conjecture. Formerly, as an adviser to Woodrow Wilson, Brandeis helped to broker the compromise that led to the adoption of the Federal Reserve Act of 1913, without which U.S. bankers could not have financed the world war.[65] Viewed from that angle one might question the purity of his anti-trust reputation. Though he should have kept his responsibilities as a Supreme Court Judge separate from the workings of the State Department, which had responsibility for all international dealings, Brandeis made his views on Palestine clear. He approached Woodrow Wilson directly on the issue of Palestine and "obtained verbal assurances" on his and the Allied policy in Palestine. In an article in the *New Statesman* and *The Nation* in November 1914, he argued that Palestine should become a British protectorate. [66] Consider that date. In November 1914, the idea that Palestine should become a British Protectorate was planted by an American Zionist three years ahead of the more general Balfour Declaration. In what depth of fertile soil did it germinate?

For many Jews who had suffered directly from Russian brutality, supporting the Allies was emotionally difficult. Many could not understand how the British in particular could fight side-by-side with the hated Romanovs. Brandeis saw beyond that hatred. Above all, he knew that America had to be involved in any international congress which would be empowered to settle the break-up of the Ottoman Empire. He looked to Chaim Weizmann, his fellow Zionist leader across the Atlantic, to help find a form of commitment which would deliver Palestine to the Jews.[67]

Weizmann had a valuable friend, the journalist and editor, C.P. Scott. Later the proprietor of the *Manchester Guardian,* Scott was an Oxford-educated man of staunch liberal leanings. He spent ten years as Member of Parliament for Leigh in Lancashire (1895-1905) and welcomed Lloyd George's courage in opposing the Boer War.[68] Their friendship endured through tumultuous times and Lloyd George trusted C.P. Scott's views.[69] The newspaper owner had befriended Weizmann when he was teaching at Manchester University and proved to be, in Weizmann's words, "of incalculable value." He pointed the Zionist leader toward the one Jewish member of Asquith's government, Herbert Samuel, whom he believed could be of great assistance.[70] Samuel was not a practicing Jew and before the war had never spoken about Zionism. Despite this apparent lack of interest he proposed, in November 1914, that Britain sponsor the establishment of a Jewish state in Palestine after the war.[71] Was it co-incidence that on both sides of the Atlantic, influential Jewish financiers and politicians – Rothschild, Brandeis, Weizmann and Herbert Samuel – looked ahead to the end of the war and appreciated the opportunity it would bring? Note the coincidence of both Brandeis and Samuel's proposals in November 1914. According to his memoirs Samuel was inspired by being the first Jew ever to sit in the British Cabinet and claimed that he turned to Weizmann for advice.[72] Consequently, he spoke to Sir Edward Grey, the Foreign Secretary, about the future of Palestine. Samuel expressed his alarm at the prospect of this part of the world falling into the hands of any of the Continental Powers and stressed the strategic importance of that region to the British Empire. He professed his enthusiasm for a Jewish State in Palestine which would be "a center of a new culture ... a fountain of enlightenment."[73]

What followed was a very curious breakfast meeting of a pro-Zionist group, including Lloyd George, on 3 December 1914. The most intriguing part of the meeting, which Weizmann described in great detail in his autobiography,[74] was that Lloyd George completely blanked that important meeting from his autobiography. In his own self-aggrandizing memoirs the Welshman explicitly dated his first meeting with Chaim Weizmann from 1916 when the Manchester chemist, by that time a Professor at the university, worked for the ministry of munitions. Indeed, the impression which Lloyd George deliberately tried to infer was that the later Balfour Declaration was a reward for Weizmann's services to the British nation for his development of acetone as a source to enhance munitions.[75] What rubbish.[76] Why did he feel it necessary to falsify his own record? Lloyd George had been introduced to Chaim Weizmann on 3 December 1914 in the company of Herbert Samuel, C.P. Scott and Josiah Wedgwood, and the sole topic of conversation, had been Palestine.[77] The then Chancellor of the Exchequer's account is so ridiculous that we have to ask, what was he trying to hide? Did later developments in Palestine embarrass Lloyd George politically? Were there other secret influences from whom he had to deflect inquiry?

Herbert Samuel proved to be an important advocate for a Zionist State in Palestine. He promoted the idea informally with fellow ministers and in January 1915 wrote a draft memorandum for the Cabinet in which he concluded that Palestine's annexation to the British Empire together with an active colonization of Jewish settlers was the best solution for Britain.[78] Prime Minister Asquith was not impressed.[79] When in March 1915 Samuel circulated his revised memorandum to all members of the Cabinet, Asquith was scathing in his dismissal, describing the proposals as "dithyrambic," an educated put-down implying a wild, over-the-top, possibly wine-fueled raving. He went further with a racist swipe which emphasized his disapproval of the very idea that "we should take Palestine, into which the scattered Jews c[oul]d swarm back from all quarters of the globe, and in due course claim Home Rule."[80] Insects swarm; not people.

Asquith also ridiculed the notion that Lloyd George cared a whit about the future of Palestine, adding: "Lloyd George ... does not care a damn for the Jews or their past or their future, but thinks it would be an outrage to let the Christian holy places pass into the possession or under the protectorate of Agnostic Atheistic France!"[81] Why did Asquith find Lloyd George's stance "curious"? Before taking office in 1906, Lloyd

George's legal firm had represented Theodore Herzl in his negotiations over the Uganda proposal. It was he who submitted Herzl's views on the offer to the British Government.[82] His association with Zionism was long-standing.

Other important politicians and Cabinet ministers who responded positively to Herbert Samuel's memorandum included Sir Edward Grey, Rufus Isaacs, Lord Chief Justice of England from 1913, Richard Haldane, who at that time was Lord Chancellor, Lord James Bryce, former Ambassador to the United States and Arthur J. Balfour,[83] who was to become Foreign Secretary when Grey was replaced in 1916.

Alfred Milner was positively predisposed towards what he himself termed, the Jewish Race. In 1902 he wrote to the President of the Zionist Federation of South Africa: "I have known the Jews as excellent colonists at the Cape, industrious, law-abiding and thoroughly loyal."[84] Herzl had written to Milner in 1903 putting forward his arguments for a Jewish National Home in Palestine and praised the bond which he believed "united us [Jews] all closely to your nation."[85] Weizmann valued the strength of Milner's support. He believed that Milner profoundly understood that the Jews alone were capable of rebuilding Palestine, and of giving it a place in the modern family of nations.[86] Such nonsense should have been summarily dismissed but Milner had more immediate concerns, among which the strategic defense of the Empire was a powerful motivator. The Secret Elite understood the natural advantage to be gained from a pliant Jewish Palestine, which would protect the western side of the Suez canal and all of the concomitant interests in Persia.

Weizmann held individual discussions with a stream of Secret Elite politicians and agents. Naturally he endowed each with qualities and perceptions which supported Zionism.[87]

He specifically targeted Lloyd George's minders in the Downing Street Garden suburb.[88] His subliminal message was hardly difficult to understand; Britain should trust in a Jewish homeland in Palestine to protect the Suez Canal and the gateway to Persia and India.

Weizmann had a further advantage. He understood the matriarchal power inside the Jewish household and sought to use it to his advantage. For example, when James de Rothschild was serving in the British army, Weizmann befriended his wife Dorothy Pinto and "won her over" to Zionism. Jessica Rothschild, wife of Nathan's second son, Charles, also proved to be a valuable asset and willingly helped the Zionist leader to widen his contacts inside London Society.

And it came to pass that the people of influence, mostly powerfully rich Jews, adopted Chaim Weizmann. The English Zionist Federation office in Fulbourne Street in the East End of London had become too small to meet the demands placed on it by 1917. Weizmann would have us believe that "after much consideration and heart-searching we decided to open an office at 175 Piccadilly." So innocuously put; so entirely misleading. From the East End to Piccadilly was a massive step on its own, but to 175 Piccadilly? To become near neighbors of their friends in "Rothschild Row"?[89] How wonderful. Yet that was not the important point. What mattered was that the English Zionist Federation was absorbed into Empire House, the home of Milner's *Round Table Quarterly Review*,[90] at the heart of the very court of influence which dominated British political thinking. Weizmann and his organization were literally embraced by the Secret Elite's inner-most think-tank. 175 Piccadilly became the hub "towards which generated everything in Zionist life."[91] Incredible. One building, two organs of political influence and a shared interest. 175 Piccadilly was a very significant address. Its importance was kept well away from public scrutiny.

Louis Brandeis and Chaim Weizmann were intimately involved in promoting Zionist intentions behind the backs of their political allies. But they hid it well. Louis Brandeis's biographer, Alpheus Thomas Mason, was authorized and approved by the Supreme Court judge himself and given full access to all his public papers, notebooks, diaries, memoranda, archived letters and personal correspondence.[92] Yet, in his 240,000-word scholarly work, only two small paragraphs, ten lines in total, cover Brandeis's feverish activities between April and June 1917.[93] The truth remains far more revealing.

The three-month period between April and June 1917 was peppered with urgent cables between Brandeis in Washington and Weizmann and James Rothschild in London, updating each other about privileged meetings, opinions and actions to be taken to advance the Zionist plan.[94] Unknown to elected politicians and Cabinet members in both countries, these men operated a clandestine cell of Zionist interest whose specific purpose was to normalize, validate and protect the idea of a Jewish homeland in Palestine. Their targets were A.J. Balfour and President Woodrow Wilson. The British Foreign Secretary was known to be sympathetic; the American president had yet to give his approval.

Even before America had formally declared war on Germany (6 April, 1917), the London cabal insisted that increased pressure be brought on the President to approve the Zionist cause. Every opportunity which presented itself had to be taken. Urged by the American ambassador at London, Walter Page, the British Government decided to send a distinguished commission to the United States on the day before America declared war on Germany.[95] America's entry profoundly altered the ground rules but not the ultimate aim to crush Germany. Lloyd George chose the near seventy-year old Arthur Balfour, former Prime Minister and current foreign secretary, to lead the charm offensive.

A.J. Balfour's mission to the United States in 1917 proved a crucial turning point. The Foreign Secretary had been primed by Weizmann to speak with Brandeis when he was in Washington. The two men were introduced at a reception in the White House on 23 April and Balfour was reported to have greeted the Judge with: "You are one of the Americans I had wanted to meet."[96] Why, other than to gauge the strength of American-Jewish support for a homeland in Palestine? They met several times, but not in the White House. Over the following days and unknown to the President, his Supreme Court judge and the visiting British Foreign Secretary had their first private breakfast together.[97] Whatever was on the menu for discussion was kept secret.

Balfour was in Washington to bolster the Allied cause and he and the President's main advisor, Mandell House, specifically discussed the terms which might be imposed on Germany once it had been destroyed. On 28 April, Balfour produced a map of Europe and Asia Minor on which was traced the results of the secret treaties and agreements with Britain and France (Sykes-Picot). They had, in House's words, "divided up the bearskin before the bear was dead."[98] Interestingly, Constantinople no longer featured as a Russian possession[99] and there was no mention of a Jewish Homeland. None. Once he was informed of this, Brandeis felt obliged to intervene. He had a forty-five minute meeting with Wilson on 6 May to assure him that the establishment of a Jewish Palestine was completely in line with the President's concept of a just peace settlement. The British Zionists wanted assurance that their American compatriots approved the general plan for a Jewish homeland in Palestine and would publicize their support. On 9 May, Brandeis sent a cable to James Rothschild in which he announced the American Zionist approval for the British program.[100] This was followed by another secret morning discussion with A.J. Balfour and on 15 May, Brandeis reported back to Weizmann and Rothschild that their objective had been achieved. The precise wording demonstrated the extent to which the leading Zionists on both sides of the Atlantic were actively influencing their respective governments. Brandeis's cable read:

> Interviews both with President and Balfour were eminently satisfactory confirming our previous impressions as to reliable support in both directions. Presented views in line with your program [but] was assured that present circumstances did not make Government utterances desirable.[101]

Private conversations between the President and the visiting Foreign Secretary were secretly passed across the Atlantic without compunction in contravention of a variety of secrecy acts.

Louis Brandeis continued to press Wilson for a public commitment on a Jewish homeland, but caution was advised. His cable to James Rothschild on 23 May stated that Balfour told him: "if we exercised patience and allowed events to take their natural course, we would obtain more." According to Brandeis, President Wilson was reluctant to make a public declaration because the United States was not at war with Turkey. So much for the notion that Judge Brandeis limited his activities to matters of law. His secret collusion with British Zionists should have raised concerns about a conflict of interest, but that paled into insignificance when compared with his involvement in destroying a clandestine American mission to Europe.

In early June 1917 an extremely concerned Louis Brandeis made an urgent call to London. He had discovered that a secret American mission, headed by the former United States Ambassador at Constantinople, Henry Morgenthau, was on its way to Switzerland. Its purpose was to convince Turkey to break away from the German-Austrian alliance, an action which would have radically altered the geo-political situation when the war ended. Indeed, if successful, it would also have shortened the war. Former ambassador Morgenthau believed that a combination of German domination and war famine was making life unbearable in Turkey. Even the Young Turks had become "heartily sick of their German masters."[102]

Henry Morgenthau thought that he understood the Turkish mind. His plan was to go to Switzerland to meet former members of the Ottoman cabinet and offer generous peace terms and "any other means" (by that he meant bribes) to encourage them to abandon their allies. Initially, Robert Lansing, the U.S. Secretary of State, had talked over the proposal with Arthur Balfour. The British Foreign Secretary suggested that since Switzerland was ridden with spies, Morgenthau should use Egypt as a base ... as if Egypt wasn't riddled with spies. It afforded the very plausible excuse that the American delegation was concerned with the condition of Jews in Palestine. Lansing agreed and an American Zionist, Felix Frankfurter, was added to the mission. The mission had been sanctioned without due consideration of its possible consequences.

Judge Louis Brandeis learned about the venture *after* the Americans had departed for a rendezvous with their Allied compatriots in Europe.[103] He immediately understood the mortal danger which any such rapprochement with the Turks would bring to their ambitions. Brandeis alerted Chaim Weizmann. They both realized that these negotiations could completely undermine their carefully constructed plans. In June 1917 there was no Jewish homeland. The very concept was at best paper-talk and had yet to be formally accepted by any of the major powers. A generous settlement for the Turks, which might have left Palestine intact, would have destroyed the Zionist ambitions before the world war had ended.

In London, Weizmann's contacts at the Foreign Office confirmed Brandeis's anxiety. He learned that the proposed British contingent contained envoys whom he did not consider as "proper persons" for such a mission.[104] Since when did unelected observers make decisions on who was or was not a "proper person" to undertake a Foreign Office assignment? Weizmann turned to C.P. Scott at the *Manchester Guardian*, and within a matter of days was invited to speak behind closed doors with A.J. Balfour, recently returned from Washington.

What emerged was an astonishing acknowledgment of Zionist complicity in scuttling the American mission. In complete secrecy, Balfour appointed Weizmann as the British representative to meet Morgenthau. Not a career diplomat. Not a Jewish member of the House of Lords or Commons. He gave the task to a "proper person." The leader of the Zionist movement in Britain, Chaim Weizmann, was formally appointed by the Foreign Office as Britain's representative to a secret mission which, had it been allowed to progress unmolested, could have radically shortened the war. Weizmann was given a formidable set of credentials, his own intelligence officer and the responsibility to stop Henry Morgenthau in his tracks.[105]

Weizmann grasped the opportunity. The Secret Elite chose to use him for their own needs. Their ultimate plan not only for Palestine, but the entire Middle East, would have been seriously compromised had Morgenthau successfully disengaged Turkey from the war. For the Zionists it was imperative that their fight for a homeland in Palestine was approved by one of the Great Powers *before* the end of the fighting. Weizmann, accompanied by Sir Ronald Graham[106] and Lord Walter Rothschild met Balfour again. They put one condition on the table. The time had come for a definitive declaration of support for a Jewish homeland in Palestine. This had to be acknowledged – urgently – in case an unexpected peace closed down the opportunity. Balfour agreed. In fact, he did more than agree. He asked Weizmann to submit a form of words that would satisfy the Zionist aspiration, and promised to take it to Lloyd George's War Cabinet.[107] Here was the golden chance which could not be missed. This was the starting point for the formal declaration which would be endorsed by the War Cabinet.

Behind the scenes in America, Louis Brandeis succeeded in completely overturning the original position held by Robert Lansing at the State Department. The plan that had been given official sanction had to be scuppered. On 25 June, while Morgenthau was en-route across the Atlantic on the SS *Buenos Aires*, an urgent telegram was sent from Washington to Balfour alerting the British to Morgenthau's arrival in Europe. Lansing specifically stated that "it is considerably important that Chaim Weizmann meet Mr. Morgenthau at Gibraltar."[108] How extraordinary. Secretary Lansing requested that his own former ambassador should meet Chaim Weizmann, the leader of the British Zionists before proceeding further. On the same day he instructed the American Ambassador (Willard) at Madrid to ensure that, as soon as he landed, Morgenthau fully understood that he was ordered to go to Gibraltar to meet Weizmann. This instruction was to be sent by "special red code strictly confidential."[109] Who was in charge of American foreign policy, Lansing or Brandeis?

While the choice of Weizmann as the main British negotiator was inspired, it was little wonder that his involvement, and indeed the whole mission, was a closely guarded secret. The Americans were halted in Gibraltar, ostensibly to agree on how the Turks might be approached. With all the weight and authority of his Zionist credentials, Weizmann pressed Morgenthau on his intentions. Why did he imagine that the Zionist organizations on either side of the Atlantic supported his actions? Did he realize that his proposals would compromise everything that Jewish organizations had been working towards? Realizing what he was up against, Morganthau abandoned the mission within two days of Weizmann's onslaught. He back-tracked to the comfort of Biarritz and left France on 12 July without informing Ambassador Willard of his future plans.[110]

His ego seriously dented, Morgenthau dispatched his own heart-felt complaint to Washington. Given the ease with which diplomatic telegrams could be intercepted, the Americans were appalled. He received a stinging rebuke from Lansing's office, which was as much for international consumption as it was for Morgenthau's. The telegram read:

> Department surprised and disturbed that your text seems to indicate you have been authorized to enter into negotiations which would lead to a separate peace with Turkey.... Final instructions were to deal solely with the conditions of Jews in Palestine ... under no circumstances confer, discuss or carry messages about internal situation in Turkey or a separate peace.[111]

The aims of the Secret Elite and the Zionist movement began to move in tandem. Consider carefully what had happened. Brandeis had interfered directly with U.S. State Department policy. Furthermore, he did not hesitate to pass secret information to Chaim Weizmann and James Rothschild in London so that Morgenthau's plans would be thwarted, nominally by the British government. Weizmann, in turn, was ushered in as the Foreign Office solution. Though by 1917 he was a naturalized British citizen, Chaim Weizmann was no diplomat or civil servant. He was a zealot for an unbending cause. By pitting a most able and skilled Jewish negotiator against a moderate (at best) American-Jewish diplomat, the Secret Elite approved an inspired appointment. Weizmann crushed Morgenthau with deep-felt passion. At an even deeper level of conspiracy Brandeis had nailed his colors, not to Old Glory, but to the Zionist flag borne by Chaim Weizmann and James Rothschild.

Weizmann the zealot lived for one purpose in 1917. His determination was absolute. He wrote to Philip Kerr, a Milner protégé and one of

Lloyd George's "secretaries": "Some Jews and non-Jews do not seem to realize one fundamental fact, that whatever happens we will get to Palestine."[112] And what of Louis Brandeis? He chose to promote and protect the Zionist vision of a Jewish homeland in Palestine in favor of an action which could well have ended the war before American troops landed in Europe. American lives or a Jewish homeland in Palestine? Did Louis Brandeis ever consider that thought?

Long after these events, in September 1922, President Warren G. Harding affirmed the establishment of a Jewish homeland in Palestine,[113] against the advice of his officials in the State Department.[114] One of but a few who spoke out against a well-organized Jewish lobby was Professor E.B. Reed of Yale, who had served as a Red Cross worker in Palestine for three and a half months in 1919. He testified that the Zionist program would bring oppression to the Arab majority in Palestine, that it was illegal and violated Arab rights.[115] In his memoirs, Chaim Weizmann recalled, incorrectly, that Professor Reed was a Senator. What annoyed him was Reed's accusation that the leaders of the Zionist movement were unworthy men, and that he (Weizmann) had prolonged the war by undermining the Morgenthau mission.[116] Strange that he remained in such deep denial.

Summary.

- Several distinguished Jewish-Israeli historians have dared to tackle the historical misrepresentations which surround the received version of Jewish history. Shlomo Sand attacked the "authorized agents of memory" who used terms like "exile," "diaspora" or "land of redemption."
- Others like Adiyah Horon and Ilan Pappe have dismissed the myth history which has grown into popular acceptance. Christians have tended to equated the bible stories with actual history even although there is no proof whatsoever for concepts like the "diaspora."
- The myth of the thirteenth tribe, the ancient Ashkenazim Jews, has been unmasked by Arthur Koestler and more recently by Peter Frankopan, as a ninth century mass conversion to Judaism. Eran Elhaik, an Israeli geneticist, has shown that their ancestral origins were not from the Middle East or indeed the Mediterranean but from a region that is now in north east Turkey.
- The point of the above is to alert readers to the fact that when the Secret Elite agents in London make reference to Palestine as a Jewish Homeland, they are using biblical terms which would be challenged today.
- The letter from the British foreign secretary, Arthur Balfour to Lord Walter Rothschild of 2 November 1917, remains one of the most contentious documents in modern history. It was the result of several years of lobbying by major British and American Zionists who used the opportunity of war to promote their long-term agenda. A Jewish state in Palestine.
- Alfred Milner was a keen supporter of a "National Home' for the Jewish Race. So too was Leo Amery and Arthur Balfour. It transpired that the

final Balfour Declaration was the end product of considerable correspondence between the British government and Walter Rothschild, Chaim Weizmann and the Zionist Federation in Britain.

- Discussions on the final wording had also been approved by President Wilson in America, supported by his Zionist Supreme Court Judge, Louis Brandeis.
- Zionism appeared on the political radar early in the twentieth century, though its roots lay earlier. Care must be taken when using the term. Initially, many Jews believed in its religious spirituality. A small but very determined group led by Chaim Weizmann in England, advocated a much more radical political solution to their perceived problem. They wanted a Jewish homeland in Palestine.
- The flag-bearer for Zionism in America was Louis Brandeis, a Boston Lawyer whom Woodrow Wilson elevated to the Supreme Court.
- When America declared war on Germany, Weizmann and Brandeis acted together to promote the Zionist ambition for Palestine. They undermined the Morgenthau mission to dislodge Turkey from Germany even though that would have shortened the war.
- Brandeis colluded with Weizmann and James Rothschild in England behind the backs of his colleagues in Wilson's administration. He ensured that they knew about secret conversations. He convinced Lansing, the American Secretary of State, to revoke his instructions to former Ambassador Morgenthau.

Chapter 29

The Balfour Declaration – Perfidious Albion

At the start of the First World War, the lands which we have come to know as the Middle East in a great sweep from the Caspian to the Red Sea, comprised a hodge-podge of factions and tribes, communities born into religious friction, wastelands and deserts, remote townships and cities with Biblical names. The Ottoman Empire had held these areas in subjugation by fear and cruelty. T.E. Lawrence, the legendary hero of the Arab rising of 1916, described the jig-saw-puzzle nature of the native peoples in his *Seven Pillars of Wisdom*.[1] He painted a detailed picture of a colorful land comprising many religions and cultures with little sense of tolerance. Ansariyas, distrustful of Islam, colonies of Syrian Christians, Armenians and Druses were to be found to the north from the Euphrates Valley down to the southern coast of the Mediterranean. Kurds populated the territory to the north-east and they hated, in order, the native Christians, then the Turks and finally all Europeans. There were settled Arabs to the east of Aleppo, semi-pastoral Muslim communities, Bedouins and some Ismaili outcasts. Between Tripoli and Beirut, Lebanese Christians, Maronite or Greek, united in their disdain for Muslims but barely tolerated each other. On the banks of the Jordan valley, Algerian refugees faced Jewish villages. These too were diverse in nature with traditional Hebrew scholars on the one hand and, on the other, recent German in-comers with European-style houses paid for from charitable funds.

Lawrence thought that the land of Palestine seemed too small, too impoverished, to absorb settlers. Galilee was apparently more tolerant of newcomers than Judea. Feuds abounded. Druses hated Maronites and indulged in periodic blood-letting. Muslim Arabs despised them with a vengeance. Around Jerusalem, the German-speaking Jews "were obliged to survive" side-by-side with "sullen Palestinian peasants" whom Lawrence described as "more stupid than the yeomen of North Syria, material as the Egyptians and bankrupt."[2] Such racist stereotyping from an upper-crust, patronizing English gentleman demands reply. Were the Felhaini, whose ancestors had worked the land for thousands of years, not entitled to be sullen when their lands were taken over by foreign strangers? There was an intrinsic difference between the old settlers, with whom the Arabs had co-operated on friendly terms for generations, and the new breed of imperialistic colonists who confronted the native Arabs with threats of violence.[3]

To the south, running along the Red Sea, was the Hejaz in which lay the holy places, Mecca and Medina. The great cities of Jerusalem, Beirut, Damascus, Aleppo, Hama and Homs had a distinctive nature and admixture of religion and history. Jerusalem had its own unique quality. As Lawrence saw it, "Jerusalem was a squalid town, which every Semitic[4] religion had made holy."[5] Behind his much-acclaimed commitment to Arab nationalism and his knowledge of Arab strengths and weaknesses, T.E. Lawrence had great sympathy for Zionism.[6]

The land known as Palestine had a population of some 500,000 Muslims, 60,000 Jews and a similar number of Christians.[7] A British War Cabinet paper written by Lord Curzon noted that under the Turkish yoke there was no country called Palestine, "because it was divided between the sank of Jerusalem and the vilayets of Syria and Beirut."[8] He estimated that there were between 600-700,000 inhabitants, of whom less than one-quarter were Jews. What he described was a patchwork of largely poor communities and tribes, disunited and distrusting, hardly a blade away from each other's throat. It was no single people's homeland but was, most certainly, predominantly Arab.

Yet the Young Turks achieved the nearly impossible feat of uniting all classes of culture and creed against the Ottomans by suppressing them with ruthless cruelty.[9] In Syria, the Arabs, the largest of the indigenous natives, were treated with contempt, their culture and language suppressed, their societies disbanded, their leaders proscribed. The Turks tried to crush Arab nationalism but the Arabs had watched what happened to the Armenians who had been isolated and systematically wiped out, and sought to establish their own sovereign land.[10] To achieve that, they needed allies who would stand by them again the hated Turk.

The importance of the Arab populations to the Allied war effort cannot be understated. Kitchener, when he was Consul-General in Cairo from 1911-14, was well aware of the desert undercurrents; the shifting sands of loyalty and treachery which his spies reported. His first priority was to safeguard British imperial interests. He knew that the Arab dream of independence was rooted in Hussein ibn Ali al-Hashimi, the Sharif of Mecca, and his sons, whose ambition was to gather a vast Arab confederacy under the suzerainty of their family and reconstitute an Arab Empire.[11] Though bogged down in the mire of the Western Front, Kitchener retained his relationship with the Husseins, custodians of Islam's holiest shrines, and when the futile attack on the Dardanelles was deliberately allowed to fail (see Chapters 9-10), they hoped that an Arab alliance with Britain would neutralize the chances of the Ottoman sultan-caliph's call to jihad. The British wanted "to rob the call to Holy War of its principal thunderbolt," by striking an agreement with the Husseins themselves.[12] Consequently, the Foreign Office instructed Sir Henry McMahon, the British High Commissioner in Egypt to offer Hussein of Mecca Britain's commitment to an independent Arab state in a "firm and

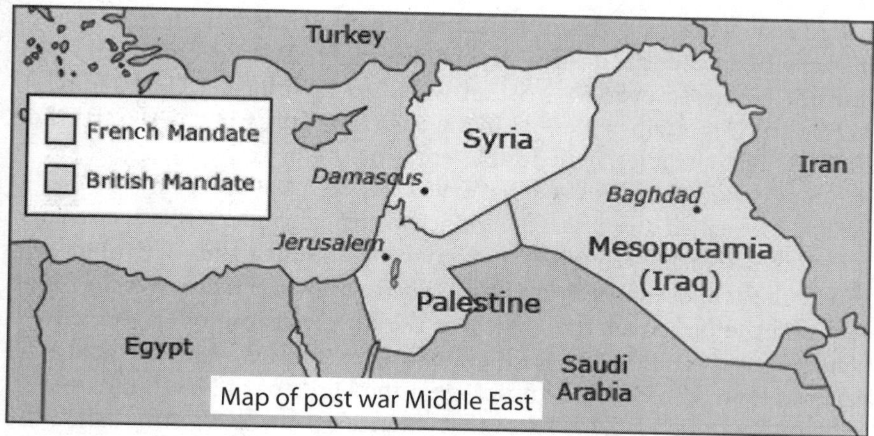

Map of post war Middle East

lasting alliance, the immediate results of which will be the expulsion of the Turks from the Arab countries…"[13] This formal promise was given in October 1915.[14] Palestine was included in the areas which the British government pledged would be an independent Arab country.[15] The Arab uprising against Turkish rule was based on that unambiguous promise.

The Foreign Office then proceeded to make a very different pact with the French. An Arab Bureau had been created in January 1916 to harmonize a wide range of political activity in the Near East to keep a watchful eye on the German-Turkish activities and co-ordinate propaganda. An interdepartmental conference agreed on the need for a single bureau stationed at Cairo to focus on Arab activities. Amongst the select group which made this decision was Captain W.F. ("Blinker") Hall, the Director of Intelligence at the Admiralty, Sir Maurice Hankey, the Cabinet secretary and Sir Mark Sykes at the Foreign Office.[16]

Britain's commitment to the Arabs was short-lived and utterly worthless. Rarely have a people been promised so much, then denied their just deserts with such callous disregard. Sir Mark Sykes was instructed by the Foreign Office to negotiate the redistribution of Turkish lands with Charles Georges-Picot, the former French consul-general in Beirut and the Quai d'Orsay's adviser on Middle Eastern affairs. They secretly agreed on the future boundaries of the Arab lands which would be dismantled and shared between them when the war was won. The Czarist Foreign Secretary Sazonov was also involved, since the Russians intended to grab a share of the rotting Ottoman carcass. Lines were drawn by Sykes and Picot to delineate a French Zone, which would include all of Syria north of Acre and west of Damascus and Aleppo, and a British Zone comprising the Tigris and Euphrates from north of Baghdad to the Persian Gulf across northern Arabia to what later became Jordan. Palestine would be a jointly controlled Allied responsibility.[17] For centuries, classical scholars had used different names and interpretations to describe the land sometimes called Asia Minor or Mesopotamia and Syria. Although no country had actually been called Palestine, the name emerged as a geographical term current in the so-called Christian world to include the "Holy Land."[18] While the Arab tribes were rising against the Turks in the desert, their faithless British Allies were double-crossing them.

Sir Edward Grey believed that Sykes had been too generous, but, vitally, he had forestalled any rift in the Franco-British alliance.[19] This is a remarkable claim. British foreign policy was never left in the hands of a minor official. If Grey believed that Sykes had avoided a rift with France over the future spoils in the Near East then that was the main purpose of the exercise. It was an agreed position whose ultimate worth would be determined once the war was won. What we do know is that the Director of Naval Intelligence, William Reginald Hall, indicated that "France's claim to Palestine cannot be justified."[20] The British government played fast and loose with all of its allies.

Thus two violently opposed arrangements were agreed to. The first was a clear pledge to the Arabs; the second was an act of betrayal which would deny them the promise of full independence. Critically, the Arabs knew nothing about the Sykes-Picot pact and remained in the dark until the Bolshevik's came to power in Russia and unmasked the secret double-cross.

The Arab cause was severely handicapped because it had no voice at the heart of the Secret Elite and no champion in Parliament. Financial and industrial powers wanted control of the resources under the sands and cared little for the indigenous population. In fact the Arabs were mere pawns in a larger game of international chess. Even at the lesser levels of power, they had no influential advocate. They were disadvantaged at every turn. T.E. Lawrence, who fought side-by-side with Faisal and the Husseins, knew that he was merely part of a conspiracy. Lawrence had personally endorsed the promises made by the British Cabinet, assuring the Arabs that their reward would be self-government. He wrote of "our essential insincerity," of his conviction that "it was better we win and break our word, than lose" the war in Arabia. His much heralded relationship with the Arabs was underpinned by fraud and he knew it.[21] Lawrence's comments were made in relation to the Sykes-Picot agreement, of which he had been fully informed. He was not party to the Balfour Declaration, but his Zionist sympathies later became apparent.

The Machiavellian intrigues which took place in London and Washington added a deeper level to this deceit. It had been argued that the British government, and A.J. Balfour in particular, did not fully realize what they were doing when they approved the fateful decision to support a Jewish homeland in Palestine. This was patently untrue. Two of the most experienced politicians in the British Empire, Lord George Curzon, former Viceroy and Governor-General of India and Edwin Montagu, the Secretary of State for India, both lobbied the War Cabinet against entering into an agreement with the Zionists without a much fuller analysis of what that would mean. Their papers on "The Future of Palestine[22] and Zionism"[23] should have been taken seriously, but were ignored. Indeed their views were presented to the War Cabinet so late in the day that they had the feel of a cosmetic device to imply some kind of balanced judgment – mere dressing.

Curzon agonized about conditions in Palestine where the Turks had broken up or dislocated Jewish colonies and warned that after the ravages of war and centuries of neglect and misrule, any revival would depend on a colossal investment. He warned that Palestine had no natural wealth. The land contained no mineral wealth, no coal, no iron ore, no copper, gold or silver. Crucially, Curzon alluded to a more immediate problem. What would happen to the non-Jewish inhabitants? He estimated that there were "over half a million Syrian Arabs – a mixed community with Arab, Hebrew, Canaanite, Greek, Egyptian and possibly Crusader blood. They and their forefathers have occupied the country for the best part of 1,500 years. They own the soil … they profess the Mohammedan faith. They will not be content either to be expropriated for Jewish immigrants or to act merely as hewers of wood and drawers of water to the latter."[24] He also informed them that anyone who glibly dreamt of a Jewish Capital in Jerusalem did not appreciate the complexity of the "holy places." Too many people and too many religions had such a passionate and permanent interest that any such outcome was not even "dimly possible." His final warning was profoundly clear: "In my judgment, it [Zionism] is a policy very widely removed from the romantic and idealistic aspirations of many Zionist leaders whose literature I have studied, and whatever it does, it will not in my judgment provide either a national, a material or even a spiritual home for any more than a very small section of the Jewish people."[25] His analysis was superb. His words were left to gather dust on the cabinet shelves and have been ignored because it destroyed the illusion which Zionists repeated about a land without people waiting for a people without land.

Edwin Montagu's Cabinet paper on Zionism was distributed at the same meeting. It included a highly perceptive report from Miss Gertrude Lowthian Bell, the acting Political Officer in Baghdad. The Oxford-educated writer and sometimes British Intelligence operative pointed out that: "Jewish immigration has been artificially fostered by doles and subventions from millionaire co-religionists in Europe; [The most prolific giver of doles and subventions was Edmond de Rothschild]…. The pious hope that an independent Jewish state may some day be established in Palestine no doubt exists though it must be questioned whether among local Jews there is any acute desire to see it realized, except as a means to escape from Turkish oppression; it is perhaps more lively in the breasts of those who live far from the rocky Palestine hills and have no intention of changing their domicile." Lord Cromer took pleasure in relating a conversation he held on the subject with one of the best known English Jews who observed: "If a Jewish kingdom were to be established in Jerusalem, I should lose no time in applying for the post of Ambassador in London."[26]

Gertrude Bell's acutely accurate observation held the key to understanding what was happening. The clarion call for a Jewish homeland in Palestine came not from the small Jewish communities which had been established there or the few more recent immigrant settlers. Naturally those Jews who, together with their Arab and Muslim neighbors, had suffered under the harsh Turkish yoke, welcomed change. What she questioned was the validity of those who canvassed for a "homeland" to which they had no intention to return. How many of those Britons or Americans who supported the idea of a Jewish homeland, actively considered packing their bags and moving to a community in Palestine? This was not the message that the Secret Elite wished to consider.

Edwin Montagu was the second British Jew to hold a cabinet post, that of Secretary of State for India. He had a keen interest in Muslim affairs and his concerns reflected an awareness of such sensitivities. Montagu made an observation about Chaim Weizmann which resonated with the evidence we have already presented. In recognizing Weizmann's services to the Allied cause and his reputation as an exceptional chemist, he reminded the Cabinet that Weizmann was a religious fanatic, a zealot for whom Zionism had been the guiding principle for a large part of his life. He saw in Weizmann's overwhelming enthusiasm, an inability to take into account the feelings of those from his own religion who differed from his view or, and herein lay a critical point, those of other religions whom Weizmann's activities, if successful, would dispossess.[27]

In an attempt to dispel the assumption that Weizmann's brand of Zionism was widely supported within the Jewish community in Britain, Montagu added a list of prominent British Jews active in public life whom he termed Anti-Zionist. It included professors, Rabbis, Jewish members of the Government (Sir Alfred Mond and Lord Reading) three Rothschilds, Sir Marcus Samuel (of Royal Dutch/Shell) and many more British Jews.[28] He begged the War Cabinet to pause and think before it ignored the British voice of the many Jews who had "lived for generations in this country, and who feel themselves to be Englishmen."[29] He countered claims that American Jews were in favor of Zionism by quoting from the Convention of the Central Conference of Jewish Rabbis held in June 1917: "The religious Israel, having the sanctions of history, must not be sacrificed to the purely racial Israel of modern times." Note how the term Israel was used. Jacob Schiff's views were included with specific emphasis on his belief that "no effort should be made to re-establish a Jewish nation…" Similar sentiments from leading French and Italian Jews were included.

These were very deep-felt pleas. Curzon's warning ought to have alerted the experienced politicians in the War Cabinet. Milner had gone to war with the Boers to protect the Empire and its gold-mines. General Smuts knew how easily native populations resented incomers who laid claim to their land. Sir Edward Carson had brought Ireland to the brink of civil war in 1914 over the rights of different communities in the North and South of that island. The Secret Elite had come to its conclusion, and no other view was welcomed. Curzon ought to have had the courage to resign, but acquiesced in silence when the vote was taken.[30]

Balfour voiced the Foreign Office view.[31] The minutes of the War Cabinet meeting on Wednesday 31 October 1917, stated that it was their unanimous opinion that:

> ... from a purely diplomatic and political point of view, it was desirable that some declaration favourable to the aspirations of the Jewish nationalists should now be made. The vast majority of Jews in Russia and America, as indeed all over the world, now appeared to be favourable to Zionism. If we could make a declaration favourable to such an ideal, we should be able to carry on extremely useful propaganda both in Russia and America.[32]

Balfour dressed the cabinet decision in the robes of diplomacy and politics. With Russia in the throes of revolution and the possibility that they might make a separate peace with Germany, every avenue of propaganda had to be activated. Chaim Weizmann had made his mark. Though there was ample evidence to the contrary, ridiculous claims which could never have been evidenced appeared to justify the War Cabinet's decision. From whose lips did the phrase "the vast majority of Jews ... all over the world" take shape? In Britain, Jewish communities were clearly divided on the issue. Edwin Montagu provided ample proof.[33] Indeed the very notion that Zionism commanded such support was a fiction. It was the message from the zealots. This was the assurance given to Balfour by Brandeis and Weizmann. It was a lie which was repeated so often within the exalted Cabinet circle that only two men spoke against it. The evidence presented was to the contrary. In modern parlance the decision was the product of smoke and mirrors, spun to create the illusion that the British Cabinet cared about the future of impoverished Jews. Impoverished Arabs did not matter.

Weizmann, like Lloyd George, wrote his memoirs through a rose-tinted, self-congratulatory prism dispensing a multi-colored light on his chosen supporters. The omissions and misrepresentations falsified history. He wrote of "those British statesmen of the old school" who were, "genuinely religious." Inside their brand of Christian morality, he claimed they "understood as a reality the concept of the Return ... of the Jewish peoples to the Holy Land. It appealed to their tradition and their faith."[34] What breath-taking nonsense. To describe the men who had approved massacres at Omdurman in Sudan, the slaughter of the Matabele tribes to create Rhodesia,[35] the men who caused the Boer War,[36] permitted the deaths of 10,000 women and children in the vile concentration camps on the Veldt,[37] and planned and caused the world war that raged across the globe as "genuinely religious," defied reason. Theirs was a very different religion. The Secret Elite aimed to control, manage and make profitable what they deemed to be a worthy civilization built through the Empire on the foundations of English ruling-class values.[38] How can we ever weigh the sins committed in the name of religious men?

These were reflections; a justification for the British government's decision. What they did not include was a recognition that, on a higher level, the money power on both sides of the Atlantic had given its approval to the Balfour Declaration. Of course the primacy of the British Empire was uppermost in the minds of Lloyd George, Milner, Curzon and the Secret Elite politicians, but their actions were predicated on the approval of financiers and bankers.

Although some historians credit Weizmann for winning over the War Cabinet to his Zionist cause,[39] the "diplomatic and political" interests to which the Secret Elite steadfastly held course were the imperial designs which underpinned their ultimate aim to dominate all other empires. It has been said that if Zionists hadn't existed, Britain would have had to invent them.[40] Palestine was the final link in a chain which would stretch from India through Persia and the Middle East, protect the Suez Canal and give them unbridled access to the sea routes to Persia, India and the Far East. French ambitions represented a serious and lasting concern. Whether or not the Sykes-Picot-Sazanov agreement would survive the final division of spoils remained unproven in 1917. Creating a Jewish-Palestinian buffer zone under some form of British control was eminently preferable to the risk of a French protectorate along the Suez.[41]

Undeterred by warnings that it was inadequately resourced to accommodate a Jewish homeland, Balfour informed his cabinet colleagues that if Palestine was scientifically developed, a very much larger population could be sustained than had endured the Turkish misrule. (You can almost hear Brandeis and Weizmann's voices). His definition of a "national home" remained significant. He understood it to mean "some form of British, American, or other protectorate under which full facilities would be given to the Jews to work out their own salvation and to build up, by means of education, agriculture and industry, a real center of national culture and focus of national life."[42]

It was a generalized, almost throw-away interpretation which appeared to avoid any threat to other communities in Palestine. Had he ended his remarks at that, there may have been a sliver of doubt about his understanding of what might follow. But Balfour clarified his thinking, and in so doing acknowledged that the establishment of a Jewish State was in fact likely. The Cabinet minute reported his claim that "it did not necessarily involve the early establishment of an independent Jewish State, which was a matter for gradual development in accordance with the ordinary laws of political evolution."[43] Consider the thought behind these words. His message to Weizmann, the international bankers and all who had direct and indirect access to the British policy, was that if they took the opportunity which Britain presented – an independent Jewish State could be within their grasp. Put very simply, the message that Jews all over the world heard was that if they supported Britain, Britain would support them. Having said that, Balfour immediately contradicted himself by adding that the suggested declaration might raise false expectations which might never be recognised.[44] It was classic double-speak.

Expectations inside the Jewish community in Britain leaped like the proverbial salmon in the first few weeks of November 1917. The Balfour Declaration was hailed as "the greatest event in the history of the Jews since their dispersion."[45] In celebratory language that brooked no qualification, claims were made that "the House of Israel is fully conscious of the high significance of the pledge of the British Government concerning its restoration." Balfour's letter to Walter Rothschild had been read aloud in synagogues and formed the text of countless sermons. Two important intertwined threads bound expectation to action. Suddenly, the Jewish community across the world, and particularly in Britain and America, valued the Allied cause, the "principles of the invincible integrity of smaller nations." The collapse of the hated Romanov dynasty in Russia had removed one obstacle from wide-scale Jewish support for the Allies and the timely British pledge unleashed a flood of enthusiasm for victory. Jews now believed that they had a vested interest of the highest order. The Zionist conference in Baltimore unanimously passed a resolution which ended: "... we and our Allies are prepared to make every sacrifice of treasure and life, until the great war shall have ended in the triumph of the high aims of the Allied nations."[46]

On Sunday, 2 December 1917, a vast meeting was held at the London Opera House with delegates sent from Anglo-Jewish communities, synagogues and societies across Britain. It was chaired by Lord Walter Rothschild and reported almost verbatim in the *Times*. He too referred to the historic importance of the government's declaration and faithfully promised that their non-Jewish neighbors in Palestine would be respected – though *he* did not use the term "Arab." Lord Robert Cecil made the word "liberation" his keynote and welcomed representatives of the Arabian and Armenian races, whom he added were also struggling to be free. His speech was proudly that of an English imperialist, dedicated to the Secret Elite cause. Cecil stressed that: "The Empire has always striven to give all the peoples that make it up the fullest measure of self government of which they are capable." Clearly the Irish nationalists imprisoned in England after the Easter Rising did not count.[47] He ended with what today reads like a chilling prophecy. "I believe it will have a far-reaching influence on the history of the world and consequences which none can foresee on the future history of the human race."[48]

One of the participants was Sir Mark Sykes of the Sykes-Picot-Sazonov agreement. Perhaps he had forgotten the various false promises which he had helped deliver. Here was the British diplomat who had been empowered by the Foreign Office to re-draw the map of the Ottoman Empire, which ceded joint ownership of Palestine to France. As a member of the Arab Bureau in Cairo he supported Faisal's Arab revolt in the desert. Now he appeared as an enthusiast for Palestine as a Jewish homeland. In each scenario, Palestine, or parts thereof, had been promised to a different party; shared ownership with France, Arab suzerainty and a Jewish homeland. Lies and false promises did not appear to concern him. Mark Sykes talked of the great mission of Zionism to bring the spirituality of Asia to Europe and the vitality of Europe to Asia. His nonsense ended in empty praise for the inclusion of "your fellows in adversity, the Armenians and the Arabs." Was anyone listening? There was one speaker who addressed the meeting in Arabic, Sheikh Ismail Abdul-Al-Akki, himself sentenced to death by the Turks for having joined the Arab nationalist movement. He appealed to the gathering not to forget that the sons of Ishmael[49] had also been scattered and confounded, but were now rising "fortified with sense of martyrs."[50] They cheered wildly; it was that kind of stage-managed event.

One week later a joyous celebration of Jewish gratitude took place in the Manchester Hippodrome. Sir Mark Sykes made a most interesting observation. His had been the only voice which cautioned care in taking serious account of native Armenians and Arabs who lived in or around Palestine. He warned that they too must be freed from oppression. His words have echoed down the century since: "It was the destiny of the Jews to be closely connected with the Arab revival, and co-operation and good will from the first were necessary, or *ultimate disaster would overtake both Jew and Arab*."[51] Unfortunately, his words were not welcomed. Chaim Weizmann objected to Sir Mark Sykes's warning: "It is strange indeed to hear the fear expressed that the Jew who has always been the victim, the Jew who has always fought the battle of freedom for others, should suddenly become the aggressor because he touches Palestinian soil."[52]

What a strange over-reaction. Weizmann and the Zionists held criticism on a short fuse. In the swelling chambers of organized celebration, Britain's commitment to "facilitate" the establishment of a national home for Jews had been translated by joyous sermon, by excited word of mouth and jubilant newspaper editorials into a fait accompli. What the faithful heard was the promised return to the Holy Land. The tragedy was that the Secret Elite had unleashed expectations they could never control. Undoubtedly, greater emphasis should have been given to the second part of the Balfour Declaration, namely: "it being clearly understood that nothing shall be done which may reduce the civil and religious rights of the existing non-Jewish communities in Palestine or the rights and political status enjoyed by Jews in any other country."[53] It was ignored.

The immediate dividend from the Balfour Declaration was its propaganda value. The Foreign Office set up a special branch for Jewish propaganda, the Jewish Bureau, in the Department of Information under a "very active Zionist,"[54] Albert Montefiore Hyamson, previously editor of the *Zionist Review*. He distributed daily copy to two Jewish daily newspapers in the United States, the *American Hebrew* and *American Jewish Chronicle*. Leaflets containing the text of the Balfour Declaration were dropped over German and Austrian territory. Pamphlets written in Yiddish were circulated to Jewish troops encouraging them to "stop fighting the Allies ... an Allied victory means the Jewish people's return to Zion."[55]

Co-incidentally, the Arab revolt against the Turks, lead by Sherif Hussein and advised by T.E. Lawrence was undermining Turkish defenses in the desert. In the wake of two failed efforts by Sir Archibald Murray to capture Gaza, General Edmund Allenby was commissioned to take charge of the desert wars. The Arabs had captured Aqaba in July; Allenby's troops, boosted by the fact that the Middle-Eastern Theatre had become the second largest campaign after the Western Front, took Beersheba and then Jaffa. On 9 December 1917, Jerusalem capitulated without a fight. On December 11, Allenby entered Jerusalem. He had the wit to understand the symbolic importance of the city both to its residents and to religious communities across the world. General Allenby chose to enter Jerusalem on foot through the Jaffa Gate giving British propaganda a wonderful photo-opportunity. His modest and respectful acceptance of the keys to the city was intended to contrast with the Kaiser's visit in 1898 when Wilhelm inadvisedly insisted on entering the old city on a white horse.[56] Charles Picot, the French political representative, had been allowed to share the cautiously triumphant entrance to Jerusalem and duly announced that he would establish the civil government under French jurisdiction. Allenby cut him dead. The civil government would be properly established after he (Allenby) judged that the military situation warranted it.[57] Britain had no intention of surrendering to France the hard-won parts of Palestine which they had captured. Imagine the message that would have been transmitted to the Zionist world had the French taken charge.

For self-evident reasons, the Balfour Declaration had not been publicized in Palestine but the news filtered through. A Foreign Office report on 20 December from Sir Gilbert Clayton at the Arab Bureau noted that

"The Arabs are still nervous and feel the Zionist movement is progressing at a pace which threatens their interests. Discussions and intercourse with Jews will doubtless calm their fears, provided [the] latter act up to liberal principles laid down by Jewish leaders in London."[58] Aye, there's the rub.

By January 1918, Lloyd George's War Cabinet realized that the unprecedented political success which had followed the announcement of the government's declaration required evidence of action. A Zionist Commission was dispatched to Palestine. Led by Chaim Weizmann, in whom the Secret Elite vested a great deal of confidence, it was accompanied by one of Lloyd George's pro-Zionist minders, William Ormsby-Gore.[59] In advance of its arrival the Foreign Office issued explicit instructions to the High Commissioner in Egypt to help create Jewish institutions "should military exigencies permit." The British government "favoured" the foundation of a Jewish University and Medical School, to which the "Jewish world attaches importance and for which large sums are coming in..."[60] From which sources were these funds flowing? Who was investing in the development of the homeland dream?

They also wanted to encourage good relations with non-Jewish communities and use the Commission as a direct link between the military and Jewish interests in Palestine. The task was enormous. Everything possible had to be done to invest credibility in the Zionist Commission in the eyes of the Jewish world and at the same time, allay Arab suspicions about the ultimate aims of Zionism.[61] Hercules would have baulked at such a task.

The military governor of Jerusalem, Ronald Storrs, did not see eye to eye with Chaim Weizmann. He refused to accept that it was Weizmann's responsibility to make sure that the Arabs and Syrians accepted the British government's policy on the future of the Jews in Palestine. He pointed to the many articles in the British Press supportive of the Zionist cause. Naturally these had unsettled Muslim confidence. Public meetings at which speakers attempted to show how the Jewish people could take over the "Holy Land" only served to exacerbate the matter. What had Weizmann expected? Storrs stressed that Palestine was a Muslim country fallen into the hands of a Christian Power, which promptly announced that a considerable proportion of its land area was to be handed over for colonization by a "nowhere very popular people."[62] The Commission had been warned in Cairo that rumors and misrepresentations were circulating throughout the region and they should make a clear statement to clarify their intentions. That, they had no intention of doing.

By late April 1918, Chaim Weizmann changed tack to offer reassurance to local Arabs. He told them that the Commission would never take advantage of low land prices caused by the war. He claimed that he wanted to improve opportunities for all and establish technical and other schools which would be open to Muslims, Christians and Jews. This spirit of conciliation had some effect, but behind the scenes Weizmann undermined the Arabs.

In a letter to Balfour at the end of May 1918, he blamed the "problems" confronting the Zionist Commission on "the treacherous nature of the Arab." Though by Weizmann's calculations there were "five Arabs to one Jew" ... he boasted that they would not be able to create an Arab Palestine because the "fellah" (the peasant laborer) was at least four hundred years behind the times and the "Effendi" (Master) was "dishonest, uneducated, greedy and as unpatriotic as he is inefficient."[63] These were not sympathies of conciliation. They were naked racist excuses for colonialism.

There was a real purpose behind these machinations. Having realized that the war might end before substantial changes could be implemented in Palestine, Weizmann urged that tangible achievements had to be registered quickly. The foundation of a Jewish University and greater autonomy for Jewish communities had to be agreed "so that when the time comes for the Peace Conference certain definite steps will have been taken which will give Zionists some right to be heard."[64] At last the truth.

Before November 1917 no public position had been taken on the future of Palestine. Thereafter there was a proposal to establish a Jewish homeland under certain conditions. But the future of Palestine was included in three radically different commitments made by the British government to the French, the Arabs and the Jews. The first could be bought off with Syria. The Arabs, well, they were considered a lesser race by the Secret Elite and, it was presumed, could be led down a different path. A distinct minority of world Jewry, by that time described as Zionists, offered a very interesting opportunity. The Empire's strategic security could be greatly enhanced by a Jewish Palestine which owed its existence to Britain.

Behind the political enthusiasm for a Jewish homeland displayed so publicly by the War Cabinet was this question: who was influencing *them*? Which of the small number of Zionist enthusiasts penetrated their inner circle and found favor with the Secret Elite? The primary answer was the House of Rothschild. Not every Rothschild, no, but over the span of 1914-1917 significant Rothschilds championed the Zionist cause and were seen by the public, especially the Jewish public, as its real leaders. Baron Edmond de Rothschild in Paris was the first of the nineteenth-century Rothschilds to help Russian victims of the vile pogroms to emigrate to Palestine between 1881-2 and throughout the prewar years, he acquired and supported several communities in Palestine. By 1903 nineteen out of twenty-eight Jewish settlements in Palestine were subsidized partly or wholly by him. It was claimed that Edmond's commitment was not aimed at the creation of a Jewish state.[65] That is convenient, for once war was underway, it was he who urged Weizmann to seize the opportunity to establish a Jewish Palestine.[66]

In London, under the patronage of Lord Nathaniel, the Rothschilds had apparently expressed no particularly strong enthusiasm for Palestine.

They were considered to be disinterested until Natty died in 1915. Described at his funeral as the "leader of his far-flung brothers ... the Prince of the Diasporas of Israel"[67] by the Chief Rabbi of the British Empire, the great "Natty" held a "quasi-monarchial status within British Jewry."[68] Yet again myth-history gave rise to extravagant titles. Suddenly, Natty Rothschild was transformed into a mythological royal figure reigning over a mythological diaspora.

If Nathaniel was King, Walter was his heir. It was to Walter Rothschild that Balfour's Declaration was sent because, for much of the preceding year, Walter had been actively promoting Zionism in company with Chaim Weizmann. Walter has long been described first and foremost as a zoologist who collected exotic birds and animals; a reluctant banker; a very shy man with a speech impediment.[69] The evidence from which we have analyzed the Balfour Declaration stands testament to a different truth. It was Walter Rothschild who drafted and re-drafted letters to Foreign Secretary Balfour in 1917.[70] He opposed the idea that power in Palestine might be shared between Britain and France and told Chaim Weizmann that Palestine must become a British Protectorate.[71]

Walter did not flinch when confronted by the many Jews opposed to political Zionism. He tackled them head-on. He wrote to the *Times* on several occasions to condemn leading Jewish opponents. When the presidents of the Jewish Board of Deputies and the Anglo-Jewish Association published what he deemed to be a manifesto against Zionism, both he and Weizmann wrote stinging letters of condemnation. Walter Rothschild then had the authors of the letter censured at the next meeting of the Board of Deputies and used his father's name to justify his position. It was generally believed that Natty Rothschild had little time for Zionists but Walter insisted that "during the latter years of his life, [his father] had frequently told him that in principle he was in favor of the establishment of a Jewish National homeland in Palestine, but not so long as Palestine was in Turkish hands."[72] Walter pressed both Lloyd George and Balfour to make a clear statement in favor of a Jewish homeland, and accompanied Weizmann when he went to persuade Balfour that a Jewish homeland had to have an expression of support before the war ended.[73] After the Declaration, Walter presided over a triumphant mass meeting at the London Opera House on 2 December and spoke eloquently. Clearly no mere zoologist, Walter Rothschild was intimately involved in the successful delivery of the Balfour Declaration.

So too was the French-born James de Rothschild, Edmond's son. James had been educated at Trinity College, Cambridge, and shared his father's enthusiasm for Jewish communities in Palestine. Chaim Weismann corresponded with him,[74] and visited his wife, Dorothy Pinto,[75] while James was serving in France. He attended a special meeting on 17 Feb, 1917, with Weizmann, Walter Rothschild, Herbert Samuel and Sir Mark

Sykes. This pressure group was specifically created to urge the British government to make a statement confirming Palestine's future.[76] James, knowing the French mentality, warned that if British Jews approached the French government for support, the French would use their own Rabbis to press for a French mandate for Palestine. He became involved in the day-to-day politics and in April and May he was an integral part of the Brandeis- Weizmann cables. He too spoke at the great rally of 2 December and quoting his father Edmond's unerring commitment to Palestine claimed that "Jewish ideals up to this time had been met at the gate, but could not get through. With one stroke of the pen the English government had flung open these gates." According to the Rothschild historian, Niall Ferguson, the meeting at Covent Garden was held to underline the Rothchilds' contributions to the historic breakthrough from which the State of Israel could be traced.[77]

This "breakthrough," this "Jewish Charter"[78] contained a delicate and labyrinthine conundrum. How could any Power which claimed to have gone to war to protect the rights of small self-determining nations bring a non-existent "country" to an international conference and claim it had greater rights to recognition than others? The first step was Balfour's Declaration of intent to support the establishment of a "homeland." An outburst of international and orchestrated approval certainly helped. But there had to be a more tangible basis; proof positive that there was a just cause. This was the reason behind the Zionist Commission. It aimed to lend credibility to the Zionist claims; give Zionists some right to be heard when the world was re-divided at the end of the war. In addition membership inside the Secret Elite began to change in a subtle manner to which Carroll Quigley made no overt reference. Perhaps a better word might be partnership.

As economic power increasingly flowed through the Morgan-Rothschild-Rockefeller-Kuhn, Loeb axis in the United States, political alliances began to firm around key issues like Palestine, but why did they go to such extraordinary lengths to realize a myth-history? The Brandeis-Weizmann connection was reflected in the Balfour-Lansing understandings. The Anglo-American Establishment began to slowly readjust its position and policy. In a sense, the drive for one-world government moved towards a shared agenda that would become clearer in the coming decades. In the new order that lay ahead was it still the British elite who were in charge? If so, how long could that continue?

Summary.

- At the start of the First World War, the lands which we have come to know as the Middle East in a great sweep from The Caspian to the Red Sea, comprised a hotchpotch of factions and tribes, communities born into religious friction, wastelands and deserts, remote townships and cities with Biblical names.

• The land now known as Palestine had a population of some 500,000 Muslims, 60,000 Jews and a similar number of Christians.

• Kitchener, who had previously commanded the army of Egypt, retained his good relationship with the Husseins, custodian of Islam's holiest shrines, and hoped that an Arab alliance with Britain would neutralize the chances of the Ottoman sultan-caliph's call to jihad. Consequently Britain pledged 'in a firm and lasting alliance', to support an independent Arab State in October 1915.

• The Foreign Office then proceeded to make a very different pact with France. Sir Mark Sykes was instructed to negotiate a secret partition of the Ottoman Empire with the French representative, Charles Georges-Picot.

• The Arab cause had no voice at the heart of the Secret Elite and no champion in Parliament. Financial and industrial powers wanted control of the resources under the sands and cared little for the indigenous population.

• The British War Cabinet was warned about the dangers implicit in accepting the Zionist claims on Palestine. Lord Curzon's paper on "The Future of Palestine" was ignored along with the warnings it contained.

• The British intelligence officer, Gertrude Bell, questioned the validity of those who canvassed for a "homeland" in Palestine to which they had no intention to return.

• Edwin Montague, the Secretary of State for India, alerted colleagues to Weizmann's inability to take into account the feelings of those from his own religion who differed from his view or, those of other religions whom Weizmann's activities, if successful, would dispossess.

• Balfour told his War Cabinet colleagues that while the declaration of support for a Jewish homeland in Palestine did not necessarily involve the early establishment of an independent Jewish State, future development would follow the ordinary laws of political evolution.

• The Jewish community celebrated the announcement of the Balfour Declaration with unbridled joy.

• No-one wanted to listen to Mark Sykes warning that co-operation and goodwill were essential from the start otherwise ultimate disaster would overtake both Jew and Arab.

• Pro-Allied propaganda went into overdrive in British and American Jewish communities. The Zionist Commission sent to Palestine was backed by moves to set up a Jewish University and Medical School.

• The real reason for such urgent input was to ensure that when the Peace Conference followed at the end of the war, definite steps will have been taken to give Zionists the right to be heard.

• The intimate role of the Rothschild dynasty in Britain and France was of great importance to the funding and promotion of a Zionist State in Palestine.

• The Secret Elite in Britain favoured a Jewish control of the east side of the Suez Canal to protect that route to their many interests in India and Persia.

Chapter 30

THE RUSSIAN REVOLUTION – PAVING THE WAY

The seizure of power by Bolshevik revolutionaries on 25 October, 1917, (O.S.)[1] brought communism to Russia and major strife to the entire world for the greater part of the twentieth century. For readers not versed in modern Russian history it is important to note that the Bolshevik Revolution was very distinct from the revolution that had taken place eight months earlier. War drained Russia literally and metaphorically. By January 1917, after two-and-a-half years of mortal combat, six million young Russians had been killed, seriously wounded or lost in action for no territorial or strategic gain. Food shortages, hunger, anti-war agitation and civil unrest increased by the day across the Czar's Empire. On 22 February, 1917, 12,000 workers at the giant Putilov manufacturing plant in Petrograd (St. Petersburg)[2] went on strike and were joined on the streets by thousands of demonstrators chanting "Down with the Czar." Soldiers from the city garrison were sent out to arrest the ring-leaders and end the protest, but they refused to open fire on the angry crowds. The Czar abdicated almost immediately, allegedly because he believed that he had lost the support of his military. The event was bloodless apart from the death of several officers shot by their own men. Thus the first Russian Revolution, known as the "February Revolution," ended 300 years of autocratic monarchical rule. A governing body was established in the Winter Palace in Petrograd by liberal deputies from the existing parliamentary body, the Duma, together with socialists and independents. Termed the "Provisional Government," it kept Russia in the war against Germany and began formulating plans for democratic rule through an elected legislative assembly of the people.

Eight months later, during the night of October 24-25, a group of armed Communists seized key areas of Petrograd, entered the Winter Palace and assumed control. The coup was led by Vladimir Lenin and Leon Trotsky, two extreme Marxist revolutionaries who had returned to Russia earlier that year from enforced exile. This was the "Bolshevik Revolution," also known as the "October Revolution." Lenin and Trotsky smothered the fledgling attempt at democratic governance, took Russia out of the war with Germany and installed a ruthless Communist system that would rule Russia for the next seventy-four years.

According to received history, the February Revolution was an entirely spontaneous uprising of the people. It was not. The Putilov strike, and the city garrison's refusal to act against the strikers, was orchestrated from abroad by well-financed agents who had been stirring unrest among the workers and soldiers with propaganda and bribery. The October Revolution was also directly influenced by the same international bankers, with vast financial and logistical support which enabled Lenin and Trotsky to seize power.

Russia had been ruled by the "divine right" of Czars from the reign of Ivan the Terrible (1547-1584) until the abdication of Nicholas II in February 1917. The Romanovs were one of the richest families in the world, on a par with the Rothschilds. They owned huge estates with elaborate palaces, yachts, a massive collection of diamonds (amounting to 25,300 carats), emeralds, sapphires and fifty-four of the priceless jewel-encrusted Fabergé eggs.[3] In May 1917, the *New York Times* estimated the total wealth of the dynasty to be in the region of $9,000,000,000,[4] a breath-taking sum today let alone a century ago. A significant number of upper-class and middle-class Russians (the bourgeoisie) included merchants, government officials, lawyers, doctors and army officers who enjoyed comfortable incomes and life styles. Urban factory workers (the proletariat) and rural agrarian workers (the peasants) comprised the vast majority of the population of 175 million in 1914. They survived on the edge of poverty and hunger, but did not generally support revolutionaries and "demonstrated a solid faith in the Czar."[5]

Alexander II had abolished serfdom in 1861 but opposed movements for political reform. Having survived several attempts on his life, he was eventually assassinated on the streets of St. Petersburg in 1881 by members of a revolutionary group, "People's Will," led by a Jew, Vera Figner. Thereafter, the Jews in the Pale of Settlement[6] were subjected to a series of terrifying pogroms (religious-ethnic massacres). Over the following decades peasants rebelled over taxes which left them debt-ridden and oppressed by hopelessness. Workers went on strike for better wages and working conditions. Students demanded civil liberties for all, and even the comfortable bourgeoisie began calling for representative government.

In 1897, in the midst of this social upheaval, a 27-year-old Marxist lawyer and intellectual Russian radical, Vladimir Ilyich Ulyanov, was arrested by Czarist secret police (the Okhrana) for subversive activities and sentenced to three years exile in Siberia. Ulyanov was treated lightly in comparison to his older brother, Alexander, who ten years earlier plotted to assassinate Czar Alexander III and was hanged for his troubles. Vladimir Ulyanov took the alias Lenin and would go on to become the most powerful man in Russia following the October Revolution.

Born in Simbirsk (renamed Ulyanovsk in his honor in 1924), a town on the Volga some 900 kilometers east of Moscow, Lenin's father was an in-

Lenin

spector of the provinces schools. His mother, the daughter of a baptized Jewish doctor, Alexander Blank,[7] bought the family a farm of some two hundred acres near Samara for 7,500 rubles. The fact that Lenin had Jewish forebears would have absolutely no relevance were it not for the fact that many consider the Bolshevik Revolution to have been a Zionist plot. Despite attacks with pejoratives such as "Anti-Semitic" or "Jew haters" (we are neither) that are likely to be made against us for broaching this, it is essential to examine the background of individuals involved in such major events without fear or favor. Powerful individuals within the Secret Elite who supported Zionism were behind the Balfour Declaration of 2 November, 1917 which led eventually to the creation of the state of Israel. Within 72 hours of that declaration, the men financed and aided by these same individuals seized control of Russia. It does not require a great leap of imagination to consider the possibility that these two seismic events in world history were connected in some way.

In March 1919, the *Times* reported, "One of the most curious features of the Bolshevist movement is the high percentage of non-Russia elements amongst its leaders. Of the 20 or 30 leaders who provide the central machinery of the Bolshevist movement, not less than 75 per cent are Jews ..."[8] Note that the *Times* differentiated between Russian and Jew, as if it were not possible to be both, while the *Jewish Chronicle* emphasized the importance of the Jewish influence on Bolshevism: "There is much in the fact of Bolshevism itself, in the fact that so many Jews are Bolsheviks, in the fact that the ideals of Bolshevism at many points are consonant with the finest ideals of Judaism."[9] Another Jewish journal, *American Hebrew*, reported:

> What Jewish idealism and Jewish discontent have so powerfully contributed to produce in Russia, the same historic qualities of the Jewish mind are tending to promote in other countries.... The Bolshevik revolution in Russia was the work of Jewish brains, of Jewish dissatisfaction, of Jewish planning, whose goal is to create a new order in the world. What was performed in so excellent a way in Russia, thanks to Jewish brains, and because of Jewish dissatisfaction and by Jewish planning, shall also, through the same Jewish mental and physical forces, become a reality all over the world.[10]

It is interesting to note that in 1920, just three years after the Balfour Declaration, Jewish journals were openly discussing the primacy of Jews in creating a new world order.

Rabbi Stephen Wise later commented on the Russian situation: "Some call it Marxism – I call it Judaism."[11] Aleksandr Solzhenitsyn, a victim of the Communist regime who spent many years exiled in Siberia and was later a recipient of the Nobel Prize in Literature, was emphatic that Jews were not involved in the first revolution: "The February Revolution was not made by the Jews for the Russians; it was certainly carried out by the Russians themselves.... We were ourselves the authors of this shipwreck."[12] Solzhenitsyn, however, added: "In the course of the summer and autumn of 1917, the Zionist movement continued to gather strength in Russia: in September it had 300,000 adherents. Less known is that Orthodox Jewish organizations enjoyed great popularity in 1917, yielding only to the Zionists and surpassing the socialist parties."[13] He observed: "There are many Jewish authors who to this very day either deny the support of Jews for Bolshevism, or even reject it angrily, or else ... only speak defensively about it.... These Jewish renegades were for several years leaders at the center of the Bolshevik Party, at the head of the Red Army (Trotsky), of the All-Russian Central Executive Committee, of the two capitals, of the Comintern..."[14] Given the repression of the Jews in Russia, it is hardly surprising that they swelled the numbers of active revolutionaries during this period. They had suffered the horror of the pogroms. They had nursed a genuine resentment for Czarist repression. They were determined to change the world.

The relationship between Jews and revolutionaries was explained by Theodor Herzl, one of the fathers of the Zionist movement in a pamphlet, "De Judenstat," addressed to the Rothschilds: "When we sink, we become a revolutionary proletariat, the subordinate officers of all revolutionary parties, and at the same time, when we rise, there rises also our terrible power of the purse."[15] On Herzl's death, his successor as president of the World Zionist Organization was the Russian-born David Wolffsohn. In his closing speech at the International Zionist Congress at The Hague in 1907, Wolffsohn pleaded for greater unity among the Jews and said that eventually "they must conquer the world."[16] He did not expand on the role that Jewish Bolshevik revolutionaries might play in this Jewish global aspiration, but from his position it seems apparent that political Zionism and the future "homeland" certainly would.[17] Wolffsohn's successor as president of the Zionist organization in 1911 was Otto Warburg, a noted scientist and relative of the Warburg banking family which features heavily in this book. Warburg later spoke of the "brilliant prospects of Palestine" and how an extensive Jewish colonization would "expand into neighboring countries."[18]

A report in 1919 from the British Secret Service revealed: "There is now definite evidence that Bolshevism is an international movement controlled by Jews; communications are passing between the leaders in America, France, Russia and England, with a view toward concerted action."[19] Hilaire Belloc, Anglo-French writer, philosopher and one time Liberal MP at Westminster, wrote: "As for anyone who does not know that the present revolutionary movement is Jewish in Russia, I can only say that he must be a man who is taken in by the suppression of our despicable Press."[20]

Years prior to the Bolshevik seizure of power, Lenin and many other young revolutionaries were sent into exile in Siberia. Among them was Leon Davidovitch Bronstein, alias Leon Trotsky, who was sentenced to four years in the frozen wilderness. Trotsky was a Marxist like Lenin and knew him well, but he initially sided with a softer faction of the socialists rather than Lenin's hard-line Bolsheviks. He later switched his allegiance to Lenin when both were financed by western bankers to seize power in October 1917. Thereafter, he became second in command of the Bolsheviks, founded the Red Army, and was every bit as infamous as Lenin.

Trotsky was born in 1879 in a small rural village, Yankova, in southern Ukraine. His father, although illiterate, was a relatively wealthy farmer. Resourceful and acquisitive, Bronstein senior owned over 250 acres of land and became a substantial employer. Both of Trotsky's parents were Jewish, but unlike his agrarian father, his mother was an educated and cultured city dweller from Odessa. Religious observance was of little importance to either, but they sent Leon to a beder, a Jewish school.[21]

In 1902 Trotsky escaped from exile in Siberia, leaving behind his wife Alexandra and their two young daughters. According to Trotsky, it was Alexandra who had insisted that he put his duty to revolution before family.[22] Trotsky blamed "fate" for their separation, but his actions suggested unbridled pragmatism and "an urge to free himself from a burden in order to move on to higher things."[23] Soon after abandoning his wife and children in Siberia he divorced Alexandra and married Natalia Sedova, daughter of a wealthy merchant.

In the early years of the century numerous other revolutionaries, who had either completed their exile or escaped from Siberia, left Russia for cities in Western Europe. Many thousands more made their way to New York where they formed a powerful revolutionary group in exile. Banned from St. Petersburg, Lenin and a fellow activist, Julius Martov, made their way to Munich in Ger-

A young Trotsky

many where they promoted the Russian Social Democratic Labor Party (RSDLP). Lenin believed the party had to be run from outside Russia. The RSDLP named its journal *Iskra* (The "Spark") believing that out of that spark, the flame of revolution would spring: "The agents would distribute it, spread party propaganda through local cells and channel information to the Central Committee. The journal would help create a cohesive party that until then had consisted of a series of independent groups."[24] Lenin firmly believed Karl Marx's dictum that capitalism would inevitably disintegrate in Russia and elsewhere because it carried within it the forces of its own destruction. Thereafter, power would be grasped by the workers, the men and women who were exploited by capital.

In late 1901, harassed by the Munich police, Lenin and the *Iskra* editors moved to Finsbury in London, where they were joined for a time by Leon Trotsky. Arguments about the best means of instigating revolution in Russia and elsewhere led to ever-increasing conflict, especially between Lenin and his friend and comrade, Julius Martov. Internal wrangling exploded at the 1903 party congress which began in Brussels in July, but was suspended after pressure by the Russian embassy led to fear of police persecution and forced the delegates to complete their business in London. It was "the first major conference that was truly representative of party delegates from Russia and all over Europe."[25] The congress was attended by representatives of 25 recognized social-democratic organizations who had two votes each. For some reason each representative of the Jewish workers organization, the Bund, had three votes "in virtue of the special status ... accorded to it by the first congress."[26]

The congress was dominated by the *Iskra* group, but Lenin realized that he could not carry the party forward in the way he desired, so he deliberately split it. Consequently, the revolutionaries divided into "hard" and "soft" factions. Lenin wanted clear-cut, perfectly defined relationships within the party, and behind the scenes there was a struggle for the support of every individual delegate. Lenin tried to convince Trotsky that he should join the "hard" faction, but he refused.[27] The "hard" was led by Lenin, who proclaimed his followers to be the *bolshinstvo*, the "men in the majority," and thereafter they became known as the Bolsheviks. Marxist intellectuals and those of a less intense ideology were attracted to the "softs," while the hard Bolshevik group, although it had its share of intellectuals, was favored more by provincial party workers and professional revolutionaries: "the bacteria of the revolution" as Lenin called them. Basically, the "softs" favored debate while the Bolsheviks were militants who considered themselves exclusively the champions of the working class of Russia.

Lenin wanted a party he was able to control tightly, and did so through a team of highly disciplined secret workers employed in a semi-military fashion. It was *his* brainchild, *his* party, and above all it was *his* aim to make it the instrument for revolution and the overthrow of the monarchy, despite the knowledge that "it could not be achieved without countless victims."[28]

Julius Martov's group, including Alexander Kerensky, was allegedly the minority (*menshinstvo*) in the RSDLP and became known as the Mensheviks. They favored the establishment of a parliamentary form of government like the French Republic. At first Mensheviks wanted to work within the system, believing that revolution in Russia would be started by the middle classes, not the proletariat. Although he flatly refused to join the Bolsheviks, Trotsky was never truly at home with the Mensheviks and sought to occupy the middle ground.[29] He was an internationalist who believed in the abolition of all territorial borders. This, of course, sat well with the long-term globalist goal of dissolution of independent nation-states and implementation of one-world government so dear to the heart of the Secret Elite. When the Mensheviks ignored Trotsky's call for reconciliation, he effectively distanced himself. Though nominally still a Menshevik, he attended the Fifth Party Congress of the Bolsheviks in London in 1907, where he met Joseph Stalin.[30]

Lenin subscribed to the consensus view within the RSDLP that revolution should lead to a "constituent assembly" elected by the whole people on the basis of "universal, equal and direct suffrage, and with secrecy of the ballot," but it was the manner in which it could be brought about that differentiated his stance from the "soft" Mensheviks. He scoffed at their call for peaceful democratic processes. "Without armed insurrection" he thundered, "a constituent assembly is a phantom, a phrase, a lie, a Frankfort talking-shop."[31] At the third all-Bolshevik congress in London in April 1905, Lenin gave a long speech on the need for an armed uprising and expressed outrage that the Mensheviks had invited the Social Democrats to take part in elections to the Czarist parliament. He considered the slow process of parliamentary reform as blasphemy and his language towards the Mensheviks grew more extreme. That in turn made party reunification impossible.[32]

Julius Martov considered ending the divisions as encouraged by Trotsky, but Lenin regarded reunification of the party as an opportunity for the Bolsheviks to swallow up the Mensheviks. In the end Martov, who wanted to retain the democratic principle within the party, would have nothing to do with it. In 1908 he wrote to his Menshevik comrade Pavel Axelrod: "I confess that more and more I think that even nominal involvement with this bandit gang is a mistake."[33] It was this same Bolshevik "bandit gang" that took control of Russia in October 1917 thanks to the international bankers. In the final analysis, the difference between the two factions boiled down to the Bolsheviks' concept of socialism on the basis of a dictatorship, and the Mensheviks' on the basis of democracy.[34] The split widened and deepened until it led to a formal separation after 1912.[35]

Lenin and Trotsky traded insults over the years. Trotsky's deeply held belief was the democratic "Westernizing" principle, but Lenin considered him evasive, underhand, and "merely posing as a leftist." Trotsky retorted that "the entire structure of Leninism is at present based on lies and falsification and carries within it the poisonous seeds of its own destruction."[36] According to Trotsky, Lenin had lost sight of the struggle for the emancipation of the working class and had become a despot who spoke of the victory of the proletariat when he really meant victory *over* the proletariat.[37] Trotsky was correct.

In February 1904, just six months after the Brussels/London RSDLP conference ended in the infamous split, Russia was inveigled into a disastrous war against Japan in the Far East. This arose through the Machiavellian machinations of the Secret Elite, including King Edward VII, Sir Ernest Cassel, and Jacob Schiff of Kuhn, Loeb bank on Wall Street.[38] Outraged by the horrendous anti-Jewish pogroms in Russia, Schiff made it a point of honor to help finance Japan in its war against Russia. To the surprise and delight of the Imperial Japanese government, he volunteered to underwrite half of the ten-million pound loan they raised in New York and London. He knew that the Japanese fleet had been built in British shipyards and their latest naval technology out gunned and outpaced the antiquated Czarist navy. Victory was not in doubt. This first of five major Kuhn, Loeb loans to Japan was approved by the Secret Elite's main agent, King Edward VII, at a luncheon with Schiff and Sir Ernest Cassel. In Germany, Under Secretary of State Arthur Zimmermann endorsed the move and authorized Max Warburg to negotiate with Japan.[39]

As the Russo-Japanese War lurched from one disaster to another for Russia, political unrest in Russia deepened. In the infamous "Bloody Sunday" atrocity of 22 January 1905, troops fired on a huge, but orderly, crowd of workers marching to the Winter Palace behind the charismatic Russian priest Father Georgii Gapon. Their intention was to present a petition to the Czar calling for universal suffrage. Around 1,000 peaceful marchers and onlookers were killed. Nicholas II had left the city the night before and did not give the order to fire personally, but he lost the respect of many Russians. 1905 was disrupted with workers' demonstrations, strikes and rebellion by sections of the army and navy. The crew of the battleship *Potemkin* mutinied, killing the captain and several officers.

Striking workers formed "Soviets," councils of delegates from workers committees, who could co-ordinate action. They sprang up in major towns and cities, including St. Petersburg, where Trotsky, then twenty-three-years old, played a major role. He had returned illegally from the safety of Finland under a false name and in the guise of a successful entrepreneur. Trotsky immediately wrote proclamations for distribution in factories and posted them throughout the city. In October 1905 a local strike by print workers flared into a national protest. Gangs of armed right-wing extremists were encouraged by the police to hold counter-demonstrations under the banners of "Holy Russia" and "God save the Czar." In response to the gang violence, the factory workers armed themselves.

In December, the Izmailovsky Regiment in St. Petersburg was ordered to arrest the entire executive committee of the Soviet in the capital. In sympathy, the Moscow Soviet declared a strike and thousands of Muscovites took to the streets in protest. Cossacks sent to break up the Moscow demonstrations twice refused orders to charge, and sympathized with the strikers. The crack Semenovsky Guards were less sympathetic, cornering protesters in Presnya, a workers' district in the city, before shelling the area for three days. Many hundreds were killed including eighty-six children.[40] 1905 had started with the Bloody Sunday massacre and ended with the Presnya massacre. Czarist forces, including the much-feared Okhrana secret police, prevailed. Later that year Trotsky and 13 other members of the St. Petersburg Soviet were arrested for political scheming and spent thirteen months as prisoners in the city jail awaiting trial. In January 1907 each was given a life sentence of exile in a small Siberian village above the Arctic Circle, 600 miles from the nearest railway station. Trotsky escaped on his journey into exile and trekked for hundreds of miles through the Urals before making his way to Finland from where, after an extremely frosty meeting with Lenin, he went on to Stockholm and then Vienna.

Nicholas II ruthlessly persecuted the insurrectionists, yet introduced measures of reform, including some basic civil liberties and the creation of a state assembly, the Duma. It was similar to a parliamentary-type elected body but, much like the British parliament in the early nineteenth century, only male property owners and taxpayers were represented. The Czar retained power over State Ministers, who answered to him, not the Duma. If he was dissatisfied with the representative body it could be dissolved at will and fresh elections held.

Unrest continued. Prime Minister and committed monarchist, Pytor Stolypin, survived an attempt on his life in August 1906 when a bomb ripped his dacha (villa) apart while he was hosting a party. Twenty-eight of his guests were killed and many injured, including his two children. In June 1907, Stolypin dissolved the Second Duma and restricted the franchise by sacking a number of liberals and replacing them with conservatives and monarchists. In a further attempt to counter the revolutionaries, he enforced a police crackdown on public demonstrations of dissent. On a more liberal note, Stolypin introduced agrarian reforms which helped many peasants desperate for land. This resulted in huge year-on-year increase in food production. Sir George Buchanan, British Ambassador at St. Petersburg, noted that though he failed to destroy the seeds of unrest which continued to germinate underground, Stolypin rescued Russia from anarchy and chaos. His agrarian policy surpassed all expectations, and at the time of his death nearly 19,000,000 acres of land had been allotted to individual peasant proprietors, by the land committees.[41]

Peasant emancipation and the consequent increase in food production were abhorrent to Bolsheviks. They intended to take all land under state control and implement co-operative food production. Trotsky had called the peasantry "a vast reservoir of potential revolutionaries," and "accepted the indispensable importance of a peasant rising as an auxiliary to the main task of the proletariat."[42] The goal was revolution and government controlled by the proletariat, that is, the working class who sold their labor for a wage, but did not own the means of production.

Peasant farmers had to be brought on board if the revolution was to succeed, but that prospect receded as ever greater numbers were enabled to own their farms. It was clear to both the Czarist regime and the Bolsheviks that the peasantry would not support a political system that would deny them ownership of their land. Stolypin's success threatened the revolution; his agrarian reforms had to be terminated. On 14 September 1911, while attending a performance at the Kiev Opera House in the presence of Czar Nicholas II, the Prime Minister was shot dead by a Jewish revolutionary, Mordekhai Gershkovich. Trotsky later commented: "Stolypin's constitution ... had every chance of surviving."[43] Exactly so. Stolypin was assassinated by the revolutionaries not because he failed to ease the hunger of the peasants or improve their lives, but because he was so successful.

Seven months later, in April 1912, miners in the Lena gold fields in northeast Siberia went on strike. The mines produced large profits for their London registered company, but workers were paid a pittance for working sixteen hours per day under atrocious conditions. The strike was savagely crushed. In what proved to be the worst massacre since Bloody Sunday, troops fired on striking workers, leaving more than 500 casualties.[44] The slaughter heralded a new era of industrial unrest, agitation and mounting tension throughout the country. Two weeks after the massacre, the Bolsheviks founded a newspaper, *Pravda.*

Despite these tragic events, preparations for the First World War gathered pace. After the humbling defeat to Japan in 1905, Russian industry recovered spectacularly thanks to the Rothschilds and other international bankers who poured massive loans into the country. The Russian economy grew at an average rate of 8.8 per cent and by 1914 there were almost a thousand factories in Petrograd alone, many devoted to producing armaments. The expansion of Russia's war industry, along with her rail network into Poland, terrified war planners in Berlin. But it came at a cost. "The pre-war Russian boom was thus highly leveraged, [and] dependent on a constant influx of foreign capital, which if it ever dried up, would leave Russia's entire economy vulnerable."[45]

Shipbuilding, railroad construction and armaments and munitions production significantly expanded. The international bankers earned large profits from substantial interest rates on their loans, at the same time they enabled Russia to conduct a major rearmament program in readiness for the Secret Elite's coming war with Germany. Bullets and artillery shells were produced by the millions. A powerful new fleet of battleships, cruisers, destroyers and submarines began rising on the stocks in shipyards across the empire. Conditions attached to large railway loans insisted that these had to be used purely for the construction of new railroads which ran towards Germany's borders. Why was this particular stipulation given priority? Mobilizing an army of millions had never been easy. It required efficient planning and careful logistical organization. A capable railway network was a prerequisite for the mobilization of the huge Russian armies which would be critical when war with Germany was declared.[46] Look again at the men who laid down the stipulation. International bankers. How odd, unless of course it was they who were planning the war.

In late July 1914, Czar Nicholas II, urged on in his recklessness by the French president, Poincaré, and secret understandings with the British government, used the pretext of protecting Serbia against Austrian retribution to force Germany to declare war. He ordered the general mobilization of Russia's armies with a massive build-up of troops along Germany's Eastern border. General mobilization was recognized by all nations as an act of war. Faced with invasion by millions of Russian troops, Germany was left with no choice but to mobilize her own forces and go to war with Russia.[47] To repay the Czar for his "loyalty," the Secret Elite dangled before him the huge carrot of Russia's ultimate dream. A solemn promise that Russia would own Constantinople and the Straits once Germany had been defeated. This had been the holy grail of Russian Czars for centuries. That was why Russia went to war in July 1914, not, as she claimed, to defend Serbia. As the years dragged on and the Russian losses on the Eastern Front approached six million dead or seriously wounded, even the Czar began to suspect that Perfidious Albion had tricked him into war with an empty promise.[48] It had.

Opposition was stifled. In the early months of fighting, five Soviet Deputies and other members of the Duma who condemned the war, were arrested and exiled in Siberia. *Pravda* was suppressed and the central Bolshevik organization in Russia was virtually broken by the authorities. Local groups inside Russia continued surreptitious propaganda, but communications with Lenin and the central committee in Switzerland were intermittent and precarious. Lenin stayed in Vienna when the war began, but moved to the comfort of neutral Switzerland where he wrote, watched and waited. The Bolshevik movement was relatively quiescent because so many leading members were either exiled abroad or had been sent to Siberia. Lenin's small émigré cabal held a conference in Berne and called on all armies to turn their weapons "not against brothers and the hired slaves of other countries, but against the reactionary and Bourgeois governments of all countries."[49] Communication with Russia was slow, but Lenin gained a growing impression that "an earthquake" was approaching because of the hardships imposed by war and the strain of constant defeats.

Lenin lived in Switzerland for the first two years of war while Trotsky spent 1915-1916 across the border in France, repeatedly irritating the French authorities. He attended the international socialist conference in Zimmerwald, Switzerland, in September 2015, which called for an end to the war and wrote inflammatory articles for a small anti-militarist Menshevik journal *Nashe Slovo* (Our Word). In September 2016 a group of Russian soldiers from a transport ship at Marseilles rioted and stoned their colonel to death. When the riot was put down and the soldiers arrested, some were found to be in possession of *Nashe Slovo,* carrying anti-war articles written by Trotsky. He claimed that the newspapers had been planted by French police to provide a reason to expel him from the country. On 30 October 1916, two gendarmes escorted him to the Spanish border from where Trotsky made his way to Madrid. On 9 November, after ten days of unrestricted freedom in that expansive city, Spanish detectives apparently tracked him down and arrested him as a "known anarchist" and undesirable alien.[50]

A mysterious benefactor arranged Trotsky's release from jail and his transfer, under police supervision, to the southern port of Cadiz. There he waited for another six weeks. On 24 November, Trotsky wrote a long and revealing letter to his comrade Moisei Uritskii in Copenhagen in which he confessed that when he arrived in Cadiz he had only about 40 francs to his name. Somehow, the Trotsky-Uritskii letter fell into the hands of the British Secret Service. British intelligence, under the control of the Admiralty's Naval Intelligence Division (NID), headed by Admiral William Reginald "Blinker" Hall[51] watched his every move.

"Blinker" Hall played a central role for the Secret Elite inside the Admiralty and among his dubious achievements he maneuvered the *Lusitania* into the jaws of a German U-Boat off the south coast of Ireland in 1915 and monitored communications between the American Embassy in London and Washington.

But who was Moisei Uritskii? A Russian lawyer, Uritskii was a member of the Jewish socialist party, the Labor Bund, and spent a period of time in exile. After the Bolsheviks seized power, Uritskii was installed as head of the Petrograd division of the feared Bolshevik secret police, the Cheka, and directly responsible for the torture and death of many innocents. In Copenhagen, Moisei Uritskii was closely associated with another revolutionary plotter, Alexander Israel Helphand-Parvus,[52] a very important player in Secret Elite intrigues. These connections cannot be explained by chance.

After a relaxing stay in Cadiz, Trotsky was taken to Barcelona to be "deported" to New York. Why Barcelona? Cadiz was an equally important seaport with closer connections to New York. According to Trotsky, "I managed to get permission to go there to meet my family."[53] Trotsky's second wife, Natalia, and their two sons were brought by "special arrangement" from Paris to join him in Barcelona where they were taken on tourist trips by the detectives. From whom did he get permission? This was not normal behavior; first class prison cell, hotels in Cadiz and Barcelona, sightseeing with his detectives? The man was not being treated as an "undesirable alien." He and his family were being pampered. At Barcelona, on Christmas Day 1916, they boarded the Spanish passenger ship, *Monserrat* to New York. Immigration Service archives relating to foreign nationals arriving at Ellis Island in 1916 indicated that the Trotsky family traveled first class to New York. Moreover, information collected by American immigration showed that the fares had been purchased for him – not by him.[54] But by whom?

A fellow passenger, one of the few with whom Trotsky engaged, was the light-heavyweight prize fighter, Arthur Cravan who had recently been defeated in a world title fight in Barcelona in front of a crowd of 30,000. The purpose behind Cravan's journey is unknown, but the intriguing possibility has been raised that he was a British agent sent to glean as much information as he could from Trotsky. On arrival in New York he would then have reported to Sir William Wiseman, head of British Intelligence in the United States.[55] There is the additional possibility that the tall, powerfully built Cravan was sent to act as Trotsky's personal bodyguard on the ship and on their arrival in the U.S. This is not as fanciful as it might first appear. He had clearly been exceptionally well protected by plain-clothes police officers throughout his time in Spain. Trotsky's expected arrival in the United States had been published in the American press at the very time anti-German propaganda and pro-war jingoism moved into overdrive. The international bankers who were to use him as one of their major pawns in their Russian intervention wanted no mishap to befall a key player before the game had even started.

Monserrat arrived in New York late at night on January 13, 1917. The passenger manifest prepared for the U.S. immigration authorities revealed that Trotsky was carrying at least $500 (an equivalent of $10,000 today). His initial residence was given as the exclusive Astor Hotel in New York. The reservation had been made for him by persons as yet unknown.[56] Trotsky failed to record in his autobiography that he and his family stayed at the Astor, but related how he "rented" an apartment in a "workers district," paying three months' rent in advance. The apartment, on Vyse Avenue in the Bronx, had every convenience, including "a gas cooking range, bath, telephone, automatic service elevator and a chute for garbage."[57] There was even a concierge. Perhaps most astonishingly of all, the family used a chauffeured limousine. Trotsky, the "impoverished, undesirable" revolutionary, had enjoyed a first-class cell in Madrid; stayed at very pleasant hotels in Cadiz and then Barcelona for six weeks; went on guided tours with his family; traveled first-class on a 13-day voyage to New York; stayed at a luxury hotel before renting an excellent apartment in New York and enjoyed stylish living standards and a chauffeur. How? In stark contrast to his immense good fortune, concurrent events in Russia precipitated disaster.

The Czar and military authorities recognized that civilian discontent was once again rampant throughout the country. They were likewise acutely aware "that gigantic forces were at work fomenting a revolutionary movement on an unprecedented scale."[58] In late December 1916 the highly controversial Russian faith-healer, Grigori Rasputin, was brutally murdered. The Czarina had fallen completely under Rasputin's influence in 1907 when she came to believe he had the power to save her hemophiliac son. Other violent events presaged the "earthquake" Lenin had predicted but the Czar hoped to ward off revolution by gaining victory in the war and seizing the great prize of Constantinople. Desperate to achieve this, Russia's most able military leaders planned a great summer offensive in 1917 with upwards of 7,000,000 troops on the Eastern Front. They intended to breach the gates of Berlin, Vienna and Constantinople. Insufficient artillery was a problem, but they were confident that Britain and America would supply it. The Russians believed that "the very pressure of this colossal army, combined with a simultaneous offensive by the British and French on the Western Front, would have beaten Germany to her knees and would have led to an overwhelming victory by September, 1917."[59]

The secret cabal in London had no need for a massive Russian offensive to win this war. From the earliest days of 1915 all that was needed to achieve victory was to stop supplies of food, oil, minerals, gun cotton and the wherewithal to produce munitions in Germany. The Secret Elite had promised the Czar that Russia would have Constantinople as a just reward at the end of the war, but were determined that it would never come to pass. The allies had sacrificed a quarter of a million men on the Dardanelles and Gallipoli campaigns in 1915, though, as explained earlier, these were deliberately set to fail in order to keep Russian out of Constantinople. The Secret Elite would certainly not allow Russia to take possession of the Ottoman capital in 1917 through a major Russian offensive that would end the war. The Secret Elite intended to carve up the Ottoman Empire for themselves, and Russia would not be permitted to interfere.

In a sense it was Gallipoli all over again. Until the United States entered the war and her troops were on the ground in Europe, Russian troops were valuable, but Russia could not be allowed to share the spoils when the ultimate victory had been secured. It was absolutely essential that the Czar be prevented from mounting a successful offensive in 1917. A conference of the allies in St. Petersburg was hastily arranged, theoretically to discuss the proposed offensive, reach an agreement for supplying vital armaments and boost Russian morale. Step forward Alfred Milner, undisputed master of the Secret Elite, to lead the British delegation. According to Cabinet papers, Milner was "authorized to give assurances on supplies to Russia *if* in his estimation the Russians could make good use of them."[60] What power. Armament supplies to Russia were crucial to the proposed offensive, yet Milner was given personal authority to decide whether or not Britain would supply them. In his hands alone lay the power to determine whether the war would end in the summer/autumn of 1917 or continue beyond. If artillery was not provided, Russia's summer offensive and consequent victory was a lost cause and the Czar's fate sealed.

Milner and the British delegation sailed from Oban in Scotland on January 20, 1917. According to Bruce Lockhart, British Consul in Moscow: "Rarely in the history of great wars can so many important ministers and generals have left their respective countries on so useless an errand." The British Mission was the largest, with Lord Milner, his political advisers Lord Revelstoke (a banker) and George Clerk, together with his military advisers Sir Henry Wilson and five other generals.[61] The French sent one politician and two generals, the Italians a politician and a general. Why was there such a ridiculously heavy presence of generals in the British delegation? The role of General Sir Henry Wilson, who was closely linked to the secret cabal, was to give military approval to the final decision. Wilson hung on Milner's every word and would never have contradicted him. In turn, few if any British generals would have dared contradict General Wilson. They had discussions with senior members of the Russian armed forces, but the generals were said to be decidedly under-impressed. It was, apparently, "a useless errand" just as the British consul had said, but in reality was completely successful in its real mission to block any Russian success in taking Constantinople.

Milner undertook the long, dangerous journey (Lord Kitchener had been killed on a similar voyage from Scotland to Russia in 1916) despite being advised not to go by a fellow member of the Secret Elite, Lord Esher.[62] On the day he arrived in Petrograd, and before he had even met or discussed the armaments proposal with the Russians, Milner made no attempt to conceal his doubt. From the very start he used "the inefficiency of the Russians" as an excuse to turn down their request for artillery.[63] He held several meetings with the Czar, warning him that if Britain was to hand over her vital heavy guns, it was necessary for Russia to prove that her own supplies were exhausted. Additionally, Milner had to be assured that Russia could defeat Germany in the proposed military operations. Milner added bluntly that it had come to his notice from many independent, "well-informed sources" that Russia had failed to fully exploit her manpower and her own vast resources.

Milner promised Nicholas II nothing. On 3 March 1917, he arrived back in London and informed the government of his decision: No guns for Russia. Three days later his formal report to the War Cabinet about the events that took place at the Allied Conference in Russia was dismissive. He felt that too many unnecessary people had attended – ironic, considering the size of the party which accompanied him – and too many personal and distracting agendas had been aired. Milner claimed to have been shocked by the lack of training in modern weaponry Russian soldiers had been given. Organization, he deemed, "chaotic." He stated that the Russian government under the Czar was "hopeless" and improvement unlikely, but in his view there was "a great deal of exaggeration about the talk of revolution."[64] He specifically denied that an impending revolution was likely. Such an astonishing assertion requires further examination.

Milner made a verbal report to a War Cabinet which included the Prime Ministers of Canada and New Zealand. All the Secret Elite political agents were present. No minutes were taken[65] and whatever was said, we will never know. His written memorandum for the Cabinet (dated 13 March) that there would be no revolution, was signed five days *after* the revolution began. To imagine that the Foreign Office did not know this, or even that Milner could not have altered the wording of his report, is ridiculous. It was a calculated comment; one meant to deflect attention from his unreported discussions with other parties. Lord Alfred Milner knew exactly what was about to happen in Petrograd because the Secret Elite was instrumental in facilitating it.

Bruce Lockhart, the British Consul in Moscow, was shocked when told of Lord Milner's conclusion that there would be no revolution. He suspected that the Foreign Office had prepared a false report, insisting that there was nothing in Milner's attitude or discussions during his visit to indicate that he had any confidence in the Czar.[66] Milner's report had been concocted in conjunction with the Foreign Office to delude his contemporaries, and doubtless later historical researchers. In his *War Memoirs*, Prime Minister Lloyd George bemoaned the fact Milner had not apparently grasped the immediate seriousness of the situation: "Having regard to the warnings which were blaring at them in every direction, it is incomprehensible that they should have been so deaf and blind."[67] Milner was neither blind nor deaf. As ever, he lived with the criticism which covered his actual purpose.

During his sojourn, Milner met with Prince Georgy Lvov, a member of the Duma, at which the possibility of revolution "within three weeks" was specifically discussed.[68] Lloyd George spouted what appeared to be criticism of Milner, but it was part and parcel of the ploy to conceal historical truth. Lloyd George was a political puppet of the Secret Elite, party to its agenda and a willing player. He had sold his soul to the international bankers for power and material riches many years before.[69] Almost three weeks to the day after Milner's private discussions with Prince Lvov, the so-called "spontaneous revolution" took place in Petrograd. Czar Nicholas subsequently abdicated, and Lvov was installed as Prime Minister.

Untangling the Secret Elite's web of intrigue during the Russian mission is no simple matter. But be certain of one thing. Alfred Milner was not a man to waste his time, let alone risk U-Boat infested seas to journey to Russia in the depth of winter, unless it was a matter of the gravest importance. It was no coincidence that he was in Petrograd less than three weeks before the revolution exploded. He saw what was happening, and he knew what was about to happen. The question of supplying Russia with artillery was most definitely *not* the reason for the visit. His presence at what was termed an Allied Conference was the perfect cover, for Milner had far more important business. Crucially, at that very time, Secret Elite agents were supplying monetary bribes to workers' leaders at the giant Putilov factory and to soldiers of the local garrisons. The ground-work for imminent revolution was in motion while Milner was in Petrograd.

We know that he had private talks with the Czar, and it is not beyond the realms of possibility that Milner warned Nicholas II that British Intelligence had sound evidence that serious disorder was about to erupt in the capital; disorder which would present an immense threat to the Czar's personal safety and that of his beloved children. The key objective of this Secret Elite exercise was to manipulate their own agents into power in Russia. Nicholas had served his purpose. Did Milner urge Nicholas to consider abdication with promises that he and his family would find a safe refuge in Britain? The speed with which the Czar abdicated and his lack of fight surprised many.

Milner's involvement is not some far-fetched theory. He was accused in Parliament of making speeches in Russia which went unreported in Britain because of press censorship. The Irish Nationalist leader, John Dillon, berated Milner for apparently supporting the Czar's regime and spouting nonsense in Moscow denying the state of popular agitation in Russia.[70] When he returned to London, Milner was reported in the *Times* as saying that "it was quite wrong to suppose that there is in Russia any controversy about the waging of the war."[71] It was of course, nonsense, but such claims served to deflect attention from what was actually happening. Two days later, the revolution began. In reply to questions in Parliament on 3 April 1917, Andrew Bonar Law, Chancellor of the Exchequer, and an associate of the secret cabal, stated: "I have seen statements emanating from our enemies that it was owing to Lord Milner that the Czar was overthrown."[72] What? Milner clearly made unreported speeches and met unreported persons. But what more did the Germans know? Where is the proof that Milner caused the overthrow of the Czar? Yet again we reach an impasse on Milner's activities. Reports and records were afterwards removed, correspondence burned on his orders and any evidence of his machinations destroyed. Whatever else, Alfred Milner was no innocent abroad. He knew what was going on because, like his Rothschild/Secret Elite friends, he had his finger on the pulse before the heart could beat.

If the received history of the First World War is true, why would he turn down the chance to offer Russia matériel support for its massive summer offensive; an offensive that would most likely have shattered the enemy forces on the Eastern Front and brought the war to a successful conclusion? Why turn down lucrative bank loans to Russia for weapons, and the substantial profits for British armaments companies which manufactured those weapons? The answer was, as always, Constantinople. The Russians could never be allowed to take possession of Constantinople.

While the Czarist authorities there were doing their utmost to dampen the revolutionary flames, the Secret Elite were fanning them. In an article in the *New York Times*, the explorer, journalist and Russian expert, George Kennan, revealed that in early 1917 Jacob Schiff of Kuhn, Loeb Bank on Wall Street financed Russian revolutionaries through an organization called the "Society of the Friends of Russian Freedom."[73] Indeed, Schiff had financed Russian revolutionaries from at least 1905.

The Czar had conferred with George Buchanan, British Ambassador in Petrograd, informing him that if the planned offensive could not proceed through lack of artillery supplies from Britain, he intended to sue for peace with Germany. Nicholas II had no inkling of the extent to which Britain was determined to prevent any dialogue between Russia and Germany. The British Ambassador in Russia himself was at the center of a scheme to overthrow the Czar if he lost his stomach for war. To that end he had gathered "a coterie of wealthy bankers, liberal capitalists, conservative politicians, and disgruntled aristocrats."[74]

Empty threat or not, the Czar had discussed signing a peace treaty with Germany, and it was patently clear to the Secret Elite that he would have to go. During and immediately after Milner's mission to Russia, many local observers, visitors and newsmen reported that British and American agents were everywhere, especially in Petrograd, providing money for insurrection. British agents were seen handing over 25-rouble notes to soldiers in the Pavloski regiment just a few hours before they mutinied against their officers and sided with the revolutionaries.[75] Subsequent publication of various memoirs and documents made it clear that this funding was provided by Milner and channeled through Sir George Buchanan. It was a repeat of the ploy that had worked so well for the cabal many times in the past. Round Table members[76] were once again operating on both sides of the conflict to weaken and topple a target government. Czar Nicholas had every reason to believe that, since the British were Russia's trusted allies, their officials would be the last on earth to conspire against him. Yet, the British Ambassador himself represented the hidden cabal which was financing the regime's downfall.[77]

Summary.

- The Russian Empire had been ruled as an autocracy by the Romanovs for 300 years. They enjoyed fabulous wealth while the vast majority of the population of 175 million lived on the edge of poverty and hunger.
- In 1881 Czar Alexander II was assassinated by members of a revolutionary group led by a Jew, Vera Figner. Thereafter, Jews in Russia were subjected to a series of terrifying pogroms. They had become the fall-guys.
- Civil unrest grew throughout the entire country for better living conditions, representative government and civil liberties.
- Thousands of young revolutionary socialists, including Vladimir Lenin and Leon Trotsky, were arrested and banished to exile in the wastelands of Siberia. Many, on their escape or release, made their way to Western Europe or the United States.
- Russian Revolutionaries exiled in Western Europe promoted the Russian Social Democratic Labour Party which split acrimoniously into two factions, the Bolsheviks and the Mensheviks.
- Bolsheviks supported an armed uprising against Czarism, but the Mensheviks argued for a peaceful transfer of power through democratic process.
- Seventy-five percent of Bolshevik leadership was Jewish. The Bolshevik movement, according to an American Jewish journal, was the product of Jewish dissatisfaction, Jewish brains and planning, and the end goal, aired at the World Zionist Congress in 1907 was to create a new world order.
- In January 1905, with Russia at war with Japan, Czarist troops killed around 1,000 peaceful protesters as they marched to the Winter Palace in Petrograd. Social unrest grew throughout that year with strikes and demonstrations.
- Striking workers formed "Soviets," councils of delegates from workers committees, and in late 1905 a local strike by print workers flared into a national protest. Revolution was possible, but Czarist forces, including the much feared secret police force, crushed the protest.
- Czar Nicholas II persecuted insurrectionists but introduced some basic civil liberties and the creation of a State Assembly – a parliamentary-type elected body called the Duma.
- Following a period of relative calm, in September 1911 the Prime Minister, Pyotor Stolypin, was shot dead by a Jewish revolutionary. A new

crack-down began. Seven months later some five hundred striking workers at the Lena gold fields, owned in part by British businessmen, were shot dead or badly wounded by government troops.

• The Lena slaughter heralded a new era of industrial unrest, but the huge international banking loans which poured into Russia to prepare for the coming war led to an economic boom and a decrease in tension.

• Spurred on by false British promises of gaining Constantinople, Czar Nicholas II ordered the general mobilization of Russia's armies in late July 1914. With this massive army drawn up along its eastern borders, Germany was forced to react and thus began the First World War.

• From December 1916, revolution became increasingly likely. Ejected from France, the "impoverished" Leon Trotsky and his family were pampered by Spanish police before they sailed first-class to New York where they initially stayed in a 5-star hotel before moving to a luxury apartment.

• Over six million war casualties in the first two years of war caused civil unrest and distress.

• The Czar began planning a major new offensive for the summer of 1917. He believed his seven million strong-army would rapidly overcome Germany, but first, artillery supplies from the Allies were required. Victory would have enabled Russia to take Constantinople, but this could never be permitted.

• Following a visit to Russia, Secret Elite leader, Alfred Milner, refused to approve their request for more guns and armaments.

• To conceal Secret Elite manipulation of revolutionary activities in Petrograd, Milner categorically stated that there would be no revolution. At the same time Secret Elite agents were preparing the ground for revolution by bribing factory workers and soldiers of the Petrograd garrison.

Chapter 31

The Rape Of Russia

The Russian Revolution began on 22 February, 1917 (O.S.) as a direct consequence of the actions of workers, leaders at the massive Putilov armaments factories in Petrograd. Portrayed as a spontaneous and leaderless uprising of the downtrodden and oppressed proletariat, it was nothing of the sort. Workers' leaders at the Putilov munitions works and other major industrial concerns in Petrograd, were bribed to stir up industrial and civil unrest.

At the Putilov factory they led some 30,000 workers out on strike after an angry and bitter tirade against the management over low wages. In the following days, workers at other factories across the city were similarly stirred to action, and encouraged to strike in support of the Putilov work force. On 22 February, management at the great armaments works locked the factory gates. Were they were forewarned of possible sabotage? It was widely known that 23 February was International Women's Day and that tens of thousands of women, many of whom were war widows or the wives of soldiers who had been badly wounded at the front, would march in protest against the war.

The Putilov work force joined the women on the streets along with 90,000 other workers. Mass crowds paraded through the city protesting food shortages, calling for an end to war and the overthrow of the monarchy. The following day numbers on the streets rapidly snow-balled. Shop windows were smashed and hungry protesters helped themselves to bread. The Petrograd police shot several protesters, but were completely overwhelmed.

Just before Petrograd "spontaneously" erupted, the British ambassador, Sir George Buchanan, took himself out of town, "safely withdrawn from the scene of a tumult that he had contributed to kindle."[1] It was an old ruse. Czar Nicholas II was some 500 miles away in Belarus in his role as Commander-in-Chief of the army. On 25 February, around thirty of the workers leaders met at the Petrograd Union of Workers Co-operative to set up a Soviet. On Sunday 26th, the Czar ordered a military crackdown. Forty, perhaps fifty, protesters were shot on the streets by troops from the city garrison, but there were increasing reports of desertion as disillusioned troops joined forces with the demonstrators.

The President of the Duma, Mikhail Rodzianko, sent urgent telegrams to the Czar. On 26 February, he sent warning of the seriousness of a situation which the government was incapable of suppressing:

> The government is paralyzed; the transport service has broken down; the food and fuel supplies are completely disorganized. Discontent is general and on the increase. There is wild shooting in the streets; troops are firing at each other. It is urgent that someone enjoying the confidence of the country be entrusted with the formation of a new government. There must be no delay. Hesitation is fatal.[2]

With exasperation bordering on despair, Rodzianko raised the level of anxiety in a second telegram on 27th February:

> The situation is growing worse. Measures should be taken immediately as tomorrow will be too late. The last hour has struck, when the fate of the country and dynasty is being decided. The government is powerless to stop the disorders. The troops of the garrison cannot be relied upon. The reserve battalions of the Guard regiments are in the grips of rebellion, their officers are being killed. Having joined the mobs and the revolt of the people, they are marching on the offices of the Ministry of the Interior and the Imperial Duma. Your Majesty, do not delay. Should the agitation reach the Army, Germany will triumph and the destruction of Russia along with the dynasty is inevitable.[3]

Nicholas read the telegram, made a derogatory comment about Rodzianko, and remained at the Front … for three short days.

On 2 March 1917, (O.S.) Czar Nicholas II abdicated, initially in favor of his 13 year-old hemophiliac son, Alexei, but quickly changed his mind to favor his brother. Grand Duke Michael declined. He was a realist. Whatever the truth, Lenin was said to have known that Michael had been in favor of the February Revolution and "had even worn a red ribbon in his buttonhole."[4] The Czar caved in without any real fight and Romanov rule came to an abrupt end after 300 years. Standard history recounts that he abdicated because he had lost the loyalty of his army, but was this put to the test? Though he announced that he would stand down in the interests of the military, he privately recorded in his diary that: "All around is betrayal, cowardice and deceit!"[5] He meekly surrendered the imperial throne, yet Rodzianko had clearly stated that the mob was marching on the Duma, not the Czar. He still commanded the army. Rodzianko warned that "*should* the agitation reach the army" Germany would win the war. The army in the field stood loyal. In addition, five squadrons of cavalry and Cossacks were available. So who had betrayed and deceived the last Czar?

What had been whispered in his ear? What role had Alfred Milner played in the Czar's decision to abdicate? What warnings or indeed assurances had been given during his private meetings with Nicholas II just weeks earlier? As we have shown, the evidence points to Milner's certain knowledge of what was about to take place before he had even departed Russia; although, once home, he tried to conceal this by making a clear statement to the contrary for public consumption. Had Nicholas been promised sanctuary in Britain, as he had previously been promised Constantinople?

On Nicholas II's abdication, a provisional government was immediately cobbled together. Most of the chosen ministers were liberals from the previous Duma with a big following among the middle class. They sought to establish a capitalist democracy similar to Britain and, most importantly, supported Russia's continuation in the war until Germany was defeated. News of the revolution and abdication was greeted in London with satisfaction by Prime Minister Lloyd George.[6] Across the Atlantic President Woodrow Wilson spoke to Congress about "those marvelous and comforting events" in Russia, where "autocracy" had finally been struck down.[7] Did the Czar ever ponder that he had talked about making peace with Germany only to be replaced with a government which promised to continue the war?

The speed with which the British government distanced itself from the Czar was breathtaking. Advised and updated by Sir George Buchanan and Hanbury-Williams [8] the War Cabinet decided to present a resolution to parliament "sending paternal greetings to the Duma, heartfelt congratulations to the Russian people" and praise for their "renewed steadfastness and vigor [in] the prosecution of the war against the autocratic militarism which threatens the liberty of Europe."[9] What? Was irony dead? For whose consumption was the notion that the Russian people, who had been subjugated to Czarist autocratic militarism, wanted to continue the war against the alleged autocratic militarism reputedly threatening Europe? These Secret Elite agents were shameless. They not only abandoned the Czar without hesitation, but instructed Hanbury-Williams to stay away from him or any member of the royal family so that Britain's good relations with the Provisional government would be seen as more important.

Discussion on the Czar's future concluded with the decision that "they were in doubt as to whether Great Britain was the right place for him to go."[10] Other opinions questioned the advisability of the Czar seeking refuge in a neutral country where he could become the center of intrigue, so the War Cabinet changed its mind within 24 hours.[11] In theory, he might have found refuge in Britain. He never did. But look what mattered to the British Elite. The Czar was instantly abandoned and no mention was made of promises like Constantinople. Both were filed in the past tense. Gone.

Prince Lvov, with whom Alfred Milner had spoken some weeks earlier, was named as the first post-imperial Prime Minister. Co-incidence? Hardly likely. Alexander Kerensky, a Menshevik, was appointed minister of war and navy. The new government, plagued with factional infighting and competition for authority, underwent several changes over the following months. The Bolsheviks had little influence on the seismic events of February-March 1917 or the new government. They were a tiny faction which had effectively been neutered by the enforced exile of their key leaders. The Mensheviks, if anything, fared worse. They "almost entirely disintegrated and became indistinguishable from other "progressives," combining a patriotic attitude towards the war with a demand for "democratic reforms."[12]

Isolated in Zurich, Lenin was allegedly "stunned" on hearing news of the Czar's abdication. He immediately cabled his trusted lieutenant Grigory Zinoviev, the alias of Hirsch Apfelbaum, son of a Jewish-Ukranian dairy farmer. Zinoviev joined Lenin in Zurich and helped plan their return. Desperate to seize control of the revolution from the provisional government, but isolated in central Europe, their first task was to get back to Russia. Promptly. The best option was to travel by rail to Stockholm, then on to Petrograd, but Germany stood in the way. Contacts were made, options considered and a strange deal made with the German government. Within days, Lenin was informed that he would soon be hearing from his old associate, Helphand-Parvus.[13]

Parvus, who assisted Trotsky in his voyage to the United States, played another significant role for the Secret Elite in spiriting Lenin safely across enemy territory and into Russia. An intriguing and mysterious individual, Parvus warrants some attention. Born to Jewish parents in Belarus in 1867, his real name was Israel Lazarevich Gelfand. When he first met Lenin in Munich in 1900 he was a brilliant young journalist and Marxist theoretician who helped by printing the early issues of *Iskra*. In 1905 he was imprisoned with Trotsky and sentenced to three years exile in Siberia. Parvus mentored Trotsky on the theory of Permanent Revolution before they both escaped. He made his way to Germany and changed his name from Gelfand to Helphand, but became better known simply as Parvus.

Around 1908 Parvus moved to Constantinople where he remained for five years. He was associated with the Young Turks, produced propaganda journals and set himself up as a grain importer and, more importantly, an arms merchant. Parvus became extremely rich, but his years in Constantinople were shrouded in mystery. His most important contact was Basil Zaharoff, the leading armaments salesman and agent of the Rothschilds and their mighty Vickers Armaments cartel.[14] Parvus earned a fortune selling arms for Zaharoff[15] and became intrinsically involved in the overthrow of the Czar.

Seventeen years after first meeting Lenin, Parvus was a grossly fat, bizarre, fantastic paradox. He was both a flamboyant tycoon, displaying the worst of bourgeois vulgarity, and yet had a brilliant Marxist mind. The millionaire Marxist became a cartoon caricature "with an enormous car, a string of blondes, thick cigars and a passion for champagne, often a whole bottle for breakfast."[16] Parvus viewed himself as kingmaker, the power behind the throne that Lenin would occupy. The association between the millionaire and Lenin horrified many socialists and revolutionaries, and Lenin claimed that he detested Parvus. Perhaps he did, but behind closed doors, they colluded happily.

Parvus had been warmly greeted by Lenin in Berne in 1915, where they held a private meeting. Its details remain clouded in mystery, yet proved to be extremely important in the history of the world. Without Parvus and his organization, through which millions of gold marks were channeled to the Bolsheviks, Lenin could never have achieved supreme power. "It was a strangely remote association in the sense that neither had direct contact with the other and both adamantly denied its existence..."[17] How convenient.

Parvus had spent a great deal of time in Germany since the early 1900s and was considered by many, including the German authorities themselves, to be a loyal German agent. Judging by his activities, however, from the time he moved to Constantinople in 1908 there can be little doubt that he was a double agent working for the British, or, to be more precise, the Rothschilds. Parvus was an extremely important player for them because he could operate freely in Germany and liaise with other important Rothschild agents such as Max Warburg. The fortune he made in Constantinople with Zaharoff's help gave him access to members of the German Foreign Ministry, Under-Secretary Arthur Zimmermann in particular. Parvus suggested that the Imperial Germans and the Russian Marxists had a common interest in the destruction of the Russian autocracy, and persuaded them to provide substantial funding to topple the Czar and bring about a separate peace with the Reich. The Germans obliged. They had supported the revolutionary movement since the war began by feeding money to Russia through Parvus in order to "create the greatest possible degree of chaos in Russia." On one day alone, 5 April 1917, the German Treasury paid more than 5,000,000 gold marks to Parvus for political purposes in Russia.[18]

Incredibly, the Allies and their German foes were playing, and paying for, the same game in Russia, but for very different reasons. The Germans thought Parvus was working to their agenda, but the Secret Elite knew he was working to theirs. While German officials believed that they were using Parvus's network as a means of putting pressure on the Czar to plea for a peace settlement, the British, supported by Ambassador Buchanan, urged him to sabotage any move towards a separate Russian-German peace. "The task facing Parvus was greatly facilitated by the helpless naivety of his secret contact, Count Brockdorff-Rantzau, German ambassador in Copenhagen."[19]

The Secret Elite had decided to spirit Lenin and Trotsky into Russia as quickly as possible. This was Parvus's masterstroke.[20] Immediately after the February Revolution he entered negotiations with the German authorities to provide a special train to transfer Lenin and his supporters safely through Germany from Switzerland. Interestingly, it was Arthur Zimmermann, by now the German Foreign Secretary, who made the initial contact by inviting Parvus to meet with him. Thereafter, Zimmermann personally supervised the arrangements.[21]

We have to question Zimmermann's actions, both here and in later activities such as his infamous and ludicrous telegram that provided Woodrow Wilson with the perfect excuse to bring the United States into the war. Was Zimmermann, in collusion with Max Warburg and other Rothschild agents such as Zaharoff, acting in the interests of Bolshevism and Zionism rather than those of Germany? He was certainly sympathetic to the Zionist cause, protected Palestinian Jews when they were threatened by the Turkish authorities and mooted the idea of a joint Turkish-German declaration in favor of colonization in March 1917.[22] Did he keep the Kaiser in the dark? Where did his true loyalty lie? Disagreements still rage over whether or not Zimmermann informed Wilhelm II about the arrangements for Lenin's transfer. Author Michael Pearson claimed that the Kaiser and his Generals approved the move in advance, whereas Professor Antony Sutton maintained that they were not informed until Lenin was safely across the border into Russia.[23]

Lenin's action could have been viewed as treason. He had, after all, accepted help from Russia's sworn enemy who benefited from his declared intention. On 9 April 1917, Lenin, together with Gregory Zinoviev, Karl Radek and other Bolsheviks and their wives, a party of thirty-two in total, boarded a Swiss train that took them from Berne to Zurich. On transferring to another train to carry them to the German border, they were subjected to abuse by a crowd of around 100 hostile Russians screaming "Spies" "Pigs" and "Traitors."[24] They then boarded a German train that was "sealed" from the outside world. Over the next three days the now famous "sealed train" took them via Frankfurt and Berlin to the port of Sassnitz in northeast Germany, from where they boarded a Swedish ferry for Trelleborg. The following day they received a warm welcome on the quayside from one Jacob Furstenberg.

Furstenberg was the alias of Yakov Stanilavovich Ganetsky, an important player in Lenin's return from exile and a key link between Parvus and Lenin in the transference of large sums of money from Germany. Furstenberg was the son of a wealthy Jewish family who owned a factory in the city, and had a range of contacts in the semi-criminal underworld. He "was seen even by Lenin's close comrades as a sinister character,"[25] but considered by Lenin as a trusted friend. Furstenberg was also Parvus's "key right-hand man," and president of a company he set up in Copenhagen during the war. The "company" comprised an espionage ring and network of agents both inside and outside Russia, that sold Russian products to the Germans and vice versa. This war-profiteering comprised merchandise like chemicals, medicines, surgical instruments and much more.[26] Some of the money raised was used to finance Lenin's propaganda from the first day of the revolution.[27] Lenin, the "pure socialist revolutionary" and "man of the people" was deeply involved with these despicable characters and benefited from the obscene profits made at the expense of men killed or horrendously maimed in the trenches. Furstenberg, indeed, was Lenin's most trusted agent.[28] They formed their own personal axis of evil.

The revolutionary and the sinister war profiteer were strange bed-fellows. In theory, Furstenberg was everything that the Bolshevik leader abhorred. He prospered by dealing in basic necessities that were in short supply: medicines, drugs and dressings for the wounded; contraceptives for the troops. His black-market business methods were equally disreputable. Furstenberg was elegant, debonair and never without a flower in his buttonhole; a dandy for whom Bolshevism seemed illogical. The two men had known each other since they met at the traumatic 1903 conference in London when Lenin split the party.[29] Furstenberg joined Lenin at Trelleborg, and he and the other Bolsheviks continued their journey to Malmo for the night train on to Stockholm. Meanwhile, in the Wilhelmstrasse in Berlin, Arthur Zimmermann followed their progress "with close interest."[30]

Sweden had dominated the market in illicit trade between the Allies and Germany since the early months of the war, and at the heart of much of that business sat a Swedish banker and businessman, Olof Aschberg and his bank, Nya Banken. Furstenberg was an associate of Aschberg's[31] and much of the money sent from both the United States and Germany for the Bolsheviks, passed through Nya Banken. Aschberg's London agent was the British Bank of North Commerce,[32] whose chairman, Earl Grey, was linked to the inner chambers of the Secret Elite in London. Another important Nya Banken connection was Max May, vice-president of J.P. Morgan's Guaranty Trust of New York, also an associate of Olof Aschberg.[33] Much of the "German" money transferred through Nya Banken to the Bolsheviks came via the Disconto-Gesellschaft bank in Frankfurt am Main.[34] When one realizes that Disconto-Gesellschaft was part of the Rothschild Group[35] and J.P. Morgan was a front for the Rothschilds on Wall Street, the hidden hand of Rothschild becomes apparent, yet again.[36]

Max Warburg, one of the most powerful bankers in Germany, was the older brother of Paul Warburg, the major force in establishing America's Federal Reserve System, which helped Wall Street fund the war in Europe. It is worth repeating that Max, himself a Rothschild agent and reputedly head of the German espionage system during the war,[37] was involved with Arthur Zimmermann in ensuring Lenin's safe passage across Germany. Max Warburg was likewise involved in the safe passage of Trotsky to Russia. A U.S. State Department file, "Bolshevism and Judaism," dated 13 November 1918, asserted that there could be no doubt that the "Jewish Firm" Kuhn, Loeb & Company and its partners "started and engineered" the revolution in Russia. The report added that Max Warburg had also financed Trotsky, and that Aschberg and Nya Banken were involved.[38] This tangled web makes little sense unless one understands just how closely all of these named bankers and banks were linked to each other, and to their common goal of international control.

Lenin's train arrived late on the evening of Easter Monday, 17 April 1917, at the Finland rail terminal in Petrograd. Both inside and outside the station, bands played "La Marseilles" and a large bouquet of flowers was thrust into Lenin's hands as a guard of honor presented arms.[39] The Bolshevik leader immediately denounced members of the provisional Government, and issued a series of ten directives in what came to be known as the "April Theses." He demanded the immediate withdrawal of Russia from the World War, and all political power placed in the hands of workers and soldiers' soviets.

Lenin's triumphant return

Lenin undoubtedly benefited from financial backing from Germany, mainly through the intrigues of men linked to the Rothschilds such as Parvus and Max Warburg, but what of Trotsky, so generously accommodated on his voyage from Barcelona to New York? Richard Spence, Professor of History at the University of Idaho, has meticulously documented the network of connections between Trotsky and international bankers,[40] and his work is required reading for those who desire a deeper understanding of the Bolshevik Revolution. His grasp of the connections between the international bankers themselves, or their globalist aims, appears less firm. Spence quoted French Intelligence reports from Barcelona in 1917 which revealed that Trotsky's benefactor was a Russian émigré, Ernst Bark, a resident of Madrid. Bark masterminded Trotsky's release from prison, his accommodation in Spanish hotels, and his first-class passage to America. He was the first cousin of Pyotor Bark, Minister of Finance in Russia from 1914. Inside these complex secret international machinations, Pyotor Bark employed Olof Aschberg as his financial agent. Having seen how Aschberg and his Nya Banken were closely linked with Parvus in facilitating Lenin's return to Russia, it comes as no surprise that they were similarly involved in ensuring Trotsky's return. Professor Spence concluded that Ernst Bark "was Parvus's cat's-paw in Spain."[41] In an interesting aside, Pyotor Bark was arrested after the Bolshevik revolution, but immediately released on higher orders. Thereafter he moved to England, became managing director of the Anglo-International Bank in London and was awarded a knighthood. He was a man with contacts in British banking circles, too.[42]

Trotsky was an old friend of Parvus and, like Lenin, he later openly criticized and distanced himself from the champagne-socialist. It seems likely, as Richard Spence suggested, that this public criticism of Parvus was to "mask a secret, on-going collaboration" between the two. It was simply part and parcel of the great game of international wheeling and dealing to deceive the masses and gain power. Certainly Parvus was intimately linked to both Lenin and Trotsky, and played a significant role in their return to Russia to seize power. Parvus, as we have seen, was likewise linked to the Rothschild agent Sir Basil Zaharoff, and that link provided yet another of many examples which confirm the relevance of G. Edward Griffin's contention that "the Rothschild formula" played a major role in shaping the Russian Revolution.

When *Monserrat* berthed in New York, Trotsky was met on the rain-swept pier by Arthur Concors, superintendent and director of the Hebrew Sheltering and Immigrant Aid Society. Concors' fellow board members, and luminaries of the American Jewish establishment, included its main financial backer, Jacob Schiff, of Kuhn, Loeb & Co.[43] Concors acted as a translator for Trotsky during an interview that had been arranged with the *New York Times*. It has never been explained why an impoverished "undesirable alien," was welcomed to America by an official of a Jewish organization who had close links to the highest echelons of the Zionist movement in the United States.

Professor Spence briefly recounted the involvement of William Wiseman, head of British Intelligence in the U.S., in relation to Trotsky's brief stay there, but unfortunately the details were sparse. Wiseman was closely linked to Woodrow Wilson's minder, Edward Mandell House and, after the war, was rewarded with a lucrative partnership in the Kuhn, Loeb & Co. Bank on Wall Street. Jacob Schiff has been the focus of much attention in Trotsky's funding, but Professor Spence urged caution in connecting him with Trotsky, stating that there was "no demonstrable direct link." Such "demonstrable" evidence may never be found, but Professor Spence was aware that men such as Schiff were adept at concealing such intrigues. Schiff was openly supportive of the Russian Revolution and in a letter published in the *New York Times* on 17 March, he "thanked the Almighty that a great and good people had been freed from their autocratic Czarist shackles."[44] Two days later he voiced his opinion that Russia would, before long, rank financially amongst the most favored nations in the money markets of the world.[45] Interestingly, that same issue of the *New York Times* reported that there had been a rise in Russian exchange transactions in London 24 hours *preceding* the revolution. Ah, the Rothschilds, as ever, a day ahead of the rest of the world. It was explained away as mere coincidence.

Jacob Schiff held a deep-rooted hatred of Czarist Russia because of its gross and frequent ill-treatment of Jews. He willingly financed revolutionary propaganda during the Russo-Japanese War and before and during the First World War.[46] The Jewish Communal Register of New York City 1917-1918 stated that "Mr. Schiff has always used his wealth and his influence in the best interests of his people. He financed the enemies of autocratic Russia and used his influence to keep Russia from the money market of the United States."[47] In 1910, Schiff was one of several Americans who campaigned to revoke a commercial treaty with the Russians over their mistreatment of Russian Jews. When the Czarist regime sought him out for loans he refused, and no one else at Kuhn, Loeb was permitted to underwrite Russian loans. After the Czar's abdication, Schiff dropped his opposition to the Russian government. His views on Zionism experienced a similar volte-face. Schiff initially opposed Zionism, believing it to be a secular, nationalistic perversion of the Jewish faith and incompatible with American citizenship. He funded agricultural projects in Palestine, however, and later favored the notion of a cultural homeland for Jews in Palestine.[48]

Schiff encouraged and financed armed revolt against the Czar. He provided financial support for Jewish self-defense groups in Russia, including

Bolshevik and other socialist revolutionaries. He was set on fomenting revolution in Russia. The America author, G. Edward Griffin, pondered the question of Schiff's involvement and unequivocally stated that Schiff "was one of the principle backers of the Bolshevik revolution and personally financed Trotsky's trip from New York to Russia."[49] Years later, Jacob Schiff's grandson admitted that his grandfather had given about $20 million for the triumph of Communism in Russia.[50]

Professor Spence agreed that Schiff "had a track record of financing revolutionaries," and was "pro-German."[51] This latter observation somewhat lets his thesis down. The German-born Schiff was *not* pro-German. He and his German-born Warburg partners in Kuhn, Loeb bank on Wall Street, and his good friend (and their brother) Max Warburg in Germany, together with their close Rothschild links in France and London, were not operating on a nationalist agenda, whether it be German, British or American, but an internationalist agenda. And that agenda was the domination of the political system of each country and the economy of the world as a whole.[52]

These international bankers of German-Jewish descent had little patriotic sympathy or support for Germany. They belonged to the secret cabal that deliberately caused the First World War in order to destroy Germany. The leading German financier, Max Warburg, was himself deeply implicated in that conspiracy. They were globalists, first and last, seeking control of the entire world. It is why the question of their support for political Zionism, and how that fitted into their agenda, is of critical importance when considering both the Bolshevik Revolution and the Balfour Declaration. The time-scale within which the Anglo-American global-elite power base moved from London to New York, and the ever-growing influence of political Zionism, has yet to be determined. If such issues are not to be addressed, the truth will remain buried.[53]

On 25 March, 1917, Trotsky, who had been living a very comfortable life-style with his family in New York for the previous eleven weeks, was issued with papers for his passage to Russia. The British consulate assured him that no obstacles would be placed in his way. "Everything was in good order," according to Trotsky;[54] but who had the power to issue such high-level permits? The surprising answer is that it reached right to the top of government in Washington. Professor Antony Sutton revealed that "President Woodrow Wilson was the fairy godmother who provided Trotsky with a passport to return to Russia to carry forward the revolution." The passport came with a Russian entry permit, a British transit visa[55] and $10,000 in cash. One first-class cabin and sixteen second-class cabins were booked for Trotsky and his party of fellow revolutionaries on the S.S. *Kristianiafjord*, of the Norwegian-America Line. They departed New York for Oslo and the onward journey to Petrograd, but failed to anticipate trouble ahead. During a scheduled stop at Halifax, Nova Scotia, Canadian officials removed Trotsky and his entire entourage from the ship and incarcerated them in an internment camp. The Halifax officials had not been advised of Trotsky's mission and naturally considered the men a danger to the Allied cause. A flurry of angry telegrams eventually descended upon them. Trotsky and the others were to be released to continue their journey to Russia.

A Canadian Intelligence officer, Lieutenant Colonel John Maclean, later wrote an article entitled, "Why did we let Trotsky go? How Canada lost an Opportunity to Shorten the War." According to Mclean, Trotsky was released "at the request of the British Embassy in Washington ... acting on the request of the U.S. State Department, who were acting for someone else."[56] Mclean did not elaborate on who that "someone else" was. The Canadian officials were instructed to inform the press that Trotsky was an American citizen traveling on an American passport, and his release was specifically requested by the State Department. Clearly, Trotsky had strong support at the highest levels of power in Britain and the U.S., and orders were issued that he must be given "every consideration."[57] Trotsky and his entourage were duly released and allowed to continue their journey.

Who was that "someone else" that held such power and took unprecedented steps to release Trotsky from the cells in Nova Scotia and allow him to continue his journey to Russia? Canada, as a Dominion of the British Empire, would have obediently complied with any instruction from the British Foreign Office, and the man in charge just happened to be Lord Arthur Balfour, member of the inner circle of the Secret Elite and the very man who would sign the Balfour Declaration.

Trotsky claimed that Pavel Miliukov, Foreign Secretary in the post-revolutionary Russian government, had initially wanted him released, but two days later "withdrew his request and expressed the hope that our stay in Halifax would be prolonged."[58] That made sense because the provisional Russian government knew that Trotsky and Lenin refused to accept their legitimacy and posed a serious threat to the government if they returned to Russian soil. Miliukov and Alexander Kerensky were determined to keep Russia in the war; Trotsky and Lenin were equally determined to sign a peace pact with Germany and take her out. The British and American authorities were fully cognizant of the fact.

In early May, Trotsky and his party arrived at Christiania (now Oslo) in Norway, and made their way by rail to Russia. On 18 May 1917, they stepped off a train at the Finland terminal in Petrograd, just as Lenin had one month earlier. Had it not been for Trotsky's unexpected delay in Nova Scotia, their arrival would have been perfectly synchronized.

The Secret Elite in London and the international bankers in the United States, with the connivance of their well-controlled governments, sent back the two men whom they knew would remove Russia from the war. Matters of great significance allowed them to adopt this change in foreign policy. They were well aware that a peace agreement between Russia and Germany would eventually release upwards of a million German troops from the Eastern Front, but there was a compensatory factor. The United States had just entered the war and the loss of Russian troops was more than recompensed by the fresh-faced young Americans who would be sacrificed in due course. Official reports showed that had it not been for the Russian treaty with Germany, "the war would have been over a year earlier,"[59] because the combined Allied strength would have been overwhelming. Millions of men died needlessly or suffered terrible wounds in 1918. The Secret Elite prolonged the war, again and again. Profits multiplied.

The "Provisional Government" in Petrograd lurched from one crisis to another. With heavy military defeats and ever-rising death toll, Russian troops and civilians called for an end to the madness. An All-Russian Peasant Congress, dominated by the socialist revolutionaries, was held in May in support of the provisional Government. A conference of Petrograd factory workers on the other hand, became the first representative body to support the Bolsheviks. It was a time of new beginnings and old grudges. The first All-Russian Congress of Soviets was held in June, with 822 vote-carrying delegates. 285 were Socialist Revolutionary Party, 248 Mensheviks and 105 Bolsheviks. The remaining 184 delegates belonged to various minority groups or had no party allegiance. Throughout the three-week conference, Trotsky solidly supported the Bolsheviks. Congress, however, passed a vote of confidence in the Government, and rejected a Bolshevik resolution demanding "the transfer of all state power into the hands of the All-Russian Soviet of Workers, Soldiers and Peasants Deputies."[60]

Women's Day march in St Petersburg

Four days of menacing street demonstrations that began on 3 July in Petrograd were widely believed to have been instigated by Lenin in an attempt to seize power. Troubles mounted. A military offensive in Galicia resulted in defeat with heavy losses. Prince Lvov resigned as premier and the Menshevik Alexander Kerensky took charge, promising that Russia would remain committed to the war. Kerensky was scathing of Bolshevism and vice versa. He dubbed it "the socialism of poverty and hunger," insisting that there could be no socialism without democracy.[61]

Trotsky, who had once sided with Kerensky, disagreed. He and around 4,000 fellow members of the *Mezhrayonka,* a faction holding an intermediate position between the "soft" Mensheviks and the "hard" Bolsheviks, sided with Lenin. Trotsky now chose to support the man he had previously attacked as a "despot"; a man whose political philosophy, he had claimed, "was based on lies and falsification." It was Trotsky himself who foresaw that Lenin's success would "lead to a dictatorship *over* the proletariat" rather than "a victory *of* the proletariat." And so it came to pass that Trotsky enabled his own prophecy. He was elected onto the Bolshevik central committee, polling a mere three votes less than Lenin himself. Strengthened by their political alliance, Lenin urged his Bolsheviks "to prepare for armed uprising." Russia, he declared, was in the hands of a "dictatorship."[62]

The irony of his words remains awesome. In August, General Lavr Kornilov, Commander-in-Chief of the provisional government's own forces, ordered his troops to march against it, but the military coup failed thanks to the Bolshevik influence on the troops. Kerensky's standing was undermined while Lenin, Trotsky and the Bolsheviks rose in popularity, winning majorities in the Petrograd and Moscow Soviets. By early October preparations were approved for an armed insurrection. Local garrisons "were bribed to remain neutral" and the Petrograd Soviet created a military-revolutionary committee under Trotsky. Bolshevik military preparations gathered pace. What had been a fringe party in May was on the point of seizing power by October.[63]

In the early hours of 25 October 1917, (7 November, in the Gregorian calendar), armed Bolshevik forces occupied key points in Petrograd, including the main telephone exchange, post office, train stations and power stations. At 2 A.M. they calmly walked into the Winter Palace, the seat of government, proclaimed victory and declared a "People's Republic." Bolshevik propaganda films produced later depicted their men fighting their way bravely through the city streets and "storming" the Winter Palace. It was all lies. Very few shots were fired all night. Prime Minister Kerensky fled, and within two days all provisional government ministers had been arrested.[64]

On 26 October 1917, Lenin signed the "Decree of Peace" which proposed the immediate withdrawal of Russia from the World War. Agreement with Germany and the Central Powers on a ceasefire on the Eastern Front was reached on 21 November, and an armistice was signed between them on 4 December. On several occasions sporadic fighting flared up, but Russia was set to sign a peace treaty at Brest-Litovsk on 3 March 1918. Peace at home, however, was an illusion. The American correspondent Eugene Lyons[65] later summarized the consequences of the Bolshevik seizure of power:

> Within a few months, most of the Czarist practices the Leninists had condemned were revived, usually in more ominous forms: political prisoners, convictions without trial and without the formality of charges, savage persecutions of dissenting views, death penalties for more varieties of crimes than in any other modern nation, the suppression of all other parties.[66]

Lenin dissolved the elected parliament and legislated through *Sovnarkom*, the Council of People's Commissars. Theoretically it was an executive branch answerable to the Soviet, but most of the members were appointed by the Bolsheviks.[67] There were no mass demonstrations on the streets when the Constituent Assembly of elected representatives was thrown out, because "it was only later that the people realized that the Bolshevik ship of state was on a straight course towards totalitarian dictatorship."[68] When reality dawned, many were prepared to resist that dictatorship, and Russia faced the bloodiest civil war in history.

The looting of the country's wealth by the Bolsheviks began in earnest. The first steps had been taken several months earlier when the Wall Street bankers used an American "Red Cross Mission" as their "operational vehicle."[69] Unwilling to use diplomatic channels, agents of the "money power" and big business had been sent to Russia disguised as Red Cross officials on what purported to be a generous act of American humanitarianism to help the suffering Russian masses. The "Red Cross" party mainly comprised financiers, lawyers and accountants from New York Banks and investment houses. Only a few doctors were involved. The international banks had bribed the American Red Cross through large financial donations and literally bought the franchise to operate in its name.[70]

In 1917 the American Red Cross depended heavily for support from Wall Street, specifically the J.P. Morgan organization. Morgan and his associated financial and business elites were determined to control Russia's vast assets after the Bolsheviks seized power. Head of the Red Cross mission to Russia, William Boyce Thompson, may have lacked the know-how to bandage a wound, but he was a director of the Federal Reserve Bank of New York and agent for J.P. Morgan's British securities operation.[71] The genuine medical professionals originally attached to the mission were sent home within a few weeks. Thompson, however, retained fifteen businessmen and bankers from the New York financial elite who made up the bulk of the "Red Cross" party. This was no mission of mercy. It might have been more accurately classified as a commercial or financial mission, but it also acted as a subversive political action group.[72]

Thompson, like Herbert Hoover, had made his fortune as a mining engineer before turning to finance and banking. He had visited Russia before the war, understood the value of its vast mineral wealth and fronted the Red Cross Mission to Russia as a vehicle for profiteering. He was interested in the potential Russian market and how this market could be influenced, diverted and captured for post-war exploitation by Wall Street.[73]

William Boyce Thompson, who was in Russia from July until November 1917, contributed $1,000,000 to the Bolsheviks.[74] His "generosity" was criticized in America but the *Washington Post* reported that he made the financial contribution "in the belief that it will be money well spent for the future of Russia as well as the Allied cause."[75] A sympathetic, controlled press has always been a prerequisite for the Secret Elite cause. Wall Street banker, Thompson, developed a close friendship with Lenin and Trotsky. He used it to gain "profitable business concessions from the new government which returned their initial investment many times over."[76] Members of the "Red Cross" mission cared nothing for humanitarian relief or Bolshevism, socialism or communism. The only "ism" they were interested in was capitalism, and how the Russian market could be influenced and manipulated for post-war exploitation. What does it tell us that Trotsky failed to mention the Red Cross mission or William Boyce Thompson or Jacob Schiff in his memoirs? When the Bolsheviks seized power, the Petrograd branch of the National City Bank of New York (of which Jacob Schiff was a director) was the only foreign bank they exempted from being nationalised.[77] Readers do not have to ask why.

When Thompson returned to the United States before Christmas 1917, he was replaced as head of the Red Cross mission by his second-in-command, Raymond Robins. Robins became the intermediary between the Bolsheviks and the American government, and was the only man Lenin was *always* willing to see.[78] Raymond Robins was an agent of the Secret Elite, a protégé of Edward Mandell House, and the President also proved an enthusiastic friend. Wilson had intervened to provide Trotsky with a passport to return to Russia to "carry forward" the revolution. He withheld American support for the Kerensky government; he expressed enthusiasm for the Bolshevik Revolution and on 28 November 1917, ordered no interference with it. Wilson's administration sent

700,000 tons of food to Russia which not only saved the Bolshevik regime from certain collapse, "but gave Lenin the power to consolidate his control."[79]

The United States could have exerted its influence to help bring about a free Russia, but it was controlled by the international bankers who would accept a centralized Czarist Russia or a centralized Marxist Russia, but not a decentralized free Russia. A corrupt system under the Czars was replaced by a corrupt system under the Bolsheviks.[80] The political hue of government, any government, was irrelevant to the bankers, provided they controlled it. And that control was considerably more straightforward through a centralized government in a highly organized state. The British wing of the Anglo-American elites gave similar support. The British government established unofficial relations with the Bolshevik regime, and close relations with the Red Cross Mission, through a young Russian speaking Scottish diplomat, Bruce Lockhart. Lockhart was chosen for the post not by the Foreign Secretary or the Foreign Office, but personally by Secret Elite supremo, Alfred Milner. Lockhart later recounted that before his departure for Russia, the great man talked to him almost every day and dined with him at Brooks's gentlemen's club in Westminster. Utterly devoted to Milner, Lockhart noted that he (Milner) "believed in the highly organized state."[81] Milner's young agent became intimately linked with Raymond Robins and the Wall Street/Red Cross mission in Petrograd.

Lockhart noted that Raymond Robins became the intermediary between the Bolsheviks and the American Government. Although Robins knew no Russian and very little about Russia, he had set himself the task of persuading President Wilson to formally recognize the Soviet regime. His assistant, Michael Gumberg, supplied him with the necessary knowledge and arguments.[82] Michael Gumberg (Gruzenberg), from Yanovich in Belarus, was a man of many aliases who was the chief Bolshevik agent in Scandinavia. He worked closely with Parvus and Furstenberg, and was "confidential adviser to the Chase National Bank in New York.... This dual role was known to and accepted by both the Soviet and his American employers."[83] When the Bolsheviks began to loot Russia in earnest, Gumberg took diamonds stitched in to his brief-case for sale in the United States.[84] He was an international agent who "worked for Wall Street *and* the Bolsheviks."[85]

Gumberg was close to the highly privileged Secret Elite agents Bruce Lockhart and Raymond Robins: "We had no difficulty in seeing the various Commissars. We were even allowed to be present at certain meetings of the central executive Committee."[86] Lockhart saw Trotsky on a daily basis, had his private telephone number and could speak to him personally at any time.[87] Professor Antony Sutton stated that Alfred Milner had primed Lockhart for the Bolshevik takeover, which begged the question as to how Milner knew in advance that there was going to be such an upheaval, when he had denied such knowledge on returning from his mission. Milner briefed the young Scot and sent him on his way with instructions to work "informally" with the Soviets.[88]

Two agents, Robins from America and Lockhart from Britain, had been sent into Russia by the Secret Elite and operated close to Lenin and Trotsky, who had also been sent in to Russia by the Secret Elite, and were admitted into the heart of the Bolshevik government. The Bolsheviks knew exactly who they were and whom they represented, and vice versa. Lockhart recounted a party he gave for embassy staff and other prominent officials in St Petersburg: "My chief guest was Robins. He arrived late having just come from Lenin.... During luncheon Robins spoke little, but afterwards ... he made a moving appeal for Allied support of the Bolsheviks."[89]

Official diplomatic representatives of the British and American governments had been neutralized and effectively replaced by unofficial agents of the bankers sent to support the Bolsheviks. The reports from these unofficial ambassadors were in direct contrast to pleas for help addressed to the West from inside Russia. Protests about Lenin and Trotsky, who had imposed the iron grip of a police state in Russia, were ignored.[90] Many Russians had experienced hunger and hardship under Czarist rule, but many millions would now die from hunger, by the bullet, or from exposure in the frozen hell of the Siberian arctic wastes. A starving wasteland loomed on the horizon as Lenin and Trotsky allowed the gold and treasures of Russia to fill the vaults of the western bankers who had financed, promoted and protected them. Whatever money came to Russia in return by way of payment was used to crush dissent and finance the "Red Terror."

The Russian writer Maxim Gorky, nominated five times for the Nobel Prize in Literature, likened it to an experiment conducted on the tormented, half-starved Russian people. "They are cold-bloodedly sacrificing Russia in the name of their dream of worldwide and European revolution. And just as long as I can, I shall impress this upon the Russian proletarian: Thou art being led to destruction! Thou art being used as material for an inhuman experiment!"[91] How right Gorky was. The corrupt, autocratic system of the Czars had been replaced by a totalitarianism that was infinitely more corrupt and evil. Having seized control from the provisional Government, the Bolsheviks won less than a quarter of the votes in the first elections for the Constituent Assembly. Lacking popular support, they knew the only means by which they could retain power was through a reign of terror. They made no attempt to justify their savagery, claiming that "the revolutionary class should attain its end by all methods at its disposal if necessary, by an armed rising: if required, by terrorism."[92]

And their dictatorship surpassed the worst nightmares of Czarism. Grigory Zinoviev, chillingly expressed what was to be done: "To overcome our enemies ... we must carry along with us 90 million out of the 100 million of Soviet Russia's population. As for the rest, we have nothing to say to them. They must be annihilated."[93] Ten million Russians were to be "annihilated" to achieve that purpose. The Bolsheviks created the feared police force, the Cheka, to conduct an utterly ruthless campaign of terror against all political dissidence. With Trotsky at the head of the Red Army, and his old friend Moisei Uritskii in charge of the Cheka, the voice of reason was choked into compliance. The Cheka put down peasant revolts in various parts of the country after the Red Army emptied their grain stores without payment. Strikes by the proletariat were mercilessly suppressed.[94] Ironically, hundreds of striking workers at the Putilov factory, where the revolution began, were executed without trial. In a nutshell, the Bolsheviks were utterly obsessed with "violence, dictatorship and coercion."[95]

The "Red Terror" went into overdrive in August 1918 when Lenin was shot and seriously wounded. The attack occurred on the same day that Chairman of the Petrograd Cheka, M. S. Uritskii, was assassinated. The numbers who were consequently slaughtered have been estimated in the millions, but no one counted. Hundreds of thousands of innocents suffered barbaric forms of torture at the hands of the Cheka, all of which was carried out with the full knowledge and support of Lenin and Trotsky. The horrors of the infamous forced-labor camps across Russia, as later revealed to an unsuspecting world by Alexander Solzhenitsyn in his *Gulag Archipelago,* began at this time. Millions died in mass famine or were shot in repeated massacres. All the while, the international bankers who had funded and enabled this savagery enjoyed the spoils.

Although they did not interfere with the National City Bank of New York's branch in Petrograd, the Bolsheviks opened the first International Bank of Foreign Commerce, the Ruskombank. It was not owned and run by the state as directed by Communist theory, but underpinned by a syndicate of private financiers. These included former Czarist bankers and representatives of German, Swedish, British and American banks. Most of the foreign capital came from England, including the British government itself. The Director of the Foreign Division of the new Bolshevik bank was Max May, Vice President of Morgan's Guaranty Trust.[96] Olof Aschberg, the Swedish agent who had facilitated Trotsky's return, and much else, was placed in charge[97] Assured of financial and political backing from abroad, the Bolsheviks and their capitalist allies proceeded to carve up Russia. On joining Ruskombank, Wall Street banker Max May stated that the United States would be greatly interested in exporting its products to Russia, taking into consideration the vast requirements of the country in all aspects of economic life. The bank was, according to May, "very important and would largely finance all lines of Russian industries." The Bolsheviks issued a steady stream of non-competitive contracts to British and American businesses owned by the Secret Elite. Loans were paid in gold, including the Czarist government's sizable reserve, which was shipped primarily to America and Britain. In 1920 alone, one gold shipment went to the U.S. through Stockholm valued at 39,000,000 Swedish kroner. Three shipments went directly to New York comprising 540 boxes of gold valued at 97,200,000 gold rubles. These were at 1920 values. The shipments were co-ordinated by Jacob Schiff's Kuhn, Loeb & Company and deposited by Morgan's Guaranty Trust.[98]

Around the same time the Wilson administration sent 700,000 tons of food to the Soviet Union. It was not Christian charity. The U.S. Food Administration, which handled this giant operation, made handsome profits for the commercial enterprises that participated. It was, of course, headed by Herbert Hoover and directed by Lewis Lichtenstein Strauss, married to Alice Hanauer, daughter of one of the partners of Kuhn, Loeb & Company. Like the British ruling class, inter-family relationships of the banking elites were labyrinthine. International profiteers grew fat on Bolshevism. Standard Oil and General Electric supplied $37,000,000 worth of machinery to the new regime. Possibly three-million slave laborers perished in the icy mines of Siberia digging ore for the British-registered Lena Goldfields, Ltd. Averell Harriman, the American railroad magnate, who became Ambassador to Russia in 1943, acquired a twenty-year monopoly over all Soviet manganese production.[99]

The totalitarian power-brokers of Bolshevism acted in partnership with, and were beholden to, the international bankers. They robbed Russia of its gold and diamonds in return for bountiful supplies of weapons with which they controlled and slaughtered the masses. Ironically, weapons that had deliberately been denied the Czar in 1917 and could have ended the war that year, were traded freely after he abdicated. International legal efforts to prevent the transfer and sale of hundreds of tons of looted Russian gold bullion and coins were easily overcome. Much of it was sent to Stockholm, where it was smelted down and reconstituted into bars set with the Swedish stamp. It was a post-war reversion to the blockade avoidance schemes which prolonged the First World War. Stockholm enjoyed a gold-laundering boom on an unprecedented scale. "The Bolsheviks were in business."[100]

Desperate for weapons, they sold gold and diamonds on the international markets at knock-down prices to fund armaments to put down civil strife against their tyranny. The Russian Civil War is beyond the scope of this book, but suffice to say that two years after seizing power, the heavily-armed Bolsheviks emerged victorious. The cost was counted in millions of dead and wounded.

By 1920 they reigned supreme over a devastated and completely bankrupt country. The pre-war population of Petrograd had been reduced by four-fifths, with the emaciated twenty per cent that remained barely surviving. Moscow suffered in like fashion. Trams and trolleys stood still; epidemic disease was rampant and the suffering people found little solace in the hospitals because the doctors and nurses were dying too. The policies of War Communism reduced the Russian people to nearly prehistoric conditions of scavenging to avoid widespread starvation.[101] Estimates of 60,000,000 Russians dying through starvation or execution in this grotesque experiment in social control were almost certainly conservative.

One of the greatest myths of contemporary history is that the Bolshevik Revolution was a popular uprising of the downtrodden masses against the hated Czars. The sheer weight of history has proven that a lie. Certainly, the planning, the leadership, and especially the finance came entirely from outside Russia, mostly from bankers in Germany, Britain, and the United States. Evidence of the role played by international bankers in both the February and October Revolutions in Russia has been laid before you, and although it would appear that the Rothschilds played no great part in them, G. Edward Griffin believed that "The Rothschild formula played a major role in shaping these events."[102] Do not dismiss Griffin out of hand.

Rothschild biographers record that men of influence and statesmen in almost every country of the world were in their pay,[103] and that most of the royalty of Europe was under their influence.[104] The Rothschilds had amassed such wealth that nothing or no one was immune to the purchasing power of their coin, and though they kept tight control of their affairs through intermarriage within the family, they offered a facility for other men to pursue great political ambition and profit. They influenced appointments to high office, had almost daily communication with the great decision makers,[105] and through them controlled politics from behind the curtain. The Rothschilds valued their anonymity and since they generally operated their businesses behind the scenes, their affairs have been cleverly veiled in secrecy through the years.[106] Their traditional system of semi-autonomous agents across the world was unsurpassed.[107] Their modus operandi was to rescue ailing banks or failing industrial conglomerates with large injections of cash, and thereafter using them as fronts for their own ends. Every banker identified in this chapter who undermined Czarist rule and financed and aided the Bolsheviks, can be closely linked to the Rothschilds: The Warburg and Disconto-Gesselschaft banks in Germany; Kuhn, Loeb & Co, J.P. Morgan bank and Guaranty Trust on Wall Street, Morgan Grenfell in London. They were all complicit.

When the Warburg bank in Hamburg was about to collapse in 1857, the Rothschilds injected vast amounts of money into it.[108] From that point in time M. M. Warburg Bank and its partners operated effectively as Rothschild fronts. Their enormous financial clout enabled the bank to grow from a tiny concern with one office and a handful of staff into one of the largest and most important banks in Germany. The Warburg brothers, who have featured heavily throughout this book, acted as covert agents of Rothschild. Max, who was their leading banker in Germany, and reputedly head of the German espionage system during the war,[109] played a major role in financing both Lenin and Trotsky and enabling the "sealed train" journey across Germany. Fritz Warburg was in Stockholm during the war as coordinator of major financial transactions between Germany and the Bolsheviks, and according to British intelligence reports he also had close contact with Parvus.[110]

Another younger brother of Max, Paul, was the senior partner with Jacob Schiff in Kuhn, Loeb & Co. Bank, which was effectively a Rothschild front. The Schiff and Rothschild forebears had actually lived in houses in the same building they shared in the Jewish ghetto in Frankfurt am Main, and Jacob Schiff was yet another Rothschild agent. A file in the U.S. State Department, "Bolshevism and Judaism," dated November 13, 1918, asserted that there could be no doubt that the "Jewish Firm" Kuhn, Loeb & Company and its partners "started and engineered" the revolution in Russia. The report added that Max Warburg had also financed Trotsky, and that Olof Aschberg and Nya Banken were involved.[111]

Jacob Schiff, who had been promoting ant-Czarist activities in Russia since the Russo-Japanese War more than a decade earlier, paid for a large proportion of the pro-Bolshevik propaganda and bribes for the workers and soldiers in the Petrograd garrison in the run-up to both the February and October Revolutions in 1917. Professor Antony Sutton believed that it was a mistake to call the Bolshevik Revolution a Jewish plot because gentiles like J.P. Morgan and William Boyce Thompson were also involved,[112] but Thompson was a loyal Morgan man and J.P. Morgan and the entire Morgan Empire were very firmly connected to Rothschild influence.[113]

Writing in 1974, Professor Sutton was clearly unaware that virtually the entire international banking cabal was linked through a complex chain that led back to the Rothschilds in London and Paris. For example, Olof Aschberg and his Nya Banken in Stockholm were closely linked to the Guaranty Trust in the United States. Guaranty Trust was closely associated with the J.P. Morgan circle, and that, in turn, was covertly under the influence of the Rothschild Empire. Aschberg and Nya Banken fed money to the Bolsheviks from these banks, and from the Warburg Bank in Germany, which was likewise under Rothschild control. Mainstream historians relate that "Germany" financed and facilitated Lenin's takeover in 1917, but it was not the German government, it was German banking institutions ultimately controlled by the Rothschilds.

Jacob Schiff, the Warburgs, the Rothschilds and the other predominantly Jewish international bankers, undoubtedly harbored considerable hatred for the Czarist regime in Russia because of the persecution of their co-religionists, but their reasons for bringing about the Bolshevik Revolution ran much deeper than religion. This was not about love for the Bolsheviks, or concern for the victims of Czarism or the ordinary downtrodden Russian Jews. This was about business and future plans for the world. Before a new world order could be created, destruction of the old order was essential. They aimed to topple the Czarist Russian Empire and bleed it dry. At the same time their friends and co-conspirators in Britain concentrated on demolishing the old order in Europe; the Ottoman Empire, the Austro-Hungarian Empire and, above all, the German Empire. The Secret Elites, including the New York money power, promoted revolution and communism for their own ends just as they promoted political Zionism for their own ends. They were but building-blocks towards their globalist dream. In the same month as the Bolshevik revolution in Russia, the Balfour Declaration was signed in London. Co-incidence? A chance happening that no-one had foreseen? If you wonder why this fact has not been widely considered in history, ask yourself: who owns history? Answer: the Secret Elite; the men of immense power and wealth who have sponsored and published the versions of history which they approve.

Louis Marshall, a leading American Zionist and legal representative of Kuhn, Loeb bank wrote in 1917 that The Balfour Declaration, with its acceptance by the Powers, is an act of the highest diplomacy. It means both more and less than appears on the surface. Zionism is "but an incident of a far-reaching plan: it is merely a convenient peg on which to hang a powerful weapon."[114] Professor Carroll Quigley was likewise very clear about this: "The powers of financial capitalism had a far-reaching plan, nothing less than to create a world system of financial control in private hands able to dominate the political system of each country and the economy of the world as a whole."[115]

Bolshevism and Zionism were funded and supported by the Secret Elite as they embarked on their "far reaching plan": their nightmare vision of a New World Order.

Summary.

- Serious industrial unrest at the massive Putilov works in Petrograd began in February 1917, encouraged by bribes given by Secret Elite agents to the workers' leaders.

• The industrial action was timed to coincide with International Women's Day on 23 February. Workers at other factories were brought out on strike and the numbers rapidly escalated.
• Some soldiers of the garrison, who had likewise been bribed, refused to act against the crowds and an ever increasing number mutinied.
• Many loyal troops were held back in reserve but it is alleged that the Czar felt that he had lost the support of the army and quickly abdicated. Within a week of the unrest a provisional government was set up which aimed to keep Russia in the war against Germany.
• British Prime Minister, Lloyd George and U.S. President, Woodrow Wilson publicly stated their approval for the revolution.
• Plans were immediately set in motion by the Secret Elite to get Vladimir Lenin and Leon Trotsky back to Russia.
• A web of international intrigue comprising mainly Jews together with international banker and Rothschild agent, Max Warburg in Germany helped Lenin.
• Trotsky was aided by Wall Street banker and Rothschild agent, Jacob Schiff, plus a large Zionist element in New York which supported him.
• He was taken off the ship in Nova Scotia by unwitting Canadian officials and imprisoned, but orders from the highest levels in both the British and U.S. governments ensured his release.
• On arrival in Russia, Trotsky joined forces with Lenin's Bolsheviks and they immediately began stirring trouble for the provisional government.
• By early October the Bolsheviks had prepared for armed insurrection. Without opposition they calmly walked into the Winter Palace, the seat of government, proclaimed victory and declared a "People's Republic."
• Lenin and Trotsky dissolved the government and formed what was effectively a Bolshevik dictatorship. On the following day Lenin signed the "Decree of Peace" which proposed the immediate withdrawal of Russia from the World War.
• The looting of Russia's gold, diamonds and other precious stones began immediately, greatly aided by a fraudulent U.S. Red Cross mission headed by a Wall Street Banker. They stripped the country of its entire wealth in return for armaments and munitions.
• Civil war began and a "Red Terror" was commenced with millions of ordinary citizens tortured or slain.
• Two agents of the Secret Elite, one American and one British, were admitted to the heart of the Bolshevik administration and had instant access to both Lenin and Trotsky.
• An international bank was set up by the Bolsheviks, and international bankers from Stockholm and New York placed in charge. Most were linked either directly or indirectly to the Rothschilds.

Chapter 32

A War Without End

We have been conveniently drawn into the belief that the First World War took place between August 1914 and November 1918. Students are taught that the First World War came to an end when an Armistice was agreed in Marshal Foch's railway carriage in the forest of Compiegne in Northern France on 11 November, 1918. Though the guns fell silent at 11 a.m. that day, and the historical strap-line 1914-1918 remains carved in stone, war against Germany continued. The brutal war to destroy her had been deliberately started and unnecessarily prolonged beyond 1915 by the hidden powers in Britain backed by their American allies, and they had no moral qualms about continuing that destruction. The instrument through which they acted was, ironically, a tightly controlled blockade on German imports of food and other supplies essential to the civilian population. The very act that would have ended the war in 1915 was ruthlessly applied *after* the armistice had been signed and caused widespread starvation and death in Germany and Austria throughout 1919. It might be some consolation if the establishment's denial of this historical fact embraced a sense of guilt or embarrassment which clashed with the myth that the Allies continued the war to save civilization. Not so. Such sentiments never found sway with Imperial Britain's ruling class.

In Britain, 11 November 1918 is still celebrated as if it brought closure to the horrors. The theatre of commemoration has marked the armistice for its annual service of remembrance for those sacrificed in the First World War. Remembrance Day services are observed annually at war memorials in every village, town and city in Britain on the Sunday closest to that date. Remembrance is more than important. It is vital. But we must clarify what should be remembered. The great lie of November 11 is matched by the lies on those war memorials – that Britain and her Empire fought in a bitter struggle to save the world from evil Germans; by the lies that millions of young men willingly laid down their lives or were horribly maimed for the greater "Glory of God" and to secure and protect "freedom" and "civilization." In reality, *they* were sacrificed; they were the unwitting victims who died for the benefit of the bankers and financiers, the secret cabals and power-mongers on both sides of the Atlantic. Remembrance is sullied by the triumphant militarism which attends these services, led still by royalty, religious leaders and the political class.

The subliminal message mocks Wilfred Owen's anti-war poem, "Dulce et Decorum Est."[1] The great lie is perpetuated; violence is seen as a means of resolving disputes while the horrors, realities and true causes of war remain buried.

Be assured, no matter the hypocrisy that surrounds Remembrance Day, war did not end with the Armistice. That is merely one of the many lies about WW1 which are still peddled as fact. Though fighting on the Western Front came to a standstill, the assault on German men, women and children continued unabated. Indeed, it became ever more extreme through a ruthless and cynical continuation of the blockade on all food supplies to Germany.

Hostilities on the Eastern Front between Germany and Bolshevik Russia had terminated unofficially in October 1917, and officially in March 1918 with the Treaty of Brest-Litovsk. By the latter months of 1918, the Allies had made some gains, but the underlying stalemate on the Western Front continued its weary, debilitating waste. The Imperial War Cabinet in London,[2] critical of the performance of senior British commanders like General Haig, was still planning advances in 1919 and 1920.[3] They saw no immediate end to the struggle. Some thought a seven-year war possible, but Germany had no reserves with which to continue. In the light of a growing number of exhausted and disgruntled troops and the fear of revolution in Germany, the Kaiser instructed Field Marshal Paul von Hindenburg to withdraw to a defensible line between Antwerp and the river Meuse.[4] Indeed, being fully aware of Woodrow Wilson's address to Congress on 8 January 1918,[5] the German government believed that the American president would guarantee an honorable outcome. Wilson had stated:

> It is our wish and purpose that the processes of peace, when they are begun, shall be absolutely open and they shall involve and permit henceforth no secret understandings of any kind. The day of conquest and aggrandizement is gone by.... What we demand in this war ... is that the world be made fit and safe ... for every peace-loving nation which, like our own, wishes to live its own life, determine its own institutions, be assured of justice and fair dealing by the other peoples of the world as against force and selfish aggression.[6]

What followed were the famous Fourteen Points by which President Wilson defined the new world in which all would be peacefully transformed. These included an end to secret treaties, the absolute freedom of navigation on the high seas, free trade and the removal of economic barriers and absolute guarantees that nations would reduce their armaments to the bare necessities of self-defense. The sovereignty of small nations and subservient colonies was to be determined through a balance of rightful claims and self-determination. Sympathy and support for Russia's political development was expressed in a plea that she be welcomed into the "society of free nations" and that Russia be given every assistance in determining her own future. Belgium merited special consideration. Her sovereignty as a free nation was to be clearly asserted and Germany had to withdraw from Belgian territory to restore confidence in justice and international law. Alsace and Lorraine, former provinces of France which had been ceded to Germany after the Franco-Prussian war in 1871, were to be "freed" and the invaded portions restored to France.

Detailed readjustments to Italy's borders, safeguards for the peoples of Austria-Hungary, territorial agreements for the Balkan states and the "Turkish portion of the Ottoman Empire" and an independent Poland were all included in Wilson's grand statement. Words like assurance, integrity, guarantees, autonomous development and rightful claims gave the Fourteen Points an implied sense of natural justice as did the final ambition of a "general association" of nations for the purpose of affording mutual guarantees of political independence and territorial integrity to great and small states alike.[7] The President appeared to have conjured a solution to the world's problems. It was a mirage.

Based on the apparent altruism of Wilson's statement to Congress nine months earlier, the recently appointed German chancellor, Prince Max von Baden sought an armistice. Baden had been appointed by the Kaiser on September 30, 1918 in anticipation of agreeing on an equitable peace. He had previously spoken out against the unrestricted use of submarine warfare and had a reputation for moderation,[8] which lent hope to the view that his appeal to President Wilson would carry some weight. Von Baden wrote directly to Woodrow Wilson accepting the program set forth "in his message to Congress of January 8th as a basis for peace negotiations," and requested an immediate armistice.[9]

Max von Baden's telegraphed message was forwarded to the U.S. President on 5 October 1918,[10] as was a similar peace overture from Austria-Hungary,[11] but Wilson said he would not negotiate as long as the German army remained on foreign soil.[12] He stated that the good faith of any discussions would depend on the willingness of the Central Powers (Germany and Austria) to withdraw their forces everywhere from invaded territory, though the President did not stipulate a deadline.[13] What followed was totally devoid of good faith.

It is often forgotten that Germany's signature to the truce was conditional. On 12 October the Kaiser's government confirmed that it wished to enter into more detailed discussions on an armistice on the understanding that it was predicated upon a joint agreement on the practical details of Wilson's Fourteen Points.[14] No-one in the German government imagined that the final demands would be left to Allied military advisors who were ordered to ensure there was no possibility of Germany's resumption of hostilities. Indeed, the Allied military commanders were ordered to resume hostilities immediately if Germany failed to concede to any of their outrageous demands. The Allies had spurned numerous German approaches to hold peace negotiations from as early as 1915, but the Kaiser's government believed that Woodrow Wilson was a man of honor. They knew that Europe was bankrupt; dependent on the United States for food supplies and financial support to stave off starvation and collapse. Negotiations in a crisis of mutual survival required cool heads and experienced decision-makers. Sadly the Allied leaders followed a different approach.

Woodrow Wilson was influenced by his Secret Elite minders in America and completely out of his depth in the political potholes of a ruined continent. Sir Arthur Willert, the British diplomat, likened President Wilson's arrival on the Parisian stage weeks after the Armistice to "a debutante entranced by the prospect of her first ball."[15] A bitterly devastated Europe offered no shelter for the starry-eyed. If he was hardly a match for cultured statesmen like Clemenceau or Balfour, Wilson was positively an innocent abroad when faced with David Lloyd George. The British economist, John Maynard Keynes, labeled Wilson a "slow-minded incompetent"[16] and wondered whether the terms of the Armistice to which he gave his approval were the product of deception or hypocrisy.[17] Either matched the Secret Elite's intention to crush Germany.

Unbeknownst to the German delegates, the British, French and Italian governments had agreed on specific armistice conditions which had not been previously outlined. The Fourteen Points were little more than live bait set to catch out the unsuspecting Germans. The Kaiser tried to leap over the Allied impasse and seek the sanctuary of a calmer pool. It proved a false hope. Perhaps the most important question in all that followed is why the Germans tholed the Allied rejection of Wilson's so-called "terms;" though having been landed on a friendless shore, they had little option.

Lloyd George continued the blockade of Germany, and France was intent on imposing severe reparations upon the "beaten" foe.[18] A major potential stumbling block to peace might have been Wilson's insistence on the abdication of the Kaiser during the pre-Armistice discussions in October, but the German Emperor stood down under protest.[19] As the German delegation "for the conclusion of the armistice and to begin peace negotiations" left Berlin,[20] they anticipated that tough decisions lay ahead, but nothing had prepared them for the shock of hearing the outrageous conditions read aloud in the presence of Marshal Foch.

The terms of the armistice required the Germans to evacuate the Western Front within two weeks. That was no surprise, but Allied forces

Words like hunger and starvation found no place in the vocabulary of the British press when Lloyd George decided to cut and run for re-election in December 1918. The supreme political predator wasted no time in calling a general election to offer the British people a "democratic" choice between his coalition partners who had latterly run the war, and either the rump of the old Liberals led by Herbert Asquith or the emerging Labour Party under Ramsay MacDonald. After all, he was the man who had won the war, was he not? Lloyd George was determined to pre-empt his loss of personal power, which would inevitably be threatened by the social and economic problems attendant on demobilization and the difficult reversion of British industry from war to peace. There was also the possibility of very awkward questions being asked about the war's causes, prolongation and mismanagement. True to Lloyd George, this was an act of political immorality totally devoid of justice.

Very few in Britain knew the true origins of the war or of Germany's innocence, and bitterness towards the Germans knew no bounds. George Barnes, the Labour member of the War Cabinet, shouted from a political platform, "I am for hanging the Kaiser."[36] Conservative Sir Eric Geddes promised to squeeze Germany "until you can hear the pips squeak."[37] The Secret Elite had always demanded that Germany be crushed. That, after all, was the raison d'etre of the war. The three-week election campaign fueled by greed, prejudice and deception ended with the Prime Minister declaring Britain's absolute right to an indemnity which covered the whole cost of the war. His supporters claimed that a vote for a Coalition candidate meant the crucifixion of the new Antichrist[38] (the Kaiser's Germany) at the ultimate behest of the real Antichrist ... the Secret Elite. Do not underestimate their capacity to ensure their priorities held sway.

The General election was held on Saturday 14 December 1918 and resulted in a landslide victory for the coalition of David Lloyd George's Liberal supporters and the Conservatives who propped up his government. There were others whose election victory in 1918 had not been anticipated by the Secret Elite. The Labour Party emerged with 57 MPs, and in Ireland, the traditional Irish Parliamentary Party was virtually wiped out by the Sinn Féin Republicans. Ironically, Sinn Féin had no connection with the Easter Rising in Dublin in 1916, but the consequent executions, murders and imprisonment of Republican Irishmen changed the political landscape. In treating Ireland with contempt, linking the long promised Home Rule Act to conscription to the British Army, and repeatedly delaying the political change which the vast majority in the south of Ireland sought, a "great disillusionment," as the Irish historian Dr. Pat Walsh termed it, set in. Sinn Féin won 73 seats but every elected member refused to take their place in Westminster. The "civilization" and "self-determination" for which thousands of Irishmen died in the war, remained an illusion whose realization the Secret Elite resisted. When the votes across Britain were counted, Lloyd George reigned supreme, and Germany was to be starved.

Lack of food was indeed the weapon of war which had ultimately brought Germany to her knees. The naval blockade, which had latterly been applied with ruthless efficiency, destroyed any prospect of a dignified recovery. But Britain could hardly provide sufficient food for her own people in 1918. All Europe faced a range of hardships from bare sufficiency to utter desperation. The controller-general was America; American surpluses; American largesse. The old-world powers were wounded, but not yet prepared to give way to the new power across the Atlantic. They were hyper-sensitive to, as they saw it, the American presumption that they could dictate Europe's economic survival without consultation and joint decision-making.[39] But America had food – and food was power.

With the authority granted to him by Congress on August 10, 1917, President Wilson had created the U.S. Food Administration.[40] He also established two subsidiaries, the U.S. Grain Corporation and the U.S. Sugar Equalization Board. The man placed in control was the same trusted agent whom the Secret Elite had charged with running the Belgian Relief scandal.[41] Herbert Hoover lobbied for, and was given, the job of head of the U.S. Food Administration. His candidature was backed by the bankers and financiers, the J.P. Morgan empire and the British political elite who had facilitated the sham Belgian Relief organization in order to feed the German army. According to the Congressional Archives, Hoover made it clear that a single, authoritative administrator should head the organization, not a board of directors. Just as in Belgium, he demanded and was given full control. As head of the U.S. Food Administration, Hoover became the food dictator.[42] The presidential powers which Wilson had been given by Congress to regulate the distribution, export, import, purchase, and storage of food were vested in Herbert Hoover. He oversaw federal corporations and national trade associations; he demanded the co-operation of local buyers and sellers. He called for patriotism and sacrifices across every state that would increase production and decrease food consumption. Above all he controlled the prices, the supply, and for as long as he could, tried to moderate the demand for food in America. Hoover was, de facto, chief-executive of the world's first multi-national food corporation.

Herbert Hoover was an astute communicator, able to call on his many friends and colleagues in the American press. Under his direction, the Food Administration, in league with the Council of Defense in the United States, urged all homeowners to sign pledge cards that testified to their efforts to conserve food. Coercion plus voluntary self-discipline produced results. By 1918 the United States was exporting three times as much breadstuff, meat and sugar as it had prior to the war. And Herbert Hoover controlled it all.

Before he left America to take charge of the food program in war-strewn Europe, Hoover announced to the press that the watertight blockade had to be abandoned and Germany stabilized, otherwise he reckoned that there would be no-one left with whom to make peace. He ended with the warning; "Famine is the mother of Anarchy."[43] Arriving in London on November 21, 1918 to supervise and control the food provision in Europe, Hoover was given instructions from his British counter-part, Sir John Beale. As director of the Midland Bank, with wide political, financial and manufacturing connections, Beale had been put in charge of Britain's Food Ministry.[44] Hoover's version of events claimed: "Sir John Beale of the British Food Ministry called on me the day after I arrived and urged that I did not discuss the food blockade on Germany publicly any more as they were opposed to relaxing it 'until' the Germans learn a few things."[45] Hoover may have thought he would be in charge, but the agents of the Secret Elite asserted their authority. The food blockade would continue until Germany had been suitably punished. The chosen instrument of "correction" was starvation. That would crush Germany. Starvation.

Having conjured the monster they called "the Hun," falsely blamed its leaders for causing the war, sacrificed an entire generation for an absurd lie, accrued vast debts to enrich themselves and continued to embellish their own propaganda into received history, sympathy for a starving people was not part of the Secret Elite agenda. Old friends played their part. Arthur Winnington-Ingram, the war-mongering Bishop of London, reminded his congregation at Westminster Abbey on December 1, 1918 that it was essential that the Germans be punished. He invoked the propaganda surrounding Edith Cavell's execution,[46] the tragic memory of the 10,000 gallant men of the merchant marine lost at sea, of hospital ships sunk, of women and children drowned and prisoners of war who had survived in half-starving conditions. His message was far from subtle. Punishment, he ranted, was warranted "for the greatest crime committed for a 1,000 years." Indeed. His bitter logic warned that should the German culprits be let off, the moral standard of the world would sink. In triumphant conclusion the good Bishop pronounced, "God expects us to exact punishment."[47] His blatant, vulgar lies were unChristian, but at least consistent with the bitter sermons he had preached since the war began.[48]

And the poisonous propaganda of the war years hardened hearts and made the final act of malice much easier for the agents of the Secret Elite. After the *Daily News* carried a report from a Swedish correspondent in late November which showed that as many as 95 per cent of the population in some parts of Germany had been living in approximate starvation for a least two years,[49] the cry of "Hun-trickery" found popular voice.[50]

Take, for example, Millicent Fawcett, trade union leader, suffragette and outspoken feminist. She made public an appeal she received from the President of German Women's Suffrage Society imploring her to use her influence to stop the blockade "because millions of German women and children will starve." Unmoved, she dismissed the request as typical of German propaganda, blaming the shortages on German submarines whose "dastardly actions had never been criticized by any German, man or woman." Fawcett quoted a claim by Herbert Hoover, "the American food expert," that "Germany still had a large proportion of this year's harvest available," and consequently, there was no likelihood of starvation for any part of the population for many months to come.[51]

Such stories abounded. It was claimed that Berlin's bread ration had been increased and "is better than in Holland."[52] The Northcliffe press railed against "impenitent" Germany and in an attempt to damn the country to further deprivations, the *Times* correspondent in Cologne described his view of the German mentality so perfectly that he unwittingly captured the truth. According to his report the Germans believed:

> Germany is beaten, but so would England have been beaten if the whole world had combined against her. The German nation from the first had been fighting in self defence, otherwise it could never have held out so long. Both France and England would have given in long ago if they had such privations to bear as the Germans have endured. We firmly believe this war has been a war of aggression against us by Russia, a force to whom England joined herself seeking an opportunity to destroy a formidable rival.[53]

Pause for a second, please. This short paragraph encapsulated the central truth. Germany *had* been fighting for its survival in self defense; Britain had been fighting to crush "a formidable rival"; it *had* been a "war of aggression" against Germany.[54] The British journalist was annoyed that he did not find "intelligent, influential Germans" disillusioned or repentant. His message was unequivocal. The German spirit remained untamed. The Northcliffe press spun the lie that the German people expected the Allies to forgive and forget and would "wipe the slate clean" of all that happened during the war. This rival, they contended, had to be crushed by fair means or foul … and all is fair to the victors of war. Let Germany starve.

Hoover realized that vindictive human nature played into the hands of his masters in Europe,[55] but dared not cross the line of open criticism. He requested a detailed breakdown of food production and health statistics from the Ebert government in Berlin, but as head of the Belgian Relief Fund, he had previously had reason to doubt the veracity of official German statements. Consequently, in December 1918, Hoover sent his own experienced officials to check the facts. According to their findings, which were subsequently relayed to Washington, the truth was appalling. Vernon Kellogg[56] reported that whereas Germany's grain production in 1913-1914 was 30,200,000 tons, in 1917-18, it had fallen to 16,600,000 tons.

Bread rationing had been cut to less than 1,800 calories per day; meat and fats had fallen from 3,300,000 tons to less than 1,000,000. The health statistics described a nation in crisis. The birth rate in Berlin had decreased from 6.1 per thousand of the population to less than 1.0, while the death rate had risen from 13.5 per thousand to 19.6. Child mortality had increased by 30 per cent, whereas in Britain it actually decreased,[57] and in adults over 70 the rise was 33 per cent. One-third of all children suffered from malnutrition, crime was rampant, demoralized soldiers were reported to be plundering farms, industry was virtually at a standstill and unemployment was enormous.[58] Kellogg's report stated that starvation had beset the lower-income groups in the major cities; that there were 800 deaths each day from starvation or disease caused by starvation. Food shortage was reportedly worse than before the armistice had been signed. Hoover concluded that the continuation of the food blockade was a crime against women and children and a blot on Western civilization. How ironic, given that Britain and the Allies had apparently gone to war to save civilization.

Hoover's conclusion may appear to convey his supposed humanitarian instincts, but records from the United States[59] demonstrated his grossly unlikeable qualities, his dishonesty, his conceit and, as in Belgium, his preoccupation with money. Hoover wanted overall control in his business dealings and spent November and December 1918 corresponding with President Wilson, his minder, Colonel House and Secretary of State Robert Lansing on that very issue. The British were particularly sensitive to any move which allowed America to take the lead in bringing relief to the civilian population in Europe,[60] and Hoover was frustrated in his bid to be the sole arbiter for food supply. He penned a memo for the President, which Wilson sent to the Supreme War Council, advocating that a Director General of Relief be created[61] to purchase and sell food to "enemy populations." On one point Wilson was insistent. Given the political necessity of American control of American resources, the Director General had to be an American.[62] He had but one American in mind.

Hoover had alerted Washington to the need for a source of working capital and temporary advances to start initial purchases in Belgium, Poland, Serbia, Yugoslavia and Bohemia. He desperately wanted to get his hands on cash. On 1 December, Hoover telegrammed Wilson from Paris suggesting that $5,000,000 of working capital could be sourced from Wilson's Presidential Fund and "I could later supplement this by dividends to you from the Sugar Equalization Board and might avoid appropriations and consequent discussions [in Congress] altogether." He wanted to operate a secret slush fund. Hoover's impertinence was underlined by a final request: "would it be possible to settle this before your departure [to Europe]?"[63] In response, the president, "very much regretted that the terms of appropriation for National Security and Defence would not justify" such action.[64] Incredible. Hoover presumed himself so secure in his appointment that he could suggest a secret and financially inappropriate action to the President of the United States, who, in turn, merely regretted that he could not break the rules. Who was the master and who the servant?

On December 10, 1918 a Conference on European Relief was held in London. Hoover led the U.S. delegation. He spelled out the American position in a manner which brooked no dissent. Given that the world food surplus was predicated on the American peoples' voluntary acceptance of continued rationing, they would not countenance either price control or the distribution of American foodstuffs organized by anyone other than their own government. He warned that any attempt by Allied buying agencies to interfere with direct trading between the United States and neutral governments would bring an end to co-operation. He proposed to construct a system similar to that which had been devised for Belgian Relief, with separate departments for purchase, transportation, finance, statistics and other aid.[65]

Old suspicions, jealousies and fears bristled with self-interest. Comrades in arms found themselves following subtly different agendas as politicians in Britain, France and the United States sought to assert their primacy on the world stage.[66] Wilson's Fourteen Points, like the fabled siren, attracted the Germans to the belief that the final settlement of the disastrous war would be based on the concept of a better, fairer world. What naivety. The British, French and Italian representatives, appointed to translate the armistice into a peace settlement, were preoccupied with selfish and vindictive priorities, with imperial designs which would enfeeble their once-dangerous foe with revenge-laden economic burdens and financial ruin.[67]

Nor had they accepted Wilson's Fourteen Points. Britain would never accept the second point on "Freedom of the Seas." This was an outright denial of the Royal Navy's God-given right to stop and board ships anywhere in the world. Point three called for the removal of trade barriers, an idea which would have ruined the imperial preference championed by many in Lloyd George's coalition government. In addition, no less than seven of the Fourteen Points dealt with "self-determination" and "autonomous development," which flew in the face of the carve-up which was about to unfold at Versailles. Did Wilson imagine that his European allies would stand aside and deny themselves the spoils of war which they considered theirs by right of victory?

The French, on whose land the most ferocious battles had been fought, focused on redrawing the boundaries of Germany without regard to nationality or historic allegiance. So much for the fabled Fourteen Points. They were also fixated on reparations, financial compensation for the physical damage which had ruined more than a quarter of France's productive capacity and 40,000 square miles of devastated cities, towns, villages and farmland.[68] It was presented as justified payback, even though it was the Allies who had forced Germany into war.

Time and again, the French Minister of Finance, Louis-Lucien Klotz, refused to contemplate an end to the blockade until the money, credits and gold which remained inside the German treasury were handed over to the Allies. They would not allow the Germans to spend their money on food. Klotz repeatedly justified his stance by asking why Germany should be allowed to use her gold and assets to pay for food in preference to other debts.[69] Keynes described Klotz in particularly cruel terms as "a short, plump, heavy-mustached Jew … with unsteady roving eye … who tried to hold up food shipments to a starving Germany."[70] He was the butt of many a deprecating joke. Woodrow Wilson wrote of "Klotz on the brain."[71] For as long as it suited, the Secret Elite cast France, its President Georges Clemenceau and Klotz, the Minister of Finance, as villains of the story. The impression given was that the French were to blame for starving Germany, not Britain.

The U.S. State Department knew otherwise. Even before the details of the armistice were made public, Secretary Lansing was in possession of an assessment of the Allied objectives which showed considerable prescience. The Americans anticipated that the U.S. and Britain would become "logical and vigorous" competitors for the world's colonial and Far Eastern trades,[72] while France would remain comparatively dependent on American imports. They correctly forecast that the blockade would continue for an indefinite period because the Allies wanted to be in a position to limit German supplies to the minimum of self-sufficiency, and, crucially, to delay for as long as possible the re-establishment of Germany's export trade. Their assessment was that peace negotiations would also be prolonged so that the British could re-establish their domestic and foreign trade well in advance of Germany and neutral countries alike.[73] They were correct on all counts.

Here, in a nutshell, was one of the Secret Elite's other objectives. Domination of world trade. They were prepared to buy the time for the recovery of their dislocated industries and reassert their pre-war primacy in international trade at the cost of the prolonged agony of the German people. Every move made to provide food to Europe had to wait until one committee or another granted its approval. What mattered was the agenda set by the Secret Elite and the old-world order still considered itself superior to the brash, overbearing Americans whose colossal power had been demonstrated to the whole world. But change was in the air.

The Americans thought they had persuaded their Allies to relax the food blockade on the neutral and liberated countries on Christmas Eve, 1918. Furthermore the Inter-Allied Trade Council proposed to allow neutral countries to trade food to Germany in exchange for commodities which did not compete with Allied exports. On Christmas Day, Hoover announced to the world press that "it is our first move towards feeding Germany." He notified all of the nations involved and announced that the British blockade authorities had confirmed the decision.[74] Unbeknownst to him, or any of the American delegation in Europe, his breakthrough was blown apart by a consortium of Allied councils and executives which met in London some six days later on December 31. They reversed the original decision and re-imposed the full blockade. Hoover described it sarcastically as "a sudden joint meeting … to which no Americans were invited." They had not even been notified.

It was a slap in the face for Hoover and another body-blow for the starving Germans. Not only had the London conspirators undermined Hoover's strategy, they had not even sufficient courage to tell him. Hoover's first concern was the financial impact this would have. It always was. The British were leading an economic revolt which would have caused an disastrous crash in the U.S. farming industries. The Grain Corporation alone had borrowed over $300,000,000 in the expectation of vast profits from sales to Europe. Hoover estimated that he already had 700,000 tons of food en-route to famine areas in Europe. Cold storage for perishable foodstuffs was already at bursting point.

At every opportunity Herbert Hoover used President Wilson to add covering letters to his dispatches, appeals and veiled threats to the Allied food agencies.[75] The Americans were justifiably aggrieved. They had taken steps to increase agricultural production on a large scale, with guaranteed prices for their farmers in order to make vast post-war profits from all and sundry, including Germany. Such guarantees extended to the 1919 crop, which meant that the U.S. producers had to be protected from deliberate price-undercuts from the southern hemisphere. At one point over 1.2 billion pounds of fats and 100 million bushels of wheat were locked down in European storage.[76] Of even greater concern were perishable foods like dairy products and pork, and the tragic fact was that vast quantities of these foodstuffs were held up in Copenhagen, Amsterdam, Rotterdam and Antwerp while millions of Germans starved.[77]

Yet, the British press were relentless in their denial of starvation in Germany. On 3 January 1919, a leading article in the *Times* dismissed the "German Hunger Bogy" as spurious. What were people to think when the trusted *Times* reported, "You don't see so many people with rolls of fat on them as you did five years ago, but you also see a healthier, harder and generally more fit population." Such twisted, pathetic logic.

Even when, by mid-January 1919, it appeared that "the Big Four" (Britain, France the United States and Italy) had agreed that Germany should be supplied with food and "if nothing else could be done" pay in gold and export a limited amount of commodities,[78] the blockade remained in place. The Allied Blockade Committee refused to issue the necessary orders and the British navy stubbornly resisted any attempt by Hoover's ships to enter German waters. The role of the Admiralty has been clearly understated in maintaining and enforcing the vicious throttling of a defeated Germany. It wasn't just that a watertight blockade was maintained; it was extended and remorselessly enforced. The Admiralty ordered the cessation of all German fishing rights in the Baltic ... an act of war, clothed in the name of the armistice. The German people were forbidden to even fish for their own food. The *Berliner Tageblatt* could not fathom why there were steamers loaded with fish from Scandinavia intended for Germany which perished in their holds "because the English had extended their hunger blockade."[79] As we have shown, had such a blockade been enforced in 1915 the war would have been over three years earlier.

Bitter voices were raised in the House of Commons demanding retribution at all costs. Commander Sir Edward Nicholl M.P., threw vastly inflated data into the equation, claiming that 23,737,080 tons of shipping had been sunk by German submarines,[80] and seventeen thousand men of the Mercantile Marine murdered "by order of Count Luxembourg," with instructions to leave no trace behind! Nicholl claimed that "the Merchant Seamen's League had sworn that they would not trade with Germany or ... sail with a German until reparation is made and compensation paid to those who have been left behind."[81] Exaggerations apart (Harold Temperley, then a British official, estimated the total tonnage sunk at over 15,000,000 tons. Lloyd's Register put the number at 13,233,672 tons). The hurt of war-loss reduced sensitivity towards the losers. While that is understandable, it is no reason to deny that the starving of Germany was deliberately maintained for ulterior motives.

The armistice of 11 November 1918 was renewed on 13 December 1918, 16 January 1919 and on 16 February 1919, with Article 26 on the blockade of Germany still in force, it was renewed indefinitely.

The Big Four: Clemenceau (left), Wilson, Orlando (back to camera) and Lloyd George.

While the blockade allowed the navy to distance itself from its consequences, the British army had to deal with the reality of hunger, starvation, poverty and misery on the streets of major German cities. The War Office in London received reports from officers in Hamburg and Hanover,[82] which described the physical deterioration of the population with alarming clarity. Shamefully, milk supplies around Hanover had dried up for children over six.[83] War continued to be waged against the innocent.

Even with his landslide election victory behind him, Lloyd George took no action to intervene until five months of misery had reduced the immune system of the German people to desperately low levels. Economic despair brought about political unrest, riots, protests and the rise of a new threat, Bolshevism.[84] Hunger and malnutrition were indeed breeding revolt. The risks to European stability merited a change of policy. The warnings sent to the War Office began to underline a growing concern about the value of the blockade. A report from fourteen ranking army officers, mainly captains with legal, business or financial backgrounds, detailed their conclusions on the critical state of Berlin, Munich, Hamburg, Hannover, Leipzig, Dresden, Magdeburg and Cassel. They stated that a disaster was imminent and "the policy of starvation (note the terminology … the *policy* of starvation) was not only senseless but harmful to ourselves … and it would be folly to suppose that the ensuing disaster would be confined to Germany."[85] Never mind the emaciated children, the fear of hunger, the sick and the dying … starvation had become a threat to stability across Europe. It was spreading disease and a new threat called Bolshevism. They had no notion that Bolshevism was being funded by the great international banks.

The War Cabinet was issued with a memorandum on these findings in February 1919[86] by the recently appointed Secretary of State for War, Winston Churchill.[87] The picture it painted was stark. Unemployment in Germany was rising at alarming rates, the cost of living had risen to dangerous levels and industry could not find a foothold because it was starved of raw materials. Malnutrition caused physical and mental inertia, with disease adding to the misery of the people. The concluding message could not have been clearer: "Revictualling Germany is really urgent because either famine or Bolshevism, or both will ensue before the next harvest."[88]

Though Britain had been struggling to import sufficient food for its population earlier in the year, by late 1918 Hoover's fleet provided a steady inflow from America to Britain. Yet the onward distribution remained completely blocked. The War Cabinet meeting of 12 February 1919 noted that British ports were stocked "to their utmost capacity," storage facilities taxed to their limit and meat supplies so strong that the civilian ration should be increased.[89] Although consideration was given to British exports to neutral countries, the government was advised that the blockade be maintained. There was to be no swift relaxation ... until, well, Herbert Hoover, the super-hero of his own legend, burst the bubble. Safe in the knowledge that he could not be contradicted, Herbert Hoover later awarded himself the pivotal role in ending the food blockade. The following story was penned by Hoover in *American Epic 2,* written in 1959.

On the evening of 7 March 1919, Herbert Hoover was summoned into Lloyd George's presence in Paris where he found a distraught General Herbert Plumer, Commander of the British Army of Occupation in Germany. Plumer insisted that the rank and file of his men could no longer cope with the sight "of skinny and bloated children pawing over the offal from British cantonments." He claimed that his soldiers were actually depriving themselves to feed these children and wanted to go home, adding that the country "was going Bolshevist." When asked by Lloyd George why he had not sent food to Germany, Hoover, in his own words, exploded in anger and detailed the obstructions put in his way. He ranted about "the three hundred million pounds of perishables," which would spoil in a few weeks, in continental ports or Belgium. He pointed to the vicious and senseless Admiralty policy which prevented the Germans fishing in the Baltic, and the inhumane tactic of starving women and children after Germany had surrendered. Hoover apparently closed this rant with the warning that "the Allies would be reduced to nothing better with which to make peace with Germany than the Germans had had with Communist Russia."[90] Truth or romanticized self-indulgence? Who can say?

Lloyd George knew all this from War Cabinet meetings he had chaired throughout February.[91] It was not news to him, but dislodging the French from their obstinate position proved difficult. On 8 March, at a joint meeting of the Allied leaders, discussions were headed towards the accustomed stalemate when, with a theatrical flourish which suggested a stage-managed prearrangement,[92] a sealed message was delivered to the British Prime Minister from the afore-mentioned General Plumer. In fact, the telegram had been sent at the Prime Minister's request.[93] Lloyd George read it aloud; despair had plummeted to such depths in Germany that "people feel that an end by bullets is preferable to death by starvation ... I request that a definite date be fixed for the arrival of the first supplies..."[94] The French finance minister, Klotz, attempted to ignore the message, but Lloyd George turned on him with unrestrained venom, pouring contempt on his miserly attitude while women and children were starving.[95] The dam broke. The French conceded that Germany's gold could be used for food, but relief was not instant. Some further headway was made on 14 March when an agreement was reached in Brussels allowing Germany to import 370,000 tons of food and 70,000 tons of fat per month. In April all blockade restrictions were removed on European neutrals, which should have allowed an increased flow into Germany.[96] In theory that should have happened, but in practice, every nation affected by the blockade had endured great hardship and either consumed the produce themselves or offered them for export at exorbitant prices which Germany could no longer pay.[97]

But the cruelty did not end there. For the remainder of the Armistice period the bickering between the Americans, led by Hoover, and the Allied decision-makers, continued to thwart the lifting of the entire blockade on Germany. Even when it was perfectly clear that the Weimar government would sign the Versailles treaty, the die-hards refused to move. And though the Allies agreed to lift the remainder of the blockade on European neutrals on 25 June, they remained stubbornly obtuse until they had proof that the Germans had fully ratified the Versailles Treaty on 12 July 1919.[98] It was as miserable as it was petty.

The formal process of agreeing on a peace treaty, predicated on the bitter Armistice, began in the Hall of Mirrors in the Palace of Versailles on 18 January 1919. From January to June, 1919, Paris was the capital of the world.[99] Complex discussions on how to punish the defeated nations involved diplomats from more than 32 countries and nationalities, but behind the scenes the true manipulators of power influenced the key decisions which determined a chain of events which go well beyond our time-scale.

History records the major outcomes from Versailles as the creation of the League of Nations; the five peace treaties with the defeated states,[100] the awarding of German and Ottoman overseas possessions as "man-

The Hall of Mirrors, Palace of Versailles, 1919

dates," chiefly to Britain and France; reparations imposed on Germany, and the drawing of new national boundaries. Critically, Section 231 of the Versailles Treaty, stated that the first World War had been caused "by the aggression of Germany and her allies."[101]

Some have supposed that Germany, by acquiescing in this charge of full and complete guilt in regard to the outbreak of war, finally clinched the argument that she had caused the war. As Professor Harry Elmer Barnes described it:

> Germany occupied the situation of a prisoner at the bar, where the prosecuting attorney was given full leeway as to the time and presentation of evidence, while the defendant was denied counsel or the opportunity to produce either evidence or witnesses. Germany was confronted with the alternative of signing the confession at once or having her territory invaded and occupied, with every probability that such an admission would ultimately be extorted in any event.[102]

By the time Article 231 was imposed, Germany was no longer in any position to resist. Her weapons and navy had been surrendered as per the Peace Treaty conditions. Do not forget that the blockade continued until the Germans signed the document which blamed them for causing the world war. Starve or sign a false testament. That was the option Germany faced. It was a travesty of truth; a cancerous lie which would reap an awful vengeance within twenty years.

The "Big Four" politicians who strutted this stage were Clemenceau, Prime Minister of France; David Lloyd George, the British Prime Minister; the President of the United States, Woodrow Wilson, and the Prime Minister of Italy, Vittorio Emanuele Orlando. They met together informally 145 times, fought their own agendas and agreed on all the major decisions which Germany had to accept in 1919. Paris became the corporate headquarters of international decision makers, the wheelers and dealers who acted as judge and jury in a kangaroo court through which new countries were created and a new order established.

The British economist John Maynard Keynes, himself present at the Versailles Peace Conference, watched the malevolent manipulators with angry contempt. The blame-shapers who knew that both the neutral countries and the German people had been shamefully damaged, pointed damning accusations at the French, at Marshal Foch for his hard-line armistice conditions, at President Clemenceau for demanding unmanageable German reparations, at finance minister Klotz for his insistence that German gold reserves could not be used to buy food, at their delaying tactics, their constant referrals to dubious committees and their unwillingness to end the hunger. Keynes was not fooled. He moved in circles whose prime motivation was to crush Germany; crush the German economy; restore British predominance in trade and industry and promote the Rhodes/Milner ideals. Unaware of the depth of their complicity, he personally blamed the intransigence of the Admiralty in Whitehall, sarcastically implying that since they had just perfected the blockade system which had taken four years to create, they did not want to dismantle it.[103] Keynes called the British Admiralty representative, Admiral Montague Browning, "an ignorant sea-dog ... with no idea in his head but the extirpation and further humiliation of a despised and defeated enemy."[104]

Keynes had considerable sympathy for the Germans. His intimate friendship during the peace talks[105] with the German financial advisor, Carl Melchior, helped find solutions to the many obstacles which blocked food for Germany. Melchior had, since 1900, been senior counsel to, and later a partner in, the Warburg Bank in Hamburg. He became Germany's representative on the Reparations Committee as was described as the country's financial director.[106] Carl Melchior was the only non-Parliamentary member of the main German Peace Delegation. His role in the Bank of International Settlements and his later chairmanship of the Financial Committee on the League of Nations is highly significant.[107] Keynes dined with Melchior and Paul Warburg, whom he described as "a German-American Jew, but one of the leading financiers of the United States, and formerly chief spirit of the Federal Reserve Board."[108] Given the bond between Melchior, the Warburgs and the Kuhn Loeb bank in New York, we need hardly ask why he was in Paris. Indeed, why were so many important bankers from the United States who were intimately linked to the Rothschilds and the Secret Elite, hovering like vultures above a stricken Germany?

For some students of history, the claim that international bankers had influenced and supported the British Secret Elite and their political agents to prolong the war will induce cognitive dissonance. It grates awkwardly against mainstream history taught in the classroom, read in the newspapers or film and television versions of the First World War. The realization that we have been lied to opens the way to a new level of appreciation of what was actually happening. It may take time. For example, take a careful look at the American and British delegations to the armistice/preparatory peace talks in Paris in 1919. When Keynes arrived in January, to be housed with the British delegation in the luxurious Hotel Majestic, "no one yet knew what the Conference was doing or whether it had started."[109] There were numerous officials who attended informal meetings, many of which were not recorded. Paris swarmed with self-interest from around the globe. Britain was formally represented by the eventual signatories to the Treaty, David Lloyd George, Arthur Balfour, Alfred Milner, Andrew Bonar Law and Georges Barnes who were all closely linked to, or approved by the Secret Elite.

Leo Amery, Milner's parliamentary Secretary, shuttled back and forth between London and Paris for five months to influence the discussions on the dismemberment of the Ottoman Empire and direct negotiations with France over the future of the Arabs and the Zionists, the latter whose cause he strongly supported.[110] William Ormsby-Gore was present, a member of the Secret Elite, who had been Alfred Milner's parliamentary private secretary and an assistant secretary to Sir Mark Sykes. Lord Robert Cecil, a cousin of Alfred Balfour, had been given charge of the Blockade from 1916 and had direct links with Herbert Hoover. He was tasked to liaise with President Wilson on his ideas for a League of Nations[111] and ensured the Empire's interests were safeguarded. Cecil was later appointed Chair of the Supreme Economic Council and drew his advice from Robert Brand, a Milner man from his Boer War reconstruction years. Brand was managing director of the merchant bank, Lazard Brothers, and a Director of Lloyd's Bank.[112] Keynes himself was the Treasury advisor appointed to assist Cecil's team, and as an outsider his observations were not colored by secret loyalties.

Consider this assembly of imperial loyalists who were committed to the ultimate victory of the English ruling class in a struggle for world domination. These heirs to Cecil Rhodes's dream marched on Versailles with serious purpose: Protect, strengthen and enlarge the Empire for "the benefit of mankind." They had a staunch ally inside the American camp, an academic historian whom Professor Carroll Quigley named as a member of the Secret Elite, George Louis Beer.[113] Beer strongly supported the Mandate system which would allow Britain to take responsibility for Palestine. He was a member of the Round Table and Milner had him named as head of the Mandate department of the League of Nations.

The official members of the American commission included President Woodrow Wilson and Colonel Edward Mandel House, Secretary of State Robert Lansing, Henry White, a former Ambassador at Rome and Paris and General Talisker Bliss.[114] Strange to relate, these men were probably the least important of the Americans in Paris. Certainly Wilson and House shared the limelight, and that, as ever, suited the real power behind the curtain. Woodrow Wilson had suffered a serious political blow in the 1918 mid-term elections for the Senate and House of Representatives in the United States. The Democrats had lost control of both Houses of Congress to the Republican Party, which did not bode well for Wilson's chance of a third term in office.[115]

Of much more importance was the entourage of vested interest from the banking community which chose to accompany him . These included Thomas Lamont a senior partner in J.P. Morgan, New York and Bernard Baruch, who left Wall Street in 1916 to advise Wilson. Baruch served on the Advisory Commission to the Council of National Defence, became the chairman of the War Industries Board in the USA in 1918, and successfully managed America's economic mobilization through which he reputedly netted a personal fortune of $200 million.[116] His origins were Wall Street and war industries and he was believed to be a Rothschild agent.[117]

Herbert Hoover hovered around the conferences, aided and advised by the team which worked with him in Belgium. Other important financiers from the U.S. Treasury Department, the Federal Reserve Board,[118] J.P. Morgan's bank in Boston, the International Harvester Company (owned from 1902 by J.P. Morgan) and several others, whose fortunes were linked to Hoover's malpractice in Belgium, became major contributors. Vance McCormick, chairman of the Democratic National Committee and chair of the American Commission to Negotiate Peace (1919) was nominally a simple politician, but he also served as chair of the War Trade Board (1916 to 1919). Links to industry and finance, mainly J.P. Morgan, dovetailed at every point.

High-level profiteering by major banks was not an exclusive American domain. One example of how rich European bankers also became, may be gauged from the post-war success of Emile Francqui's Société Générale. Having made an exorbitant fortune through its link with Herbert Hoover's Belgian Relief program and its internal association with the Bundesbank during the occupation of Belgium,[119] from 1919 onwards it flourished as never before. It's London branch, the Banque Belge pour L'Etranger was the financial center for all of the Société Générale's affairs outside occupied territories. In the immediate post-war period it benefited greatly from the influx of capital which followed the signing of the armistice. It created a series of new companies to accommodate the immense reconstruction in Belgium and extended and modernized the country's infrastructure. Banque Belge pour L'Etranger opened new international branches in New York (1917), Paris, Manchester and Cologne (1919), Bucharest (1920) and Constantinople (1924).[120] While the poor in Belgium remained needy and impoverished, its banks flourished. In wars, all wars, billions of dollars are made through profits accruing from the manufacture of warships, airplanes, weapons, and munitions. At war's end, they reap a second dividend through reconstruction of cities, towns and villages shattered by the conflict. War is good business for banks; very good business.

As has been said repeatedly, no event "just happens" as if by mystical or divine intervention. Two important Americans who made their way to Paris were Supreme Court Judge, Mr. Justice Brandeis, and his close associate, Felix Frankfurter. Brandeis openly "went abroad on Zionist missions" and had three "busy and profitable days" in Paris where he "lunched effectively" with Mr Balfour and breakfasted with the American Peace Commissioners.[121] The only item on his agenda was Palestine. Indeed, most of the leading Zionists went to Paris during the conference. Chaim Weizmann maintained his high-pressure tactic of interviews and meetings with the powerful and the influential,[122] the most important of which was held at the French Foreign Office at the Quay D'Orsay on February 27, 1919. Britain was represented by Arthur Balfour, Alfred Milner, Maurice Hankey and William Ormsby-Gore, each handsomely pro-Zionist. The American delegation that day was limited to Robert Lansing and former Ambassador White, while the Zionist delegation was headed by Chaim Weizmann.[123] He presented a Statement of the Zionist Organization regarding Palestine which supported a British Mandate. Weizmann claimed to speak in the name of a million Jews "who, staff in hand, waited for the signal to move."[124]

A French-Jewish historian, Sylvain Levi, was included in the French delegation. He was not a Zionist, and questioned the validity of the ingrained idea of a "country of their ancestors" and warned that the eastern European migrant Jews would include many who "would carry with them into Palestine, highly explosive passions conducive to very serious trouble in a country which might be likened to a concentration camp of Jewish refugees." He stated that "nations could not be created at will ... and that the realization of a certain number of aspirations would not suffice to create a national identity..."[125] Levi warned that it was dangerous to create a precedent whereby people who already possessed citizenship in one country would be called upon to govern and exercise other rights of citizenship in a new country.[126] To the Zionist ear, this was heresy.

Weizmann was stunned, frozen with anger. Lansing stepped in to ask him for clarification about the correct meaning of a "Jewish national home." Weizmann prevaricated. The Zionists, he said, did not want to set up an autonomous Jewish government, merely set up, under a Mandate, an administration "not necessarily Jewish," to send 70-80,000 Jews per year into Palestine – that they would build up gradually a nationality that would be as Jewish as the French nation was French and the British nation, British.[127]

If the Zionist agenda later became self-evident and openly contentious, little attention has been paid to the J.P. Morgan/Warburg/Rockefeller/Wall Street assault on Versailles. What brought that legion of damned bankers to Paris? Their presence had the feel of an exclusive conference for sales executives, for in many ways that was their agenda. War was opportunity and so was its consequence. In America, the January 1919 *Bankers Magazine* reported a high-level conference held in Atlantic City. Entitled, "A Reconstruction Congress," it was spearheaded by Rockefeller Jr., banker, William Cox Redfield (President Wilson's Secretary of State for Commerce form 1913-1919) and James A. Farrell of the U.S. Steel Corporation, part of the Morgan Empire. Rockefeller opened the Congress by stating: "Never was there such an opportunity as exists today for the industrial leader with clear vision ... to establish a solid foundation for industrial prosperity."[128]

This prosperity was to be had on the back of reconstruction and reparation in Europe. The Reconstruction Congress stressed that "there seems no reason why enterprise should not move forward with confidence in the great work of reconstruction." The marketplace was the new world of post-war investment, reparations and reconstruction, but this new-world order embraced its old-world mentor as a partner.

In the same edition of *Bankers Magazine*, the U.S. financial elites advocated the re-union of "the two great English-speaking countries of the world" whose language, faith in democracy and concern for human liberty "derives from the same source." Put aside the grand lie of meaningful democracy and concern for humanity. These were the weasel-words behind which the Secret Elite had always protected themselves. One can almost hear Cecil Rhodes speaking. Magnanimously, the Americans accepted that Britain had spread civilization; that differences between the English-speaking nations had become less marked and wider financial co-operation "will be welcome by the English bankers." At which point the *Bankers Magazine* announced a new alliance: "The people of these two great English Speaking democracies have made their minds definitely to pull together hereafter – and no propaganda engendered either in hell or in Germany can change this purpose."[129]

And there it was. A statement from the heart of American banking that categorically announced the merger of Britain's Secret Elite and the U.S. Money power in a united design to "pull together hereafter," for these were the people about whom the article was talking. Not ordinary people; powerful bankers and financiers. It was as if the birth of a new world order had been announced in their columns. It was to be a marriage of like purpose and all that remained to be ironed out were the pre-nuptial agreements. The Anglo-American establishment was to be in their joint control. What makes this all the more galling is the fact that in both Britain and America the ordinary man and woman was close to despair. High prices, low wages and industrial disputes became the order of the day. General strikes took place in Seattle and Winnipeg.[130] In Glasgow, troops from England had to be rushed into the fray carrying rifles with bayonets. Tanks were brought into the streets and union leaders beaten and thrown into prison.[131] The new Anglo-American establishment rose above such working-class protest. It always has.

The Treaty of Versailles, signed eventually on 28 June 1919, was uncompromising. Germany lost nearly one-seventh of its territory and one-tenth of its population. Half the iron ore and one-quarter of the coal production as well as one-seventh of agricultural production were taken from her. German colonies and all foreign possessions of the Reich were lost. Most of her commercial fleet had to be handed over and long-term economic discrimination endured.

The army and navy were considerably reduced. The Rhineland was de-militarized, split in three zones and occupied by Allied forces for five to fifteen years. The Saarland was put under the mandate of the League of Nations. The coal mines went to France. Gdansk and its surrounding area was turned into a Free City of Poland with special rights. The independence of Austria, whose National Assembly had voted to accept the connection to the German Reich, was to be guaranteed in perpetuity. The amount of reparations was to be determined at a later time. That the sum to be compiled would be very high, was beyond doubt. The murdered Kitchener must have spun in his watery grave. This was not a just peace.

Before the signing of the treaty, President Wilson said that if he were a German, he would not sign it. His Secretary of State Lansing considered the conditions imposed on Germany as unutterably hard and abasing, many of them impossible to comply with. His adviser, Mandell House, wrote in his diary on 29 June that the treaty was bad and should never have been concluded; its execution would bring no end of difficulties over Europe.[132] The real victors would not be swayed. The final Treaty stands testament to how little real influence Woodrow Wilson wielded in Europe.

The Versailles Peace Settlement was a stepping-stone to future wars. Diplomat-historian George F. Kenan later wrote that the peace treaty "had the tragedies of the future written into it as if by the devil's own hand."[133] As we have pointed out, by accepting Article 231, Germany was obliged to bear the burden of guilt for causing the war. Old Empires were dismantled and choice pickings reallocated. Gone was the German Empire and Queen Victoria's grandson, the Kaiser. The Imperial Russian Empire was no more, its Czar Nicholas II, cousin of Britain's King George V, executed by the very Bolsheviks whom American and British bankers had financed. The Ottoman Empire, ripped apart by the victors, offered the opportunity to redraw the Middle East with the lure of oil and prime strategic locations. The British Empire survived, but at a cost. Britain had sold off at least a quarter of its dollar investments and borrowed over £1,027,000,000 from the United States.[134] Consequently, the flow of capital from America to Europe reversed the pattern which had dominated the previous century. These immense changes represented a long-term financial realignment in favor of Wall Street.

The conclusion to the First World War was not the beginning of the end, but a building-block towards disasters that were to come. A new Elite intended to control the peace and exert its influence through organizations which it created specifically to determine how that would be done. During the Peace Conference in Paris, Alfred Milner's chief acolyte, Lionel Curtis, organized a joint conference of British and American "experts" on foreign affairs at the Hotel Majestic.[135] The British contingent came almost exclusively from men and women identified by Professor Carroll Quigley as members of what we have termed The Secret Elite.[136] The American "experts" came from banks, universities and institutions dominated by J.P. Morgan and members of the Carnegie Trust.[137] This alliance of international financial capitalism and political thinkers and manipulators began a new phase in the life of the secret cabal as they continued their drive to establish a new world order.

They took the successful Round Table Group and remodeled it into The Institute of International Affairs. Smothered in words which when decoded meant that they would work together to determine the future direction of a fast-changing world, Lionel Curtis advocated that "National Policy ought to be shaped by a conception of the interests of society at large."[138] By that he meant the interests of the Anglo-American Establishment. He talked of the settlements which had been made in Paris as a result of public opinion in various countries, and spelled out the need to differentiate between "right" and "wrong" public opinion. With chilling certainty, he announced that "Right public opinion was mainly produced by a small number of people in real contact with the facts who had thought out the issues involved."[139] He talked of the need to "to cultivate a public opinion in the various countries of the world" and proposed the creation of a "strictly limited" high-level think-tank comprising the like-minded "experts" from the British and American Delegations. A committee of selection, dominated entirely by Secret Elite agents was organised[140] to avoid "a great mass of incompetent members." What quintessential British ruling-class thinking. A new Anglo-American Elite of approved membership was self-selected.

Thus the Institute of International Affairs, also known as Chatham House, was formally established in July 1920 and was granted a Royal charter in 1926.[141] Its first decision was to write a history of the Peace Conference. A committee to supervise these writings, in other words, to ensure that the official history recorded only their version of events, was funded by a gift of £2,000 from Thomas Lamont of J.P. Morgan. Follow the money and you will always trace the power behind the politicians. At the same time the Institute's sister organization, the Council on Foreign Relations (CFR), was created with J.P. Morgan money. Acting in close co-operation and funded by similar sources, the CFR and Chatham House ensured that the Britain and the United States followed similar foreign policies.

It is important to bear in mind that Curtis and his new updated organization invited speakers to discuss and develop the "right" opinion. That would have been why the first fully recorded meeting which was published in *The Round Table Journal*[142] in 1921 was given by D.G. Hogarth who served on the Arab Bureau during the war. He was a friend of T.E. Lawrence and Sir Mark Sykes, the men who betrayed the Arabs. Hogarth spoke on the Arab States as an indication that this was one specific area for which the "right" opinion had to be endorsed.[143] In 1922, Chaim Weizmann gave an address on Zionism.[144] His must have been the "right" opinion too.

One final task was required before these elites could safely move forward. They had to ensure that all the evidence of their complicity in deliberately starting the war in 1914 and prolonging it beyond 1915, was removed. The task fell to Herbert Hoover, who also had a proprietary interest in hiding his own fraudulence in the Commission for Relief in Belgium. On the basis that his involvement was kept "entirely confidential," Ephraim Adams, professor of history at Stanford University, a close friend of Hoover's from their student days, was called to Paris to co-ordinate a great heist of documentary evidence from countries across Europe pertaining to the war and its true origins, and dress it in a cloak of academic respectability. Adams resolved to keep a diary, but stopped after a week on the spurious excuse that he was making too many contacts and the work was too interesting "to suffer interruption by recording them."[145] The task had to be undertaken immediately. Speed was of the essence. Adams was in Paris by 11 June with no plan of action, other than to follow Hoover's instructions that all the stolen or illegally procured documentation was sent to Stanford University in California. It was about as distant a destination from the European Theatre as could be imagined.

Nothing was too unimportant. Decisions about relevance were left to a later date. Two years later Adams still hadn't even begun the process of creating a catalogue of the treasures he had siphoned off, on the rather spurious basis that doing so too early led to "disappointment and vexation."[146] In Belgium, for example, access to government records was facilitated by "M. Emile Francqui, mining engineer and a banker of world reputation."[147] Of course it was. Who else knew where all of the skeletons from the Belgian Relief scandal were buried? Francqui, whose all-powerful Belgian bank, the Société Générale, ended the war cash-rich and thriving beyond its dreams,[148] was the one man who knew exactly what evidence had to be removed immediately. Why have historians and investigative journalists failed to unmask this charade? Hoover and Francqui orchestrated the removal of documents that enabled the myth of Belgian Relief to flourish while masking its sinister role.

Hoover had many powerful friends. He persuaded General John Pershing to release fifteen history professors and students serving in various ranks of the American Expeditionary Force in Europe and sent them, in uniform, to the countries his "humanitarian" relief agency was feeding. With food in one hand and reassurance in the other, these agents faced little resistance in their quest. They were primarily interested in material relating to the war's origins and the workings of the Commission for Relief of Belgium. They made the right contacts, snooped around for archives and found so many that Hoover "was soon shipping them back to the U.S. as ballast in the empty food boats."[149] He recruited an additional 1,000 agents whose first haul amounted to 375,000 volumes of the "Secret War Documents" of European governments.[150] Hoover allegedly donated a $50,000 "gift" for the task. That would only have paid for around seventy of these agents for a year. It has not proved possible for us to discover from what source the remaining nine-hundred men were paid.

Hoover's backers claimed that there would only be ten years within which the most valuable material could be "acquired." According to Ephraim Adams, Hoover himself estimated that the process of "collecting" would go on for twenty-five years[151] but it could take "a thousand years" to catalogue the material. The collection was accelerated to a "frenzied pace."[152] How convenient. The official propaganda insisted that the work was urgent, but it would take a millennium to catalogue. The secret removal and disposal of incriminatory British and French material posed little or no problem for the Secret Elite, and, once the Bolsheviks had taken control, access to Russian documents proved straightforward. Professor Pavel Miliukov, foreign minister in the old Kerensky regime, informed Hoover that some of the Czarist archives from the origins of the war had been concealed in a barn in Finland. Hoover later boasted that "Getting them was no trouble at all. We were feeding Finland at the time."[153]

The Secret Elite thus took possession of a mass of evidence from the old Czarist regime that undoubtedly contained hugely damaging information on Sarajevo and Russia's secret mobilization. Likewise, damning correspondence between the Russian foreign ministry and its representatives in Paris and Belgrade has been "lost" to posterity. All Russian diplomatic papers from 1914 were removed from their archives by an unknown person. These were documents of momentous importance that would have proved that Germany had not caused the First World War.

It might at first appear strange that the Bolsheviks cooperated so willingly by allowing Hoover's agents to remove 25 carloads of material from Petrograd.[154] According to the *New York Times*, Hoover's team bought the Bolshevik documents from a "doorkeeper" for $200 cash,[155] but there were darker forces at play. As we have documented in Chapter 31, the Bolshevik leaders were beholden to American bankers closely linked to the Secret Elite and were in the process of selling off the best of Russian resources to them.

The removal of documents from Germany presented few problems. Fifteen carloads of material were taken, including "the complete secret minutes of the German Supreme War Council," a "gift" from Friedrich Ebert, first president of the post-war German Republic. Hoover explained that Ebert was "a radical with no interest in the work of his predecessors,"[156] but the starving man will exchange even his birthright for food. Hoover's people also acquired 6,000 volumes of court documents covering the complete official and secret proceedings of the Kaiser's preparations for war should France and Russia mobilize against her. Where then is the vital evidence to prove Germany's guilt? Had there been proof it would have been released immediately. There was none.

By 1926, the "Hoover War Library" was so packed with documentary material that it was legitimately described as the largest in the world dealing with the First World War.[157] In reality, this was no library. While the documents were physically housed within Stanford, the collection was kept separate and only individuals with the highest authorization and a key to the padlock were allowed access. In 1941, 22 years after Hoover began the task of secreting away the real history of the First World War, selected documents were made available to the public. What was withheld from view or destroyed will never be known. Suffice to say that no First World War historian has ever reproduced or quoted any controversial material housed in what is now known as the Hoover Institution on War, Revolution and Peace. Indeed, it is a startling fact that few if any war historians have ever written about this illicit theft of European documents relating to arguably the most crucially important event in European and world history, and their concealment in California. Why? They were stealing history to protect themselves.

In a sense this whole protracted world war, justified by lies, prolonged by profiteers and politicians with hidden agendas, subjected to false histories, suffered by nations in debt and by ordinary people through irreparable loss, did not end. All of the consequences of war were sucked into the vortex of a grossly unfair peace. Furthermore, the "hidden powers," the "money-power," "the power behind the curtain" who had ordained the war were more secure in their control of the developed world by the end of 1919. Versailles did not mark the end. It provided a forum for the new elite to regroup and draw breath. Worse was to come.

Summary.

- Although the guns on the Western Front fell silent on November 11th 1918, the war did not end because the food blockade of Germany continued to be tightened and the country starved.
- Woodrow Wilson had presented to Congress, a Fourteen Point solution to war which promised justice and fair dealing, in January 1918.
- On 12 October the German government confirmed that it wished to enter into more detailed discussions on an armistice on the understanding that it was predicated upon a joint agreement on the practical details of Wilson's Fourteen Points.
- The terms of the Armistice were unexpectedly severe. The British and French military authorities demanded harsh retribution which crippled Germany's capacity to transport what meager food it had around the country.
- Lloyd George called an election in Britain in December 1918 and his campaign used bilious anti-German slogans to whip up support for his election. Though he won by a coalition landslide, a new political party in Ireland, Sinn Fein, swept away the former Irish National Party.
- America was the source of food for Europe and the importation of food was centered on one controller, Herbert Hoover.
- When he arrived back in Europe in 1918, Hoover was summoned to London to be told that the blockade of Germany was none of his business and

that the British government would not relax it until "the Germans learn a few things." Germany was to be crushed by starvation, by order of the Secret Elite.

• Official statistics from the German government and quoted by Hoover's own agents showed Germany in crisis by December 1918, with a lack of food and consequent malnutrition, crime and desperation in the country.

• As ever Hoover demanded to be in sole control of food administration and the Allies objected to the belief that they were being saved by the Americans.

• The French were particularly bitter about their humiliation and loss over the war years and demanded that Germany handed over its reserves of gold, rather than spend it on food for the populous.

• The armistice of 11 November 1918 was renewed on 13, December 1918, 16 January 1919 and on 16 February 1919, with Article 26 on the blockade of Germany still in force, it was renewed indefinitely.

• The British contingency at the Versailles peace talks was dominated by members and associates of the Secret Elite, especially Alfred Milner's acolytes.

• The American contingency was dominated by the influential bankers and financiers who controlled Congress and the presidency. JP Morgan's influence was paramount.

• The Belgian Banks, especially Emile Francqui's Société Générale blossomed in the post war years.

• Chaim Weizmann and the Zionist lobby was supported by the British delegation. He presented a Statement of the Zionist Organization regarding Palestine which supported a British Mandate. Weizmann claimed to speak in the name of a million Jews "who, staff in hand, waited for the signal to move."

• At a specially convened conference in January 1919 at Atlantic City, the top bankers in the United States declared that prosperity would be Allied to reconstruction in Europe and declared their faith in the re-union of the 'two great English-speaking countries of the world.'

• During the Peace Conference in Paris a joint conference of British and American 'experts' was held at the Hotel Majestic. The British contingent came almost exclusively from men and women we have identified as The Secret Elite. The American "experts" came from banks, universities and institutions dominated by J P Morgan and members of the Carnegie Trust. This alliance of international financial capitalism and political thinkers and manipulators began a new phase in the life of the secret cabal which sought to establish a new world order.

• To ensure that all of the evil fascinations which had caused and prolonged that awful war, Herbert Hoover was charged to collect every scrap of evidence which would have incriminated the Secret Elite which remained on the European continent an ship it to safety in California.

• The conclusion to First World War was not the beginning of the end but a building block towards further struggles that were to come.

Postscript

The War to End ...

A decade ago, when we first took up Professor Carroll Quigley's challenge to look for the evidence of Rhodes's secret cabal[1] and how they grew into the Secret Elite, we were stunned by the facts which had been ignored, amazed by the ease with which important figures had been air-brushed from history and angered by the repetition of old lies about the causes and conduct of the First World War. Researchers are still denied access to records and official papers which remain under lock and key or have been burned or shredded. Yet, after many years of dogged research we have proved without doubt that the Secret Elite caused the war against Germany and, in conjunction with their associated international bankers and political allies in London and New York, deliberately prolonged the carnage beyond 1915. They were determined to break up forever the old empires which threatened the imperial power of Great Britain. Germany had to be destroyed. As the Romans had insisted that Carthage had to be destroyed to ensure the primacy of Rome, so the Secret Elite and their agents focused their might on the destruction of Germany. For almost a century the myth that Germany deliberately started that war has been repeated like a mindless mantra. Over the last few years there has been a noticeable move towards a softer approach, the most recent of which being Christopher Clark's interpretation that Europe sleepwalked into war.[2] Not so. We cannot repeat too often, the hard fact that millions of men were sacrificed by evil profiteers and malignant power-brokers in a determined effort to bring about their new world order.

Chapter by chapter we have produced clear evidence that the war was prolonged, deliberately and unnecessarily. This accusation was made repeatedly in the British parliament, in the French assembly and in contemporary reports. Such protestations were ignored, rejected or deemed groundless. The misery of the war in Europe, in the Dardanelles and Gallipoli, on the high seas and in the air, was justified by propaganda and lies, while those who suffered the deprivations and agony were sacrificed to a dark cause about which they knew nothing.

The United States, though posturing as a neutral, was essentially an active ally for the British and French governments from the early days of the conflict. The money-power and the presidential minders who controlled U.S. foreign policy would never have allowed Germany to succeed.

J.P. Morgan and his Rothschild backers, the Rockefellers, Kuhn Loeb and Warburgs made unprecedented profits on the back of the sheer hell of the trenches and poverty and deprivation on the home front. Though Britain was assured of support from the Anglo-American banking fraternity from the first day of the war, it was no easy task to turn the average American citizen from isolation and a deeply entrenched anti-war sentiment to active involvement. The financial clout of the American banks, the munitions industries and the essential food producers unquestionably ensured an Allied victory, though, for most of the war the American people had no inkling of their government's complicity.

The lies and deceit continued unabated. Cleverly staged propaganda justified the loss of civil liberty which was imposed by government. The Secret Elite have no respect for democracy. We live in a strange era of alternative fact and fake news, but do not imagine that this is some new invention. Woodrow Wilson was re-elected in 1916 on the boast that "he kept America out of the war"; barely three months after his second inauguration he completely reversed his policy and effectively ended any chance of Germany's success. This is precisely how elites have always worked. Given all that she was up against, Germany could never have won once the Kaiser's armies had failed to take Paris in the first few months of the war.

Should any doubt remain about the power, largely unelected power, exercised by the men identified at the end of the nineteenth century by Professor Quigley as Rhodes' secret cabal, consider the following. By the year 1912, Rhodes and W.T. Stead were dead, but Cecil Rhodes' fortune had been placed in the hands of Alfred Milner and his associates, and the press in Britain was dominated by the Secret Elite-approved, Lord Northcliffe. Natty Rothschild succumbed to ill health in 1915, but his successors, and in particular, his son Walter and nephew James de Rothschild had been thrust to the fore of an emerging force called Zionism. Above all was Alfred Milner. The man who saved Rothschild's gold and diamond mines in South Africa became the unelected permanent member of the War Cabinet under Lloyd George.

Milner the mastermind; Milner the "Race Patriot"; Milner who commanded the loyalty of the senior ranks in the British Army; Milner, who had given Lloyd George his support to lead the government; Milner, whose acolytes controlled Lloyd George's policy from their Downing Street offices; Milner, the man who personally bade farewell to the last Czar. A man so important to the creators of the new world order that his influence has been airbrushed from history. Had you previously heard of Alfred Milner? Was his name ever mentioned in the classroom or lecture hall when you were studying history? Has his place in all that happened been acknowledged by those who control the organized commemorations for the First World War? No. It was he who had the steel to "disregard the screamers" and hold out for the destruction of Germany.

What too of the imposter, Herbert Hoover? He was re-invented as a great humanitarian between 1914-1919, but his success was backed by the men who wanted to prolong the war. The Commission for Relief in Belgium was not his great achievement; nor was his role as Food Administrator for the American government. While the Germans will be remembered for the burning of Louvain, and its historic library in 1914, a crime against civilization, they said, Hoover literally stole the history of Europe from before the war until 1919, and took it half-way round the world to place it under lock and key. Ah, but he was a good-guy. He did it for posterity, did he not? What a shame that the evidence, or what remains of it, has been condemned to eternal darkness; that all of his shipping and distribution papers have disappeared; that the entire narrative of Belgian Relief has been left exclusively to Hoover's apologists. It is disgusting to admit that the secret papers concerning the causes of the war in Europe were exchanged by desperate men for food. That is the level to which the man who would be 31st President of the United States of America sank.

So many questions remain unanswered. You will have your own. Do not give up on them. An issue which needs considerable examination is Woodrow Wilson's "Fourteen Points." With hindsight it ranks as one of the greatest mirage's of all time, for it never was anything more than a clever deception, the lure which the Kaiser and his advisors swallowed. They made the devastating mistake of trusting the American government. What were they thinking? The Germans knew about Britain and France's dependence on America, of the blatant lies about the sinking of the *Lusitania*, and every other scandal, yet they were apparently willing to put their faith in Woodrow Wilson. Certainly the Americans had kept them fed through the Belgian Relief program, and the Rockefeller/Rothschild axis ensured that their oil supply was not interrupted, but once the United States joined the war against Germany, surely the blinkers should have fallen?

But desperate times demanded desperate action. The promise of a just peace was too powerful for the Kaiser's government to ignore. The German offensive from March to June 1918 is said to have pushed the Allied armies on the Western Front closer to disaster than at any time since the first battle of the Marne in 1914,[3] but this last throw of Ludendorff's dice was frustrated by "the enormous acceleration of the arrival of American troops."[4] Like exhausted prize fighters who had fought to a standstill, the Allies and Germany stood in their corners feigning a readiness for the next round. But while Britain and France had almost limitless reserves on hand from America, Germany was truly spent. Wilson's Fourteen Points appeared as the basis for a just and honorable settlement. It was a triumph of deceit over justice.

The truth is that Germany had sought a just peace many times since December 1914. The Allies simply did not want to know in 1915, 1916 and 1917. In fact, they did not want to know in 1918. There is ample evidence that preparations for war on the Western Front in 1919 and 1920 was discussed and anticipated by the British War Cabinet. The American presence changed every dynamic. Time was on the Allied side.

The failure of Woodrow Wilson's Fourteen Points to find international support sucked the last breath of hope from the German leaders. Wilson had no power to stop his proposals being picked apart at Versailles, and returned to America a sick and disillusioned man. He had fulfilled his mission for the Elites by revoking his election stance of 1916 and then abruptly bringing America into the war. He had confused the German leadership with his "idealism" and upset his political enemies in America by proposing a League of Nations,[5] which was nominally adopted in the eventual Treaty of Versailles. Though the troubled, one might say dysfunctional, history of the League of Nations extends beyond our timescale, its very proposal caused the U.S. Congress to twice reject the Versailles Peace Treaty.[6] A cross-section of American Senators were so determined to have no truck with Wilson's League of Nations that they declared the Treaty "dead to stay dead."[7] These words might well have served as an epitaph for Wilson's political career. Having suffered a devastating stroke in October 1919, his candidacy for a third term in office was rejected by the Democratic Party.

What too of Russia? When one considers the sacrifices made by the Russian people in their war against Germany, their absence at Versailles ought to have caused some embarrassment. For three long years Russia had battled the Germans and Austrians, inflicting great losses but absorbing even more.[8] The long-standing promise that Russia would annex Constantinople and the Straits once Germany was destroyed was effectively and conveniently annulled when the Bolshevik government made peace with Germany in 1918. Lloyd George raised the hitherto unasked question of Russian involvement in the peace process in January 1919,[9] but there was no coherent or consistent agreement from a divided Supreme Council. Alarming tales circulating in Paris of the barbaric Red Terror unleashed by the Bolsheviks, were dismissed as exaggeration by Lloyd George.[10] Of course. The British Prime Minister was a master at dissembling. The all-embracing role of the British and American bankers was another factor which was not to be mentioned. What mattered in the end was that Constantinople remained outside Russian control and Russia no longer threatened Persia, India or a redrawn map of the Middle East.

History is not just a series of eras or neatly constructed time lines within which commentators try to explain events or construct their own given narrative. History lives and breathes and never stands still. It is our past and determines much of our future. Events, decisions and consequences ensure that it will always remain a fascinating basis through which we better understand where we currently are, and how we got here. But the historical record is incomplete. It has been tampered with, remastered and abused by those with much to hide. Where there are gaps, suspect the motivation. Do not fall prey to the subtle weasel words of those who throw their hands in the air and claim that our narrative cannot be entirely proved because the evidence is no longer available. We know how these people work. Their operative DNA is now so transparent that any knowledgeable person will dismiss their protestations on the volume of circumstantial evidence alone. But they hide behind the pejorative cry of "conspiracy theory," a convenience which protects the guilty. Year by year, even as we worked on this book, acknowledgments have been quietly conceded about Edith Cavell's spy ring, on the RMS *Lusitania's* real cargo-manifest, of the gross over-exaggerations of the Bryce Committee. Yet the great lies persist and are regurgitated in the mainstream media.

Our books cover a period between 1890-1919, because within that time-scale a group of elite politicians, influential power-brokers, rich financiers, determined opinion-moulders and their academic entourage made a concerted move to create a new world order under their control. In 1890 it was driven by upper-class English values and British domination of world trade, politics and influence. By 1919 clearer bonds between the Anglo-American Establishment, and the exhausting, deliberately prolonged war, had moved the new world order towards an Atlantic Alliance and the enduring "special relationship" between Britain and the United States.

It is essential that everyone understands that 1919 was not an end-point. There was no sense of "job done." Indeed not. What happened in 1919 was just another stepping stone, a building-block towards a new order in the world. National boundaries changed in many parts of Europe. New territorial responsibilities (the talk was of Mandates) were allocated to the victors. New countries were shaped. Economic interests were, as ever, to the fore. Old disputes re-emerged around lucrative parts of the dismembered Ottoman Empire. Germany had been defeated and humiliated, but Germany survived. The politicians who disgraced humanity by claiming that the world war had saved civilization escaped the scrutiny of justice. They wrote their memoirs, accepted their rewards, and lived well on the profits that ensued. Above them, the controllers of real power did not break step. They simply marched unnoticed along their chosen route.

If you feel that you now have a keener sense of who these people were and are, engage in Quigley's challenge. He stated that "the evidence of their existence is not hard to find, if one knows where to look."[11] They remain behind the scenes, influencing politicians and policy, buying public opinion, rewarding their own, falsifying media reports and protecting themselves from public scrutiny. History will continue to be controlled by them for as long as criticism can be ignored. You can shake this comfortable establishment set-up by continuing to question official versions and never allowing yourself to be easily satisfied with so-called truth.

Everything that we have described is a series of building blocks. The Secret Elite has metamorphosed into a much more modern phenomenon with the same objective – to be that new world order. The evidence of their existence is not hard to find.

References

PROLONING THE AGONY

CHAPTER 1: THE ORIGINS REVISITED

1. Ronan McGreevy, *The Irish Times*, 2 January 2014.
2. Gerry Docherty and Jim Macgregor, Hidden History, *The Secret Origins of the First World War*, p 11.
3. www.sahistory.org.za › politics and society › 20th Century South Africa.
4. Carroll Quigley, *The Anglo-American Establishment*, p. 4
5. Ibid., p. 3.
6. Ibid., p. 197.
7. W.T. Stead, *The Last Will and Testament of Cecil John Rhodes*, p. 59.
8. These included Edmund Garrett (*Cape Times*), E.T. Cook (editor of the *Pall Mall Gazette* and the *Westminster Gazette*) and Geoffrey Dawson (editor of *The Times*), all members of the secret society's inner circle and personal friends and colleagues of the leader, Lord Alfred Milner.
9. W.T. Stead, *The Last Will and Testament of Cecil John Rhodes*, p. 55.
10. See the official James Lees-Milne website at http://www. jamesleesmilne.com/books.html
11. Carroll Quigley, *Tragedy and Hope: A History of the World in Our Time*, p. 137.
12. Niall Ferguson, *The House of Rothschild*, vol 11. p. 251.
13. Derek Wilson, *Rothschild: The Wealth and Power of a Dynasty*, pp. 98-9.
14. Ferguson, *House of Rothschild*, p.xxvii..
15. Ibid., p. 319.
16. Quigley, *The Anglo-American Establishment*, pp. 52–83.
17. Stead, *The Last Will and Testament*, p. 108.
18. Quigley, *Anglo-American Establishment*, pp. 16-17.
19. John S. Ewart, *The Roots and Causes of the Wars*, vol. II, p. 681.
20. Keith Hitchins, *Romania, 1866-1947*, p. 192.
21. Will Podmore, *British Foreign Policy Since 1870*, pp. 11-20.
22. Pat Walsh, *The Events of 1915 in Eastern Anatolia*, p. 4.
23. Niall Ferguson, *Pity of War*, p. 41.
24. Nicholas d'Ombrain, *War Machinery and High Policy Defence Administration in Peacetime Britain, 1902–1914*, p. 125.
25. Docherty and Macgregor, *Hidden History*, pp. 194-202.
26. Keith Jeffery, *Field Marshal Sir Henry Wilson: A Political Soldier*, p. 39.
27. D'Ombrain, *War Machinery and High Policy*, pp. 142–3.
28. Ibid, pp. 142–3.
29. David Lloyd George, *War Memoirs*, p. 27.
30. Quigley, *The Anglo-American Establishment*, p. 25.
31. Hansard, House of Commons, Debate, 12 July 1906, vol. 160, cc1074– 171.
32. Baron John Arbuthnot Fisher, *Memories and Records*, vol. II, pp. 134–5.
33. Cabinet Papers, CAB/ 38/113/1907, p. 12.
34. Quigley, *Anglo-American Establishment*, pp. 311-2.
35. Ibid., p. 102.
36. Ibid., p. 115.
37. In fact, the War Office presented a paper on this action to the Committee of Imperial Defence in September 1905. CAB 38/10/ 1905, no. 73.
38. CAB 38/9/ 1905, no. 65.
39. Sir Frederick Maurice, *Haldane*, p. 175.
40. Confidential report of General Ducarne to the Belgian minister of war, 10 April 1906, as quoted by Dr Bernhard Demburg in *The International Monthly*, New York, at http://libcudl.colorado.edu/wwi/pdf/ i73726928.pdf
41. Ibid.
42. Ewart, *Roots and Causes of the Wars*, Vol. I, pp. 542-6.
43. Albert J. Knock, *The Myth of a Guilty Nation*, p. 37, ebook at http:// library.mises.org/books/Albert%20Jay%20Nock/The%20Myth%20of%20a%20Guilty%20Nation.pdf
44. Friedrich Stieve, *Isvolsky and the World War*, p. 117.
45. Sidney Bradshaw Fay, *The Origins of the World War*, vol. I, p. 329.
46. Albert J Nock, *Myth of a Guilty Nation*, p. 60.
47. Docherty and Macgregor, *Hidden History*, pp. 242-251.
48. Isvolsky to Sazonov, 31 July 1914, in Fay, *Origins of the World War*, vol. II, p. 531.
49. Fay, *Origins of the World War*, vol. II, p. 532.
50. Lawrence Lafore, *The Long Fuse: An Interpre-*

tation of the Origins of World War, p. 261.
51. George Malcolm Thomson, *The Twelve Days*, p. 152.
52. Fisher, *Memories and Records*, vol.1, p. 21.
53. Ferguson, *The House of Rothschild*, vol. 11, p. 319.
54. An in-depth analysis of the extent of this control can be found in our blogs of 18-19 June 2014: https://firstworldwarhiddenhistory.wordpress.com/2014/06/18/
55. D'Ombrain, *War Machinery and High Policy*, p. xiii.
56. https://firstworldwarhiddenhistory.wordpress.com/2014/08/25/
57. firstwordlwarhiddenhistory.wordpress.com.

CHAPTER 2: THE FIRST VICTIMS TRUTH AND THE PEOPLE

1. *Manchester Guardian*, 5 August, 1914, p. 4.
2. Jonathan Reed Winkler, (2008). *Nexus: Strategic Communications and American Security in World War I.*
3. House of Commons Debate 05 August 1914 vol 65 cc1986
4. House of Lords Debate 05 August 1914 vol 17 cc384-5384.
5. Christopher Andrew, *Secret Service*, p. 181.
6. House of Commons Debate 07 August 1914 vol. 65 cc2191-3.
7. House of Lords Debate 05 August 1914, vol. 17 cc374-84.
8. National Archives, PRO CAB 16/18A p.93.
9. House of Lords Debate 05 August 1914, vol. 17 cc374-84.
10. David Lloyd George, *War Memoirs*, p. 61.
11. Ibid.
12. David Lloyd George, House of Commons Debate, 5 August, 1914 vol.65 cc1991-2000.
13. House of Commons Debate, 06 August 1914 vol. 65 cc2101-7.
14. House of Lords Debate 05 August 1914, vol. 17 cc374-84.
15. House of Lords Debate 08 August 1914, vol. 65 cc2212-22.
16. After the embarrassment of the 'Curragh Mutiny' in 1914, John Seeley resigned from his post as Secretary of State for War. Asquith failed to appoint anyone in his Cabinet to the post and took over of both the government and the War Office. See *Hidden History, the Secret Origins of the First World War* pp. 309-11
17. Michael and Eleanor Brock, HH Asquith, Letters to Venetia Stanley, p. 157.
18. Grey of Fallodon, *Twenty-Five Years* vol.II, pp286-287.
19. Milner had been very annoyed by Kitchener's willingness to accept compromises with the Boer leaders in 1901.
20. J Lee Thomson, *Forgotten Patriot*, p.309.
21. Tony Heathcote, *The British Field Marshals 1736–1997*. p.195.
22. Stephen Roskill, *Hankey, 1877-1918*, p. 134.
23. Winston Churchill, *The World Crisis, 1911-1918*, p190.
24. A M Gollin, *Proconsul in Politics*, p. 240.
25. He was the military correspondent for the Secret Elite's *Times* newspaper. He had his own desk at the War Office.
26. Brock, HH Asquith, *Letters to Venetia Stanley*, p. 152.
27. *The Times*, 4 August, 1914, p.5.
28. Ibid.
29. Leopold Amery, *My Political Life, Vol. II*, pp. 21-23.
30. Brock, HH Asquith, *Letters to Venetia Stanley*, pp. 157-8
31. National Archives, CAB 21/ 1/ 1.
32. Max Arthur, *Forgotten Voices of the Great War*, p. 16.
33. Churchill, *The World Crisis, 1911-1918*, p.191.
34. Hansard, House of Lords Debate, 25 Aug 1914 vol. 17 cc501-4.
35. Brock, HH Asquith, *Letters to Venetia Stanley*, p.154 and *Grey of Fallodon, Twenty-Five Years*, vol. II p. 279.
36. Arthur, *Forgotten Voices of the Great War*, p. 9.
37. Brock, HH Asquith, *Letters to Venetia Stanley*, p.154.
38. Hansard, House of Commons Debate, 06 August 1914 vol.65 cc2073-100.
39. Ibid.
40. Arthur Ponsonby, *Falsehood in Wartime*, p. 15.
41. Sidney B Fay, *The Origins of the World War*, vol. 1. p.3.
42. M L Sanders, "Wellington House and British Propaganda in the First World War," *The Historical Journal*, vol. 18, No1. (March 1975), p. 119.
43. Hansard, HC Deb 27 August 1914 vol. 66 c123.
44. In the pre-war years Northcliffe commissioned William le Queux to write The Invasion of 1910, a scare serial published in the *Daily Mail*. It was utter drivel, badly written but meticulously researched.
45. Jonathan Reed Winkler, (2008). *Nexus: Strategic Communications and American Security in World War I.*
46. Patrick Beesley, *Room 40, British Naval Intelligence 1914-18*, p. 2.
47. H C Peterson, *Propaganda for War*, p. 13.
48. Rear Admiral Sir Douglas Brownrigg, *Indiscretions of the Naval Censor*, pp. 2-4
49. F E Smith, later Lord Birkenhead, was a close friend of Alfred Milner and Sir Edward Carson of the Secret Elite.

50. Hansard, HC Deb 07 August 1914 vol. 65 cc2153-6.
51. J. S. Ewart, *Roots and Causes of the Wars,* p.30.
52. HC Deb 10 September 1914 vol. 66 cc726-752.
53. Dillon, *The Times and the Press Censor,* House of Commons Debate 31 August 1914, vol. 66, cc454-511.
54. Irene Cooper Willis, *England's Holy War*, p. 179.
55. John F Lucy, *There's a Devil in the Drum,* p.74.
56. C R Cruttwell, *A History of the Great War* 1914-1918, p. 23.
57. Ibid.
58. Special edition of the *Times*, 30 August 1914.
59. Hansard, HC Debate 31 August 1914, vol. 66 cc497-8.
60. *The Times* 31 August 1914, p.9.
61.Paul Greenwood, *The British Expeditionary Force August-September 1914.* http://1914ancien.free.fr/bef_1914.htm
62. Hansard, HC Debate 31 August 1914, vol. 66 cc498-9.
63. Hansard, HC Debate 31 August 1914, vol. 66 cc372-4.
64. Quigley, *The Anglo-American Establishment*, p. 197.
65. *The Times*. 1 August 1914, p. 6.
66. S.J.D. Green and Peregrine Horden *All Souls and the Wider World*, p 171.
67. The Oxford Pamphlets, 1914-15
68. https://archive.org/stream/27to54oxfordpam00londuoft#page/n1/mode/2up
69. *The Round Table, Special War Number, Germany and the Prussian Spirit* p.15.
70. Ibid., p.30.
71. Quigley, *The Anglo American Establishment*, p. 85.
72. *The Round Table, Special War Number, Germany and the Prussian Spirit*, p.37.
73. Quotation credited generally to Arthur Ponsonby MP.
74.The School History was hailed as the chief literary event of the coronation year by the Church Family Times and as a most pernicious influence on the minds of children by the *Manchester Guardian. Oxford Dictionary of National Biography*.
75. Quigley, *The Anglo-American Establishment*, p. 312.
76. Ibid.
77. Green and Horden, *All Souls and the Wider World* p. 176
78. https://archive.org/stream/27to54oxfordpam00londuoft#page/n5/mode/2up
79. Quigley, *The Anglo-American Establishment*, p. 197.
80. HH Asquith, *Letters to Venetia Stanley,* p.221.
81. Gary Messinger, *British Propaganda and the State in the First World War*, p. 38.
82. H C Peterson, *Propaganda for War*, p. 18.
83.Carroll Quigley, *The Anglo-American Establishment*, p. 313.
84. John Buchan, *Memory Hold The Door,* pp. 169-70 and pp 205-8.
85. M L Sanders, "Wellington House and British Propaganda in the First World War," *The Historical Journal*, vol. 18, No1. (March 1975), pp. 120-1.
86. Phillip Taylor, *British Propaganda in the 20th Century: Selling Democracy*, p. 11.
87. Quigley, *Anglo-American*, p. 313.
88. Ibid., p. 27.
89. Ibid., p. 312.
90. Gareth S Jowett and Victoria O'Donnell, *Propaganda and Persuasion*, p. 218.
91. *Report of the Central Committee for National Patriotic Organisations*, (London 1916) p. 18 ff.
92. Peterson, *Propaganda for War*, p. 19.
93. Quigley, *Anglo-American Establishment*, p. 313.
94. Messinger, *British Propaganda and the State in the First World War*, p. 40.
95. *First Report of the Work of Wellington House*, 7 June, 1915, Inf. 4/5 (PRO) p.1.
96. Carnegie Endowment for International Peace, *Official German Documents relating to the World War*, vol. II, p.1315.
97. Printed in *Harper's Magazine* in 1917.
98. Bertrand Russell, *These Eventful Years*, Vol. 1. p.381.
99. Gabriel Hanotaux, *Historie Illustre de la Guerre de 1914*, vol. 9, p. 56.
100. Niall Ferguson, *The Pity of War*, p. 212.
101. http://www.gwpda.org/wwi-www/BryceReport/bryce_r.html
102. *The Daily Mail*, 28 August 1914.
103. J Lee Thompson, Northcliffe, *Press Baron in Politics, 1865-1922*, p.231.
104. Verax, Truth, *A Path to Justice and Reconciliation*, p.151.
105. Ibid., pp.151-2.
106. Barbara Tuchman, *The Guns of August*, pp. 130-132.
107. C R M F Cruttwell, *A History of the Great War*, p.16.
108. Carroll Quigley, *The Anglo-American Establishment*, p 24.
109. "Warrant of Appointment," *Report of the Committee on Alleged German Outrages, 1915*, p2.
110. *Report of the Committee on Alleged German Outrages, 1915*, pp. 3-4.
111. Ibid., p. 7.
112. Ibid., pp. 4-7.
113. Ibid., pp. 60-1.
114.*New York Times*, 15 May 1915.

115. Irvin S Cobb, *Paths of Glory*, p 154.
116. Thomas Fleming, *The Illusion of Victory: America in World War I*, as quoted in *The Journal of* History, http://hnn.us/articles/1489.html
117. Verax, *A Path to Justice and Reconciliation*, p. 154.
118. *Report of the Committee on alleged German Outrages, 1915*, p. 26.
119. H C Peterson, P*ropaganda for War*, p. 53.
120. D J Cardinal Mercier, *Cardinal Mercier's Own Story*, p 24.
121. Ibid., p. 34.
122. Letter from von Bissing to Cardinal Mercier, 20 April 1915, quoted in *Cardinal Mercier's Own Story*, p. 109.
123. *The Times* 17 July 1917, p.3. (Maude Roythen)
124. *The Times*, 31 August, 1914, p.4.
125. Albert Marrin, *The Last Crusade: The Church of England in the First World War*. p. 179.
126. Kevin Christopher Fielden, "The Church of England in the First World War." (2005). Electronic Theses and Dissertations. Paper 1080. http://dc.etsu.edu/etd/1080
127. Hugh McLeod,. *Religion and Society in England, 1850-1914*. p.20.
128. Marrin, *The Last Crusade*. p. 12.
129. *Christian Times*, 11 July 1914.
130. Henry Newbold, *War Trust Exposed*, pp. 14–15.
131. Quigley, *The Anglo-American Establishment*, p. 25.
132. J. G. Lockhart, *Cosmo Gordon Lang (1949)* p. 246.
133. Oxford Pamphlets, 1914-1915; To Christian Scholars of Europe and America; A Reply from Oxford to German Address to Evangelical Christians by Oxford Theologians.
134. *The Times* 12 October 1914, p.5.
135. Arthur Marwick, *The Deluge; British Society and the First World War*, p.33.
136. *The Times*,16 March 1916, p. 9.
137. *The Times*, 10 February 1915, page 5.
138. Ibid.
139. Fielden,, "The Church of England in the First World War."
140. C.H.W. Johns, "Who is on the Lord's Side?" Sermons for the *Times* no. 9 (1914), p.14.
141. *Oxford Dictionary of National Biography* Jeremy Morris, 'Ingram, Arthur Foley Winnington [http://www.oxforddnb.com/view/article/36979.
142. Marrin, *The Last Crusade: The Church of England in the First World War*. p.181.
143. *The Times*, 10 February, 1915, p.5.
144. Annette Becker, *A Companion to World War 1*, pp., 237-238.
145. Winnington-Ingram, *The Potter and the Clay*, p. 42.
146. Ibid., p. 229.
147. Fielden, , "The Church of England in the First World War. p. 42.
148. F P Crozier, 'A Brass Hat in No-Man's Land' p.43. https://archive.org/stream/brasshatinnomans00fran#page/42/mode/2up/search/blood-lust

CHAPTER 3: THE SCANDAL OF BRIEY

1. Sidney B Fay, *Origins of the World War*, Vol. II, p. 532
2. Harry Elmer Barnes, *Genesis of the World War*, p. 354
3. Fernand Engerand, *La Battaille de la Frontiere, Briey*, (Aout, 1914), Preface, p.ix
4. Clarence K Streit, *Where Iron Is, There Is The Fatherland*, pp. 1-2
5. Engerand, *La Battaille de la Frontiere, Briey*, p. 4
6. There is a terrific description of this in Eric Ambler, *Journey Into Fear*, p. 77
7. Engerand, La Battaille de la Frontiere, Briey, pp.1-2
8. Comite des Forges de France, Circulaire no. 655, p.13
9. Philip Noel-Baker, *The Private Manufacture of Armaments*, p. 45
10. Maurice Barres, *L'Echo de Paris*, 25 February to 8 March, 1918.
11. Engerand, *La Battaille de la Frontiere, Briey*, p. 36
12. Pierre Renouvin, *The Immediate Origins of the War*, p. 244
13. So described by Louis Loucher, French Minister of Munitions.
14. Engerand, *La Battaille de la Frontiere, Briey*, preface, p.x
15. After the war Sir Edward Grey used the same argument to belittle Rear Admiral Consett who had criticised the British naval blockade of Germany between 1914-1916.
16. Engerand, *La Battaille de la Frontiere* preface, pp. xiv-xv.
17. Ibid., pp. 145-178.
18. Ibid., p. 7.
19. Ibid., p.11.
20. *Journal Officiel de la République Française*, 31 January, 1919, Paris.
21. Noel-Baker, *The Private Manufacture of Armaments*, p. 43.
22. *Officiel de la République Française*, 24 January, 1919, Paris.
23. Donald McCormick, *The Mask of Merlin*, p. 206.
24. Jean Noel Jeanneney, *Francois de Wendel en Republique, L'Argent et le Pouvoir, Revuie Historique*, T. 257, Fasc. 2 (522) Avril-Juin 1977, pp. 495-498.
25. Congressional Record for March 6 and 12, 1934, Text of the *Nye Resolution to Investigate*

America's Armament Makers, United States Government Printing Office Washington: 1934; 52620 – 10175. Article from *Fortune Magazine,* 22 May 1934, "A Primer on Europe's Armament Makers who prolong War and disturb Peace."
26. Carroll Quigley, *Tragedy and Hope*, p. 518.
27. David Stevenson, *Armaments and the Coming of War: Europe, 1904-1914*, p. 29.
28. Ibid., p. 30.
29. Michael J Rust, *The Journal of Economic History, Vol. 37*, issue 2, June 1977, p. 531.
30. The Demanchy Bank was controlled by the Comite des Forges.
31. Streit, *Where Iron Is*, pp. 24-25.
32. Ibid.
33. Harold James, *Family Capitalism*, p. 185.
34. Ibid., p. 186.
35. Streit, *Where Iron Is,* pp.29-32.
36. James, *Family Capitalism*, p.187.
37. Streit, *Where Iron Is,* pp. 42-3.
38. *Le Matin,* 14 February, 1919.
39. Streit, *Where Iron Is*, pp.46.
40. Congressional Record for March 6 and 12, 1934, Text of the *Nye Resolution to Investigate America's Armament Makers*, United States Government Printing Office Washington : 1934; 52620 – 10175. Article from *Fortune Magazine,* 22 May 1934, *A Primer on Europe's Armament Makers who prolong War and disturb Peace,* p. 14.
41. Major General Smedley Darlington Butler, *War is a Racket,* page 1.
42. Matthew White, Source List and Detailed Death Tolls for the Primary Megadeaths of the Twentieth Century.http://necrometrics.com/20c5m.htm#WW1
43. Gerry Docherty and Jim Macgregor, *Hidden History, The Secret Origins of the First World War* pp.11-16.

CHAPTER 4: THE MYTH OF THE GREAT BLOCKADE

1. M Parmalee, *Blockade and Sea Power: The Blockade, 1914-199*, p. 7.
2. George F.S. Bowles, *The Strength of England,* p. 162.
3. *The Times*, 16 Feb, 1915.
4. Winston Churchill, *World Crisis*, pp. 38-9.
5. Hew Strachan, *The First World War* vol.1, pp. 394-5.
6. Ibid.
7. Ibid.
8. http://www.naval-history.net/WW1NavyBritishDestroyers.htm#1914
9. Hansard, House of Commons Debate, 18 February 1914, vol. 58 cc 961.
10. *The Times*, 10 November, 1914.
11. Rear-Admiral M. W. W. P. Consett, *The Triumph of Unarmed Forces (1914-1918)*, preface, p. vii.
12. George F.S. Bowles, *The Strength of England,* p. 162.
13. C. Paul Vincent, *The Politics of Hunger, The Allied Blockade of Germany, 1915-1919.* p. 36.
14. ibid., p. 37.
16. Norman Bentwich, *The Declaration of London, 1911*, http://www.archives.org. eBook and Texts, California Digital Library.
17. *The Great War,* ed. Hammerton and Wilson vol. 7. p. 122.
18. Consett, *Triumph of Unarmed Forces*, p. 23.
19. Hansard, House of Commons Debate, 29 June 1911 vol 27 cc574-696.
20. Hansard, House of Lords Debate, 12 December 1911 vol 10 cc809-95.
21. Bowles, *The Strength of England,* p.163.
22. National Archives, Cabinet Papers PRO CAB16/18A
23. PRO CAB16/18A, p. 429.
24. Ibid., pp. 429-30.
25. Ibid., p. 74.
26. Ibid., p. 45.
27. Carroll Quigley, *The Anglo-American Establishment,* p. 158.
28. Viscount Milner, Cotton Contraband, *New York Times*, 21 August 1915.
29. Barbara Tuchman, *The Guns of August,* p. 333.
30. Thomas Baty and John Hartman Morgan, *War: Its Conduct and Legal Results,* p. 538.
31. Arthur J Marder, *From the Dreadnought to Scapa Flow*, Vol. 11. pp. 372-3.
32. E Keble Chatterton, *The Big Blockade*, p. 33.
33. Ibid., pp. 56-7.
34. Burton J Hendrick, *The Life and Letters of Walter H Page*, vol. 1 p. 380.
35. Chatterton, *The Big Blockade,* p. 5.
36. Ibid., p. 53.
37. Tuchman, *The Guns of August,* p. 337.
38. Ibid.
39. Ibid.
40. Marder, *From the Dreadnought to Scapa Flow,* Vol. 11. pp. 374-5.
41. Gerry Docherty and Jim Macgregor, *Hidden History, The Secret Origins of the First World War,* p. 221-2.
42. Webster Tarpley and Anton Chaitkin, *George Bush, The Unauthorised Biography*, p. 330.
43. Docherty and Macgregor, *Hidden History*, p. 222.
44. Joseph Ward Swain, *Beginning the Twentieth Century*, p. 472.
45. http://encyclopedia.1914-1918-online.net/pdf/1914-1918-Online-Sweden-2014-10-08.pdf
46. Consett, *The Triumph of Unarmed Forces,* p. xv.
47. Ibid., p. vii.

48. George F S Bowles, *The Strength of England*, p. 173.
49. Chatterton, *The Big Blockade*, p. 279.
50. Ibid., pp. 43-46.
51. Ibid., p. 25.
52. Bowles, *The Strength of England*, p. 173.
53. Ibid., p. 176.
54. Chatterton,*The Big Blockade*, p. 214.
55. Docherty and Macgregor, *Hidden History*, pp. 215-217.
56. Bowles, *The Strength of England*, p. 179.
57. Docherty and Macgregor, *Hidden History*, p. 114.
58. Chatterton, *The Big Blockade*, p. 61.
59. Ibid., p. 73.
60. Marder, *From the Dreadnought to Scapa Flow*, vol. 11, p. 373.
61. Consett, *The Triumph of Unarmed Forces*, p. 221.
62. Lord Sydenham of Combe, *Studies of An Imperialist*, London 1928 p. 3.
63. Hansard House of Commons Debate 12 July 1915, vol. 73, cc719-20.
64. Chatterton, *The Big Blockade*, p. 167.
65. Bell, *A History of the Blockade.*
66. Chatterton, *The Big Blockade*, pp. 166-167.
67. Bell, *A History of the Blockade.*
68. *The Times* 20 July 1915, p. 7.
69. Ibid., 21 July, 1915, p. 8.
70. Lord Lansdowne House of Lords Debate, 22 February 1916 vol 21 cc97-98.
71. Consett, *The Triumph of Unarmed Forces*, pp. 264-5.
72. Docherty and Macgregor, *Hidden History*, p. 53.
73. Hansard House of Commons, 12 July, 1915 vol. 73 cc712-13.
74. Bell, *A History of the Blockade.*

CHAPTER 5: THE MYTH OF THE GREAT BLOCKADE 2. SHAMEFUL PROFITS

1. Bowles, *The Strength of England*, p. 193.
2. Consett, *Triumph of Unarmed Forces*, pp. x-xvi.
3. Ibid., pp. 113-4.
4. Ibid., p. 118.
5. Ibid., p. xiii.
6. Ibid., pp. 119–122.
7. Ibid., pp. 127-8.
8. *The Times*, 18 February, 1915.
9. Hansard, House of Commons Debate, 22 July, 1915, vol. 73, cc1674-1794.
10. House of Commons Debate 19 July 1915, vol. 73, cc1196-272.
11. House of Commons Debate, 27 July 1915, vol. 73, cc2159-84.
12. House of Common Debate 19 July 1915, vol. 73, cc1196-272.
13. Consett, *Triumph of Unarmed Forces*, p. 119.
14. Ibid., p. 130.
15. Ibid., pp. 131-2.
16. Hew Strachan, *The First World War*, vol. 1, pp. 1018-9.
17. Consett, *The Triumph of Unarmed Forces*, p. 80.
18. George Seldes, *Iron, Blood and Profits*, p. 89.
19. Consett, *The Triumph of Unarmed Forces*, p. 80.
20. Ibid., pp. 190-93.
21. Ibid., p. 141.
22. Ibid., pp. 84–85.
23. Ibid., p. 201.
24. Ibid., p. 198.
25. Seventh Report from the Select Committee on National Expenditure, 21. December, 1920.
26. Consett, *The Triumph of Unarmed Forces*, pp. 197-199.
27. Ibid., p. 199.
28. Ibid.
29. *The Times*, 24 January, 1918, p. 8.
30. *Daily News*, 1 January 1915.
31. C Paul Vincent, *The Politics of Hunger, The Allied Blockade of Germany 1915-1919*, p. 40.
32. https://archive.org/details/unarmedforces00consuoft
33. Consett, *The Triumph of Unarmed Forces*, pp. 268-293.
34. Ibid., p. 288.
35. Ibid., pp. 210-217.
36. Ibid., p. 168.
37. Hansard House of Lords Debate 20 December 1915 vol. 20 cc696-744.
38. Consett, *The Triumph of Unarmed Forces*, pp. 134-136.
39. Ibid., pp. 140-2.
40. Ibid., p. 148.
41. Martin Daunton, 'Henderson, Alexander, first Baron Faringdon (1850–1934)', *Oxford Dictionary of National Biography*, Oxford University Press, 2004 http://www.oxforddnb.com/view/article/47784
42. Hansard House of Commons, Speech by Sir Edward Grey, 26 January, 1916 in a pamphlet entitled, *Great Britain's Measures Against German Trade*, published by Hodder and Stoughton.
43. http://archive.org/stream/greatbritainsmea00greyuoft/greatbritainsmea00greyuoft_djvu.txt
44. Hansard, House of Commons Debate 24 February, 1916, vol. 80. c783.
45. Consett, *The Triumph of Unarmed Forces*, p. 254.
46. Ibid., 253.
47. Ibid.,
48. The history of the Belgian Relief Commission will be fully examined later. This in itself was one of the war's major scandals successful-

ly hidden from the public. Suffice for the moment to say that between 1915-17, huge quantities of foodstuffs were being redirected from Belgium to feed the German people and army.
49. Hansard, House of Commons Debate, 26 January, 1916.
50. Winston Churchill, *The World Crisis, 1915*, p. 295.
51. Hansard, House of Commons Debate, 27 March 1917 vol. 92. cc226-80.
52. Hansard House of Commons Debate 22 June 1915 vol. 72 cc1094-1131.
53. Ibid., p. 163.
54. Hansard, House of Lords Debate, 22 February 1916 vol 21 cc72-128.
55. Hansard House of Commons Debate, 21 March 1918 vol. 104 cc1231-57
56. Andrew S. Thompson, 'Croft, Henry Page, first Baron Croft (1881–1947)', *Oxford Dictionary of National Biography*, Oxford University Press, 2004; online edn, Jan 2008 [http://www.oxforddnb.com/view/article/32633]
57. Hansard House of Commons Debate, 21 March 1918 vol. 104 cc1231-57.
58. Foreign Office 21 March, 1916. Secret Note on the Blockade of the North Sea, Printed for the Committee of Imperial Defence. G-67.
59. Ibid.
60. Bowles, *The Strength of England*, p. 173.
61. Ian Cobain, *The Guardian*, 18 October 2013.
62. Julian Thompson, The Imperial War Museum, *Book of The War At Sea, 1914-1918*.
63. Hansard, House of Lords Debate 27 June 1923 vol 54 cc647-54.
64. Ibid
65. Ibid.
66. see Chapter 32.

CHAPTER 6: THE OTTOMAN ENIGMA 1 – SAVING CONSTANTINOPLE

1. David Fromkin, *A Peace to End All Peace, The Fall of the Ottoman Empire and the Creation of the Modern Middle East,* p. 138; Niall Ferguson, *The Pity Of War,* p. 61.
2. Friedrich Stieve, *Izvolsky and the World War,* p. 44.
3. Sean McMeekin, *The Russian Origins of the First World War,* p. 28.
4. Pat Walsh, *Remembering Gallipoli,* p 15.
5. *Willy-Nicky Letters,* 22 August 1905 and Sidney B. Fay, *Origins of the World War, Vol. 1*, p. 175.
6. Encyclopaedia Britannica, *These Eventful Years, Vol. 2,* pp. 130-132.
7. Alan Moorhead, *Gallipoli*, pp. 11-12.
8. J Laffin, *The Agony of Gallipoli.* p. 4.
9. Geoffrey Miller, *Straits*, Ch.X1
10. Robert Rhodes James, *Gallipoli*, p. 8.
11. Hew Strachan, *The First World War*, p. 102.
12. Stieve, *Isvolsky and the World War,* p. 177.
13. W W Gottlieb, *Studies in Secret Diplomacy,* p. 34.
14. Ronald P Bobroff, *Roads to Glory, Late Imperial Russia and the Straits,* p. 93.
15. McMeekin, *The Russian Origins of the First World War*, pp. 30-34.
16. Ibid., p. 102.
17. W S Churchill, *The World Crisis*, pp. 221-2.
18. Dan Van Der Vat, *The Dardanelles Disaster,* p. 28.
19. L A Carlyon, *Gallipoli*, p. 42.
20. Gottlieb, *Studies in Secret Diplomacy*, p. 42.
21. David Fromkin, *A Peace to End All Peace,* p. 57.
22. Sidney B, Fay, *Origins of the World War*, vol 11, p. 531.
23. Harry Elmer Barnes, *The Genesis of the World War*, p. 534. Kennan,Fateful Alliance, p. 161. Marc Trachtenberg, *The Meaning of Mobilization in 1914*, International Security, vol 15, issue 3.
24. Fay, *Origins of the World War*, vol 11, p. 532.
25. Fromkin, *A Peace to End All Peace*, p. 61.
26. Alan Moorhead, *Gallipoli*, pp. 25-26.
27. Fromkin, *A Peace to End All Peace*, p. 59.
28. J S Ewart, *The Roots and Cause of the Wars (1914-1918*), p. 207.
29. Sean McMeekin, *The Russian Origins of the First World War*, p. 103.
30. Ibid., p. 106.
31. Moorehead, *Gallipoli*, p. 26.
32. Arthur J Mader, *From the Dreadnought to Scapa Flow*, vol II, pp., 20-21.
33. Peter Hart, *Gallipoli*, p. 9.
34. C.R.M.F. Crutwell, *A History of the Great War, 1914-1918*, pp. 69-72.
35. Marder, *From the Dreadnought to Scapa Flow*, p. 21.
36. Van der Vat, *The Dardanelles Disaster,* p. 32.
37. Churchill, *The World Crisis, 1911-1918*, vol. p. 209.
38. Barbara Tuchman, *The Guns of August,* p. 137.
39. Ibid., p.150.
40. When it was pointed out that there was a one hour time difference between London and Berlin, this was changed to 11.pm GMT.
41. Martin Gilbert, *Winston S. Churchill,* vol III, p. 30.
42. Edmond Delage, *The Tragedy of the Dardanelles,* p. 2.
43. Tuchman, *Guns of August,* p. 146.
44. Moorehead, *Gallipoli*, p. 26.
45. Marder, *From Dreadnought to Scapa Flow*, p 23.
46. Tuchman, *Guns of August*, p. 152.
47. Hew Strachan, *The First World War, Volume 1; To Arms*, p. 650.
48. War was not declared between Britain and

Austria until 12 August.

49. Tuchman, *Guns of August*, p. 153.
50. CRMF Crutwell, *A History of the Great War*, p 71.
51. Ulrich Trumpener, "The Escape of the Goeben and Breslau," *Canadian Journal of History*, September 1971, p 171.
52. Strachan, *The First World War*, Volume 1, p. 648.
53. Barbara Tuchman, *The Guns of August*, p. 150.
54. John Laffin, *The Agony of Gallipoli*, pp. 6-7.
55. Ulrich Trumpener, "The Escape of the Goeben and Breslau," *Canadian Journal of History*, September 1971, pp. 178-9.
56. Geoffrey Miller, *The Straits*, ch. 16.
57. Alberto Santini, *The First Ultra Secret: the British Cryptanalysis in the Naval Operations of the First World War*, Revue internationale d'histoire militaire, vol 63 1985, p. 101.
58. Sean McMeekin, *The Russian Origins of the First World War*, p. 109.
59. Ibid.
60. Trumpener, "The Escape of the Goeben and Breslau," *Canadian Journal of History*, September 1971, pp. 181-7.
61. Docherty and Macgregor, *Hidden History*, p. 64.
62. Trumpener, "The Escape of the Goeben and Breslau," *Canadian Journal of History*, 1971, pp. 179-183.
63. Ibid.
64. Ibid., p. 181.
65. Ibid., p. 175.
66. Geoffrey Miller, *Superior Force*, Chapter 11.http://www.superiorforce.co.uk
67. CRMF Crutwell, *A History of the Great War*, p. 72.
68. Churchill, *The World Crisis*, p. 209.
69. Crutwell, *A History*, p. 72.
70. Hew Strachan, *The First World War*, p. 674.
71. WW Gottlieb, *Studies in Secret Diplomacy*, p. 45.
72. Ibid.

CHAPTER 7: The Ottoman Enigma – Neutral till It Suits

1. Gottlieb, Studies in *Secret Diplomacy during the First World War* pp. 47ff and passim.
2. McMeekin, *The Russian Origins of the First World War.* p. 106.
3. Trumpener, "The Escape of the Goeben and Breslau," *Canadian Journal of History*, September 1971, p. 171.
4. Gilbert, *Winston S Churchill*, vol III, p. 194.
5. Michael and Eleanor Brock, *HH Asquith, Letters,to Venetia Stanley*, p. 171.
6. McMeekin, *The Russian Origins*, pp. 99-100.
7. Ibid., pp. 105-106.
8. Djamal Pasha, *Memories of a Turkish Statesman*. http://archive.org/details/ memoriesofturkis00ahmeuoft
9. Brock, *HH Asquith, Letters*, p. 179.
10. Joseph Heller, "Sir Louis Mallet and the Ottoman Empire, The Road to War," *Middle Eastern Studies, Vol.12*, No. 1 (Jan., 1976), p. 36.
11. Fromkin, *A Peace to End All Peace*, p. 101.
12. Brock, *HH Asquith, Letters*, p. 171.
13. Heller, Sir Louis Mallet and the Ottoman Empire, Middle Eastern Studies, Vol.12, No. 1 (Jan., 1976), p. 36.
14. For example, when Sir Alfred Milner decided that war with the Boers was unavoidable he deliberately 'bounced' Kruger into making the first move. (Docherty and Macgregor, *Hidden History*, p. 40.)
15. Michael Hickey, *Gallipoli*. p. 27.
16. Travers, *Gallipoli*, pp 20–21.
17. Hickey, *Gallipoli*. p. 27.
18. Heller, Sir Louis Mallet and the Ottoman Empire, Middle Eastern Studies Vol.12, No. 1 (Jan., 1976), p. 36.
19. Gilbert, *Winston S Churchill, vol III*, p. 194.
20. Strachan, *The First World War vol. 1; To Arms*, p. 675.
21. Sazonov to Girs, 8 August, 1914, telegram, 1746, MO 6.1 no.33.
22. Bobroff, *Roads to Glory, Late Imperial Russia and the Straits*, p 101.
23. Ibid.
24. McMeekin, *The Russian Origins of the First World War*, p.107.
25. Gottlieb, *Studies in Secret Diplomacy*, p. 60.
26. Heller, Sir Louis Mallet and the Ottoman Empire, Middle Eastern Studies, Vol.12, No. 1 (Jan., 1976), p. 12.
27. Ibid., p. 14.
28. *Daily Telegraph*, 3 October 1914.
29. A.L. Macfie, "The Straits Question in the First World War," *Middle Eastern Studies*, July 1983, p. 49.
30. Heller, SSir Louis Mallet and the Ottoman Empire, Middle Eastern Studies, Vol.12, No. 1 (Jan., 1976), p. 20.
31. Robert Rhodes James, *Gallipoli* p. 112.
32. Tuchman, *The Guns of August*, p. 67.
33. Carlyon, *Gallipoli*, p. 45.
34. McMeekin, *The Russian Origins*, pp. 110-11.
35. Fromkin , *A Peace to End all Peace*, p.72.
36. Gilbert, *Churchill, vol III*, p. 215.
37. Gottlieb, *Studies*, p. 62.
38. Heller, *Sir Louis Mallet*, p.21.
39. Pat Walsh, *The Great Fraud of 1914-1918*, p. 31.
40. Strachan, *The First World War,Vol 1*, p. 680.
41. Pat Walsh, *Remembering Gallipoli*, p. 25.

42. Edward David, *Inside Asquith's Cabinet*, p. 205.
43. Bobroff, *Roads to Glory*, pp. 115-116.
44. McMeekin, *The Russian Origins*, p. 113.
45. Ibid., p. 114.

CHAPTER 8: DARDANELLES 1: THE RUSSIAN DREAM

1. Harvey Broadbent, *Gallipoli, One Great Deception?*http://www.abc.net.au/news/2009-04-24/30630%5D
2. Ibid.
3. Ronald P Bobroff, *Roads to Glory, Late Imperial Russia and the Straits*, p. 122.
4. *The Times*, 10 November 1914, p. 9.
5. Sean McMeekin, *The Russian Origins of The First World War*, p. 123.
6. Martin Gilbert, *Winston S Churchill*, p. 221.
7. McMeekin, *The Russian Origins*, p. 123.
8. W.W. Gottlieb, *Studies in Secret Diplomacy*, pp. 68–70.
9. Ibid., pp 74-75.
10. Bobroff, *Roads to Glory*, pp. 120-121.
11. Gottlieb, *Studies*, p. 75.
12. Winston Churchill,*World Crisis*, p. 296.
13. Sir Alfred Knox, *With the Russian Army, 1914-1917*, 1 December 1914, p. 193.
14. Ibid., p. 213.
15. Ibid., p. 217.
16. Ibid., p. 220.
17. Ibid., pp. 352-3.
18. Churchill, *The World Crisis, 1911-1918*, vol. 1., pp. 296-298
19. Carroll Quigley, *The Anglo-American Establishment*, pp.153-160 and p. 313.
20. Stephen Roskill, *Hankey, Vol.1 1897-1918*, p. 148.
21. Bobroff, *Roads to Glory, Late Imperial Russia and the Straits*, p 125.
22. Fromkin, *A Peace to End All Peace*, p. 127.
23. Quigley, *The Anglo-American Establishment*, p. 312.
24. Roskill, *Hankey*, p. 150.
25. Terence O'Brien, *Milner*, p. 267.
26. Quigley, *The Anglo-American Establishment*, p. 312.
27. Ibid., p. 52 and 56.
28. John Hanbury-Williams, *The Emperor Nicholas II As I Knew Him, Diary in Russia*, pp. 22-5.
29. Ibid., p. 24.
30. McMeekin, *The Russian Origins of the First World War*, p. 129.
31. Hanbury-Williams, *The Emperor Nicholas II*, p. 24.
32. Docherty and Macgregor, *Hidden History*, p. 280.
33. Graham T Clews, *Churchill's Dilemma*, p. 60.
34. Churchill, *World Crisis 1915*, p. 94.
35. Hart, *Gallipoli*, p. 15.
36. Churchill, *World Crisis 1915*, p. 93.
37. James, *Gallipoli*, p. 27.
38. Travers, *Gallipoli*, p. 22.
39. Delage, *The Tragedy of the Dardanelles*, pp. 27-28.

CHAPTER 9: THE DARDANELLES 2 – THE IMPOSSIBLE QUEST

1. Nevison, *The Dardanelles Campaign*, p. 25.
2. Liddell Hart, *History of the First World War*, p. 213.
3. Moorehead, *Gallipoli*, p. 60.
4. Harvey Broadbent, *Gallipoli, The Fatal Shore*, p. 21.
5. John Laffin, *The Agony*, p. 9.
6. Memorandum by the General Staff, 19 December 1906, National Archives, PRO. CAB/4/2/92.
7. Hickey, *Gallipoli*, p. 28.
8. James, *Gallipoli*, pp. 3-4.
9. Robin Prior, *Gallipoli, The End of The Myth*, p. 18.
10. Alan Moorehead, *Gallipoli*, p. 40.
11. J Laffin, *The Agony of Gallipoli*, p. 15.
12. Moorhead, *Gallipoli*, p. 41.
13. Graham T Clews, *Churchill's Dilemma*, p. 117-19.
14. Moorehead, *Gallipoli*, p. 46.
15. Peter Hart, *Gallipoli*, p. 23.
16. Clews, *Churchill's Dilemma*, pp. 119-20.
17. Ibid.
18. Ibid.
19. WW Gottlieb, *Studies in Secret Diplomacy*, pp. 88-89.
20. Ronald P Bobroff, *Roads to Glory, Late Imperial Russia and the Straits*, p. 126.
21. Gottlieb, *Studies*, p. 90.
22. Clews, *Churchill's Dilemma*, pp. 124-26.
23. Laffin, *The Agony of Gallipoli*, p. 22.
24. Ibid., p. 24.
25. Robin Prior, *Gallipoli, The End of The Myth*. p. 23.
26. Churchill letter 12 January 1915; pp. 326-7 *World Crisis, 1911-1918*.
27. Gilbert, *Winston S Churchill*, p. 279.
28. Prior, *Gallipoli*, pp. 28-29.
29. G Aspinal-Oglander, *Roger Keyes*, p. 126.
30. Van der Vat, *The Dardanelles Disaster*, p. 88.
31. Prior, *Gallipoli*, p. 31.
32. Laffin, *The Agony of Gallipoli*, p. 26.
33. Prior, *Gallipoli*, p. 30.
34. Gilbert, *Churchill*, pp. 287-8.
35. Prior, *Gallipoli*, p. 31.
36. Gilbert, *Churchill*, p. 288.
37. Ibid., pp. 296-302.
38. Moorehead, *Gallipoli*, p. 55.
39. Steel and Hart, *Defeat at Gallipoli*, p. 14.

40. Gilbert, *Winston S Churchill*, pp. 304-5.
41. Laffin, *The Agony of Gallipoli*, p. 27.
42. Moorehead, *Gallipoli*, pp. 56-57.
43. Laffin, *The Agony*, p. 3.
44. Gilbert, *Winston S Churchill*, vol. III, p. 321.
45. Bobroff, *Roads to Glory, Late Imperial Russia and the Straits*, p.131.
46. McMeekin, *The Russian Origins of The First World War*, pp. 130-131.
47. Harvey Broadbent, *The Fatal Shore*, p. 28.
48. Marder, *From the Dreadnought to Scapa Flow*, vol II, pp. 235-6.
49. Churchill, *The World Crisis, 1915*, p. 214.
50. Roskill, *Hankey*, vol I, p. 156.
51. Steel and Hart, *Defeat at Gallipoli*, pp. 16-17.
52. Moorehead, *Gallipoli*, p. 60.
53. Prior, *Gallipoli*, p. 53.
54. Carlyon, *Gallipoli*, p. 50.
55. C Aspinal-Oglander, *Roger Keyes*, p. 136.
56. Robert Burns, "To A Mouse," *The Canongate Burns*, pp. 95-6.
57. Travers, *Gallipoli*, p. 29.
58. Marder, *From the Dreadnought to Scapa Flow*, vol II, p. 247.
59. Ibid., p. 248.

CHAPTER 10: GALLIPOLI 1 – PREPARE TO FAIL

1. Les Carlyon, *Gallipoli*, p. 72.
2. Alan Moorehead, *Gallipoli*, p. 116.
3. Ellis Ashmead-Bartlett, *The Uncensored Dardanelles*, p. 14 and pp. 247-8.
4. Robin Prior, *Gallipoli*, p. 67.
5. Peter Hart, *Gallipoli*, p. 63.
6. John Laffin, *The Agony of Gallipoli*, p. 43.
7. Sir Ian Hamilton, *Gallipoli Diary, Vol 1*, Chapter 1, 14 March 1915. http://www.gutenberg.org/files/19317/19317-h/19317-h.ht.8. Harvey Broadbent, *Gallipoli, The Fatal Shore*, p. 37.
9. Laffin, *The Agony*, p. 34.
10. Carlyon, *Gallipoli*, p. 60.
11. Ibid., p. 54.
12. Carlyon, *Gallipoli*, p. 86.
13. Laffin, *The Agony*, p. 34.
14. Carlyon, *Gallipoli*, p. 87.
15. Laffin, *The Agony*, p. 35.
16. Sir Ian Hamilton, *Gallipoli Diary, Vol 1*, Chapter 1, 14 March 1915.
17. John North, *Gallipoli, The Fading Vision*, p. 247.
18. Moorehead, *Gallipoli*, pp. 82-83.
19. Laffin, *The Agony*, p. 35.
20. Michael Hickey, *Gallipoli*, p. 28.
21. T R Moreman, *Callwell, Sir Charles Stewart, 1859-1928*, Oxford Dictionary of National Biography, 2008.
22. Laffin, *The Agony*, pp. 12-13.
23. Moorehead, *Gallipoli*, p. 83.
24. Laffin, *The Agony*, p. 30.
25. Hickey, *Gallipoli*, p. 68.
26. John Hargrave, *The Suvla Bay Landing*, p. 29.
27. Harvey Broadbent, *The Fatal Shore*, p. 38.
28. Dan Van Der Vat, *The Dardanelles Disaster*, p. 145.
29. Robin Prior, Gallipoli, *The End of The Myth*, p. 68.
30. Alan Moorehead, *Gallipoli*, p. 88.
31. Ibid.
32. Prior, *Gallipoli, The End of The Myth*, p. 68.
33. Hamilton, *Gallipoli Diary, vol. 1*, 15 March, 1915 http://www.gutenberg.org/files/19317/19317-h/19317-h.htm#Page_127,
34. Robert Rhodes James, *Gallipoli*, p. 21.
35. Ellis Ashmead Bartlett, *The Uncensored Dardanelles*, pp. 39-40.
36. Michael Hickey, *Gallipoli*, p. 77.
37. Prior, *Gallipoli*, p. 242.
38. Hamilton, *Gallipoli Diary, vol. 1*, 5 April 1915http://www.gutenberg.org/files/19317/19317-h/19317-h.htm#Page_127,
39. James, *Gallipoli*, p. 80.
40. Laffin, *The Agony of Gallipoli*, p. 258-9.
41. James, *Gallipoli*, p. 79.
42. L A Carlyon, *Gallipoli*, p. 105.
43. Moorehead, *Gallipoli*, pp. 117-118.
44. Arthur J Marder, *From Dreadnought to Scapa Flow*, vol 11, p. 258.
45. Robert Rhodes James, *Gallipoli*, p. 79.
46. Laffin, *The Agony of Gallipoli*, p. 40.
47. Hickey, *Gallipoli*, p. 87.
48. Marder, *From Dreadnought to Scapa Flow*, Vol. 11, p. 212.
49. Peter Hart, *Gallipoli*, p. 56.
50. Laffin, *The Agony*, p. 35.
51. Edmond Delage, *The Tragedy of the Dardanelles*, p. 109.
52. Hickey, *Gallipoli*, pp. 57-58.
53. Denis Winter, *Haig's Command*, p. 140.
54. Prior, *Gallipoli*, p. 80.
55. Laffin, *The Agony*, p. 31.
56. Martin Gilbert, *Winston S Churchill*, vol 111, p 297.
57. Moorehead, *Gallipoli*, p. 90.
58. Marder, *From Dreadnought to Scapa Flow*, Vol. 11, p. 238.
59. Laffin, *The Agony*, p. 44.

CHAPTER 11: GALLIPOLI 2 – WHAT DID THEY CARE?

1. Sir Ian Hamilton, *Gallipoli Diary*, vol. 1, 31 March, 1915 http://www.gutenberg.org/files/19317/19317-h/19317-h.htm#Page_127,]
2. John Hargrave, *The Suvla Bay Landing*, pp. 39-40.
3. L A Carlyon, *Gallipoli*, pp. 119-122.
4. John Laffin, *The Agony of Gallipoli*, p. 55.

5. Ibid., p. 56.
6. Robin Prior, *Gallipoli, The End of The Myth*, p. 101.
7. Carlyon, *Gallipoli*, p. 120.
8. Moorehead, *Gallipoli*, pp. 145-148.
9. Hamilton, *Gallipoli Diary, vol. 1*, 26 April, 1915 http://www.gutenberg.org/files/19317/19317-h/19317-h.htm#Page_127
10. Prior, *Gallipoli*, p. 114.
11. Ibid., pp. 31-33.
12. Travers, *Gallipoli*, p. 101.
13. Hart, *Gallipoli*, pp.104-5.
14. Ellis Ashmead-Bartlett, *The Uncensored Dardanelles*, p. 81.
15. Hargrave, *The Suvla Bay Landing*, p. 41.
16. Baron John Arbuthnot Fisher, *Memories and Records*, Vol. 1. p. 77.
17. Gilbert, *Winston S Churchill*, pp. 448-9.
18. Carroll Quigley, *The Anglo-American Establishment*, p. 312.
19. Ashmead-Bartlett, *The Uncensored Dardanelles*, p. 81.
20. Ibid., pp 163-4.
21. Carlyon, *Gallipoli*, p. 120.
22. Ashmead-Bartlett, *The Uncensored Dardanelles*, pp.162-3.
23. Robert Rhodes James, *Gallipoli*, p. 210.
24. Hargrave, *The Suvla Bay Landing*, p. 66.
25. Rhys Crawley, *Climax at Gallipoli, The Failure of the August Offensive*, p. 58.
26. Hamilton, *Gallipoli Diaries, Vol II*, 6 August, p. 53.
27. Hargrave, *The Suvla Bay Landing*, pp. 75-76.
28. James, *Gallipoli*, p. 262.
29. Laffin, *The Agony of Gallipoli*, p. 153.
30. Michael Hickey, *Gallipoli*, p. 240.
31. Laffin, *The Agony of Gallipoli*, p. 154.
32. James, *Gallipoli*, p. 279.
33. Hargrave, *The Suvla Bay Landings*, p. 115.
34. Ibid., p. 131.
35. Hamilton, *Gallipoli Diary*, Vol. II, p. 51.
36. Ibid., p. 95.

CHAPTER 12: GALLIPOLI 3 – THE COVER-UP

1. James, *Gallipoli*, p. 222.
2. Robert Rhodes James, *'Birdwood, William Riddell, first Baron Birdwood(1865–1951)'*, ref. *Oxford Dictionary of National Biography*, Oxford University Press, 2004; online May 2009 [http://www.oxforddnb.com/view/article/31898.
3. Delage, *The Tragedy of the Dardanelles*, pp. 216-7.
4. Hickey, *Gallipoli*, p. 319.
5. Delage, *The Tragedy*, p. 222.
6. James, *Gallipoli*, p. 222.
7. Travers, *Gallipoli*,p. 273.
8. Roskill, *Hankey*, p. 189.
9. Ibid., pp. 198-9.
10. Guy Payan Dawnay had been a student at the Staff College at Camberley. His imperialist credentials were celebrated in his co-founding the Chatham Dining Club in 1910, [Richard Davenport-Hines, 'Dawnay, Guy Payan (1878–1952)', *Oxford Dictionary of National Biography*, Oxford University Press, 2004;] a seed-bed for those who shared the Secret Elite philosophy of British Race supremacy. Guest speakers between 1910 and 1914 included many of the most senior members of the Secret Elite including Leo Amery, Robert Brand, William Waldergrave Palmer, Earl of Selborne, Walter Long and George Lloyd. Maurice Hankey was amongst the first club members. http://www.chathamdiningclub.org.uk/speakers/
11. Hamilton, *Gallipoli Diary*, Vol.II, chapter XVII, 19 August 1915. http://www.gutenberg.org/files/22021/22021-h/22021-h.htm#Page_144
12. National Archives PRO CAB 42/3.
13. Roskill, *Hankey*, p. 207.
14. Hamilton, *Gallipoli Diary, Vol.II*, chapter XVII, 30 August 1915. http://www.gutenberg.org/files/22021/22021-h/22021-h.htm#Page_144
15. Richard Davenport-Hines, *Dawnay, Guy Payan* (1878–1952), *Oxford Dictionary of National Biography*, Oxford University Press, 2004.
16. Laffin, *The Agony of Gallipoli*, p. 189.
17. Denis Winter, *Haig's Command, A Reassessment*, p. 291.
18. Moorehead, *Gallipoli*, p. 305.
19. http://adb.anu.edu.au/biography/murdoch-sir-keith-arthur-7693%5D
20. A M Gollin, *Proconsul in Politics*, pp. 136-7.
21. The Round Table was the name given to Milner's organisation which promoted imperial ideals and aimed to influence the Dominions and other territories.
22. Desmond Zwar, *In Search of Keith Murdoch*, p. 20.
23. Ibid., p. 22.
24. Hamilton, *Gallipoli Diary Vol. II*, 2 September, 1915.
25. Zwar, *In Search of Keith Murdoch*, p. 25.
26. Ibid., p. 28.
27. Ashmead-Barlett, *The Uncensored Dardanelles*, p. 239.
28. Ibid., pp. 240-243.
29. Moorehead, *Gallipoli*, p. 309.
30. Travers, *Gallipoli*, p. 274.
31. Quigley, *The Anglo-American Establishment*, p. 312.
32. Carlyon, *Gallipoli*, p. 599.
33. Broadbent, *Gallipoli, The Fatal Shore*, p. 246.
34. Carlyon, *Gallipoli*, p. 496.
35. Docherty and Macgregor, *Hidden History*, pp. 146-7.
36. Zwar, *In Search of Keith Murdoch*, pp. 40-41.
37. Ashmead-Barlett, *The Uncensored Darda-*

nelles, pp. 254-5.
38. Hansard, House of Lords Debate 14 October 1915 vol 19 cc1045-62.
39. Travers, *Gallipoli*, p. 275.
40. Carlyon, *Gallipoli*, p. 502.
41. Ibid., p. 503.
42. Ibid., 504.
43. Ibid., p. 619.
44. Moorehead, *Gallipoli*, p. 327.
45. Milner Papers, Bonar Law to Milner, 25 July 1916.
46. A M Gollin, *Proconsul in Politics*, pp. 350-1.
47. Roger Owen, *Lord Cromer: Victorian Imperialist, Edwardian Proconsul*, pp. 388-9.
48. Macleod, *Reconsidering Gallipoli*, p.27.
49. Stephen Roskill, *Hankey*, p. 294.
50. Macleod, *Reconsidering Gallipoli*, pp. 28-9.
51. Martin Gilbert, *Winston S Churchill*, p. 248.
52. Moorehead, *Gallipoli*, p. 40.
53. Carlyon, *Gallipoli* p. 646.
54. Macleod, *Reconsidering Gallipoli*, p. 33.
55. Ibid.
56. Kevin Fewster, Vecihi Bagram, Hatice Bagram, *Gallipoli, The Turkish Story*, pp. 10-11.

CHAPTER 13: LUSITANIA – LOST IN A FOG OF LIES

1.Jonathan Reed Winkler *Nexus: Strategic Communications and American Security in World War* 1, pp. 5-6
2. Patrick Beesley, *Room 40, British Naval Intelligence 1914-1918*, p. 2.
3. H C Peterson, *Propaganda for War*, p.13.
4. Rear Admiral Sir Douglas Brownrigg, *Indiscretions of the Naval Censor*, pp 2-4.
5. It may come as a surprise to readers that the author John Buchan was in the outer circle of the Secret Elite in London. [Carroll Quigley, *The Anglo-American Establishment*, p 313.] Buchan wrote Nelson's *History of the Great War* and served as Director of Information for the War Office. Famed for his Richard Hannay series of adventure stories, Greenmantle, *The Thirty-Nine Steps* and *The Three Hostages*, these books shamelessly reflect Secret Elite values and British propaganda.
6. Beesley, *Room 40*, p. 3.
7. Christopher Andrew, *Secret Service*, p. 88.
8. Colin Simpson, *Lusitania*, p. 67.
9. Julian Thompson, *The War at Sea, 1914-1918*, p. 85.
10. Count Benckendorff, *Half A Life, The Reminiscences of a Russian Gentleman*, pp. 158-160.
11. Winston S Churchill, *The World Crisis 1911-1918*, pp. 414-5.
12. Public Record Office, ADM 137/4156.
13. Beesley, *Room 40*, p.6. footnote.
14. Diana Preston, *Wilful Murder, The Sinking of the Lusitania*, p. 184.
15. Beesley p. 20.
16. Ibid., p. 7.
17. Ibid.
18. Hansard, House of Commons Reports, 03 August, 1903, series 4 vol. 126 cc1272-3.
19. Hansard, House of Commons Reports, 02 August, 1904, vol. 139, cc673-4.
20. David Ramsay, *Lusitania, Saga and Myth*, pp 12-17.
21. John V Denson, *A Century of War: Lincoln, Wilson and Roosevelt*, p. 135.
22. *Jane's All the World Fighting Ships*, 1914.
23. Report of the Formal investigation into the circumstances attending the foundering on 7th May 1915, of the British Steamship *Lusitania*, Presented to both Houses of Parliament, 17th July 1915. [http://www.rmslusitania.info/primary-docs/mersey-report/
24. *New York Times*, May 10, 1915.
25. Julian Thomson, *The Imperial War Museum's Book of the War at Sea*, 1914-1918, p. 195.
26. Patrick Beesly, *Room 40*, p. 113.
27. *New York Times*, 9 May, 1915.
28. Mitch Peeke, *The Lusitania Story*, published 2003.
29. lusitania.net, Report and Manifest, confirmed by Wood Niebuhr and Co. Customs Brokers, New York.
30. Receipt Nos. 170-72.
31. Gerry Docherty and Jim Macgregor, *Hidden History, The Secret Origins of the First World War*, pp. 312-317.
32. Report of the Formal investigation into the circumstances attending the foundering on 7th May 1915, of the British Steamship Lusitania, Presented to both Houses of Parliament, 17th July 1915. [http://www.rmslusitania.info/primary-docs/mersey-report/ Mersey Inquiry, Day 3 evidence.
33. http://www.lusitania.net/deadlycargo.htm
34. Michael and Eleanor Brock, *HH Asquith, Letters To Venetia Stanley*, 11 May 1915, p. 590.
35. The Times, 11 May 1915, p. 9.
36. Arthur J Marder, *From Dreadnought to Scapa Flow*, Vol 11, pp. 342-3.
37. Winston S Churchill, *The World Crisis 1915*, p. 283.
38. Marder, *From Dreadnought to Scapa Flow*, Vol 11, pp. 342-3
39. *The Times*, February 16, 1915, p.8.
40. *The Times*, 19 February, 1915, p. 9.
41. From *The Times* Washington correspondent, *The Times*, 6 February 1915, p. 9.
42. Walter Millis, *Road To War – America, 1914-1917*, pp. 134-5.
43. Churchill, T*he World Crisis 1915*, p. 284.
44. Ibid., pp. 291-2.

45. Martin Gilbert, *Churchill on America*, p. 57.
46. *New York Tribune,* 1 May 1915
47. *The Washington Times* 1 May 1915, page 1.
48. United States Library of Congress: http://chroniclingamerica.loc.gov/lccn/sn83030214/1915-05-01/ed-1/seq 3/#words=-German+EMBASSY+WARNS+GERMAN+Embassy+warning+GERMANY
49. Preston, *Wilful Murder, The Sinking of the Lusitania*, p.133.
50. Patrick Beesly, *Room 40*, p. 102.
51. These special service ships were heavily armed merchantmen with hidden guns whose purpose was to lure a submarine into view before revealing her heavier guns, open fire and sink them.
52. Beesly, *Room 40*, p. 95.
53. Colin Simpson, *Lusitania*, pp. 136-7.
54. Preston, *Wilful Murder*, pp. 205-6.
55. Colin Simpson, pp. 127-8.
56. Gerry Docherty and Jim Macgregor, *Hidden History, The Secret Origins of the First World War,* p. 222.
57. Edward Mandell House and Charles Seymouur, *The Intimate Papers of Colonel House,* vol.1, p. 432.
58. *The Scotsman*, 8 May p. 10.
59. *The Times*, Saturday 8 May, 1915, p. 9.
60. Ibid., p. 10.
61. Simpson, *Lusitania*, pp.173-4.
62. http://www.rmslusitania.info/people/deck/william-turner/#bluebell
63. Report of the Coroner's Inquiry at Kinsale, *The Scotsman*, p. 5, Tuesday 11 May 1915.
64. Martin Gilbert, *Winston S Churchill, Companion Volume III*, p. 852.
65. Ibid., Maurice Brett letter to Lord Esher, 8 May 1915.
66. Hansard, House of Commons Debate 12 May 1915, vol. 7, cc1656.67. Mic
hael and Eleanor Brock, *HH Asquith, Letters to Venetia Stanley*, p. 487.
68. *The Times* and *The Daily Mail,* 21 May 1915.
69. Public Records Office., ADM/137/1058/3621/143.
70. Simpson, *Lusitania*, p. 182, citing Lord Mersey's papers.
71. Ibid., p. 200.
72. Eric Saunder and Ken Marschall, *RMS Lusitania, Triumph of the Edwardian Age*, pp. 46-7.
73. http://www.rmslusitania.info/people/saloon/oliver-bernard/
74. Simpson, *Lusitania*, p. 168.
75. http://www.titanicinquiry.org/Lusitania/
76. PRO ADM/137/1058. Webb's career blossomed. By the end of the war he had been promoted to Rear-Admiral, made Assistant High Commissioner at Constantinople and knighted in 1920.
77. Mersey Report Day 1, In Camera, Testimony of Captain Turner http://www.titanicinquiry.org/Lusitania/
78. Beesly, *Room 40*, p. 97.
79. PRO ADM/137/1058
80. The Mersey Inquiry, Day 4 (Continued) [http://www.titanicinquiry.org/Lusitania/04Header3.php]
81. Simpson, *Lusitania*, p.232.
82. The Lusitania Inquiry, *The Times* 19 July 1915.
83. Winston Churchill, *World Crisis, 1911-1918,* p. 448.
84. Ibid., p. 447.

CHAPTER 14: *LUSITANIA* - PROTECTING THE GUILTY

1. Carrol Quigley, *The Anglo-American Establishment,* published 1981, Books In Focus.
2. Gerry Docherty and Jim Macgregor, *Hidden History, The Secret Origins OF The First World War,* p. 18.
3. Lewis Einstein, The *United States and the Anglo-German Rivalry*, National Review, LX, Jan. 1913.
4. Ibid., pp. 736-50
5. Quigley, *The Anglo-American Establishment,* p. 168.
6. Robert E Osgood, *Ideals and Self Interest in America's Foreign Policy,* pp.114-34; and 150-54.
7. Bryan to JP Morgan and Co. 15 August, Library of Congress, Foreign Relations, Supplement 580.
8. Daniel M Smith, *Lansing and the Formation of American Neutrality Policies, 1914-1915*, Mississippi Valley Historical Review, vol.43 No. 1, p. 69.
9. Kathleen Burk, *War And The State, The Transformation of British Government, 1914-1919*, p. 89.
10. Kathleen Burk, *Britain, America and the Sinews of War*, pp. 18-19.
11. Colin Simpson, *Lusitania*, pp. 49-51.
12. http://notorc.blogspot.co.uk/2013/02/dudley-field-malone-1-courage-of-his.html
13. lusitania.net
14. Simpson, *Lusitania*, p. 59.
15. "The United States and War: President Wilson's Notes on the Lusitania and Germany's reply," *Brooklyn Daily Eagle*, vol. XXX (1915).
16. Simpson, *Lusitania*, pp. 172-3.
17. "The United States and War: President Wilson's Notes on the Lusitania and Germany's reply," *Brooklyn Daily Eagle*, vol. XXX (1915) p. 47.
18. Our thanks to Colonel Robert A Lynn, Florida Guard, from personal communication.
19. Mitch Peeke, *The Lusitania Story – The Struggle for The Truth*.20. *The Times*, Saturday 15 May,

1915, p. 7.
21. "The United States and War: President Wilson's Notes on the Lusitania and Germany's reply," *Brooklyn Daily Eagle*, vol. XXX (1915) p. 47.
22. Ibid., p. 48.
23. Simpson *Lusitania*, p. 168.
24. Charles E Lauriat, *The Lusitania's Last Voyage.*
25. Burton J Hendrick, *The Life And Letters Of Walter Page*, vol. 1. p. 436.
26. Edward Mandell House and Charles Seymour, *The Intimate Papers of Colonel House, vol.1*, p. 432.
27. Reported in a letter from George Booth to Alfred Booth, 25 September 1914.
28. Thomas A Bailey, *A Diplomatic History of the American People*, p. 626.
29. New York *Nation*, 13 May, 1915.
30. H C Peterson, *Propaganda for War,* p. 170. and footnote 6.
31. Julian Thompson, *The Imperial War Museum's Book of The War at Sea, 1914-1918*, p. 195.

CHAPTER 15: THE RELIEF OF BELGIUM 1 – THE GREAT HUMANITARIAN

1. George I Gay and H H Fisher, *Public Relations of the Commission For Relief In Belgium*, published in 2 volumes by Stanford University in 1929. It remains the official version, and is widely quoted as a valuable source.http://net.lib.byu.edu/estu/wwi/comment/CRB/CRB1-TC.htm Gay was on the executive staff as a statistician and promoted to Assistant Director in the London office of the CRB from 1918 onwards. He was sent to California in 1923 to ' work on the the records of the Belgian Relief commission. [*New York Times* Archives, 26 October, 1964.] Hoover's official biographer, George H Nash, published a 3 volume life of the man who would one day be President of America. seehttp://net.lib.byu.edu/estu/wwi/comment/CRB/CRB1-TC.htm The book written by Tracey Barrett Kittredge, *The History of the Commission for Relief in Belgium 1914-17 – Primary Source Edition*, was pulped by order of Herbert Hoover, even though she was member of the Commission who served in Belgium and France. The American diplomat Hugh Gibson's *A Journal From Our Legation in Belgium*, was rewritten and amended to glorify Hoover.http://www.ourstory.info/library/2-ww1/Legation/Gibson8.html
2. Expériences et représentations de la pénurie alimentaire durant la Guerre 14-18. Allemagne-Belgique', chaired by Professor Laurence Van Ypersele; Brussels 6/11/2014.
3. Michael Amara and Hubert Roland, *Gouverner en Belgique occupee: Oscar von der Lancken-Wakenitz – Rapports d'activite 1915-1918* collection, Comparatisme et Societe, no.1, 2004, introduction, p. 39.
4. George H Nash, *Herbert Hoover The Humanitarian, 1914-1917*, preface, p. x.
5. *The Commission for Relief in Belgium, Balance sheets and Accounts*, by joint liquidators, Edgar Rickard and W. B. Pollard https://archive.org/stream/executivepersonn00comm#page/n7/mode/2up
6. Measuring worth.com http://www.measuringworth.com/uscompare/relativevalue.php
7. Edwin W. Morse; *America in the War, Part V. Relief Work in Belgium and Northern France; Herbert Hoover and Engineering Efficiency*, p. 175.
8. David Lloyd George, *War Memoirs*, and Viscount Grey of Fallodon *Twenty-Five Years, 1892-1916.*
9. Micheal and Eleanor Brock, *HH Asquith, Letters to Venetia Stanley.*
10. *New York Times*, 17 July, 1921.
11. John Hamill, *The Strange Case of Mr Hoover Under Two Flags*, pp. 48-9.
12. Walter W Liggett, *The Rise of Herbert Hoover,* pp. 68-70.
13. *The Straits Times*, 3 March 1903. [http://eresources.nlb.gov.sg/newspapers/Digitised/Article/straitstimes19030303.2.3.aspx]
14.*The Times*, 19 January 1903, p. 3.
15. Liggett, *The Rise of Herbert Hoover*, pp. 111-12.
16. *The Times*, 2 March 1905, p. 9.
17. Carroll Quigley, *The Anglo-American Establishment*, p. 312.
18. Nash, *Herbert Hoover, 1914-1917*, p. 148.
19. Grey to Hoover, 9 June 1914, cited in Nash, op. cit. p.148.
20. Gay & Fisher, *Public Relations of The Commission for Relief in Belgium*, document 190, Dec 1914.
21. Nash, *Herbert Hoover*, p.127.
22. Ibid., p. 3.
23. http://rbkclocalstudies.wordpress.com/2012/10/25/elegy-for-the-red-house/
24. Fred I Kent Papers (1901-1954).http://findingaids.princeton.edu/collections/MC077
25. Nash, *The Life of Herbert Hoover*, p. 4.
26. *Chicago Tribune*, 6 Aug 1964. http://archives.chicagotribune.com/1964/08/06/page/123/article/widow-recalls-husbands-voyage-on-gold-ship-u-s-s-tennessee
27. Nash, *Herbert Hoover*, p.7.
28. CRB Miscellaneous files, H1. Nash, op. cit., reference 22 page 386.
29. *New York Times*, 8 August 1914, p. 3.
30. Nash, *Herbert Hoover*, p. 10.
31. Ibid., p. 10.
32. Hoover to Page, 23 September, 1914. Reference 52, as cited in Nash, *Herbert Hoover*, p. 387.

33. Burton J Hendrick, *The Life and Letters of Walter H Page*, vol. 3, p.136.
34. Ferdinand Lundberg, *America's 60 Families*, p. 142.
35. Ray Stannard Baker, (Pulitzer Prize winning journalist and confidante of Woodrow Wilson), *The Life and Letters of Woodrow Wilson*, VI, pp. 33-4.
36. Antony Sutton, *The Federal Reserve Conspiracy*, p. 78.
37. Lundberg, *America's 60 Families*, p. 142-3.
38. *The Papers of Woodrow Wilson, vol, 32.* Princeton NJ, as quoted in Nash, *Herbert Hoover, The Humanitarian*, p. 96.
39. Nash, *Herbert Hoover*, preface, p. x.
40. Ibid., p. 16.
41. John Hamill, *The Strange Career of Mr Hoover Under Two Flags*, p. 318.
42. *The Mining Magazine*, July 1916, p. 9.
[43] Elena S Danielson, *Historical Note on the Commission for Relief in Belgium, in United States in the First World: An Encyclopaedia*, edited by Anne Cipriano Venzon http://www.oac.cdlib.org/findaid/ark:/13030/tf6z09n8fc/entire_text/
44. *The Times*, 23 December 1914, p. 14.
45. *The Mining Magazine*, July 1916, pp. 42, 103, 168, 232.
46. Tracy Barrett Kittredge, *The History of the Commission for Relief in Belgium, 1914-1917*. Primary Source Edition, p. 7.
47. Lipkes J. (2007) *Rehearsals: The German Army in Belgium, August 1914*, Leuven University Press suggests a figure of around one and a half million.
48. Kittredge, *The History of the Commission*, p. 1.
49. *Rapport sur l'activite du Bureau Federal des Co-operatives Intercommunales de Revitaillement*,in General Report on the functioning and operations of the Comite National de Secours et Alimentation – Quatrieme Parte, p. 267.
50. Kittredge, *The History of the Commission*, p. 1.
51. Louis Delvaux, *Annals of the American Academy of Political and Social Science*, vol. 247, *Belgium in Transition* (September 1946) p. 144.
52. *Rapport sur l'activite du Bureau Federal des Co-operatives* – Quatrieme Parte, p. 267.
53. http://www.hoover.archives.gov/exhibits/Hooverstory/gallery02/index.html
54. *Heures de Detress, l'oeuvre du comite national de secours et d'alimentation et de la Commission for Relief in Belgium, 1914-1915*, p. v. http://uurl.kbr.be/1007553?bt=europeanaapi
55. Michael Amara and Hubert Roland, *Gouverner en Belgique Occupee*, p. 39.
56. Kittredge, *The History of the Commission*, p. 7.
57. Nash, *The Life of Herbert Hoover, The Humanitarian*, p.18.
58. Niall Ferguson, *The House of Rothschild: The World's Banker, 1849-1999*, vol. II, p. xxvii.
59. Francis Neilson, *How Diplomats Make War*, p.179.
60. *Banque Nationale de Belgique, The Centenary of the Great War – the National Bank in wartime*. http://www.nbbmuseum.be/fr/2013/11/wartime.htm
61. *Rapport sur les Petites Abeilles, Auot 1914* – December 1918, p.20.http://www.14-18.bruxelles.be/index.php/fr/vie-quotidienne/femmes-et-enfants/textes-femmes-et-enfants/book/94/Array
62. Kittredge, *The History of the Commission*, p. 17.
63. Ibid., p. 12.
64. *Physics Today* (15) 3. 1962. Obituary for Dannie Heineman.
http://scitation.aip.org/docserver/fulltext/aip/magazine/physicstoday/15/3/1.3058089.pdf?expires=1438164099&id=id&accname=guest&checksum=99F881D-F2AA9139F38DDD426F550985A
65. Nash, *Herbert Hoover*, p. 18.
66. *Letters and Journal of Brand Whitlock, The Journal, Chapter II.* http://www.ourstory.info/library/2-ww1/Whitlock/bw02.html
67. Kittredge, *The History of the Commission*, p. 78.
68. Ibid., p. 34.
69. Nash, *Herbert Hoover*, p. 18.
70. Kittredge, *The History of the Commission*, p. 35.
71. While the Report (page 18) refers to them as Ambassadors, technically Brand Whitlock was Head of the American Legation. Many writers simply blur the issue and refer to Whitlock as Ambassador.
72. Michael Amara and Hubert Roland, *Gouverner en Belgique Occupee*, p. 39
.73. Bryan to Gerard, 7 October 1914, *The American Journal of International Law*, p. 314.
74. Walter W Liggett, *The Rise of Herbert Hoover*, pp. 87-8.
75. *The Times*, 19 January 1905, p. 3.
76. Kittredge, *The History of the Commission*, p. 37.
77. Nash, *Herbert Hoover*, p.19.
78. Ligget, *The Rise of Herbert Hoover*, p. 223.
79. John Hamill, *The Strange Case of Mr Hoover Under Two Flags*, pp. 150-60.
80. Nash, *The Life of Herbert Hoover: The Engineer, 1874-1914*, pp. 5-11.
81. Kittredge, *The History of the Commission*, p. 37.
82. Nash, *The Life of Herbert Hoover: The Engineer*, pp. 390-1.
83. Gay and Fisher, *Public Relations for the Com-*

mission for Relief in Belgium, Page's letter to Hoover, 25 February 1916. Photostat copy opposite page http://net.lib.byu.edu/estu/wwi/comment/CRB/CRB1-TC.htm
84. Nash, *The Life of Herbert Hoover: The Engineer*, p. 21.
85. *New York Herald*, 15 October 1914.
86. Kittredge, *The History of the Commission*, p. 40.
87. *New York Times*, 1 November 1914.
88. Ibid.
89. *The Times*, 13 Oct 1914.
90. There are many pertinent examples. A number can be found in the *New York Times* throughout July 1916, from which those mentioned in the text are drawn.
91. Nash, *The Life of Herbert Hoover, The Humanitarian, 1914-1917* p. 52.
92. Ibid., p. 49.
93. Ibid.
94. Hoover to Bates, 13 November 1914, Nash, *The Life of Herbert Hoover,* p. 54.
95. Nash, *The Life of Herbert Hoover*, p. 55.
96. Whitlock to Bryan, 16/10/14, Gay and Fisher. Doc. 8, cited in the *American Journal of International Law*, p. 314.
97. Quigley, *The Anglo-American Establishment,* p. 31.
98. Kittredge, *The History of the Commission for Relief in Belgium* – Primary Source Edition, p. 56.
99. Brand Whitlock, Letters and Journals 10 December 1914 http://www.ourstory.info/library/2-ww1/Whitlock/bw05.html
100. Nash, *The Life of Herbert Hoover*, p. 80.
101. A perusal of Brand Whitlock's Letters and Journals shows just how involved and useful the Marquis was on a daily basis in Brussels. http://www.ourstory.info/library/2-ww1/Whitlock/bw05.html102. Gay and Fisher, *Public Relations for the Commission for Relief in Belgium,* p.13 Letter from Sir Arthur Nicolson, 20 October 1914 to Ambassador Page. http://net.lib.byu.edu/estu/wwi/comment/CRB/CRB1-TC.htm
103. *Norddeutsche Allgemeine Zeitung*, 4 March, 1915, p. 1.
104. Nash, *The Life of Herbert Hoover*, p. 34.
105. The Commission for Relief in Belgium, Balance Sheet and Accounts, http://babel.hathitrust.org/cgi/pt?id=coo1.ark:/13960/t04x5vs3b;view=1up;seq=7
106. Gay and Fisher, *Public Relations of the Commission for Relief in Belgium*, p. 5. http://net.lib.byu.edu/estu/wwi/comment/CRB/CRB1-TC.htm

CHAPTER 16: THE RELIEF OF BELGIUM 2: A GENEROSITY OF BANKERS

1. Nash, *The Life of Herbert Hoover, The Humanitarian*, pp. 49-52.
2. Ibid., p. 57.
3. Manfred Pohl and Sabine Freitag, *Handbook on the History of European Banks*, p.84.
4. King Edward VII had a very close relationship with Sir Edward Cassell, whom he trusted and valued. Interestingly, Cassell was the last visitor whom Edward saw before his death in 1910.
5. R Brian et J.L. Moreau, *Inventaire Des Archives de la Banque d'Outremer S.A., 1899-1957,* pp. VII- VII. http://www.avae-vvba.be/PDF/Banque_%20d_Outremer.pdf
6. Ibid.
7. Marie Therese Bitsch, *La Belgique Entre La France et d'Allemande, 1905-1914*, p. 134.
8. *The Times* 22 Feb. 1915.
9. Gabriel Tortella and Gloria Quirega, *Entrepreneurship and Growth: An International Historical Perspective*, pp. 78-81.
10. E.D. Morel, *Affairs of West Africa*, p. 331.
11. *The Times,* 2 March 1905, p. 9.
12. Neal Ascherson, *The King Incorporated, Leopold and the Congo*, p.199.
13. Charles D'Ydewalle, *Albert King of the Belgians*, p. 147.
14. Kittredge, *The history of the Commission for Relief in Belgium – Primary Source Edition*, p. 77.
15. Charles de Lannoy, *L'Alimentation de la Belgique par le comite national* (published 1922) p. 32. https://archive.org/details/lalimentationdel00lann
16. *The Times* 22 February 1915.
17. Gay and Fisher, *Public Relations of the Commission for Relief in Belgium,* pp. 245-250, Documents 135-138.
18. Nash, *The Life of Herbert Hoover*, pp. 86-7.
19. Gerry Docherty and Jim Macgregor, *Hidden History, The Secret Origins of the First World War.* pp. 214-5.
20. Gay and Fisher, *Public Relations of the Commission*, p. 245, Document 135.
21. Ibid., p. 247, document 136.
22. Bernhard Huldermann, *Albert Ballin*, p. 215.
23. Ibid., pp. 223-228. http://www.archive.org/stream/albertballin00hulduoft/albertballin00hulduoft_djvu.txt
24. Gay and Fisher, *Public Relations of the Commission*, p. 248, Document 137.
25. Ibid., Document 138.
26. Manfried Pohl and Sabine Freitag, *Handbook on the History of European Banks.*
27. Brand Whitlock, *Belgium Under German Occupation*, p. 214.
28. Charles D'Ydewalle, *Albert King of the Belgians*, p. 147.
29. Whitlock, *Belgium Under German Occupation*, p. 217.
30. Ibid., p. 215.

31. *New York Times*, 21 December 1916, p.8.
32. Nash, *The Life of Herbert Hoover*, p.197.
33. *New York Times*, 31 January 1917.
34. Hamill, *The Strange Case of Mr Hoover*, pp. 322-3.
35. *New York Times*, 10 May 1917.
36. Nash, *The Life of Herbert Hoover*, p. 196. [143] Kittredge, *The History of the Commission for Relief in Belgium 1914-1917*, p. 81.

CHAPTER 17: THE RELIEF OF BELGIUM 3 – PROLONGING THE WAR

1.Tracy Barrett Kittredge, *The History of the Commission for Relief in Belgium 1914-1917 – Primary Source Edition*, p. 81.
2. He was a German aristocrat, Major Frankenburg and Ludwigsdorf, personal adjutant to the military governor of Antwerp.
3. Kittredge, *The History of the Commission*, p. 81.
4. Ibid., p. 82.
5. Edward David, *Inside Asquith's Cabinet*, pp. 201-2.
6. Gay and Fisher, *Public Relations of the Commission for Relief in Belgium, vol. I* p. 308, Document 189.
7. Ibid., pp. 308-9, Document 190.
8. Alfred Emmott was Chair of the Committee on Trading with the Enemy and Director of the War Trade Department from 1915-1919.
9. Quigley, *The Anglo-American Establishment*, p. 57 and 313
10. Gay and Fisher, Public Relations, pp. 232-235, Document 129.
11. Ibid., p. 263, Document 146.
12. The Germans were concerned about the amount of spying that was taking place in mid-1915. Oscar von der Lancken, Head of the German Political Department in Belgium, made particular reference to some members of the CNSA sending illegal information to Britain in the month before Edith Cavell was arrested. Ref. Micheal Amara and Hubert Roland, *Gouverner En Belgique Occupee*, p. 99.
13. Gay and Fisher, *Public Relations*, p. 264, Document 146.
14. Ibid., paragraph 4. p. 265.
15. Gay and Fisher, *Public Relations of the Commission for Relief in Belgium, Vol.1*. p. 52, Document 33.
16. Ibid.
17. Gay and Fisher, *Public Relations*, p. 309, Document 190.
18. The appointment of American Rhodes Scholars from Oxford University was altogether appropriate for the Secret Elite. The scholarships had been created by Cecil Rhodes, the man whose imperial dream was to create a world dominated by the best of English culture. The reality of a one-world Anglo-Saxon-based cabal developed from this into the Secret Elite who had caused the First World War . [Gerry Docherty and Jim Macgregor, *Hidden History, The Secret Origins of the First World War*, pp. 17-30.] The American Rhodes Scholars were thus presumed to be an outstanding choice to support the CRB in their work, though they were in fact completely inappropriate for the task, had it been genuine.
19. Hamill, *The Strange Career of Mr Hoover*, p. 318.
20. Kittredge, *The history of the Commission for Relief in Belgium 1914-1917*, p. 90.
21. Whitlock to Page, 19 December 1914.
22. Gay and Fisher, *Public Relations*, pp. 48-49, Document 31.
23. Ibid., p. 49.
24. Ibid., pp. 73-74, Document 43.
25. Ibid.
26. Michael Amara et Hubert Roland, *Gouverner En Belgique Occupee*, p. 99.
27. Ibid.
28. Ibid., p. 214.
29. Ibid.
30. Ibid., p. 334. Report August 1916 – January 1917.
31. Ibid., p. 298. Report February-July 1916 – January 1917.
32. Hansard, House of Commons Debate, 10 July 1916 vol. 84 c7.
33. Hansard, House of Commons Debate, 18 July 1916 vol. 84 c818.
34. Micheal Amara et Hubert Roland, *Gouverner en Belgique occupee*, pp 55- end.
35. Gay and Fisher, *Public Relations for the Commission for Relief in Belgium*, Percy to Hoover, 26 January 1916, Document 46, p.79.
36. Ibid., Document 48, pp. 80-81.
37. Ibid., Document 49, pp. 81-82.
38. Ibid., Document 50, pp. 82-83.
39. *Rapport General sur le functionement et les operations du Comite National de Secours et Alimentation, 1914-1919*, p. 35.
40. Hansard, House of Commons Debate, 20 July 16 vol. 84 cc1158-60.
41. Ibid.
42. Hansard, House of Commons, Debate, 27 July1916 Vol. 84 cc1841-2.
43. Mr Evelyn Cecil MP, Hansard, House of Commons Debate, 10 August 1916 vol. 85. cc1201-2.
44. Ibid.
45. Hansard, House of Commons Debate, 23 Nov 1916, Vol. 87 cc1547-8.
46. Hansard, House of Commons Debate, 31 Dec 1916, Vol. 88 cc1588-9.
47. Brand Whitlock, *The Letters and Journal*,

Chapter VII, 17 November, 1916, http://www.ourstory.info/library/2-ww1/Whitlock/bw07.html48. Ibid., 6 November 1916.
49. Ibid.
50. Ibid.
51. Ibid., 1 August 1916.
52. Nash, *Herbert Hoover, The Humanitarian*, p. 219.
53. Memorandum drafted to Walter Hines Page, 3 May, 1916.
54. Nash and Fisher, *Herbert Hoover*, p. 204.
55. Kittredge, *The history of the Commission for the Relief in Belgium, 1914-1917*, p. 364.
56. Ibid., p. 371.
57. Ibid., p. 374.
58. Whitlock, *Letters and Journal*, Chapter VII, 17, 6 November, 1916. [202] Nash, *Herbert Hoover, The Humanitarian*, p. 298.
59. Ibid., p. 300.
60. Gay and Fisher, *Public Relations for the Commission for Relief in Belgium*, Document 158, p. 278.
61. Ibid.
62. *Hawara and Normanby Star*, Vol. LXXII, 6 January, 1917, p. 4.
63. *Sydney Morning Herald*, 20 February, 1934 in the obituary for William A Holman, President of the New South Wales Belgian Relief Fund.
64. Hamill, *The Strange Career of Mr Hoover*, p. 348.
65. Nash, *The Life of Herbert Hoover*, p. 311.
66. Gay and Fisher, *Public Relations for the Commission for Relief in Belgium*, Documents 134 -137, pp. 241-248.
67. Nash, *The Life of Herbert Hoover*, p. 312.
68. Gay and Fisher, *Public Relations for the Commission for Relief in Belgium*, Document 240, p. 361.
69. Ibid., p. 354.
70. *The Times*, 17 March 1917, p. 8.
71. Sir Maurice de Bunsen statement to the Associated Press, *New York Times*, 6 March 1917.
72. Hamill, *The Strange Career*, p. 348.
73. Hoover cable 93 to CRB-London office, 13 February 1917.
74. Nash, *The Life of Herbert Hoover*, p. 320.
75. *New York Times*, 14, February, 1917.
76. Nash, *The Life of Herbert Hoover*, p. 326.
77. Whitlock, *Letters and Journals*, 4 March, 1917.
78. Ibid., 13 March, 1917.
79. Kittredge, *The History of the Commission for Relief in Belgium*, p. 418.
80. Nash, *The Life of Herbert Hoover*, p. 339.
81. Kittredge, *The History of the Commission for Relief in Belgium*, pp. 435-442.
82. Amara et Roland, *Gouverner En Belgique Occupee*, p. 298.
83. Nash, *The Life of Herbert Hoover*, p. 358.
84. Gay and Fisher, Document 168, p. 286.
85. *New York Times*, 4 May 1917.
86. The Times, 20 July 1917, p. 5.
87. George I Gay and H H Fisher, *Public Relations of the Commission for Relief in Belgium*, Document 18, p. 19.
88. Nash, *Herbert Hoover, The Humanitarian*, pp. 69-70.
89. Gay and Fisher, *Public Relations of the Commission for Relief in Belgium*, Document 147 , p. 266.
90. Ibid., Document 134, pp. 241-2.
91. Ibid., Document 140, pp. 252-255.
92. Nash, *Herbert Hoover*, p. 176.
93.The Massacre at Amritsar in 1919 was known also as the Jallianvala Bagh Massacre. http://www.sikh-history.com/sikhhist/events/jbagh.html
94. Nash, *Herbert Hoover*, p. 270.
95. Liggett, *The Rise of Herbert Hoover*, p. 209.
96. Ibid., pp. 210-211.
97. http://www.encyclopedia.com/topic/Anglo_American_Corp._of_South_Africa_Limited.aspx
98. *The Commission for the Relief in Belgium, Balance Sheet and Accounts*, published 1921 p. 86 http://libcudl.colorado.edu/wwi/pdf/i71185215.pdf
99. Nash, *Herbert Hoover*, p. 274.

CHAPTER 18: THE MARTYRDOM OF EDITH CAVELL

1. *Secrets and Spies*, BBC Radio 4, broadcast on 15/09/2015
2. Possibly the worst of the propaganda hagiographies is William Thomson Hill's *The Martyrdom of Nurse Cavell: The Life Story of the Victim of Germany's Most Barbarous Crime*. London: Hutchinson & Co., 1915.
3. H.C. Peterson, *Propaganda for War*, p. 61.
4. Diana Souhami, *Edith Cavell*, p.105.
5. Ibid., p. 19.
6. *The British Journal of Nursing*, May 1924, p. 112.
7. Helen Judson, "Edith Cavell". *The American Journal of Nursing*, July 1941, p. 871.
8. *Nursing Mirror and Midwives' Journal*, vol. XXI no. 526
9. Hoehling, A. (1957). "The Story of Edith Cavell"; *The American Journal of Nursing*, 1320-1322.
10. Kenneth Bertrams, Nicholas Coupain, Ernest Homburg, *Solvay, History of a Multinational Family Firm*, p. 2.
11. *New York Times*, April 27, 1915.
12. Paragraph 58 of the German military code.
13. Princess Marie De Croy, *War Memories*, pp.

100- 211.https://archive.org/details/warmemories00croyuoft
14. Debruyne, Emmanuel: *Patriotes désintéressés ou espions vénaux? Agents et argent en Belgique et en France occupées, 1914-1918, in: Guerre mondiales et conflits contemporains,* 2008/4, no. 232, p. 25-45.
15. Christopher Andrew, *Secret Service, The Making of the British Intelligence Service,* p. 45.
16. Marie de Croy, *War Memories*, p. 117.
17. Ibid., p. 111.
18. Harry Beaumont, *Old Contemptible*, p. 148.
19. Marie de Croy, *War Memories*, p. 106.
20. Ibid., p.111.
21. Ibid.
22. George Gay and HH Fisher, *The Public Relations of the Commission for Relief in Belgium,* Document 33, pp. 52-3 http://www.gwpda.org/wwi-www/CRB/CRB1-TC.htm
23. Marie de Croy, *War Memories,* p.131.
24. Ibid.
25. Ibid., p.118.
26. *The Times,* 15 Aug, 1914, p.8.
27. *Nursing Mirror and Midwives' Journal*, vol. XXI no. 526, p. 57.
28. Diana Souhami, *Edith Cavell,* pp 200-203.
29. Ibid., p. 248.
30. Ibid., p. 259.
31. *Nursing Mirror and Midwives' Journal*, vol. XXI no. 526, p. 57.
32. Ibid., p. 63.
33. Ibid., p. 64.
34. Ibid.
35. Harry Beaumont, *Old Contemptible*, p. 154.
36. Souhami, *Edith Cavell*, p. 221.
37. Beaumont, *Old Contemptible*, p. 95.
38. Ibid., p. 181.
39.Souhami, *Edith Cavell*, p. 271.

CHAPTER 19: CAVELL? SEEMINGLY NO-ONE KNEW

1. Marie de Croy, *War Memories*, p. 127.
2. Brand Whitlock, *Belgium under the German Occupation, a personal narrative,* vol.2, p. 46.
3. Diana Souhami, *Edith Cavell,* p. 199.
4. *La Libre Belgique*, issue 30, June 1915.
5. Phil Tomaselli, *BBC History Magazine*, September 2002, p. 6.
6. Public Records Office papers released in 2001-2 and quoted in the above.
7. Tomaselli, *BBC History Magazine*, September 2002, p. 6.
8. Ibid.
9. Ibid.
10. Our thanks to our colleague in Belgium, Hugo Lueders, who shared his personal research with us. Hugo does sterling work on centenarynews.com https://www.academia.edu/9532093/EDITH_S_WONDERLAND_IN_MEMORIAM_OF_EDITH_CAVELL_12_OCTOBER_1915#signup/close
11. Harry Beaumont, *Old Contemptible*, p. 192.
12. Ibid., p. 172.
13. Emmanuel Debruyne and Jehanne Paternostre, *"La résistance au quotidien 1914-1918, Témoignages inédites"*, Racine, Brussels, 2009: *'Trois échelons vers la Hollande'*, pp. 45-51 (here: page 51) as cited by Hugo Leuders, see below.
14. Dame Stella Rimington, BBC Radio 4, Secrets and Spies, broadcast on 15/09/2015.
15. Hugo Lueders, *Edith's Wonderland*, footnote 35 p. 15. https://www.academia.edu/9532093/EDITH_S_WONDERLAND_IN_MEMORIAM_OF_EDITH_CAVELL_12_OCTOBER_1915#signup/close
16. Undated hand-written note by Capiau, private archives Herman Capiau, Centre de documentation, Musée Royal de l'Armée et d'Histoire militaire, Brussels.
17. See relevant page from website below. whitlockfamilyassociation.com.s3amazonaws.com/sources/newspapers/NP0261.pdf
18. Dame Stella Rimington, BBC Radio 4, *Secrets and Spies*, broadcast on 15/09/2015.
19. Brand Whitlock, *Belgium under the German Occupation, a personal narrative*, vol.2, pp. 138-9.
20. Ibid., p. 183.
21. Ibid., pp. 225-6.
22. Hoover to Whitlock, 6 March 1916, Document 33, Gay and Fisher, *The Public Relations of the Commission for Belgian Relief,* p. 52.
23. *New York Times*, 18 March, 1915.
24. *Nursing Mirror and Midwives' Journal*, vol. XXI no. 526, p. 64.
25. George H Nash, *The Life of Herbert Hoover, The Great Humanitarian, 1914-1917*, p. 136.
26. *The Times*, 15 August 1914, p. 8.
27. Diana Souhami, *Edith Cavell*, p. 271.
28. Project Gutenberg, *A Journal From Our Legation in Belgium,* by Hugh Gibson, *The Case of Miss Edith Cavell.* http://net.lib.byu.edu/estu/wwi/memoir/legation/Gibson8.htm
29. First World War Primary Documents, *Maitre Gaston de Leval on the Execution of Edith Cavell* http://www.firstworldwar.com/source/cavell_deleval.htm
30. Tracey Kittredge, *The history of the Commission for Relief in Belgium*, p. 97.
31. Harry Beaumont, *Old Contemptible*, pp. 173-4.
32. Souhami, *Edith Cavell,* p. 271.
33. Marie de Croy, *War Memories*, p.192.https://archive.org/details/warmemories00croyuoft
34. Charles F Horne, *Source Records of the Great War, Vol. III,* ed., National Alumni, 1923. first-

worldwar.com – Primary Documents – *Maitre G. de Level on the Execution of Edith Cavell*
.35. Jacqueline Van Til, *With Edith Cavell in Belgium,* pp.125-131.https://archive.org/details/withedithcavelli00vant%5D
36. Souhami, *Edith Cavell,* p. 313.
37. *The Times*, Friday 22 October 1915, p. 9.
38. First World War.com – Primary Documents – *Hugh Gibson on the Execution of Edith Cavell*
39. John Hamill, *The Strange Career of Mr. Hoover, Under Two Flags*, p. 333.
40. Charles Tytgat, *Nos Fusilles* (raconteurs et espions) p. 67.http://www.bel-memorial.org
41. *La Belgique et la guerre.* Georges Rancy Edition Henri Bertels 1927 http//www.1914-1918.be/photo.php?image=photos2/president hoover/president hoover 006.jpg
42. Brand Whitlock to von Der Lancken, 31 August 1915 as quoted in Brand Whitlock, *Belgium Under the German Occupation vol. 2*, p. 4.
43. Baron von Der Lancken to Mr Whitlock, 12 September, 1915 as quoted in *Brand Whitlock, Belgium Under the German Occupation Vol. 2*, p. 5.
44. Tytgat, *Nos Fusilles*, pp. 68-69
45. Sadi Kirschen, *Devant les Conseils de Guerre Allemandes*, p.54.
46. ibid., p. 136.
47. Kirschen, *Devant les Conseils de Guerre Allemandes,* p.55.
48. firstworldwar.com – Primary Documents, *Maitre G. de Leval on the execution of Edith Cavell,* 12 October 1915.
49. Brand Whitlock, *Belgium Under German Occupation, vol. 2,* p. 2.http://www.firstworldwar.com/source/cavell_deleval.htm
50. Ibid., p. 3.
51. Marie de Croy, *War Memories*, pp. 127-8. https://archive.org/details/warmemories00croyuoft
52. Antoine Redier, *La Guerre des Femmes, Histoire de Louise de Bettignes et de ses compagnes,* p. 30.
53. Ibid., p. 186.
54. Diana Souhami, *Edith Cavell*, p. 325.
55. Marie de Croy, *War Memories*, p. 176.
56. Brand Whitlock, *Belgium Under German Occupation, Vol. 2*, p. 11.
57. Katie Pickles, *Transnational Outrage – The Death and Commemoration of Edith Cavel,* p. 29.
58. Souhami, *Edith Cavell,* p. 249.

CHAPTER 20: CAVELL – THE UNEDIFYING CIRCUS

1. Marie de Croy, *War Memories*, p. 179.
2. Ibid., p.190.
3. Brand Whitlock, *Letters and Journals*, 11 October, 1915.http://www.ourstory.info/library/2-ww1/Whitlock/bw05.html
4. Ibid.
5. Whitlock, *Belgium under the German Occupation, vol. 2.*, p 15.archive.org/stream/belgiumundergerm02whit#page/68/mode/2up/search/edith+cavell
6. Ibid.
7. Ibid., p 19.
8. Hugh Gibson, *'A Journal from our Legation in Belgium'.*
9. firstworldwar.com Primary Documents – *The Rev H. Stirling Gahan on the execution of Edith Cavell.* Source Records of the Great War, Vol. III, ed. Charles F. Horne, National Alumni 1923.
10. *Exchange Telegraph*, Paris, 2 November 1915.
11. firstworldwar.com- Primary Documents-*Alfred Zimmern on the execution of Edith Cavell*
12. Ibid.
13. Marie de Croy, *War Memories*, p. 165.
14. Ibid., p. 176.
15. *New York Times,* 10 July 1917.
16. Harry Brittain, *Pilgrim Partners, Forty Years of British American Fellowship*, pp. 110-11.
17. Charles Tytgat, *Nos Fusilles (recruiters et espions)*, p. 66
18. *The Times,* 16 May, 1919.
19. Brand Whitlock, *Belgium under the German Occupation, vol. 2.*, p. 49.
20. Ibid., p. 51.
21. Amara et Roland, *Gouverner En Belgique Occupee*, p.124.
22. Whitlock, *Belgium under the German Occupation*, vol. 2., p. 55.
23. George H Nash, *Herbert Hoover the Humanitarian*, p. 201.
24. Whitlock, *The Letters and Journals,* Chapter 6. (7 February 1916.)
25. Ibid., note 7, chapter 6.
26. George H Nash, *Herbert Hoover the Humanitarian*, p. 201.
27. Richard Norton Taylor, *The Guardian,* 12 October 2005.
28. *The Times,* 20 October 1915, editorial and Page 9.
29. Ibid.
30. Hansard, House of Lords Debate, 20 October 1915, cc. 1100-1104.
31. William Thomson Hill, *The Martyrdom of Nurse Cavell, The Life Story of the Victim of Germany's Most Barbarous Crime* (With Illustrations).
32. *The Times,* 16 May 1919 pp. 13-14.
33. Ibid., p. 14.
34. Phil Tomaselli, *BBC History*, September 2002, p. 6.
35. Hugo Lueders, https://www.academia.edu/9532093/EDITH_S_WONDERLAND_IN_

MEMORIAM_OF_EDITH_CAVELL_12_OCTOBER_1915#signup/close

36. A G Gardner, *The Guardian,* 23 October 1915; quoted in Irene Cooper Willis, *England's Holy War*, p. 231.

37. Dame Stella Rimington, Secrets and Spies, BBC Radio 4, broadcast on 15/09/2015. http://www.bbc.co.uk/programmes/b069wth6

38. National Archives, PRO / CP 1813, p. 424.

39. Ibid., p. 428.

40. Hansard, House of Lords Debate, 20 October 1915, vol. 19 cc. 1100-1104.

41. Brand Whitlock, *The Letters and Journals of Brand Whitlock*, Chapter V, 6-9 October 1915.

42. Souhami, *Edith Cavell*, p. 346.

43. Ibid., p. 320.

44. Whitlock, *The Letters and Journals*, Chapter 5, 11 October 1915. http://www.ourstory.info/library/2-ww1/Whitlock/bw05.html

45. *New York Times,* 2 November 1915.

46. Sophie Schaepdrijver, *Gabriel Petit, The Death and Life of a Female Spy,* p. 92.

47. Brand Whitlock, *Belgium Under German Occupation*, p. 198.

48. Vernon Kellogg, *Fighting Starvation*, p. 66.

49. Ibid.

50. Schaepdrijver, *Gabriel Petit,* p. 92.

51. *The Times*, 18 June 1962, p.14; Rhodri Jeffreys-Jones, *Sir William Wiseman*, Oxford Dictionary of National Biography; Christopher Andrews,*Secret Service, The Making of the British Intelligence Service*, p. 209.

52. Rimington, *Secrets and Spies*, BBC Radio 4, broadcast 15/09/2015.

53. Gay and Fisher, *Public Relations of the Commission for Relief in Belgium*, Documents, 46-50 pp. 79-84.

54. Marie de Croy, *War Memories*, p. 204.

CHAPTER 21: OIL – THE UNEVEN PLAYING-FIELD.

1. See Chapter 3 - Briey,

2. See Chapter 5 - Blockade.

3. See The Commission for Relief in Belgium chapter, p. ??

4. Hew Strachan, *The Morale of the German Army, 1917-18*, in, Hugh Cecil and Peter H Liddle, *Facing Armageddon*, p. 383.

5. B S McBeth, *British Oil Policy 1919-1939*, p. 20.

6. Gerry Docherty and Jim Macgregor, *Hidden History, The Secret Origins of the First World War,* pp. 12-16.

7. Carrol Quigley, *The Anglo-American Establishment*, p. 311.

8. Docherty and Macgregor, *Hidden History* p. 158 and 362.

9. Hansard House of Lords, *Anglo – Persian Oil Co. Acquisition of Capital (Bill)*, House of Lords, 7 August 1914, series 5, Vol 17, cc461-2.

10. John Howard Morrow, *The Great War – An Imperial History*, p. 26.

11. Keith Jeffrey, *The British Army and the Crisis of Empire*, p. 36.

12. Dr F C Gerretson, *History of the Royal Dutch, Volume III*, p. 65.

13. David S Landes, *The Unbound Prometheus*, p. 327.

14. William Engdahl, *A Century of War*, p. 25.

15. Ibid.

16. Alison Frank, "The Petroleum War of 1910: Standard Oil, Austria, and the Limits of the Multinational Corporation," *The American Historical Review*, 114 (1)pp. 16-41.

17. *Neue Freie Presse* (Vienna) 24 September 1910.

18. Frank, *The Petroleum War,* p. 17.

19. Ibid., p. 28.

20. Ibid., p. 41.

21. *The Tablet*, 1 June 1912, p. 32.

22. *The Times*, 14 November 1916, p. 3

.23. Alison Frank, *Oil Empire, Visions of Prosperity in Austrian Galicia*, pp. 171-173.

24. Ibid., p. 173.

25. *150 Years of Oil in Romania.* http://www.150deanidepetrol.ro/history.html

26. Ibid.

27. Keith Hitchins, *Rumania 1866-1947*, p. 192.

28. Daniel Yergin, *The Prize, The Epic Quest for Oil, Money and Power.* p.163.

29. 61st Congress, 2nd Session, Senate Document 593, *National Monetary Commission, the Economic Development of Germany* by Dr J Reisser. http://babel.hathitrust.org/cgi/pt?id=uc2.ark:/13960/t7cr5qn19;view=1up;seq=432

30. *New York Times* 16 May 1911. Articles explain the decision of the Supreme Court. http://query.nytimes.com/gst/abstract.htmlres=9900E5DA1431E233A25755C1A9639C946096D6CF

31. MYM Babayev, *Baku Baron* Days,http://www.azer.com/aiweb/categories/magazine/ai122_folder/122_articles/122_foreign_investment.html

32. Professor Robert W Tolf, *The Russian Rockefellers*, pp. 90-92.

33. Ron Chernow, Titan, p. 246.

34. Ibid.

35. Ibid., p. 247.

36. Ibid., p. 248.

37. Ibid.

38. Gerretson, *History of the Royal Dutch,* Vol III, pp. 80-81.

39. Ibid., p. 123.

40. Yergin, *The Prize*, p. 116.

41. Niall Ferguson, *The House of Rothschild,* p. 242.

42. Landes, *The Unbound Prometheus*, p. 290.

43. Docherty and Macgregor, *Hidden History*, p. 14.
44. *New York Times*, 10 February, 1902.
45. 61st Congress, 2nd session, Senate Document 593, *National Monetary Commission, the Economic Development of Germany* by Dr J Reisser.
46. Ibid., p. 412.
47. Ibid.
48. Fritz Stern, *Gold and Iron: Bismarck, Bleichröder and the Building of the German Empire*, pp. 9-11.
49. Gerretson, *History of the Royal Dutch*, Vol. III, p. 119.
50. Ibid., p. 82.
51. Landes, *The Unbound Prometheus*, pp. 235-7.
52. Alfred Dupont Chandler, *Scale and Scope: The Dynamics of Industrial Capitalism*, p. 438.
53. Ferguson, *The House of Rothschild*, p. xxvii.

CHAPTER 22: OIL 2 – BRITAIN FIRST

1. Engdahl, *A Century of War*, p. 20.
2. In 1912, retired Admiral Jackie Fisher was appointed chairman of the Royal Commission to enquire into Liquid Fuel, with a view to converting the entire fleet to oil. Classified 'Secret', Fisher's Commission reported on 27 November 1912, with two following reports on 27 February 1913 and 10 February 1914. See National Archives.
3. Gerretson, *History of the Royal Dutch*, Vol. 1, p.214.
4. *The Times*, 1 July 1908. Gerretson, *History of the Royal Dutch*, Vol. 2, pp. 197-8.
5. Gerretson, *History of the Royal Dutch*, Vol. 2, p. 303.
6. Glyn Roberts, *The Most Powerful Man in the World, The Life of Sir Henri Deterring*, p. 106.
7. Engdahl, *A Century of War*, p. 63.
8. Gerretson, *History of the Royal Dutch*, vol III, p. 228.
9. Ibid.
10. R W Ferrier, The *History of the British Petroleum Company*, p. 5.
11. Engdahl, *A Century of War*, p 20.
12. Ferrier, *The History of the British Petroleum Company*, p. 97.
13. Ibid., p. 105.
14. Engdahl, *A Century of War*, p 93.
15. Chief amongst these was Donald Smith, Lord Strathcona a Scottish-born Canadian businessman, financier and philanthropist. Donna McDonald, Lord Strathcona, p. 467.
16. http://www.measuringworth.com/ukcompare/relativevalue.php Dr FC Gerretson, History of the Royal Dutch states that D'Arcy was paid £170,000 in shares, while Ferrier, see below, cites 170,000 shares.
17. Ferrier, *The History of the British Petroleum Company*, p. 112.
18. Gerretson, *History of the Royal Dutch*, p. 231.
19. Donna McDonald, *Lord Strathconna*, pp. 507-526.
20. Yergin, *The Prize*, p. 159.
21. Ibid., p. 158.
22. *The Times*, 18 June 1914, p. 12.
23. Yergin, *The Prize*, p. 161.
24. *The Times*, 23 June 1914, p. 19. Company Meetings, Shell Transport and Trading Co. (Ltd)
25. *The Times*, 18 June, 1914, p. 12. Mr Ramsay MacDonald's Views.
26. Hansard, House of Commons Debate, 10 August 1914 vol 65 cc2308-35.
27. John Pilger, *The New Rulers of the World*, p. 101.
28. Engdahl, *A Century of War*, p. 20.
29. Yergin, *The Prize*, p. 163.
30. Hansard, House of Commons Debate, 5 August 1914, vol 65 c2001.
31. http://www.measuringworth.com/ukcompare/relativevalue.php.
32. Churchill was later to claim, without a moment's hesitation, that the sums realised from this venture meant that the cost of all the great ships laid down between 1912-1914 were added to the British navy at no cost to the taxpayer. Winston Churchill, *The World Crisis 1911-1918*, p. 77.
33. *The Times*, 18 June 1914, p. 12.
34. Gerretson, *History of the Royal Dutch*, vol. Four, inset pp. 174-5 details the complex interlocking of the giant Royal Dutch/Shell 's organisation in the Western Market in 1914.
35. Ibid., p. 282.
36. Hansard, House of Commons Debate, 17 July 1913, vol 55 cc1465-583.
37. See Chapters 4 /5
38. Hansard, House of Commons Debate, 17 November 1914, vol 68 cc314-7.
39. Rear-Admiral M W W P Consett, *The Triumph of Unarmed Forces* p.180.
40. Ibid.
41. Pierre de la Tramerye, *The World Struggle for Oil* p. 103.
42. Consett, *The Triumph*, pp. 180-189.

CHAPTER 23: OIL 3: PROLONGING THE WAR AGAIN

1. E Keble Chatterton, *The Big Blockade*, p. 73.
2. The United States and War: President Wilson's Notes on the Lusitania and Germany's reply, *Brooklyn Daily Eagle*, vol. XXX (1915) p. 47.
3. Paul Konig, *Voyage of the Deutschland, The First Merchant Submarine*, p. 19. Konig was the Captain of the Deutschland.
4. Dwight Messimer, *The Baltimore Sabotage*

Cell, German Agents, American Traitors and the U-boat Deutschland During World War 1, p. 139.
5. Quigley, *The Anglo-American Establishment*, p. 38.
6.Hansard, House of Commons Debate, 31 July 1916, vol 84 cc 2044-6.
7. See Blockade chapter
8. Time and again questions were asked in Parliament about Romanian oil and its ownership, who owned shares in various companies and where the war profits were going. One example of this can be appreciated from Hansard, House of Commons Debate, 06 January 1916, vol 77 cc1079-80.
9. Yergin *The Prize*, p. 163.
10. C R M F Crutwell, *A History of the Great War* p. 292.
11. Churchill, *The World Crisis 1911-1918*, pp. 675-9.
12. Lloyd George, *War Memoirs*, vol 1, p. 548.
13. Ibid., p. 549.
14. Sir William Robertson, *Soldiers and Statesmen 1914-1918,* vol II, p. 127.
15. Lloyd George, *War Memoirs*, vol. I, p. 549.
16. Ibid.
17. *The Times*, 11 December, 1916, p. 8.
18. Yergin, *The Prize*, pp. 164-5.
19. David Stevenson, *With Our Backs to the Wall: Victory and Defeat in 1918*,p. 225.
20. Liddell Hart, *History of The First World War,* p. 350.
21. George, *War Memoirs*, vol.II, p.1921.
22. Ibid.
23. Ferrier, *History of the British Petroleum Company*, Table 6.9, p. 236.
24. Ibid., Table 6.6, p. 231.
25. *New York Times*, 24 July 1919.
26. Ibid.

CHAPTER 24: LLOYD GEORGE – OPEN FOR BUSINESS

1. For detailed information about the Roberts Academy, the privileged post-Boer War clique which dominated military strategy and planning in the year before the First World War, see Gerry Docherty and Jim Macgregor, *Hidden History, The Secret Origins of the First World War*, pp. 194-202.
2. *Ministry of Munitions*, vol. 1. pt. 1, p. 21.
3. Hew Strachan, *The First World War, vol.1: To Arms*, p. 997.
4. Hansard House of Commons Debate, 13 June 1911, vol. 26, cc1459-97
5. Lloyd George, *Memoirs*, pp. 76-7.
6. Strachan, *The First World War*, vol.1, p. 1000.
7. Lloyd George, *Memoirs*, p.84.
8. Strachan, *The First World War*, p. 998.
9. Nicholas A Lambert, "Our Bloody Ships", *Journal of Military History,* 1998, p. 36.
10. *Ministry of Munitions,* vol 1, pt. 1. p. 96.
11. Jon Tetsuro Sumido, British Naval Operational Logistics, 1914-1918, *Journal of Military History*, vol. 57, no. 3, July 1993, p. 453.
12. Strachan, *The First World War*, p. 1001.
13. Lloyd George, *Memoirs*, p. 89.
14. Michael and Eleanor Brock, *HH Asquith, Letters to Venetia Stanley*, p. 267.
15. Kathleen Burk, *Britain, America and the Sinews of War*, p. 14.
16. Gerry Docherty and Jim Macgregor, *Hidden History, The Secret Origins of the First World War,* p. 312.
17. Kathleen Burk, *War and the State, The Transformation of British Government 1914-18*, p. 89.
18. David Lloyd George, *War Memoirs*, Vol. 1, p.70.
19. Kathleen Burk, *Britain, America and the Sinews of War*, p. 14.
20. J P Morgan, New York, to E C Grenfell, 11 November 1914, PRO LG/C/1/1/32.
21. Edward Grenfell to Mr Lloyd George, 13 November, 1914, PRO, LG/C/1/1/33.
22. Lloyd George to Mr Grenfell, PRO LG/C/1/1/34.
23. Chris Wrigley, *The Ministry of Munitions* in Kathleen Burk, *War and the State*, p. 41.
24. Kathleen Burk, *Britain, America and the Sinews of War*, p. 18.
25. Docherty and Macgregor, *Hidden History,* pp. 212-214.
26. Kathleen Burk, *War and the State, The Transformation of British Government 1914-18*, p. 90.
27. Hansard House of Commons Debate. 20 April 1915, vol. 71, cc175-6.
28. David Lloyd George, *War Memoirs,* vol. 1, pp. 79-80.
29. Richard Toye, *Lloyd George and Churchill,* p. 133.
30. Lloyd George, *Memoirs*, p. 82.
31. Ibid., pp. 86-7.
32. Ibid., p. 89.
33. A M Gollin, *Proconsul in Politics*, pp. 45-49.
34. Defence of the Realm Act (D.O.R.A.) No. 2 Act, 16 March 1915.
35. Defence of the Realm Act, 4 and 5 Geo. 5 c. 29, 8 August, 1914.
36. D.O.R.A. No. 2 Act, 16 March 1915 section 2E.
37. Ibid., section 6A.
38. http://www.theodora.com/encyclopedia/m2/munitions_of_war.html
39. Rudolf G Binding, *A Fatalist At War,* p. 22.
40. House of Lords Debate, 15 March 1915 vol 18 cc719-24.
41. Michael and Eleanor Brock, *HH Asquith, Letters to Venetia Stanley* pp. 488-9; and *David Lloyd George, War Memoirs*,vol. 1, pp. 113-5.

42. Reginald Pound and Geoffrey Harmsworth, Northcliffe, p. 474.
43. Lloyd George, *War Memoirs*, p. 116.
44. Ibid.
45. Hansard, House of Commons Debate. 21 April 1915, vol. 71 cc 864-926.
46. Ibid., vol. 71 cc 918-9.
47. Harry J Wilson, Inspector of Factories, 3 April 1915, cited in http://www.inverclydeshipbuilding.co.uk/home/general-history/drink-absenteism
48. *The Times*, 1 April, 1915, p. 8.
49. The battle is variously known as Festubert, Givenchy and Fromelles. See A M Gollin, *Freedom or Control in the First World War, Historical Reflections*, 1976, p. 148.
50. http://www.1914-1918.net/bat11.htm
51. Hugh Cecil and Peter H Liddle, *Facing Armageddon, The First World War Experienced*, p. 42.
52. Trevor Royle, *The Kitchener Enigma*, p. 292.
53. Ibid., p. 290.
54. Cecil and Liddle, *Facing Armageddon*, p. 42.
55. Royle, *The Kitchener Enigma*, p. 290.
56. Gerry Docherty and Jim Macgregor, *Hidden History, The Secret Origins of the First World War*, p. 50.
57. Quigley, *The Anglo-American Establishment*, p. 13.
58. Milner Papers, Milner to Birchenough, 13 May, 1915.
59. A. M. Gollin, *Proconsul in Politics*, p. 253.
60. Reginald Pound and Geoffrey Harmsworth, *Northcliffe*, p. 477.
61. *Daily Mail*, 21 May 1915. See also *Daily Mail* Historical Archives at http://gale.cengage.co.uk/daily-mail-historical-archive/subjects-covered.aspx
62. John Pollock, *Kitchener*, pp. 443-4.
63. Pound and Harmsworth, *Northcliffe*, p. 478.
64. Ibid.
65. Alex Brummer, *Daily Mail*, 28 Dec 2012, citing research from Professor Richard Roberts, Kings College, London.
66. Pound and Harmsworth, *Northcliffe*, p. 479.
67. Edward David, *Inside Asquith's Cabinet*, p. 242.
68. Donald McCormick, *The Mask Of Merlin*, p. 102.
69. J. Lee Thompson, *Forgotten Patriot*, p. 315.
70. Milner to Gwynne, 10 May1915; in Thompson, *Forgotten Patriot*, p. 315.
71. David Lloyd George, *War Memoirs of David Lloyd George*, p. 144.
72. George H Cassar, *Kitchener, Architect of Victory*, p. 343.
73. Donald McCormick, *The Mask of Merlin*, pp. 100-101.
74. Hew Strachan, *The First World War, Vol. 1 The Rush To Arms*, p. 1077.
75. McCormick, *The Mask of Merlin*, p. 102.
76. Rodger Davidson, *Oxford Dictionary of National Biography* http://www.oxforddnb.com/view/article/36147
77. Kathleen Burk, *Britain, America and the Sinews of War*, p. 18.
78. *Daily Mail*, 26 May, 1915.
79. J. Lee Thomson, *Northcliffe, Press Baron in Politics*, 1865-1922, p. 242.
80. George A B Dewar and J H Boreston, *Sir Douglas Haig's Command*, vol. 1, p.69.
81. *Ministry of Munitions*, vol. 1 , Pt. 1 p. 150.
82. Strachan, *The First World War, Vol. 1*, p. 1069.
83. Keith Grieves, *Oxford Dictionary of National Biography*, http://www.oxforddnb.com/view/article/33360
84. Chris Wrigley, *The Ministry of Munitions: An Innovatory Department, in War and the State*, edited by Kathleen Burk, p. 39.
85. David Lloyd George, *War Memoirs*, p. 150.
86. Strachan, *The First World War, Vol. 1*, pp. 1079-80.
87. *The Times*, 1 June 1915, p. 5.
88. Ibid., 4 June, p.9.
89. Ibid., 11 June, p. 9.
90. Ibid., 14 June, p. 8.
91. Ibid., 18 June, p. 5.
92. R J Q Adams, "Delivering The Goods: Reappraising the Ministry of Munitions: 1915-1916," *Albion: A Quarterly Journal Concerned with British Studies*, Vol.7 no. 3 (autumn 1975) pp.232-244.
93. Rules For The Limitation of Profits In Controlled Establishments, PRO MUN /5/100/360/13.
94. http://sites.scran.ac.uk/redclyde/redclyde/rceve5.htm
95.T C Smout, *A Century of the Scottish People*, 1830-1950, pp. 268-9.
96. *The Times*, 27 December, 1915, p. 3.
97. Hansard, House of Commons Debate 7 November 1921 vol 148 cc17-18.
98. Richard Lewinsohn, Sir Basil Zaharoff, pp. 21-2.
99. Robert Neumann, *Zaharoff the Armaments King*, p. 9.
100. Donald McCormick, *The Mask of Merlin*, p. 201.
101. *The Times* 6 July 1918, p. 9.
102. Lewinsohn, *Zaharoff*, p. 110.
103. Ferguson, *The House of Rothschild*, p. 354.
104. D.G. Paterson, "Spin Off" and the Armaments Industry, *Economic History Review*, vol 24. issue 3 pp. 463-468.
105. Guiles Davenport, *Zaharoff, High Priest of War*, p. 154.
106. William Stewart, *J. Keir Hardie*, p. 340.

107. Discours de Jean Jaures, Lyon-Vaise, 25 July 1915. atelier-histoire.ens-lyon.fr/Atelier-Histoire/episodes/.../5
108. Stewart, *J Keir Hardie*, p. 340.
109. John T Flynn, *Men of Wealth*, p. 372.
110. McCormick, *The Mask of Merlin*, p. 202.
111. Jean-Marie Moine, Basil Zaharoff (1839-46) 'Le Marchand de Canons' Ethnologie française nouvelle serie, T. 36, No. 1, De la censure à l'autocensure (Janvier-Mars 2006), p. 143.
112. Donald McCormick, *The Mask of Merlin*, p. 206.
113. Ibid.
114. Moine, Basil Zaharoff (1839-46) 'Le Marchand de Canons' Ethnologie française nouvelle serie, T. 36, No. 1, *De la censure à l'autocensure* (Janvier-Mars 2006), p. 144.
115. Ibid., p. 140.

CHAPTER 25: THE FATE OF A FIELD MARSHAL

1. *The Times*, 12 November, 1915, p. 9.
2. Trevor Royle, *The Kitchener Enigma*, p. 338.
3. See firstworldwarhiddenhistory.wordpress.com Munitions 4: Lloyd George And Very Secret Arrangements. Posted on 24 June 2015.
4. Carroll Quigley, *The Anglo-American Establishment*, p. 313.
5. Stephen Roskill, *Hankey*, Vol. 1, 1877 – 1918. p. 237.
6. Sir George Arthur, *Kitchener* vol. III, p. 299.
7. Thomas Pakenham, *The Boer War*, p. 570.
8. Ibid., p. 551.
9. Lord Derby, Edward George Villiers Stanley, 17th Earl of Derby aided Kitchener in promoting recruitment. In October 1915, as Director General of Recruitment, he introduced a scheme which included enlistment and conscription. Asquith made him Under-Secretary of State for War after Kitchener's death. Derby was one of the few politicians whom Kitchener trusted.
10. Randolph S Churchill, *Lord Derby, King of Lancashire*, p. 210.
11. Ibid.
12. The complete history of the Secret Elite's drive to create a war with Germany is contained in Gerry Docherty and Jim Macgregor's *Hidden History, The Secret Origins of the First World War*, published 2013.
13. PRO 30/57/53 Kitchener Papers.
14. Royle, *The Kitchener Enigma*, p. 348.
15. Edward Mandell House was President Wilson's eminence grise in the White House. closely associated with the Morgan financial empire in New York, House was very much an anglophile who advised the President on all aspects of the war in Europe.
16. Grey of Fallodon, *Twenty-Five Years*, Vol III, p 63.
17. Ibid., pp. 68-71.
18. George Casssar, *Kitchener: Architect of Victory*, p. 474.
19. *The Times*, 1 June, 1916, p. 10.
20. Churchill, *Lord Derby*, p. 210.
21. Pollock, *Kitchener*, p. 471.
22. Randolph Churchill, *Lord Derby, King of Lancashire*, pp. 209-10.
23. Churchill, *Lord Derby*, p. 210.
24. Stephen Roskill, *Hankey* Vol. I, 1877-1918, p. 268.
25. Ibid. p. 269.
26. Cabinet Papers CAB 42/13 4/5/16.
27. Carroll Quigley, *The Anglo-American Establishment*, pp. 153-60 and p. 313.
28. That it suddenly became Kitchener's idea is promoted by several historians including Trevor Royle, *The Kitchener Enigma* p. 356 , and in John Pollock, *Kitchener*, p. 469.
29. Sir John Hanbury-Williams was Lord Milner's military secretary in South Africa before becoming secretary to the Secretary of State for War in 1900. He acted as Chief of the British Military Mission to Russia (1914-1917) and was instrumental in requesting that Britain attacked the Dardanelles on behalf of the Czar's government.
30. PRO 30/ 57/ 67.
31. Pollock, *Kitchener*, p. 469.
32. Ibid., p. 470.
33. Royle, *The Kitchener Enigma*, p. 357.
34. This was an unexpected request which temporarily took Lloyd George out of the equation for the proposed trip to Russia. He had absolutely no experience of Irish matters. He had always voted in favour of Home Rule and his strange intervention in 1916 changed nothing. According to the Irish historian, Jonathan Brandon, his duplicity sealed the fate of the Irish Parliamentary Party.
35. Lloyd George, *War Memoirs*, p. 420.
36. Royle, *The Kitchener Enigma*, p. 357.
37. PRO 30/57/67, 27 May 1916.
38. Randolph Churchill, *Lord Derby*, p. 210.
39. Sir John Hanbury-Williams, *The Emperor Nicholas II, as I knew him*, p. 98.
40. Ibid., p. 99.
41. Ibid., pp. 98-99.
42. Royle, *The Kitchener Enigma*, p. 358.
43. Sir George Arthur, *The Life of Lord Kitchener*, pp. 349-50, is typical of the misleading notion that the Secretary of State for War was invited by the Czar to go to visit him in Russia.
44. *The Times* 1 June 1916, p. 10.
45. John Pollock, *Kissinger*, p. 475.
46. *The Times*, 3 June 1916, p. 8.
47. Nicholas A Lambert, "Our Bloody Ships or

Our Bloody System? Jutland and the loss of the Battle Cruisers, 1916." *Journal of Military History*, vol. 62, no. 1, January 1998, p. 47.
48. http://www.battle-of-jutland.com/jutland-gains-losses.htm
49. S W Roskill, "The Dismissal of Admiral Jellicoe," *Journal of Contemporary History*, vol.1, no. 4 (October 1966) p. 69.
50. Arthur Balfour was at that point First Lord of the Admiralty. His Secret Elite credentials placed him in the inner core of the secret society. See Carol Quigley, *The Anglo-American Establishment*, pp.17-18 and 312.
51. George H Cassar, *Kitchener, Architect of Victory*, p. 476.
52. Ibid.
53. Alexander McAdie, 'Fate and a Forecast', *Harvard Graduate Magazine*, September 1923, p. 46.
54. Trevor Royle, *The Kitchener Enigma*, p. 364.
55. Rev C H Hamilton, *The Times*, Letters to the Editor, 9 June 1916, p. 9.
56. Hansard, House of Commons Debate, 18 February 1914 vol 58 cc961-3W
57. Both vessels were listed in Churchill's lists of 252 ships to be oil-fired.
58. *The Times*, 10 August, 1926, p. 9.
59. Trevor Royle, *The Kitchener Enigma*, p. 367.
60. ref Chapter X
61. Patrick Beesly, *Room 40 British Naval Intelligence 1914-1918*, pp. 21-33.
62. National Archives ADM137 / 4105.
63. Royale, *Kitchener Enigma*, pp. 369-70.
64. George H Cassar, *Kitchener, Architect of Victory*, p.476. or Royle, *Kitchener Enigma*, p. 480.
65. Jane E Storey.http://www.bjentertainments.co.uk/js/THE%20Orcadian.htm *The Arcadian, New Light On Hampshire Tragedy*.
66. Philip Magnus, *Kitchener, Portrait of an Imperialist*. p. 373.
67. Trevor Royle, *The Kitchener Enigma*, p. 374.
68. Joe Angus, Stromness, 'World War One', Orkney Public Library, Kirkwall, interview for Sound Archive by Eric Marwick.
69. Jane E Storey.http://www.bjentertainments.co.uk/js/THE%20Orcadian.htm *The Arcadian, New Light On Hampshire Tragedy*.
70. The timings used are at Greenwich Mean Time (GMT) which is used throughout the world. British Summer Time (BST) , or delight saving time, is one hour in advance of that, viz GMT+1.
71. Royle, *Kitchener Enigma*, p. 372.
72. Evidence of Petty Officer Samuel Sweeney. All of the following statements were sent by telephone from O.C.W.P. at 2.pm on 6 June 1916.
73. The precise number may never be known, Royle puts it at 655 (p. 375). Orkney Heritage Society put the number at 737 to include men killed in the loss of the Laurel Crown. http://www.orkneycommunities.co.uk/ohs/index.asp?pageid=592610
74. The Carley float was formed from a length of copper or steel tubing surrounded by a buoyant mass of cork. The American produced raft was rigid and could remain buoyant, floating equally well with either side uppermost. The floor of the raft was made from a wood or webbed grating. Commonly used on British warships in World War 1.
75. *The Great War- I Was There*, Walter Farnden, part 15. pp. 604-7.
76. Royle, *Kitchener Enigma*, p. 375.
77. W. S. Chalmers, 'Brock, Sir Osmond de Beauvoir (1869–1947)', rev. *Oxford Dictionary of National Biography*, Oxford University Press, 2004 http://www.oxforddnb.com/view/article/32079
78. Jane Storey; http://www.bjentertainments.co.uk/js/THE%20Orcadian.htm
79. Ibid.
80. *The Times*, 7 June 1916. p. 10.
81. *The War Illustrated, Volume 4*, 17 June 1916, p. 410.
82. *The Times*, 10 June, p. 8.
83. *The Times*, 9 June 1916, p. 9.
84. The Royal Naval Cemetery at Lyness on the island of Hoy is the resting place for 445 Commonwealth naval personnel, 109 of whom died in the First World War.
85. National Archives ADM 53/66480 and ADM 53/67364.
86. Royle, *Kitchener Enigma*, p. 371.
87. Viscount Jellicoe, *The Grand Fleet (!914-1916): Its Creation, Development and Work*, p. 427, where he states that had he ordered the seas ahead of HMS Hampshire swept, Kitchener would have lost three days in consequence. Alas it was his life that was lost.
88. Hansard, House of Commons Debate, 6 July 1916 vol 83 cc1796-813.
89. In Scottish Law a fatal accident inquiry would have been the appropriate means of investigation. This legal process would take place before a Sheriff and does not require a jury.
90. House of Commons Debate 22 June 1916 vol. 83 cc316-3.
91. Wesson's service number was PO201136(-PO). A full list of survivors and their identification number was published.
92. *Sunday Express*, 8 July, 1934.
93. Jane Storey, HMS Hampshire, Survivors and Their First Statements, http://www.bjentertainments.co.uk/js/survivors.htm%5D
94. Hansard, House of Commons Debate, 6 July

1916 vol 83 cc1813.
95. Ibid.
96. Ibid.
97. http://www.channel4.com/programmes/jutland-wwis-greatest-sea-battle
98. Hansard House of Commons Debate, 27 June 1916 vol 83 cc732-3.
99. *The Times*, 10 February, 1926, p.10.
100. Ibid.
101. Cmd. 2710.
102. Fregattenkapitän Oskar Groos. Der Krieg zur See 1914-18, Nordsee Band V pp. 201-2.
103. National Archives ADM 137/3138.
104. Groos, Der Krieg zur See 1914-18, Nordsee Band V.
105. Footnote information https://www.google.co.uk/url?sa=t&rct=j&q=&esrc=s&source=web&cd=1&ved=0ahUKEwj6-fzEvfrMAhVLDsAKHU30Am4QFggdMAA&url=http%3A%2F%2Fwww.rbls-kirkwall.org.uk%2Fmemorials%2FBur%2FGeorgePetrie.doc&usg=AFQjCNFPMO_PWaZWiQp6oJ3o_ONhNn72lg&sig2=XPyFHttCwB_DkKyUPnrp_Q
106. National Archives ADM 137/3138
107. Henry Newbolt, *History of the Great War,* Based on Official Documents. Naval Operations, Vol IV, pp. 1-21.
108. David Lloyd George, *War Memoirs*, vol.1, p. 456.
109. Stephen Roskill, *Hankey*, Vol. I, p. 269.
110. Hankey Diary 6 June 1916, quoted in Roskill, *Hankey* Vol 1, pp. 279-80.
111. Lloyd George, *War Memoirs*, p. 456.
112. J Lee Thomson, *Politicians, the Press and Propaganda, Lord Northcliffe & The Great War, 1914-1919*, p. 101.
113. *The Times*, 14 June 1914.
114. Boris L Brasol, *The World At The Crossroads*, pp. 80-81.
115. Lord Lansdowne , Hansard, House of Lords Debate, 20 June 1916 vol 22 cc315-22.
116. House of Commons Debate, 21 June 1916 vol 83 cc145-51.
117. John Buchan, *Episodes of the Great War*, pp. 246-7.
118. *The Times* 14 June 1914.

CHAPTER 26: The Great British Coup 1916

1. David French, The Rise and Fall of Business as Usual', in Kathleen Burk, *War and the State, The Transformation of the British Government, 1914-1919*, p.10.
2. Perhaps the most interesting and puzzling scandal of the First World War was Herbert Hoover's Commission for Relief in Belgium which ensured that war was prolonged by providing supplies, especially foodstuffs, to Germany from 1914-1917.
3. Kathleen Burk, *War and the State, The Transformation of British Government 1914-18*, p. 90.
4. Michael Amara et Hubert Roland, *Gouverner En Belgique Ocuppee*, p. 99 and p. 214.
5. David French, *The Rise and Fall of Business as Usual'*, p. 7.
6. David Lloyd George, *War Memoirs*, p. 70.
7. J Lee Thompson, *Forgotten Patriot*, p. 483.
8. Henry Campbell-Bannerman died in 10 Downing Street on 22 April 1908 from a heart attack.
9. A. Bonar Law to Asquith, 17 May 1915.
10. David Lloyd George, *War Memoirs*, p. 137.
11. Ibid., p. 135.
12. Roy Jenkins, *Asquith*, pp. 360-1.
13. Hansard, House of Commons Debate, 19 May 1915 vol 71 cc2392-3.
14. Michael and Eleanor Brock, *HH Asquith, Letters to Virginia Stanley*, p. 598
15. Brian P Murphy, *Patrick Pearse and the Lost Republican Ideal*, p. 45.
16. Pat Walsh, *The Great Fraud of 1914-18*, p. 25.
17. Lloyd George, *War Memoirs*, p. 142.
18. Founded in 1902, this exclusive association of politicians and financiers, ambassadors and businessmen in New York and in London, aimed to preserve the bonds of the english-speaking peoples and promote the Anglo-Saxon race values.
19. Anne Pimlott Baker, *The Pilgrims of America*, p. 4.
20. Roosevelt to Lloyd George, 1 June 1915, reproduced in full on p.145 of his *War Memoirs*.
21. Quigley, *Anglo-American Establishment*, p. 313.
22. Stephen Roskill, *Hankey, Man of Secrets, 1877-1918*, pp. 179-185
23. Hansard, House of Lords Debate, 20 December 1915 vol 20 cc696-744.
24. A M Gollin, *Proconsul in Politics*, p. 320.
25. Maurice Hankey, Diary entry 28th October 1916, quoted in Stephen Roskill, *Hankey: Man of Secrets*, p. 312.]
26. Ibid.
27. For a detailed examination of the influence which Lords Roberts exerted over the British Military Establishment see Gerry Docherty and Jim Macgregor, *Hidden History, The Secret Origins of the First World War*, chapter 15, The Roberts Academy, pp. 194-203.
28. Gollin, *Hankey*, p. 313.
29. Ibid., pp. 323-4.
30. F. S. Oliver, *Oxford Dictionary of National Biography*, author, Richard Davenport-Hines.
31. Alfred Milner, Leo Amery, Philip Kerr, Waldorf Astor and Geoffrey Dawson were specifically placed inside what Carroll Quigley

called The Society of the Elect in his work, *The Anglo-American Establishment*, while Leander Starr Jameson was placed in the outer circle. [pp. 311-313.] We have enlarged the group under the collective title of the Secret Elite.

32. Thomas Pakenham, *The Boer War*, Prologue, pp. 1-5.

33. Sentenced to fifteen months imprisonment for his involvement in the infamous Jameson Raid, he served barely three before being pardoned. His career flourished thereafter. From 1904-1908 Jameson was Prime Minister of the Cape Colony. He returned to England in 1912 and remained one of Alfred Milner's trusted confidantes.

34. Gollin, *Hankey*, p. 324.

35. Davenport-Hines, *Oxford Dictionary of National Biography*. See above.

36. It is often interesting to consider the manner in which historians entitle events. In A.M. Collin's *Proconsul in Politics*, he boldly christened Milner's group as The Monday Night Cabal – which it certainly was, while Terence O'Brien, in his work, Milner, stepped away from controversy by calling it the Monday Night Group, thus omitting any hint of conspiracy. [Terence O'Brien, *Milner*, p. 266.]

37. Amery Papers, "Notes for Monday's Meeting, 19th February 1916."

38. Gollin, *Hankey*, p. 325.

39. *The Times*, 14 April, 1916, p. 9.

40. *The Times*, 1 December 1916, p. 9.

41. Tom Clarke, *My Northcliffe Diary*, p.107.

42. Docherty and Macgregor, *Hidden History*, chapter 12, Catch a Rising Star, pp. 161-171.

43. Later Viscount Lee of Farnham. Typical of many Secret Elite associates, his loyalty was rewarded with political appointments including Director General of Food Production from 1917-18, President of the Board of Agriculture, 1919-21 and first Lord of the Admiralty, 1921-22. He donated Chequers, still the country residence of British Prime Ministers, for that purpose.

44. Gollin, *Hankey*, p. 348 and p. 354.

45. A Clark, *A Good Innings: the private papers of Viscount Lee of Fareham*, p. 92.

46. Ibid., p.140.

47. David Lloyd George, *War Memoirs*, p. 346.

48. V. W. Baddeley, 'Lee, Arthur Hamilton, Viscount Lee of Fareham (1868–1947)', rev. Marc Brodie, *Oxford Dictionary of National Biography*.

49. Edward Mandell House and Charles Seymour, *The Intimate Papers of Colonel House, 1915-1917*, p.175.

50. By this time there were daily examples of the horrendous waste of life on the Western Front. one example amongst hundreds can be found in *The Times* 1 February, 1916, p.10.

51. Alfred Milner and his associates in the Round Table group in Britain had from 1905 onwards worked tirelessly to promote the Empire and indeed prepare the Empire of 'the coming war'. See Gerry Docherty and Jim Macgregor, *Hidden History, The Secret Origins of the first World War*, pp. 153-160.

52. Stephen Roskill, *Hankey*, Volume 1, 1877-1918, p. 245.

53. This secretive committee was originally formed in 1902 to advise the Prime Minister on matters of military and naval strategy. Maurice Hankey had been Assistant Secretary since 1908 and was the immensely authoritative Secretary from 1912 onwards.

54. The nerve centre of British intelligence was in Room 40 at the Admiralty where the highly secretive Captain (later Rear- Admiral) William 'Blinker' Hall monitored radio and telegraphic messages from Germany and German ships. Britain had had possession of all German codes from the first months of the war. See Blog; *Lusitania 1: The Tale of there Secret Miracles*, 28 April 2015.

55. *House and Seymour, The Intimate Papers*, p. 135.

56. Ibid., p. 170.

57. Allegedly, Hankey visited Hall on 27 January 1916 to discuss a ploy to put false German banknotes into circulation and the conversation just happened to wander into Mandell House's visit to Sir Edward Grey. So they would have us believe. Roskill, *Hankey*, p. 247.

58. CAB 42/14/12.

59. CAB 42/18/ 8.

60. CAB 42/18/ 7.

61. CAB 42/18/10.

62. See Blog; Commission For Relief in Belgium 13: *As If It Had Never Happened*. posted on 25 November 2015.

63. FO 899 Cabinet Memoranda 1905-1918, Memorandum by Lord Eustace Percy, 26 September 1916.

64. Harold Kurtz," The Lansdowne Letter," *History Today*, Volume 18 issue 2 February 1968.

65. Randolph S Churchill, *Lord Derby, King of Lancashire*, p. 210.

66. Asquith had lost his son Raymond, on 15 September 1916, at the Somme. It was a crushing personal blow.

67. Hansard, House of Commons Debate, 11 October 1916, vol 86 cc95-161.

68. *The Times*, 29 September 1916, p. 7.

69. Hankey, Diary 10 November 1916.

70. *The Times* 27 May 1915.

71. Roy Hattersley, *David Lloyd George, The Great Outsider*, p. 402.

72. David Lloyd George, *War Memoirs,* p. 574.
73. Stephen Roskill, *Hankey,* Volume I, 1877-1918, p. 319.
74. Carroll Quigley, *The Anglo-American Establishment*, p. 313.
75. Roy Jenkins, *Asquith; portrait of a man and an era*, p. 421.
76. *The Times*, 4 December 1915, p. 9.
77. Lloyd George, *War Memoirs*, p. 592.
78. Gollin, *Proconsul*, p. 295.
79. Library of the House of Commons, Prime Ministers, SN/PC/4256. p. 5.
80. John Turner, "Cabinets, Committees and Secretariats: The Higher Direction of War," in Kathleen Burk, *War and the State*, p. 59.
81. C E Caldwell and Marshal Foch, *Field Marshal Sir Henry Wilson VI: His Life and Diaries*, pp. 304-5.
82. Terence H O'Brien, *Milner*, pp. 266-9.
83. David Lloyd George, *War Memoirs*, p. 620.
84. Hankey, Diary 10 December 1916.
85. War Cabinet 1, CAB 23/1/1 discussed the cost of loans from America which were running at $60 million per week. Messrs. Morgan, Grenfell and Co. continued as the conduit for all American payments. Hankey also recorded in these minutes that the Press had been informed that the War Cabinet would meet every weekday.
86. Lord Vansittart recorded that Hankey 'progressively became secretary of everything that mattered..He grew into a repository of secrets, a chiefInspector of Mines of information.' Robert Gilbert Vansittart, *The Mist Procession*, p. 164.
87. While Lloyd George spends many pages expressing his opinion on most of his colleagues, he curiously omits a pen-picture on Lord Milner. Possibly the Censor removed it. Either way it is interesting to note how carefully Milner's contribution to Lloyd George's ascent to the premiership has been airbrushed.
88. Lloyd George, *Memoirs*, p. 596.
89. *The Times* estimated that Lord Northcliffe's lengthy article in praise of Lloyd George had been carried in one thousand American, Australian, Canadian, South African, French, Italian and other journals. [*Times* 11 December, 1916.]
90. A M Gollin, *Proconsul in Politics*, p. 329.
91. *The Times*, 11 December 1916, p. 4.
92. Gollin, *Proconsul*, p. 376.
93. Ibid., p. 329.
94. Gerry Docherty and Jim Macgregor, *Hidden History, The Secret Origins of the First World War,* pp 164-5.
95. Carroll Quigley, *The Anglo-American Establishment*, pp. 6-9 and pp.140- 47.
96. The place of All Souls college at Oxford as the centre of the Secret Elite intelligentsia in Britain was identified by Professor Quigley. See *The Anglo-American Establishment* pp. 20-26.
97. In August 1914 Arthur Henderson had been outspoken in his objection to war, but he changed his position absolutely within weeks.
98. Gollin, *Proconsul*, p. 391.
99. E S Montagu was both a friend of Asquith's and respected colleague of Lloyd George. To most observers his omission from Asquith's cabinet in 1916 spelled the end of his political career. But this is not how the Secret Elite work. In stepping down temporarily, Montagu earned the right to be promoted to the prestigious position of Secretary of State for India in 1917.
100. Thomas S. Legg, Marie-Louise Legg, 'Cave, George, Viscount Cave (1856–1928)', *Oxford Dictionary of National Biography*.
101. Lord Ernle, Whippingham to Westminster, p. 248.
102. Quigley, *Anglo-American Establishment*, p. 27.
103. Ibid., p. 312.
104. Ibid.
105. President of the Board of Trade was Lloyd George's first cabinet post in 1906. During his tenure there he became popular with the business class whose interests he often championed.
106. Lloyd George, *Memoirs*, p. 61.
107. Ibid., pp. 688-95.
108. Richard Davenport-Hines, 'Kearley, Hudson Ewbanke, first Viscount Devonport (1856–1934)', *Oxford Dictionary of National Biography.*
109. John Williams, 'Thomas, David Alfred, first Viscount Rhondda (1856–1918)', *Oxford Dictionary of National Biography*.
110. Geoffrey Jones, Westman Pearson, 1st Viscount Cowdrey, *Oxford Dictionary of National Biography.*
111. Gordon H Boyce, *Co-operative Structures in Global Business*, pp. 84-5.
112. Rear Admiral MWWC Consett, *The Triumph of Unarmed Forces*, p. 201.
113. Hansard House of Commons Debate, 14 January 1918 vol. 101 cc5-6.
114. *Maurice Hankey, Supreme Command*, vol. II, p. 590.
115. John Turner, *Lloyd George's Secretariat*, p.1.
116. Carroll Quigley, *The Anglo-American Establishment*, p. 313.
117. Ibid., pp. 91-93. All Souls College in Oxford has been closely associated with the Rhodes / Milner group so integral to the Secret Elite in England.
118. The title Milner's Kindergarten was given to the group of young Oxford University graduates whom Milner attracted to help him rebuild South Africa after the Boer War. They subsequently enjoyed stellar careers in journalism, politics, banking and finance every area of Secret Elite influence. Further reading – Walter

Nimocks, *Milner's Young Men.*
119. Milner to Lloyd George 17 January 1917, in the Lloyd George Papers.
120. H W Massingham, *The Nation* 24 February, 1917.

CHAPTER 27: American Mythology - He Kept Us Out oF War

1. Anthony Sutton, *Federal Reserve Conspiracy*, pp. 82-3.
2. Carroll Quigley, *Tragedy and Hope*, p. 76.
3. Paolo Enrico Coletta, *The Presidency of William Howard Taft*. pp. 154–157.
4. http://uselectionatlas.org/RESULTS/national.php?year=1912
5. Albert Shaw, *President Wilson's State Papers and Addresses*, p. 150.
6. Hans P. Vought, *The Bully Pulpit and the Melting Pot, American Presidents and the Immigrant, 1897-1933*, p. 96.
7. Thomas A Bailey, *A Diplomatic History of the American People*, p. 611.
8. Roger Casement was at that time a hero of the Irish Republican movement because of his support for and involvement in, the Easter Rising in Dublin in 1916.]
9. Edward Cuddy, "Irish Americans and the 1916 Election," *American Quarterly*, vol. 21, no. 2, Part 1, Summer 1969, pp. 229-231.
10. *Irish World*, 24 June, 1916.
11. For example, the New York Times urged the U S Senate to throw out Brandeis's nomination *New York Times*, 29 January 1916. p. 3
12. See See chapter 28.
13. Bailey, *A Diplomatic History of the American People*, p. 622.
14. Paul Birdsall, "Neutrality and Economic Pressures," *Science and Society*, Vol. 3, no. 2, (Spring 1939) p. 221.
15. Cuddy, "Irish Americans and the 1916 Election," *American Quarterly* vol. 21, no 2, Part 1 p. 235.
16. Walter Millis, *Road to War, America 1914-17*, p. 352.
17. *The Times*, 8 Nov. 1916, p. 9.
18. *The Times*, 18 Nov. 1916. p. 7.
19. Millis, *Road to War, America 1914-17*, p. 353.
20. Foley, Ballot Battles: *The History of Disputed Elections in the United States*, p. 202.
21. *New York Times*, 11 November 1916.
22. Foley, *Ballot Battles:* p. 431.
23. *The Times*, 13 November, 1916, p. 9.
24. H. C. Peterson, *Propaganda for War*, p. 281.
25. Woodrow Wilson: Address to the Senate of the United States; World League for Peace, 22 January, 1917.
26. Ibid.
27. *New York Times*, 23 January, 1917, Scenes in the Senate .
28. *New York Times*, 23 January, 1917. Wilson's Senate Speech - Press comments
29. Alfred Carter Jefferson, *Anatole France: The Politics of Skepticism*, p. 195.
30. http://www.firstworldwar.com/source/wilson1917inauguration.htm
31. Papers of Woodrow Wilson, Address to a Joint Session of Congress Requesting a Declaration of War against Germany, 2 April, 1917. http://www.presidency.ucsb.edu/ws/index.php?pid=65366
32. Papers of Woodrow Wilson, Presidential Proclamation 1364 http://www.presidency.ucsb.edu/woodrow_wilson.php
33. H C Peterson, *Propaganda for War*, pp. 321-2.
34. American Press Resume (A.P.R.) issued by the War Office and Foreign Office. "For Use of the Cabinet", 18 April, 1917.
35. A.P.R. 30 May, 1917.
36. Peterson, *Propaganda for War*, p. 325.
37. A.P.R. 6 June, 1917.
38. Peterson, *Propaganda for War*, p. 324. footnote.
39. 65th Congress, Session 1, CH. 15 1917. H.R. 3545.
40. Patrick Beesly, *Room 40*, pp. 207-8.
41. http://www.firstworldwar.com/source/zimmermann.htm
42. Rodney Carlisle, *The Attacks on US Shipping that Precipitated American Entry into World War 1.* http://www.cnrs-scrn.org/northern_mariner/vol17/tnm_17_3_41-66.pdf
43. Telegram to SS Carvalho, 2 March 1917.
44. *New York Times* 11 December 1918.
45. Peterson, *Propaganda*, p. 314.
46. Bailey, *A Diplomatic History*, p. 643, note 28.
47. Beesly, *Room 40*, p. 223.
48. Charles Seymour, *American Diplomacy During the World War*, p. 210.
49. Paul Birdsall, "Neutrality and Economic Pressures 1914-1917," *Science and Society* vol. 3, No. 2. (Spring 1939) p. 217.
50. Bailey, *A Diplomatic History of the American People*, p. 641.
51. Millis, *Road to War*, p. 400.
52. Peterson, *Propaganda*, p. 318.
53. Carlisle, "Attacks on American Shipping that Precipitated the War," *The Northern Mariner*, XVII, no. 3, p. 61. http://www.cnrs-scrn.org/northern_mariner/vol17/tnm_17_3_41-66.pdf
54. New York Times, 19 March 1917.
55. Congressional Record, 64th Congress of the United States, February 9 1917, p. 2947.
56. Ibid.
57. Charles Tansill was Professor of History at the American University. He prepared the official volume on World War I responsibility for

Congress and in 1927 edited another volume for the Library of Congress entitled "Documents on the Formation of the American Union. His America Goes to War was considered the officially accepted view.
58. Charles Cannon Tansill, *America Goes to War*, p. 657.
59. Bailey, *A Diplomatic History*, p. 644.
60. Nomi Prins, *All The President's Bankers*, p. 47.
61. Ibid.
62. letter from JP Morgan to President Wilson April 4, 1917, Wilson Papers vol. 41.
63. *New York Times*, 25 April 1917.
64. Hearings before the Special Committee Investigating the Munitions Industry, US Senate S.Res. 206.
65. W. G. Carr, *Pawns in the Game*, p. 60.
66. Hearings before the Special Committee Investigating the Munitions Industry, US Senate S.Res. 206. exhibit 2040, p. 7505.
67. David Lloyd George, *War Memoirs*, p. 70.
68. Ray Stannard Baker, *The Life & Letters of Woodrow Wilson*, p.181. This was cited in evidence against J P Morgan in Hearings before the Special Committee Investigating the Munitions Industry, US Senate S.Res. 206, p. 7566.

CHAPTER 28: BALFOUR DECLARATION 1: MYTHISTORY

1. Emeritus professor of History at Tel Aviv University and much published author
2. Shlomo Sand, *The Invention of the Jewish People*, p. xi.
3. Ibid., p. 131.
4. Ibid. pp.134-5.
5. Ibid. p. 130.
6. Illan Pappe is an Israeli historian and socialist activist. He is a professor at the College of Social Sciences and International Studies at the University of Exeter.
7. Illan Pappe: *History of Israel, Stolen Land of Palestine* on youtube. https://www.youtube.com/watch?v=dKGA48MptlY&t=965s
8. Arthur Koestler, *The Thirteenth Tribe*.
9. Peter Frankopan, *The Silk Roads*, pp. 111-114.
10. Eran Elhaik, geneticist and former John Hopkin's University post-doctoral researcher, currently lecturer at University of Sheffield.
11. A term coined by Zionists who seek to denigrate those members of the Jewish faith or Israeli citizens who question their orthodox mythistory.
12. CAB 23/4 WC 261, p. 6.
13. The original quotation from which this observation is taken was made by Arthur Koestler, in *Promise and Fulfilment, Palestine 1917- 1949*, p. 4.
14. National Archives, War Cabinet Memorandum GT 2406.
15. CAB 24/30 ; GT 2406, p.1.
16. See chapter 26
17. CAB 23/4, WC 261 p. 5.
18. *The Times* 26 October 1917, p.7.
19. CAB 23/4 WC 261, p. 6.
20. Letter from A J Balfour to Lord Rothschild, 2 November 1917.
21. Great Britain, Palestine and the Jews. Jewry's Celebration Of Its National Charter - Anonymous pamphlet, 1917.
22. Sol M. Linowitz, "Analysis of a Tinderbox: The Legal Basis for the State of Israel," *American Bar Association Journal*, Vol. 43, 1957, p. 523.
23. Arthur Koestler, *Promise and Fulfilment, Palestine 1917- 1949*, p. 4.
24. CAB 23/4/19 WC 245, p. 6.
25. A M Gollin, *Proconsul in Politics*, p. 401.
26. CAB 23/4/19 WC 245, p. 6.
27. GT - 2015.
28. GT - 2158.
29. CAB 23/4/19 p. 5.
30. CAB 23/4/1. WC. 227, p. 1.
31. GT-1803 - *The Zionist Movement*.
32. Ibid.
33. Ibid.
34. CAB 24/24/4.
35. CAB 23/4/1. WC 227, p. 2.
36. Jessie Ethel Sampter, *A Guide to Zionism*, p. 59.
37. Ibid., p. 64.
38. letter from Sir Clement Hill, chief of Protectorate Department, Foreign Office to Mr. L J Greenberg, 14 August 1903.
39. Chaim Weizmann, *Trial and Error*, pp. 120-1.
40. Ibid., p. 121.
41. for example, no mention is made of Weizmann in Hankey's Diaries. GBR/0014/HNKY or in Roskill's masterly volume on Hankey up to 1918.
42. The 1906 election produced a landslide victory for Campbell-Bannerman's Liberal party and expelled A J Balfour from office until 1915.
43. Niall Ferguson, *The House of Rothschild, The World's Banker, 1849-1999*, pp. 417-8.
44. Weizmann, *Trial and Error*, p. 143.
45. http://www.jta.org/1931/08/20/archive/baron-edmond-de-rothschild-86
46. Weizmann, *Trial and Error*, p. 189.
47. Carroll Quigley, *The Anglo-American Establishment*, pp. 311-5.
48. Sampter, *A Guide to Zionism*, p. 71.
49. Ibid, p. 73.
50. Donald Neff, *Fallen Pillars*, Chapter 1, http://www.washingtonpost.com/wp-srv/style/longterm/books/chap1/fallenpillars.htm
51. Ibid.
52. http://www.washingtonpost.com/wp-srv/

style/longterm/books/chap1/fallenpillars.htm
53. Warren and Brandeis, *Harvard Law Review*, Vol. IV December 15, 1890 No. 5, The Right To Privacy.
54. Muller v. Oregon, 208 U.S. 412 (1908).
55. George R Conroy, editor of the ironically titled magazine, *Truth* penned a much quoted and often re-quoted allegation against Brandeis that linked him to the Jewish banker Jacob Schiff. It was one of many wild allegations made against Louis Brandeis to discredit him.
56. Jonathan D Sarna, "Louis D Brandeis: Zionist Leader," *Brandeis Review*, winter 1992.
57. Sampter, *A Guide to Zionism*, p. 81.
58. Neff, *Fallen Pillars*, Chapter 1, http://www.washingtonpost.com/wp-srv/style/longterm/books/chap1/fallenpillars.htm
59. Donald Lloyd Neff was an American historian and journalist. Originally from Pennsylvania, he spent 16 years working for *Time*, and was a former *Time* bureau chief in Israel. He also worked for the *Washington Star*. It is said that his work was erased from history for reporting on Palestine.
60. *New York Times*, 29 January 1916. p.1.
61. Ibid. p. 3.
62. Alphas Thomas Mason, *Brandeis - A Free Man's Life*, p. 451.
63. *New York Times* 5 June 1916.
64. Ibid.
65. Gerry Docherty and Jim Macgregor, *Hidden History, The Secret Origins of the First World War*, pp. 220-21.
66. Mason, *Brandeis - A Free Man's Life*, p. 452.
67. Ibid., pp. 451-2.
68. Trevor Wilson, Scott, Charles Prestwich (1846–1932)', *Oxford Dictionary of National Biography*, Oxford University Press, 2004.
69. They did fall out for a year in1920-21 over Ireland.
70. Weizmann, *Trial and Error*, p. 190.
71. Bernard Wasserstein, 'Samuel, Herbert Louis, first Viscount Samuel (1870–1963)', *Oxford Dictionary of National Biography.*
72. Viscount Samuel, *Memoirs*, p. 139.
73. Ibid., pp. 140-142.
74. Weizmann, *Trial and Error*, p. 191.
75. David Lloyd George, *War Memoirs*, p. 348-9.
76. Oscar K Rabinowicz, *Fifty Years of Zionism*, p. 69.
77. Weizmann, *Trial and Error*, p. 192.
78. Viscount Samuel, *Memoirs*, p.142.
79. Micheal and Eleanor Brock, *HH Asquith, Letters to Venetia Stanley*. p. 406.
80. Ibid., p. 477.
81. Ibid.
82. http://www.jta.org/1931/01/15/archive/mr-lloyd-george-was-legal-adviser-to-dr-herzl-on-uganda-project-and-submitted-dr-herzls-views-to
83. Viscount Samuel, *Memoirs*, pp.143-4.
84. Vladimir Halpern, *Lord Milner and the Empire*, p. 169.
85. Ibid., p. 170.
86. Weizmann, *Trial and Error*, p. 226.
87. Ibid., p. 241.
88. J A Turner, *The Historical Journal* vol.20, No 1 (March 1977) p. 165-184.
89. Fredric Bedoire and Robert Tanner, *The Jewish Contribution to Modern Architrecture, 1830-1930*, p. 131.
90. Walter Nimmocks, *Milner's Young Men*, p.166.
91. Weizmann, *Trial and Error*, p. 232.
92. Mason, *Brandeis - A Free Man's Life*, p. vii.
93. Ibid., p. 452-3.
94. Richard Neb Lebow, Woodrow Wilson and the Balfour Declaration, *Journal of Modern History*, Vol. 40. No. 4 (Dec 1968) pp 501-523.
95. https://wwi.lib.byu.edu/index.php/XXII_THE_BALFOUR_MISSION_TO_THE_UNITED_STATES
96. Blanche E C Dugdale, *Arthur J Balfour, Vol II*, p. 231.
97. Richard Neb Lebow, Woodrow Wilson and the Balfour Declaration, *Journal of Modern History*, Vol. 40. No. 4 (Dec 1968) p. 507 footnote 22.
98. Charles Seymour, *Mandell House vol.II* pp. 42-3.
99. What an enlightening insight. The Tzar having been deposed, all promises to Russia could be abandoned with all haste.
100. Richard Neb Lebow, Woodrow Wilson and the Balfour Declaration, *Journal of Modern History*, Vol. 40. No. 4 (Dec 1968) p. 508 footnote 26.
101. Ibid.
102. Nevzat Uyanik, *Dismantling the Ottoman Empire: Britain, America and the Armenian Question*, pp. 62-63.
103. Memorandum of Henry Morgenthau's Secret Mission, 10 June 1917, Robert Lansing Papers, Box 7, Folder 2. Quoted in Uyanik, *Dismantling the Ottoman Empire*, p. 63.
104. Weizmann, *Trial and Error*, p. 246.
105. Ibid., p. 247.
106. The British chief of staff in Egypt responsible for the safety of the Suez Canal. Married to daughter of Viscount Milner's great friend, Lord Midleton. [I. S. Munro, 'Graham, Sir Ronald William (1870–1949)', rev. *Oxford Dictionary of National Biography*, [http://www.oxforddnb.com/view/article/33505]
107. Weizmann, *Trial and Error*, p. 256.
108. United States Department of State, Papers

Relating to the Foreign Relations of the United States 1917, (FRUS) Supplement 2, The World War (1917) p. 109.
109. Ibid.
110. Ibid., p. 127.
111. Ibid., p. 129.
112. Weizmann, *Trial and Error*, p. 227.
113. S.J. Res. 191, 67th Congress, 2 Session, Congressional Record, Vol. LX11, part 5, p.5376.
114. The Lodge-Fish Resolution, Herbert Parzen, *American Jewish Historical Quarterly*, Vol. 60. no. 1 *Zionism in America*, (September 1970, p. 71.
115. Irwin Oder, "American Zionism and the CongressionalResolution of 1922 on Palestine," *Publications of the American-Jewish Historical Society*, Vol. 45, No.1 (September 1955.) p. 44.
116. Weizmann, *Trial and Error*, p. 251.

CHAPTER 29: THE BALFOUR DECLARATION 2: PERFIDIOUS ALBION

1. T E Lawrence, *Seven Pillars of Wisdom*, pp. 256-260.
2. Ibid., p. 259.
3. Jeremy Wilson, *Lawrence of Arabia, The Authorised Biography*, pp 606-7.
4. The three main Semitic religions are Judaism, Islam and Christianity, They are related by a common belief in God, the hereafter and the constant battle between good and evil.
5. Lawrence, *Seven Pillars*, p. 260.
6. [http://www.nationalreview.com/article/418688/lawrence-arabia-was-zionist-benjamin-weinthal
7. Doreen Ingrams, *Palestine Papers*, p.1.
8. CAB /24/30 *The Future of Palestine*, p. 2.
9. Robert Fisk, *The Great War for civilisation, The conquest of the Middle East*, pp. 400-401.
10. Lawrence, *Seven Pillars*, p. 24.
11. Liddell Hart, *T E Lawrence*, p. 61.
12. Dr Peter Shamrock, "A Lapse into Clarity. The McMahon-Hussein Correspondence Revisited," paper given at the Balfour Project conference October 2015, http://www.balfourproject.org/the-mcmahon-hussein-correspondence-revisited/
13. http://www.balfourproject.org/translation-of-a-letter-from-mcmahon-to-husayn-october-24-1915/
14. CAB 27/24
15. Doreen Ingrams, *Palestine Papers*, p. 48.
16. FO 882/2; ARB/15/3 p. 6.
17. Liddell Hart, *Lawrence*, pp. 69-70.
18. Fromkin, *A Peace to End All Peace, The Fall of the Ottoman Empire and Creation of the Modern Middle East*, p. 48.
19. Lawrence James, 'Sykes, Sir Mark, sixth baronet (1879–1919)', *Oxford Dictionary of National Biography.*
20. Mayir Verete, "The Balfour Declaration and its Makers," *Middle Eastern Studies*, 6 (1), January 1970, p. 54.
21. Lawrence, *Seven Pillars*, pp. 5-6.
22. CAB 24/30.
23. CAB 24/28.
24. CAB 24/30 p. 2.
25. Ibid., p. 3.
26. Ibid., p.4.
27. GT 2263 p. 1.
28. CAB 24/28, GT 2263.
29. Ibid., p. 2.
30. Ibid., p. 3.
31. War Cabinet no. 261 p. 5.
32. Ibid.
33. Ibid.
34. GT 2263.
35. Weizmann, *Trial and Error*, p. 226.
36. Will Podmore, *British Foreign Policy since 1870*, p. 21.
37. Thomas Pakenham, *The Boer War*, p. 115.
38. W T Stead, quoted in Hennie Barnard, *The Concentration Camps 1899-1902.*
39. One example being Leonard Stein, *The Balfour Declaration.*
40. Mayir Verete, "The Balfour Declaration and its Makers," *Middle Eastern Studies*, 6 (1), January 1970. p. 50.
41. Ibid., pp. 54-57.
42. *War Cabinet* 261, p. 5.
43. Ibid.
44. Ibid., p. 6.
45. Great Britain, Palestine and the Jews: Jewry's celebration of its national charter, Preface v. https://archive.org/details/greatbritainpale00unse
46. Ibid. p. 13.
47. At one stage around 1,800 Irishmen had been imprisoned at Frongoch in Wales in the aftermath of the British over-reaction to the Easter Rising. Most were released in December 1916 when Lloyd George became Prime Minister.
48. *The Times* December 1917, p. 2.
49. Muhammad, the prophet of Islam, traced his lineage to Ishmael through his first born son, Nabaioth : Genesis 25:6 12-18.
50. *Great Britain, Palestine and the Jews*: pp. 50-51.
51. Ibid., p. 66.
52. Ibid., p. 75
53. CAB 23/4 WC 261, p. 6.
54. FO 395/ 202.
55. Doreen Ingrams, *Palestine Papers*, p. 19.
56. David B Green, The Balfour Project http://www.balfourproject.org/this-day-in-jewish-historygeneral-allenby-shows-how-a-mor-

al-man-conquers-jerusalem/
57. Lawrence, *Seven Pillars*, p. 360.
58. FO 371/3054
59. Ormsby-Gore, was Parliamentary Private Secretary to Alfred Milner and as assistant secretary in the war cabinet, and to Sir Mark Sykes. Chaim Weizmann was a personal friend and he later approved Ormsby-Gore as the British military liaison officer with the Zionist mission in Palestine.
60. CAB 27/23.
61. Doreen Ingrams, *Palestine Papers, pp. 21-22.*
62. FO 371/3398
63. Doreen Ingrams, *Palestine Papers*, p. 32.
64. FO 371/3395.
65. Ferguson, *The House of Rothschild*, p. 280.
66. Weizmann, *Trial and Error*, p. 189.
67. Memorial Sermon given by The Very Rev. Dr. J. H. Hertz, 19 April, 1915, https://archive.org/stream/rthonlordrothsch00hert#page/n3/mode/2up
68. Ferguson, *The House of Rothschild*, p. 450.
69. https://en.wikipedia.org/wiki/Walter_Rothschild,_2nd_Baron_Rothschild
70. GT 1803 and CAB 24/24/4.
71. Niall Ferguson, *The House of Rothschild*, p. 450.
72. *The Times* 18 June 1917.
73. Weizmann, *Trial and Error*, p. 256.
74. Ibid., p. 201.
75. Ibid., p. 206.
76. Ibid., p. 238.
77. Ferguson, *The House of Rothschild*, p. 452.
78. The title 'Charter' appears to have been invented by the English Zionist Federation, whose pamphlet, Great Britain, Palestine and the Jews: *Jewry's Celebration of its National Charter*, published anonymously after December 1917 repeats the concept of a 'Charter' almost as if it was the Magna Carta, talking of ' a National Charter', 'The Charter of Zionism' and the 'British Charter of Zionism'

CHAPTER 30: THE RUSSIAN REVOLUTION 1 PAVING THE WAY

1. The date, October 25, 1917, was in the Julian calendar then still in use in Russia – the Old Style (O.S. calendar). In the Gregorian calendar used elsewhere in Europe and the United States it was November 7, 1917, That is, the O.S was 13 days behind the Gregorian.
2. The Russian capital, St Petersburg, was renamed Petrograd at the beginning of WW1 to give it a less German sounding name. It reverted to St Petersburg on the fall of communism.
3. Sean McMeekin, *History's Greatest Heist, The Looting of Russia by the Bolsheviks*, p. xix.
4. *New York Times*, 12 May, 1917.
5. Peter Waldron, *The End of Imperial Russia, 1855 – 1917*, p. 22.
6. The Pale of Settlement was territory within the borders of czarist Russia wherein Jews were legally authorised to live. It included present day Belarus, Ukraine, Poland, Moldova and much of Latvia and Lithuania.
7. Dmitri Volkogonov, *Lenin, Life and Legacy*, p. 5.
8. *The Times*, 29 March, 1919.
9. *Jewish Chronicle*, 4 April, 1919.
10. *American Hebrew*, 20 September, 1920.
11. Rabbi Stephen Wise, *The American Bulletin*, 5 May, 1935.
12. Aleksandr Solzhenitsyn *Juifs et Russes pendant la periode soviétique*, Volume 2, pp. 44–45
.13. Ibid., p. 54.
14. Ibid., p. 91.
15. https://archive.org/details/bub_gb_7cN-JAAAAMAAJ16. *New York Times*, September 17, 1914, David Wolffsohn obituary.
17. Zionism in Europe and America proved to be a comparatively slow-burning evolution. Between 1900 -1917 there was a serious divergence between Zionists who promoted a faith based assimilist belief, and the political Zionists who had one aim - a return to what they claimed as their former homeland in Palestine.
18. Jewish Telegraphic Agency, July 14, 1929. http://www.jta.org/1929/07/14/archive/german-zionists-celebrate-seventieth-birthday-of-otto-warburg
19. Scotland Yard, *A Monthly Review of the Progress of Revolutionary Movements Abroad*, July 16, 1919.
20. Hilaire Belloc. *G.K's Weekly*, 4 February, 1937.
21. Dmitri Volkogonov, *Trotsky, The Eternal Revolutionary*, pp. 2-3.
22. Leon Trotsky, *My Life*, p. 132.
23. Volkogonov, *Trotsky*, pp. 11-12.
24. Michael Pearson, *The Sealed Train, Journey to Revolution*, p. 26.
25. Ibid., p. 30.
26. E.H.Carr, *The Bolshevik Revolution 1917-1923*, p. 26.
27. Trotsky *My Life*, p. 160.
28. Dimitri Volkogonov, *Lenin, Life and Legacy*, p. xxxii.
29. Pearson, *The Sealed Train*, p. 31,
30. Volkcogonov, *Trotsky*, p. 47.
31. E. H. Carr, *The Bolshevik Revolution*, p. 86.
32. Volkcogonov, *Lenin*, p. 84.
33. Volkogonov, *Lenin*, pp. 85-86.
34. Ibid.
35. E. H Carr, *The Bolshevik Revolution*, p.26.
36. Volkogonov, *Trotsky*, pp. 30-31.
37. Pearson, *The Sealed Train*, p. 32.
38. Gerry Docherty and Jim Macgregor, *Hidden*

History, The Secret Origins of the First World War, pp. 86-87.]
39. Ron Chernow, *The Warburgs*, p. 110.
40. Pearson, *The Sealed Train*, p. 34.
41. George Buchanan, *My Mission to Russia and Other Diplomatic Memories, vol. 1*, p. 77.
42. Carr, *The Bolshevik Revolution*, p. 60.
43. Trotsky, *My Life*, p. 208.
44. Carr, *The Bolshevik Revolution*. P. 65.
45. McMeekin, *History's Greatest Heist*, p. xvii.
46. Docherty and Macgregor, *Hidden History*, p 297.
47. Ibid, p. 239.
48. Guido Preparata, *Conjuring Hitler*, p. 27.
49. Carr, *The Bolshevik Revolution*, p. 66.
50. Richard B Spence, *Hidden Agendas; Spies, Lies and Intrigue surrounding Trotsky's American visit of January-April 1917*. https://www.scribd.com/doc/124323217/HIDDEN-AGENDAS-SPIES-LIES-AND-INTRIGUE-SURROUNDING-TROTSKY-S-AMERICAN-VISIT-OF-JANUARY-APRIL-1917
51. Ibid.
52. Ibid.
53. Trotsky, *My Life*, p. 267.
54. Richard B Spence, *Hidden Agendas; Spies, Lies and Intrigue surrounding Trotsky's American visit of January-April 1917*.
55. Ibid.
56. Ibid.
57. Ibid.
58. Boris L. Brasol, *The World at the Crossroads*, p. 58.
59. Ibid., pp. 62-64.
60. CAB 23/1 War Cabinet 37, 18 January 1917. P.3.
61. R H Bruce Lockhart, *Memoirs of a British agent*, p. 162.
62. J Lee Thompson, *Forgotten Patriot*, p. 335.
63. R H Bruce Lockhart, *Memoirs of a British agent*, p. 163.
64. CAB/ 24/3/36 Lord Milner's Memorandum of 13 March, 1917 (G - 131).
65. CAB 23/2 War Cabinet 88.
66. R H Bruce Lockhart, *Memoirs of a British Agent*, pp. 168-169.
67. Lloyd George, *War Memoirs vol 1.*, p. 943.
68. R H Bruce Lockhart, *Memoirs of a British Agent*, pp. 164.
69. Docherty and Macgregor, *Hidden History*, pp. 161-163.
70. House of Commons Debate 27 March 1917 vol 92 cc295-318
71. *The Times*, 6 March 1917, p. 6.
72. House of Commons Debate 03 April 1917 vol 92 c1120.
73. *New York Times*, March 24, 1917.
74. Preparata, *Conjuring Hitler* pp 28-29.
75. G. Edward Griffin, *The Creature from Jekyll Island*, p. 274.
76. The Round Table was an influential think-tank pressure group which was built around Alfred Milner and his acolytes. Its prime aim was to spread his ideas of expanding the Empire to encompass the entire world.
77. G. Edward Griffin, *The Creature from Jekyll Island*, p. 274.

CHAPTER 31: THE RAPE OF RUSSIA

1. Guido Preparata, *Conjuring Hitler*, p. 29.
2. http://www2.stetson.edu/~psteeves/classes/rodzianko.html
3. Ibid.
4. Dimitri Volkogonov, *Lenin*, p. 106.
5. http://www.smithsonianmag.com/history/abdication-nicholas-ii-left-russia-without-tsar-first-time-300-years-180962503/
6. Preparata, *Conjuring Hitler*, p.29
7. Ibid.
8. National Archives FO telegram 514, dated 19 March 1915, and the reply FO telegram 514 dated 20 March 1917.
9. CAB/23/2 WC 100, 21 March 1917. p. 4.
10 Ibid., p. 5.
11. CAB 23/40/2, WC 101. 22 March,1917.
12. E. H. Carr, *The Bolshevik Revolution*, p. 67.
13. Pearson, *The Sealed Train*, p. 57.
14. See chapter 24.
15. Pearson, *The Sealed Train*, pp. 57- 8.
16. Ibid., pp. 58-59.
17. Ibid., p. 64.
18. Preparata, *Conjuring Hitler*, pp. 30-31.
19. Ibid., pp. 32-33.
20. Ibid. p. 33.
21. Pearson, *The Sealed Train*, p. 65.
22. Isaiah Friedman, *The Question of Palestine: British-Jewish-Arab Relations, 1914-1918*, p. 145.
23. Antony Sutton, *Wall Street and the Bolshevik Revolution*, p. 40.
24. Pearson, *The Sealed Train*, p. 83.
25. Ibid., p. 49.
26. Ibid, p. 61.
27. Volkognov, *Lenin*, p. 115.
28. Ibid., p. 114.
29. Pearson, *The Sealed Train*, pp. 101-102.
30. Ibid., p. 83.
31. Sean McMeekin, *History's Greatest Heist*, p. 225.
32. Sutton, *Wall Street and the Bolshevik Revolution*, p. 57.
33. Ibid., p. 67.
34. McMeekin, *History's Greatest Heist*, p. 59.
35. Niall Ferguson, *The House of Rothschild*, p. 384.
36. The convoluted and intricate means by which the Rothschilds and their associates on

Wall Street funded the Bolsheviks are beyond the scope of this chapter, and we would point interested readers to the late Antony Sutton's powerful book, *Wall Street and the Bolshevik Revolution*. Professor Sutton revealed exactly how Guaranty Trust, American International Company and the Kuhn, Loeb bank of Jacob Schiff and Paul Warburg gave large sums of money not merely to Bolsheviks, but to the German espionage system.

37. A.N.Field, *All These Things*,vol.1.http://www.yamaguchy.com/library/field_an/things_01.html

38. Sutton, *Wall Street and the Bolshevik Revolution*, pp. 186 -7.

39. Pearson, *Sealed Train*, p. 128.

40. Richard B Spence, *Hidden Agendas; Spies, Lies and Intrigue surrounding Trotsky's American visit of January-April 1917.*

41. Ibid.

42. Obituary. Sir Peter Bark, Bernard Pares *The Slavonic and East European Review* Vol. 16, No. 46 (Jul., 1937).

43. Ibid.

44. *New York Times*, March 18, 1917.

45. *New York Times*, 20 March, 1917.

46. *New York Times*, 24 March, 1917.

47. The Jewish communal register of New York city, 1917-1918, p. 1019. https://archive.org/stream/jewishcommunalr00marggoog#page/n953/mode/2up/search/money+market+of+the+48. E. Slater and R. Slater, *Great Jewish Men*, pp. 274-276.

49. G. Edward Griffin, *The Creature from Jekyll Island*, p. 210.

50. Cholly Knickerbocker, *New York Journal American*. As quoted by Griffin, p. 265.

51. Spence, *Hidden Agendas.*

52. Carroll Quigley, *Tragedy and Hope*, p. 324.

53. The Austrian philosopher, Guenter Jaschke, wrote recently to co-author Jim Macgregor, 'How can it happen that a minority of idiots, psychopaths and madmen rule the world, while the silent majority is paralysed?

54. Trotsky, *My Life*, p. 279.

55. Sutton, *Wall Street and The Bolshevik Revolution*, p. 25.

56. Ibid., pp. 32-33.

57. Ibid., pp. 33-34.

58. Trotsky, *My Life*, p. 284.

59. Sutton, *Wall Street and the Bolshevik Revolution*, p. 32.

60. Carr, *The Bolshevik Revolution*, p. 89.

61. Volkogonov, *Lenin*, p. 131.

62. Ibid., p. 141.

63. Preparata, *Conjuring Hitler*, p. 36.

64. Griffen, *Creature from Jekyll Island*, p. 286.

65. Eugene Lyons began his journalistic career in Russia in the 1920s as an enthusiastic supporter of the new order in Russian society, but in witnessing the outrageous excesses of Stalin's terror, the American writer came to loathe the regime.

66. Eugene Lyons, *Workers Paradise Lost*, p. 29.

67. Sean McMeekin, *History's Greatest Heist*, p. 54.

68. Volkogonov, *Trotsky*, p. 95.

69. Sutton, *Wall Street and the Bolshevik Revolution*, p. 71.

70. Griffin, *The Creature from Jekyll Island*, p. 274.

71. Ibid., p. 275.

72. Antony Sutton, *Wall Street and the Bolshevik Revolution*, p. 80.

73. Ibid., 97.

74. Ibid., p. 83.

75. Ibid.

76. Griffin, *The Creature from Jekyll Island*, p. 283.

77. Sutton, *Wall Street and the Bolshevik Revolution*, p. 83.

78. Bruce Lockhart, *Memoirs of a British Agent*, pp. 222-223.

79. George F Kennan, *Russia and the West under Lenin and Stalin*, p.180.

80. Sutton, *Wall Street*, p. 19.

81. Lockhart, *Memoirs of a British Agent*, p. 206.

82. Ibid., pp. 222-223.

83. Sutton, *Wall Street* p. 36.

84. Ibid., p. 115.

85. Ibid., p. 171.

86. Bruce Lockhart, *Memoirs of a British Agent*, p. 256.

87. Ibid., pp. 228-229.

88. Sutton, *Wall Street and the Bolshevik Revolution*, p. 94.

89. Lockhart, *Memoirs of a British Agent*, p. 224.

90. Sutton, *Wall Street and the Bolshevik Revolution*, p. 103.

91. Maxim Gorky, *The New Life*, April 1918.

92.Trotsky, *Terrorism and Communism*.https://www.marxists.org/archive/trotsky/1920/terrcomm/ch04.htm

93. George Leggett. *The Cheka: Lenin's Political Police*, p. 114.

94. Robert Conquest, *Reflections on a Ravaged Century*, p 101.

95. Dimitri Volkogonov, *Trotsky*, p. 394.

96. Sutton, *Wall Street and the Bolshevik Revolution*, p. 57.

97. Ibid., p. 63.

98.. U.S. State Dept., Decimal File, 861.51/815, 836, 837, October, 1920. Also Sutton, *Revolution*, pp. 159-60, 165.

99. Griffin, *The Creature from Jekyll Island*, p. 293.

100. Sean McMeekin, *History's Greatest Heist*, p. 136.

101. McMeekin, *History's Greatest Heist*, pp. 138-

139.
102. G Edward Griffin, *The Creature from Jekyll Island*, p. 263
103. E.C. Knuth, *The Empire of the City*, p. 70.
104. Griffin, *Creature from Jekyll Island*, p. 233.
105. Gerry Docherty and Jim Macgregor, *Hidden History, The Secret Origins of the First World War*, pp. 23-25.
106. Derek Wilson, *Rothschild: The Wealth and Power of a Dynasty*, pp. 98–9.
107. Knuth, *Empire of the City*, p. 68.
108. Ferguson, *House of Rothschild*, p. 65.
109. Chernow, *The Warburgs*, p. 12.
110. A.N Field, *All These Things*, vol.1. http://www.yamaguchy.com/library/field_an/things_01.html
111. Spence, *Hidden Agendas;*
112. Sutton, *Wall Street and the Bolshevik Revolution*, p. 189.
113. Ibid.
114. Louis Marshall in a letter to Max Senior, dated New York, September 26, 1917. Quoted in B. Jensen, *The Palestine Plot*, https://www.scribd.com/document/16563284/Jensen-The-Palestine-Plot-Quote-History-of-Zionism-1987
115. Carroll Quigley, *Tragedy and Hope*, p. 324.

CHAPTER 32: A WAR WITHOUT END?

1. Wilfred Owen, *Dulce Et Decorum Est*, is the best known English anti-war poem from the First World War. It essentially attacks the old lie that it is a great and glorious thing to die for one's country.http://www.warpoetry.co.uk/owen1.html
2. The Imperial War Cabinet comprised the Prime Ministers of Britain, Canada, Australia, New Zealand, Newfoundland and South Africa, represented by Jan Smutts.
3. Minutes of the Imperial War Cabinet, 32B, August 16 1918, CAB 23/44A/13.
4. Ex-Kaiser William II, *My Memoirs: 1878-1918*, pp. 268-9.
5. President Wilson's Message to Congress, January 8, 1918; Records of the United States Senate; Record Group 46; Records of the United States Senate; National Archives.
6. https://www.ourdocuments.gov/doc.php?doc=62&page=transcript
7. There are many sources for the exact wording. The Yale Law School site at http://avalon.law.yale.edu/20th_century/wilson14.asp can be accessed at this address.
8. http://www.firstworldwar.com/bio/maxvonbaden.htm
9. Erste deutsche Note an Wilson – Friedensersuchen (The First German Note to Wilson – Request for Peace), in Erich Ludendorff, ed., Urkunden der Obersten Herresleitung über ihre Tätigkeit 1916/8 (Records of the Supreme Army Command on its Activities, 1916/18). Berlin: E. S. Mittler und Sohn, 1920, p. 535.)
10. C Paul Vincent, *The Politics of Hunger*, p. 61.
11. David Lloyd George, *War Memoirs*, vol. 2, p. 1934.
12. *The Times*, 10 October 1918, p. 7.
13. Robert Lansing to Swiss Charge d'Affaires at Washington 8 October 1918.
14. J M Keynes, *The Economic Consequences of the Peace*, p. 27.
15. Arthur Willert, *The Road to Safety: A Study in Anglo-American Relations*, p. 166.
16. Keynes, *The Economic Consequences of the Peace* pp. 20-1.
17. Ibid., p. 29.
18. http://www.firstworldwar.com/features/armistice.htm
19. Ex-Kaiser William II, *My Memoirs: 1878-1918*, pp. 280–84.
20. David Lloyd George, *War Memoirs Vol. 2*, Appendix, pp 2044-2050.
21. Ibid., p. 2045
22. Randolph S Churchill, *Lord Derby, King of Lancashire*, p. 210.
23. National Archives, ADM 1/88542/290.
24. Vincent, *The Politics of Hunger*, p. 67.
25. Keynes, *The Economic Consequences of the Peace*, p. 50.
26. Lloyd George, *War Memoirs*, pp. 1983-4.
27. Herbert Hoover, *An American Epic 2*, p. 319.
28. Lloyd George, *War Memoirs*, p. 1985.
29. Vincent, *The Politics of Hunger*, p. 70.
30. http://www.todayinhistory.de/index.php?what=thmanu&manu_id=1561&tag=26&monat=8&year=2016&dayisset=1&lang=en] The murderers fled abroad after the assassination but returned after the National Socialists granted an amnesty for all crimes committed 'in the fight for national uprising'.
31. *The Times* 27 August 1921, p. 7.
32. *The Times* 29 August, 1921 p. 9.
33. Keynes, *The Economic Consequences of the Peace*, p. 65.
34. *The Times*, 30 November 1918, p. 9.
35. Lloyd George: speech at Newcastle, 29 Nov. 1918.
36. *The Times*, 2 December 1918. p. 9.
37. Keynes,*The Economic Consequences of the Peace*, p. 68.
38. Ibid., p. 69.
39. Vincent, *The Politics of Hunger*, pp. 77-8.
40. Woodrow Wilson, Executive Order 2679-A http://www.conservativeusa.net/eo/wilson.htm
41. See Chapter 15.
42. Lawrence E Gelfand, *Herbert Hoover, The Great War and its Aftermath, 1914-1923*, p. 48.
43. *Christian Science Monitor* November 18,

1918.
44. Kathleen Burk, *War and the State*, p. 139.
45. Herbert Hoover, *American Epic 2*, p. 319.
46. See Chapter 20. The myth of Edith's innocence was routinely abused by the British propagandists.
47. *The Times* 2 December 1918, p. 5.
48. Hailed by the military and the War Office, Arthur Winnington-Ingram, the war-mongering Bishop of London, was a jingoists xenophobic who was influential in recruitment drives. Awarded as a Knight of the Royal Victorian Order by King George VI and the Grand Cross of the Order of the Redeemer (Greece) and the Order of St. Sava, 1st Class (Serbia).
49. *The Daily News*, 22 November 1918.
50. Vincent, *The Politics of Hunger*, p. 79.
51. *The Times*, 2 December 1918, p. 9.
52. *The Times*, 10 December 1918, p. 7.
53. *The Times*, 30 December 1918, p. 7.
54. Indeed this quotation could sit at the heart *of Hidden History, The Secret Origins of the First World War.*
55. Herbert Hoover, *An American Epic 2*, p. 318.
56. Kellogg spent two years (1915 -1916) in Brussels as director of Hoover's Commission for the Relief of Belgium. He was a loyal servant to Herbert Hoover.
57. http://www.bclm.co.uk/ww1/childhood-in-ww1/49.htm
58. Herbert Hoover, *An American Epic 2*, p. 320.
59. FRUS vol. 2. Papers relating to the Foreign Relations of the United States, The Paris Peace Conference 1919.
60. Ibid., pp. 636-7, House to Lansing, 27 November 1918.
61. Ibid., House to Wilson, 28 Nov. 1918.
62. Ibid., p.639.
63. Ibid., Hoover to Wilson, 1 December 1918, p. 645.
64. Ibid., Wilson to Hoover, 5 December 1918, p. 648.
65. FRUS vol. 2. Papers relating to the Foreign Relations of the United States, The Paris Peace Conference 1919, pp. 649-653.
66. Vincent, *The Politics of Hunger*, pp. 60-61.
67. Roy Hattersley, *David Lloyd George, The Great Outsider*, p. 490.
68. Ibid., pp. 492-3.
69. Hoover, *An American Epic* vol.2. pp. 323-4.
70. J M Keynes, *Dr. Melchior, Two Memoirs*, p. 61.
71. FRUS, vol 13, p. 205.
72. FRUS, U.S. Department of State / Papers relating to the foreign relations of the United States, 1919, Paris Peace Conference - The Blockade and regulation of Trade, p. 729.
73. Ibid., p. 731.
74. Hoover, *American Epic 2*, pp. 303-4.
75. FRUS vol 2. Papers Relating etc pp. 695-7.
76. Hoover, *Memoirs, Vol 1*. pp. 332.
77. Ibid., p. 333.
78. Ibid., p. 339.
79. *Berliner Tageblatt*, 13 December 1918, p. 2.
80. House of Commons Debate 02 April 1919 vol 114 cc1304-49.
81. Ibid., cc1311.
82. Reports by British Officers on the Economic Conditions Prevailing in Germany, December 1918-March 1919 , Cmd.52, HMSO 1919. (Period 12 January-12 February 1919, in CAB/ 24/ 76)
83. Ibid., pp. 57-8.
84. Hoover, *Memoirs, Vol. 1*, pp. 340-1.
85. Reports by British Officers, Cmd.52, HMSO 1919. p. 84.
86. CAB/ 24/76/22
87. Winston Churchill was returned to high office on 9 January 1919 as Secretary of State for War.
88. CAB/ 24/76/22.
89. War Cabinet 531, p. 2. War Cabinet Minutes 12 February 1919. CAB /23/ 9/18.
90. Herbert Hoover, *American Epic 2*, pp. 337-8.
91. http://filestore.nationalarchives.gov.uk/pdfs/large/cab-23-9.pdf
92. Vincent, *Politics of Hunger*, p. 121 footnote.
93. Keynes, *Dr. Melchior*, p. 59.
94. Bane and Lutz, *Blockade of Germany After the Armistice*, p. 214.
95. Keynes, *Dr. Melchior, Two Memoirs*, pp. 60-61.
96. Eric W Osborne, *Britain's Economic Blockade of Germany, 1914-1919*, p.188.
97. Bane and Lutz, *The Blockade of Germany after the Armistice*, pp. 549-50.
98. Ibid., pp. 558-9.
99. Margaret Macmillan, *Peacemakers, Six Months That Changed The World*, p. 1
100. These were ; the Treaty of Versailles, 28 June 1919 with Germany; the Treaty of Saint-Germain, 10 September 1919 with Austria; the Treaty of Neuilly, 27 November 1919 with Bulgaria; the Treaty of Trianon, 4 June 1920 with Hungary; the Treaty of Sèvres, 10 August 1920, later revised by the Treaty of Lausanne, 24 July 1923 with Turkey.
101. http://net.lib.byu.edu/~rdh7/wwi/versa/versa7.html
102. Harry Elmer Barnes, *The Genesis of the World War*, pp. 34-35.
103. Keynes, *Dr. Melchior*, p. 24.
104. Ibid., p. 13.
105. Ibid., pp. 49-50.
106. A. N. Field, *The Truth About the Slump*, p.35.
107. Ibid., p. 57.
108. Keynes, *Dr. Melchior*, p. 70.

109. Ibid., p. 12.

110. J Lee Thompson, *Forgotten Patriot*, p. 359.

111. The League of Nations came into being on 10 January 1920. It was the first international organisation which theoretically aimed to maintain world peace, prevent wars through collective security and disarmament. International disputes were to be solved through negotiation and arbitration. It failed because those who wielded real power ensured that it did not succeed..

112. Kathleen Burk, 'Brand, Robert Henry, Baron Brand (1878–1963)', *Oxford Dictionary of National Biography.*

113. Carroll Quigley, *The Anglo-American Establishment*, p. 168.

114. https://www.loc.gov/law/help/us-treaties/bevans/m-ust000002-0043.pdf

115. www.usmidtermelections.com/midterm_summary.php?year=1918_1918&chart...

116. Mujahid Kamran, *The International Bankers, World Wars 1, II and Beyond*, p. 146.

117. Ibid., p. 63.

118. Minutes of the Federal Reserve Board, 20 January 1919, https://fraser.stlouisfed.org/files/docs/historical/nara/bog_minutes/19190120_Minutes.pdf

119. See Chapter 17.

120. Manfred Pohl, *Handbook on the History of European Banks,* pp 84-5.

121. Brandeis: *A Free Man's Life*, p 529.

122. Margaret Macmillan, Peacemakers, *Six Months That Changed The World.* p. 429.

123. FRUS vol. IV, p. 159.

124. Ibid., p. 165.

125. Ibid., p. 167.

126. Ibid., p. 168.

127. Ibid., p. 169.

128. *The Bankers Magazine* Vol. 49, No 1, January 1919, p. 8.

129. Ibid., p. 7.

130. https://libcom.org/history/1919-winnipeg-general-strike.

131. Chanie Rosenberg, http://pubs.socialistreviewindex.org.uk/sr226/rosenberg.htm

132. Professor Hans Fenske, *A Peace to End All Peace* https://firstworldwarhiddenhistory.wordpress.com//?s=Fenske&search=Go

133. Adam Hochschild, *To End All Wars: A Story of loyalty and Rebellion*, p. 357.

134. David S Landes, *The Unbound Prometheus,* pp. 362-3.

135. The inaugural meeting to establish the Institute took place on 30 May 1919.

136. Docherty and Macgregor, *Hidden History,* p.18.

137. Carroll Quigley, *The Anglo-American Establishment*, pp. 182-183.

138. M. L. Dockrill, "The Foreign Office and the 'Proposed Institute of International Affairs 1919'" International Affairs (Royal Institute of International Affairs 1944-), Vol. 56, No. 4 (Autumn, 1980), pp. 667.

139. Ibid., p. 666.

140. All of the senior organisers have been identified as members of the Secret Elite many times over; Lord Robert Cecil, Valentine Chirol, foreign editor of *The Times*, Geoffrey Dawson, G. W. Prothero etc.

141. Dockrill, The Foreign Office and the 'Proposed Institute of International Affairs 1919' International Affairs (Royal Institute of International Affairs 1944-), Vol. 56, No. 4 (Autumn, 1980), pp. 671.

142. Docherty and Macgregor, *Hidden history,* chapter 11, pp. 153-160.

143. Both Hogarth and T E Lawrence were largely responsible for *The Bulletin*, a secret magazine of Middle East politics. Lawrence edited the first number on 6 June 1916 and thereafter sent numerous reports to it, enabling readers to follow, week by week, the Arab Revolt, which ended Ottoman domination in the Arabian peninsula. The British Foreign Office described it as: 'A remarkable intelligence journal so strictly secret in its matter that only some thirty copies of each issue were struck off... Nor might the journal be quoted from, even in secret communications. http://www.archiveeditions.co.uk/titledetails.asp?tid=7

144. Quigley, *The Anglo-American Establishment*, p. 185.

145. Ephraim Adams, *The Hoover War Collection at Stanford University, California*; a report and an analysis, (1921), p. 7. https://archive.org/details/cu31924031034360.

146. Ibid.

147. Adams, *The Hoover War Collection*, (1921), p. 36.

148. http://www.fundinguniverse.com/company-histories/generale-bank-générale-de-banque-history/

149. Whittaker Chambers, Hoover Library http://whittakerchambers.org/articles/time-a/hoover-library/%5D

150. *New York Times,* 5 February 1921.

151. Adams, *The Hoover War Collection*, p. 5.

152. Cissie Dore Hill, *Collecting the Twentieth Century*, p. 1 at http://www.hoover.org/publications/hoover-digest/article/8041.

153. Whittaker Chambers, Hoover Library at http://whittakerchambers. org/articles/time-a/hoover-library/

154. Ibid.

155. *New York Times*, 5 February 1921.

156. Whittaker Chambers, Hoover Library, as above.

157. *New York Times*, 5 February 1921.

Postscript

1. Carrol Quigley, *The Anglo-American Establishment*, p. x.
2. Christopher Clark, *The Sleepwalkers, How Europe Went To War in 1914.*
3. Report of the Committee of Prime Ministers. Preliminary Draft. appended to the minutes for the Imperial War Cabinet 32B, 16 August 1918. p. 167.
4. Ibid.
5. The League of Nations was an international organisation, created in 1920 as part of the Treaty of Versailles. Though first proposed by President Woodrow Wilson as part of his Fourteen Points for a just peace in Europe, Congress refused to endorse the proposal.
6. Firstly on 19 November 1919, then again on 19 March 1920.
7. *New York Times*, 20 March 1920.
8. Margaret Macmillan, *Peacemakers, Six Months That Changed the World*, p. 71.
9. FRUS, vol. 3 pp. 581-4.
10. National Archives, CAB 29/ 28.
11. Quigley, *The Anglo-American Establishment*, pp ix-x.

Bibliography

Primary Sources

Papers relating to the Committee of Imperial Defence. National Archives, Kew.

Papers relating to the Foreign Relations of the United States Government. (FRUS)

Papers relating to the Foreign Relations of the United States, The Paris Peace Conference 1919. FRUS vol. 2.

Papers of Woodrow Wilson

Private archives Herman Capiau, Centre de documentation, Musée Royal de l'Armée et d'Histoire militaire, Brussels.

Congressional Record of the United States Government.

First World War Primary Documents, Maitre Gaston de Leval on the Execution of Edith Cavell http://www.firstworldwar.com/source/cavell_deleval.htm

Hansard, House of Commons, Debates.

Hansard, House of Lords, Debates.

Milner Papers, Bodliean Library, Oxford.

National Archives Public Records Office, Cabinet Papers - PRO / CAB reference

National Archives Public Records Office, Admiralty Papers - PRO / ADM

National Archives Public Records Office, Cabinet Memoranda 1905-1918.

Oxford Dictionary of National Biography.

Record Group 46; Records of the United States Senate; National Archives.

Seventh Report from the Select Committee on National Expenditure, 21. December, 1920.

United States Library of Congress.

Newspapers, Magazines & Journals

American Bulletin

American Hebrew

American Journal of International Law

BBC History Magazine.

Chicago Tribune

Christian Times

Daily News

Daily Telegraph

Exchange Telegraph

Fortune Magazine.

Guardian

Irish World

Irish Times

International Monthly, New York.

Jewish Chronicle

Kolnische Volkrientung

L'Echo de Paris

La Libre Belgique

Journal Officiel de la République Française.

Le Matin

Neue Freie Presse (Vienna)

New York Herald

New York Nation

New York Times

New York Tribune

New York World

Norddeutsche Allgemeine Zeitung.

Nursing Mirror and Midwives' Journal

Philadelphia Public Leger

Scotsman

Straits Times

Sydney Morning Herald

Tablet

The British Journal of Nursing

Times

Washington Post

Washington Times

Articles / Pamphlets / Reports

American Press Resume (A.P.R.) issued by the War Office and Foreign Office. "For Use of the Cabinet".

Angus, Joe, Stromness, "World War One," Orkney Public Library, Kirkwall, interview for Sound Archive by Eric Marwick.

Balfour Project, The, http://www.balfourproject.org/427/

Banque Nationale de Belgique, *The Centenary of the Great War – the National Bank in Wartime*. http://www.nbbmuseum.be/fr/2013/11/wartime.htm

Birdsall, Paul, *Neutrality and Economic Pressures, Science and Society, Vol. 3, no. 2,* (Spring 1939)

British Wreck Commissioner's Inquiry, http://www.titanicinquiry.org/Lusitania/lucy01.php

Broadbent, Harvey, *Gallipoli: One Great Deception?* http://www.abc.net.au/news/2009-04-24/30630

Burk, Kathleen, *History Today, Volume 43, Issue 3,* March 1993. http://www.historytoday.com/kathleen-burk/money-and-power-america-and-europe-20th-century

Carlisle, Rodney, "Attacks on American Shipping that Precipitated the War," *The Northern Mariner, XVII, no. 3,* p. 61. http://www.cnrs-scrn.org/northern_mariner/vol17/tnm_17_3_41-66.pdf]

Comité des Forges de France, Circulaire no. 655.

Commission for Relief in Belgium, Balance sheets and Accounts, by Joint Liquidators, Rickard, Edgar, and Pollard, W. B. https://archive.org/stream/executivepersonn00comm#page/n7/mode/2up

Crammond, Edgar, "The Cost of War," *Journal of the Royal Statistical Society, Vol. LXXVIII, Part III,* May 1915.

Cuddy, Edward, "Irish Americans and the 1916 Election," *American Quarterly, vol. 21, no. 2, Part 1, Summer 1969.*

Danielson, Elena S., "Historical Note on the Commission for Relief in Belgium," in *United States in the First World: An Encyclopaedia*, edited by Anne Cipriano Venzon

Delvaux, Louis, *Annals of the American Academy of Political and Social Science, vol. 247,* "Belgium in Transition" (September 1946).

Dockrill, M. L., "Historical Note: The Foreign Office and the 'Proposed Institute of International Affairs.'" *Royal Institute of International Affairs 1944, Vol. 56, No. 4* (Autumn, 1980).

Einstein, Lewis, "The United States and the Anglo-German Rivalry," *National Review,* LX, Jan. 1913.

Fielden, Kevin Christopher, *The Church of England in the First World War.* (2005). Electronic Theses and Dissertations. Paper 1080. http://dc.etsu.edu/etd/1080

Fitzgerald, John J., "The Task of Financing the War," *The Annals of the American Academy of Political and Social Studies,* Vol. 75.

Frank, Alison, "The Petroleum War of 1910: Standard Oil, Austria, and the Limits of the Multinational Corporation," *The American Historical Review,* 114.

Great Britain's Measures Against German Trade, published by Hodder and Stoughton.

"Great Britain, Palestine and the Jews. Jewry's Celebration of Its National Charter" - Anonymous pamphlet, 1917.

Heller, Joseph, "Sir Louis Mallet and the Ottoman Empire, The Road to War," *Middle Eastern Studies, Vol.12, No. 1* (Jan., 1976)

Heures de Detress, l'oeuvre du comite national de secours et d'alimentation et de la Commission for Relief in Belgium, 1914-1915. http://uurl.kbr.be/1007553?bt=europeanaapi

Hill, Cissie Dore, *Collecting the Twentieth Century.* http://www.hoover.org/research/collecting-twentieth-century

Horne, Charles F., Source Records of the Great War, Vol. III, ed., National Alumni, 1923. firstworldwar.com – Primary Documents – Maitre G. de Level on the Execution of Edith Cavell. Hoehling, A. (1957). "The Story of Edith Cavell"; *The American Journal of Nursing,*

Jeanneney, Jean Noel, Francois de Wendel en Republique, L'Argent et le Pouvoir, *Revuie Historique*, T. 257, Fasc. 2 (522) Avril-Juin 1977.

Judson, Helen, "Edith Cavell". *The American Journal of Nursing,* July 1941.

Kurtz, Harold, "The Lansdowne Letter," *History Today,* Volume 18, issue 2 February 1968.

Lambert, Nicholas A., "Our Bloody Ships or Our Bloody System? Jutland and the loss of the Battle Cruisers," *Journal of Military History,* vol. 62, no. 1, January 1998.

Lebow, Richard Neb, "Woodrow Wilson and the Balfour Declaration," *Journal of Modern History,* Vol. 40. No. 4 (Dec 1968)

Linowitz, Sol M., "Analysis of a Tinderbox: The Legal Basis for the State of Israel," *American Bar Association Journal,* Vol. 43, 1957.

Lueders, Hugo, "Edith's Wonderland." https://www.academia.edu/9532093/

Macfie, A.L., "The Straits Question in the First World War," *Middle Eastern Studies,* July 1983.

McAdie, Alexander, "Fate and a Forecast," *Harvard Graduate Magazine,* September 1923.

Mersey Report Day 1, In Camera, Testimony of Captain Turner

http://www.titanicinquiry.org/Lusitania/

Bernard Pares, Sir Peter Bark, *Slavonic and East European Review* Vol. 16, No. 46 (Jul., 1937).

Physics Today (15) 3. 1962. Obituary for Dannie Heineman.

Rapport sur l'activite du Bureau Federal des Co-operatives Intercommunales de Revitaillement. General Report on the functioning and operations of the Comite National de Secours et Alimentation – Quatrieme Parte.

Reisser, Dr. J., "National Monetary Commission, the Economic Development of Germany."

61st Congress, 2nd Session, Senate Document 593.

Report of the Committee on Alleged German Outrages, 1915. (Bryce).

Rimington, Dame Stella, BBC Radio 4, *Secrets and Spies,* broadcast on 15/09/2015.

Roskill, S. W., "The Dismissal of Admiral Jellicoe," *Journal of Contemporary History,* vol.1, no. 4 (October 1966).

Round Table, Special War Number, "Germany and the Prussian Spirit," 1914.

Rust, Michael J., *The Journal of Economic History,* Vol. 37, issue 2, June 1977.

Sanders, M. L., "Wellington House and British Propaganda in the First World War," T*he Historical Journal,* vol. 18, No1. (March 1975)

Santini, Alberto, "The First Ultra Secret: the British Cryptanalysis in the Naval Operations of the First World War," *Revue Internationale D'Histoire Militaire,* vol 63 1985.

Sarna, Jonathan D., "Louis D Brandeis: Zionist Leader," *Brandeis Review,* winter 1992.

Shamrock, Dr. Peter, "A Lapse into Clarity. The McMahon-Hussein Correspondence" revisited, paper given at the Balfour Project conference October 2015, http://www.balfourproject.org/the-mcmahon-hussein-correspondence-revisited/

Sizer, Roseanne, "Herbert Hoover and the Smear Books," 1930-32, *State Historical Society of Iowa,* Vol. 47, (Speing 1984) no. 4.

Smith, Daniel M., "Lansing and the Formation of American Neutrality Policies, 1914-1915," *Mississippi Valley Historical Review,* vol.43 No. 1, p. 69.

Storey, Jane E., http://www.bjentertainments.co.uk/js/THE%20Orcadian.htm *The Arcadian,* "New Light On Hampshire Tragedy."

"The United States and War: President Wilson's Notes on the Lusitania and Germany's reply," *Brooklyn Daily Eagle,* vol. XXX (1915).

Trachtenberg, Marc, "The Meaning of Mobilization in 1914," *International Security,* vol. 15, issue 3.

Trumpener, Ulrich, "The Escape of the Goeben and Breslau," *Canadian Journal of History,* September 1971.

Verete, Mayir, "The Balfour Declaration and its Makers," *Middle Eastern Studies,* 6 (1), January 1970.

Warburg, Paul, A *Plan for a Modified Central Bank. The Federal Reserve System: Its Origins and Growth, Vol. 2,*

Warren and Brandeis, *Harvard Law Review,* Vol. IV December 15, 1890 No. 5, "The Right To Privacy."

Wilson, Woodrow,: Address to the Senate of the United States; World League for Peace, 22 January, 1917. http://www.presidency.ucsb.edu/ws/?pid=65396]

Secondary Sources

Adams, Ephraim, The Hoover War Collection at Stanford University, California; a report and an analysis, (1921), p. 7.https://archive.org/details/cu31924031034360

Adam-Smith, Patsy, *The Anzacs.*

Aldington, Richard, *Lawrence of Arabia.*

Amara, Michael and Roland, Hubert, Gouverner en Belgique occupee: Oscar von der Lancken-Wakenitz – Rapports d'activite 1915-1918.

Ambler, Eric, *Journey Into Fear.*

Amery, Leopold , *My Political Life, Vol. II.*

Anderson, Scott, *Lawrence of Arabia, War, Deceit, Imperial folly and the Making of the Modern Middle East.*

Andrew, Christopher, *Secret Service.*

Arthur, Sir George, *The Life of Lord Kitchener.*

Arthur, Max, *Forgotten Voices of the Great War.*

Ascherson, Neal, *The King Incorporated, Leopold and the Congo.*

Ashmead-Bartlett, Ellis, *The Uncensored Dardanelles.*

Aspinal-Oglander, G., *Roger Keyes.*

Babayev, Mir, *Baku Baron Days.*

Baker, Anne Pimlott, *The Pilgrims of America.*

Baker, Ray Stannard, *The Life and Letters of Woodrow Wilson, VI.*

Ballard, Robert, with Spencer Dunmore, *Robert Ballard's Lusitania.*

Bane, Suda Lorena, and Lutz, Ralph Haswell, *Blockade of Germany After the Armistice.*

Bailey, Thomas A., *A Diplomatic History of the American People.*

Bardon, Jonathon, *A History of Ireland in 250 Episodes.*

Barnes, Harry, Elmer, *In Quest of Truth and Justice.*

Barnes, Harry Elmer, *The Genesis of the World War.*

Barnes, Harry Elmer, *Who Started the First World War?*

Barr, James, *A Line in the Sand, Britain, France and the Struggle that Shaped the Middle East.*

Barr, James, *Setting the Desert on Fire, T.E. Lawrence and Britain's Secret War in Arabia, 1916-1918.*

Barnett, Correlli, *Studies in Supreme Command in the First World War.*

Baty, Thomas, and Morgan, John, *War: Its Conduct and Legal Results.*

Beaumont, Harry, *Old Contemptible.*

Beesley, Patrick, *Room 40, British Naval Intelligence 1914-1918.*

Bell, Archibald, *A History of the Blockade of Germany.*

Benckendorff, Count Constantine, *Half A Life, The Reminiscences of a Russian Gentleman.*

Bentwich, Norman, *The Declaration of London, 1911.*

Bertrams, Kenneth, Coupain, Nicholas, Homburg, Ernest, Solvay, *History of a Multinational Family Firm.*

Binding, Rudolf G., *A Fatalist at War.*

Birkenhead, *Earl of, Churchill, 1874-1922.*

Birmingham, Stephen, *Our Crowd.*

Bitsch, Marie Therese, *La Belgique Entre La France et d'Allemande, 1905-1914.*

Bobroff, Ronald P., *Roads to Glory, Late Imperial Russia and the Straits.*

Bowles, George F.S., *The Strength of England.*

Brasol, Boris L., *The World at the Crossroads.*

Brian, R., et Moreau, J.L. *Inventaire Des Archives de la Banque d'Outremer S.A., 1899-1957.*

Brittain, Harry, *Pilgrim Partners, Forty Years of British American Fellowship.*

Broadbent, Harvey, *The Fatal Shore.*

Brock, Michael and Eleanor, H.H. Asquith, *Letters to Venetia Stanley.*

Brown, James, Anzac's Long Shadow, *The Cost of Our National Obsession.*

Brownrigg, Rear Admiral Sir Douglas, Indiscretions of the Naval Censor.

Buchan, John, *Episodes of the Great War.*

Buchan, John, *Greenmantle.*

Buchan, John, *Memory Hold The Door.*

Buchan, John, *Nelson's History of the Great War.*

Buchanan, George, *My Mission to Russia and Other Diplomatic Memories, Vol. 1.*

Buchanan, George, *My Mission to Russia and Other Diplomatic Memories, Vol. 2.*

Buchanan, Meriel, *The Dissolution of an Empire.*

Burk, Kathleen, *Britain, America and the Sinews of War.*

Burk, Kathleen, *War and the State, The Transformation of British Government, 1914-1919.*

Butler, Major General Smedley Darlington, *War is a Racket.*

Cafferky, John P., *Lord Milner's Second War, The Rhodes-Milner Secret Society, The Origins of World War 1and the Start of the New World Order.*

Caldwell, C. E. and Marshal Foch, *Field Marshal Sir Henry Wilson VI: His Life and Diaries.*

Carlyon, L. A., *Gallipoli.*

Carr, E. H., *The Bolshevik Revolution 1917-1923.*

Carr, W. G., *Pawns in the Game.*

Casement, Roger, *The Crime against Europe, The Writings and poetry of Roger Casement.*

Casssar, George, *Kitchener: Architect of Victory.*

Cecil, Hugh, and Liddle, Peter H., *Facing Armageddon: The First World War Experienced.*

Chandler, Alfred Dupont, *Scale and Scope: The Dynamics of Industrial Capitalism.*

Chapman, Stanley, *The Rise of Merchant Banking.*

Chatterton, E. Keble, *The Big Blockade.*

Chernow, Ron, *The House of Morgan.*

Chernow, Ron, *Titan, The Life of John D. Rockefeller.*

Chernow, Ron, *The Warburgs.*

Churchill, Randolph S., *Lord Derby, King of Lancashire.*

Churchill, Winston S., *World Crisis 1911-1918.*

Clark, A., A *Good Innings: the private papers of Viscount Lee of Fareham.*

Clarke, Tom, *My Northcliffe Diary.*

Clews, Graham T., *Churchill's Dilemma.*

Clifford, Brendan, *Alsace-Lorraine and the Great Irredentist War.*

Clifford, Brendan, *Connolly and German Socialism.*

Coletta, Paolo Enrico, *The Presidency of William Howard Taft.*

Cobb, Irvin S., *Paths of Glory.*

Combe, Lord Sydenham of, *Studies of an Imperialist.*

Conquest, Robert, *Reflections on a Ravaged Century.*

Consett, Rear Admiral M.W.W.P., *The Triumph of Unarmed Forces.*

Cooper, Duff, *Haig,* vol. 1.

Cowles, Virginia, *Winston Churchill.*

Crankshaw, Edward, *The Shadow of the Winter Palace.*

Crawley, Rhys, *Climax at Gallipoli, The Failure of the August Offensive.*

Crozier, Brig.-General F.P., *A Brass Hat in No man's Land.*

Crutwell, C.R.M.F., *A History of the Great War, 1914-1918.*

Davenport, Guiles, *Zaharoff, High Priest of War.*

David, Edward, *Inside Asquith's Cabinet.*

Debruyne, Emmanuel, and Paternostre, Jehanne, "La résistance au quotidien 1914-1918, Témoignages inédites".

De Croy, Princess Marie, *War Memories.*

De Groot, *Douglas Haig, 1861-1928.*

Delage, Edmond, *The Tragedy of the Dardanelles.*

Denson, John V., *A Century of War: Lincoln, Wilson and Roosevelt.*

Denton, Kit, *Gallipoli, One Long Grave.*

Dewar, George A.B., and Boreston, J.H., *Sir Douglas Haig's Command.*

Dixon, Norman, *On the Psychology of Military Incompetence.*

Docherty, Gerry, and Macgregor, Jim, *Hidden History, The Secret Origins of the First World War.*

D'Ombrain, Nicholas, *War Machinery and High Policy Defence Administration in Peacetime Britain, 1902–1914.*

Dugdale, Blanche E. C., *Arthur J Balfour,* vol. II.

D'Ydewalle, Charles, *Albert King of the Belgians.*

Edward, David, *Inside Asquith's Cabinet.*

Engdahl, William, *A Century of War.*

Engelbrecht, H.C. and Hanighen, F.C., *The Merchants of Death.*

Engerand, Fernand, *La Battaille de la Frontiere, Briey.*

Esher, Viscount Reginald, *The Tragedy of Lord Kitchener.*

Ewart, John S., *The Roots and Causes of the Wars,* vol. II.

Farrer, David, *The Warburgs.*

Fay, Sidney Bradshaw, *The Origins of the World War,* vol. I.

Fahey, Rev. Denis, *The Rulers of Russia.*

Feis, Herbert, Europe, *The World's Banker 1870-1914.*

Ferguson, Niall, *The House of Rothschild,* vol II.

Ferguson, Niall, *The Pity of War.*

Ferrier, R. W. *The History of the British Petroleum Company.*

Fewster, Kevin, Bagram, Vecihi and Bagram, Hatice, *Gallipoli, The Turkish Story.*

Field, A.N., *All These Things,* vol. 1.

Finkelstein, Israel, and Silberman, Neal Asher, *The Bible Unearthed, Archeology's New Vision of Ancient Israel and the Origin of its Sacred Texts.*

Fisher, Baron John Arbuthnot, *Memories and Records,* vol. II.

Fisher, Irving, *The Money Illusion.*

Fleming, Thomas, *The Illusion of Victory, America in World War 1.*

Flynn, John T., *Men of Wealth.*

Foley, Edward, *Ballot Battles: The History of Disputed Elections in the United States.*

Foy, Michael, and Barton, Brian, *The Easter Rising.*

Frank, Alison, *Oil Empire, Visions of Prosperity in Austrian Galicia.*

Frankopan, Peter. *The Silk Roads.*

French, David, *The Rise and Fall of Business as Usual.*

Fromkin, David, *A Peace to End All Peace, The Fall of the Ottoman Empire and the Creation of the Modern Middle East.*

Fromm, Erich, *The Anatomy of Human Destructiveness.*

Gay, George I. and Fisher, H. H., *Public Relations of the Commission For Relief In Belgium.*

Geiss, Immanuel, *July 1914.*

Gelfand, Lawrence E ,*Herbert Hoover, The Great War and its Aftermath, 1914-1923.*

George, David Lloyd, *The Truth About Reparations and War-Debts.*

George, David Lloyd, *War Memoirs,* vols. I & II.

Gerretson, Dr. F. C. *History of the Royal Dutch,* vol. III.

Gibson, Hugh, *Journal From Our Legation in Belgium, The Case of Miss Edith Cavell.*

Gilbert, Martin, *Churchill on America.*

Gilbert, Martin, *Winston S. Churchill,* vol. III.

Goldston, Robert, *The Russian Revolution.*

Gollin, A. M. *Proconsul in Politics.*

Gottlieb, W. W. *Studies in Secret Diplomacy.*

Green, S.J.D., and Horden, Peregrine, *All Souls and the Wider World.*

Greenwood, Paul, *The British Expeditionary Force August-September 1914.*

Griffin, Des, *Descent Into Slavery.*

Griffin, G. Edward, *The Creature from Jekyll Island.*

Grigg, John, Lloyd George, *The People's Champion.*

Grey, Mary, *Chaim Weizmann (1874-1952).*

Grey of Fallodon, Viscount, *Twenty-Five Years, 1892-1916.*

Groos, Fregattenkapitän Oskar, *Der Krieg zur See 1914-18, Nordsee Band V.*

Guehenno, Jean-Marie, *The End of the nation State.*

Haldane, Richard Burdon, *An Autobiography.*

Halpern, Paul, *A Naval History of World War 1.*

Halperin, Vladimir, *Lord Milner and the Empire, The Evolution of British Imperialism.*

Hamill, John, *The Strange Career of Mr. Hoover Under Two Flags.*

Hamilton, Sir Ian, *Gallipoli Diary,* vol. 1.

Hammerton and Wilson, ed. *The Great War.*

Hankey, Maurice, *Supreme Command,* vol. II.

Hanbury-Williams, John, *The Emperor Nicholas II As I Knew Him.*

Hanotaux, Gabriel, *Historie Illustre de la Guerre de 1914,* vol. 9.

Hargrave, John, *The Suvla Bay Landing.*

Hart, Liddell, *History of the First World War.*

Hart, Liddell, *T. E. Lawrence.*

Hart, Peter, *Gallipoli.*

Hattersley, Roy, *David Lloyd George, The Great Outsider.*

Heathcote, Tony, *The British Field Marshals 1736–1997.*

Hedges, Chris, *American Fascists, The Christian Right and the War on America.*

Hendrick, J., *The Life and Letters of Walter H Page,* vol. I.

Hill, William Thomson, *The Martyrdom of Nurse Cavell: The Life Story of the Victim of Germany's Most Barbarous Crime.*

Hickey, Michael, *Gallipoli.*

Hitchins, Keith, *Romania, 1866-1947.*

Hochschild, Adam, *To End All Wars, A Story of Protest and Patriotism in the First World War.*

Hoover, Herbert, *An American Epic 2.*

Hoover, Herbert, *Memoirs,* Vol 1.

Hopkirk, Peter, *The Great Game, On Secret Servive in High Asia.*

House, Edward Mandell, *Philip Drue: Administrator.*

House, Edward Mandell, and Seymouur, Charles, *The Intimate Papers of Colonel House,* 1915-1917.

Huldermann, Bernhard, *Albert Ballin.*

Hyam, Ronald, *Britain's Imperial Century, 1815-1914, A Study of Empire and Expansion.*

Ingrams, Doreen, *Palestine Papers: 1917-1922: Seeds of Conflict.*

James, Harold, *Family Capitalism.*

James, Robert Rhodes, *Gallipoli.*

Jefferson, Alfred Carter, *Anatole France, The Politics of Skepticism.*

Jeffrey, Keith, *The British Army and the Crisis of Empire.*

Jeffery, Keith, *Field Marshal Sir Henry Wilson: A Political Soldier.*

Jenkins, Roy, *Asquith; Portrait of a Man and an Era.*

Jellicoe, Viscount John, *The Grand Fleet (1914-1916): Its Creation, Development and Work.*

Jensen, B., *The Palestine Plot.*

Jowett, Gareth S., and O'Donnell, Victoria, *Propaganda and Persuasion.*

Kamran, Mujahid, *The International Bankers, World Wars 1, 11, and Beyond.*

Kaufman, Richard, *The War Profiteers.*

Kennan, George F., *Russia and the West under Lenin and Stalin.*

Keynes, J. M., *The Economic Consequences of the Peace.*

Keynes, J. M., *Two Memoirs: Dr. Melchior; A Defeated Enemy and My Early Beliefs.*

Kirconnell, Robert, *American Heart of Darkness, vol. 1, The Transformation of the American republic into a Pathocracy.*

King, Peter, *The Viceroy's Fall, How Kitchener Destroyed Curzon.*

Kirschen, Sadi, *Devant les Conseils de Guerre Allemandes.*

Kitson, Sir Arthur, *The Bankers' Conspiracy, with the Money Question.*

Kittredge, Tracey Barrett, *The History of the Commission for Relief in Belgium 1914-17.*

Knox, Sir Alfred , *With the Russian Army, 1914-1917.*

Knuth, E.C. *The Empire of "The City", The Secret History of British Financial Power.*

Koestler, Arthur, *Promise and Fulfilment, Palestine 1917- 1949.*

Koestler, Arthur, *The Thirteenth Tribe.*

Kollerstom, Nick, *How Britain Initiated Both World Wars.*

Konig, Paul, *Voyage of the Deutschland, The First Merchant Submarine.*

Laffin, J., *The Agony of Gallipoli.*

Lafore, Lawrence, *The Long Fuse: An Interpretation of the Origins of World War 1.*

Lake, Marilyn, and Reynolds, Henry, *What's Wrong with Anzac? The Militarisation of Australian History.*

Landes, David S., *The Unbound Prometheus.*

Langewiesche, Dieter, *Liberalism in Germany.*

Lannoy, Charles de, *L'Alimentation de la Belgique par le comite national.*

Lauriat, Charles E., *The Lusitania's Last Voyage.*

Lawrence, T. E., *Seven Pillars of Wisdom.*

Leggett, George, *The Cheka: Lenin's Political Police.*

Lenin, V.I., and Stalin, Joseph, *The Russian Revolution.*

Lewinsohn, Richard, *Sir Basil Zaharoff.*

Lichnowsky, Prince, *Heading for the Abyss.*

Liggett, Walter W., *The Rise of Herbert Hoover.*

Lipkes, J., *Rehearsals: The German Army in Belgium, August 1914.*

Lockhart, R.H. Bruce, *Memoirs of a British Agent.*

Long, Walter Hume, *Memories.*

Lucy, John F., *There's a Devil in the Drum.*

Ludendorff, Erich, ed., Urkunden der Obersten Herresleitung über ihre Tätigkeit 1916/18.

Lundberg, Ferdinand, America's 60 Families.

Lyons, Eugene, *Workers Paradise Lost.*

Macleod, Jenny, *Reconsidering Gallipoli.*

Macdonald, Lyn, *Somme.*

Macmillan, *Margaret, Peacemakers, Six Months That Changed The World.*

Magnus, Philip, *Kitchener, Portrait of an Imperialist.*

Mair, Craig, *Britain at War 1914-1919.*

Manchester, William, *The Arms of Krupp.*

Marder, Arthur J., *From the Dreadnought to Scapa Flow, Vol. 11.*

Marrin, Albert, *The Last Crusade: The Church of England in the First World War.*

Marwick, Arthur, *The Deluge; British Society and the First World War.*

Masefield, John, *Gallipoli.*

Mason, Alphas Thomas, *Brandeis - A Free Man's Life.*

Massie, Robert, *Castles of Steel: Britain, Germany and the winning of the Great War at Sea.*

Maurice, Sir Frederick, *Haldane.*

Maxton, James, *Lenin.*

McBeth, B. S. *British Oil Policy 1919-1939.*

McCormick, Donald, *The Mask of Merlin.*

McDonald, Donna, *Lord Strathcona.*

McLeod, Hugh, *Religion and Society in England.*

McMeekin, Sean, *History's Greatest Heist, The Looting of Russia by the Bolsheviks.*

McMeekin, Sean, *The Russian Origins of the First World War.*

McNeal, Shay, *The Plots to rescue the Tsar, The Truth behind the Disappearance of the Romanovs.*

Mercier, D. J. Cardinal, *Cardinal Mercier's Own Story.*

Messimer, Dwight, *The Baltimore Sabotage Cell, German Agents, American Traitors and the U-boat Deutschland During World War 1.*

Messinger, Gary, *British Propaganda and the State in the First World War.*

Miller, Geoffrey, *Straits.*

Millis, Walter, *Road to War – America, 1914-1917.*

Milner, Viscount Alfred, *Cotton Contraband.*

Moody, John, *The Masters of Capital: A Chronicle of Wall Street.*

Moorhead, Alan, *Gallipoli.*

Morel, E.D., *Affairs of West Africa.*

Morel, E.D., *Truth and the War.*

Morgan, J.H., *The German War Book.*

Morrow, John Howard, The Great War – An Imperial History.

Morse, Edwin W., America in the War, Part V. Relief Work in Belgium and Northern France; Herbert Hoover and Engineering Efficiency.

Murphy, Brian P., *Patrick Pearse and the Lost Republican Ideal.*

Nash, George H., *Herbert Hoover The Humanitarian, 1914-1917.*

Nash, George H., *The Life of Herbert Hoover: The Engineer.*

Neff, Donald, *Fallen Pillars.*

Nevison, Henry Woodd, *The Dardanelles Campaign.*

Newbold, J.T. Walton, *How Asquith Helped the Armaments Ring.*

Newbold, J. T. Walton, *The War Trust Exposed.*

Newbolt, Henry, *History of the Great War, Based on Official Documents. Naval Operations, Vol IV.*

Nimmocks, Walter, *Milner's Young Men.*

Nock, Albert J., *Myth of a Guilty Nation.*

Noel-Baker, Philip, *The Private Manufacture of Armaments.*

North, John, *Gallipoli, The Fading Vision.*

O'Brien, Terence, *Milner.*

Osgood, Robert E., *Ideals and Self Interest in America's Foreign Policy.*

O'Sullivan, Tim, *The Casement Diary Dogmatists.*

Owen, Robert L., *The Russian Imperial Conspiracy, 1892-1914.*

Owen, Roger, *Lord Cromer: Victorian Imperialist, Edwardian Proconsul.*

Pakenham, Thomas, *The Boer War.*

Pappe, Illan, *The Ethnic Cleansing of Palestine.*

Parmalee, M., *Blockade and Sea Power: The Blockade, 1914-1919.*

Pasha, Djamal, *Memories of a Turkish Statesman.*

Passmore, Kevin, *The Right in France from the Third Republic to Vichy.*

Pearson, Michael, *The Sealed Train, Journey to Revolution, Lenin-1917.*

Peeke, Mitch, *The Lusitania Story.*

Perris, George Herbert, *The War Traders: An Exposure.*

Peterson, H. C., *Propaganda for War.*

Peterson, H.C., and Fite, Gilbert C., *Opponents of War, 1917-1918.*

Pickles, Katie, *Transnational Outrage – The Death and Commemoration of Edith Cavell.*

Pilger, John, *The New Rulers of the World.*

Piper, Richard, *Communism: A History.*

Pitt, Barrie, *1918, The Last Act.*

Pohl, Manfred, *Handbook on the History of European Banks*

Pollock, John, *Kitchener.*

Pound, Reginald, and Harmsworth, Geoffrey, *Northcliffe.*

Powell, Anne, *A deep Cry, First World War Soldier-poets killed in France and Flanders.*

Powell, E. Alexander, *Fighting in Flanders.*

Preparata, Guido Giacomo, *Conjuring Hitler, How Britain and America Made the Third Reich.*

Preston, Diana, *Wilful Murder, The Sinking of the Lusitania.*

Prins, Nomi, *All the Presidents' Bankers.*

Prior, Robin, *Gallipoli, The End of The Myth.*

Podmore, Will, *British Foreign Policy Since 1870.*

Ponsonby, Arthur, *Falsehood in Wartime.*

Pohl, Manfred, and Freitag, Sabine, *Handbook on the History of European Banks.*

Quigley, Carroll, *The Anglo-American Establishment.*

Quigley, Carroll, *Tragedy and Hope: A History of the World in Our Time.*

Rabinowicz, Oscar K., *Fifty Years of Zionism.*

Rait, Robert S., *Critical Moments in British History.*

Ramsay, David, *Lusitania, Saga and Myth.*

Redier, Antoine, *La Guerre des Femmes, Histoire de Louise de Bettignes et de ses compagnes.*

Renin, Ludwig, *War.*

Renouvin, Pierre, *The Immediate Origins of the War.*

Roberts, Glyn, *The Most Powerful Man in the World, The Life of Sir Henri Deterring.*

Robertson, Sir William, *Soldiers and Statesmen 1914-1918.*

Rose, Norman, *The Cliveden Set, Portrait of an Exclusive Fraternity.*

Roskill, Stephen, *Hankey, Man of Secrets, vol.1 1897-1918.*

Roth, Cecil, *The Sasson Dynasty.*

Royle, Trevor, *The Kitchener Enigma.*

Russell, Bertrand, *These Eventful Years*, vol. 1.

Sachar, Abram Leon, *A History of the Jews.*

Sampter, Jessie Ethel, *A Guide to Zionism.*

Samuel, Herbert, *Memoirs, Viscount Samuel.*

Sand, Shlomo, *The Invention of the Jewish People.*

Sand, Shlomo, *The Invention of the Land of Israel, From Holy Land to Homeland.*

Sand, Shlomo, *The Words and the Land, Israeli Intellectuals and the Nationalist Myth.*

Saunder, Eric, and Marschall, Ken, *RMS Lusitania, Triumph of the Edwardian Age.*

Sazonov, Serge, *Fateful Years, 1909-1916, The Reminices Of.*

Schaepdrijver, Sophie, *Gabriel Petit, The Death and Life of a Female Spy.*

Schechtman, Joseph B., *The Life and Times of Vladimir Jabotinsky: Rebel and Statesman.*

Schneer, Jonathon, *The Balfour Declaration, The Origins of the Arab-Israeli Conflict.*

Seldes, George, *Iron, Blood and Profits.*

Seymour, Charles, *American Diplomacy During the World War.*

Shartle, Samuel G., *Spa, Versailles, Munich.*

Shaw, Albert, *President Wilson's State Papers and Addresses.*

Shaw, Stanford J., and Shaw, Ezel Kural, *History of the Ottoman Empire and Modern Turkey.*

Sheffield, Gary, *Forgotten Victory, The First World War Myths and Realities.*

Sheridan, Owen, *Propaganda as Anti-History.*

Simpson, Colin, *Lusitania.*

Slater, E. and Slater, R., *Great Jewish Men,*

Smout, T.C., *A Century of the Scottish People, 1830-1950.*

Solzhenitsyn, Aleksandr, Juifs et Russes pendant la Periode Soviétique, vol. 2.

Stead, William T., The Last Will and Testament of Cecil John Rhodes.

Steel, Nigel, and Hart, Peter, Defeat at Gallipoli.

Stern, Fritz, Gold and Iron: Bismarck, Bleichröder and the Building of the German Empire.

Stevenson, David, *Armaments and the Coming of War: Europe, 1904-1914.*

Stevenson, David, *With Our Backs to the Wall: Victory and Defeat in 1918.*

Stevenson, David, *1914-1918, A History of the First World War.*

Stewart, William, *J. Keir Hardie.*

Stieve, Friedrich, *Isvolsky and the World War.*

Stone, Oliver, and Kuznick, Peter, *The Untold History of the United States.*

Strachan, Hew, *The First World War* vol.1.

Streit, Clarence K., *Where Iron is, There is the Fatherland.*

Souhami, Diana, *Edith Cavell.*

Sutton, Antony, *The Federal Reserve Conspiracy.*

Sutton, Antony, *Wall Street and the Bolshevik Revolution.*

Swain, Joseph Ward, *Beginning the Twentieth Century.*

Sydenham of Combe, Lord, *Studies of An Imperialist.*

Tansill, Charles Cannon, *America Goes to War.*

Tarpley, Webster, and Chaitkin, Anton, *George Bush, The Unauthorized Biography.*

Taylor, A.J.P., *Essays in English History.*

Taylor, A.J.P., *Lloyd George, Rise and Fall.*

Taylor, Phillip, *British Propaganda in the 20th Century: Selling Democracy.*

Terraine, John, *General Jack's Diary, War on the Western Front, 1914-1918.*

Terraine, John, *The Road to Passchendaele.*

Thomson, George Malcolm, *The Twelve Days.*

Thomson, J. Lee, *Forgotten Patriot.*

Thomson, J. Lee, *Northcliffe, Press Baron in Politics, 1865-1922.*

Thomson, J. Lee, *Politicians, the Press and Propaganda, Lord Northcliffe & The Great War, 1914-1919.*

Thompson, Julian, The Imperial War Museum, Book of The War At Sea, 1914-18.

Tolf, Robert W., *The Russian Rockefellers.*

Tooley, T. Hunt, *Merchants of Death Revisited.*

Tortella, Gabriel, and Quirega, Gloria, *Entrepreneurship and Growth: An International Historical Perspective.*

Toye, Richard, *Lloyd George & Churchill, Rivals for Greatness.*

Tramerye, Pierre de la, *The World Struggle for Oil.*

Travers, Tim, *Gallipoli.*

Travers, Tim, *The Killing Ground, The British Army, The Western Front and the Emergence of Modern Warfare, 1900-1918.*

Trotsky, Leon, *My Life, An Attempt at an Autobiography.*

Tuchman, Barbara, *The Guns of August.*

Tumulty, Joesph, *President Wilson as I Knew Him.*

Turner, John, *Lloyd George's Secretariat.*

Tytgat, Charles, *Nos Fusilles (raconteurs et espions).*

Uyanik, Nevzat, *Dismantling the Ottoman Empire: Britain, America and the Armenian Question.*

Van Der Vat, Dan, *The Dardanelles Disaster.*

Van Til, Jacqueline, *With Edith Cavell in Belgium.*

Verax, *Truth, A Path to Justice and Reconciliation.*

Viereck, George Sylvester, *The Strangest Friendship in History: Woodrow Wilson and Colonel House.*

Vincent, C. Paul, *The Politics of Hunger, The Allied Blockade of Germany, 1915-1919.*

Volkognov, Dmitri, *Lenin, Life and Legacy.*

Volkognov, Dmitri, *Trotsky, The eternal Revolutionary.*

Von Bulow, Prince Bernhard, *Imperial Germany.*

Vought, Hans P., *The Bully Pulpit and the Melting Pot, American Presidents and the Immigrant, 1897-1933.*

Waldron, Peter, *The End of Imperial Russia, 1855 – 1917.*

Walsh, Pat, *The Events of 1915 in Eastern Anatolia.*

Walsh, Pat, *The Great Fraud of 1914-1918.*

Walsh, Pat, *Remembering Gallipoli.*

Weizmann, Chaim, *Trial and Error.*

Whitlock, Brand, *Belgium under the German Occupation, a personal narrative*, vol.2.

Whitlock, Brand, *Letters and Journal of Brand Whitlock, The Journal, Chapter II.*

Willert, Arthur, *The Road to Safety: A Study in Anglo-American Relations.*

Willis, Irene Cooper, *England's Holy War.*

Wilson, Derek, *Rothschild: The Wealth and Power of a Dynasty.*

Wilson, Jeremy, *Lawrence of Arabia.*

Wilson, Mairead, *Roger Casement: A Reassessment of the Diaries Controversies.*

Wilson, Sir Henry, *Diaries.*

Wilson, Trevor, *The Myriad Faces of War.*

Winkler, Jonathan Reed, *Nexus: Strategic Communications and American Security in World War 1.*

Winnington-Ingram, Arthur F., *The Potter and the Clay.*

Winter Denis, *Death's Men, Soldiers of the Great War.*

Winter, Denis, *Haig's Command.*

Woodbury, Martha Liggett, *Stopping The Presses, the Murder of Walter Liggett.*

Wright, Peter E., *At the Supreme War Council.*

Yergin, Daniel, *The Prize, The Epic Quest for Oil, Money and Power.*

Zwar, Desmond, *In Search of Keith Murdoch.*

Zweig, Arnold, *Outside Verdun.*

Index

C

D

H

L

M

N

O

P

Q

R